History of the Holocaust

History of the

HOLOCAUST

A Handbook and Dictionary

Abraham J. Edelheit &
Hershel Edelheit

Westview Press

BOULDER • SAN FRANCISCO • OXFORD

Copyright © 1994 by Westview Press, Inc.

Published in 1994 in the United States of America by Westview Press, Inc., 5500 Central Avenue, Boulder, Colorado 80301-2877, and in the United Kingdom by Westview Press, 36 Lonsdale Road, Summertown, Oxford OX2 7EW

Library of Congress Cataloging-in-Publication Data
Edelheit, Abraham J.
   History of the Holocaust : a handbook and dictionary / Abraham J.
Edelheit and Hershel Edelheit.
     p.   cm.
   ISBN 0-8133-1411-9 — ISBN 0-8133-2240-5 (pbk.)
   1. Holocaust, Jewish (1939–1945).   2. Holocaust, Jewish
(1939–1945)—Dictionaries—Polyglot.   3. Dictionaries, Polyglot.
I. Edelheit, Hershel.   II. Title.
D804.3.E33   1994
940.53'18—dc20   93-47316
                                                                                              CIP

Printed and bound in the United States of America

(∞) The paper used in this publication meets the requirements
of the American National Standard for Permanence of Paper
for Printed Library Materials Z39.48-1984.

10   9   8   7   6   5   4   3   2   1

Dedicated to
David and Phyllis Edelheit
with love

CONTENTS

PART 2
DICTIONARY OF HOLOCAUST TERMS

Table of Major Entries

ILLUSTRATIONS

Tables

Graphs

Maps

Illustrations

ABBREVIATIONS

A	=	Austria	I	=	Italy/Italian
Br	=	Belorussia	La	=	Latvia
Bu	=	Bulgaria/Bulgarian	Li	=	Lithuania
Cz	=	Czech	NA	=	Not Available
Du	=	Dutch	P	=	Poland/Polish
E	=	Estonia	PN	=	Proper Name
En	=	England	R	=	Russia/Russian
Fr	=	France/French	Ro	=	Romania/Romanian
G	=	Germany/German	Sl	=	Slovak
Gr	=	Greece/Greek	Tr	=	Transnistria
H	=	Hebrew	Uk	=	Ukraine
Ho	=	Holland	Y	=	Yiddish
Hu	=	Hungary/Hungarian	Yu	=	Yugoslavia

PREFACE

Language, the symbols, terms, and concepts we use to communicate, can play an important role in the way we understand the past. Language is the means by which humans give context and meaning to their experiences. The way an order is framed, the way a report is written, the way records are kept, impact directly on the ability of historians to reconstruct events that, by and large, they know only by means of orders, reports, and records. This is true of any period of history, but it is most especially true of the Holocaust era.

As the world passes the fifty-year mark — half a century since the launching of the Final Solution — we may ponder the importance of language for our understanding of the history of the Holocaust. We must, furthermore, dig below the surface of language as it was used to understand the sense and context of what we are describing. We must also, it seems, keep in mind the counsel of Karl Kraus, a Viennese Jewish writer of the fin de siècle: "Die deutschen sind nicht nur ein Volk der Dichter und Denker, sondern auch der Richter und Henker" (The Germans are not only a nation of poets and thinkers, but also of judges and hangmen).

The Final Solution, after all, was to be the great unwritten chapter of German history. The Nazis operated best when they could operate in secrecy. Their plans for world conquest and for the elimination of world Jewry were to be shrouded in mystery. Code words or euphemisms that sanitized reality replaced terms considered too forward, too clear, too inappropriate. Thus, the Nazis had no fewer than nineteen different terms to replace murder: *Aufgelöst, Ausgemerzt, Ausgeraumt, Auslöschen, Ausschaltung, Beseitigung, Entjudung, Entlaust, Erledigt, Erleichtert, Evakuiert, Gesonderte Unterbringung, Gesundung, Hingerichtet, Judenreinigung, Sauberung, Sonderbehandlung, Umgelegt, Vernichtung.* One should add *Aktionen, Aussiedlungen,* and *Endlösung,* three broad, almost meaningless terms, always used in some way to cover direct murder or any activity that led to eventual murder. These terms were designed not only to cover up the Holocaust but also to deceive the victims, the bystanders, and even (to a degree) the perpetrators.

Nevertheless, everything had to be done in an orderly fashion — to the extent that order was possible. Of course, in an ordered world every undertaking had to be legal. Even in a totalitarian state the veneer of legality had to be maintained. The task at hand required bureaucratization and legislation. Once the proper laws were passed, then action might proceed.

Language presumes communication. Yet meaningful communication is the bane of secrecy. The utilization of propaganda became, therefore, a cardinal precept of Nazi rule. Propaganda had to be couched in the proper vocabulary. Dr. Joseph Goebbels, the Nazi propaganda minister, thus invented the concept of a "Big Lie": a lie of such massive magnitude and repeated so often with firm conviction that its hearers could only conclude the lie must be true. Repeated often enough, this lie took on a life of its own; by the time a lie becomes a "Big Lie," its truth or untruth no longer matters. The lie, in effect, becomes an article of faith for the believer.

Antisemitism was just such a lie. It was (and remains) a lie that has had nearly two thousand years of repetition. The importance of traditional forms of Jew hatred cannot be underestimated. From the "Jewish wizard" of early medieval stereotype, to the Jewish Antichrist, to the Jewish conspiracy theory exemplified by the *Protocols of the Elders of Zion*, demonization of the Jew has provided charlatans, rabble-rousers, and demagogues with a weapon to rally the masses. Hitler himself is reputed to have said that without antisemitism there was no Nazism.

A criminal state has its victims. The more powerful the state, the more victims. Places of confinement, punishment, and execution had to be established. The Nazi SS state had an intricate network of camps — *Konzentrationslager* (KL) — created for the sole purpose of inflicting pain and suffering on the incarcerated victims, thereby breaking their spirit and will to live. Here too a new set of rules, coded in KL language, had to be created.

The Jewish victims also needed their own language. Whether in closed or open ghettos, in slave-labor or concentration camps, or hiding among the Gentiles, masquerading as an Aryan, the victims had to create an old-new language to place their experiences into some new context. Like their adversaries, the victims had to innovate and utilize a host of coded terms. Where there is life, there is hope. And yet, the Jews eventually came to understand what the Nazis planned for them; they knew, but they had no real response. How could an unarmed civilian population ever have a response to cold-blooded murder on a scale so unprecedented that — fifty years later — it still sends a chill down the spine of anyone contemplating the history of the Holocaust and its implications? The dimensions are almost beyond belief, if not almost beyond words.

Almost beyond belief, but not completely. As long as survivors remain alive, the direct experience of the Holocaust shall not be forgotten. But as the generation of survivors passes on, the possibility exists that a new generation will arise that neither knows of the Holocaust nor understands its implications. This possibility, which must be fought with every means available, is already apparent in the efforts of distorters of the Holocaust to open a "public debate" on the facts of the twentieth century's greatest crime. The "Big Lie," it would seem, is still alive and well.

The purpose of this handbook and dictionary is threefold: to provide the reader with a general overview of Jewish history during the Nazi era, to tabulate all data on the Holocaust that can possibly be reduced to tabular or graphic form, and to gather in one source as many terms dealing directly or indirectly with the Holocaust as possible. To that end, we have organized this book into two sections. Part 1 offers an overview of Jewish history in the first half of the twentieth century, with emphasis on the causes, course, and results of the Final Solution. This part is based primarily on secondary sources and seeks nothing more, nor less, than a synthesis of the work of previous generations of Holocaust historians. Still, it must be emphasized that the nine chapters of Part 1 offer only an introductory overview. The writing of anything approaching a definitive history of the Holocaust is still many years in the future.

Part 2 provides an alphabetical review of terms related to the Holocaust as viewed from the perspectives of perpetrators, victims, and bystanders. In this section as well, we have included larger entries that not only define but also quantify a subject and relate pertinent information on that subject in tabular, graphic, or illustrative form. Here too, we must note the incomplete nature of much of the data. A large measure of anti-Jewish legislation, for example — extensively covered under the entry *Legislation, Anti-Jewish* — was promulgated by almost every country allied to or occupied by the Nazis. Nevertheless, much of the raw data on antisemitic legislation remains untapped. In most cases, no compilation exists of anti-Jewish laws; to uncover such laws a reader must pore over the official state journals for virtually every country in Europe.

We hope that our efforts have contributed a useful new tool for educators, students, and researchers in the field of Holocaust studies. The present volume also reflects a turning point in our own scholarly manifestation, for it is the first work to be published by Westview Press under the imprint of the Edelheit Research Institute for Contemporary History (ERICH), a nonprofit, family research institute dedicated to providing a framework for the study of the contemporary

Jewish experience.

Nevertheless, a work of this magnitude could not have been completed by us alone. We would like to take this opportunity to thank the following individuals and institutions for their help in completing this book: Seth Bowman; Dr. Randolph L. Braham; Dr. Lucjan Dobroszycki; Dr. Luba K. Gurdus; Col. Irving Heymont (U.S. Army, ret.); Isaac Kowalski; Dr. David Kranzler; Professor Robert Laurenty; Dr. Abraham J. Peck; Dr. Monty N. Penkower; Marc Rose; Dr. and Mrs. Nessim Roumi; Allen Wollman; Ms. Evelyn Zimmerman; Dr. Susan Zuccotti; Terri Anderson and the staff of the Fred R. Crawford Witness to the Holocaust Project of Emory University; Mrs. Adaire Klein, Ms. Cheryl Miller, and the staff of the Simon Wiesenthal Center; Dr. Brewster Chamberlain, Jacek Novakowski, Genya Markon, and the staff of the U.S. Holocaust Memorial Museum; Dina Abramovich, Zachary Baker, and the staff of the YIVO Institute, New York; Dr. Tuvia Friling and the staff of the Ben-Gurion Research Center, Sde Boker, Israel; Dr. Yitzhak Arad and the staff of Yad Vashem, Jerusalem; Dr. Daniel Greenberg and the staff of the Jewish Historical Institute, Warsaw; Mrs. Batya Leshem and the staff of the Central Zionist Archives, Jerusalem; Mrs. Amira Stern and the staff of the Jabotinsky Institute Archive, Tel Aviv; Mr. Yerucham Meshel and the staff of the Lavon Institute/Histadrut Archive, Tel Aviv; the staff of the Leo Baeck Institute, New York; and the staffs of the New York Public Library Jewish and Slavic Divisions. Thanks as well to Susan L. McEachern, Jane Raese, Marian Safran, and the staff at Westview Press for their professionalism in preparing a difficult manuscript for publication. Special thanks go to Rabbi and Mrs. Amos Edelheit, and finally, Mrs. Ann D. Edelheit, mother, wife, and proofreader extraordinaire.

Abraham J. Edelheit
Hershel Edelheit

PART 1

HISTORY OF THE HOLOCAUST

East European scholar on the eve of World War II
Authors' Collection

1

ANTECEDENTS

The Jews of Europe

If it had not been for the terrible events that unfolded between 1933 and 1945, the Jews of Europe would, in all probability, have continued to live as they had for nearly a millennium. Arriving on the continent after the conquest of the then-known world by Alexander the Great (ca. 333 B.C.E.), European Jewish communities developed primarily after the Roman destruction of the Second Temple (70 C.E.) and the failure of the Bar-Kokhba revolt (ca. 132–135 C.E.). Despite the fact that Jews in Europe thus predated the arrival of many of the ethnic groups associated with European countries, Jews did not become prominent until after the ninth or tenth century.[1]

Thereafter, Jews had to endure repeated periods of hatred, persecution, and, at times, almost daily violence. Jews were confined to designated areas called ghettos and were forced to wear distinctive marks upon their clothing. At times, entire communities were obliterated by pogroms or expulsion.[2] Jewish history was not, however, only a history of tears. Judaism survived and even thrived wherever it found fertile soil. A vibrant and varied social, political, and intellectual life developed in both ghettos and villages. Jewish institutions — *kehilot* (community councils), synagogues, *yeshivot* (academies), and *hevrot* (societies) — flourished, as did the greatest of all Jewish institutions, the family.[3]

Although Jewry had previously weathered numerous crises, the period after 1500 witnessed an increasing fragmentation of the Jewish world. The mass conversion of Spanish Jews who, under duress, officially adopted Christianity while continuing some Jewish observances in secret — so-called Marranos — created a class of Jews by birth who no longer had an attachment to traditional norms of Jewish life.[4] A further series of crises, beginning with the Chmielnicki massacres in 1648–1649 and ending with the Shabbatean heresy of the late 1660s, very nearly rent asunder the Jewish community.[5] In response, the Hasidic movement, which emphasized piety and articulated an optimistic worldview, arose to fill the vacuum left by the crises. The Hasidic masters, the *tzadikim*, followed Israel ben Eliezer, the Baal Shem Tov, in emphasizing *devekut* (devotion) and *hitlahavut* (joy) — both seen as being as important as, if not more important than, book learning. Hasidism, moreover, represented the apotheosis of the communal crisis in post-Shabbatean Jewry. Combining mystical piety with a de-activated form of messianism that emphasized the cosmic importance of *halacha* (Jewish law), Hasidism spoke to the Jewish everyman and soon spread from the steppes of the Ukraine to the foothills of the Carpathians and even to central Poland and beyond.[6]

Only in Lithuania did the *Mitnagdim*, those who opposed Hasidism, retain a foot-hold. The *Mitnagdim* were especially strong in and around Vilna, the "Jerusalem of Lithuania." Here the *yeshivot* reigned. For the further glory of Judaism, students spent days and nights studying Talmudic tomes replete with ancient law and lore. These Talmudic academies rivaled those of Babylonia and Eretz Israel, if they did not in fact surpass them. In Mir, Slobodka, Volozhin, Vilna, and Brisk some of the greatest Jewish minds were honed to perfection.[7]

Sephardi Jewry

Jewish communities also flourished throughout the Mediterranean lands and in Southeast Europe. Among these communities perhaps the largest were those of the Sephardim, Jews who had been expelled from Spain in 1492 and their descendants. As was the case with Ashkenazi Jewry (Jews who had settled in the Germanic lands), the Sephardim and their offspring were able to rebound into a cohesive and well-organized community.[8]

After 1492 Sephardim spread far and wide. A majority of the exiles went east to the Ottoman Empire. Briefly, it seemed that the expulsion might lead to a renewed settlement in the Land of Israel. This possibility, in turn, led to renewed messianic speculation and the aforementioned controversy surrounding the false messiah Shabbetai Zevi. Others from among the exiled of Spain came to the New World to establish what was to become the largest and richest Jewish community in history. Still other Sephardim sought refuge in the North, reestablishing Jewries in the Netherlands, England, and France. The largest concentration of Sephardim by far was in the Balkans. Their distinctive culture clearly identified them as originating in Spain, which affirms the unique cultural symbiosis of the "golden age" of Spanish Jewry.[9]

Enlightenment and Emancipation

The latter half of the eighteenth century spawned a series of ideological changes in Western Europe. Although not directly related to Jews, two particular developments had impact on the status and fate of European Jewry. The first of the two developments was the Enlightenment, generally identified with cultural and intellectual trends in France. The Enlightenment represented the systematic application of rationalist and "scientific" principles to humanity, and particularly to politics. Connected with the Enlightenment, although independent of the intellectual movement, was the rise of the absolutist state, one that encompassed all citizens or subjects. For Jews these two movements augured a change in status, since the absolutist nation-state could no longer tolerate autonomous national entities — states within a state — within its borders.[10] As a result, concerned thinkers proposed the "civic improvement" of the Jews by granting emancipation and citizenship to Jews willing to become part of the host nation. Thus, from the mid-eighteenth century on, a grand debate raged over the idea of emancipation, but the Ancien Régime proved unable to reform in so radical a fashion.[11] Further impetus was given to the European debate in the aftermath of the American Revolution (1776–1783), the ratification of the U.S. Constitution, and the granting of citizenship to American Jewry.

Within the Jewish world a new spirit was also kindled during the middle of the eighteenth century. Small numbers of Jews became aware of the "backwardness" of Jewish society and proposed remedies for all ills that kept Jews in what they saw as a cultural ghetto even while the walls of the physical ghetto were crumbling. The modernizers adopted the name of *Maskilim* (Enlighteners) and called their movement the Haskala (Enlightenment). Ideologically, this group owed its background to the writings and teachings of Moses Mendelssohn, a German Jewish philosopher. The primary goal of the Haskala was to reeducate Jews so that they could fit into modern society. With the emancipation, the *Maskilim*, at least in Western Europe, led the way in creating "good" Jewish citizens. Thus, adaptation of Jewish mores to the larger society became the goal. "Be a Jew in your home and a man in the street" was their motto.[12]

The French Revolution (1789) brought the debate on Jewish status to a crescendo. During the next century civil rights were granted to Jews in virtually all of Western Europe: in France (1791), Italy (1869), Great Britain (1858–1871), and Germany (1871).[13] Tension often accompanied the emancipation, however, especially in France and Germany. Civil status was accorded to Jews as individuals, not to Jewish communities. In return for civil rights, Jews were asked to surrender their national identity and assimilate into the larger society.[14]

Under the circumstances, adaptation to and assimilation into the larger environment appeared the only means to resolve the paradox of Jewish survival and also proved that Jews had made strides in "improving" themselves in order to become deserving citizens — Israelites of French or German nationality. With the internalization by Jews of new liberal ideas, religious Judaism also became more diverse. In Germany, a number of Jews sought to reform Judaism in order to make it more compatible with modern society. A different group saw the need for some changes but were only willing to make changes for which they found precedents in Jewish history. Yet a third group saw no need for changes in the tradition, although they too adopted a more modern worldview.

In Germany, England, and the United States, the most liberal group of the *Maskilim* crystallized into the Reform movement, which was formulated by leaders such as Abraham Geiger, Samuel Holdheim, and David Friedlander. The middle group, under the guidance of luminaries including Zechariah Frankel and Solomon Schechter, became the Positive Historical school, better known as Conservative Judaism. The most traditional group, led by Rabbis Shimshon Raphael Hirsch, Isaac Breuer, and Azriel Hildesheimer, developed into Neo-orthodoxy, which combined strict adherence to Jewish law with a modern *Weltanschauung*.[15]

Closely related to the religious sphere was the development of modern Jewish studies.

Applying modern historical principles to Judaism, practitioners of *Wissenschaft des Judentums* (Science of Judaism) offered both proofs for religious polemics and a more relevant way of understanding the Jews' role in society. In this way the liberal scholars, such as Geiger and Leopold Zunz, could meet traditionalists like Nachman Krochmal, Shlomo Yehuda Rapoport, and Shmuel David Luzzatto. The result was an almost-unprecedented flourishing of Jewish scholarship.[16]

Wissenschaft des Judentums also bore fruit in Eastern Europe. Scholars trained in scientific historiography who made seminal contributions to Jewish scholarship included Meyer Balaban, Ignac Schipper, and Emmanuel Ringelblum. Their dean was Simon Dubnow, the historian and political activist.[17] Jewish literature also developed significantly with the likes of Haim Nahman Bialik, Saul Tchernikovsky, Isaac Leib Peretz, Judah Leib Gordon, Abraham Mapu, Mendele Mokher Seforim (Shalom Jacob Abramowitsch), and Shalom Aleichem (Shalom Rabinovitz) who depicted — in verse and prose — the life of a civilization.[18]

Post-Emancipation German Jewry

With the final decree of emancipation dated January 12, 1871, German Jewry entered a new stage of history. At least officially, German Jews now became full citizens of the German Empire, permitted to participate in all aspects of economic, political, and cultural life. German Jewry became a shining example of both the best and worst aspects of modern Jewry: great wealth coupled with intense materialism; religious freedom coupled with an attempt to flee Judaism; civic equality and intense antisemitism in many circles. Throughout the nineteenth century and well into the twentieth, German Jewry remained a compact, highly urbanized middle-class or upper-middle-class element in German society. It has been estimated, for example, that 70 percent of German Jews made their living in commerce (primarily in small- and medium-scale retailing), banking, and manufacture. Jewish professionals — lawyers, doctors, dentists —

represented the next largest group of gain-fully employed Jews. In both cases, the percentage of Jews in these fields was disproportionate to their total population.[19] When Jewish urban concentration is considered, the amount of disproportion declines and it becomes clear that Jews did not dominate any field of economic activity.[20] The same may be said of Jewish political orientations in pre–World War I Germany: They tended to the center and left primarily because the right-wing parties had been opposed to emancipation in the first place.[21]

Internally as well, emancipation resulted in a major transformation of German Jewry. In addition to the aforementioned rise of multiple Jewish denominations, German Jewry experienced an intense period of secularization. Increasingly, German Jews did not identify themselves as Jews, but as Germans. When they did discuss religious affiliation, they did so as "Germans of the Mosaic faith."[22]

As a direct result, radical assimilation — which may be defined as an attempt to flee Judaism — became rampant in many segments of German Jewry.[23] Even assimilation had its limits: In particular, Germans viewed the "new" Germans with suspicion and considered them to be Jews, even if they converted.[24] At best, the Jew was considered a parvenu, at worst, a pushy pariah seeking to force himself on an unwilling but irresistible world.[25]

In turn, the fact that Jews sought entry into an ambivalent environment created a tension within German Jewish society that obtained throughout the years between 1870 and 1914. In most cases, the internal tension was transformed into creative energy that culminated in some of the greatest artistic and literary creations of the pre–World War I era. This creative tension also resulted in a systematic, although initially amorphous, effort to redefine Jewry's role in the modern world — a pursuit that eventually culminated in the rise of Zionism and Jewish nationalism.

Failure of Emancipation in Eastern Europe

Socially and politically, however, East European Jewry faced much harder conditions than their Western counterparts for most of the nineteenth century. In the territory of the Russian Empire, civic emancipation never progressed beyond rudimentary stages, despite a number of half-hearted efforts early in the century to assimilate Jews.[26] The Jewish experience in the Duchy of Warsaw, the remnant of the Polish commonwealth that was absorbed into the Russian Empire in 1795 (effectively ceasing to exist as a result of the Congress of Vienna in 1815), was similar. Despite efforts to grapple with the Jewish problem, the Sejm (parliament) failed to achieve a consensus on Jewish rights, and proposals to effect emancipation along French lines collapsed.[27]

The failure of emancipation in Eastern Europe was more apparent after 1880. Most particularly, the pogroms that spread throughout Russia in 1881 and 1882 in the wake of Czar Alexander II's assassination by Narodnik (Populist) terrorists proved to be a watershed. The government response to the pogroms — which were neither planned nor supported by the authorities in Petersburg (unlike later outbursts, which were government sponsored) — included a series of laws designed to further limit Jewish rights.[28] In response, Russian Jews turned to emigration as an immediate solution for their problems. By this means the Jewries of Western Europe, the United States, and Palestine were reinvigorated.[29]

For Russian *Maskilim*, however, the pogroms proved to be a double shock. Expecting to find an ally in the Russian intelligentsia, the *Maskilim* were disappointed to discover that the educated elements of society strongly supported the pogromchiks. As a result, the Jewish intelligentsia began to turn elsewhere for salvation and to seek means of self-emancipation.[30]

Ultranationalism and National Egotism

A new phase in Jewish and European history

began after 1870. A number of historians have argued that Jews were drawn into the storm center of events that were only remotely of their concern. Increasingly, European power politics impinged upon the security of the European Jewish communities. In particular, the unification of Germany in 1870–1871 shook the foundations of the European balance of power and brought with it a rise of hypernationalism. Whereas in 1789 nationalism had been a progressive movement, by 1848 ultranationalism had become a highly conservative and even reactionary force in national affairs.[31]

A new ideological trend, usually subsumed under the term *national egotism*, developed from the notion that one's own nation represents the pinnacle of all that is good and pure. National egotism also acted as the justification for national demands for respect from other nations and for attempts by the nation to "find its place in the sun" through a policy of territorial expansion. National egotism, thus, also justified a jingoistic and militaristic form of hyperpatriotism. At the same time, and paradoxically, the same roots of national egotism also created the sense of imperfection within certain elements, primarily the intelligentsia. Given the premise that the nation is perfect, a premise that flows naturally from an egotistical analysis of one's own nation, then the analyst must take pains to explain why mundane reality has continued, especially if one perceives the creation of a nation-state in messianic terms.[32]

In Germany, radical illiberalism developed directly from four anomalous features of German unification: First, Germany was unified as a political entity, but not all Germans lived under the sovereignty of the Kaiser. Austria, Bohemia-Moravia, and Switzerland, all areas identified with German culture, remained outside of the new German state, which was dominated by Prussia. Second, Germany controlled a significant non-German ethnic population, primarily composed of Poles in Silesia and a small but prominent Jewish minority. Third,

the territorial conflict with the French, who sought revenge for their defeat in 1870, continued. Finally, the state created by Chancellor Otto von Bismarck and its foreign policy owed much to his personal style of rule. In particular, Bismarck's system used contradictory defensive alliances with Austria (against Russia) and with Russia (against Austria) to thwart French revanchism.[33]

The direct result of these anomalies was the rise of German hypernationalism, associated with the "Germanic critics," Paul de Legarde, Julius Langbehn, Arthur Möller Van den Bruck, and Richard Wagner, who offered a new picture of what was wrong with Germany. For Germany to gain its "place in the sun" it first had to become pure. Foreign influences — democracy, liberty, constitutions — had to be done away with. So too, Germany had to purge itself of the inner enemy — the Jews. Even Christianity would undergo reform: It would develop into a new "Germanic" form. Although their ideas were not officially accepted, the critics, especially Wagner, exerted a good deal of influence among German intellectuals.

The critics' position was strengthened by a heavy dose of *völkisch* romanticism that suffused German nationalism in the fin de siècle. Almost all German nationalists viewed the nation as an organic being that was more than "merely" the sum of its citizens. Therefore, the critics concluded that the new Reich was neither a worthy heir of the traditions of Teutonic greatness nor a proper vehicle for expressing the national will of the German *Volk*. Rather, the Second Reich was a philistine state influenced by a cancerous foreign body that had been permitted to fester within the German body politic: the Jews.[34]

A similar ultranationalist spirit developed in fin de siècle France, although in this case the rallying cry was for revenge against Germany. The Third Republic, born in the ashes of the Second Empire at the Paris Commune (1871), was beset for most of its existence by numerous discordant relationships: between workers and employers; between urban and rural elements; between Monarchists, Bonapartists, and Republicans; and between true Frenchmen and those perceived to be foreigners, once again primarily Jews.[35] These various trends may be seen as having come together, with a passion, during the Dreyfus Affair.

Captain Alfred Dreyfus — a French Jewish artillery officer — was falsely accused of espionage in 1893 and was convicted and punished for that crime by banishment to the French prison colony on Devil's Island. Although continuing to profess his innocence, Dreyfus was widely assumed guilty, even within the Franco-Jewish community. As the wheels of justice slowly turned, however, it became increasingly clear that Dreyfus was indeed innocent, the victim of an antisemitic officer corps wishing to blame a scapegoat for failure on the battlefield in order to avoid admitting defeat at the hands of a better-prepared enemy.

After years of advocacy by the pro-Dreyfusards, justice was finally served; in no small measure thanks to the efforts of the writer Emile Zola, whose essay *J'accuse* forced the case to be reopened, and the Socialist leader Jean Jaurès, whose humanistic spirit was offended by the very act of injustice. Nevertheless, the anti-Dreyfusards were not swept away in defeat but rather were forced underground. The position of those opposed to reopening the case must also be kept in mind, for it indicates much about the crisis of French society at the time. Many of the anti-Dreyfusards were willing to admit, in the face of overwhelming evidence, that Dreyfus could actually be innocent. Yet, they argued, the best thing for France would be to continue the charade of his guilt so that the army's reputation would remain untainted. For the anti-Dreyfusards, as for the German critics, an imperfect society had to be brought to apocalyptic perfection, even against its will.[36]

Continental Europe's three other major kingdoms — Italy, Russia, and Austria-Hungary — also suffered greatly in this era of social malaise. Political and social crises, exacerbated by periodic economic difficulties and the costs of maintaining an international system based on mistrust, created a disheartening atmosphere among certain social and political groups. Increasingly, these groups sought an outlet for the frustrations created by unfulfilled expectations. Most of these groups sought war as a means of finding relief from the mundane world and righting what was wrong with government and society. Regardless of their standing on international issues, however, all sought a scapegoat on whom to blame the ills of society; invariably that scapegoat was the Jew.[37]

The Jewish Problem

In such a milieu the Jew — seen as the quintessential modern — was almost immediately identified with the worst aspects of modern society. The result was the development of a "Jewish problem" in the minds of many Europeans. The reasons that continued Jewish existence was seen as a problem are clear and may be subsumed into three broad categories. First, Jews had traditionally been both demonized and victimized by Christian societies seeking a scapegoat for their imperfections. Second, although the Enlightenment reduced religious antisemitism to a fringe element, the philosophes retained considerable antipathy toward Jews. This antipathy was partly rooted in the philosophes' critique of organized Christianity, which was seen as the ultimate victory of Judaism's morality over Greece's aesthetic sense. The philosophes' hatred of Jews, however, also contained a good proportion of traditional antisemitic rhetoric, paradoxically taken straight from the teachings of the same Christian church that the philosophes publicly scorned. This was especially true of Voltaire's condemnation of Jewish usury but may also be discerned in the writings of other members of the French and German Enlightenment. Third was the inescapable appearance of Jewish "success" in the modern world. Whereas Jews had previously been outsiders, they had been emancipated as a result of the changes in European politics in the eighteenth and nineteenth centuries and had now entered into the very bosom of European society. In the view of the aforementioned social critics, emancipation, which was supposed to lead to a disappearance of the Jews, had only resulted in the "Judaization" of society. In order to reach the millennium, the critics argued, society had to be "de-Judaized," that is, returned to its pristine pre-Christian form by the creation of a "new" ghetto, through legislation strictly segregating Jews and protecting society at large from their harmful effects, and through a return of the old pagan Nordic values. The result of such agitation was that antisemitism became an element on the political agenda in Germany and France during the last decades of the nineteenth century.

Between 1870 and 1900 antisemitism also took on a quasi-scientific element. Antisemitism merged with a new and popular pseudo-science, Social Darwinism. Although most antisemites adopted racism because of their *a priori* antisemitism, and not vice versa, they adopted an ideology that had developed over the nineteenth century and turned it into a eugenic science. In general, the racists argued, humanity was not a totality that originated from a common root. Rather, they assumed the existence of different races, much as there are different breeds of animals linked by a common genus, with one, the Aryan (Nordic) race, being superior and the others inferior. Society was seen as being ill from racial intermingling, whose prime result was the Jewish rise to prominence. Jews, however, were not merely a lower race, but represented an anti-race. Jews were actually identified with bacilli or with cancers; just as the bacillus infects the victim, Jews infected European society. Just as the only response to physical disease is to attempt to exterminate the bacilli, so too the only response to the crisis of European society was to eliminate the cause, the Jews.[38]

The novelty of the Jewish problem must, however, be questioned. The phenomenon of antisemitism long predated use of the term, which was coined by Wilhelm Marr in 1879. Clearly, hatred, fear, and dislike of Jews are as ancient as the Jewish people.

Even in the relatively tolerant Greco-Roman world, Jew hatred became a matter of public policy at times of economic and social upheaval. Nevertheless, pagan antisemitism arose primarily from a lack of a common cultural ground between Jew and non-Jew and ultimately led nowhere. Christian antisemitism arose out of a different set of motives. Whereas paganism lacked a common religious ground with the Jews, Christianity rejected them. Judaism had been surpassed and was no longer relevant, and Jews were deicides who had to pay for their sins. They could no longer even bear the title of Israel, for they were no longer the chosen people. Antisemitism, based upon the very foundations of Christian rejection of Judaism and the attempt to co-opt the Bible for Christian purposes, could thus be seen as almost inherent in Christianity.[39]

To be sure, a variety of factors — political, social, economic, and intellectual — with different emphasis in different eras, ensured that Judaism was never completely extirpated. Even the Catholic Church, although it recommended pressuring the Jews, recognized their role in society. Under the Doctrine of Testimony, Jews were to be downtrodden but not destroyed, eternal testimony for Divine justice.[40]

To better understand the modern problem, the premodern background must be kept in mind. In the twelfth century, a diabolical view of the Jew emerged. It was widely believed that Jews knew the truth of Christianity but stubbornly rejected salvation. In a superstitious world, this view of Jewish perversity and the belief in the imminent, daily existence of Satan were soon linked. The Jews' perversity was therefore explained as a sign of Jewish cooperation with the Devil. Ultimately, Jews were seen as the Antichrist, whose sole purpose was to fight against the Divine order and to destroy all Christians.[41] As the incarnation of pure evil, the Jews would stop at nothing to achieve their nefarious goals: the ritual slaughter of Christian children, the use of Christian blood in baking *matzot* (unleavened bread used for the Passover festival), desecration of the Host, the murder of Christian patients, and the poisoning of wells.[42] One need only to read the anti-Jewish rantings of Martin Luther to obtain a clear perception of the issue. The leading founder of Protestantism suggested his own solution to the Jewish problem in his work *Concerning the Jews and Their Lies* (1543). In a seven-point program Luther called for the complete outlawing of Judaism: Expropriation of Jewish property, the burning of their prayer books and synagogues, and the reduction of Jews to slavery were key elements of this plan, as was the possibility of the expulsion of Jews from Germany.[43]

The modern Jewish problem arose from slightly different origins. From the period of the Enlightenment on, it was no longer acceptable to hate Jews on religious grounds. Jews were no longer the "damned, rejected race" that Luther had fulminated against; their religion per se was no longer an issue. "Jew" or "Christian," they were still a problem, albeit for a host of new reasons: economic competition, disloyalty to the state, lack of cultural assimilation into the body of the nation, and racial differences. The Doctrine of Testimony, furthermore, which had guaranteed Jewish survival, was simply forgotten.

When combined with racism and Social Darwinism, antisemitism became a potent and potentially violent ideology. At the turn of the twentieth century a further justification was added to this ideology: the so-called Jewish conspiracy theory. As developed by the authors of *The Protocols of the Elders of Zion*, this theory holds that Jews seek world dominion, using both liberal capitalism and revolutionary socialism as tools to manipulate the political life of Europe. In addition, according to believers in this theory, Jewish financiers attempt to centralize control of Europe's finances. Together, the ultimate goal of this conspiracy, variously attributed to the Rothschilds, the Bleichroders, and Theodor Herzl, was to create and cement Jewish domination over the entire world.[44]

The Jewish conspiracy theory may be seen as the ultimate development of the position of the German critics regarding the "Judaization" of society. However, one major difference existed. Whereas the critics held that society had already been "Judaized," since even Christianity (as then organized) represented the victory of Jewish morality, the conspiracy theorists held that the process of Judaization had not yet been completed. Regardless, both positions held that de-Judaization was still possible, if not morally imperative. Doing so, however, required the adoption of a conscious program designed to remove the Jews from all influential positions in politics, the economy, and culture and to encourage them to emigrate (preferably to Palestine). The creation of such a program itself required that antisemitism become the operative ideology of a government and resulted in the growth of antisemitic political parties as well as the rise of professional antisemitic rabble-rousers.[45]

In Western Europe this antisemitic agitation, although intense at times, did not turn especially violent and emphasized emigration and the creation of a "new" ghetto instead. In Czarist Russia, however, the new antisemitism did turn violent, especially during the years of upheaval after the assassination of Czar Alexander II (1881) and after the Russo-Japanese War (1903–1905). In both cases pogroms broke out. In addition, the process of scapegoating may be seen in Russia, especially in the 1911 Beilis trial. Not unlike the Dreyfus trial, this was a case of the conscious distortion of justice. Mendel Beilis, a Jewish factory worker in Kiev, was accused of ritual murder when a young Christian boy was found killed. Eschewing a proper investigation, the local police authorities on orders from the Interior Ministry arrested Beilis and soon placed him on trial. Almost immediately the show-trial nature of the Beilis case became obvious, with the Russian prosecutors attempting to prove the truth of the traditional antisemitic accusation that Jews use the blood of Christians in the process of baking *matzot*. As with the Dreyfus trial, the Beilis case ended with the accused being cleared of all charges.[46]

Thus, in the modern era, antisemitic rhetoric became secularized. No longer a matter of religious intolerance, the European Jewish problem was one of race and nationality. Raul

Hilberg summarized this process succinctly by noting that in Christian Europe Jews were told, "You cannot live among us as Jews;" in nineteenth century Europe they were told, "You cannot live among us;" and in Nazi Europe the Jews were told, "You cannot live."[47] However, a common denominator remained: As it had been for nearly seven hundred years, the antisemites' motto remained, "Die Juden sind unser Unglück" (The Jews are our misfortune). Heinrich von Treitschke's phrase found an echo in almost every country in and outside of Europe. Jews were seen as the root of all evil and, therefore, had to be fought with every possible weapon. Moreover, the secularization of antisemitism meant that the last support system was lost: Jews could no longer have the option of conversion; there could no longer be any escape for the Jewish masses on any grounds. Antisemitism sought a Final Solution.

Jewish Responses to Antisemitism

Under the circumstances, Jews were forced to respond to an ever-increasing crescendo of antisemitic voices. It would, however, be a mistake to conclude that the Jewish community was besieged and that, logically, no solution short of mass evacuation existed. Such was not the case, although distressed East European Jews turned to mass emigration: Between 1881 and 1914 more than 2 million Jews emigrated to Western Europe, the Americas, and Eretz-Israel.[48]

In general, Jews responded to the crisis in one of four ways. In Germany, France, Great Britain, and the United States, Jews tried to assimilate into their surroundings by abandoning the distinctive cultural and religious traits that were identified with Jewishness. Rather than identifying as Jews, these assimilators preferred to be citizens of the Mosaic faith or, at best, Israelites, and they denied any political or social connection between Jews living in different countries. Judaism, according to them, was only a religious community with no political

overtones; there could be no world Jewish conspiracy since world Jewry did not exist.[49]

Although there were Jews who advocated assimilation into the Eastern European environment, their efforts were doomed to failure by the czarist governmental policy. Unwilling to permit Jews to live in Russia as Jews, the czarist autocracy also was unwilling to take the steps necessary to assimilate Jews. The result was a policy of brutal and violent repression coupled with scapegoating. Rather than emphasize emancipation and assimilation, the three movements that became dominant in Eastern Europe emphasized self-emancipation and Jewish identification: Folkism, Bundism, and Zionism.

The ideology of Folkism, developed in large part by the historian Simon Dubnow, may be summarized as follows: Jews, according to Dubnow, are indeed a nation and all Jews are connected by bonds of nationality. However, Jews are a spiritual nation and their national consciousness requires no specific territory. The upshot of Dubnow's position, a form of diaspora nationalism, was to emphasize the need for Jews to reorganize their communal structure on a regional and international scale while also attaining recognition of Jewry's right to cultural autonomy in Eastern Europe.[50]

Whereas Folkism had no specific economic agenda, Bundism was a form of Jewish revolutionary socialist nationalism. Although the early founders of the Bund thought that Jewish nationalism was transitory in nature and that Jews were fated to assimilate out of existence after the advent of socialism, by the late 1890s most Bundists had adopted a position of unqualified advocacy of their form of diaspora nationalism. According to the Bundists, Jews are a nation whose destiny is to be an ever-present minority in European society. Cultural and communal autonomy — the centerpiece of the Folkist agenda — would be necessary to guarantee Jewish national self-expression; however, true justice for the Jews could be attained only by overthrowing the capitalist system and replacing it with the type of socialist society predicted by Karl Marx. The Bund, therefore, exerted much of its energy on preparing Jews for revolutionary activity.

Nevertheless, there were two potential inconsistencies to the Bundist approach; neither of them was apparent in the 1890s, and the second became clear only considerably later. First was the issue of how other socialists responded to Jewish requests for autonomy. In August 1903, a meeting of the Central Committee of the All-Russian Social Democratic Party (held in Brussels) rejected requests for autonomy from the Poles and the Bund, meaning that for the foreseeable future the main nationalist part of the Bundist agenda was unattainable even under the best circumstances. Second, and even more basic to the problem posed by Bundist ideology, was the tension between nationalism and socialism that derived from the fact that a nationalist party must represent all elements of the national group, irrespective of their class consciousness. As a socialist revolutionary party, however, the Bund was committed to a policy of class warfare and the overthrow of all capitalists. Left unstated was the Bund's attitude toward Jewish capitalists, although the problem would not become apparent until after the 1917 Bolshevik Revolution in Russia. In 1917 many Bundists defected to the ranks of the victorious Communist Party and abandoned all pretense of a nationalistic orientation.[51]

In contrast to both the Folkists and the Bundists, who retained a primary Jewish presence in the diaspora, Zionists despaired of a diaspora foundation for the Jewish people. Based on the premise that Jews form a single nation and that a territorial base was needed to anchor world Jewry, Zionism set as its goal the creation of a renewed Jewish society in Palestine, Jewry's ancestral homeland. To be sure, Zionism was not a monolithic ideology, although all Zionists agreed on basic principles. Beyond that, issues including religion, cultural orientation, political activism, and economics divided Zionists into a multiplicity of political parties that often competed against one another in violent terms. Such disputes notwithstanding, Zionism did represent the movement for Jewish national rebirth and offered a clear solution to two distinct problems — that of Jews seeking a safe haven and that of Judaism seeking an accommodation with current modes of thought.[52]

Zionism could not, however, offer an immediate solution to Jewish distress for two reasons: Jews represented a minority of Palestine's population and Zionism could not, initially, sway even a plurality of the diaspora Jewish communities. To many European Jews, Zionist goals seemed a dream that could never be fulfilled. Furthermore, although antisemitic agitators sought to besiege European Jewry, as long as society remained stable, their rabble-rousing was held in check. Indeed, the German anti-semitic political parties — established with much fanfare in the 1890s — were resoundingly defeated in 1906.[53] Thus, there appeared no need for mass Jewish evacuation, even from Eastern Europe. Only developments after World War I would radically change conditions for the Jewries of Eastern Europe that, in 1939, numbered two-thirds of world Jewry.

Notes

1. Haim H. Ben-Sasson, פרקים בתולדות היהודים בימי הביניים (Chapters in the history of the Jewish people in the Middle Ages), Tel Aviv: Am Oved, 1962, ch. 1.

2. Léon Poliakov, *The History of Antisemitism*, New York: Schocken Books, 1974, vol. 1, pts. 2–3.

3. Ben-Sasson, פרקים, ch. 5–8.

4. Cecil Roth, *A History of the Marranos*, New York: Meridian Books, 1959, ch. 1, 7.

5. Bernard D. Weinryb, *The Jews of Poland*, Philadelphia: JPS, 1973, ch. 9–10, Gershom Scholem, "Redemption Through Sin," in his *The Messianic Idea in Judaism*, New York: Schocken Books, 1971, pp. 78–141.

6. For the ideological history of Hasidism, see G. Scholem, "The Neutralization of the Messianic Element in Early Hasidism," and "*Devekut*, or Communion with God," in *Messianic Idea*, pp. 176–227, Samuel H. Dresner, *The Zaddik*, New York: Schocken Books, 1960, ch. 1; regarding the spread of Hasidism and its history after 1800, see Jacob S. Minkin, *The Romance of Hasidism*, New York: Macmillan, 1935.

7. Cf. Gedalia Alon, "Yeshivot Lita," in מחקרים בתולדות ישראל (Studies in Jewish history), Tel Aviv: Hakibbutz Hameuchad, 1973, pp. 1–11.

8. Roth, *Marranos*, ch. 8–11.

9. Meir J. Benardete, *Hispanic Culture and the Character of the Sephardi Jews*, New York: Sepher-Hermon Press, 1982; Daniel J. Elazar, *The Other Jews*, New York: Basic Books, 1989, ch. 1.

10. Cf. Howard M. Sachar, *The Course of Modern Jewish History*, New York: Dell, 1977, ch. 1–2.

11. Arthur Hertzberg, *The French Enlightenment and the Jews*, New York: Columbia University Press, 1968, ch. 4.

12. Cf. Michael A. Meyer, *The Origins of the Modern Jew*, Detroit: Wayne State University Press, 1979, ch 1–2.

13. Sachar, *Course*, ch. 3, 5–6.

14. On this aspect of the emancipation, a statement by Stanislaus de Clermont-Tonnerre has often been quoted: "All should be refused the Jews as a nation, but everything granted to them as individuals." Hertzberg, *French Enlightenment*, p. 360.

15. Joseph L. Blau, *Modern Varieties of Judaism*, New York: Columbia University Press, 1964.

16. Morris R. Cohen, "Philosophies of Jewish History," *Jewish Social Studies* [hereafter *JSS*], vol. 1 (1939), 39–72.

17. Philip Friedman, "Polish Jewish Historiography Between the Two Wars, 1918–1939," *JSS*, vol. 11 (1949), 373–408.

18. Israel Zinberg, *A History of Jewish Literature*, New York: Ktav, 1978, vols. 11–12.

19. Jacob R. Marcus, *The Rise and Destiny of the German Jew*, reprint ed., New York: Ktav, 1973, pp. 106–120; 325.

20. Ibid. ch. 9.

21. Ibid. ch. 7.

22. George L. Mosse, *German Jews Beyond Judaism*, Bloomington: Indiana University Press, 1985.

23. Werner E. Mosse, "Problems and Limits of Assimilation: Hermann and Paul Wallich, 1833–1938," *Leo Baeck Institute Yearbook* [hereafter *LBIYB*], vol. 33 (1988), 43–65.

24. Ibid. pp. 57–58.

25. Cf. Hannah Arendt, "The Jew as Pariah: A Hidden Tradition," *JSS*, vol. 6 # 2 (1944), 99–122; and Werner Jochmann, "The Jews and German Society in the Imperial Era," *LBIYB*, vol. 20 (1975), 5–11.

26. Cf. Louis Greenberg, *The Jews in Russia: The Struggle for Emancipation*, New York: Schocken Books, 1976, vol. 1, ch. 3.

27. John Stanley, "The Politics of the Jewish Question in the Duchy of Warsaw, 1807–1813," *JSS*, vol. 44 (1982), 47–62.

28. Greenberg, *Jews in Russia*, vol. 2, ch. 2.

29. Mark Wischnitzer, *To Dwell in Freedom*, Philadelphia: JPS, 1948, ch. 2–4. It may be useful to note, however, that the new immigrants were not always perceived in a positive light. See Steven Ascheim, *Brothers and Strangers: The East European Jews in German Jewish Consciousness*, Madison: University of Wisconsin Press, 1982.

30. See the documents cited in Arthur Hertzberg (ed.), *The Zionist Idea*, New York: Atheneum, 1976, pp. 142–198.

31. Hannah Arendt, *The Origins of Totalitarianism*, new ed., New York: Harcourt, Brace, and Jovanovich, 1973, ch. 2–3.

32. Cf. Eugen Weber and Hans Rogger (eds.), *The European Right*, Berkeley: University of California Press, 1965, pp. 1–28, 575–589; J. L. Talmon, *Political Messianism: The Romantic Phase*, Boulder, CO: Westview Press, 1985, pt. 2.

33. Cf. Fritz Stern, *The Politics of Cultural Despair*, Berkeley: University of California Press, 1961, pp. xi–xxx; Hajo Holborn, *A History of Modern Germany, 1840-1945*, Princeton: Princeton University Press, 1969, ch. 6–8.

34. Stern, *Cultural Despair*, ch. 1–2, 7, 11.

35. For political conditions in France at the turn of the century, see Eugen Weber, *Action Française*, Stanford: Stanford University Press, 1962, pp. 1–88.

36. Norman Finkelstein, *Captain of Innocence: France and the Dreyfus Affair*, New York: Putnam, 1991, is the most recent complete account of the affair and its implications.

37. cf Arendt, *Origins*, ch. 5.

38. George L. Mosse, *Toward the Final Solution: A History of European Racism*, New York: Harper Colophon Books, 1978, ch. 6–8.

39. For a general survey of medieval antisemitism, see Poliakov, *History of Antisemitism*; for the origins of Chrisitian antisemitism, see James Parkes, *The Conflict of Church and Synagogue*, New York: Atheneum, 1974, pp. 371–378.

40. Guido Kisch, *The Jews in Medieval Germany: A Study of their Legal and Social Standing*, New York: Ktav, 1970, pp. 145–153.

41. Cf. Joshua Trachtenberg, *The Devil and the Jews: The Medieval Conception of the Jew and Its Relation to Modern Antisemitism*, Philadelphia: JPS, 1961, pt. 1.

42. Ibid., ch. 7-10.

43. Luther is quoted in Poliakov, *History of Antisemitism*, pp. 216–226.

44. Norman Cohn, *Warrant for Genocide*, New York: Harper and Row, 1966.

45. Peter Pulzer, *The Rise of Political Antisemitism in Germany and Austria*, rev. ed., Cambridge: Harvard University Press, 1988.

46. Cf. Maurice Samuel, *Blood Accusation*, New York: Knopf, 1966.

47. Raul Hilberg, *The Destruction of the European Jews*, student ed., New York: Holmes and Meier, 1986, pp. 3–4.

48. Wischnitzer, *Dwell in Freedom*, app. 1 and 2, pp. 288–296.

49. Cf. Rubin Gotesky, "Assimilationism," in Feliks Gross and Basil Vlavianos (eds.), *Struggle for Tomorrow: Modern Political Ideologies of the Jewish People*, New York: Arts, Inc., 1954, pp. 215–231.

50. Cf. Koppel S. Pinson's introductory notes to Simon Dubnow, *Nationalism and History: Essays on the Old and New Judaism*, Philadelphia: JPS, 1958, pp. 40–65.

51. A general review of Bund ideology is Emanuel Scherer, "Bundism," in Gross and Vlavianos, *Struggle for Tomorrow*, pp. 135–196; cf. Nora Levin, *While Messiah Tarried: Jewish Socialist Movements, 1871–1917*, New York: Schocken Books, 1977.

52. David Vital, *The Origins of Zionism*, New York: Oxford University Press, 1975.

53. Richard S. Levy, *The Downfall of the Antisemitic Political Parties in Imperial Germany*, New Haven: Yale University Press, 1975, ch. 9.

2

WORLD WAR I
AND ITS AFTERMATH

World War I

The international system based on mutual fears and suspicions that derived from unchecked ultranationalism could not function forever. By 1900 rival imperial claims in Africa and Asia, economic competition, and political conflict in Europe had divided the continent into two rival armed camps: the Central Powers (Austria-Hungary, Germany, and Ottoman Turkey) and the Triple Entente (France, Great Britain, and Russia). Nevertheless, peace in Europe allowed for the outward facade of stability.[1] Only the Russo-Japanese War (1903–1905) broke this pattern. An abortive revolutionary upheaval, born in defeat, further weakened the czarist autarchy, although in the end the principle of absolutist monarchy was upheld for the time being. No other European state suffered so much turmoil as Russia did, although again it must be emphasized that in most cases stability was just a facade.[2]

World War I changed the situation entirely. It has been said that no war has ever been as long expected as World War I. Yet, at the same time no war has ever caught the combatants as unprepared over the long run as World War I. On a number of occasions between 1890 and 1914, war appeared imminent. Therefore, all the European powers took the precaution of maintaining massive military capabilities, which resulted in an arms race of then-astronomical proportions. The economic strain of such a system would have been enormous, however, and almost every country relied on a reserve force of trained men — conscription being mandatory in all European states but Great Britain — who would be called to the colors in an emergency (often by telegraph). As was to be proved in 1914, however, this system of rapid deployment via road and rail had one flaw: Once deployed, the army could not demobilize without threatening national security, because no reserve existed. Deployment, therefore, virtually sealed the fate of the soldiery; only a short war would prevent chaos. Yet, although each of the European armies prepared for a short war, new weapons technology made a long, drawn-out conflict likely. Germany deployed more that 1,300,000 troops on the Western Front alone; these faced slightly more than 1,000,000 French troops, the entire Belgian army, and the British Expeditionary Force.

The immediate cause of long-awaited war was the assassination of Austrian Archduke Francis Ferdinand and his wife, Sofie, by Gabriel Princip — a Serbian nationalist — on June 28, 1914. The Austrians, who suspected that Serbian intelligence officers were involved, demanded revenge. A diplomatic impasse ensued, with each side preparing for the worst. Austria-Hungary declared war on Serbia on July 28, and within a week almost all of Europe became involved. The Germans pursued a pre-existing strategy, the so-called Schlieffen Plan, designed to defeat France in a rapid campaign before Russia could fully deploy its military might. The Schliefen Plan, however, required traversing Belgium, which was invaded by German armies on August 4. Britain, which had guaranteed the territorial integrity of Belgium, was thus drawn into a war that was clearly avoidable.[3]

World War I, was the largest European war since the days of Bonaparte. Fought not only on land but also on the sea and in the air, it was the deadliest war of its time: Ten million soldiers perished in the trenches and battlefields. In the trench warfare that followed a brief mobile phase, both sides suffered grievous losses in futile frontal assaults. Thereafter, in 1915 and 1916, machine guns, artillery, barbed wire, and poison gas ruled an essentially deadlocked battlefield. By 1917 both sides had attempted every possible gimmick: naval blockade, unrestricted submarine warfare, and aerial bombing.[4] Then too, new fronts were opened. Italy joined the Entente in 1915, attacking its former allies in an attempt to retrieve Trieste, Fiume, and other parts of *Italia Irredenta*. The Italians were hampered, however, by the poor state of communications in the Alpine front, by poor leadership, and by an army not fully prepared for war. Stalemate soon occurred on both the Southern and the Western fronts. A British attempt to outflank the Central Powers by invading Turkey (which also would provide a supply route to Russia) failed in the crucible of the battle of Gallipoli. Although both sides were nearing exhaustion, the war continued and became more bloody. As 1917 began, the military situation remained deadlocked. In April the United States joined the Entente, goaded on by the Germans' renewal of unrestricted submarine warfare.[5]

The Armenian Massacres

World War I also witnessed the first modern act of genocide.[6] Turkey was in a state of disarray well before joining the war as an ally of the Central Powers. Nationalist agitators of various stripes had been advocating dismantling the Ottoman Empire from the 1840s on. The Turks had resisted these centrifugal forces to the best of their ability, in an attempt to maintain the empire's territorial integrity. Beginning in 1890, however, an active nationalist movement in Anatolia seemed to threaten Turkey itself: The Armenians, a highly urbanized, Christian minority living on the borderlands between the Ottoman and Russian empires, demanded autonomy. Given the Armenians' role in Turkish trade and retail, in addition to the fact that Armenia was located on the border, the Turks rejected all demands that appeared to tear Armenia away from the rest of Turkey.

Imperial forces and even the Young Turks, who took over the reins of government in 1908, sought to fight the perceived Armenian menace. In 1894 nearly 20,000 Armenians were murdered by Turkish troops in Sassun, Turkey. Turkish pressure on the Armenians increased after 1913, when Russia declared its intention to act as the protector of this persecuted minority.[7] In turn, the Turkish authorities concluded that only the extermination of the Armenians could save Turkey. In February 1915, therefore, the Young Turk movement (known as the Jemiyet) decided "to exterminate all Armenians living in Turkey, without allowing a single one to remain alive and to this end [gave] the government extensive authority."[8]

Two months later, systematic measures began with the disarming, segregation, and execution of all Armenian troops in the Turkish army. In village after village, prominent Armenians, along with the young and healthy, were arrested and shot. Finally, a series of forced marches into the desert resulted in the mass deaths of the old, the young, and the women. Only conversion to Islam offered a slim possibility of survival. The few able to survive by their own wits often succumbed to attacks by marauding tribesmen, who sought booty.

Estimates of the number of victims vary, but it is clear that at least 1 million Armenians perished as a direct result of Turkish persecution during World War I. In its defense, the Turkish government declared that the Armenians were plotting with the Russians to dismember Turkey. Armenian acts of self-defense and the actions of a few Armenian hotheads were exaggerated as further evidence of an immediate threat, although even Turkey's German and Austrian allies recognized these arguments as specious. In reality, the Turks defined all Armenians as "the enemy" because they were Armenians.[9]

The Armenian massacres represented a watershed: A perceived enemy of the state could easily be isolated, rendered defenseless, and ultimately destroyed. Ultranationalism and its concomitant belief that any act undertaken on behalf of the organic integrity of the nation was justified had reached their ultimate development: An ethnic minority that was "inconvenient" could henceforth be demonized, isolated, and then destroyed. Adolf Hitler himself expressed an understanding of these implications when, in reference to his plans for mass eugenic genocide in Europe, he asked rhetorically, "Who today speaks of the annihilation of the Armenians?"[10] Still, there was a difference between this case of genocide and the later Nazi attempt to exterminate European Jewry: Armenians could save their lives by conversion to Islam. Nevertheless, although not a case of total annihilation, the Armenian massacres were a precedent for further acts of genocide in the twentieth century.

The Politics of War and Peace

While the war remained stalemated on the fronts, events of long-term importance transpired in Russia. On March 17, 1917, Czar Nicholas II abdicated as a result of food riots in Russia's major cities; overnight, Russia became a democratic state led by a provisional government under Alexander Kerensky. Kerensky attempted to transform Russia into a Western-style democracy while the country remained in the war. Those goals proved incompatible. Finally, in October (actually November, since the Russians still used the Gregorian calendar) the Bolsheviks, led by Vladimir I. Lenin,

seized power. In creating a one-party state based on his interpretation of Marxism, Lenin was faced with numerous problems — civil war at home, continued fighting against the Germans, and an economy that had been reduced to shambles. In response, Lenin withdrew from the war against Germany, preferring to concentrate on his internal foes, and surrendered a large mass of territory to the Germans in the Treaty of Brest-Litovsk. For the next two years the Red Army, led by Leon Trotsky, fought the White counterrevolutionaries, finally emerging victorious at the end of 1919. The country was not fully under control until the early 1920s, by which time Lenin had already created the institutions of a vast police state; these institutions would later form the core of Joseph Stalin's terror apparatus and are one of the more unfortunate parts of the Leninist legacy.[11]

The entry of the United States into the war, along with the increasingly successful Allied blockade of Germany, finally brought the Central Powers to a submissive stance. On November 11, 1918, the guns fell silent: An armistice was signed that brought World War I to a military close, although peace negotiations took close to a year to complete. The war had been devastating. In addition to direct military casualties, many civilian losses also occurred. The economic life of virtually every country in Western and Central Europe was shattered. Morale also was shattered among both the victors and the vanquished. More than anything else, World War I destroyed the Old World while also destroying the sense of optimism that had characterized European thought during the nineteenth century.[12]

Nevertheless, a veneer of the old world order remained, at least for public consumption. When the United States entered the war in April 1917, it officially did so only in response to German aggression as represented by the resumption of unrestricted submarine warfare. Additionally, U.S. President Woodrow Wilson sought to give the war a moral meaning. In his declaration of war, Wilson elucidated the Fourteen Points for which the United States was going to war, all of which fit under the general rubric of "making the world safe for democracy."[13] In general, these points called for a fair peace as well as a solution to the nationalities problem in Eastern Europe. Interested in gaining U.S. support, the Entente powers all officially accepted the Fourteen Points, although in practice they intended to undermine many (if not all) of Wilson's idealistic pronouncements. The Germans believed that Wilson's Fourteen Points were a fair basis for negotiations and hoped to gain some advantages from Allied idealism.

In 1919 peace negotiations began in Versailles, France. French intention for revenge, in addition to the narrow self-interests of each Allied state, all of which pressed their demands to the maximum, rendered Wilson's hope for a fair peace based on his Fourteen Points meaningless.[14] Instead of a peace without territorial gains, France demanded the return of Alsace-Lorraine, Italy demanded Tyrol and other territories, and Britain seized Germany's African colonies. Moreover, Germany was forced to accept the premise of its war guilt, was saddled with demands for reparations, and was obliged to considerably curtail its armed forces. The German army was to include only 100,000 troops, with no tanks, heavy guns, or aircraft. The German navy was to be reduced similarly to simply a coastal defense force with no battleships and no submarines.[15]

Naturally, many Germans saw the Treaty of Versailles as grossly unfair. Those who opposed the treaty viewed it as a betrayal, seeing the German signatories as traitors who had stabbed Germany in the back.[16] In particular, the defeat was blamed on Jews, Communists, and pacifists, who imposed their will on Germany to the detriment of German national interests.

The only small consolation that could be drawn from the treaty was the creation of the League of Nations. The League was based on the idea of collective security, and its proponents hoped to use negotiations and legal action to defuse conflicts, avoid war, and deter aggression. The League had no real power, however. Although many countries joined the League, others,

including the United States, declined to do so. Then too, the League assembly had no means to enforce its decisions: The League charter left no possibility of mobilizing forces to prevent, quell, or (at the least) mitigate wars. Only voluntary economic sanctions could be invoked by member states. As a result, the League had no power to impose its will on rogue members — for instance, on Italy for its 1935 invasion of Ethiopia. If only for those reasons, the League was to prove a disappointment for its supporters and, with only a few notable exceptions, failed at its primary international tasks.[17]

The Successor States

World War I swept away three mighty empires. In place of the Romanovs, Habsburgs, and Hohenzollerns, smaller successor states arose — less powerful, less secure, all trying to cope with the vacuum in the balance of power, massive debts, and demoralized populations. No economy was secure, no state safe from a putsch. Almost all turned to the Right for solutions to their national problems.

After a century of foreign occupation, Poland was reborn, and Yugoslavia, Czechoslovakia, Latvia, Lithuania, and Estonia all gained independence under the terms of the Treaty of Versailles. These states shared common goals and problems. All were in favor of the maintenance of the status quo through restoring the balance of power and collective security. All these states had border disputes with their larger neighbors as well as with each other. All were saddled with huge national minorities problems, which presented the threat of foreign subversion through the "fifth column." Only in Czechoslovakia did a semblance of democracy thrive.[18]

In each of the other successor states, social, economic, and political conditions that discouraged democracy and encouraged autocratic forms of government prevailed. The Polish case is instructive. Reborn in 1919, Poland began its period of renewed sovereignty with a democratic constitution and with all the institutions of parliamentary democracy. Wars fought

Europe After World War I
Authors' Collection

against Ukrainian revolutionaries and the Soviet Union almost immediately undermined the central government's authority. Although Poland stabilized after the wars, the country remained fractured and political conditions worsened. In 1926 Marshal Jozef Pilsudski, one of the founders of modern Poland, took matters into his own hands, leading a *coup d'état* that effectively ended democratic government in Poland.[19] After Pilsudski's death in 1935, the regime adopted overtly authoritarian forms, becoming a military dictatorship that leaned toward fascism.[20]

Similar scenarios occurred in other Eastern European states including Yugoslavia — which was deeply divided between Serbs and Croats — Romania, and Hungary. The latter two states were ruled for all or part of the 1930s by Fascist governments. In both cases authoritarian governments arose out of the exigencies of failed royalism: Petty monarchs gave way to even pettier dictators, such as Hungary's Miklos Horthy and Romania's Alexandru Cuza and Octavian Goga.[21]

The Soviet Union, born in the throes of the collapse of the Romanov empire, the creation of a provisional government, and the subsequent Bolshevik *coup d'état*, faced many problems that were similar to those of the successor states. Economic recovery was a foremost priority and led Lenin to advocate a temporary step back from pure communism, the New Economic Program (NEP). NEP permitted a limited amount of profit taking by industrial managers, thus giving them an incentive to operate their factories in an efficient manner. It is clear that the NEP was planned as only a temporary gesture, even though Lenin died before ending it. Stalin, who succeeded Lenin in 1928, built on the police state that Lenin had created, abandoning NEP and embarking on a program of forced collectivization and industrial development. Resistance was met with the means of a modern totalitarian dictatorship. In the Ukraine, for example, food supplies were cut off to break resistance to collectivization; in the interim

millions of innocents died or were murdered by the secret police. Although not Fascist in the traditional sense of the term, the Leninist-Stalinist Soviet Union developed beyond Czarist authoritarianism into a totalitarian state that, in many ways, paralleled Nazi Germany and Fascist Italy.[22]

East European Jewry on the Brink

In each of the successor states a Jewish problem existed to one degree or another. Again, the Polish example is indicative. Violent antisemitism was most prevalent in Poland, which also had the largest Jewish population in Europe (3.5 million). Both organized pogroms and random attacks on Jews were relatively common, as were political, religious, and economic discrimination. In general, four eras of Polish-Jewish relations in the interwar period are discernible: During the first era, between 1919 and 1922, in the immediate aftermath of the founding of the Polish republic, Jews suffered from considerable physical violence that derived in large part from unstable conditions in the country. In the second era, between 1922 and 1925, the years of the "Sejmocracy," anti-Jewish violence abated slightly. Nevertheless, Jews found numerous obstacles placed in the path of full citizenship by an unfriendly Polish government that sought to limit the role of national minorities. In this era Jewish suffering was primarily economic, since the government sought to eliminate Jews — by direct or indirect means — from the economic life of the country. The third era, between 1925 and 1935, for the most part, the years after Pilsudski's coup, represented a respite from public manifestations of antisemitism — reflected in a reduction in pogroms and swift police action to quell anti-Jewish violence — but the respite did not improve the socioeconomic position of Polish Jewry.[23]

The fourth era began after Pilsudski's death in 1935, when the reins of power were taken over by a troika — President Ignacy Mościcki, Marshal Edward Rydz-Śmigly, and Foreign Minister Józef Beck — and continued until the outbreak of World War II. In this era Polish

Scenes of Jewish life in a small *shtetl* in Poland on the eve of World War II
Authors' Collection

Jewry was besieged. In almost every sphere, the government, its supporters of the Sanacja movement ("Recuperation," a term coined by Pilsudski, when, after the coup, he established a military regime and named himself minister of defense, but used to signify the colonels' clique that held the actual power and operated behind the scenes), and the nationalist opposition — primarily the National Democracy Party, the Narodowa Demokracja (Endecja), better known as Endeks — operated from a clearly antisemitic program. Only the small Polish Socialist movement defended the Jews, whenever possible.[24] In this period Jewish economic life was systematically undercut; Jews were treated as second-class citizens; their political rights were ignored; and the minority treaties were reduced to a sham. Whether the issue was the anti-*shechita* (ritual slaughter) bill of 1937 or "ghetto benches" in universities, the Poles pursued one policy: "Rzeczypospolita Polska dla Polakow, Żydzi do Palestini" (Poland for Poles, Jews to Palestine).

This last point must be remembered, for Polish antisemitic policy had an ironic sidelight: Poland was one of the staunchest supporters of the Jewish national home — the Yishuv represented a potential target for Jewish emigration and for Polish exports — and of Jewish migrationy rights throughout the world. In both cases, Polish support for Jewish rights derived from the hope to increase Jewish emigration.[25] Furthermore, Polish antisemitism derived not from racist considerations, but from nationalistic and religious ones. Thus, August Cardinal Hlond, the Primate of Poland, issued a pastoral letter on February 29, 1936 that read in part:

A Jewish problem exists, and will continue to exist as long as Jews remain Jews. . . . One does well to prefer his own kind in commercial dealings and to avoid Jewish stores and Jewish stalls in the markets. . . One ought to fence oneself off against the harmful moral influences of Jewry, to separate oneself against its anti-Christian

culture, and especially to boycott the Jewish press and the demoralizing Jewish publications.[26]

A similar problem arose in Lithuania, although there the economic and social pressures made antisemitic sentiments less direct. However, Lithuanians saw Jews as a Polonizing group and especially blamed the Jews for Poland's seizure of Vilna in 1926.[27] In both Czechoslovakia and Yugoslavia, Jews found themselves caught between two rival ethnic groups vying for control of the state. The stability of Czech democracy and the personal goodwill of President Tomas G. Masaryk kept antisemitism in check. Antisemitic feelings did exist, however, and were particularly strong in Slovakia. Jews were much less secure in Yugoslavia, where they were caught between Serbs and Croats. Both ethnic groups viewed Jews as an untrustworthy element, and both were willing to eliminate their Jews at the proper moment.[28]

Hungarian and Romanian Jewry also found themselves besieged. The Hungarian Jewish problem may be dated to the White Terror that followed the fall of Bela Kuhn's abortive Communist state. To be sure, antisemitism had existed in nineteenth century-Hungary — as it had throughout Central Europe — but had been more muted. After 1920, however, the Hungarian elite held Jews to be collectively guilty of treason because of the acts of one man who was only marginally Jewish.[29] Conditions in Romania were much the same, but they derived from factors that existed well before World War I. When the Congress of Berlin created Romania in 1878, the new state was forced to guarantee the civil rights of Jews. From that time on, however, the government sought to limit Jewish rights — which were seen as deriving from foreign intrusions upon Romanian sovereignty.[30] Conditions for Jews in Romania worsened after World War I and became especially difficult with the rise of the Garda de Fier government, led by Octavian Goga, in December 1937.[31]

Even in the Soviet Union, dedicated to creating a classless, international society, the fate of Jews was paradoxical. During the 1920s the USSR was the only country in which antisemitism was outlawed. Yet, Joseph Stalin had a deep antipathy to Jews — many of whom formed a loyal opposition to his positions in the Communist Party — that would become more pronounced during the 1930s and 1940s. Overall, the Jewish situation was based on a paradox: outward manifestations of anti-Jewish bias ceased, but the Jewish community was rendered less secure than it had been before the revolutions. Thus, for example, all restrictions on Jewish residency rights and employment opportunities — which had existed during the czarist regime — were removed. Simultaneously, all traces of an independent Jewish community were also eliminated. Jews, Stalin had long argued, were fated to assimilate out of existence and ought to be encouraged to do so. Any manifestation of Jewish nationalism, especially Zionism, was to be strongly discouraged. Here too, the paradox is clear: In seeking to uproot Zionism, Stalin offered the Jews an alternate Zion in the form of the Birobidjzhan Jewish Autonomous Region. Nevertheless, by decade's end Birobidjzhan was Jewish in name only; the majority of Soviet Jewry continued to reside in the European segments of the country, principally in the Ukraine, Crimea, and Belorussia.[32]

Efforts to guarantee Jewish rights by international agreement met with only partial success. Following up on the legal formula established at the Congress of Berlin, the League of Nations induced most of the successor states to sign national minorities treaties. In theory, the treaties guaranteed the civil rights of all national minorities. Theory did not always accord with practice, however. Each of the successor states sought to limit international intrusions into "internal affairs" while also undermining the terms of the treaties. The Poles, for example, succeeded in undercutting some aspects of the treaty by holding census counts on Saturdays. Since a majority of Polish Jews would neither write nor answer family-related questions on the Sabbath, there was an undercount of the Jewish population. As a result, the Polish government could "legitimately" set aside less money for Jewish schools or communal institutions.[33]

The national minorities treaties thus were, much like other aspects of the League of Nations, a noble experiment doomed to failure. East European Jewry survived a series of social, political, and economic crises during the 1920s and entered the 1930s largely beleaguered, possessing few avenues of possible escape, and supported by virtually no allies. Already in 1933 Yitzhak Ben-Zvi, one of the leaders of the Labor Zionist movement in Palestine, stated that "Jewish distress [in Eastern Europe] was reaching much the same proportions as that in Germany."[34]

From Ultranationalism to Fascism

Although the experience of the successor states may offer the impression of a continuous political crisis — an impression that is largely (but not completely) accurate — the crisis was not limited to Eastern Europe. Many countries, including the United States, France, and Great Britain, began the process of slow but steady arms reduction. It seemed that stability had returned and with it the facade of civility that had been lost during the war. The United States, for example, "returned to normality" after its brief experience as a key player in international affairs. Although leaders were still interested in economic trends throughout the globe, the general mood favored isolationism and uninterest in other peoples' politics. Great Britain and France, too, again focused on their imperial concerns, although France also maintained a watchful eye on Germany. Many French citizens were appalled at the thought that a new war might break out, and fear led to paralysis so that, in the mid-1920s the French no longer acted but rather reacted to events in other countries. Then too, many voices argued for the purge of foreign elements — mainly Jews — from the French body in order to restore the nation to its vigor. Economic weakness, political collapse, war weariness, and a general malaise turned the 1920s into the aptly nicknamed "devil's decade" and created a field ripe for agitators and rabble-rousers in the 1930s.

Italy emerged from World War I in less than satisfactory condition both economically and politically. The Risorgimento (revival), completed in 1870, had not solved all of Italy's manifold economic and social problems. Whereas many nationalists had hoped that unification would restore Italy's greatness, in reality, the country was riven by deep divisions: between North and South, between Liberals and Conservatives, and between rich and poor. The feeling that Italy had not yet lived up to its potential was exacerbated by the conviction that Italy should have gained greater compensation for its sacrifices during the war. Many Italian nationalists bridled at the thought that World War I resulted in a "mutilated victory." Those who dreamed of re-creating the great Roman Empire further fanned these flames by their words and their deeds. Moreover, the government appeared unable to cope with all these problems and was accused of being dedicated solely to maintaining power at all costs. As matters became worse, radical politicians increasingly advocated a *coup* to replace the ineffective government.

In 1919 one such group advocating the replacement of the current Italian government crystallized into the Fascist movement, adopting the name Partito Nazionale Fascista (PNF) on November 7, 1921. Combining the muscle of the black-shirted *Squadristi* with the ideological orientation of right-wing Italian intellectuals, the PNF sought to create a new, "corporate" state. Just one year later, the Blackshirts' leader, Benito Mussolini, marched his private army, the Fasci di Combatimento, to Rome. A Socialist until 1915, Mussolini was, with the march on Rome in October 1922, consciously aping Julius Caesar. The immediate result was about the same: Before the Blackshirts reached Rome, the government caved in and Mussolini was appointed prime minister. For the first time a Fascist government took over and began

to rule.[35]

Initially, Mussolini was somewhat successful in creating an effective government. In the long run, however, his use of strong-arm tactics, combined with the Fascist effort to uproot Italy's other traditional centers of power, was not successful. Despite Fascist attempts, Italian society was not fully recast into the totalitarian state that Mussolini hoped to develop.[36] Nevertheless, Mussolini's power base was secure in the 1920s, as was his role in international affairs. Such opposition as existed was swept aside with relative ease. Moreover, Mussolini's Italy became a model for Fascists worldwide, further enhancing Mussolini's prestige.

Mussolini's ideology was, however, at least as important as his actions. Broadly, Mussolini saw fascism as a "third way," one between the polar extremes of capitalism and communism. The goal of "corporatism," was the creation of a centralized nation, more disciplined than a democracy, and revitalized through military vigor and foreign conquests. Centralization was not only a political concept, however; it embraced cultural and economic unification as well. Mussolini described fascism as "form, inner law, and discipline of the whole person." He said, "It permeates the will and intellect."[37] In essence, therefore, Italian fascism emphasized action for action's sake, a doctrine that also animated radical syndicalists and anarchists. Fascism also emphasized history — especially the need for the nation to find its "place in the sun." Finally, Italian fascism saw the state as the all-encompassing entity that gave expression to the organic nation. The Fascist personifies "the nation and patria, moral law which links individuals and generations together in tradition and vocation."[38] In common with other totalitarian movements, Italian fascism developed a leadership cult, centered on Mussolini and expressed in slogans such as "The Duce is always right" and "Believe, obey, fight."

Opposition to fascism — to the movement that declared itself to be the repository of the national will — was thus viewed exclusively as personal egotism and, ultimately, a form of slavery. Fascism sought to fight against and to liberate Italy from this slavery, a philistine attachment to material benefits whose clearest expression was in supposedly democratic structures that benefited only a few vested interests. After the victory of fascism a new Italian empire, greater than even Rome at its height, would arise and bring about the perfection of all aspects of Italian civilization.

Despite Mussolini's use of concepts associated with egotistical nationalism, his seizure of power did not initially alter the status of Italian Jewry. As Europe's oldest Jewish community, Italian Jewry was well integrated into the Italian nation. As a result, antisemitism never became a mass movement in modern Italy and Jews did not become the butt for Italian frustrations. Jews were not turned into the scapegoats for an ill society and were thus able to participate fully in the Fascist movement; many did so, although most remained outside of politics. Until 1938, when his alliance with Nazi Germany brought about an abrupt change in Fascist Jewish policy, Mussolini also played an important role in international Jewish politics. He was seen as a potential counterweight to Britain's colonial government in Palestine and was courted as a potential ally by such Zionist leaders as Chaim Weizmann, Ze'ev Jabotinsky, and Nahum Goldmann.[39]

Although his program was initially somewhat successful, Mussolini's ultimate failure must be scored. Efforts to establish a unitary society were effectively checked by the resilience of social institutions, including the Church and the family, as well as the underdeveloped state of much of the hinterland. Additionally, despite a few successes, the Fascists were unable to overcome the overwhelming importance placed on local and regional loyalties. Unintentionally, therefore, Italians of all political orientations resisted Fascist efforts to create an autarkic state.[40] Nevertheless, only the defeats suffered in World War II eventually drove the Fascists from the reins of government.[41]

The Balfour Declaration and the Mandate

The interwar era also represented an important watershed for Jewry. As World War I spread throughout Europe, Britain was led into a search for new allies to aid in the war against Germany and its allies. In particular, the failure of the Gallipoli operation led to the concern that Britain's position in the Middle East might be in danger. Therefore, Britain entered into secret discussions with the French over partitioning the Ottoman Empire, which culminated in the Sykes-Picot Agreement. The British also sent T. E. Lawrence (Lawrence of Arabia) to stir up an Arab revolt, to weaken Ottoman resistance. To further fan the flames of the revolt, Henry McMahon, British minister resident in Cairo, promised Emir Faisal that Britain would assist in the creation of an Arab state in the Levant. Unfortunately, the British failed to inform the Arab leaders of the agreement with France, even though the idea of an independent Arab state contradicted the planned partition of the Ottoman Empire into British and French zones.[42]

Simultaneously, the British turned to the Jews, hoping to trade support of Zionist goals for the aid of "international Jewry." Accepting the premise that some form of Jewish world government existed — even if it was more benign than antisemites claimed — the British hoped to use Jewish financial power and the Jewish urge to resettle their ancestral homeland as a means of defending the Suez Canal. Representing this new attitude was the Balfour Declaration, issued on November 2, 1917:

His Majesty's Government view with favor the establishment in Palestine of a national home for the Jewish people, and will use their best endeavours to facilitate the achievement of this object, it being clearly understood that nothing shall be done which may prejudice the civil and religious rights of existing non-Jewish communities in Palestine, or the rights and political status enjoyed by Jews in any other country.[43]

With the Balfour Declaration Britain committed itself to help fulfil the Zionist endeavor in Palestine. Again, however, the territory was already promised — or appeared to be promised — to the Arabs as part of the McMahon-Faisal agreement. Thus, in the span of three years, Britain laid the foundations for many of the complexities of the Middle Eastern conflict that continues to plague the world. At the San Remo Conference (1922) the League of Nations granted a Mandate for Palestine to Great Britain; the Mandate recognized that Jews migrating to Palestine did so by right, not by sufferance. These diplomatic developments permitted the creation of a small but vibrant Yishuv, an avant-garde of Jewish nationalism that grew from just under 50,000 in 1914 to 174,610 in 1933.

This growth did not come without resistance, however. In essence, the Arabs attempted to destroy the Jewish national home through local violence. The first Arab riots began in 1921; violence broke out again in 1929, 1930, and 1936. In each case the Arabs used violence to convince the British that continued support for Jewish rights was not cost-effective. The 1929 riots belied the Arab claim that they opposed only Zionists, since the main victims of Arab outrages were anti-Zionist members of Palestine's Ultraorthodox community, primarily in the city of Hebron.

Still, the Yishuv represented the only secure hope for an increasingly insecure European Jewry. Despite its own insecurity, and its weak economy, the Yishuv was a destination for increasing numbers of Jews unable to find a home in an unfriendly European environment. The Yishuv's role as a haven would increase after 1933 and would, by 1948, mean the creation of a sufficiently strong entity that crystallized into the State of Israel.[44]

Notes

1. J. M. Roberts, *Europe 1880–1945*, New York: Holt, Rinehart and Winston, 1967, ch. 8.
2. Barbara Tuchman, *The Proud Tower*, New York: Macmillan, 1966.
3. Roberts, *Europe*, pp. 263–264, 270–284.
4. Ibid., pp. 265–270.
5. Ibid., pp. 285–288, 290–291, 294–303.
6. This section is summarized from Helen Fein, *Accounting for Genocide*, New York: Free Press, 1979, pp. 10–18.
7. Djemal Pasha, *Memoirs of a Turkish Statesman*, London: Hutchinson, 1922, p. 276.
8. Cited in Fein, *Genocide*, p. 15.
9. Fein quoted Talaat Bey, then prime minister of Turkey, saying that even innocent Armenians had to be killed since "those who are innocent today might be guilty tomorrow." Ibid., p. 17.
10. Quoted in Jack N. Porter (ed.), *Genocide and Human Rights: A Global Anthology*, Washington, DC: University Press of America, 1982, p. 98.
11. Cf. Hugh Seton-Watson, *From Lenin to Khrushchev: The History of World Communism*, New York: Praeger, 1960, ch. 2.
12. Roberts, *Europe*, ch. 10–11.
13. The Fourteen Points are cited in full in Louis L. Snyder (ed.), *Fifty Major Documents of the Twentieth Century*, Princeton: Van Nostrand Company, 1955, pp. 26–28.
14. Harold Nicholson, *Peacemaking 1919*, New York: Grosset & Dunlap, 1965, pt. 1.
15. "Extracts from the Treaty of Versailles," in Snyder, *Major Documents*, pp. 44–51.
16. Cf. Gordon A. Craig, *The Politics of the Prussian Army, 1640–1945*, London: Oxford University Press, 1955, pp. 364–381.
17. F. S. Northedge, *The League of Nations: Its Life and Times, 1920–1946*, New York: Holmes and Meier, 1986. It should be noted that the League was not an unequivocal failure; indeed, it did have many successes that were not fully appreciated at the time. However, the League's successes were fleeting, whereas its shortcomings had a more immediate and disastrous impact on European affairs.
18. Hugh Seton-Watson, *The East European Revolution*, London: Methuen, 1961, ch. 1–2.
19. Cf. Richard M. Watt, *Bitter Glory: Poland and Its Fate, 1918–1939*, New York: Simon and Schuster, 1982, ch. 4–10.
20. Ibid., ch. 16.
21. See Seton-Watson, *East European Revolution*, pp. 46–69, and his *Eastern Europe Between the Wars, 1918–1941*, New York: Harper Torchbooks, 1967.
22. Cf. Mikhail Heller and Aleksandr M. Nekrich, *Utopia in Power: The History of the Soviet Union from 1917 to the Present*, New York: Summit Books, 1986, ch. 2–4.
23. Celia Heller, *On the Edge of Destruction*, New York: Schocken Books, 1977, ch. 3–4; Ezra Mendelsohn, *Zionism in Poland*, New Haven: Yale University Press, 1981, ch. 7.
24. Joel Cang, "The Opposition Parties in Poland and Their Attitude Towards the Jews and the Jewish Problem," *JSS*, vol. 1 (1939), 241–257.
25. "Colonies for Poland," *World Review*, vol. 2 (1936), 60–61.
26. Cited from Heller, *Edge of Destruction*, p. 113.
27. Dov Levin, "On the Relations Between the Baltic Peoples and Their Jewish Neighbors Before, During, and After World War II," *Holocaust and Genocide Studies*, vol. 5 (1990), 53–66.
28. On Czechoslovakia see Ezra Mendelsohn, *The Jews of East Central Europe Between the World Wars*, Bloomington: Indiana University Press, 1983, pp. 146–168; on Yugoslavia see Harriet P. Friedenreich, *The Jews of Yugoslavia*, Philadelphia: JPS, 1979.
29. Cf. Nathaniel Katzburg, *Hungary and the Jews, 1920–1943*, Ramat Gan: Bar Ilan University Press, 1981, ch. 2.

30. Mendelsohn, *Jews of East Central Europe*, pp. 183–189, 202–204.

31. Report by Gershom Agronsky, Protocols of the Jewish Agency Executive, January 16, 1938, pp. 1–4. Central Zionist Archives S100/23.

32. Cf. Nora Levin, *The Jews in the Soviet Union Since 1917: The Paradox of Survival*, New York: New York University Press, 1988, vol. 1; and Abraham J. Edelheit, "The Soviet Union, the Jews, and the Holocaust," *Holocaust Studies Annual*, vol. 4 (1990), 113–116.

33. Cf. Oscar I. Janowsky, *The Jews and Minority Rights*, New York: AMS Press, 1966; Nathan Feinberg, האגודות היהודיות למען חבר הלאומים (The Jewish League of Nations Societies), Jerusalem: Magnes Press, 1967, ch. 4.

34. Minutes of an interview between the High Commissioner and Ben-Zvi, September 13, 1933, p. 3. Central Zionist Archive, S25/17/I.

35. F. L. Carsten, *The Rise of Fascism*, Berkeley: University of California Press, 1967, pp. 63–73.

36. Mussolini was one of the first to use the term "totalitarian state." On his use of the term, see ibid., p. 73. On the failure of Italian fascism see Christopher Leeds, *Italy Under Mussolini*, London: Wayland Publishers, 1972, and Alexander DeGrand, "Cracks in the Facade: The Failure of Fascist Totalitarianism in Italy, 1935-1939," *European History Quarterly*, vol. 21 # 4 (1991), 515–535. For a broader analysis of Totalitarianism that also offers a comparison of the three major totalitarian states of the twentieth century, see Carl J. Friedrich, *Totalitarianism in Perspective: Three Views*, New York: Frederick A. Prager, 1969.

37. Benito Mussolini, "Fascismo," *Encyclopedia Italiana*, vol. 14, p. 848A.

38. Ibid., p. 850B. Cf. Mussolini's *The Political and Social Doctrine of Fascism*, New York: Carnegie Endowment for International Peace, 1935.

39. Meir Michaelis, *Mussolini and the Jews*, Oxford: Clarendon Press, 1978, ch. 1–2.

40. The example of Ferrara is indicative. Without the grass root support in Northern Italy, it is unlikely that the PNF would ever have come to power. Yet, long-term support for fascism remained shallow. Cf. Paul Corner, *Fascism in Ferrara, 1915–1925*, New York: Oxford University Press, 1975.

41. Leeds, *Italy*, ch. 5.

42. Elie Kedourie, *England and the Middle East*, London: Bowes and Bowes, 1956, pp. 29–66.

43. "The Balfour Declaration," in Walter Laqueur (ed.), *The Israel–Arab Reader*, rev. ed., New York: Bantam Books, 1970, p. 18.

44. Cf. Abraham J. Edelheit, "The Yishuv in the Shadow of the Holocaust: Palestinian Jewry and the Emerging Nazi Threat, 1933–1939," Ph.D. dissertation, City University of New York Graduate School, 1992, Ch. 1.

3

THE NAZI TOTALITARIAN STATE

From Crisis to Stabilization

Totalitarian movements had gained control of both the Soviet Union and Italy by the middle of the 1920s; it was Germany, however, that experienced the most concerted crisis in the aftermath of World War I. Many Germans felt that the Versailles Treaty was unfair; these groups also claimed that Germany had been betrayed by its internal enemies. The new Germany was unable to pay its debts, especially reparations owed to the Allies, and soon was faced with a French occupation of the Saar and abortive revolts by radicals on both the left (the Spartacists) and the right (the Kapp putsch).

As a result, the newly created Weimar Republic, ruled by a coalition of Social Democrats and other left-center parties, was not established on a very secure foundation. Indeed, the suppression of the Spartacist uprising proved to be a pyrrhic victory: The government was forced to call on right-wing paramilitary groups (Freikorps and Stahlhelm) to eliminate the rebellion. This decision would be costly to the republic in later years, for these paramilitary groups could not be eliminated.[1]

Nevertheless, the new republic did coalesce, and as long as the economy held stable, a certain degree of democracy flourished. But when the economy slackened even temporarily — for example, during the "great inflation" of 1923–1924 — support for the fledgling republic waned rapidly. Concurrently, tremors were felt, as parties of both the Left and the Right proceeded to cut away the foundations of law and order. Increasingly the republic turned to suppression in order to secure peace and quiet in the streets. Curiously, only the Left was treated seriously. Judges often gave right-wing agitators token sentences for crimes that would bring Communists to the gallows.

Similarly, rule by decree had to be invoked in order to finesse the increasingly splintered Reichstag. The administration was rapidly collapsing under its own weight and was unable to sustain the daily demands of governing a state.[2]

Antisemitism, which had lain dormant during the war, returned with a passion in Weimar Germany. Parties of the Right routinely denounced the republic as a "Jew republic." They accused Communists, Jews, and liberals of having stabbed Germany in the back, of treachery and treason that had led to defeat. At the same time that they were accusing Jews of being Communists willing to sell Germany's soul for the sake of their world domination plans, and with a degree of inconsistency not uncommon for bigots, the radical right also accused Jews of being the capitalists who had profited from the war. Calls for action did not go unheeded. Individuals who were unhappy with the state of affairs in Weimar soon joined together into mass movements, especially during the inflation of 1923–1924. *Soldatenverbände*, roaming bands of rowdy and disenchanted veterans, appeared, as did dozens of private armies. Each offered the solution to Germany's problems: revenge for the disgrace of Versailles; justice against traitors, Jew and Communist alike; the creation of a new Reich that would restore Germany to its rightful place in the sun.[3]

On June 24, 1922, Consul, a secret right-wing organization led by Captain Ludwig Ehrhardt, assassinated Germany's Jewish foreign minister, Walter Rathenau.[4] Also making his appearance at this time was an almost unknown rabble-rouser named Adolf Hitler, who led the Nationalsozialistische Deutsche Arbeiterpartei (NSDAP) — the Nazi Party — in an abortive putsch. On November 8, 1923, members of the NSDAP, led by Hitler, met in a Munich beer hall for a political gathering. Thinking that a bold act could achieve the destruction of the hated "Jew republic," Hitler and his storm troopers aimed to seize the government of Bavaria and from there topple the Berlin government. The fact that a constitutional crisis regarding the status of the Weimar constitution had erupted in Bavaria in the months before Hitler's actions still seemed to preclude resistance. In fact, the acrimony of the dispute appears to have convinced Hitler that he would get considerable support. As is well known, the opposite happened. The Bavarian police quickly suppressed the putsch, killing one Nazi, Horst Wessel.[5]

Shortly thereafter, Hitler himself was arrested and tried for treason. Found guilty he was nevertheless given a token sentence of only five years' imprisonment. Of this sentence — for actions that surely would have brought Socialists or Communists to the executioner — Hitler served only nine months. While in prison Hitler crystallized his ideology; he wrote his main ideological work, *Mein Kampf*, at this time. Still, the failure of the putsch was a major setback. Furthermore, as the economic dislocations caused by the inflation dissipated, the Nazis, as well as other right-wing anti-republican groups, were weakened.

Adolf Hitler and the NSDAP

In Adolf Hitler the NSDAP, as well as many of the roaming *Soldatenverbände* had found their man. An Austrian by birth, Hitler was not the only right-wing agitator in Weimar Germany. As we have seen, there were the Freikorps, units of demobilized soldiers who became involved in political street violence. Stahlhelm, the Deutschnationale Volkspartei (DNVP), and other similar organizations all opposed the Weimar Republic. The small Nazi party, however, was different. Whereas most of the other agitators were only rabble-rousers, Hitler mesmerized ever-widening segments of the population with his stirring, passionate speeches. In speech after speech, Hitler called for restoration of German pride and revenge for the ignominy of Versailles. He aspired to be Germany's messiah, who would create a Thousand-Year Reich, restore that which properly was due Germany, and settle accounts with those who had betrayed Germany in 1918, especially the Jews. Hitler depicted a secure, peaceful, and powerful Germany — a far cry from the rapidly disintegrating Weimar Republic.[6]

Moreover, Nazis were masters of psychological techniques. Using triumphal marches, many held at night under the light of torches, the Nazis hoped to tap into the *volkisch* spirit that had developed over the previous century. Everything the Nazis did was "German"; their very ideology called for a return to the glorious days of Teutonic heroism. Additionally, anti-semitism played a central role in Nazi ideology. Mixing racial, political, and demonic anti-semitism, Hitler blamed all the difficulties that faced Germany upon the Jews. In Hitler's estimation, the Jew was the enemy par excellence. In *Mein Kampf* he wrote:

> If at the beginning of the War and during the War twelve or fifteen thousand of these Hebrew corrupters of the people had been held under the poison gas, as happened to hundreds of thousands of our best German workers in the field, the sacrifice of millions at the front would not have been in vain.[7]

Using the *Dolchstosslegende* (Stab-in-the-back myth) to the fullest, Hitler also posited that "there was no coming to terms with the Jew, there was only the harsh either-or."[8] In this propaganda campaign, Hitler was once again helped by the existence of other parties arguing the same thing, a fact that lent the antisemitic lies an air of legitimacy, and by the extensively organized NSDAP propaganda machine.

Additionally, Hitler — or his handlers — recognized early on the potentialities posed by other media, including radio and film. In fact, in 1932 Hitler became the first German politician to conduct his campaign across Germany by air: The speed with which he was thus able to move from one part of Germany to another conferred significant, if short-term, advantages.[9] Hitler clearly grasped the importance of propaganda, noting in *Mein Kampf*:

The art of all truly great national leaders has at all times consisted of this: not to divide the attention of the people, but to concentrate that attention on a single enemy. The more unified the fighting spirit of a nation, the greater the magnetic attraction of a movement, the more forceful the power of its thrust.[10]

This was to be a mass campaign. Although this did not imply that no intellectuals supported Hitler, it indicates the narrowly oriented quasi-intellectual ideology that suffused Nazism and attracted disaffected members of the lower-middle classes. Anything that could not be gained by conversion of the masses could be gained by coercion. The NSDAP had its own private army, the Sturmabteilungen (SA), which rapidly wrested control of the streets from the Communists.

Here too, the Nazis were masters in a struggle that was not exclusively theirs. All the right-wing parties and the Communists used "street politics," that is, limited public combat, as a means to attain their goals. Each of the parties maintained a self-defense militia and used a cadre of uniformed thugs to disrupt opponents' rallies. These private armies slowly but surely sapped the power of the Weimar police.[11]

Again, however, Nazi use of political violence reflected a unique synthesis. Whereas Stahlhelm was exclusively a party of street fighters and DNVP almost exclusively a "legitimate," if radical, parliamentary party, the NSDAP's strategy employed both: limited violence, to gain physical control of Germany's streets; and the Weimar constitution, especially its election laws, to undermine democracy and constitutional government.

Still, for the most part, Hitler's strategy was a failure during the mid-1920s. With the German economy stabilized and steady political progress, both at home and abroad, being made by statesmen and chancellors such as Gustav Stresemann (who served briefly in 1923, but remained as foreign minister until his death in 1929), Wilhelm Marx (1923–1924 and 1926–1928), Hans Luther (1925–1926), and Hermann Müller (1928–1930), Nazism could not take root.

The Road to Power

Stymied for most of the 1920s, the NSDAP got a second chance in the form of the stock market crash in New York on October 24, 1929. The resulting depression destroyed all vestiges of economic stability in the United States and throughout the world. Once again the Weimar Republic was beset by internal strife, as both Nazis and Communists vied for control. This battle was played out on the streets as well as in the voting booths, and in both, the Nazis eventually gained the upper hand. Significantly, the depression splintered the already fragmented party structure of the republic, as can be seen in Table 3.1.

TABLE 3.1 German Election Results, 1930–1932, by Number of Seats

Party	1930	July 1932	November 1932
NSDAP	107	230	196
DNVP	41	37	51
Deutsche Volkspartei	31	7	11
Bayerische Volkspartei	19	22	20
Zentrum	68	75	70
Sozialdemokratische Partei Deutschlands	143	133	121
Kommunistische Partei Deutschlands	77	89	100
Other Right	78	11	13
Other Center	20	4	2

Source: J.C.G. Röhl, *From Bismarck to Hitler*, New York: Barnes and Noble, 1970, p. 129.

More simply put, in 1930 the Nazis held 18 percent of the seats in the Reichstag. In July 1932 their proportion rose to 38 percent, as the Nazis became Germany's largest party. In the interim, the republic was collapsing under its own weight. In the Reichstag, coalition governments rose and fell without a decisive majority being established. The republic briefly rallied in 1930 when a center-right coalition was created by Franz von Papen. This coalition was soon broken, however, and von Papen began to rule by decree. Indeed, at this point von Papen seriously considered the possibility of launching a *coup d'état* and establishing a dictatorship. Von Papen and General Kurt von Schleicher approached Reichspräsident Paul von Hindenburg, seeking to convince him that "he might be justified in placing the welfare of the nation above his oath to the constitution."[12]

Hitler's electoral victory in July put an end to von Papen's plans for dictatorship but did not end the crisis. Although the Nazis were the largest single party in the Reichstag, they failed to get a clear majority and still required a coalition to rule. Unwilling to accept a coalition, Hitler, supported by the Reichswehr, demanded new elections, which were held in November.[13] At this point the Nazis actually lost ground, tallying only 34 percent of the vote but still remaining the largest single party in the Reichstag. Intense negotiations in

December 1932 and January 1933 finally led to Hitler's appointment as chancellor on January 30, 1933, by President von Hindenburg, albeit as head of a government that had a minority Nazi representation.[14]

Creating the Nazi Totalitarian State

With the Nazi victory came an almost immediate effort to recast Germany in the framework of Hitler's ideology. Initially, street battles with the Communists continued. Now, however, that the police openly supported the rightist elements, the Nazis rapidly won control of the streets. On the night of February 27–28, 1933, a mysterious fire in the Reichstag gave Hitler a further opportunity to extend his control over all of Germany. Conveniently blamed on the Communists (although it has since become clear that the Nazis staged the fire), the Reichstag fire gave the Nazis an excuse to outlaw the Kommunistische Partei Deutschlands altogether and to severely circumscribe the activities of the Sozialdemokratische Partei Deutschlands as well.[15] On March 20, 1933, the first official concentration camp — as opposed to SA *wilde lager* (wild camps) — opened at Dachau with a capacity of 5,000 inmates. Other concentration camps were added to this system; it has been estimated that, by July 31, 1933, the system held some 30,000 inmates.[16] Finally, when the rump Reichstag met on March 23, 1933, Hitler demanded that it approve his use of the *Ermächtigungsgesetz* (Enabling Law). The Reichstag approved the decree, in effect abdicating its constitutional powers and providing Hitler and the Nazis with virtually unlimited powers; his prediction that he could use the Weimar constitution to subvert democracy had indeed come true.[17]

One limit to total Nazi control of Germany still remained: By the terms of the Weimar constitution, the chancellor was not the nation's chief executive. That status fell to the president, who was elected independently of the Reichstag for a four-year term. In 1932, in a close election, Hitler had been defeated for the presidency of the Reich by Field Marshal Paul von Hindenburg, a World War I military hero. With a clear popular mandate, von Hindenburg could have represented a balance against Hitler's totalitarian tendency. In reality, however, von Hindenburg's age and infirmity led him to eschew opposition. Moreover, von Hindenburg's point of view was similar to Hitler's — although perhaps more moderate in tone.[18] In any event, von Hindenburg died on August 2, 1934. At this point Hitler assumed the newly created title of *Führer*, a position that fused the functions of both chancellor and president. The new title also symbolized Hitler's assumption of total control over Germany.[19]

Hitler sought to formulate his new totalitarian state on a number of conceptual foundations. Of all the concepts that animated Nazism, three stand out: *Blut und Boden* (blood and soil), a quasi-populism; *Führerprinzip* (worship of the leader); and *Gleichschaltung* (coordination).[20] These concepts were not unique to Nazism, they formed part of almost every fascist ideology, but the way that Hitler and other Nazi leaders used their ideology proved unique.[21]

Blut und Boden, which the Nazis claimed was central to their program, argued that a society was healthy only as long as its people (*Volk*) were racially united and possessed their own soil. Corollaries that emanated from this idea included the search for *Lebensraum* (living space) and *Eindeutschung* (re-Germanization); taken

together, these concepts also justified Nazi imperialism and aggression. Additionally, these concepts also justified Nazi plans for a racial apocalypse that would end with the elimination of all "lower" races (*Untermenschen*).

The *Führerprinzip* and *Gleichschaltung* implied the centralization of all authority, political or otherwise, in the party. The concepts were supposed to create a completely new society, to fuse individual, family, state, and party into one entity, all sublimated to the existence and power of one man — Adolf Hitler. On a national level, *Gleichschaltung* implied the total realignment of the Reich to bring the civil service in line with the requirements of the regime. This aspect of coordination extended into the economic sector as well, with less overall success, for the purpose of synchronizing the economy with Hitler's long-term war aims. On this level, *Gleichschaltung* had parallels in other totalitarian movements (most noticeably with the concept of "democratic centralism" in Communist regimes).[22] *Gleichschaltung* also extended down to an individual level. In one way or another, virtually every German was connected with the party and, through the party, with Hitler. By that means, the Nazis sought the creation of a totalistic *Volk* that would, of necessity, develop into a master race and subjugate the world.

Taken together, these concepts were to lead Germany to its destiny, the New Order, whose primary actor was to be the Thousand-Year Reich. The purpose of the New Order was to create, or rather to re-create, a purely Teutonic civilization. The New Order would expurgate all Jewish influence, even in Christianity, and transmute all Western values. A key element in this New Order called for the reorganization of Europe. Most Western and Scandinavian countries would be nazified and "coordinated." Barriers separating them would be destroyed. The Slavic *Ostmensch*, although retaining the status of "Aryan," would be reduced to slavery and would do all the hard labor that his German masters required. A very different fate awaited the Jews: Their complete extinction was to signal the end of racial strife and announce the messianic era. The destruction of the "Jewish vermin" was to be the first and most glorious (but strictly secret) phase of the Nazi apocalypse.[23]

The Nazi use of terror, however, extended beyond the Jews to almost every phase of life. Through the all-inclusiveness of the SS apparatus, the Nazis sought to create a truly totalitarian state — the SS state. That they did not completely succeed at this task may be attributed to two considerations: Hitler's penchant for encouraging internal disputes over authority (as a means to ensure that his subordinates were always dependent upon his final approval) and the relatively short time available for completion of the task — although Nazi leaders talked about the Thousand-Year Reich, their program lasted only twelve years.[24] Even so, virtually every institution in German society was co-ordinated: the labor unions, the schools, and the universities. Even the army, the pride of the old Prussian Junkers, surrendered its independence, swearing an oath to the *Führer* rather than to the state and thereby becoming accomplices in Nazi crimes.[25]

Through the *Kraft durch Freude* (Strength through Joy) program, the SS state strictly regimented leisure time, as well as the everyday lives of youth and families.[26] Nazism touched, tainted, and corrupted every element of German society. No one was safe. Random denunciations could easily land one in a concentration camp, as could even the most casual anti-Nazi remark. The crippled, infirm, and mentally retarded might have been consigned to a holocaust of their own, had public and Church resistance not stopped the Euthanasia Program (Operation T4) after only a short duration. Still, approximately 275,000 mentally ill Germans and other victims within this category were gassed to conform with Nazi eugenic dogma.[27]

The Third Reich: An Institutional Overview

Institutions also played a significant role in Nazi totalitarianism. Among the most important, of course, was the NSDAP itself. The party was the body that lent meaning to

National Socialism. Arranged pyramidically from Hitler down, the NSDAP directly controlled agencies for racial and political activities; a treasury; the propaganda and press offices; the youth division; and its own internal court system.[28] Within Germany, the party was organized by region, with each district (*Gau*) possessing its own party organization. The *Gau* party agencies, in turn, answered to the central party chancellery run by the deputy *Führer* (Rudolf Hess until 1941 and Martin Bormann thereafter). In 1938 Germany was divided into 30 *Gaugebiete* that were further subdivided into 822 *Kreise*, 28,000 *Ortsgruppen*, 93,000 *Zellen*, and 480,000 *Blöcke*.[29] Owing to territorial accretions, the number of *Gaugebiete* was increased to 42 in 1944.[30]

Furthermore, an entire parallel party micro-organization, known as the Auslands-organization der NSDAP (AO, the Nazi Party Foreign Organization) existed for Germans living outside the Reich; its internal structure was parallel to the NSDAP organization up to the *Gauleiter* (district leader) level; the regional leaders' titles were changed (*Landleiter* rather than *Gauleiter*, for example) to reflect the external nature of the AO.[31]

Four other agencies also operated under the tutelage of the NSDAP but were autonomous within the party hierarchy: the National-sozialistisches Kraftfahrkorps (NSKK, National Socialist Motor Transport Corps), the Hitler-jugend (HJ, Hitler Youth), the Sturm-abteilungen (SA), and the Schutzstaffel (SS, Protection Squads). Each of them formed part of Hitler's plans to nazify Germany and thus secure the future of the Thousand-Year Reich. The NSKK was officially created to teach proper motor skills to German youth. This goal was actually a cover for providing training in the use of motor vehicles for military purposes and played a role in the training of the Wehrmacht's (and Waffen-SS's) armored formations.[32]

The HJ was organized as a quasi-military group intended to produce a future generation of SS and party leaders. More broadly, HJ was supposed to also create the "new Nazi man" who would represent the Reich's new values and mores. In this case, the paramilitary purpose of the organization was apparent and quite public. To further its goals, the HJ was assisted by two networks of schools: the so-called Adolf Hitler Schulen and the Nationalpolitische Erziehungsanstalten (NAPOLA), both directly sponsored by the NSDAP and organized to train the new generation of party leaders.[33]

Albeit unofficially, the SA, headed by Ernst Röhm, and the SS, headed by Heinrich Himmler, saw themselves as the *corps d'elite* of the party. Both the SA and SS aimed to be the central institution of the Thousand-Year Reich and the key to the creation of the New Order. The SS sought to be more than that. Under Heinrich Himmler's leadership, the black-shirted SS developed from a minor organ of the party into a state within a state. The SS removed the SA during the blood purges — the so-called Röhm affair of June 30, 1934 — known as the *Nacht der langen Messer* (Night of the Long Knives). In this power struggle Himmler showed his tenacity, intelligence, and uninhibited lust for power.[34] Whereas the rank-and-file SA member was not an intellectual, the SS tended to attract a more educated membership. Similarly, whereas members of the SA took Hitler's quasi-populist rhetoric seriously, the SS made loyalty to Hitler the Nazis' foremost obligation. Indeed, the SS — not the SA — displayed the total, unwavering brutality that would terrorize all of Europe during the war. In effect, the SS thus possessed wide powers within the Reich; these powers transformed the SS into Hitler's private revolutionary army.[35]

Himmler, at one time an unsuccessful chicken farmer and provincial village schoolteacher, organized his fiefdom into twelve main branches, with further subdivisions (*Ämter*) to carry out specific functions.[36] The Reichssicherheitshauptamt (RSHA), the State Security Main Office, created in 1939, was charged with administrative control of Himmler's far-flung empire. The Wirtschafts- und Verwaltungshauptamt (WVHA), the SS Economic and Administrative Office,

complemented the work of the RSHA. The Rasse- und Siedlungshauptamt (RUSHA) served as the SS watchdog bureau for racial purity and the resettlement of ethnic Germans. The Volksdeutsche Mittelstelle (VOMI) was responsible for the welfare of ethnic Germans in foreign lands. Finally, aiding in the racial reorganization of Europe was the Reichskommissariat für die Festigung des deutschen Volkstums (RKFdV), the Reich Commission for the Strengthening of the Germanic Peoples, established in 1939.

For internal security, as chief of the German police (*Chef der deutschen Polizei*), Himmler ruled in each region of the SS state through the Höherer SS- und Polizeiführer (HSSPF), the Higher SS and Police Leaders. He was also the keeper of the largest and most sophisticated prison system in Western history — the concentration camps. The camps were, in turn, controlled by the Inspectorate of Concentration Camps, under Theodor Eicke, and guarded by members of the SS-Totenkopfverbände.[37] The SS Central Office controlled many other agencies, including a variety of lucrative business enterprises that employed slave labor from the camps. During World War II, when literally thousands of the *Zivilarbeitslager* flourished in all parts of occupied Europe, the SS enterprise took in a tidy sum from renting out slave laborers of all nationalities to the German or ethnic-German private companies that ran the camps.

Of all the aforementioned agencies of the SS, the RSHA was probably most important. Divided into seven departments, its offices were charged with all matters relating to national security. The RSHA maintained the SS police organs: Geheime Staatspolizei, or Gestapo (the Secret State Police); Kriminalpolizei, or Kripo (the Criminal Police); and Sicherheitspolizei, or Sipo (the Security Police), which combined both Gestapo and Kripo. RSHA also controlled the Reichsführer's intelligence service, the Sicherheitsdienst (SD). Under the leadership of Reinhard Heydrich, and Ernst Kaltenbrunner after Heydrich's assassination, the RSHA directed and oversaw the *Endlösung der Judenfrage*, the Final Solution, in cooperation with other SS organizations.[38]

In 1939, on the outbreak of the war, Hitler ordered the recruitment of SS-Verfügungstruppen, special duty troops, under Himmler's exclusive command. In 1940 the Verfügungstruppen units were merged with the Leibstandarte-SS Adolf Hitler (the Nazi Praetorian Guards, commanded by Sepp Dietrich) and other units to form the Waffen-SS. Organized into standard divisions, the Waffen-SS constituted the core of an independent army under Himmler's personal command.[39]

The Nazi Mentality

Any survey of National Socialism, no matter how brief, raises complex questions about the Nazis, and about the Germans in general.[40] In light of the wartime atrocities, the Nazis might seem to be a band of sadists who achieved almost sexual pleasure from seeing their victims tormented. Careful study appears to show the opposite. With the possible exception of the Sturmabteilungen (SA), many of whose members were professional ruffians, most of the Nazis were of lower-middle-class origin. Few were unusual before their nazification and almost none had previous police records. Indeed, recent studies portray them as bland, banal, ordinary, lacking strong personalities, and — to a great extent — failures in "normal" life.[41]

Nazism was, nevertheless, able to call upon a deep-seated core of violence that turned ordinary middle-class citizens into fanatical murderers. Although no single explanation is presently available to completely explain why this was so, psychological studies done during the 1960s — generally associated with Theodore Adorno's hypothesis about the existence of an "authoritarian personality" — offer some applicable generalizations. In particular, Adorno suggested that some traits, identified in "normal" times as mild eccentricities, could lead to extreme violence in "abnormal" circumstances. Among other things, the list included: submissivness to authority, rigid adherence to conventional behavior, stereotyping of outsiders, noncreativity, superstition, cynicism, and an unusual concern with "manliness" and sexuality.[42]

Yet the banal and ordinary citizens were not the only ones attracted to Nazism; the educated elite also felt a deep attraction to Nazi doctrine. Long a seedbed for German arch-conservatism and hypernationalist agitation, by 1933 Germany's universities had adopted the nineteenth-century critics' views regarding the past, present, and future almost entirely.[43] As a result, lawyers, physicians, historians, educators, and scientists all lent a hand to Hitler's grand undertaking. A case in point was Gerhard Kittel. Born in September 1889, he was the son of Rudolf Kittel, a biblical scholar and author of *Biblia Hebraica*. Gerhard Kittel, a scholar in his own right, author of *Die Probleme des Palestiner Spätjudentums*, was professor of theology at the University of Tübingen. Before the advent of the Thousand-Year Reich, he frequently associated with Jewish scholars of the day. In 1933, after the *Machtergreifung* (seizure of power), Kittel wrote a short book, *Die Judenfrage* (The Jewish Question), in which he showed that the emancipation had been an error and ought to be undone. Later, during the period of extermination, Kittel used his knowledge of Judaism to justify the destruction of European Jewry.[44]

Kittel, of course, was not an exception. "Hitler's professors," some of them the best in their respective fields, were able to come up with precedents that gave legal sanction to the most brutal measures that any criminal state has ever undertaken.[45]

One example may suffice: Historian Walter Frank used his considerable talents to expose "international Jewry" on every possible occasion. Not surprisingly, Frank wrote his doctoral dissertation (1927) on the court chaplain and well-known antisemite, Adolf Stöcker.[46] On October 19, 1935, Frank was tapped by the NSDAP to create a new research institute, the Reichsinstitut für Geschichte des neuen Deutschlands (State Institute for the History of the New Germany). Among his patrons — members and honorary members of the institute — were many of the most famous historians and academicians of contemporary Germany.[47]

The Nazi regime also co-opted medical science for its purposes. Nazi doctors committed numerous crimes in the name of science. Viktor Brack, in the forefront of the nazification of German medicine, attempted to justify the gruesome "medical experiments" that were carried out on unwilling victims with fatal results. Dozens of other doctors, all sworn by the Hippocratic Oath to alleviate human suffering, also participated in the Nazi experiments, committing atrocious crimes on healthy human specimens: injecting into their tormented bodies all kinds of poisonous chemicals; cutting out pieces of flesh without the benefit of anesthesia; and abandoning the subject to fight infections without antibiotics. If the subject survived, there would be more experiments. If not, it mattered little because plenty of other subjects were readily available.[48]

None of these "doctors of doom" is more infamous than Joseph Mengele, the "purveyor of death" at Auschwitz, perhaps the most pernicious mass murderer of all time. Mengele almost single-handedly played god over millions of innocent souls, selecting arbitrarily those who would forfeit their lives and those who might stay alive, by his grace, a while longer. He was not, however, alone. In every extermination camp, a "Doctor Mengele" selected a few from the wretched masses of the ever-arriving transports to stay alive a while longer.[49]

A similar personality profile could, with some modifications, fit the other key Nazis as well. Hans Frank, the governor-general of Poland, was a member of the party from 1923 — he joined in time to participate in the beer hall putsch — and earned a doctorate of law in 1924. He was but twenty-four years old at the time.[50] Deputy Foreign Minister Martin Luther was widely perceived as a suave speaker and a self-confident defender of Germany's national interests. Besides his famous ancestor's name, however, Luther inherited a genteel anti-semitism in his diplomatic mission.[51]

Those very same Nazis who consigned millions to their deaths were also loving husbands and parents. Many of them were fond of animals, keeping pets in their homes. Quite a few were even vegetarians. What made them unique was that they could divorce murder, rape, and pillage from their personal lives. Their banality makes them even more frightening. Clearly, the National Socialist rot had eaten deeply into the root of German society.

Notes

1. Erich Eyck, *A History of the Weimar Republic*, Cambridge: Harvard University Press, 1967, vol. 1, ch. 5–6.

2. The inflation began as a result of the French occupation of the Ruhr, a punishment for German delay in paying reparations. Henri Lichtenberger, *The Third Reich*, New York: Greystone Press, 1937, p. 28.

3. See the documents cited in Henry C. Meyer (ed.), *The Long Generation: Germany from Empire to Ruin*, New York: Walker, 1973, pp. 128–137; and, more generally, Donald I. Niewyk, *The Jews in Weimar Germany*, Baton Rouge: Louisiana State University Press, 1960, ch. 3.

4. Eyck, *Weimar Republic*, pp. 210–215.

5. Harold J Gordon, Jr., *Hitler and the Beer Hall Putsch*, Princeton: Princeton University Press, 1972, ch. 12–14.

6. Lichtenberger, *Third Reich*, pp. 29–31.

7. Adolf Hitler, *Mein Kampf*, Boston: Houghton Mifflin, 1971, p. 679.

8. Ibid., p. 295.

9. Z.A.B. Zeman, *Nazi Propaganda*, Oxford: Oxford University Press, 1973, ch. 1.

10. Hitler, *Mein Kampf*, p. 129. Zeman provided a number of examples of Nazi use of scapegoats, primarily Jews: Cf. *Nazi Propaganda*, p. 31, for an example of a Nazi election poster. In this, Hitler paralleled Mussolini: both made careful use of all available media to spread their message.

11. An extensive history of the street battles during the Weimar Republic's waning years was provided by J. M. Diehl, *Paramilitary Politics in Weimar Germany*, Bloomington: Indiana University Press, 1977.

12. Quoted from the *Memoirs of Franz von Papen*, as cited in J.C.G. Röhl, *From Bismarck to Hitler*, New York: Barnes and Noble, 1970, p. 138.

13. Ibid., pp. 139–140. The Nazis received 196 Reichstag seats as a result of the November 1932, election. Although that was a net loss of 34 seats, most of those losses were due to the downsizing of the Reichstag from 599 members in June to 572.

14. William L. Shirer: *The Rise and Fall of the Third Reich*, New York: Simon and Schuster, 1960, pp. 183–187.

15. Ibid., pp. 191–195.

16. Falk Pingel, "The Concentration Camps as Part of the National-Socialist System of Domination," in Israel Gutman and Avital Saf (eds.), *The Nazi Concentration Camps: Structure and Aims, the Image of the Prisoner, the Jews in the Camps*, Proceedings of the Fourth International Yad Vashem Historical Conference, Jerusalem: Yad Vashem, 1984, p. 7.

17. Shirer, *Rise and Fall*, pp. 198–199.

18. Karl D. Bracher spoke of Hindenburg's role in government as a "substitute monarchy" and especially emphasized the similarities in their policies. See his *The German Dictatorship*, New York: Holt, Rinehart and Winston, 1970, p. 340.

19. Lichtenberger, *Third Reich*, pp. 55–63.

20. Cf. Eberhard Jäckel, *Hitler's Weltanschauung: A Blueprint for Power*, Middletown, CT: Wesleyan University Press, 1969, pp. 75–86; Hilde Kammer and Elisabet Bartsch, *Nationalsozialismus*, Hamburg: Rowohlt Taschenbuch, 1992, pp. 80–82.

21. One of the best comparative studies on Nazi and Fascist ideology was provided in Ernst Nolte, *Three Faces of Fascism*, New York: Dell, 1966; for a more recent comparison, see Michael Curtis, *Totalitarianism*, New Brunswick, NJ: Transaction Books, 1979.

22. Hannah Arendt, *The Origins of Totalitarianism*, new ed., New York: Harcourt, Brace and Jovanovich, 1973, pp. 401–404.

23. Morris E. Opler, "The Bio-social Basis of Thought in the Third Reich," *American Sociological Review*, vol. 10 (1945), 776–786; and Joseph Tenenbaum, *Race and Reich: The Story of an Era*,

New York: Twayne, 1956.

24. Albert Speer, *Inside the Third Reich*, New York: Macmillan, 1970, ch. 14–18, to be read, of course, with all due cautions, since Speer's memoir was one of the most self-serving regarding his actual role in the Reich hierarchy. Cf. Matthias Schmidt, *Albert Speer: The End of a Myth*, New York: St. Martin's Press, 1985.

25. Cf. Robert J. O'Neill, *The German Army and the Nazi Party, 1933–1939*, New York: Heineman, 1966, ch. 5.

26. Richard Grunberger, *The Twelve Year Reich: A Social History of Nazi Germany, 1933–1945*, New York: Holt, Rinehart and Winston, 1971, pp. 197–198.

27. Philippe Aziz, *Doctors of Death*, Geneva: Ferni, 1976, vol. 1, ch. 3, vol. 4, ch 2.

28. A useful schematic presentation of NSDAP structure is provided in Michael Freeman (comp.), *The Atlas of Nazi Germany*, New York: Macmillan, 1987, pp. 62–63; cf. Grunberger, *Twelve Year Reich*, ch. 4.

29. Ibid., pp. 66-67.

30. Ibid.

31. Donald M. McKale, *The Swastika Outside of Germany*, Kent, OH: Kent State University Press, 1977, ch. 3–4.

32. cf Kammer and Bartsch, *Nationalsozialismus*, pp. 90–94, 143.

33. Ibid., pp. 12–13, 131–133.

34. Cf. Richard Breitman, *The Architect of Genocide: Himmler and the Final Solution*, New York: Knopf, 1991, pp. 33–35.

35. Gerald Reitlinger, *The SS: Alibi of a Nation*, new ed., Englewood Cliffs, NJ: Prentice Hall, 1981.

36. Hans Bucheim, "The SS — Instrument of Domination," in Helmut Krausnick et al., *Anatomy of the SS State*, New York: Walker, 1968, pp. 143–254.

37. Martin Broszat, "The Concentration Camps," in ibid., pp. 436–446.

38. Helmut Krausnick, "The Persecution of the Jews," in ibid., pp. 1–124.

39. Cf. John Keegan, *Waffen SS: The Asphalt Soldiers*, New York: Ballantine Books, 1970, pp. 8–19.

40. Léon Poliakov, "The Mind of the Mass Murderer: the Nazi Executioners – and those who stood by," *Commentary*, vol. 12 # 5 (1951), 451–459.

41. Studies on the Nazi's personalities have multiplied in recent years and become more sophisticated. For an example of the Nazi hierarchy, see Breitman, *Architect of Genocide*, pp. 12–13, which detailed Himmler's unsuccessful agricultural career. For a study on a middle-level Nazi bureaucrat, see Peter Malkin and Harry Stein, *Eichmann in My Hands*, New York: Warner Books, 1990, passim. And for a study on the lowest levels of Nazi control, see Christopher Browning, *Ordinary Men: Reserve Police Battalion 101 and the Final Solution in Poland*, New York: HarperCollins, 1992, ch. 18.

42. Theodore Adorno, *The Authoritarian Personality*, New York: Harper and Row, 1950, pp. 222-279.

43. Max Weinreich, *Hitler's Professors: The Part of Scholarship in Germany's Crimes Against the Jewish People*, New York: YIVO, 1946, pp. 10–17.

44. Robert Eriksen, "Theologian in the Third Reich: The Case of Gerhard Kittel," in *Journal of Contemporary History*, vol. 12 # 3 (1977), 595–622.

45. Weinreich, *Hitler's Professors*, pp. 17–22.

46. Ibid., p. 45.

47. Ibid., pp. 46–50.

48. Cf. Robert J. Lifton, *The Nazi Doctors: Medical Killings and the Psychology of Genocide*, New York: Basic Books, 1986.

49. A number of recent biographies have appeared on Mengele, all deriving from the mysterious

circumstances surrounding his presumed death. Regarding his activities in Auschwitz, see Gerald Posner, *Mengele: The Complete Story*, New York: McGraw-Hill, 1986, ch. 2.

50. Robert Wistrich, *Who's Who in Nazi Germany*, New York: Macmillan, 1982, pp. 78–79.

51. Ibid., pp. 200–201.

4

THE SHOA

Overview

The ink on President von Hindenburg's signature — designating Hitler as the new German chancellor — had hardly dried when the Nazis began to institute their platform. Now, with legal means at their disposal, the Nazis' long-pent-up rage against Communists, Jews, and all other opponents gave vent to a campaign of harassment, assault, and terror against real or perceived enemies. Foremost on their hit list was German Jewry. This seemingly annoying beginning would, within less than a dozen years, culminate in the murder of some 6 million European Jews and millions of others.

In recent years two schools of thought regarding the nature and the development of the Nazis' genocidal plans have emerged. The "intentionalists" emphasize the roles that Hitler, his virulent antisemitism, and the totalitarian ideology espoused by Nazism played in the formulation of the Final Solution. Intentionalists thus argue that mass murder of Jews was always the Nazi intent, and they view the Final Solution as the culmination of Nazi plans conceived in the 1920s.[1] "Functionalists," in contrast, argue that the extermination program was more an example of bureaucracy run amok than an example of long-held Nazi intent. Functionalists, therefore, tend to emphasize the fluid situation in Germany during the 1930s and the different solutions offered by Nazi functionaries short of total extermination — for example, sterilization, expulsion, and/or economic expropriation.

Both schools have strengths and weaknesses. Most notably, the intentionalists have great difficulty in explaining the often-contradictory policies carried out by the Nazis before extermination began en masse in 1941, and the functionalists can explain neither the ideological background of Nazi antisemitism nor the fixation with the pursuit of a racial millennium that led the Nazis to place a higher priority on killing Jews than on winning the war.[2]

In the interim, a third school — which may be termed "eclectic" — has emerged. The eclectics emphasize the positive elements of both schools while avoiding their pitfalls. Eclectics thus accept the functionalist argument that the Nazis began with only a very general goal, termed *Entjudung*, but lacked a specific plan for attaining that goal. However, unlike many functionalists, eclectics also accept the intentionalist emphasis on ideology: Although the *Endlösung* emerged only after other policies were tried but did not achieve the stated goal, both the goal of *Entjudung* and the ideology that dehumanized Jews to the extent that they could be seen as vermin worthy of extermination were adhered to without deviation for the entire existence of the NSDAP.

In any case, intentionalists, functionalists, and eclectics all agree that Nazi antisemitic policy was carried out in a number of phases, each of which set the stage for further developments in the next phase, and each successive phase presupposed those policies previously implemented. In every case, succeeding phases represented a generally stricter or more brutal policy toward Jews, with decreasing possibilities for escape with each passing year. Most historians divide the Holocaust into four phases: (1) from the *Machtergreifung* on January 30, 1933, to the Nuremberg rallies of September 15, 1935; (2) from the Nuremberg rallies to the outbreak of World War II on September 1, 1939; (3) from the outbreak of war to the invasion of the Soviet Union on June 22, 1941; and (4) from the invasion of the Soviet Union to the end of World War II in Europe on May 8, 1945.

Incubation: 1933–1935

The first phase of the Holocaust began with the *Machtergreifung* on January 30, 1933, and continued through mid-September 1935. During this time German Jewry was isolated by effective Nazi antisemitic propaganda and was turned into a "leprous community" with which Aryans had no contact.[3] Anti-Jewish violence was limited to sporadic, random assaults. The precise level of violence varied according to place and time but never reached mass proportions. Instead, the Nazis concentrated on legislation issued in a relatively steady stream and designed to severely circumscribe the areas of economic activity and social contact permitted to Jews. In order to encourage emigration, economic warfare was waged on those areas of activity still permitted to Jews. At the same time, there was an anti-Jewish propaganda campaign and an attempt to blunt worldwide protests against Germany's antisemitic actions.

The legislative program began on April 7, 1933, with the publication of the Law for the Restoration of the Professional Civil Service.[4] Also enacted on that day was a law establishing a *numerus clausus* on Jews for admission into the legal profession. Both decrees were designed to bar Jews from important professions, but both contained loopholes whereby Jewish war veterans or

the relatives of Jews who were killed during World War I received the "privilege" of retaining their profession. Between April 1933 and September 1935 more that fifty other decrees were enacted, all of which followed the same general pattern and each of which covered a different profession. Included in this set of decrees was one Against the Overcrowding of German Public Schools, passed on April 25, 1933, which introduced a *numerus clausus* in universities and technical schools. Published on July 14, 1933, was the Law Regarding Revocation of Naturalization and the Annulment of German Citizenship — which became the legal basis for the denial of citizenship to all Jews from Eastern Europe living on German soil. The decree was followed up on March 23, 1934, by the actual revocation of citizenship. The stateless families in the newly created category were not, however, immediately deported from Germany. Two other laws passed in May and June 1935 precluded Jews from serving in the armed forces and from employment through the German Labor Front.

Just before the legislative campaign began, some Nazis gave vent to their antisemitic feelings in a series of sporadic attacks on Jews. The earliest of them started in Thuringia in February 1933 and spread throughout Germany intermittently during February and March 1933.[5] Unexpectedly, press reports in neighboring countries and worldwide concern about these and other attacks brought about an immediate response from Jewish communities and anti-Nazi leaders, including a massive protest rally on March 27 called by the American Jewish Congress in New York.[6] In retaliation, the Nazis declared a one-day anti-Jewish boycott for Saturday, April 1, 1933. Under the sponsorship of Julius Streicher, armed guards of the SA were posted at Jewish shops with orders to keep out all Aryan customers, by whatever means necessary.[7] Although the one-day boycott did not have an immediate impact on German Jewry per se, it did play an important role in internal Nazi politics, allowing the SA to release tension without harming the economy.[8] Jewish institutions throughout the world were also placed on

The public burning of un-German books in the Opernplatz, Berlin,
on the night of May 10, 1933
Courtesy of the National Archives/U.S. Holocaust Memorial Museum

the defensive in relation to Nazi anti-semitism, fearing a further worsening of living conditions for German Jewry resulting from any of their actions that might provoke the Nazis. The same goal was promoted by a thinly veiled, but carefully orchestrated, propaganda campaign that claimed that German Jews were not being persecuted at all. Both the boycott and propaganda campaign succeeded in retarding the anti-Nazi response of Jewish communities in the free world, especially the United States and Great Britain. At the same time, poisonous antisemitic propaganda was drummed into the German citizenry in order to further isolate the Jewish community from the larger society. To cement the Aryan culture of the state, a thorough purge of German-

Jewish, pacifist, socialist, and anti-Nazi books was undertaken, culminating in the mass bonfires of May 10, 1933.[9]

Formulation: 1935–1939

In mid-September 1935, Nazi policy reached another important turning point for German Jewry. During the Nazi Party rallies held in Nuremberg, two specific laws were enacted on September 15, namely the State Citizenship Law (*Reichsbürgergesetz*) and the Law for the Protection of German Blood and German Honor (*Gesetz zum Schutze des deutschen Blutes und der deutschen Ehre*). Better known as the Nuremberg Laws, they brought about a shockwave of epic proportions for German and, indirectly, for world Jewry. The two rulings served the dual purpose of defining who was considered a Jew and of revoking the Jews' few remaining rights. The statutes included a clear racial definition of who was a Jew, who was a German, and who was a *Mischling*, the intermediate category of persons of mixed Jewish and German ancestry. The State Citizenship Law defined the *Reichsbürger* as a pure-blooded German citizen with full political rights; and the *Staatsangehöriger* as a subject of the Reich, to which status German Jewry was now reduced.[10] At least 121 further laws, decrees, and ordinances were published between the rallies of September 1935 and the outbreak of war on September 1, 1939; these finalized the Jews' fallen status and utterly destroyed whatever foundations may have still survived to continue Jewish life in Germany.

Operating alongside the Nazi legislative program was a policy of *Arisierung* — that is, the aryanization of Jewish property. Although it began in 1933, the process of aryanization became systematic only after the start of the rearmament campaign of 1935 and 1936. Until that time the Nazis adopted a policy of economic self-restraint regarding German Jewish businessmen (as opposed to laborers or professionals), primarily for fear of unemployment. After 1937, however, the campaign to create a *judenrein* (Jew-free) economy began to speed up. Nevertheless, this antisemitic campaign was not fully completed until the months just before the outbreak of World War II.[11]

The Nazis initiated similar measures upon their takeover in Austria on March 12, 1938. Austrian Nazis greeted the *Anschluss* with anti-Jewish violence, especially in Vienna, where they forced Jews to scrub the streets with their bare hands.[12] Hitler's string of bloodless victories was made simpler, and the suffering of his victims more pronounced, by the policy of appeasement adopted by the Western states. The height of appeasement came during the Munich Conference (September 28–30, 1938), when Britain and France agreed to the dismemberment of Czechoslovakia in return for Hitler's vague promise that this was his last territorial demand. In return, the Nazis demanded the Sudetenland, the segment of Czechoslovakia that was ethnically German.[13] Of course, Hitler never meant to honor his promise, and as of March 16, 1939, the Nazis occupied the rest of Czechoslovakia. With the dismembering of Czechoslovakia, a bitter fate befell Prague Jewry. The Nuremberg Laws and the subsidiary laws emanating from them placed all Czech Jews outside the law: As with German and Austrian Jewry, no Czech Jews, therefore, would have any recourse within the established legal system, no matter what was done to them.[14]

Throughout this period the Nazis sought a solution to the Jewish problem through mass emigration. Despite all the difficulties in gaining admission to safe havens, 315,000 Jews managed to escape the Grossreich before the outbreak of the war. Almost 80,000 of those who left managed to enter the Yishuv, despite British demurral, and an equal number were able to gain entry into the United States.[15] The Yishuv took in a large number of young people through its Youth Aliyah program. Another 60,000 immigrants entered Palestine under the *Ha'avara*, or Transfer, agreement.

In August 1933 German Jewry was able to reach an agreement with the Gestapo whereby any Jews who left Germany for Palestine would place a percentage of their capital into an account with the Palestine Trust and Transfer Company (PALTREU). Upon their arrival in Palestine the immigrants received the equivalent of their deposit in German goods or services. The *Ha'avara* agreement officially remained in existence until September 1939, although as Jews became more desperate to leave Germany, the Nazis allowed a smaller percentage of Jewish money to leave the country. Many Jewish organizations in both the United States and Europe opposed the agreement because the American Jewish Congress had declared a worldwide Jewish boycott of German goods in August 1934. They feared that the transfer of German goods to Jewish Palestine would undercut the boycott and render it worthless. These conflicting

ואתם עוד קונים סחורה גרמנית?

‏... והמצב בגרמניה...‏   ‏אצלנו בארץ - ישראל‏

"And you still buy German products?" Anti-*Ha'avara* poster from the Yishuv
Courtesy of the Jabotinsky Institute Archives, Tel Aviv

approaches to the Nazis were taken to the World Zionist Congress (WZC) in 1935. Approving the *Ha'avara* by a wide majority, the WZC placed the agreement under stricter national control by the Jewish Agency Executive, which acted on behalf of the Yishuv. Despite the controversy, the *Ha'avara's* single greatest contribution was the timely removal of some Jews and part of their capital from Nazi Germany.[16]

Efforts at Self-Defense

Soon after the Nazi takeover, under the slogan Wear the Yellow Badge with Pride, members of almost all the factions of German Jewry united into a representative body comprising Zionists and non-Zionists, Orthodox and assimilationists. Under the aegis of scholars such as Martin Buber, they formed a *Kulturbund* and attempted to reconstruct their lives by establishing Jewish cultural and social circles. Say Yes to Our Judaism became their battle cry.

Efforts to reshape German Jewry were based, in some senses, on the long-standing critique of assimilation. German Jews, it was argued, had gone too far in attempting to be Germans and had almost completely abandoned their Jewish identity.[17] Yet this policy was also based on the assumption that the German Jews could weather the storm. Proponents assumed that eventually Nazi antisemitism would lose its appeal. They argued that the regime could not last long and that better days were ahead.[18] The nature of the threat must be kept in mind: Until 1938, most German Jews believed that Nazi actions, although greatly distressing, could be tolerated, since Jews were still permitted an amount of economic survival within what was widely perceived as a "new ghetto."[19] Despite efforts to protect German Jewish rights, emigration increasingly became the choice means of defense, especially after 1938. The Reichsvertretung der Juden in Deutschland (Reich Representation of Jews in Germany, a voluntary association of German Jewish organizations founded in 1933) and other German Jewish organizations, however, opposed flight, condemning it as an effort to escape from communal responsibilities.[20] Although German Jewish organizations modified their approach thereafter, they continued to oppose mass flight until 1938, when it became clear that no *modus vivendi* was possible.[21]

In the summer of 1938 the major German Jewish institutions turned from advocating limited emigration to urging evacuation, stating that the German Jews could no longer bear their suffering. Even in 1938 and 1939, however, the German Jewish leaders opposed flight, preferring an organized and orderly exodus. Despite this policy, a total of 315,000 German and 118,000 Austrian Jews left the Grossreich before the outbreak of World War II.[22]

Another effort to defend Jewish rights was undertaken through the League of Nations. Since Jews were considered a "national minority," and since the rights of national minorities had been regulated by the League in a series of Minorities Treaties signed with Eastern European states in the early 1920s, it seemed reasonable to assume that Jews in Germany could benefit by using the League to pressure the Nazis into canceling their antisemitic campaign.[23] On this basis a number of Jewish organizations planned to petition the League for redress. Since Germany had not signed any of the broad Minorities Treaties and was thus not bound by any legal precedent, this line of operation unfortunately proved futile. Moreover, German Jewry had not been considered, nor did it consider itself, a national minority during the 1920s. As a result these initial efforts to place the Jewish issue on the League's spring agenda failed, as did efforts to persuade Great Britain to sponsor a pro-Jewish resolution.[24]

At this point a change in tactics became necessary. Although Germany was not a signatory to any of the broad Minorities Treaties, the nation was bound by a little used-provision of the 1922 convention on Upper Silesia signed by Germany and Poland.[25] Five articles of this convention (numbers 66, 67, 75, 80, and 83) promised full equality for all German citizens living in Upper Silesia "without distinction of birth, nationality, language, race or religion."[26] Based on this convention, Franz Bernheim, a Silesian Jew, presented a petition to the League Council on May 12, 1933. Despite strong German objections, the League took up the petition and on May 31 concluded that Bernheim's protest was valid. Because of Germany's interest in maintaining the Silesian convention, the Nazis deferred to the League of Nations on this issue and exempted Silesian Jewry from all antisemitic legislation, including the *Arisierung* campaign, until 1937, when the treaty was not renewed.[27]

Although Jewish defenders had won a small victory, they proved unable to gain any further advantage from the League of Nations' action. Primarily, that resulted from the limited scope of the Silesian convention; its terms could not easily be applied to the rest of Germany. Furthermore, no member state of the League was willing to support Jewish efforts at defense. The European powers certainly preferred appeasement to confrontation and therefore shied away from aggressively pursuing Jewish claims regarding German human rights abuses.

Kristallnacht

The expansion of Germany's territory through bloodless conquests heightened Nazi hopes for a full solution to the Jewish question. In late 1938, therefore, the Nazis accelerated forced emigration. In Vienna, SS-Obersturmbannführer Adolf Eichmann created the Zentralstelle für jüdische Auswanderung (Central Office for Jewish Emigration). Eichmann used what may be fairly described as a carrot-and-stick approach, with emphasis on the stick: the open threat of incarceration in a concentration camp, torture, and even death.[28] To a degree, Eichmann succeeded in expanding Jewish emigration, and his approach was adopted — in January 1939 — in the guise of the Reichszentralstelle für jüdische Auswanderung, also headed by Eichmann, but headquartered in Berlin. Eichmann's methods were extended to Prague after the occupation of Czechoslovakia.

Well before that, the Nazis found a simpler

Kristallnacht: Burning of the Rostock Synagogue
Courtesy of the Simon Wiesenthal Center Beit HaShoah Museum of Tolerance Archives/Library, Los Angeles, CA

Response of the *Palestine Post* to *Kristallnacht*
Courtesy of the New York Public Library Jewish Division

method of reducing Germany's unwanted Jewish population. They dumped thousands of East European Jews at border points between Germany and Poland. One well-known case included some 17,000 former Polish Jews who were stripped of German citizenship and dumped on the Polish border near Zbąszyn on October 28, 1938. Not permitted to enter Polish territory, they endured hard conditions, barely existing in the no-man's-land between the two states.[29] Herschel Grynszpan, the son of one of the unfortunates, reacted by assassinating the third secretary of the German embassy in Paris, Ernst vom Rath.[30]

Twenty-four hours later came the Nazi revenge — pogroms throughout Germany, Austria, and Bohemia. That night, November 9–10, 1938, has become known as *Kristallnacht*, the Night of Broken Glass. Over the course of the evening's array of destruction, Jewish homes and shops were looted, scores of synagogues and Jewish communal centers — some hundreds of years old and containing priceless ritual objects — were burned, and ninety-seven Jews were murdered by the mobs. This night marked the beginning of further radicalization and violence. Although the pogrom had actually been planned well in advance, the Nazis used the initial attack as a conveniently timed pretext. Following *Kristallnacht*, the Nazis rounded up as many as 30,000 German Jews and incarcerated them in various concentration camps. These new inmates could buy their freedom only by showing proof that they would emigrate in the span of weeks. The Nazis would no longer permit a slow and orderly emigration; flight was the only escape. In addition, Hermann Göring saw fit to levy a collective fine of 1 billion Reichsmarks on German Jewry to cover insurance company expenses for the Nazi destruction of Jewish property.

Kristallnacht, the bloody pogrom systematically directed at German, Austrian, and Bohemian Jewry the evening of November 9–10, 1938, clearly represented a further decline in the German Jewish position and also demonstrated for the first time that the Nazis sought to solve the "Jewish Question" through violence.[31]

Nazi Plans for Aggression

Jewish affairs were only part of the Nazi regime's policies. Foreign policy, notably concern with territorial expansion and rearmament, also played a crucial role during this period. Foreign policy considerations also affected the condition of German Jewry — the events leading up to *Kristallnacht* are but one notable example — and are thus worthy of attention. In this area of the history of the Third Reich too, a historiographical dispute among historians has developed since 1945: in this case between intentionalists and structuralists.

The intentionalists, whose ranks include H. R. Trevor-Roper and William Shirer, posit that Hitler had a clear set of foreign policy goals, a master plan, and a timetable for conquest and, ultimately, for war.[32] Structuralists, especially A.J.P. Taylor, agree that Hitler had a clear set of goals but deny any master plan or time-table.[33] They point to the fact that the Nazis faltered in their first major foreign policy effort, the assault on Austria following the assassination of Chancellor Engelbert Dollfus.[34]

Structuralists also note that Hitler's goals formed a historical continuum with previous German foreign policy, notably with the secret rearmament policy pursued by the Reichswehr, and the so-called Schwarze Reichswehr, during the Weimar era.[35]

In any case, it is clear that Nazi Germany pursued a policy of rearmament and territorial expansion simultaneously with its persecution of the Jews.[36] Throughout the 1930s, Hitler's foreign policy emphasized slow steps that would not elicit a response from Britain or France. To that extent, Hitler's moves after the abortive events in Vienna in 1934 were moderate in tone and were calculated to elicit maximum benefit for minimum resources. The Reichswehr began secret rearmament in 1934. Only in 1935 did the program become public, and then it was linked to the repudiation of the Versailles Treaty. On February 13, 1934, the Saar region was rejoined to the Reich and on March 7, 1936, the Rhineland was reoccupied. Having already repudiated the Versailles Treaty, Hitler now repudiated the Locarno Pact as well.[37]

Hitler's fears that a British or French response would lead to war proved unfounded. Far from wishing to confront Nazi Germany, both countries feared confrontation, especially if that would lead to war, and preferred to appease Hitler. The British even sought to divert the Nazis' attention from expansion in Europe, a virtual guarantee of conflict, by returning some or all of the German colonies seized in 1918.[38] The policy of appeasement did have its critics, for instance, Winston Churchill, who said, "Unless we take warning in time, we may someday be the victims."[39] But appeasement was popular, since it avoided war and most West Europeans feared mass bloodshed more than they feared immorality.

Of course, appeasement merely emboldened Hitler's voracious appetite. In due course, Austria was reunited with Germany, and Nazi activists, as we have seen, turned to Czechoslovakia, demanding that the Sudetenland, with its Volksdeutsch population, be handed over to Germany. The Munich agreement surrendering Czechoslovakia signaled to Hitler that England and France would not confront him.[40] Munich was not, however, fated to bring peace. The Nazis' territorial quest now turned toward the free city of Danzig and the "Polish corridor," which they considered to be part of Greater German Pomerania. Germany had long sought *Lebensraum* in the East. The Nazis added racial and messianic overtones to this expansionist ideology. Danzig and the Polish corridor were to be Germany's final demand. Peace could still be maintained, Hitler declared, if only Britain and France would cooperate. This time they refused: British Prime Minister Neville Chamberlain was now, belatedly, ready to confront the Nazis. Both Britain and France pledged assistance to Poland if independence was threatened.[41]

World War II and the New Order

By dawn on September 1, 1939, the outlines of a more radical solution were becoming visible. Having secured a non-aggression treaty with the Soviet Union through the Ribbentrop-Molotov pact, signed on August 23, 1939 — much to the surprise of the Western powers — Hitler now felt confident that he could pursue his blitz on Poland with impunity.[42] The *Blitzkrieg* enabled the Wehrmacht to occupy the greater part of Poland within three weeks, and under the terms of the German-Soviet agreement, the Red Army occupied eastern Poland to the San and Bug rivers. In a further series of lightning campaigns, the Nazis occupied in succession Denmark (April 9, 1940), Norway (April 10, 1940), Belgium (May 10, 1940), Holland (May 10, 1940), Luxembourg (May 10, 1940), France (May 10, 1940), Yugoslavia (April 6, 1941), and Greece (April 7, 1941). Through promises, insinuations, and threats, Hitler persuaded some of the other petty European Fascist dictators — Mussolini, Horthy, Antonescu, Tiso, Pavelić, and King Boris of Bulgaria — to join the Nazi cause. With the blitz on the Soviet Union (June 22, 1941), Germany established an empire that, at its height in 1942, stretched from the Atlantic to the Caucasus and from the Arctic to North Africa.[43]

Almost immediately the Nazis began to establish their New Order. In each occupied country they introduced Nazi legislation and administration, including the entire array of anti-Jewish laws. According to Nazi dogma, however, and their perception of the Reich's vital interests, not every country was to be treated the same way. Western countries, such as Denmark, Norway, Belgium, Luxembourg, and Holland, were to be treated kindly and eventually converted to the Nazi philosophy. The Nazis encouraged collaboration and fraternization and aimed to crush resistance to the regime, but with only the minimum force necessary. To a degree, the Nazis applied the same principle to France. This policy derived from two facts: First, discounting Alsace-Lorraine (which area the Nazis had arbitrarily reincorporated into the Reich), France did not have any significant territorial disputes with Germany.[44] Second, a nazified French empire — controlling Madagascar, North Africa from Morocco to Tunisia, and Syria — would almost naturally provide a counterweight to the British Empire. The French would thus force the British, who continued to resist when the rest of Europe had fallen into Hitler's grip, to maintain in their colonies military resources to protect their interests from French encroachment that would be better used elsewhere.[45] To ensure that France would become a useful ally, the Nazis made all-out efforts to encourage collaboration. They left southern France unoccupied (until November 1942) under the collaborationist Vichy government of Marshal Philippe Pétain and Pierre Laval.[46]

In all the occupied countries collaborationists, who can be classified into four types, arose: Opportunists, who saw the Nazis as a vehicle for gaining power; ideologues, largely from Fascist or quasi-Fascist parties; administrative collaborators, members of the former government who remained at their posts initially to help their compatriots but — in many cases — who continued to work for the occupiers long after national interest was no longer served by their assistance to the Nazis; and ad hoc collaborators, the common folk — especially shopkeepers — who had little alternative but to accept the reality and do business with the Germans. The last named were usually the least committed to collaboration and the first to switch allegiance when the tide of war turned.[47]

The collaborators moved by opportunism and ideology were largely one and the same. Men like Vidkun Quisling (Norway), Joseph Darnand (France), and Anton Mussert (Holland) and their associated parties saw fascism as the only solution to the problems of Europe. Working with Nazi Germany, primarily in the anti-Bolshevik and anti-Jewish crusades, seemed to them the only way to save their countries. Many of these men ended up in the non-German volunteer legions of the Waffen-SS, which fought on the Eastern Front. The opportunists also included such men as Marshal Pétain, the president of Vichy, and General Andrei Vlasov, a Russian renegade who threw in his lot with the Nazis, as well as thousands of anonymous Dutch, Latvians, Lithuanians, Ukrainians, Estonians, Cossacks, Flemish, and others. We will probably never fully penetrate the psyche of the collaborators, who believed that Nazism was the only way to save Europe. They were what we might term patriotic traitors, helping the enemy for what seemed to them to be the greater good of the nation.[48]

In general, the same policy of encouraging collaboration in order to avoid resistance was applied to Eastern Europe, although in practice the Nazis were considerably less restrained in their response to resistance in the east. It was recognized, for instance, that peace in Czechoslovakia was vital to the prosecution of the war. However, a unified Czechoslovakia would resist Nazi occupation. Therefore, the Nazis turned to a policy of divide and conquer to ensure Czech quiescence. The former Czech Republic was divided into two: the Reichs Protectorate of Bohemia and Moravia, ruled by a resident Nazi "protector," and an independent Slovak Republic, ruled by Josef Tiso. In fact, the Slovak Republic was little more than a thinly disguised puppet regime with only limited authority. The Nazis implemented similar policies in Yugoslavia, exploiting ethnic rivalries between Croats and Serbs to cement Axis rule and weaken potential resistance. The Croat minority was granted self-determination in the guise of a puppet republic led by Ante Pavelić, whose Ustaša, the Fascist militia, was the principal perpetrator of the crimes committed there, against both the Jews of Yugoslavia and others.[49]

A very different fate awaited the Slavic nationalities, particularly the Poles and the Russians. Although the Nazis would allow some collaboration, their policy was not only to crush all resistance but also to reduce these Slavic groups to a state of abject slavery through the expropriation of property and through cultural and political genocide. The Slavs were to lose their national and cultural identity, their political independence, and even their personal self-respect and to become slaves for the master race — "two-legged cattle," in Reinhard Heydrich's terminology. This, in turn, was to provide Germany with *Lebensraum* to expand its population to the fullest. In this manner the dream of the Thousand-Year Reich stretching from the foothills of the Urals to the Atlantic would be realized. The policy also would provide cheap labor and plentiful food for the Reich, which would insure Germany's security in the future utopian era.[50] Even the Slavs' children could be taken from them. Under the concept of *Lebensborn*, Nazis could kidnap children younger than nine years old who possessed Aryan features and, in fact, send them to special orphans' homes to be brought up in the way of the Hitlerjugend.[51]

Jews were considered to exist in a class unlike any other. No thought of permitting Jewish collaboration was ever entertained by the Nazis, since there could be no compromise with the racial enemy. Indeed, in a Reichstag speech on January 30, 1939, marking the sixth anniversary of the *Machtergreifung*, Hitler said:

If the international Jewish financiers in and outside Europe should succeed in plunging the nations once more into a world war, then the result will not be the Bolshevizing of the earth, and thus the victory of Jewry, but the annihilation of the Jewish race in Europe![52]

To this end, some limited anti-Jewish *Aktionen*, especially associated with the so-called Brennkommandos — the mobile SS units that used arson as a means of sowing terror in the Polish and Polish-Jewish population — were undertaken. The purpose of these acts of random violence was to divide Poles and Jews and to terrorize both populations.[53]

With the occupation of the rest of Europe, however, the Nazis were faced with a considerably larger Jewish population. The goal of *Entjudung* remained unchanged, although the program's scale would now have to be much larger. Wartime realities meant, however, that mass emigration was no longer possible, although those Jews who could get out would — to a limited degree — still be permitted to leave. Two small exits remained open: first, from Vichy France to Spain or Portugal (both neutral states), thence to the United States, South America, or Canada; second, from Vilna (transferred to the independent Lithuania by the Soviets under the terms of the Ribbentrop-Molotov agreement and later incorporated with the Baltic Republics into the USSR) across Russia to China (Shanghai), Japan, or Australia with the ultimate destination being the United States.[54] The Nazis considered two alternative solutions (described below) to the Jewish problem; their failure and the incarceration of the Eastern European Jewish masses in ghettos presaged the Final Solution that emerged in 1941.

"Phantom" Solutions to the Jewish Problem

Initially, the Nazis prepared to settle Jews into a reservation — parallel to the Indian reservations in the United States — to be located in the Lublin-Nisko region of southeast Poland. In concert with the Germanization of the Warthegau and eastern Upper Silesia, both incorporated into the Reich rather being than part of the Generalgouvernement (General Government), the SS began a series of expulsions, of which the deportation of Jews to the Lublin area was to be a major part. Jews from western Poland, Austria, the Protektorat, and the Reich were deported there between October 1939 and February 1940.[55]

The first transport — 600 Jews from Czechoslovakia — left on October 26, 1939, and the last — a transport 1,200 Jews from Pomerania — left in early February. Between these two dates an estimated 78,000 Jews were deported to the reservation.[56] Upon arrival, however, the deportees discovered that no preparations had been made for them. A small number were housed in the Lublin-Lipowa and Majdanek camps; the rest had to fend for themselves in terms of shelter, food, and other living necessities. Thousands died during the bitter cold of the winter 1939–1940. Thereafter, the effort lapsed because of German administrative and tactical considerations. Although advocates of the plan hoped to deport a further 400,000 Jews in 1940, the rolling stock for such mass deportations was simply not available: The trains were needed to transport troops to the West in preparation for operations in the Low Countries and France. Furthermore, the occupation authorities in the General Government protested continued deportations on economic and administrative grounds. The governor of the Lublin province went so far as to declare that he "refuse[d] to bear any responsibility for these steps or their consequences."[57] In any event, a more radical solution to the European Jewish problem made all talk of a reservation moot.

Instead, the Nazis revived a Polish proposal to exile Europe's Jews to Madagascar and keep them there as hostages to ensure the "proper" behavior of free-world Jewry. This proposal was by no means a new one. In 1937, when the Polish government first investigated its feasibility, the proposal was already almost fifty years old. Madagascar was a French colony, but the Poles investigated the matter and concluded that mass Jewish colonization was feasible, but only with great difficulty.[58] Despite some international support, for various reasons, the Polish plan was dropped.

In the summer of 1940, however, the Nazis turned to Madagascar as a realistic solution to the Jewish problem. In effect, two difficulties associated with their plan had been removed. The Nazis controlled France — even if through the Vichy government — and could get the island if they wished. Similarly, the feasibility or suitability of the island for mass migration did not really interest the Nazis, who could hardly have cared less if the Jews flourished or perished as long as they were removed from Aryan Europe and were placed under strict SS control. Therefore, serious planning proceeded and by August 15, 1940, a memorandum on the scheme was presented to Hitler.[59]

The Madagascar plan, however, hinged on one of two possibilities: either the British agreed to Hitler's June 1940 peace plan and joined him in an anti-Bolshevik crusade, or Britain succumbed to superior Nazi forces and was occupied.[60] In both cases, the Madagascar plan was contingent upon gaining access to the Royal Navy and British merchant marine. In fact, the Germans proved incapable of transporting their proposed invasion force across the English Channel. They certainly could not transport all of Europe's Jews, approximately 4 million persons in all, with their small fleet. Thus, when neither British surrender nor German victory occurred, the Madagascar plan no longer represented a feasible policy and was abandoned.

Preparation: 1939–1941

In the interim, the Nazi bureaucracy took a number of steps designed to simplify any long-term solution that was adopted. In Poland the Nazis incarcerated Jews in ghettos. Some of the ghettos located in large cities were sealed with walls, barbed wire, and guard posts. Jews lived in appalling conditions in these closed ghettos. In Warsaw nearly half a million Jews resided in an area adequate for less than 100,000; similar conditions existed in Lodz, Krakow, Tarnow, and Lublin. In addition to over-crowding — and even more important — the ghettos were given a totally inadequate supply of food, medicine, and fuel. In some instances, even clean drinking water became scarce. Sanitary conditions declined rapidly as over-crowding, starvation, dysentery, typhus, and other diseases took hold.

In many of the smaller Jewish communities, the Nazis chose to leave the Jewish population intact for the time being. These communities were designated "open" ghettos. In places where Jews were allowed to remain in their previous homes without having to relocate, conditions were somewhat better. Still, even in those places, Jewish families who happened to live at the fringes of town or in predominantly Christian neighborhoods had to find living space within the "Jewish street" or were ordered to move into the larger closed ghettos. Nevertheless, these were but temporary havens, because the open ghettos were the first to undergo *Aussiedlungsaktionen* and, as a rule, almost all of them were made *judenrein* all at once.

In 1940 and 1941, however, the Nazis opted for what may be seen as a natural solution to the Jewish problem. Instead of murdering Jews outright, they waited for conditions in the closed ghettos to take their toll. Nearly 100,000 Jews, representing 20 percent of the Jewish population in Warsaw, perished in that city during the winter of 1940–1941. The numbers were similar in other locations. In both open and closed ghettos Jews were systematically starved and worked to death.[61]

The severity of conditions in the ghettos may also be seen in mortality statistics for Polish Jewry. Before World War II, the mortality rate for Polish Jewry was 9.6 per 1,000. By the end of 1940, the rate had risen to 39.2 per 1,000, and one year later to 75.7 per 1,000. In 1942 the estimated mortality rate — adjusted to take into account deaths by direct Nazi murder actions — was 159.8 per 1,000.[62] At this mortality rate, the Nazis could have eliminated East European Jewry in approximately a decade, even without resorting to direct murder, just by maintaining their ghetto policy.

Within the ghettos, the Nazis thoroughly reorganized Jewish life to fit their own

Homeless child sleeping on a street in the Warsaw ghetto
Courtesy of the Simon Wiesenthal Center Beit HaShoah Museum of Tolerance Archives/Library, Los Angeles, CA

ideology, plans, and needs. Thus began the process of deassimilation, the reversal of the previous century of European Jewish history. In every community, the Nazis selected the members for a Jewish council, the Judenrat, and appointed a *Judenälteste* to run the council. The purpose of these institutions was to facilitate Germany's Jewish policy on the local level. From the Nazi point of view, the Judenrat had three basic functions: To provide the Nazi authorities with updated lists of Jews and their possessions; to pay levies; and to provide Jewish laborers for Nazi-sponsored work projects.[63] In almost every community the Nazis also established a Jewish auxiliary police, the Ordnungsdienst, the role of which was to ensure compliance with Nazi regulations and to help round up Jews for "relocation."[64]

Initially, the Jewish communities welcomed these entities. The councils and police seemed to reflect the possibility of accommodation and survival even under the Nazis.[65] These institutions played a controversial role in the life and death of the ghettos. Objectively, the Judenräte facilitated Nazi extermination policy. Although not always willingly, the *Judenältesten* were forced to provide lists of deportees to be sent "eastward." Not all *Judenältesten* cooperated with the Nazis, but most did initially. A small proportion even continued to cooperate after their discovery that "relocation" actually meant deportation to a death camp.[66] We must, however, note that this was not the intent of the council members, elders, or policemen. They saw themselves in the unenviable position of having no recourse but to carry out Nazi orders. In their estimation it was likely that the Germans would have proceeded without their "help" and might have been infinitely more brutal without it. In the interim they hoped to maintain morale and keep their communities intact. Moreover, they reasoned that if they acted properly, at least a remnant of their communities could be saved, although this would mean sacrificing some Jews to the Nazis. Not all the *Judenältesten* were willing or able to bear the pressure. Adam Czerniakow, of Warsaw, refused to accommodate any further deportations when he discovered that what the Nazis termed "relocation" meant death in the gas chambers of Treblinka. Czerniakow took his own life rather than be party to the Nazi crimes.[67] Other elders did not follow his example. Leaders such as Jacob Gens, of Vilna; Mordechai Chaim Rumkowski, of Lodz; and Moses Merrin, of Sosnowiec, developed into quasi-messianic figures. In their view survival made it necessary for Jews to work hard for the Nazis in order to become vital to the Nazi war machine; some sacrifice was unavoidable until the Allied victory would signal the liberation of at least part of the community.[68]

Their tragedy was that they imputed some rationality to the Nazis: Would Germany exterminate even those who could be useful workers in the war industries? The elders' hopes to mitigate the conditions under which Jews lived proved futile — as futile in the long run as the social and cultural activities — for ultimately the Nazi Moloch would only be satisfied with a completely *judenrein* Europe.

Life and Death in the Ghettos

For Jews, this phase of Nazi persecution posted a new challenge for survival. Virtually all of European Jewry was united under the heel of Nazi oppression. Yet individual Jewish communities were increasingly isolated from one another. Because of Nazi laws severely curtailing Jewish movement from one place to another without permission, on penalty of imprisonment or death, hardly any Jew knew what was going on in the next community, even if they were separated by only a few kilometers. Further obstacles also existed. East European Jewry in particular was doubly isolated: from the general environment and from each other. Whereas aggression by the common enemy should have instilled a sense of solidarity, in reality Jews felt abandoned by the local non-Jewish populations. Within the Jewish community itself was the possibility that communal

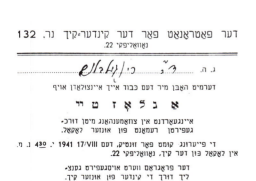

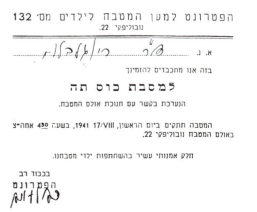

Dr. Emmanuel Ringelblum's invitation to a charity tea party in the Warsaw ghetto
Courtesy of the Żydowski Instytut Historyczny/U.S. Holocaust Memorial Museum

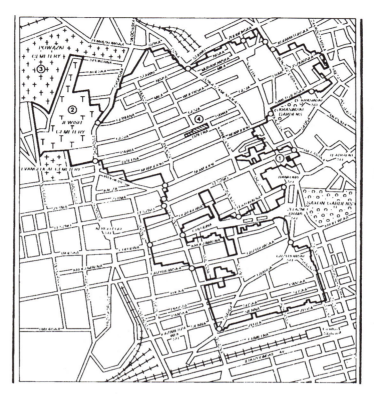

Above: The Warsaw Ghetto
Authors' Collection

Below: The Lodz Ghetto
Courtesy of Dr. Lucjan Dobrozsycki

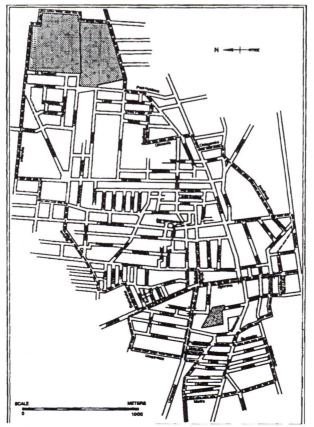

anarchy would take hold — that instead of working collectively, each individual would attempt to save him/herself and immediate family members. Although such cases did exist on a limited scale, anarchy did not reign. Jewish communities lost much of their cohesion, but they did not collapse.

Despite the numerous obstacles, moreover, the Jews did not surrender their human dignity. They opened soup kitchens to feed the hungry and maintained clandestine schools, synagogues, and cultural activities to feed Jewish souls. The prewar Jewish political parties continued to operate in the underground, publishing a secret Jewish press and preparing the young members for the day of the battle. Although at first glance it would appear that Jewish disunity was maintained — each party operated on its own — a trend toward unification was also perceptible. In particular, the debate over Jewish nationalism ceased to animate as passionate an ideological struggle as it had in the prewar era.[69] In Warsaw a small group of young historians, led by Emmanuel Ringelblum, set up a secret archive, code-named *Oneg Shabbat*, in which they painstakingly documented Jewish life and suffering. Similar secret archival undertakings were conducted in Bialystok, Kovno, Krakow, Terezin, and other ghettos. Dozens of other individuals documented the torment of Jewish Europe in diaries and personal journals.[70]

Indicative of the Jewish will to live were the ingenious methods Jewish children used to smuggle food and medicine into the ghettos. Jews were incarcerated like vermin; they were tired, cold, and hungry; they were hounded, hunted, and mistreated by almost everyone. Yet the suicide rate in the ghettos was relatively small. "M'hot zei in drerd di rotzchim" (We shall yet live to see these murderers in their graves) and "A sho gelebt iz oichet gelebt" (An hour of life is a lifetime) represented the battle cry of these eternally optimistic Jews. Jews did not lose their sense of humor and even mocked their tormentors, waiting, hoping, and praying for the day of vengeance.[71]

From World War to Ideological Crusade

In the aftermath of the Madagascar plan's failure, the Nazis sought the means for an encompassing solution to the Jewish problem. To be sure, their biological policy — starving the inhabitants of the ghettos and slowly working them to death — was taking its toll. Indeed, in a retrospective statement in August 1942 on rations for Jews, Hans Frank, the Nazi governor general of Poland, noted bluntly that the rations were meant to be a death penalty.[72] Still, Jews had managed to supplement their meager rations, and as a result, the program was moving too slowly. Moreover, what served as a policy in Eastern Europe could not be applied elsewhere: Jewish communities in Western, Central, and Southern Europe were too small to make ghettoization feasible.

Two additional elements entered into the Nazis' calculations. First, with each new victory, another Jewish community came under Nazi control. In April 1941 Greece and Yugoslavia were occupied, and it seemed plausible that Britain — which remained defiant — would ultimately capitulate. Afrika Korps advances in North Africa brought yet further Jews under the Nazi heel: In Cyrenaica and western Egypt

Janusz Korczak with a group of children from the Warsaw ghetto orphanage, 1940

Courtesy of the Simon Wiesenthal Center Beit HaShoah Museum of Tolerance Archives/Library, Los Angeles, CA

Theatrical performance in the Warsaw ghetto, 1941
Courtesy of the Simon Wiesenthal Center Beit HaShoah Museum of Tolerance Archives/Library, Los Angeles, CA

at the very least; by the summer of 1942 even the Yishuv was under direct Nazi threat.[73] Clearly, the policy of *Entjudung* could not proceed. And Hitler had made *Entjudung* one of his main political and military goals.

By October 1940 a second consideration influenced Nazi policies. In that month Hitler, tiring of the direct — but unsuccessful — air assault on Great Britain began to contemplate an assault on the Soviet Union. The attack would not merely be another military operation. Despite representing the reversal of two years of German foreign policy, an attack on the Soviet Union actually had been a centerpiece of Hitler's *Weltanschauung*. Not only would occupation of the vast territories of the Soviet Union give the German people *Lebensraum*, but the successful destruction

of the Soviet state would also eliminate the final bastion of the Jewish threat: Bolshevism. Thus, the Nazis, ever in pursuit of an apocalyptic struggle, moved from a global war to an ideological crusade.[74]

In light of the crusading nature of the planned operations, conventional norms of military behavior could no longer apply. The commanders of the Wehrmacht were duly instructed — and passed on these instructions as well — that brutal behavior toward the enemy was, henceforth, to be the order of the day on the Eastern Front. Red Army soldiers who resisted too much, political commissars, resisters, and "all life unworthy of being lived" were to be eliminated. Included in the latter category were all Jews, their physical elimination being considered of paramount importance.[75]

To be sure, no single document has ever come to light specifically ordering the extermination of European Jewry. Historians have even argued over the date and context of the decision to slaughter the Jews.[76] Yet, it is clear to all — from the available evidence — that the decision to move from passive persecution to active extermination of Jews was coterminous with the decision to invade the Soviet Union. It could hardly have made sense — in Hitler's mind or in the minds of his henchmen — to fight against an ideological enemy abroad while allowing that same enemy to fester in the occupied territory. As justification, the army officers and SS and NSDAP leaders explained that the extermination was "the *Führer's* wish."[77]

By spring 1941 the decision to exterminate the Jews moved from theory to practice. A recruiting call yielded volunteers from all the branches of the SS — the Sicherheitsdienst, Gestapo, and Kriminalpolizei. From these volunteers 3,000 men were selected and assembled into four Einsatzgruppen: Einsatzgruppe A, with 1,000 men, was commanded by SS-Brigadeführer Franz W. Stahlecker (until mid-March 1942) and operated in Estonia, Latvia, Lithuania, and parts of Belorussia; Einsatzgruppe B, with 655 men, was commanded by SS-Brigadeführer Arthur Nebe (until November 1941) and operated in the Russian Republic and parts of Belorussia; Einsatzgruppe C, with 750 men, was commanded by SS-Standartenführer Dr. Emil Otto Rasch (until October 1941) and operated in central and northern Ukraine and — among other massacres — was responsible for the Babi Yar massacre, outside of Kiev; Einsatzgruppe D, with 600 men, was commanded by SS-Gruppenführer Professor Otto Ohlendorf (until June 1942) and operated in southern Ukraine, the Crimea, and the Caucasus. The four Einsatzgruppen were further subdivided into nineteen Sonderkommandos/Einsatzkommandos, each of which reported to its Einsatzgruppe, which, in turn, reported to one of the four regional Higher SS and Police Leaders (HSSPF), who reported to the Reichssicherheitshauptamt (RSHA) in Berlin, under whose overall authority this criminal operation functioned.[78]

Starting with June 22, 1941, the four Einsatzgruppen followed the Wehrmacht deep into Soviet territory, seeking out and destroying Jewish communities along the way. Throughout the Eastern Front they took the same action: Before dawn, the men of an Einsatzkommando would surround a town or village with the assistance of local volunteers — *Hilfswillige* — made up mostly of Ukrainians, Latvians, Lithuanians, or Estonians (depending on location). On many occasions (when they had to deal with large numbers of Jews) they would also be assisted by Wehrmacht military police, units of the Waffen-SS, or even sharpshooters from Wehrmacht line units. The Jews would be ordered to assemble in the village center; most of the unsuspecting Jews would comply. Jews trying to hide would be ferreted out by the *Hilfswillige* and killed. A selection would take place with a few Jews being left temporarily behind to gather up Jewish belongings and do the cleanup. The rest would be driven or marched out of town to prepared pits, anti-tank ditches, ravines, or other sites. They would be ordered to undress and marched off ten at a time to the edge of the pit, where they would be shot. Occasionally the Nazis took no chances and tied their victims' hands before shooting them in the back of the neck.[79]

In the short time of their first sweep, from June 22 through December 1941, the Einsatzgruppen performed their mission well, killing close to 1 million Jews and numerous others.[80] The daily toll of murder, however, soon affected some of the men, many of whom took to drink. Even HSSPF General Erich von dem Bach-Zelewski, responsible for the Einsatzgruppen, suffered a breakdown. Moreover, the process was neither fast enough nor secret enough for the murderers. It also could not be applied to other territories under Nazi control where life had, to a degree, been stabilized.

Planning for a Final Solution

For all these reasons, the Nazi hierarchy sought new means to accomplish the now definitive goal of making European Jewry extinct.

Babi Yar: Soldier masking the truth by distributing rations to Jews about to be killed
Courtesy of the Simon Wiesenthal Center Beit HaShoah Museum of Tolerance Archives/Library, Los Angeles, CA

As early as July 1941 — even before it was clear that continued Einsatzgruppen operations would be difficult — Göring ordered Heydrich to make "all necessary preparations with regard to organizational, practical, and financial aspects for an overall solution to the Jewish Question in the German sphere of influence in Europe."[81] Actual planning began in October 1941. In the interim, the Einsatzgruppen received a number of experimental gas vans. As a short-term solution, the gas vans worked, but they did not represent a long-term solution: The vans, built on captured French military vehicles, continually broke down. Furthermore, the murderers still had to face their victims, a fact that had led to psychological problems to begin with.[82]

The culmination of Nazi planning was the Wannsee Conference, which took place on January 20, 1942. During the eighty-five-minute conference the plan for an *Endlösung* was finally put into place: The Einsatzgruppen would continue to operate in places where their style of operation was practical. To handle the anticipated 14,723,468 Jewish victims, special camps — *Vernichtungslager* — were to be set up for the sole purpose of murder.

After intense discussion the Nazis decided to deal first with Polish Jewry and to spread the Final Solution from there. Starting in spring 1942, under the pretense of "resettlement," they transported the majority of Polish Jews in closed cattle wagons to the newly established death camps. The daily transports of Jews were met on their arrival to the seemingly peaceful camp by a small number of strange-looking prisoners in striped pajamas, who had been selected to take part in the Sonderkommando. A few of the arriving victims in the four

Vernichtungslager were chosen for work; the rest were sent immediately, or almost immediately, to the gas chambers. Depending on location and method, it took the victims from ten to thirty minutes to expire. Members of the Sonderkommando took the bodies from the chamber — examining each body closely for any hidden valuables previously overlooked and tearing out any gold fillings or crowns from their teeth — moving them into crematoria, where the bodies were burned, or burying them in giant pits. In most cases, after a short period of time, the Sonderkommando was disposed of too and was replaced by a newly selected group. Meanwhile, other crews — also potential candidates for the gas chamber — sorted, stored, and packed the victims' personal belongings for shipment to the Reich.[83]

Jews in every country would ultimately face their turn at a railroad platform or other impromptu *Umschlagplatz* (assembly place). *Aussiedlung*, the Nazi code word for deportation, became the byword for death. Only a few Jews, primarily those needed for the German war effort, were given a temporary respite. After Poland, the Grossreich was rendered *judenrein*. The Jews of Holland, Belgium, and France were the hunters' next targets. South European Jewry and the Jews of North Africa soon followed, as did the Jews of Slovakia. Finally, the Jews of the Axis-allied states — Italy, Romania, and Hungary — were liquidated. In all, 6 million Jews were done in by the murderous designs of the Nazis and their henchmen.[84]

Notes

1. Lucy S. Dawidowicz, *The War Against the Jews*, 10th anniversary ed., New York: Macmillan, 1986. Ch. 1–2 offers the standard intentionalist account.
2. Abraham J. Edelheit, "Historiography of the Holocaust," in Israel Gutman (editor in chief), *The Encyclopedia of the Holocaust*, New York: Macmillan, 1989, vol. 2, pp. 666–672 reviewed both schools.
3. On the Nazi use of medical terminology see Erich Goldhagen, "Pragmatism, Function and Belief in Nazi Antisemitism," *Midstream*, vol. 18 # 10 (1972), 52–62.
4. Cf. *American Jewish Yearbook*, vol. 35 (1934/1935), 38–40. A fuller list of Nazi laws, as promulgated in the pages of the official *Reichsgesetzblatt*, is provided herein in Part 2, "Dictionary of Holocaust Terms."
5. In addition to the daily press for those days, see ibid., pp. 29–31.
6. Ibid., pp. 31–32.
7. Cf. Karl A. Schleunes, *The Twisted Road to Auschwitz*, Urbana, IL: University of Chicago Press, 1970, pp. 63–84.
8. Ibid., pp. 84–91.
9. Cf. Philip Friedman, "The Fate of the Jewish Book," in his *Roads to Extinction: Essays on the Holocaust*, Philadelphia: JPS, 1980, pp. 88–99.
10. "Legal Status of the Jews Defined in Orders Issued by Nazis," *Congress Bulletin*, vol. 2 # 4 (1935), 1, 4.
11. Schleunes, *Twisted Road*, ch. 5.
12. On the *Anschluss* see William L. Shirer, *The Rise and Fall of the Third Reich*, New York: Simon and Schuster, 1960, ch. 11; on the treatment of Jews see B. Z. Pinot, "Hitler's Entry into Vienna," *Yad Vashem Bulletin*, # 3 (1958), 15–16.
13. Shirer, *Rise and Fall*, ch. 12–13.
14. Cf. John G. Lexa, "Anti-Jewish Laws and Regulations in the Protectorate of Bohemia and Moravia," in *The Jews of Czechoslovakia*, Philadelphia: JPS, 1983, vol. 3, pp. 75–103.
15. Cf. Werner Rosenstock, "Exodus 1933–1939: A Survey of Jewish Emigration from Germany," *LBIYB*, vol. 1 (1956), 373–390.
16. This section is summarized from Abraham J. Edelheit, "The Yishuv in the Shadow of the Holocaust," Ph.D. dissertation, City University of New York, 1992, ch. 5.
17. The most famous expression of this self-defense formula is contained in Robert Weltsch's essay, "Tragt ihn mit Stolz, den gelben Fleck," *Jüdische Rundschau*, April 4, 1933, p. 1.
18. Cf. Abraham Barkai, *From Boycott to Annihilation*, Hanover, NH: University Press of New England, 1989, p. 37.
19. Ibid., pp. 47–54; Edelheit, "Yishuv," pp. 43–44.
20. For an example of this line of reasoning see Alfred Wiener's statement in *CV Zeitung*, April 27, 1933, p. 1.
21. Abraham Margaliot, "The Problem of Rescue of German Jewry During the Years 1933–1939; the Reasons for the Delay in Their Emigration from the Third Reich," in Y. Gutman and E. Zuroff (eds.), *Rescue Attempts During the Holocaust*, Jerusalem: Yad Vashem, 1977, pp. 256–259.
22. Ibid., p. 263.
23. For a study on the legal and political context of the national Minorities Treaties, see Oscar I. Janowsky, *The Jews and Minority Rights*, New York: Columbia University Press, 1966.
24. Nathan Feinberg, ‫המערכה היהודית נגד היטלר על בימת חבר הלאומים:הפטיציה של ברנהיים‬ (The Jewish struggle against Hitler at the League of Nations: The Bernheim Petition), Jerusalem: Magnes Press, 1957, pp. 31–35.
25. "The Bernheim Petition to the League of Nations," *AJYB*, vol. 35 (1934/1935), 74–101.
26. Article 66 of the Silesian convention, quoted in ibid., p. 74.

27. Feinberg, *המערכה היהודית*, passim.

28. A melodramatic, but compelling, example of Eichmann's approach was provided by William Perl, *The Four Front War*, New York: Crown, 1979, pp. 11–13.

29. Rita Thalmann and Emmanuel Feinermann, *Crystal Night: 9–10 November 1938*, London: Thames and Hudson, 1974, pp. 25–32.

30. Ibid., pp. 41–43.

31. Ibid., ch. 3–5.

32. Shirer, *Rise and Fall*, pp. 279–308.

33. A.J.P. Taylor, *The Origins of the Second World War*, New York: Atheneum, 1961, pp. 9, 13–14.

34. On the Nazi defeat in Austria, see G. Kindermann, *Hitler's Defeat in Austria, 1933–1934*, Boulder, CO: Westview Press, 1988.

35. Klaus Hildebrand, *The Foreign Policy of the Third Reich*, Berkeley: University of California Press, 1973, pp. 1–12.

36. Cf. Dawidowicz, *War Against the Jews*, ch. 6. Although somewhat overstating the case, especially given her intentionalist interpretation of the course of events, Dawidowicz does provide a basic outline of the events.

37. Shirer, *Rise and Fall*, pp. 281–303.

38. Martin Gilbert and R. Gott, *The Appeasers*, Boston: Houghton Mifflin, 1963, pp. 80–101.

39. Speech of March 19, 1935, cited in Winston Churchill, *The Gathering Storm* (History of the Second World War, vol. 1), Boston: Houghton Mifflin, 1948, p. 122.

40. Gilbert and Gott, *Appeasers*, pt. 2.

41. Peter Calvocoressi and Guy Wint, *Total War: The Story of World War II*, 1st ed., New York: Pantheon Books, 1972, p. 84.

42. Ibid., ch. 5.

43. See the map in Gordon Wright, *The Ordeal of Total War*, New York: Harper and Row, 1968, p. 109.

44. Cf. Norman Rich, *Hitler's War Aims*, New York: Norton, 1974, vol. 2, ch. 5–8.

45. The classic application of this Nazi policy was in French-controlled Syria: During the summer and autumn of 1941 the British felt the need to remove Vichy influence in Syria, thus weakening Allied forces deployed in North Africa. See Barrie Pitt, *The Crucible of War*, New York: Paragon House, 1986, pp. 290–293, 310–314.

46. Robert Aron, *The Vichy Regime, 1940–1944*, Boston: Beacon Press, 1958, pp. 121–133.

47. David Littlejohn, *The Patriotic Traitors*, London: Heineman, 1971, and Werner Rings, *Life with the Enemy*, Garden City, NY: Doubleday, 1982, are the most extensive histories of European collaboration, a subject that remains a raw nerve in most European countries to this day. Cf. the recent report on French collaboration in the *New York Times*, April 7, 1993, pp. 1, 6.

48. P. Buss and A. Mollo, *Hitler's Germanic Legions*, London: Macdonald and Jane's, 1978.

49. Cf. Rich, *War Aims*, ch. 3, 9.

50. Ibid., ch. 4, 11.

51. A journalistic account of *Lebensborn* is provided in Marc Hillel and Clarissa Henry, *Of Pure Blood*, New York: McGraw-Hill, 1976.

52. Hitler's now-infamous speech is excerpted in Jeremy Noakes and Geoffrey Pridham (eds.), *Documents on Nazism*, 1st ed., New York: Viking Press, 1974, pp. 485–486.

53. Examples of early Nazi mistreatment of Jews in Poland are contained in Shimon Huberband, *Kiddush Hashem: Jewish Religious and Cultural Life in Poland During the Holocaust*, Hoboken, NJ: Ktav, for Yeshiva University Press, 1987, pp. 34–38.

54. On escape via Vichy see Varian Fry, "Operation Emergency Rescue," *New Leader*, vol. 48 #25 (1965), 11–14. On Vilna see Zorach Warhaftig, *פליט ושריד בימי השואה* (Refugee and Remnant during the Holocaust), Jerusalem: Yad Vashem, 1984, ch. 5–6, and Yehuda Bauer, "Rescue Operations Through Vilna," *Yad Vashem Studies* [hereafter *YVS*], vol. 9 (1973), 215–233. On

refugees in general, see Michael R. Marrus, *The Unwanted: European Refugees in the Twentieth Century*, New York: Oxford University Press, 1985, pp. 203–207.

55. Philip Friedman, "The Lublin Reservation and the Madagascar Plan: Two Aspects of Nazi Jewish Policy During the Second World War," in *Roads to Extinction*, pp. 34-37.

56. Ibid., p. 39.

57. General Government Administrative report, March 28, 1940, cited in ibid., p. 40.

58. Friedman, "Lublin Reservation," pp. 44–46. On the Polish aspects of the plan, see Marrus, *Unwanted*, pp. 186–187.

59. Friedman, "Lublin Reservation," pp. 46–49.

60. Ibid., pp. 50–52. See also Leni Yahil, "Madagascar — Phantom Solution for the Jewish Question," in B. Vago and G. Mosse (eds.), *Jews and Non-Jews in Eastern Europe*, Jerusalem: Israel Universities Press, 1974, pp. 315–334.

61. Cf. Philip Friedman, "The Jewish Ghettos of the Nazi era," in his *Roads to Extinction*, pp. 59–87.

62. These statistics are cited from Lucjan Dobroszycki (comp.), *Chronicle of the Lódz Ghetto*, New Haven: Yale University Press, 1984, pp. l–li.

63. Isaiah Trunk, *Judenrat*, New York: Stein and Day, 1977, ch. 1–2.

64. Ibid., ch. 18.

65. Ibid., ch. 15.

66. Ibid., ch. 11, 16.

67. Arye Tartakower, "Adam Czerniakow — the Man and His Supreme Sacrifice," *YVS*, vol. 6 (1967), 55–82. Emmanuel Ringelblum's evaluation of Czerniakow was much less positive. See his *Notes from the Warsaw Ghetto*, New York: Schocken Books, 1974, p. 316. On Czerniakow's diary see Raul Hilberg et al. (eds.), *The Warsaw Diary of Adam Czerniakow*, New York: Stein and Day, 1979.

68. See Friedman, *Roads to Extinction*, ch. 11–13.

69. Nathan Eck, "The Place of Jewish Political Parties in the Countries Under Nazi Rule," in *Jewish Resistance During the Holocaust*, Jerusalem: Yad Vashem, 1971, pp. 132–138; and Joseph Kermish, "The Land of Israel in the Life of the Ghetto as Reflected in the Illegal Warsaw Ghetto Press," *YVS*, vol. 5 (1963), 105–131.

70. Joseph Kermish (ed.), *To Live with Honor and Die with Honor*, Jerusalem: Yad Vashem, 1986, presents edited selections from the *Oneg Shabbat* archive.

71. For example, see *The Warsaw Diary of Chaim A. Kaplan*, ed. by Abraham I. Katsh, rev. ed., New York: Collier Books, 1973, pp. 130–132.

72. Speech by Frank, August 24, 1942, cited in Léon Poliakov, *Harvest of Hate*, New York: Holocaust Library, 1979, p. 40. Nevertheless, the date of Frank's speech must be kept in mind; by then the Nazis had already converted to a policy of mass extermination.

73. On the widening war in Europe, see Calvocoressi and Wint, *Total War*, ch. 8.

74. Cf. Omer Bartov, *The Eastern Front, 1941–1945: German Troops and the Barbarization of Warfare*, New York: Macmillan, 1986, and his *Hitler's Army: Soldiers, Nazis and War in the Third Reich*, New York: Oxford University Press, 1991.

75. Three of the most important extant documents regarding Nazi extermination policy on the Eastern Front are contained in Yitzhak Arad et al. (eds.), *Documents on the Holocaust*, New York: Ktav, 1981, pp. 375–377.

76. For a functionalist and intentionalist perspective on the problem, see (respectively): Christopher Browning, *Fateful Months: Essays on the Emergence of the Final Solution*, New York: Holmes and Meier, 1985, ch. 1, and Gerald Fleming, *Hitler and the Final Solution*, Berkeley: University of California Press, 1982, ch. 3.

77. Fleming, *Hitler*, p. 128.

78. Yitzhak Arad et al. (eds.), *The Einsatzgruppen Reports*, New York: Holocaust Library, 1989, pp. v–xiii.

79. A typical Einsatzkommando operation primarily resulted in the mass murder of Jews, along with Communist officials, snipers, and resisters. See, e.g., Arad et al., *Einsatzgruppen Reports*, pp. 10–12.

80. This number is based on an estimate of total losses incurred by Soviet Jewry and including Jews in formerly Polish territories that remained administratively part of the Nazi Reichskommissariat Ostland. For a recent survey of estimates see Gutman, *Encyclopedia of the Holocaust*, app. 6, vol. 4, pp. 1797–1802.

81. Göring to Heydrich, July 31, 1941, in Arad et al., *Documents on the Holocaust*, p. 233.

82. Cf. Browning, *Fateful Months*, ch. 3.

83. Cf. the Wannsee Conference Protocol in Arad et al., *Documents on the Holocaust*, pp. 249–261.

84. The standard figure cited by all historians is 6 million but it is not an exact figure. Given limited record keeping by the Nazis (who wanted to keep the Final Solution secret) and the imprecise nature of prewar Jewish population figures (especially in Eastern Europe), the exact number of victims will never be known with any certainty. Estimates on the actual number of victims vary, although the best estimate is 5,700,000 European Jews murdered, excluding those from the territories of the former Soviet Union. This number is based on the so-called Kohrer Report that was produced in 1943 by Richard Kohrer, the chief of statistics for the SS, at Himmler's orders. Adding the estimated 1.5 million Soviet Jews murdered makes a total of 7.2 million victims, and recently uncovered evidence suggests that the number may be even higher. For the complete text of the Kohrer Report see G. Wellers, "The Number of Victims and the Kohrer Report," in S. Klarsfeld (ed.), *The Holocaust and Neo-Nazi Mythomania*, New York: Beate Klarsfeld Foundation, 1978, pp. 139–211. For a more recent attempt to estimate the number of victims, see Gutman, *Encyclopedia of the Holocaust*, app. 6.

5

THE GEOGRAPHY OF
THE HOLOCAUST

The Concentration Camps

Terror played a key role in Nazi rule. Routine seizures of hostages, summary executions, and imprisonment all kept occupied peoples in line. This system of applied terror operated through a spiderweb of camps established throughout Europe by the SS state. As early as February 1933 the Gestapo rounded up political enemies into *Schutzhaftlager* (protective-custody camps), the so-called *wilde Lager* (wild camps) that the SA had set up. These were, in many instances, set up in abandoned factories, warehouses, or the barns of neglected farms. These camps lacked central command, and the prisoners subsisted in impossible conditions, with beatings, torture, unproductive work, and starvation being the rule. As the SS gained the upper hand in its ideological struggle with the SA, culminating in the June 30, 1934, *Nacht der Langen Messer* (Night of the Long Knives), Himmler assumed the key internal security position in the Reich and reorganized the entire camp system.

An Inspectorate of Concentration Camps was created within the SS on July 4, 1934, headed by the *Lagerführer* of Dachau, SS-Gruppenführer Theodor Eicke. Eicke immediately undertook an intensive program to restructure the camp system. In particular, the new system emphasized the strict and proper training of camp guards, who were organized into an elite SS unit, the Totenkopfverbände.[1] In 1936 a camp order, serving as the model for all camps, was introduced. The order was based on a system of brutal punishment and the complete organization of the inmates' daily life. Thereafter, the camp system was vastly enlarged to accommodate thousands of new inmates.

By September 1, 1939 — when the Wehrmacht blitzed its way into Poland — Germany had established a full-fledged concentration camp system, composed of seven *Stammlager*, or main camps: Dachau, Buchenwald, Sachsenhausen, Flossenburg, Mauthausen, Neuengamme, and Ravensbrück. All the camps had numerous subcamps, and all operated uniformly, with a well-drilled central command. With the subsequent occupation of most of Europe, these SS camps were expanded into a network of thousands of camps that crisscrossed the continent.[2]

Most of the new camps — especially in Eastern Europe — were organized similarly to the early camps, except that now the SS made the prisoners their chattel, renting them out as labor gangs to German industry. Under this arrangement, close to 9,000 *Zivilarbeitslager* and *Judenlager* were established in the Reich and throughout the occupied countries. Most of these camps operated only for the duration of a single labor project, some with only dozens of inmates and others with thousands. Once the work was completed — unless a new project appeared in the same region — the camp was liquidated and its Jewish inmates were either transferred or murdered. Non-Jewish inmates in camps made up of different nationalities were, in some cases, released but, in most cases, were sent into Germany as "volunteer" laborers. During the deportation period — from late 1941 through mid-1943 — Jewish camp inmates, whether a project was completed or not, were transported to the death camps to be killed, the project being completed by non-Jews.[3]

After the Nazi defeat, hundreds of these private companies professed total ignorance of, and responsibility for, the bestial acts and behavior toward concentration camp inmates they so utterly abused. Yet during the war these same companies had offered shares of stock and profit sharing to many a camp commandant and SS cartel for supplying them with a steady stream of personnel paid for with pennies a day.[4]

Cruelty was the order of the day in all the SS camps, although the camps not belonging to the concentration camp system, the so-called unattached camps, tended to be among the worst. Through this terror, violence, and sadism, the Nazis aimed to break the human spirit of the victim; not to convert him or her to the Nazi way of thinking, but merely to dehumanize, to reduce the victim to human refuse. The Nazis sneeringly referred to their victims as Muselmänner, a reference to prisoners who had lost all will to live, bent over like Muslims at prayer.

In all, forty-three different categories of camps existed. Each category appertained to at least one camp, although most referred to more than one. In most cases, camps — especially *Stammlager* (main camp) — were officially listed in more than one category. In addition, almost all the camps shared certain characteristics: Hard work, poor diet, overcrowded and unsanitary living conditions, and SS cruelty. The SS would utilize to the utmost, in the shortest time possible, production by free Jewish slave labor to enrich its treasury. Thus, in the *Judenarbeitslager* (JAL) — used as holding pens pending transportation of Jews to death camps and extermination sites — excruciating labor coupled with starvation diets was the norm,

to reap financial benefit from the victims before their extermination.

Similar conditions, the specifics varying from camp to camp but not the generality of mistreatment *en masse*, existed in all nineteen of the major concentration camps (KLs). All except Bergen-Belsen had numerous *Nebenlager* (subcamps), in addition to *Aussenkommandos*, *Unterkommandos*, and *Baubrigaden*. In all the KLs living conditions were below what would be considered necessary for bare survival.

Brutality, horror, and human degradation were the benchmarks of the slave-labor camps. Of the thousands crisscrossing Europe — although they were similar in composition — few were alike. Depending on the whim of the *Lagerführer*, the absolute camp master, the *Lagerältesten*, the camp guards — whether SS, Ukrainian, or other *Hilfswillige* (*Hiwis*) — the Oberkapo, the Kapo, or other petty camp functionary, the life of the inmate was sheer hell. The prisoner had no individual rights at all. Prisoners were no longer even known by their names; they were identified solely by the number tattooed on their arm, belly, and/or on their striped, pajama-like, uniform (the only piece of clothing allowed the inmate). Nothing belonged to the inmates, not even their souls. The prisoners had no time for themselves, not even after putting in a twelve-to-fourteen-hour workday — during daylight or nighttime — on a Saturday, Sunday, legal, civil, or religious holiday; not even while gulping down that miserable bit of ersatz soup called lunch or supper.

The inmates were forced to stand for hours on all kinds of *Appells* (rollcalls), fallouts (unofficial rollcalls), secondary *Appells*; they were forced to witness the meting out of punishment, beatings and hangings. For the amusement of the SS, *Hiwis*, or others, they were forced to engage in all kinds of tedious and humiliating "sports." The most common were frog jumping, running a 50 to 100–meter gauntlet, and running up 100 steps loaded with at least 100 pounds of stones. But spraying the prisoners with cold-water hoses in the middle of freezing winter while setting dogs upon those trying to escape the spray was the

Labor detail
Authors' Collection

cruelest of all.

The major concentration camps were populated by prisoners from most European countries and included some from Asia, Africa, the Americas, and Australia as well. Most of the inmates suffered from hunger, malnutrition, overwork, cold, and fatigue; the majority lacked sanitary conditions and medical help. They fell by the thousands; many welcomed an early death that released them from all the miseries of the slave labor camp. Some fought a brave but mostly a losing battle for survival. Jews who thought that they would somehow survive, especially after all the suffering and after witnessing the destruction of most of their families, were removed from the camps by the thousands and shipped to Auschwitz or to one of the other extermination sites to be gassed and incinerated.

Not all the inmates, however, were destined to the same fate. Many of the incarcerated non-Jewish Germans or Austrians, who were professional criminals, and some others had the run of the camps, especially as far as internal administration was concerned. These murderers, robbers, rapists, and swindlers — including some who were certified criminally insane — enjoyed complete freedom (and were almost always encouraged by the SS administration)

to do what they pleased to further brutalize, berate, and demoralize the other prisoners. This especially held true when they dealt with Jews and, to a lesser degree, with Communists.

The work details were driven relentlessly under blows and curses from early in the morning when they left camp and during the long hours of hard, and often, useless, labor. Flogging and/or vicious dogs awaited the returning work commandos in the evening; hungry, thirsty, filthy, and extremely tired, the inmates were forced to stand for the night *appell* until all work details returned to camp. For the Nazi technocrat everything had to click: The number of prisoners in the evening had to be exactly the same as the number that had left in the morning. All inmates out on work detail that died of exhaustion or were "shot while trying to escape" or succumbed from other causes had to be carried back to camp and left on the *Appellplatz* to be counted in the evening. Any prisoner who escaped and evaded recapture would first have to be caught and brought back to camp dead or alive before the *Appell* would be completed, even if the other inmates would have to stand on the *Appellplatz* until the next day. They would furthermore have to witness, first, the flogging, then the reading of the sentence, and, finally, the hanging. There was hardly a work commando that left camp in the morning that returned intact by evening.

Of all the camps, none is more infamous than Auschwitz-Birkenau. A conglomerate of some forty subcamps, Auschwitz was home for prisoners of war, political prisoners, Polish and Czech intellectuals, convicted German and Austrian criminals, a-socials, Gypsies, and Jews. Most Jews brought there from all parts of occupied Europe hardly had time to get acquainted with the place; for them, Auschwitz served only as an exit point via gas chamber and crematorium. As such, they were never officially registered as camp arrivals in any of the well-kept records of the camp. Buna, industrial Auschwitz, where the large plants of I.G. Farbenindustrie, Deutsche Aus-rüstungswerke (DAW), Bunawerke, Krupp, and others were situated, employed thousands in slave labor, and slave labor was also parceled out from there by the thousands. Even though relatively small in area (circa forty square kilometers), Auschwitz is, most likely, the largest cemetery in the entire world. It has been estimated that as many as 4 million victims, including between 1,200,000 and 2,500,000 Jews, perished there.[5] Auschwitz (especially Birkenau), it must be reemphasized, was considered both a KL and a *Vernichtungslager*; it shared this dual status with only KL Lublin-Majdanek and Sajmište (Semlin) in Croatia.[6]

The *Vernichtungslager*

Unlike Auschwitz, Lublin-Majdanek, and Sajmište, the four Aktion Reinhard (Operation Reinhard) camps — Belzec, Chelmno, Sobibór, and Treblinka — were strictly classified as *Vernichtungslager*, camps set up solely for the murder of Jews. For camouflage reasons, each camp had a few workshops, mainly repair shops to service the camp's SS contingent and their Ukrainian helpers. Between 1,500,000 and 2,000,000 Jews perished in these four extermination centers. Another 110,000 to 200,000 Jews perished in the fifth death camp, Majdanek. All five of these *Vernichtungslager* and

Auschwitz were located in occupied Poland. Belzec served as the terminus for Galician Jews and Jews from eastern Poland; Chelmno for the Warthegau and Silesia; Sobibór for central and eastern Poland; Treblinka for Warsaw and northern Poland. Thousands of Jews from other parts of Europe were also transported to the Aktion Reinhard camps.[7]

Each death factory used a different method, although all with the same ultimate goal: to eliminate as many Jews in the shortest, most economical way. In Auschwitz II (Birkenau) and Majdanek, once the victims were packed into the hermetically sealed gas chamber, an SS orderly dropped pellets of Zyklon B (manufactured and supplied by two German firms: DEGESCH and Tesch und Stabenow) into an air vent. When the chemical oxidized, it turned to gas. Depending on the level of humidity, all those in the gas chamber were killed in ten to twenty minutes. Death was due to suffocation and was accompanied by sensations of fear, dizziness, and vomiting. In Treblinka the victims were asphyxiated by carbon monoxide pumped into the chamber from a captured Soviet tank located on the premises. In Belzec and Sobibór the victims were killed by carbon monoxide pumped into the chambers by diesel engines. In Chelmno, mobile gas vans took the victims from a reception building dubbed the "palace" on a ride to meet their maker. In the seventh extermination camp — Sajmište — the killing process was through gas vans and by machine-gunning thousands of Jews and non-Jews, whose bodies were then dumped into giant pits.

In most of these camps, no selection took place. All the members of a transport were sent straight down the *Himmelstrasse*, the heavenly road. In Auschwitz, some Jews were selected for labor — a chance for temporary survival. The Nazis made each victim pass singly before an SS doctor who decided who would go right, to the gas chamber, and who would go left, to work. The number of prisoners kept alive was very small, never more than one-third of a transport and often considerably less. Often those selected for work were chosen arbitrarily by a doctor who had never even looked at them. At times, when

Toward the crematorium
Courtesy of Dr. Luba K. Gurdus

there seemed to be too large a backup of Jews in quarantine, a supplementary selection ensued, with most sent to the gas chambers as soon as it was cleared of gassed victims.

The victims were transported to their final destination in various ways. Jews from Eastern Europe, including those from the General Government (Poland), were transported in closed freight cars — at least a hundred to a car — most of the time without any food or water. Passengers in these transports were deprived of all sanitary facilities. The overcrowded, bolted cars were heavily lined with a residue of lime. By the time a given transport arrived at its destination and the doors were opened for the first time, scores of victims had already died. In contrast, some of the victims from parts of the Grossreich and some Western countries were transported by regular passenger trains. As a result, most of them were bewildered on arrival, as they were totally unprepared for what was in store for them.

The first sight that greeted the Jewish prisoners was a well-kept station, part of the Nazi ruse to lull the victims into a false sense of security. While the dark chimney stacks of the ever-burning crematoria constantly belched out a thick, smelly smoke, an orchestra made up of half-starved musicians dressed in striped pajamas played. De-

pending on the location of the camp and temperament of the *SS-Lagerführer* and his staff, once the "formal niceties" were over, the victims destined for the incinerator pile were ordered to strip naked (on the pretense that they would be examined, deloused, taken to the showers, and given clean clothes) and led from station to station (hair-cutting, final rectal examination for hidden gems or foreign currency, and so on). As the victims came nearer and nearer to the last station, the SS men and their collaborationist helpers dropped the pretense completely. They lashed into the mass of prisoners, whipping them mercilessly, and setting upon them specially trained dogs who tore into their naked flesh. In the less "sophisticated" death camps, such as Sobibór, the Ukrainian guards raised geese in order to mask the death cries of those in the gas chambers.[8]

The Destruction of Soviet and Polish Jewry

With the Final Solution duly in place, the Nazis began their systematic, methodical campaign to annihilate European Jewry. Following the decisions of the Wannsee Conference, this campaign was to be carried out in the East and its first victims were to be the Jews of the occupied Soviet and Polish territories. Of the Jews in what the Nazis now styled the Reichskommissariat Ostland, that is, the occupied territory of the Soviet Union and the Baltic Republics, most had already been murdered during the first sweep of the Einsatzgruppen. The remnants barely existed in a small number of ghettos and a few camps that had been created as holding pens pending further *Aktionen*. Of these ghettos, the five major ones were Minsk and Lvov, in the Ukraine; Vilna and Kovno, in Lithuania; and Riga, in Latvia. In 1942 and 1943 these ghettos all experienced the continuing paroxysms of deportation and extermination by gunfire.[9] Added to that experience, at least in Minsk and Riga, was the deportation of German and Austrian Jews to the ghetto, followed by a brief respite as they were allowed to acquaint themselves with their new locale. Before they could become too comfortable, however, they too were deported and never returned.[10]

Conditions in Poland differed and resulted in a different Nazi approach. In the aftermath of the Wannsee Conference, a staff of 450 "technicians of death" was assembled in Lublin under the command of HSSPF Odilo Globocnik. Among this group, a large number were expert killers, freshly transferred from the euthanasia staff.[11] Detailed and elaborate plans were designed for the construction of *Vernichtungslager* and for the procedure to be adopted during deportation.[12] Geographical location — places removed from the public eye, yet easily accessible by rail — played a major role in this planning. With the machinery of destruction in place, deportations began in spring 1942.

In the interim, the anti-Jewish campaign received a further ideological and personal ingredient in June 1942. Czech agents working for the British Special Operations Executive (SOE) assassinated *Reichsprotektor* and RSHA chief Reinhard Heydrich on May 27, 1942. In retaliation, the Nazis murdered the population of Lidice — innocent civilians uninvolved in the assassination — and took revenge on suspected enemies of the Reich throughout the Protectorate of Bohemia-Moravia.[13] To honor Heydrich's

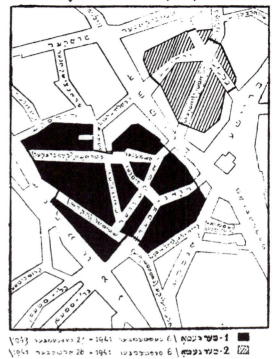

The Vilna Ghetto
Authors' Collection

memory, the SS staff of the murder operation in Poland named the operation Aktion Reinhard. They saw destruction of the Reich's ultimate enemy — the Jew — as a fitting tribute to its third most powerful leader.

Aktion Reinhard began on a massive scale with the liquidation of the Polish ghettos in the spring and summer of 1942. The initial deportations began in Lublin, where Globocnik's headquarters were located, on March 16, 1942. The deportations — a catchword that in reality meant transporting Jews to an extermination center — soon spread throughout the Lublin district. Jews in smaller, open ghettos were dealt with first. During an initial *Aktion* the Jewish population was divided between those to be murdered immediately (the majority) and those to be spared for a time (the minority). Survivors of these *Aktionen* were transferred to larger ghettos, from which they, together with the Jews of those ghettos, were deported to a death camp. In some cases, certain ghettos that were completely emptied of Jews in a single or a series of *Aktionen* were reopened and filled beyond their capacity with other Jews — mostly consisting of broken families, individual Jews, stragglers, Jews turned over to the Gestapo or police by would-be rescuers, Jews from work details, and others.

Only those with valid work permits — signifying their vital contribution to the German war effort — were spared at this juncture.[14] Even for the few lucky ones that were chosen for work and thus left behind in a makeshift camp or ghetto/camp, survival was not a simple matter. Nazi policymakers rapidly realized that the Jewish labor force could be pared to a minimum and

used a policy of ever-changing colors for the work passes that guaranteed life. The color or format of the *Arbeitsschein* that was valid in the morning when setting out to work was, at times, no longer valid at midday or toward the evening, when a *Razzia* (raid) was in progress. In that way the work force was kept off balance, and resistance to Nazi deportations was kept to a minimum.

In some instances, primarily where transportation facilities were not available, the process of transportation and deportation to death camps was abandoned. In these localities Einsatzgruppen, now dubbed Aussiedlungskommandos, composed of personnel from the Reichssicherheitshauptamt (RSHA) and supplemented by detachments of *Freiwillige* (Ukrainians, Latvians, Lithuanians, and/or Estonians) and (in Poland) by the Polish Blue police, the Granatowa Policja, were used to

Forcing the crowd into boxcars
Courtesy of Dr. Luba K. Gurdus

Deportation from the Krakow ghetto
Courtesy of the Main Crimes Commission/U.S. Holocaust Memorial Museum

eliminate entire Jewish communities in a one- or two-day orgy of murder.[15] This method was mainly used in the Lublin district, where the principal murder unit was Reserve Police Battalion 101, and in eastern Galicia.[16] In the latter, the Aussiedlungs-kommandos followed the well-established Einsatzgruppen procedure: A small group of Jews were selected to form a cleanup commando to gather up, sort, pack, and prepare for shipment to the SS treasury all of the goods the assembled Jews were forced to leave behind at the impromptu *Umschlagplatz* — usually in the village square — the *rynek*. Some of the very old, the feeble, the bedridden, and the very young, were loaded on trucks and driven to the Jewish cemetery grounds or to a prepared pit dug in a nearby forest where they were disposed of by small-arms fire. The remainder was forced to march and (depending on the number of

victims) were murdered in the same general area. Similar proceedings were conducted in townships with a larger Jewish population, except for two additional steps: Some of the stronger young adults that were still left in the community were selected and separated from the rest of the assembled; there was an arbitrary selection of the middle-aged and others, who were lined up five abreast and marched off to a railroad spur five-to-twenty kilometers away. All those who could not keep up were shot on the way. It has been estimated that from 30 to 60 percent lost their life before being loaded on the freight cars.[17] From mid-March 1942 through September 1942, at least sixty-eight major *Aktionen* of this type occurred in Nazi-occupied Poland.

Next, the Nazis turned their attention to the Warsaw ghetto. Considering that Warsaw still had the largest Jewish population — in 1942 close to 400,000 Jews still resided there — the

Deportation of Jews from the Krakow area
Courtesy of Main Crimes Commission/USHMM

SS undertook numerous precautions to maintain the secrecy of the operation. In particular, the Nazis preyed on the rampant hunger of the ghetto inmates. To ensure smooth deportations, Jews appearing at the *Umschlagplatz* voluntarily received an extra ration of bread and jam.[18] The actual *Aussiedlungsaktion* began in Warsaw on July 22, 1942 — corresponding to the Ninth of Av on the Jewish calendar, a fast day commemorating the destruction of the First and Second Temples in Jerusalem (586 B.C.E. and 70 C.E.) — and continued for some seven weeks, ending September 12. During that period nearly 300,000 Jews were deported to Treblinka and murdered. Here again, only those engaged in productive work for German firms, in addition to members of the Judenrat and the Jüdischer Ordnungsdienst and their immediate families were temporarily exempted from deportation.[19]

In addition to inducements of food, the Nazis used two other tactics in Warsaw.

First, they used the Jüdischer Ordnungsdienst to search for, find, and transport Jews to the *Umschlagplatz*. This tactic was used both to sow dissension within Jewish ranks and to provide a veneer of normality that would calm Jewish fears and avert possible resistance. Second, the Nazis used blockades — called *sperre* (derived from the German word Gesperre) in the local Polish and Jewish jargon — in effect, a cordon-and-search policy, to locate all Jews in the ghetto who did not have *Arbeitsscheinen*.[20] In the end, even the Judenrat and Ordnungsdienst were "pruned," the former being reduced by almost 60 percent.[21] By these means only an estimated 70,000 Jews remained in Warsaw after the deportations, about half of them considered "illegal" by the Germans, since they lacked *Arbeitsscheinen*. Of the legals, more than half were men and the overwhelming majority were between twenty and thirty-nine years old.[22]

With Warsaw thus reduced, in September and October 1942 the Nazis began deportation operations in the Bialystok district and in the Lodz ghetto. Jews from ghettos in the occupied Soviet territory, primarily Minsk, were also deported. Again, some Jews were permitted to survive for a time, and the rest were sent to extermination camps — where the gas chambers worked overtime — to be *sonderbehandelt*.[23] Some forty additional *Aktionen* were carried out between October 1942 and the end of the year. During the winter of 1942–1943 deportations were slowed down — they never completely ceased — as Jewish victims were shipped to the Polish death camps from the rest of occupied Europe.

In January 1943 the Nazis began the final elimination of Polish Jewry. This time there were delays: The Jews in Warsaw defended their lives as best they could and refused to come to the *Umschlagplatz* voluntarily. Even so, the uprising in the Warsaw ghetto and in some other localities were only temporary setbacks in the Nazi assault on Polish Jewry. Jews in Lvov, Radom, Grodno, Krakow, and other localities were butchered by the tens of thousands. On November 3, 1943, the SS launched Aktion Erntefest (Operation Harvest Festival) to liquidate the remnants of Polish Jewry. By the end of the operation, there were no Jews legally living in Poland; only a few survivors, members of partisan units in hiding or incarcerated in concentration camps, remained on blood-soaked Polish soil.[24]

The Course of Deportations: Grossreich

Deportations of Jews from Greater Germany to extermination sites in the East began in September 1941, simultaneously with the planning phase of the Final Solution. The territory involved in this deportation scheme included Germany, Austria, the Protectorate of Bohemia and Moravia, Danzig, the Grand Duchy of Luxembourg, and territories incorporated from both Poland (the Warthegau) and France (Alsace-Lorraine). A number of Jews from Germany, Austria, the Protectorate, and Danzig had been deported to Polish territory as early as fall and winter 1939–1940. These deportations, however, were just that: There was no hidden connotation attached to them, and they were not synonymous with extermination. The deportations brought thousands of German Jews to ghettos in Eastern Europe, primarily, Lodz, Minsk, and Riga. Yet there was still a small avenue of escape for German Jewry: emigration. In October 1941 further Jewish emigration from the Reich was banned; henceforth, European Jewry was trapped in the Nazi death grip.[25]

A new round of deportations eastward — in this case primarily to Aktion Reinhard death camps — took place in the summer of 1942. At this time almost all of the *hachsharot* (agricultural training centers) in Germany were closed; their students were deported and murdered shortly thereafter.[26]

In some cases, however, direct deportations to murder sites proved inconvenient for the Nazis. With plans ready to deport Czech Jewry to Poland, preparatory to their liquidation, a temporary way station was established in the fortress town of Terezin (Theresienstadt). On November 24, 1941, the first inmates — a construction commando — was dispatched to the newly created Terezin ghetto. During the next two years Terezin became the Nazis' model ghetto — Hitler's "gift" to the Jews — in addition to serving as an antechamber to Auschwitz. Among the deportees to Terezin were those considered too well known for regular treatment — because of their fame or other considerations. Included in the latter category were elderly German and West European Jews, who were sent to Terezin, settled there briefly, and then continued on their final journey.[27]

As in Poland, the process of deportations from the Grossreich was continuous, operating at a slow but steady pace. By the end of 1942, 155 transports had brought 109,000 Jews to Terezin. Approximately 50,000 of the deportees survived in the fortress ghetto; 40,000 were taken from Terezin to Auschwitz; the remainder perished in Terezin.[28] Between February and June 1943 the majority of German Jews were deported. Berlin was officially declared *judenrein* on June 16, 1943. By the end of September only about 14,000 Jews remained in Germany; almost all of them were Jews by Nazi racial definition, and they were largely protected because of either their marriage to Aryan spouses or because of special work skills they possessed.[29]

The Course of Deportations: Western Europe

Conditions in Western Europe were much the same as in Germany. Forced under the Nazi heel by the military occupations of 1940, Western Jewry had to contend with the anti-Jewish laws and restrictions of the SS regime. Still, prevailing conditions for Jews in Western Europe can hardly be compared to the impossible ones for Jews in Poland from the start of the German occupation. In particular, Jews were not herded into overcrowded, closed ghettos. The German policy vis-à-vis West European Jewry did not derive from the fact that the Nazis disliked the Jewries of the West less than East European Jewry, but from more practical considerations: There were fewer Jews in Western Europe, they were much less concentrated in specific areas and neighborhoods, and, through assimilation, they were much more integrated into the local culture. Although antisemitism was not lacking in Western Europe, the norm of the Gentile populations was to consider their countries' Jews as fellow citizens. As a result, an attempt to concentrate all Jews in one ghetto along the lines of Nazi-occupied Poland would not be cost-effective.

Instead, Jews were carefully registered and marked for the purpose of an eventual "evacuation" to an as-yet-undecided destination. The Nazis did, however, impose Judenräte on West European Jewry: the Union Générale des Israélites de France (UGIF), Association des Juifs en Belgique (AJB), and the Joodse Rad, in Holland. As

with the East European Jewish councils, all were forced to obey Nazi orders to the letter, to pay various fines and penalties, and to provide a quota of laborers for the Wehrmacht. The councils were also commissioned to register all Jewish-owned properties — both business and private — the former for aryanization, the latter for appropriation at the proper time. Unlike their Eastern counterparts, whose authority was limited to one locality, the Western councils operated on a nationwide scale.[30] In light of the dual nature of occupied France — the northern zone under direct German military occupation and the southern zone under the collaborationist Vichy government — the UGIF was divided into two autonomous segments; they combined, however, to

Provincial Dutch Jews forced to move to the Jewish quarter in Amsterdam
Courtesy of the Rijksinstituut Voor Oorlogsdocumentatie (Netherlands)
U.S. Holocaust Memorial Museum

form a single imposed Jewish governing body. Additionally, small numbers of Jews living in provincial Dutch and Belgian communities were ordered to move to Amsterdam and Brussels respectively. Over the course of 1941 the Nazis sought to aryanize and expropriate Jewish property and severely limited all Jewish activities. Until the Wannsee Conference, that was approximately the extent of the persecution of West European Jewry.

In late April or early May 1942 members of Adolf Eichmann's staff began working on detailed plans for the deportations from Western Europe. These plans were completed by June 11, 1942, when all of Eichmann's subordinates met in Berlin for a briefing on the impending deportations.[31]

The arrests prior to deportation began in France on July 16 and 17, 1942. Some 13,000 Jews, including 4,000 children, were caught in a joint dragnet of French police and Gestapo agents. Most were incarcerated at the now infamous Vélodrome d'Hiver sports complex, with no food, water, or sanitary facilities. By the end of August, 25,000 Jews had been deported; by the end of the year, the number reached 42,000.[32] Eichmann's original plan, however, was to deport an initial 100,000 Jews through December 1942 and to complete the deportations by mid-1943. Technical difficulties, including somewhat successful Jewish evasion tactics and the lack of wholehearted French support, slowed down the process. The occupation of the Vichy zone in November 1942 speeded up deportations slightly, but the pace was still considered too slow and was increased beginning in July 1943. Nevertheless, by liberation, only one-third of French Jewry had been deported.[33]

Similarly difficult were the deportations from Belgium. In this case, the Belgians proved un-cooperative: The Queen Mother sought to have the deportation order nullified altogether, and other members of the Nazi-imposed Belgian administration tried to mute its impact. Even so, on July 15, 1942, the Gestapo ordered the AJB to set up a special *Arbeitseinsatz* (work command) to oversee deportation of Belgian Jews to "labor camps," the usual Nazi cover term camouflaging the true meaning of deportation. At the same time other anti-Jewish measures were undertaken by the Nazis, including forbidding Jews to frequent public places. These measures were designed to make evasion by Belgian Jews, especially in Antwerp and Brussels, more difficult.

The first transport departed from Belgium on August 2, 1942. Nazi efficiency was such that the initial Belgian quota of 15,000 was exceeded by October 1942, when a total of 16,600 Jews had been deported.[34] Jewish efforts to obstruct the deportations — for example by the destruction of the AJB card files — met with mixed success, as did Jewish efforts to "disappear" before arrest. Jewish defense efforts were more successful in 1943 and 1944: Slightly under 9,000 Jews were deported from Belgium in twelve transports during the next two years.[35] Finally, the rapid Allied advance into Belgium in August and September 1944 halted the deportations altogether.

In Holland, the first deportation train left for Auschwitz from Westerbork on July 15, 1942. Two days before, on July 13, all non-Jewish refugees in the camp had been ordered out by the Gestapo, who had taken over the refugee camp (originally run by the Dutch), reclassifying it as a *Polizeiliches Durchgangslager* (Police Transit Camp). Westerbork thus became an assembly point for Dutch Jews on their way to the Polish extermination camps. Twelve additional transports were dispatched from Westerbork within the next six weeks (two transports per week), totaling more than 10,000 victims. The Nazis planned to eliminate half of Dutch Jewry before December 1942 — some 50,000 persons in all.[36] In reality, that quota was not quite reached: Only 38,000 Jews had been deported when a temporary halt to the deportations was called.

In Holland, Jewish efforts to escape and Dutch rescue efforts were, however, almost complete failures. When the deportations resumed in January 1943, an initial transport of 8,000 Jews was easily filled. Continued attempts at evasion were met by the Nazis with increasingly successful dragnets. Thus, although only 500 Jews voluntarily appeared as ordered in late June 1943, 5,500 more were captured in a dragnet in Amsterdam that month.[37] By June 30, the Nazis could satisfactorily report to Berlin that 100,000 Jews had been deported.[38] Seven thousand additional Jews were deported between July 1 and the suspension of deportations in September 1943.[39]

The Nazi policy toward the small Jewish community of Luxembourg was initially geared toward forced emigration. Almost half of Luxembourg's 4,000 Jews had escaped to France even before the German invasion. Another 1,150 were deported to France in 1940 and 1941. Of the remaining Jews, 127 managed to leave Nazi-occupied Europe via Portugal in January 1942. The others were deported to Poland in a single *Aussiedlungsaktion*; only 35 survived the ordeal.[40]

In sum, French Jewry had been reduced by almost one-third, Belgian Jewry by nearly half, and Dutch Jewry by three-quarters. Nazi plans to eliminate the remaining Jews of the three West European communities faltered because of attempts at escape and evasion, which prevented the completion of deportations before the Allied armies liberated those territories. Had the Allied invasion of Western Europe not happened when it did, it is certain that casualty figures for the West European communities would have been much higher. As it was, Dutch Jewry was not completely liberated until 1945: Westerbork, the Nazi transit camp for Jews, was not finally liberated until April 12, 1945 (although the last transport for Auschwitz actually left on September 3, 1944, carrying, among others, Anne Frank and her family).[41]

Deportation and Rescue in Scandinavia

Characteristically, the Nazis had laid plans for the deportation and extermination of every single Jew in Europe. Uncharacteristically, their plans went almost completely awry in Scandinavia. As in France and the Low Countries, planning for the deportations was undertaken by Eichmann's office during the early spring of 1942. Here too, great emphasis was to be placed on the cooperation of local collaborators and on swift operations so that no response by the Jews or friendly Gentile populations would be possible. The small number of Jews in Scandinavia, their almost complete assimilation (and consequently the low intensity of antisemitism), and the distances that needed covering for transportation delayed the deportation plans for a year, but in late 1942 the first move to deport Scandinavian Jewry began.

The first operation occurred in Norway on November 6, 1942. Supported by Norwegian police, the Gestapo and members of the Sicherheitsdienst began searching for Jews, arresting some 800. On November 26, 1942, half were forced to board the German freighter *Donau*; the remaining Jews followed aboard the *Monte Rosa*, which sailed in February 1943. The two ships sailed to the port of Stettin, on the Baltic coast; from there the victims were transported to Berlin and thence to Auschwitz. A number of Jews were selected upon arrival to work in the Silesian coal mines. From the initial transports of 800, all but 24 eventually perished. Thereafter, the Gestapo experienced much difficulty in arresting Jews: Word had leaked out that deportation was to death and not to labor camps, which Nazi propaganda claimed. As a result, the better half of Norwegian Jewry, almost 900 persons, was secreted across the border to Sweden.[42]

A more basic rejection of Nazi plans occurred in Finland. Despite the Finns' close alliance with the Third Reich, manifested in intensive Finnish military operations against the Soviets in the Leningrad region, the Finns refused to hand over their Jews to the Gestapo. Even when the Nazis toned down their demands — asking only for the "extradition" of the few dozen Jewish refugees that had arrived in Finland in 1938 — the Finns refused. Finnish Jews continued to serve in the armed forces throughout the war, the only Jews to serve in any of the Axis states, and a number were, ironically, granted awards for heroism from the Wehrmacht. As an overt symbol of support, moreover, Field Marshal Carl Gustav von Mannerheim, Finland's head of state, attended independence day ceremonies in 1944 at the Helsinki synagogue. The Final Solution simply never began in Finland, and thus the small Finnish Jewish community was spared.[43]

The classic case of rescue in Scandinavia, however, transpired in Denmark, where 7,700 Jews resided before World War II. Scandinavia's largest Jewish community fell under the Nazi heel, along with the rest of the country, in April 1940. Technically, Denmark was not at war with Germany when invaded and did not declare war even after the occupation. In order not to upset the Danes, the Nazis did not at first molest Danish Jewry, although a crude and largely ineffective antisemitic propaganda campaign was begun.[44] Over the course of 1943, however, relations between the Danes and the Germans soured, resulting in the imposition of a harsher (but still not very harsh) occupation regime. Finally, in September 1943, plans were laid for the complete deportation of Danish Jewry.

The plan went awry almost from the beginning. Although the Nazis planned to carry out the roundup and deportation in complete secrecy, and over the course of a single night, members of the Danish government were surreptitiously informed of the impending operation. This news soon spread throughout Copenhagen and galvanized the Danish underground to action. Jews who could flee their homes were advised to do so and were provided with safe houses. By the end of the initial roundup, most Jews had evaded the Nazis.[45] Further searches failed to achieve substantive results but did alert the underground that a more permanent haven was needed. At this point the decision to transport Danish Jewry to safety in neighboring, neutral, Sweden was made. This heroic operation was carried out with great success: Seven thousand Danish Jews were transported to safety.[46] In all the Nazis caught only approximately 700 Jews. Moreover, the Danish government demanded information regarding the deportees' fate.

Again, to avoid possible difficulties, the Nazis assented and sent all the Danish deportees to Terezin. There they were visited by two Danish representatives in February 1944. None of the Danish inmates were directly murdered by the Nazis; those who perished succumbed to disease, malnutrition, old age, or ill health.[47]

Southern Europe and the Balkans

Even before the beginning of mass deportations to death camps, the Jews in Yugoslavia suffered greatly. Beset by antisemites in both Serbia and Croatia, Yugoslav Jewry was largely under siege even before the Nazi occupation. After the Nazi occupation in April 1941, conditions worsened in the territories under Nazi or Nazi collaborationist puppet regimes. This policy did not, however, hold true in the Italian zone of occupation (along the Dalmatian coast and in the Northwest).

Croat nationalists, the so-called Ustaša, already began to slaughter their enemies in the summer of 1941. Primary victims were Serbs, of whom between 70,000 and 100,000 may have been butchered, and Jews.[48] In April 1941 the Croat regime under Ante Pavelić enacted a series of anti-Jewish laws modeled on the Nuremberg Laws. In May, the Croats — with Nazi "technical" assistance — established their first concentration camp, Danica, near the village of Koprivnica. Between May 16, 1941, when the first roundup of Jews began, and July 1941, nearly 25,000 Jews (more than 60 percent of the Jewish population in Croatia) were murdered. The only escapees from Croat terror were those who found a refuge in Italian-occupied territory.[49]

Given the nature of their occupation in Serbia, the Nazis were able to proceed to the murder of Jews more directly than in other countries. In this case, the already existing Nazi policy regarding retaliation for acts of resistance — that 100 civilians were to be shot for every German soldier killed by the partisans — was interpreted specifically to refer to racial enemies. This policy clearly derived from Hitler's racial and political ideology: Since the Jews were the progenitors of Bolshevism, and since much of the resistance activity in Yugoslavia derived from Tito's partisans, it stood to reason that eliminating Jews would eliminate resistance. As a direct result, the Wehrmacht undertook the elimination of virtually all male Jews in Serbia during autumn 1941.[50] The remaining Jews in Serbia, women, children, and older men not killed during the reprisal operation, were systematically deported to the Sajmište (Semlin) concentration camp, beginning in December 1941. Although the initial intention was to transport these Jews to the death factories in Poland, a shortage of rolling stock made that plan impractical. Instead, in January 1942 a number of gas vans — improvements on the vehicles used by the Einsatzgruppen in the Soviet Union — were dispatched to Sajmište. By May 1942 all the inmates were exterminated; even the Jewish concentration camp prisoners transferred to Sajmište from camps in Germany to form the inner camp "administration" were killed. The Nazis did spare some non-Jewish spouses of the victims — they were released at the end of May, although they were sworn to secrecy.[51]

Given the similarities in the occupation regime — divided between German, Bulgarian, and Italian zones — conditions in Greece were similar to those in Yugoslavia. Although the early days of the Nazi occupation were tranquil, relatively speaking, all anti-Jewish laws were introduced into the German zone as part and parcel of their military regime. Nevertheless, the Nazis proceeded relatively slowly at first. On April 15, 1941, all Jewish institutions in Greece were ordered closed. The Chief Rabbi, Zvi Koretz, was removed to a Gestapo prison in Vienna, but other Jewish leaders were freed. One year later, in July 1942, forced labor for Jews was introduced with an initial corvee of 9,000.[52] In December the Jewish community was reorganized, with a Judenrat headed by Rabbi Koretz imposed on the community.[53]

At this stage, the Nazis took no further action. In February 1943, Greek Jewry in the Nazi zone was ghettoized while detailed plans for their deportation were being laid

by Eichmann's staff. The deportations commenced on March 15, 1943, when a transport of 2,800 Jews departed for Auschwitz. Deportations to Auschwitz — and later to Treblinka as well — continued until May 1943, despite unsuccessful efforts to rescue even a small number of Jews. By May, nearly 50,000 Jews had been deported, with 80 percent of the deportees murdered in the death camps. The SS did, however, agree to a temporary respite for some 3,000 Jewish slave laborers working for the Organisation Todt.[54]

In fact, only two avenues of escape existed: flight into the hills to join the partisans, difficult for Salonica Jews, but an acceptable option elsewhere in Greece, and evasion. In the latter case, only those possessing Spanish or Italian nationality — several hundred Jews in all — could successfully evade the Nazi dragnet. The issue was not so simple, however, and a series of multilateral negotiations culminated in the deportation of Spanish nationals to Bergen-Belsen and thence to Spain.[55] The length of the negotiations proved to be of no benefit to those holding Italian passports; by then Italy had surrendered and was under Nazi occupation. The Greek Jews of Italian nationality thus joined their compatriots murdered in Auschwitz.

The same fate awaited the Jews in the other former Italian zones in Yugoslavia (Dalmatia) and Greece (Epirus, Athens, and the Dodecanese Islands). Efforts to avert deportations from Athens failed, although the process was delayed until March 1944; in the interim many Jews took the opportunity to escape from Athens and join the partisans. Those who did not — or could not — escape did not fare well. By the spring of 1944 only 4,000 Jews were living legally in Greece, and they all resided on Corfu and Rhodes. In June and July 1944 even these Jews were deported: first by boat to the mainland and thence by rail to Auschwitz.[56] In all, 80 percent of Greek Jewry, approximately 68,000 souls, perished in the crematoria.

The minuscule Albanian Jewish community fared only marginally better. Numbering only 200 Jews in 1930, the community had been augmented by a small number of Jewish refugees from Germany and Austria. On April 7, 1939, the Italians occupied Albania, but this did not alter the Jews' status. Their fate changed only after the Italians surrendered and the Wehrmacht occupied Albania. At that point the Nazis began a roundup that resulted in the arrest of virtually all the Albanian Jews, all the Central European Jewish refugees, and about 100 Croat Jews who had fled Yugoslavia in 1941. In all, the SS deported 400 Jews in a single transport that was sent to Bergen-Belsen. From there, the Albanian Jews were shipped to labor camps or to Auschwitz; only 100 returned after the war.[57]

A far different fate awaited the Jews of Bulgaria and Italy, although that could hardly have been anticipated at the outset. Because of the close alliance between Bulgaria and Germany, antisemitism rose distinctly after 1933. By 1939 the Bulgarian royal government had adopted an intense antisemitic orientation. As a result, strict regulations were enacted that culminated in the adoption of antisemitic legislation — virtually a Bulgarian copy of the Nuremberg Laws — in 1941.[58] Between 1941 and 1943 further limitations were placed on Jews in Bulgaria. Moreover, in March 1943 the Bulgarian army actively assisted in the deportations of Jews from Macedonia and Thrace — Greek territories under Bulgarian occupation — to the death camps in Poland.[59] Simultaneously, plans were laid to deport the Jews in Bulgaria proper and the SS brought considerable pressure to bear on the Bulgarians to comply.[60] Indeed, briefly the Bulgarians did agree to deport all the Jews — except for a few under royal protection — beginning with those in Sofia.[61]

At this point, the Bulgarians apparently had a change of heart. Deporting Jews, even those holding Bulgarian nationality, to labor camps in Bulgaria was one thing. Handing them over to the Germans for deportation to an unknown fate was an entirely different matter. During the spring and summer of 1943 various elements of Bulgarian society, notably the Eastern Orthodox Church, began to advocate a lessening of anti-Jewish

pressure. Still, the Bulgarian government agreed in May 1943 to exile all Jews from the capital, as a first step toward ghettoization and eventual deportation. Abruptly in September all talk of further deportations was canceled.[62] All elements of Bulgarian society — except for an overtly antisemitic fringe element — had protested the persecution of the Jews. These protests convinced King Boris and members of the government to step back from the persecution. Resistance to further deportations was strengthened when the ultimate destination of Jewish deportees became known: The Bulgarians had proven willing to persecute the Jews, but cold-blooded murder was not acceptable.[63] In 1944 Bulgaria left the Axis altogether, and the Communist-inspired Government of National Salvation actively protected Jews from further persecution.

Conditions in Italy were similar in many ways. Italy was a very close ally of the Third Reich, and antisemitic legislation had been introduced before World War II — as an outward symbol of the close alliance between the two Fascist states. Again, however, the Italian government and people largely refused to cooperate in the Final Solution.

Unlike in Bulgaria, conditions in Italy were much more complicated. For one, Italy, because of its role as a buffer between the Allied Powers and the Third Reich, was for Germany of greater strategic importance than Bulgaria. When the latter withdrew from the Axis, no German forces of any consequence were in the country and the Bulgarian surrender (to the Soviets) was a relatively straightforward affair. This was not the case in Italy. Between Mussolini's fall and the Allied invasion of mainland Italy — that is, between July and September 1943 — the Badoglio government was involved in a double game: negotiating with the Allies secretly while officially professing an intention to remain in the Axis. In reality the Germans were not fooled; they poured men and matériel into Italy. Thus, when the Allies did invade the mainland, the Wehrmacht and the SS were able to impose a German occupation on northern and central Italy: a front line on the Volturno River stabilized by mid-October 1943.[64]

This reality was quickly impressed upon Jews in northern Italy and in territories formerly occupied by the Italian army. In Italy proper, some Jews managed to escape by making their way southward, where they found safety in Allied-occupied territory. Others, trapped in Nazi-occupied territory, were luckily forewarned by their Italian neighbors and went into hiding with their assistance. Local clergy and — in some cases — total strangers opened their homes to them; a majority of Italian Jews were able to survive the storm in this way.[65] Between 7,000 and 10,000 Italian Jews were not so fortunate: They were seized either by the SS or by fanatical Fascist police of the reconstituted Sálo Republic. Almost all of them were deported to Auschwitz between autumn 1943 and spring 1944. Other victims were murdered in Italy proper, including 77 Jews murdered by the SS (along with 258 non-Jews) at the Ardreatine Caves in retaliation for a partisan attack on Wehrmacht troops in Rome.[66]

In the former Italian zones of occupation in southern France (Nice), Yugoslavia (Dalmatia), and Greece (Athens, Epirus, and the Dodecanese Islands), the same pattern was repeated. A few Jews managed to escape, but most were caught in the Nazi dragnet, deported, and executed. As a result, the Jews of Southern Europe joined their Northern, Western, and Eastern European brethren in the crematoria and murder pits of Poland.

Slovakia, Romania, and Hungary

As a subsidiary to the deportations from the Greater Reich, the Nazis also undertook a series of *Aussiedlungsaktionen* in concert with the Slovak government. In this case, the impetus for deportation derived from both German and Slovak desires to be rid of Jews. The likelihood of Slovak cooperation with the Final Solution was specifically mentioned at the Wannsee Conference. Therefore, Slovakia became a testing ground for the deportation experts in Adolf

Eichmann's office: The methods used there were applied, modified for local conditions, in every country in Nazi-occupied Europe. And the Slovaks proved enthusiastic in their support of the deportations, at least initially, agreeing to pay RM 500 for each deported Jew.[67]

The first Slovakian transport departed in April 1942. Deportations continued until July 1942, by which time nearly 60,000 Jews had been deported. In July the deportations were halted — strangely, at German request — and were not resumed until summer 1944. In the interim two separate strands of activity came together to slow down the process of deportation. Although the Slovakian collaborationist regime of Josef Tiso had supported the deportations, pressure by influential religious leaders in Slovakia, including the papal nuncio, caused the government to move more slowly on Jewish affairs.[68]

As a result, deportations were halted — as much from German considerations as from Slovak. But the halt allowed Slovak Jewry to reorganize in order to better face the new conditions. A Jewish group, the Pracovna Skupina (Working Group), was created by Rabbi Dov Baer Weismandel, one of the spiritual leaders of the Nitra Yeshiva, and Gisi Fleischmann, a Labor Zionist activist. Their goal was to avoid any further deportations of Slovak Jews, and to this end they sought to bribe the Nazis responsible for the deportations and thereby rescue a remnant of Slovak Jewry. As negotiations began, the Jewish advocates sensed a willingness among certain SS officers to be bribed. It is not clear, however, if these SS officials ever intended to keep their part of any deal made. Still, some innuendos, hints, and half signs dropped by Eichmann's deputy, SS- Hauptsturmführer Dieter Wisliceny, the SS chief negotiator, at intervals during the negotiations gave the Working Group greater incentive to expand the negotiations to include all the remaining Jews of Europe. To this end about $50,000 was advanced by the Pracovna Skupina negotiators to Wisliceny.[69]

The reprieve proved to be temporary, however. The Slovak government, in collusion with the RSHA and the German Foreign Office, intended to resume deportations in April 1943, but these plans did not materialize. In August 1944 new plans were laid to resume the deportations. At that point, Weismandel and Fleischmann redoubled their efforts to bribe the Nazis. By end of August 1944 it became clear that the negotiations had failed, and the remnant of Slovak Jewry was soon deported along with all the members of the Pracovna Skupina. Very few of them were to survive the ordeal.[70]

As with other Jewries in the Danube basin, the Jews in Romania faced considerable hostility — from both the government and local Fascist groups — even before the war. In particular, the antisemitic government of Alexandru Cuza and Octavian Goga that rose and fell in 1938 set the stage for an intense and combative antisemitism. When the National Legionary government of Ion Antonescu came to power in September 1940, living conditions for Romanian Jewry worsened considerably. The Romanians — who invaded the Soviet Union in conjunction with the Nazi onslaught (June 22, 1941) — also participated, from the start, in massacres of Jews in cooperation with Einsatzkommandos or other Nazi and volunteer-killer task forces. On June 27 (only five days after the start of hostilities) Antonescu gave the green light to his Iron Cross legionnaires to stage a bloody pogrom in Jassy. He also invited the Germans to witness the pogrom and to participate if they wished. Thousands of Jewish men, women, and children were brutally butchered, and some of Jassy's streets literally ran red with blood.[71] A similar picture was painted in Odessa when the city fell after a prolonged siege: Thirty-five thousand Jews were killed outright in retaliation for a partisan attack on a Romanian divisional headquarters.[72]

In late August 1941 Romania was given administrative control of Bessarabia — which had been Romanian until seized by the Soviets in 1940 — and the territory between the Dniester and Bug rivers. This area, dubbed Transnistria by the Romanians, was fated to become a death zone for Romanian Jewry: A reservation was established along the lines of the Nazi-planned (but never fully implemented) Lublin Reservation. From September 1941 on villages, towns, cities, and entire regions of Romania were cleared of Jews, who were deported to camps in Transnistria. During the first two months alone, 120,000 Jews were deported; by the time deportations ended, over 300,000 Jews were incarcerated there.[73]

Unlike the Nazis, however, the Romanian deportations were neither as methodical nor as immediately sinister. First, not all Jews were deported. Most notably, a Jewish community was permitted to exist in Bucharest — albeit after being "pruned" of potential troublemakers and living in precarious conditions.[74] Second, deportations to Transnistria were not initially part of a further deportation process to the German death camps in Poland. To be sure, these differences should not minimize the suffering of the deportees in Transnistria; it does, however, explain why many of them were able to survive.

Plans were, in due course, laid for the further deportation of Romanian Jewry to the death camps. Here, however, the Nazis met with an extremely inconsistent Romanian response. On the one hand, Romanian Legionnaires undertook periodic murder rampages, slaughtering thousands of Jews while "liberating" or retreating from large stretches of territory in the Ukraine. In fact, the Romanian secret service even went as far as to create its own Einsatzgruppe in 1941.[75] Similarly, in late 1942 and early 1943 some Jews were deported before Eichmann's representatives had a chance to make all the necessary arrangements. On the other hand, the Romanian government firmly refused to abide by German "suggestions" regarding policy toward Jews. For example, on September 3, 1941, the Romanians agreed to institute the wearing of the Jewish star, only to rescind the decision four days later. The star was eventually implemented in some localities but not in others.[76] Then too, the Romanians proved susceptible to bribery — the Antonescu government even proposed ransoming 70,000 Jews previously deported to Transnistria for a $3,500,000 payment.[77]

In 1943, moreover, the Romanian government further undercut the Final Solution by agreeing to allow the few surviving internees of Transnistria to return to Romania. Antonescu's reasoning appears to have been simple and was certainly opportunistic: The persecution of Romanian Jewry, although a goal of the government, had to be considered in the context of the military and political realities on the Eastern Front. Romania had already experienced the topsy-turvy nature of Hitler's treatment of Axis allies and had temporarily lost Bessarabia. If the Nazis won the war, Romania's sovereignty could be at risk; but if the Nazis lost, Romania would definitely suffer the consequences of its alliance with the Third Reich. Thus, in 1942, the Jews became a touchstone of Romanian independence and could not be handed over. In 1943, Nazi defeat and a consequent Soviet victory became increasingly likely. Therefore, Antonescu halted the further persecution of the Jews as a means of saving his government, if not his life. Paradoxically, this decision was based on an antisemitic analysis of the world situation, since the Romanian dictator "knew" without need of further proof that the Jews controlled all three of the Allied governments.[78]

Hungarian Jewry, the last Jewish community to suffer under the Nazi heal, had also experienced intense antisemitism derived from a quasi-Fascist government. After 1920 antisemitism entered into the public sphere of the Hungarian state, culminating in efforts between 1938 and 1941 to legislate on the Jewish problem.[79] In 1941 this campaign reached its height with the incorporation of Hungarian racial laws patterned on the Nuremberg Laws.[80] With Hungary's entry into the anti-Soviet war, the government further hardened conditions for Jews. In particular, thousands of Jewish men were conscripted for forced labor on behalf of the army — under the *Munkaszolgálat* (Labor Service) program. Although initially permitted to wear military uniforms, the laborers were treated worse than prisoners of war. In addition, they were not permitted to bear arms and thus could not defend themselves when attacked. Ironically, Jewish laborers captured by the Soviets on the Eastern Front were systematically mistreated twice: by their Soviet captors, who considered them enemy soldiers, and by fellow Hungarian prisoners of war.[81]

A further worsening of conditions for some Jews in Hungary — primarily refugees — occurred during the summer of 1941. In July, the Hungarian military began the roundup of nearly 18,000 Jewish refugees, most of whom were handed over to German authorities. Imprisoned in Kamenets-Podolski (Ukraine) those stateless Jews were murdered together with another 5,000 local Jews during an Einsatzkommando *Aktion* on September 27–28. Other atrocities against Jews took place near Déldivék in Hungarian-occupied Yugoslavia during the course of antipartisan operations.[82] All these atrocities had two elements in common: First, Hungarian participation in massacres was only indirect — the Germans, with Ukrainian help, murdered the Kamenets-Podolski victims, and Jews were not the official target of the operations in Déldivék, although that should not be construed as absolving Hungarian complicity in war crimes. Second, neither operation was directed at Hungarian Jews per se. After these operations — not counting the mistreatment of the Jewish labor battalions by their non-Jewish officers — antisemitism faded to the background of Hungarian wartime policy, although the overall Jewish conditions did not improve.[83] Externally, however, despite German pressure, the Hungarians resisted inclusion in the Final Solution, at least during 1942 and 1943.[84] Indeed, Hungary was considered relatively safe and became a destination for a small number of Jewish survivors able to escape from the Polish death camps making their way through Slovakia to Hungary under the Tiyul (trip) program.[85]

Conditions in Hungary changed rapidly in 1944. The Hungarian government, much like that of Romania and Bulgaria, sought to withdraw from its alliance with Nazi Germany. In so doing, the Hungarians sought an honorable means to withdraw from the war at a time when the Red Army was rapidly approaching Hungary's borders. Unlike the case in Bulgaria or Romania, however, talk of withdrawal proved premature: Since Soviet troops were not even remotely near Budapest, the Nazis were able to occupy most of the country. On March 19, 1944, the Nazis forced Regent Miklos Horthy to install a government composed of Fascists and Nazi sympathizers led by Ferenc Szálasi and the Arrow Cross.[86]

Along with Wehrmacht units that entered Hungary on that day, armed columns of Einsatzkommando Eichmann — elements of the Aussiedlungskommandos responsible for deporting Jews to the death camps and headed by Adolf Eichmann — simultaneously entered Hungary. Between that date and December 1944, 107 anti-Jewish laws, aimed at the complete physical elimination of Hungarian Jewry, were promulgated. In short order, Hungarian Jewry was ghettoized and prepared for deportation. Having refined their techniques, the Nazis were able to operate systematically and methodically. Losing no time, the Nazis reactivated the Auschwitz gas chambers and crematoria, and on May 2 the first transport of more than 1,000 Hungarian Jews was immediately gassed at Birkenau. Over the course of August 1944, with the eager help of the new Szálasi government, almost all Hungarian Jews — except the Jews of Budapest — were deported to Auschwitz and murdered.[87] Before year's end, when the gas chambers were finally blown up on Himmler's orders, some 400,000 Hungarian Jews were murdered.

Unlike the murder of Polish Jewry, which was accomplished in relative secrecy, the deportation and extermination of Hungarian Jewry was known to the public in the Allied countries almost from the very beginning.[88] Despite public pressure on Allied governments, only half-hearted rescue measures were undertaken initially; by the time attitudes changed, only 100,000 remained: those incarcerated in the Budapest ghetto.[89]

Even more controversial was the response of the Jewish leadership in Budapest. Many leaders of Hungarian Jewish organizations were aware that deportation meant death. In particular, they were in possession of a detailed report about the true meaning of

Auschwitz written some time before by two escapees, Rudolf Vrba and Alfred Wetzler.[90] Yet these leaders — in particular the chairman of the Va'ad ha-Ezra veha-Hatzala, Rezsö (Rudolf) Kasztner — decided to keep silent, hoping to bargain for Jewish lives with the Nazis.[91] As had been the case in Slovakia, some Nazis, Eichmann included, appeared ready to accept a bribe in order to save at least part of Hungarian Jewry. Since the negotiations did not proceed, it is not clear if these Nazis were sincere about their willingness to permit Jews to flee; what is clear is that members of the SS hierarchy had an ulterior motive in the negotiations.[92]

On April 27, 1944, Eichmann approached Kasztner and another Va'ad member, Joel Brand, with a proposal. Brand would be permitted to leave Hungary for Turkey in order to contact Allied representatives with a proposal to ransom 1 million Jews in return for 10,000 trucks and other goods. As a sign of good faith, Eichmann permitted Kasztner to select a small number of Budapest Jews who would be transported to safety rather than to Auschwitz. Left unsaid by Eichmann was the fact that Brand would be traveling with a Hungarian Jew, Bernard (Bandi) Grosz, who was considered "reliable" by the Gestapo. It now appears that Brand's mission was little more than a cover for Grosz's: to negotiate a separate peace with the Western Allies that would bring the United States and Great Britain into the Nazis' anti-Bolshevik crusade.[93] In any event, the Allies proved unwilling to consider anything less than Germany's unconditional surrender, and the negotiations to save Hungarian Jewry collapsed. Despite this setback, most of Budapest's Jews were rescued due to the timely intervention of diplomats representing neutral states including Sweden (Raoul Wallenberg), Switzerland (Karl Lutz), and Spain (Giorgio Perlasca). Nevertheless, by the time Soviet troops finally liberated Hungary (January 1945), more than two-thirds of Hungary's Jews had been murdered.

Balance Sheet

After this brief examination of the geography

of the Holocaust, it is important to consider two facts: By the time Budapest was liberated by the Red Army, most of Festung Europa was smashed, with the would-be Thousand-Year Reich a mere shadow of what it had been some twelve years earlier when it had set out to conquer the world and institute its New Order. It is also a fact that the larger part of European Jewry had been, by this time, decimated.

Although intentionalists and functionalists disagree fundamentally on the origins of the Final Solution, all Holocaust historians agree that once begun, the Nazi campaign to exterminate Jews was pursued systematically, methodically, and with vigor. The Nazis sought the extinction of European — if not world — Jewry, and they very nearly achieved that goal.

The realities of Jewish history under Nazi impact raise a four-part question that we must consider: The state of the Jews and their attitude toward their destruction; the lukewarm response to the predicament of the Jews by most of their non-Jewish neighbors; the almost cold indifference by the official church and by most of the neutral powers; and, finally, the cool response to and minimum consideration of the Allied Powers to the Jewish quandary.

Notes

1. Martin Broszat, "The Concentration Camps," in H. Krausnick et al., *The Anatomy of the SS State*, New York: Walker, 1968, pp. 421–428.
2. Ibid., pp. 399–504. Although there is no single comprehensive history of the Nazi concentration camp system, Konnilyn Feig, *Hitler's Death Camps*, New York: Holmes and Meier, 1981, and Israel Gutman and Avital Saf (eds.), *The Nazi Concentration Camps*, Jerusalem: Yad Vashem, 1984, provide incisive overviews.
3. Krzysztof Dunin-Wasowicz, "Forced Labor and Sabotage in the Nazi Concentration Camps," in Gutman and Saf, *Concentration Camps*, pp. 133–142.
4. Joseph Borkin, *The Crime and Punishment of I.G. Farben*, New York: Free Press, 1978, ch. 6; Bernard P. Bellon, *Mercedes in Peace and War*, New York: Columbia University Press, 1990, pp. 246–247.
5. Hermann Langbein, "Auschwitz: The History and Characteristics of the Concentration and Extermination Camp," in Gutman and Saf, *Concentration Camps*, pp. 273–290.
6. Sajmište, the seventh camp built for the sole purpose of mass murder, was located in Nazi-occupied Serbia. Cf. Menahem Shelah, "Sajmište — An Extermination Camp in Serbia," *Holocaust and Genocide Studies*, vol. 2 # 2 (1987), 243–260.
7. Yitzhak Arad, *Belzec, Sobibór, Treblinka: The Operation Reinhard Death Camps*, Bloomington: Indiana University Press, 1987, ch. 17–19. Further data on deportations may be found in the later sections of this chapter and in Part 2, s.v. *Aktionen*.
8. Jean-Claude Pressac, *Auschwitz: Technique and Operations of the Gas Chamber*, New York/ Paris: Beate Klarsfeld Foundation, 1990. No comparable work exists for other death factories. Cf. Arad, *Belzec, Sobibór, Treblinka*, ch. 16.
9. On Minsk, see Hersh Smolar, *The Minsk Ghetto*, New York: Holocaust Library, 1989, pp. 71–75; on Vilna, see Yitzhak Arad, *Ghetto in Flames*, New York: Holocaust Library, 1982, ch. 13; on Kovno, see Samuel Gringauz, "The Ghetto as an Experiment of Jewish Social Organization," *JSS*, vol. 11 # 1 (1949), 3–20; on Riga, see Gertrude Schneider, *Journey into Terror*, New York: Ark Home, 1979.
10. Cf. Avraham Barkai, "German-speaking Jews in Eastern European Ghettos," *LBIYB*, vol. 34 (1989), 247–266.
11. The euthanasia program, code-named Operation T4, was a systematic Nazi effort to eliminate Germans with mental or physical handicaps. Undertaken at six facilities in Germany and German-occupied Poland, these killing operations commenced in late 1940. The program officially ended in 1941, because of the outcry of the German public, although such killings continued until 1945 on a smaller scale. Thereafter, the T4 staff shifted to the Final Solution, providing the core of killers in the death camps. Cf. Philippe Aziz, *Doctors of Death*, Geneva: Ferni Publishers, 1976, vol. 4, ch. 1–2.
12. Arad, *Belzec, Sobibór, Treblinka*, pp. 16–19.
13. Callum McDonald, *The Killing of SS-Obergruppenführer Reinhard Heydrich*, New York: Macmillan, 1989, and John Bradley, *Lidice: The Sacrificial Village*, New York: Ballantine Books, 1972.
14. Arad, *Belzec, Sobibór, Treblinka*, pp. 54–59.
15. See, for example, Christopher Browning, "One Day in Józefów: Initiation to Mass Murder," in Peter Hayes (ed.), *Lessons and Legacies: The Meaning of the Holocaust in a Changing World*, Evanston, IL: Northwestern University Press, 1991, pp. 169–209.
16. On the Lublin district, see Christopher Browning, *Ordinary Men: Reserve Police Battalion 101 and the Final Solution in Poland*, New York: Harper Collins, 1992.
17. Much of the data on Galicia is from Hershel Edelheit's as-yet-unpublished diary, "Journal from a Lost World."

18. Arad, *Belzec, Sobibór, Treblinka*, pp. 61–62.

19. Israel Gutman, *The Jews of Warsaw, 1939–1943*, Bloomington: Indiana University Press, 1982, pp. 197–218.

20. This process is graphically described in Emmanuel Ringelblum, *Notes from the Warsaw Ghetto*, New York: Schocken Books, 1975, pp. 311–316.

21. Ibid., p. 314. The Warsaw Judenrat had as many as 7,000 employees in 1942 but the number was reduced to only 3,000 as a result of the deportations.

22. Gutman, *Jews of Warsaw*, pp. 270–272.

23. Arad, *Belzec, Sobibór, Treblinka*, ch. 18.

24. Browning, *Ordinary Men*, ch. 15.

25. Cf. Ruth Zariz, "Officially Approved Emigration from Germany After 1941: A Case Study," *YVS*, vol. 18 (1987), 275–291.

26. Werner T. Angress, *Between Fear and Hope: Jewish Youth in the Third Reich*, New York: Columbia University Press, 1988.

27. Terezin had the status of both a concentration camp (in 1941 and 1942) and a ghetto (after 1942). On the history of Terezin, see Hans-Günther Adler, *Theresienstadt, 1941–1945: Das Antlitz einer Zwangsgemeinschaft. Geschichte, Soziologie, Psychologie* (Theresienstadt, 1941–1945: The face of a forced community. History, sociology, psychology), Tübingen: J.C.B. Mohr, 1960.

28. Ibid., p. 59.

29. Leni Yahil, *The Holocaust*, New York: Oxford University Press, 1990, pp. 406–408.

30. On the UGIF see Cynthia J. Haft, *The Bargain and the Bridle: The General Union of Israelites in France*, Chicago: Dialog Press, 1983; on Holland and Belgium, see (respectively) Dan Michman, "The Controversy Surrounding the Jewish Council in Amsterdam," and Maxime Steinberg, "The Trap of Legality: The Association of the Jews in Belgium," in Israel Gutman and C. J. Haft (eds.), *Patterns of Jewish Leadership in Nazi Europe, 1933–1945*, Jerusalem: Yad Vashem, 1979, pp. 235–265 and 353–376.

31. Cf. Raul Hilberg, *The Destruction of the European Jews*, 1st ed., Chicago: 1961, pp. 405–406.

32. Michael R. Marrus and Robert O. Paxton, *Vichy France and the Jews*, New York: Schocken Books, 1983, pp. 255–261.

33. Ibid., pp. 329–339.

34. Hilberg, *Destruction*, p. 388.

35. Steinberg, "Trap of Legality," pp. 370–376.

36. Hilberg, *Destruction*, p. 376.

37. Jacob Presser, *Ashes in the Wind*, Detroit: Wayne State University Press, 1988, pp. 184–195, 209.

38. Ibid., pp. 209–213, 221.

39. Ibid., pp. 214–220.

40. Cf. Felix Gut, "The Jewish Star over Luxembourg," *South African Jewish Affairs*, vol. 42 # 11 (1987), 29–30.

41. Conditions in Holland from September 1944 to April 1945 have remained unclear since the end of World War II. Allied military operations, notably Operation Market-Garden of September 1944, seem to have permanently disrupted the deportation machinery but did not result in the liberation of the concentration camps located in Holland. It appears that one camp, a labor camp near Arnhem — the main focus of the fighting — was temporarily captured by British paratroopers but had already been emptied of inmates. Thus, the issue requires further elucidation.

42. Samuel Abrahamsen, *Norway's Response to the Holocaust: A Historical Perspective*, New York: Holocaust Library, 1991.

43. Hannu Ruatkallio, *Finland and the Holocaust*, New York: Holocaust Library, 1987.

44. Leni Yahil, *The Rescue of Danish Jewry*, Philadelphia: JPS, 1969, pp. 87–93.

45. Ibid., pp. 168–195.

46. Ibid., ch. 7.

47. Harold Flender, *Rescue in Denmark*, New York: Simon and Schuster, 1963, pp. 215–223, 249–250.

48. Cf. Menachem Shelah, "Genocide in Satellite Croatia During the Second World War," in Michael Berenbaum (ed.), *A Mosaic of Victims*, New York: New York University Press, 1990, pp. 74–79.

49. Cf. Léon Poliakov and Jacques Sabille, *Jews Under the Italian Occupation*, Paris: Editions du Centre, 1955.

50. Christopher Browning, *Fateful Months: Essays on the Emergence of the Final Solution*, rev. ed., New York: Holmes and Meier, 1993, pp. 39–56. Browning contended that these shootings were not part of the Final Solution, even though they were clearly antisemitic in nature. Instead, he placed them as preparatory to the emerging decision to murder European Jewry. Cf. Yahil, *The Holocaust*, p. 351.

51. Shelah, "Sajmište," pp. 243–260.

52. Michael Molho and Joseph Nehama, *In Memoriam: Hommage aux Victimes Juives des Nazis en Grèce*, Salonika: Imp. N. Nicolaides, 1948–1953, vol. 1, pp. 40–46.

53. Joseph Ben, "Jewish Leadership in Greece During the Holocaust," in Gutman and Haft, *Patterns*, pp. 335–351.

54. Molho and Nehama, *In Memoriam*, vol. 1, pp. 77–90.

55. Haim Avni, *Spain, The Jews and Franco*, Philadelphia: JPS, 1982, ch. 5.

56. Molho and Nehama, *In Memoriam*, vol. 1, pp. 222–224.

57. Hilberg, *Destruction*, pp. 450–451.

58. Haim Kechales, קורות יהודי בולגריה (The history of Bulgarian Jewry), Tel Aviv: Davar Press, 1969, vol. 3, ch. 2–3.

59. Ibid., ch. 5.

60. See, for example, the collection of telegrams cited by Kechales, in ibid., pp. 99–117.

61. Ibid., p. 151.

62. Ibid., ch. 6–7.

63. Frederick B. Chary, *The Bulgarian Jews and the Final Solution*, Pittsburgh: University of Pittsburgh Press, 1972, pp. 184–199.

64. Cf. David Mason, *Salerno: Foothold in Europe*, New York: Ballentine Books, 1972, p. 150.

65. For a classic example of such aid, see Alexander Ramati, *The Assisi Underground*, New York: Stein and Day, 1978.

66. Susan Zuccotti, *The Italians and the Holocaust*, New York: Basic Books, 1987, pp. 192–193. See also her note # 12 (p. 312), where she detailed the varying claims regarding the number of Jewish victims.

67. Livia Rothkirchen, *The Destruction of Slovak Jewry: A Documentary History* (Hebrew/English), Jerusalem: Yad Vashem, 1961, pp. 140–141.

68. John Morely, *Vatican Diplomacy and the Jews During the Holocaust*, New York: Ktav, 1980, pp. 89–98.

69. Wisliceny further intimated that $200,000 could ransom all of European Jewry. These demands for money, and the hopes for rescue that they engendered, cannot be taken at purely face value. Cf. Yehuda Bauer, *The Jewish Emergence from Powerlessness*, Toronto: University of Toronto Press, 1979, pp. 14–15.

70. One of the few who survived was Weismandel, who later wrote a stirring condemnation of free-world Jewry's response to the Holocaust. Michael Dov Weismandel, שאלות ותשובות מן המצר (Responsa from the depths), New York: The Author, 1953, passim.

71. On the Jassy pogrom, see Jean Ancel, "The Jassy Syndrome," *Romanian Jewish Studies*, vol. 1 # 1 (1991), 35–52.

72. Cf. Dora Litani, "The Destruction of the Jews of Odessa in the Light of Romanian Documents," *YVS*, vol. 6 (1967), 135–154.

73. Joseph B. Schechtman, "The Transnistria Reservation," *Yivo Annual*, vol. 8 (1953), 178–196.

74. Bela Vago, "The Ambiguity of Collaborationism: The Center of the Jews in Romania (1942–1944)," in Gutman and Haft, *Patterns*, pp. 287–309.

75. Jean Ancel, "The Romanian Way of Solving the 'Jewish Problem' in Bessarabia and Bukovina, June–July, 1941," *YVS*, vol. 19 (1988), 227–231.

76. Cf. Theodore Lavi, "Documents on the Struggle of Romanian Jewry for Its Rights During the Second World War," *YVS*, vol. 4 (1960), 261–315.

77. Dina Porat, "The Transnistria Affair and the Rescue Policy of the Zionist Leadership in Palestine, 1942–1943," *Studies in Zionism*, vol. 6 # 1 (1985), 27–52.

78. Theodore Lavi, "The Background to the Rescue of Romanian Jewry During the Holocaust Period," in B. Vago and G. L. Mosse (eds.), *Jews and Non-Jews in Eastern Europe*, Jerusalem: Israel Universities Press, 1974, pp. 177–186.

79. Nathaniel Katzburg, *Hungary and the Jews*, Ramat Gan: Bar Ilan University Press, 1981, ch. 3–7.

80. Ibid., ch. 8.

81. Randolph L. Braham, *The Hungarian Labor Service System, 1939–1945*, Boulder, CO: East European Quarterly, 1977.

82. Randolph L. Braham, *The Politics of Genocide*, 1st ed., New York: Columbia University Press, 1981, pp. 199–216.

83. Ibid., pp. 226–229.

84. Ibid., pp. 229–249.

85. Giles Lambert, *Operation Hazalah*, Indianapolis: Bobbs–Merrill, 1974, pp. 60–69.

86. For the general background to the Nazi occupation, see C. A. Macartney, *October Fifteenth: A History of Hungary*, New York: Praeger, 1957, passim; for a perspective on the Jewish response to the Nazi occupation, see Lambert, *Operation Hazalah*, ch. 16–17.

87. Braham, *Politics*, ch. 19–22.

88. Cf. "Hungarian Jews Doomed: Planned Extermination," *Jewish Chronicle*, July 14, 1944, pp. 1, 7.

89. Braham, *Politics*, ch. 24.

90. The complete Auschwitz protocol is provided in John Mendelsohn (editor in chief), *The Holocaust: Selected Documents in Eighteen Volumes*, New York: Garland, 1981, vol. 11; for a more personal perspective on the report, see Rudolf Vrba and Alan Bestig, *I Cannot Forgive*, New York: Grove Press, 1984.

91. Braham, *Politics*, ch. 23.

92. The negotiations are detailed in André Biss, *A Million Jews to Save*, New York: A. S. Barnes, 1973. Biss adopted a more pro-Kasztner orientation than seems prudent in light of currently available evidence. Cf. Braham, *Politics*, pp. 933–976.

93. Still controversial, the Kasztner affair has led to numerous publications, most of which are sensationalized and partisan. Two articles appear, however, to have clarified the issue beyond any further doubt, and they have been closely followed in the preceding section: Bela Vago, "The Intelligence Aspects of the Brand Mission," *YVS*, vol. 10 (1974), 111–128, and Yehuda Bauer, "The Mission of Joel Brand," in his *The Holocaust in Historical Perspective*, Seattle: University of Washington Press, 1978, pp. 94–155.

6

JEWISH RESPONSES TO PERSECUTION

As Sheep to the Slaughter?

In light of the grave threat the Nazis posed to Jewish survival, the question of Jewish responses to persecution is an important and timely one. Unfortunately the issue has been rendered complex, without any true elucidation, by authors who have created a bogus theory regarding the issue of death with dignity. Thus, for example, child psychologist Bruno Bettelheim wrote:

> If, today, Negroes in [South] Africa march against the guns of a police that defends apartheid — even if hundreds of them will be shot down . . . their march, their fight, will sooner or later assure them of a chance for liberty and equality. Millions of Jews . . . could at least have marched as free men against the SS, rather than to first grovel, then wait to be rounded up for their own extermination, and finally walk themselves to the gas chambers.[1]

Raul Hilberg appeared — at least during the 1960s — to take this thesis of the Jews' collaboration in their own murder a step further in his discussion of a "Jewish compliance reaction."[2]

In response, accusations of Jewish passivity led to an initially apologetic response, followed by a later emphasis on objective scholarship. Apologists attempted to defend the honor of the victims who stood accused of going to their deaths like sheep.[3]

Moreover, it is becoming increasingly clear that the accusation that Jews did not die with dignity fails to address the daily reality of life in the ghettos and concentration camps. This is true because it is impossible to die with dignity unless one has lived with dignity. At every turn, however, the Jewish victims sought to defend their humanity; they never surrendered their self-respect even in the most dire conditions. As victims of an unprecedented Nazi hatred, they can be said to have died with dignity precisely because they lived with dignity both before and during the war.

Another element must also be kept in mind. When the accusers — Bettelheim was especially guilty in this regard — stated that Jews "went as sheep to the slaughter," they were using a meaningless phrase that distorted not only the history of the Holocaust but also much of previous Jewish history. First, it must be remembered that Jews *went* nowhere in Nazi-occupied Europe. They may (or may not) have been led as sheep, but Jews (with the exception of a few members of the Judenräte or Jewish police) were never active actors in the process of deportation. More significantly, the term "sheep to the slaughter" plays an honored role in the history of Jewish martyrology. The phrase originated with the prophet Isaiah and his "suffering servant" prophecy.[4] During the Greco-Roman eras and into the Middle Ages Jewish commentators and biblical exegetes interpreted that prophecy as an allegory of Jewish history and particularly of the history of *Kiddush ha-Shem* (martyrdom).

Examples may be drawn from almost every era in Jewish history, from the well-known story of Rabbi Akiva to lesser-known pronouncements cited in the Talmud, such as elucidated in those teachings of Rabbi Hiyya bar Abba: "If one comes to you and demands, 'Give your life for *Kiddush ha-Shem*,' respond, 'I give [it]!'"[5] Furthermore Jewish law is clear on this issue: In normal times one is permitted to martyr oneself only to avoid the three cardinal sins, idolatry, sexual license, and murder. But in a time of persecution, a Jew is to accept martyrdom regardless of how trivial the persecutors' demands may be.[6]

It must also be pointed out that martyrdom is the last resort. Before one is allowed to sacrifice one's own life, one must attempt to physically defend it as best one can. On the whole, Jews subscribed to this *halacha*. It may well be that during the Crusades, acts of self-defense were numerically more prevalent than acts of martyrdom. Certainly all able-bodied men fought to whatever degree was possible. In Šla (Bohemia), 500 armed Jews with the help of Imperial Knights fought off the enemy.[7] The same was to recur later. For this reason Polish synagogues were designed to be fortresses, not only for architectural adornment but also for very utilitarian considerations: Envisioning the need for defense, their builders designed them as fortresses, and they were the only hope of survival for many a community in its hour of need.[8]

Furthermore, martyrdom and self-defense are not contradictory: One complements the other, since an individual is bidden to do everything to preserve life for as long as possible. Rabbi Menachem M. Ziemba of Praga (a Warsaw suburb, which had a large Jewish community before World War II) framed the issues best when, on January 14, 1943, he declared to a council of the Warsaw ghetto's Jewish political undergrounds:

Of necessity, we must resist the enemy on all fronts. . . . We shall no longer heed his instructions . . . as it is now we have no choice but to resist . . . *Halacha* demands that we fight and resist to the very end with unequalled determination and valor for the sake of the Sanctification of the Divine Name.[9]

The Jews' Spiritual Stand

Such sentiments were implicitly or explicitly echoed by groups of Jewish intellectuals, political activists, and members of youth movements. From the earliest days of Nazi occupation these small groups continued to operate surreptitiously, crystallizing into a political underground that sought to mute the effects of Nazi persecution.

Since the initial goal of Nazi persecution appeared to be the psychological degradation and physical debilitation of the Jewish victims, the initial responses of these undergrounds were geared to protecting morale, educating youth, and supplementing the meager rations available to most ghetto inmates. The goal of such activities was not to subvert the Nazi stranglehold on the ghettos — or on the occupied lands — but to maintain the spirits of Nazism's special victims. Since the war, most historians have denoted such forms of activity as spiritual resistance, which may be exemplified by three broad spheres of activity:[10]

1. The opening of soup kitchens and the systematic smuggling of food and medicine into the ghetto. Such activity was not the exclusive province of Jewish undergrounds; many individuals also engaged in such activity. Furthermore, in 1939, 1940, and 1941, the establishment of soup kitchens sponsored by the American Jewish Joint Distribution Committee (JDC) proceeded quite openly. Since the JDC was a private agency from a neutral country, its employees were able to operate with relatively few external impediments until the United States entered World War II in December 1941.[11]

2. The publication of a widely ramified underground press. Three main ideological trends may be discerned in the Polish Jewish underground press: the Zionists, the Bundists, and the Communists. They published at least

twenty-one different titles on a fairly regular basis. Scores of others appeared on an irregular basis or as one-time publications.[12] Most of these publications — in typed form, stenciled, or hand written — appeared in Hebrew, Yiddish, or Polish or in a combination of those languages and served both a morale-building and an educational purpose. Typically, an issue included news about the course of the war, party-related topics, and articles, illustrations, or poems related to the date of appearance.[13] The Zionist-oriented underground press paid particularly close attention to news from the Yishuv. Such articles were considered vital to the training of young members who, it was hoped, would be emigrating after liberation. Additionally, the continued security of the Yishuv was seen as vital for long-term Jewish survival. "As long as there is a Jewish Eretz-Israel," one underground paper editorialized, "the Jewish people will not be exterminated."[14]

3. Various educational, cultural, and intellectual activities — including art exhibits, musical recitals, and poetry readings.[15] Here again, not all activities were clandestine; in some ghettos (for example, Vilna) schools were permitted to operate openly. These activities served three purposes: to build morale, to maintain a sense of normalcy in ghetto life, and to provide an opportunity for artists and individuals interested in the arts to channel their creative energies. All such activities also served an ideological purpose as well. Specifically, this form of spiritual resistance has been subsumed under the title of *Kiddush ha-Hayim* (the Sanctification of Life) — the act of *Kiddush ha-Hayim* being the act of outliving the Nazis. Rabbi Yitzhak Nissenbaum, a leader of the Mizrachi (religious Zionists) movement in Poland, explained *Kiddush ha-Hayim* thus:

It is a time for *Kiddush ha-Hayim*, the sanctification of life, and not *Kiddush Hashem*, the holiness of martyrdom. In the past the enemies of the Jews sought the soul of the Jew, and so it was proper for the Jew to sanctify the name of God by sacrificing his body in Martyrdom, in that manner preserving what the enemy sought to take from him. But now it is the *body* of the Jew that the oppressor demands. For this reason it is up to the Jew to defend his body, to preserve his life.[16]

There was an additional element of the Jews' spiritual stand against the Nazis. In virtually every ghetto and camp, individuals or small groups began to collect materials of historical importance. Many also kept diaries. Their purpose was to preserve some form of Jewish documentation in order to ensure that even if the Nazis silenced all Jews, they would never silence the victims' voices. This too was an act of defiance; for the Nazis, in their use of coded terms, euphemisms, and oblique references, sought to ensure that the Final Solution would be the great, unwritten, chapter in the Thousand-Year Reich's history.[17]

The most systematic effort to document Jewish suffering was undertaken in the Warsaw ghetto. A young historian, Dr. Emmanuel Ringelblum, took the first steps to organize the secret archive as early as October 1939. From May 1940 on, Ringelblum engaged the assistance of a number of scholars in their own right (among others, Rabbi Simon Huberband) to further expand the project. As described by Ringelblum, the archive, called *Oneg Shabbat*, was set up with three goals: (1) to document the suffering of Warsaw Jewry and, to the greatest extent possible, Polish Jewry, under the Nazis; (2) to preserve items of historical significance, including Jewish underground newspapers, minutes of meetings of Warsaw's clandestine Jewish political parties, and data on Warsaw Jewry; and (3) to collect and preserve oral testimonies of Jews who had witnessed aspects of the Holocaust and reported on what they saw. Also included in the archive were German documents relating to Jews and the diaries kept by *Oneg Shabbat* archivists.[18] A subsidiary *Oneg Shabbat* archive was established in Bialystok; Vilna, Krakow, Lodz, Lvov, and Riga had similar underground archives.[19]

Consciously or subconsciously, archivists and diarists were also following in a rich Jewish tradition of using history as a means of

Page from Dr. Emmanuel Ringelblum's Warsaw ghetto diary
Courtesy of the Żydowski Instytut Historyczny/U.S. Holocaust Memorial Museum

ensuring memory. It has been, in fact, reported that the last words of Jewish historian Simon Dubnow, as he was being led to his death in the Riga ghetto, were, "Yidn, farshraibt" (Jews, write it down).[20]

Resistance and Collaboration in Europe

Two wars were fought on the European continent during the Nazi occupation. One was the conventional struggle waged by the Allied armies to liberate Europe. The other was a struggle for national liberation and for national honor, waged by patriotic civilians of almost every Nazi-occupied country. Since World War II, the European resistance has been elevated to the status of a myth, in which even the German masses (as opposed to the few bona fide anti-Nazi Germans) are considered resisters. In reality, neither resisters nor collaborators were in the majority. Wartime realities led civilians to emphasize either collaboration with or resistance to the Nazi occupation authorities, based on the course of the war. Thus, a few highly motivated diehards notwithstanding, collaboration appeared the best course early in the war — especially in 1940 and 1941 — and resistance thereafter, accelerating to a mass movement in 1944.[21]

Still, one fact must be kept in mind. In every occupied country, stout-hearted men and women for whom duty, honor, and country meant more than life itself arose to fight the Nazis. Even some Germans looked forward to the demise of Nazism, opposed everything the Hitlerite regime stood for, and prepared themselves, abortively in most cases, to do battle with the SS state. Ultimately these altruists and visionaries, not the realists who collaborated with the Nazis, won the day. By their sacrifice, the resisters proved that one does not have to surrender to evil, but that evil can be resisted and eventually defeated.

In the both Soviet Union and Yugoslavia resistance activities were primarily manifested in operations by bands of partisans operating for months and years in the enemy rear. In Yugoslavia both Communist and non-Communist resistance movements arose, led respectively by Josip Tito (Broz) and Draza Mihailović. At times their anti-Nazi struggle took on the aspect of a civil war, which Tito's Communist partisans eventually won. By late 1944 the partisans, who numbered nearly 400,000, were able, with Soviet, British, and U.S. assistance to liberate Belgrade.[22]

The Soviet partisan movement was more unified. Initially composed of large numbers of Red Army troops who had been bypassed during the Nazi blitz during the summer of 1941, by 1943 most partisans were civilians fighting out of a patriotic sense. Although fighting with great fervor, the first Soviet partisan groups were poorly organized and received little more than encouraging words from the unoccupied territories. As the partisan movement grew in strength, however, operations became better organized, until, in 1943 and 1944, the partisans became a fourth arm of the Soviet ground forces. In particular, partisan operations were coordinated with parachute drops and with conventional operations. And once they were liberated, the partisan units were absorbed into the ranks of the regular armed forces.[23]

Nazi measures against the partisans were, to say the least, ruthless and included the destruction of entire villages suspected of aiding resisters.[24] Less well known is the fact that the SS Einsatzgruppen often used the pretext of internal security needs as a cover for the mass extermination of Jews.[25] Such operations were only partly successful in eliminating the partisans; some historians have argued that the Nazis' ruthlessness may have actually contributed to partisan recruitment since the killing of civilians — in retaliation for attacks on Wehrmacht or SS troops — instilled hatred of the occupying regime and a thirst for revenge rather than fear.[26] As an example, Wehrmacht Army Group Center — whose operational zone lay between Kiev in the South and Vitebsk in the North and ranged from the Bryansk-Orel-Kursk region — logged more than 11,000 partisan operations in August 1943, as against a mere 26 operations by the Soviet air force.[27]

In Poland and Western Europe resistance activities included both partisans in mountainous and forested areas and urban guerrilla operations in large cities. In Poland, resistance movements began to operate almost immediately after the Nazi occupation. Recognizing that an open battle against the Germans would be suicidal, however, the Poles adopted a slower operational strategy that emphasized building up strength for an eventual national insurrection.[28] As the Soviet army approached the Polish borders in late 1943, however, the main underground movement — the Armia Krajowa (AK) — began Tempest, the code name for a series of small-scale anti-Nazi strikes.[29]

Tempest, in turn, led to Typhoon, an uprising by the entire population of Warsaw on August 1, 1944. Although they held the initiative, the Poles were soon disappointed. Armia Krajowa units operating in conjunction with groups from the Communist-led Armia Ludowa (AL) and sundry Polish Fascists were not able to overwhelm the German garrison. In particular, the Poles failed to capture Warsaw's airport and could do no more than besiege the Wehrmacht and Gestapo headquarters. Furthermore, anticipated Soviet military assistance did not materialize. As a result, the Armia Krajowa was ground to dust during a brutal two-month battle; approximately 200,000 Poles died during the fighting.[30]

France experienced a similar pattern of development. The first resistance cells were created in late 1940. Unlike the Poles, however, the French resisters had to fight against two foes: The Nazis who occupied northern France and the collaborationist Vichy regime in the south. Initially, resistance cells were widely scattered and extremely disorganized. By 1943 a measure of unity was instilled in the resistance groups, especially by leaders such as Jean Moulin. Thus, the resistance movements consolidated into two broad groups, the Communist Francs-Tireurs et Partisans (FTP), and the non-Communist Forces Francaises de l'Intérieur (FFI). Both these groups, in turn, were responsible to the Armée Secrète, for military affairs, and to the Conseil National pour la Résistance, for political issues.[31] Overall control of underground activities was provided by the French National Committee led by General Charles de Gaulle. Initially headquartered in London, de Gaulle moved to Algiers in 1943 in anticipation of the invasion of France.[32]

As in Poland, French resistance movements concentrated on small-scale sabotage activities in 1941 and 1942. Maquis activity was stepped up in late 1943 and continued to build in anticipation of aiding the Allied invasion of France, which occurred on June 6, 1944.[33] Here too, the Allied invasion signaled the beginning of the French national uprising; in contrast to the case in Poland, the end result was a victory for the underground that culminated in the self-liberation of Paris.[34] The success of the French resistance was, of course, not unequivocal and certainly did not come cheap. Outright Maquis defeats, such as that in the Vercors, and Nazi atrocities, such as the massacre at Oradur-sur-Glâne, meant that, as in the rest of Europe, much blood was spilled before liberation was achieved.[35]

Resisters throughout Europe had similar experiences. Thousands of Europeans, from France to Russia and from Norway to North Africa, representing every political movement, answered the call to arms of the clandestine armies. Many brave souls gave their lives for liberty.[36] In this connection, mention, albeit brief, must be made of the Allied secret service agents, the British Special Operations Executive, the American Office of Strategic Services, and the Soviet NKVD (secret police), who aided the resisters at every turn.[37]

Conditions for Jewish Resistance

Many Jews also participated in the European struggle for freedom. The Jewish war, however, was fundamentally different. No other people faced *Ausmerzung*. The Nazis planned to enslave all of Europe but never planned to murder all Europeans. Yet National Socialism would accept nothing less that the total eradication of all Jews throughout the world. No quarter would be given. The simple fact must be stated: The majority of European Jewry did not actively resist the Nazis; neither did all other Europeans under Nazi occupation. This does not, however, mean that Jews collaborated in their own destruction. The majority of Jews could not resist for a variety of reasons. Eight major factors came together to inhibit Jewish resistance: lawfulness; time; lack of arms; lack of trained men; lack of an outside source of aid; lack of a suitable place to fight; the Jewish view of the Germans; and collective responsibility. We will summarize each one briefly.

Lawfulness is the tendency to obey laws. Most human beings tend to obey authority; that is human nature. But though this would not lead to problems for a Gentile under Nazi occupation during World War II, it would for the Jew. Thus, for instance, when Jews were ordered to wear the distinctive Jewish star, most obeyed and by doing so — even those who would not otherwise be identifiable as Jews — became easy targets. Again, when Jews were ordered to register with the Judenrat or other authorities, most obeyed and registered themselves, their families, and all of their belongings. By obeying this law, Jews inadvertently gave the Nazis lists that could later be utilized by Aussiedlungskommandos to empty one Jewish community after the other with ease. In sum, when Jews obeyed laws, they died; when they refused to obey, their chances for survival were greatly enhanced. Still, a Jewish legal principle is *dina malhuta dina* — the law of the land is the law — and even though the law was evil, the Jewish masses chose to obey.

Time, of course, could have made the difference. The Poles, French, and Norwegians all had to overcome the same psychological problem. The difference was that no one was murdering 30,000 Frenchmen a day, everyday.

Forged Aryan identity papers (top) and a ration booklet (bottom)
Courtesy of Isaac Kowalski

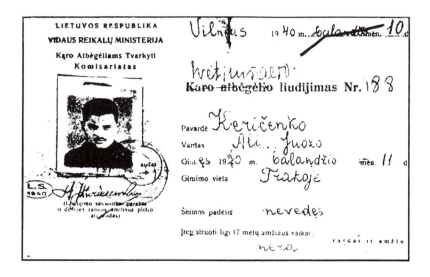

Jews, thus, found themselves not only at a disadvantage, but at a severe disadvantage: They had to overcome the psychological barriers to resistance and had to do it quickly. The longer they tarried, the less it would matter; the Nazis' main objective to render Europe *judenrein* took precedence above all. In comparison with the Final Solution, all other goals became secondary. To beleaguered Jewry time was thus of the essence, since to the Nazis, the destruction of European Jewry was more important than the defense of the Reich itself.

The lack of arms was also a problem. We have been told, after the fact that, they "should have fought with anything." Perhaps! Reality, points to different conclusions, however: If outside of Britain, the organized armies of Europe's independent states could hardly stand up to the might of Nazi Germany, succumbing one by one in short order, how then could a handful of Jews without any arms at all? Although the Allied armies supplied and helped stockpile some weapons for most of the European resistance groups, no weapons were ever offered to the beleaguered Jews. The pitiful number of pistols, rifles, some hand grenades, and the few rounds of ammunition provided to Jews in Poland by some of the undergrounds were given begrudgingly and then were often found to be damaged or unusable. In many instances, Jewish fighters that managed to secure a weapon or two were ambushed in the forests by non-Jewish guerrillas while the Jews were trying to join the partisan ranks. Again, of course, conditions were better in Western Europe and Jews did receive arms from Allied stockpiles.

The lack of trained men was almost as debilitating as the lack of arms, for the one is dependent upon the other. Although this was a trans-European problem, it was a greater problem for Jews. In the general European underground a trained cadre of troops from the former national armies existed. The Jews had had no army or any collective national military experience for many hundreds of years, at least since the Chmielnicki pogroms of 1648–1649. To be

sure, there were Jewish soldiers in the various armies of Europe; some of them played significant roles in the resistance. The vast majority, however, when taken as prisoners of war, were separated and incarcerated in special Gestapo-run camps from where many — in due time — were dispatched to their deaths. The Nazis and their collaborators did not wish to take the chance that Jewish soldiers might become future leaders of a Jewish underground. Furthermore, many of the Jewish leaders that had trained Polish youth for self-defense and future *aliya* left Europe just before or with the outbreak of war. As a result, many of youth movements that eventually became the backbone of the Jewish resistance were initially left with only an ad hoc leadership that was not up to par.

Regarding outside aid, two important points need to be made: First, European antisemites, especially those in Eastern Europe, had a vested interest in being rid of their Jews. It is, therefore, no surprise that large segments of the non-Jewish populace hardly exerted themselves to save Jews, even if they were not directly involved in the genocide process. Second, no other practical source of aid was available. Western Allied aid to resistance was controlled by the British in coordination with the various governments in exile. There was no Jewish state at the time and, therefore, no Jewish government in exile to look after Jewish interests; the Yishuv was itself governed by Great Britain. As mentioned above, the Allies trained and supplied most of the European undergrounds; Jews, as separate resistance bodies, were not even considered undergrounds by the Allies and were therefore entirely ignored.

This problem was further exacerbated by the place in which most Jews fought. A successful guerrilla movement needs to be mobile. The Jews turned some of the ghettos into fortresses, but without a relieving force, the besieged could hardly expect to be victorious. As it happens, Jewish resistance is one of the classic examples that proves the failure of the so-called national redoubt concept of resistance so popular during World War II. Under this concept, resistance movements sought to seize and hold a region until it was liberated by Allied ground forces. Except for Paris in August 1944, no application of this concept succeeded. For Jews this failure was even more pronounced, since there was no force coming to the rescue to begin with.

Of course, we assume that the Jews knew what fate was awaiting them. But this hardly is so! The Jewish masses deluded themselves into believing that no German — viewed as the liberator only thirty years before — even a Nazi, would murder innocent civilians. Germans might well be antisemites, but they would not stoop down to brutal, wanton murder. Oppress, yes; they might even kill some Jews during pogroms, but resort to mass murder, never.

Then too, the majority view of the Jewish leadership, especially in Nazi-occupied Eastern Europe, was that if the Jews would work hard and diligently — thus contributing to the Nazi war machine — their lives and that of their families would be spared. Even though a minority viewed this line of reasoning to be erroneous, the Jewish masses went along with this notion until it was too late.

Finally, we come to collective responsibility. The resistance was continually plagued by this moral dilemma. The Nazis, knowing the strength of the Jewish ideal of brotherhood, made one Jew responsible for the other in fact. Thus, for instance, if one Jew dared to resist, all Jews in the community would be held responsible. This moral dilemma was foremost in the mind of potential resistance fighters, perhaps more so than all the above problems combined. For by the act that offered their chance for survival they were virtually guaranteeing the destruction of their loved ones, friends, and neighbors. The example of Abba Kovner, one of the commanders of the Faraynikte Partizaner Organizatzye in the Vilna ghetto, is indicative of the dilemma: As he was about to leave the ghetto for the forests with a group of Jewish partisans, his mother came to him and asked what she should do. He answered that he did not know and left. Many years later, Kovner was still asking

whether he deserved to be hailed as a hero of the resistance or vilified as an unfaithful son.[38]

Despite these impediments to resistance, as well as other obstacles designed to keep Jews quiescent, Jews never surrendered. Even in death they walked with their pride intact. Lacking a state, Jews could not hope to fight for liberation. For European Jewry, resistance was a struggle to survive, a fight to choose the time and place of one's death, a war to sell Jewish blood at a high price. The statement of the Jewish will to live and fight for survival was implicit in the Jewish struggle.

Under the circumstances, it is clear that Jewish resistance movements would be most likely to develop from the Jewish political undergrounds that had been established in 1939 and 1940. In this area, Jews paralleled developments in the general environment, although Jews had generally less time to form their movements before becoming active. However, Jewish resisters had little to fear from Jewish collaborators, who never represented a major threat to the resistance movements, and thus had slightly more internal freedom of action than their European counterparts.[39] Still, the Jewish situation was unique and resulted in unique patterns of resistance activity.

In particular, spontaneous acts of active resistance played a much greater role in the early history of Jewish resistance than they did among the general European undergrounds. This spontaneous resistance took many forms: Small numbers of Jews, two or three at the most, might find an opportunity to jump from a deportation train heading to a death camp.[40] In another typical case, a Jew (or a small group of Jews) would attack members of an Einsatzkommando as they were in the process of shooting their intended victims. A case in point is the anti-Jewish *Aktion* in the Lithuanian village of Kedainiai: The Jewish victims were already in the murder pit, about to be slaughtered, when the village's ritual butcher jumped from the pit, grabbed one of the would-be killers and, sinking his teeth deep in the murderer's throat, bit him to death while the butcher was cut down by rifle fire.[41] A similar example is the poignant story told of two French Jews, brothers, incarcerated in the

Unit of Jewish partisans from the "Grynspan Group" operating in the Parczew Forest.
Back row (from left): Dudkin Rubinstein, Jurek Pomeranc, Lonka Feferkorn, Lova,
Chil Grynspan (leader), Janek, Wojo.
Front row (from left): Two unknown partisans, Pacan Rubinstein.
Courtesy of Mr. Samuel Gruber/U.S. Holocaust Memorial Museum

Mauthausen concentration camp, who committed suicide by jumping into that camp's infamous quarry. As they took their leave of their friends and of the guards (who, incidentally encouraged them to jump), the two brothers grabbed two SS men and died with them.[42]

Although heroic in themselves, these spontaneous acts of resistance — all save escape attempts — did not appreciably affect the course of the Final Solution. Saving Jewish lives required acts of collective resistance and, especially, required a generally unavailable amount of aid for Jewish resistance from the local non-Jewish population.

Jewish Resistance in Eastern Europe

The earliest manifestations of organized active resistance took place in the East. Spontaneous acts of resistance have been recorded in response to Einsatzkommando *Aktionen*; one typical case has already been cited. In other instances, Jewish survivors of murdered communities and escapees who fled before or during Nazi *Aktionen* took to the forests. These individuals banded together to form units of Jewish partisans. Moreover, young Jews incarcerated in some of the ghettos systematically escaped to the forest, with or without weapons, and tried to form additional partisan units. In turn, these partisan units attached themselves to battalions or brigades of Soviet partisans operating in the Belorussian, Lithuanian, and Ukrainian forests.[43] As they developed, Jewish partisan units became the focal point of Jewish rescue efforts: Whenever possible, the units established family camps composed of non-combatants — including entire families — protected by partisans. In return for protection, the non-fighters provided various support services to the fighters. In response to Nazi antipartisan sweeps, both partisan units and family camps repeatedly changed location, often keeping only a step ahead of the SS, German military police, or local collaborators' "protective battalions," the so-called Schumas.[44]

The best-known family camp, nicknamed Jerusalem, operated in the Naliboki Forest, situated between Lithuania and northern Belorussia, from 1941 through 1944. Commanded by the four Bielski brothers — Tuvia, Zusya, Aharon, and Asael — the camp included almost 1,300 fighters and in 1944 nearly five times as many civilians. Despite intense Nazi efforts, including a major antipartisan sweep launched in July and August 1943, Jerusalem tenaciously fought and moved from place to place, outflanking the Nazis, until liberated by the Red Army. Thereafter, Bielski and his men, officially known as the Kalinin Battalion, participated in the liberation of Novogrodek and in conventional operations — after being absorbed into the Red Army — in Poland, Pomerania, and East Prussia.[45]

Jewish partisan units, some smaller, some larger, operated throughout Eastern Europe: in Lithuania, in Belorussia, in the Ukraine, and in Galicia (southeastern Poland). In the USSR, however, Jewish partisans — both units and individuals — were faced with a tripartite problem: First, the Soviet partisans refused to accept unarmed civilians. The Bielski brothers actually disobeyed their superiors in order to protect their family camp but were able to do so because of a sympathetic brigade commander; other Jews were less fortunate. In most cases, Jews without arms were turned away from

partisan units, generally to their deaths.[46] Second, antisemitism did not disappear even among Soviet or pro-Soviet partisans. Isaac Kowalski, who provided Jewish and non-Jewish partisans in the Lithuanian forests with propaganda material from his printing press, was a typical example: An antisemitic Ukrainian partisan shot him "accidentally," but Kowalski was only wounded.[47] Third, and most important, Soviet policy did not permit the continued existence of independent Jewish partisan units. The groups that existed were forced to integrate into general units by the partisan high command. Soviet reasoning has never been fully explained but may be summarized thus: Cognizant as they were of the intense antisemitism of many partisans and of the general population, Stavka (the Soviet chiefs of staff) sought to "hide" Jewish partisans so as not to appear to favor Jews and thereby justify Nazi propaganda. In truth, Jews were not alone in being made invisible by the Soviet high command. All partisan detachments were Soviet rather than "Ukrainian," "Russian," or "Belorussian."[48]

Jewish partisans operating in southeastern Poland also experienced numerous difficulties, but of a different nature. Here too, the Jewish partisans had to fight a dual war, against Nazis and against local antisemites, but, unlike the USSR, Poland had no sizeable partisan movement until 1943 and 1944, that is, after most Jews had already been murdered.[49] Furthermore, Poland's flat, mountainless terrain did not encourage partisan operations. Therefore, most Jewish fighters in Poland concentrated on fighting in the ghettos.

Jewish resistance activities culminated in rebellions in seventeen East European ghettos: Będzin, Bialystok, Brody, Częstochowa, Krakow, Lvov, Lutsk, Minsk, Mir, Riga, Sielce, Sosnowiec, Stryzow, Tarnopol, Tarnow, Vilna, and Warsaw. Of these revolts, none is better known than the Warsaw ghetto uprising. Jewish prewar political parties had organized into underground political cells with the Nazi occupation of Poland, some of them as early as October 1939; other reorganized and expanded through 1940. The Germans purposely looked away for a time, their policy being that some clandestine political activity would lull the Jewish community into a false sense of normality. The Nazis did not initially attempt to uproot these Jewish political cells and thereby emboldened some of them into expansion.[50] Until the Nazi invasion of the Soviet Union, almost all the political undergrounds were preoccupied with day-to-day matters — principally, to alleviate the immediate needs of their members, both physically and mentally — and little thought was given to prepare for the battle for their lives. With the beginning of Operation Barbarossa, some information filtered into the Warsaw ghetto (and from there to the larger Jewish communities) regarding the massive Nazi atrocities in eastern Poland and the Soviet Union committed by the Einsatzgruppen and their local helpers. As a result, Jewish underground activities were heightened, but not fundamentally changed.[51]

A degree of inter-party unity was established in January 1942, when Jewish Communists and a number of Socialist Zionist groups created a united anti-Fascist bloc in the ghetto.[52] Around the same time, the Nazis started implementing their Final Solution in full gear. Village after village, town after town, and ghetto after ghetto were emptied of Jews. In Warsaw, too, the Nazis began the systematic application of their deportation and murder policy. Between July 22 and September 7, 1942,

approximately 300,000 Warsaw Jews were deported. The anti-Fascist bloc did not respond because, at the time, it did not possess even one firearm. On July 28, 1942, however, the anti-Fascist bloc officially ceased to exist, converting itself into the Żydowska Organizacja Bojowa (ŻOB, the Jewish Combat Organization). Between July and September 1942, ŻOB grew to include all Jewish parties except the Bund and the Revisionist Zionists.[53] Despite its wider representation, ŻOB still remained weak; its stock of weapons was especially poor since the organization had little outside aid. Moreover, on September 3, 1942, ŻOB's entire arsenal was discovered and captured by the Nazis.[54]

Shortly thereafter, the deportations ended temporarily. The remaining 70,000 Jews of the Warsaw ghetto used the respite to prepare to defend themselves. Between September 1942 and January 1943, arms were acquired and 611 bunkers were prepared. In October, the Bund joined the ŻOB, agreeing to unity only after the "political" aspect of ŻOB's operations was taken over by the newly created Żydowski Komitet Narodowy (ŻKN, the Jewish National Committee).[55] The Revisionist Zionists, who in the interim had created their own combat organization — the Żydowski Związek Wojskowy (ŻZW, the Jewish Military Union) — agreed to coordinate operations with the ŻOB and the ŻKN.[56] Thus, by the end of 1942, the structure of Warsaw's Jewish underground was something like this:

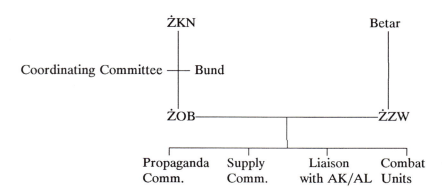

Graph 6.1: Structure of the Warsaw Ghetto Underground

ŻOB's key weakness, and to an extent this held true for the ŻZW as well, was the lack of firearms; most armed combatants had only pistols or homemade grenades. The ŻOB arsenal included a small number of rifles, and the ŻZW had a single light machine gun — in effect the heaviest weapon in the ghetto.[57] Still, the Jewish fighters had one element in their favor: that of surprise. German unpreparedness for resistance was used to good effect between January 18 and 22, 1943, the period of the so-called Small Revolt. The Nazis came to liquidate the ghetto. Encountering resistance, they were forced to call off the *Aktion* after only 8,000 Jews had been deported.[58]

It was clear, however, that the Germans would return. On April 18, 1943, the Nazis did return, intending to undertake a three-day *Grossaktion* that would eliminate the last Jews of Warsaw in time for the *Führer's* birthday. Again, the SS received more than they bargained for: The initial assault on the morning of April 19, 1943, was repulsed by the Jews, who stoutly resisted from strongpoints throughout the ghetto. At one point in the fighting, Jewish insurgents waved two flags — the blue and white Zionist flag and the red and white Polish flag. The Nazis resumed the attack on the afternoon of April 19, only to be again repulsed. Despite their overwhelming firepower, they could not overpower the few hundred fighters, whose heaviest weapon was a light machine gun. After three days, the Nazis altered tactics. Instead of trying to engage the Jewish fighters in setpiece battles, the commander of the operation, SS-General Jurgen Stroop, decided to simply burn down the ghetto.

From the Stroop Report:
Jewish resistance members in the hands of SS troops
during the Warsaw ghetto uprising
Courtesy of the National Archives/U.S. Holocaust Memorial Museum

Ruins of the Warsaw ghetto after the uprising
Courtesy of the Simon Wiesenthal Center Beit HaShoah Museum of Tolerance Archives/Library, Los Angeles, CA

Eventually, the disparity in firepower was telling. Outnumbered and outgunned, the Jewish fighters still held on for twenty-eight days (longer than the entire Polish army did in 1939). They too changed tactics, changing to hit-and-run-operations in order to be less easy targets. On May 8, 1943, an SS patrol discovered ŻOB's command bunker at 18 Ulica Mila; during the ensuing firefight the Jewish fighters killed themselves rather than surrender to the enemy. Among the dead was Mordechai Anielewicz, the Warsaw ghetto's 24 year-old commander. On May 16, the Germans declared the revolt to be over. As a symbol of their victory, Stroop ordered that the last remaining synagogue building in Warsaw, the Tlomacki Street Synagogue, be demolished.[59]

Only a small number of ŻOB and ŻZW fighters were able to escape through the sewers; they continued to fight, however. Indeed, 1,000 Jewish fighters served with Polish Socialist and Communist underground groups during Operation Typhoon in August and September 1944.[60] Never-

theless, the "twenty-eight days of absolutely hopeless, absolutely heroic revolt provide," in the words of M.R.D. Foot, "a passionate denial of the other popular stereotype, of Jews who shambled off unprotesting to the slaughter-house."[61] Quite naturally, the Warsaw ghetto uprising has become a modern symbol of heroic struggle against unsurmountable odds.

Jewish undergrounds operated in a number of concentration, slave labor, and death camps as well; in at least three there were full-scale uprisings: Jews rose up in Sobibór, Treblinka, and Auschwitz-Birkenau. The Birkenau uprising, a desperate October 1944 attempt by the Sonderkommando to halt murder operations of newly arrived Hungarian Jews, by trying to blow up the gas chambers and crematoria, failed. Although one crematorium was completely destroyed, the rebels only slowed the destruction process but could not stop it. Ironically, one of the elements that delayed the Sonderkommando uprising was the Polish underground in the camp: The Poles did not consider an earlier revolt to be "timely," and failed to offer sufficient support. [62] At least twelve other camps had undergrounds, and resistance activities culminated in revolts and mass escapes in eleven of them: Budzyn, Jastkow, Kielce, Krasnik, Kruszyna, Krychów, Minsk Mazowiecki, Ostrowiec Swietokrzyski, Pionki, Skarzysko-Kamienna, and Wolanow. At the SS training camps of Trawniki and Poniatow — where Jewish inmates did forced labor and Ukrainian and other *Hiwi*s were trained as camp guards — Jewish underground activity was brutally suppressed, although it is not possible to discern the exact course of events.[63] Additional plots and small-scale fighting took place in dozens of towns, villages, and camps.

Jewish Resistance in Western Europe

Jews in Western Europe experienced the same process of slowly organizing for resistance once it became clear that the Nazis sought the complete extermination of the entire Jewish people. The relatively small Jewish population of Western Europe, however, meant that Jewish resistance activities would, of necessity, be organized differently than in the East. Most significant, the lack of closed ghettos in Western Europe meant that no revolt on a par with the Warsaw ghetto uprising could ever occur. Then too, the relative openness of West European resistance movements to Jews — in contradistinction to the antisemitism displayed by many members of the East European undergrounds — meant that most Jews participated actively in the general undergrounds and not in specifically Jewish organizations.

The reality of the Jews' being a minuscule minority population in Western Europe and the resulting change that reality wrought upon Jewish resisters has, in fact, led some historians to question whether Jewish participation may be considered Jewish resistance. Henri Michel, for instance, asked whether "action by Jews within the Resistance can properly be called Jewish resistance?"[64] Some Jewish members of the French resistance have gone even farther:

"There was no Jewish Resistance movement in France," declared André Manuel, former adjutant to Colonel Passy in the BCRA in London, on 13 November 1968, going on to declare that a large number of Jewish men and women had fought in the Resistance but had done so for motives that had no bearing on the fact that they were Jews. "There was no Jewish Resistance in France," reiterated Jerome Stroveis of the *Interallié* networks, F2 and others, one of the first to organize the setting up of transmitting stations on a large scale in Occupied France.[65]

Indeed, it is plausible to argue that during the most significant act of West European resistance relating to the Jews — the Danish rescue operation of October 1943 — the Jews remained almost totally passive: They were "merely" rescued by the Danish underground; except as individuals, they did not undertake any resistance activities.[66] But this question most singularly pertains to French Jewry, which numbered about 350,000 in 1940. Almost 8.5 percent of the French Jewish population, some 30,000 men and women in all, participated in the resistance. Of them, however, no more than 3,000 ever served in all-Jewish units — 2,000 in the Zionist Armée Juive (later known as the Organisation Juive de Combat) and 1,000 in Communist underground cells organized by and for immigrants. Of the latter, 500 Jewish fighters in one Main-d'ouvre immigree (MOI) combat group were the largest single all-Jewish Communist resistance group in Western Europe.[67]

Nevertheless, viewed in its broader context, Jews operating in the resistance throughout Western Europe can justifiably be considered Jewish resistance. Since all Nazi and Nazi-inspired actions and measures after 1941 were oriented toward one goal — the total physical elimination of the Jew — all Jewish activity in opposition to Nazism may be justifiably considered Jewish resistance. Thus, despite protestations to the contrary emanating from the resisters, they were predisposed to oppose Nazi Germany precisely because they were Jews. It follows then, that their resistance derived,

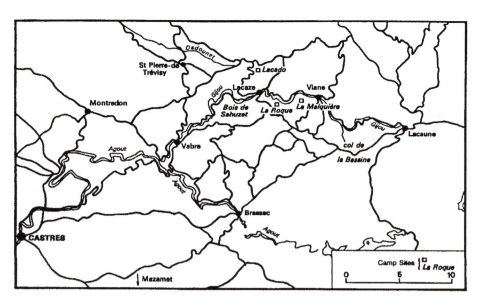

The Location of Jewish Maquis in Southern France
Courtesy of Holocaust Publications

even subconsciously, from a Jewish source. Moreover, a unique situation existed in Nazi-occupied Europe: A non-Jew who took up arms against the Nazi occupiers, by the very fact of doing so, increased his or her chances of getting killed. In contrast, a person of French, Dutch, Polish, or other nationality — even if the conditions under the occupying power were not ideal — as long as that person stayed within the law, though Nazi law, he or she was not in danger of being physically done away with. The Jewish situation, however, was in a category entirely by itself: The Jew, as the enemy *extraordinaire* of the Third Reich, and thus earmarked for the incinerator, had nothing to lose. The Jews who fought could be killed just as dead as the Jews who meekly surrendered. In fact, by taking up arms, the Jews increased their chances of survival; they were no longer such easy prey for the Nazis and their collaborators.

Similar observations appertain to Jewish resistance activities throughout Western Europe. Every European country had some form of anti-Nazi underground. In each, Jews were represented; invariably, Jewish representation was out of proportion to the actual number of Jews living in the country. It may be added that the Nazis and their collaborators paid an inadvertent compliment to the Jewish resistance. Throughout the war, Nazi propagandists sought to use antisemitism as a means of weakening the resistance. This was cleverly done, by using propaganda posters and short films proving that the moving force behind the resistance was the Jew, whether in his Wall Street capitalist or Red Communist garb.

One example of this were the Red Posters (so-called because of their color). The Nazis posted them at various locations, so that large numbers of the French could see them. A typical one (1941) read: "Des Libérateurs? La Libération par l'Armée du Crime!" The poster then listed ten Jewish maquis who were to be hanged.[68] Similar techniques were used in radio and film propaganda: "At the same time movie houses featured films . . . Documentaries were put on showing ruined houses and mangled bodies — allegedly, the work of our people."[69] Radio Paris continually repeated:

Is Greiswachs, the perpetrator of two outrages, a Frenchman? No, he is a Jew, a Polish Jew. Is Elek, who was responsible

One of the Nazis' "red posters" attacking
the French resistance as "Jewish"
Courtesy of the U.S. Holocaust Memorial Museum

for eight derailments and the deaths of
dozens of people, a Frenchman? No, he is
a Hungarian Jew. Is Weisbrod? . . . The
other terrorists are also Jews: Lifshitz,
Fingerweiss, Stockwerk and Reiman.[70]

We now know that this propaganda policy
backfired: If anything, it brought new
recruits for the resistance.[71] Even so, and
giving due consideration to the Nazi
penchant for declaring all opponents to be
Jews or the Jews' lackeys, it is clear that
Jewish resisters played a prominent role in
the secret war against Nazism waged between 1940 and 1945.

The Jewish War Effort

Hundreds of thousands of Jews fortunate
enough to live outside of Nazi terror also

resisted. They did so by actually participating in
the war against the new Haman, knowing that
only thus could Jews live in peace. The Jews
fielded an army more than 1.5 million strong,
fighting on all battle fronts, in every campaign,
in every corps and regiment. Of course, this
Jewish army did not serve under the colors of
a sovereign Jewish state, since a Jewish state
did not yet exist. Instead, most Jewish servicemen and servicewomen served in the armed
forces of the country whose citizenship they
held. In doing so, Jews served in every army
fielded by the Allies.

In particular, both Great Britain and the
Soviet Union fielded military forces composed
of personnel from the occupied countries and
associated with their respective government in
exile. Among them, the Poles and Czechs had
extensive military forces under both British and
Soviet command; the Free French and other
Western European states also raised considerable forces under British command; and a
number of East European states — notably
Bulgaria and Romania — created small forces
under Soviet command. In the latter cases, the
forces were created just after the entry of Red
Army troops into the national territory.[72] Within the ranks of these forces, Jews and Jewish
refugees played a crucial role. Although exact
figures are unavailable, it appears that as many
as 10 percent of the soldiers in the exile armies
were Jews. Among them, a majority were refugees who, having fled the Nazi terror, decided
to join the continuing anti-Nazi struggle for
personal, ethnic, or national reasons.[73]

The Jewish soldiers, like their compatriots in
the resistance, generally had to fight a two-
fronted war: against the Nazis and against in-
grained antisemitism in the troops among
whose ranks they stood. Antisemitism was a
special problem within the Polish armed forces,
although it must be noted that some form of
Jew hatred was not completely absent from the
Allied forces themselves.[74] Conditions were
especially bad in the Polish armed forces.
Initially raised in the Soviet Union, the Polish
Second Corps — commanded by General
Wladyslaw Anders — moved through Persia,
Iraq, Syria, Palestine, and Egypt until finally
arriving for combat duty in Italy in 1943.

Although thousands of Jews volunteered for service, relatively few were accepted, and when the corps arrived in Palestine, Jewish enlisted men were encouraged to desert. Despite such efforts, many Jews remained in the ranks; some eventually requested transfers to British, imperial, or other units, including the Jewish Brigade.[75] Furthermore, antisemitism followed Jewish troops to every location where Polish troops were concentrated; antisemitism even penetrated to the Polish First Corps, operating under Soviet supervision in Eastern Europe. The army-sponsored, London-based daily, *Jestem Polakiem* (I am a Pole) published such glaringly antisemitic articles that it provoked a British parliamentary inquiry.[76]

The problem of antisemitism in Allied armed forces — as troubling a reality as it was — should not detract from the heroism of Jewish troops, many of whom fought under dire conditions, knowing that if captured, they would face — unlike non-Jewish prisoners of war — "special treatment," similar to that of their captive brethren in Nazi-occupied Europe. The imminent reality of mortal danger was also true for Jews serving in Allied special forces. For that reason, most who served in such units as Great Britain's Number 10 Inter-Allied Commando or who served in Allied secret services changed their names and — at least during the war — assumed non-Jewish identities.[77] British secret service historian M.R.D. Foot has concluded: "If ever the clandestine history of the war gets treated in the detail it deserves, it will be found that many Jews who . . . well knew what the barbarous torturer had ready for them, were ready to go back into Europe on secret missions; some did astounding things."[78]

Special mention must be made of the Yishuv's war effort. On September 3, 1939, David Ben-Gurion announced before a meeting of the Jewish Agency Executive, "We shall fight Hitler as if there was no White Paper and we shall fight the White Paper as if there was no Hitler."[79] Thirty-five thousand Palestinian Jews followed the Jewish Agency's call to the colors, serving in the British army. Among them, it might be noted, were two of Israel's presidents (Chaim Herzog and Ezer Weizman) and many of the commanders who later served in the Hagana and the Israel Defense Forces.[80] In September 1944 the British established the independent Jewish Brigade, which saw service in Italy (on the Senio River front) and later participated in the postwar Allied occupation forces in Germany, Austria, and Italy.[81] From 1945 until demobilization, the Jewish Brigade also served an unofficial, Jewish, function: to assist Jewish refugees and displaced persons in finding safety and then to set up Briha (flight) and Aliya Bet ("illegal" immigration) operations as part of the Zionist struggle to establish a Jewish state.[82]

Evaluating Jewish Resistance

How, then, should Jewish resistance be evaluated? Although not all Jews resisted, accusations regarding a Jewish "compliance reaction" may be ignored in light of actual conditions and in light of the greater extent of Jewish resistance than was assumed in the immediate postwar years. Then too, we must consider that the armed resistance that the Jews finally did effect received almost no aid from the Allies and, in Eastern Europe, little from their neighbors. Nevertheless, Jewish resisters won a moral victory, for although doomed, they dared to declare that world Jewry was not yet ready to die — that it would live. The Jewish struggle in World War II was a stage in the Jewish emergence from powerlessness. Ultimately the Jewish war that began in April 1943 ended in May 1948. The process begun by the resistance ended with the establishment of the State of Israel.

Jewish resistance — whether in the ghettos, camps, or forests — was also a reaffirmation of Jewish history. Throughout their long history the Jewish people had been attacked countless times merely for being born Jewish and for stubbornly adhering to their forefathers' faith. They had to endure the early persecutions of the Catholic Church; the ravages of the Crusades; desecration of the Host and blood libels, accusations of being the poisoners of wells and carriers of the Black Plague; the Inquisition; the Chmielnicki massacres; and countless pogroms. They were tortured, burned at the stake, expelled, made to wander from place to place — always forced to rely on the whim of the ruling bishop or prince. Yet in many instances throughout their long journey, Jewish men and women defended themselves with whatever means were available to them and acquitted themselves honorably. Despite the harsh reality, the Jews managed to survive. So too it was during the Holocaust. Reality declared that the Jews should not resist their murderers or survive them — but the Jews did both.

Notes

1. Bruno Bettelheim, *The Informed Heart: Autonomy in a Mass Age*, New York: Avon Books, 1971, p. 263.

2. Raul Hilberg, *The Destruction of the European Jews*, 1st ed., Chicago: Quadrangle Books, 1961, pp. 14–16, 662–669. Hilberg has muted his position in his latest book, *Perpetrators, Victims, Bystanders: The Jewish Catastrophe, 1933–1945*, New York: Harper Collins, 1992, but still remained skeptical about the Jewish resistance. Cf. Jeffrey M. Masson, "Hilberg's Holocaust," *Midstream*, vol. 32 # 4 (1986), 51–55.

3. Karl Shabbetai, *As Sheep to the Slaughter?* New York: World Association of Bergen-Belsen Survivors, 1963.

4. Isaiah 53.

5. Cited from Israel Halpern (ed.), ספר הגבורה (The book of Jewish heroism), Tel Aviv: Am Oved, 1940, vol. 1, p. 22.

6. The most authoritative discussion of the *halachic* norms is contained in Rabbi Joseph Caro's שלחן ערוך, יורה דעה (*Shulhan Aruch, Yore Deah*), § 157.

7. Halpern, ספר הגבורה, p. 91.

8. In ibid., p. 143, there is an illustration of one such synagogue.

9. Cited in H. J. Zimmels, *The Echo of the Nazi Holocaust in Rabbinic Literature*, New York: Ktav, 1975, pp. 63–64.

10. Cf. Joseph Rudavsky, *To Live with Hope, To Die with Dignity*, Lanham, MD: University Press of America, 1987, ch. 3–5.

11. Yehuda Bauer, *American Jewry and the Holocaust: The American Jewish Joint Distribution Committee, 1939–1945*, Detroit: Wayne State University Press, 1981, ch. 3.

12. Joseph Kermish, "The Underground Press in the Warsaw Ghetto," *YVS*, vol. 1 (1957), 85–123.

13. For instance, all May 1 issues of publications associated with Socialist or Socialist-Zionist parties contained articles on Marxist theory and other issues related to Socialism. Thus, see, for example, the May 1, 1941, issue of *Neged ha-Zerem*, Ringelblum Archive, AZIH I/698. This document and other selections from the Ringelblum Archive are currently deposited in the United States Holocaust Memorial Museum in Washington, DC. Our thanks to Mr. Jacek Nowakowski, who provided us with copies of this document.

14. *Unzer Weg*, May 1, 1942, cited by Joseph Kermish, "The Land of Israel in the Life of the Ghetto as Reflected in the Illegal Warsaw Ghetto Press," *YVS*, vol. 5 (1963), 105.

15. Rudavsky, *To Live with Hope*, pt. 4.

16. Ibid., p. 5.

17. Regarding the care needed in using terminology related to the Holocaust, see the Introduction to our *Bibliography on Holocaust Literature: Supplement*, Boulder, CO: Westview Press, 1990, pp. 20–21.

18. "O.S. [Oneg Shabbat]," cited in Joseph Kermish (ed.), *To Live with Honor and to Die with Honor: Selected Documents of the Warsaw Ghetto Underground Archives, "O.S." (Oneg Shabbat)*, Jerusalem: Yad Vashem, 1986, pp. 2–21. This document was, presumably, written by Ringelblum.

19. Cf. Zvi Shner, "On Documentation Projects as an Expression of Jewish Steadfastness in the Holocaust," in Moshe Kohn (ed.), *Jewish Resistance During the Holocaust*, Jerusalem: Yad Vashem, 1971, pp. 191–201. Similar Jewish documentary projects, it may be noted, existed in France, Italy, and the Low Countries.

20. Numerous different versions of this basic story exist; as a result, even if the quote is not precise, it carries the spirit of Dubnow's actual words (which are open to some disagreement). For one of the earliest versions of the story, see E. Gekhman, "Simon Dubnov: How the Famous Jewish Historian Died," *Jewish Chronicle*, # 3950 (1944), 1, 7.

21. Werner Rings, *Life with the Enemy: Collaboration and Resistance in Hitler's Europe*, Garden

City, NY: Doubleday, 1982.

22. Cf. David Mountfield, *The Partisans: Secret Armies of World War II*, London: Hamlyn, 1979, pp. 129–149. The Allied role in Yugoslavia's first civil war was reviewed in David Martin's apologetic book, *The Web of Disinformation: Churchill's Yugoslav Blunder*, San Diego: Harcourt, Brace, Jovanovich, 1990.

23. Mountfield, *The Partisans*, pp. 171–190.

24. Matthew Cooper, *The Nazi War Against Soviet Partisans, 1941–1944*, New York: Stein and Day, 1979, ch. 1–4, 6.

25. Hilberg, *Destruction*, p. 243.

26. Cooper, *Nazi War*, ch. 8–9.

27. Ibid., p. 136.

28. Stefan Korbonski, *The Polish Underground State*, New York: Hippocrene Books, 1978, pp. 150–153.

29. Ibid., ch. 22; Józef Garlinski, *Poland in the Second World War*, New York: Hippocrene Books, 1985, ch. 17, 19–20.

30. Stefan Korbonski, *Fighting Warsaw*, New York: Funk and Wagnalls, 1956, ch. 19.

31. David Schoenbrun, *Soldiers of the Night: The Story of the French Resistance*, New York, Dutton, 1980, ch. 17.

32. Ibid., pp. 299–303.

33. Ibid., ch. 22–23.

34. Cf. Larry Collins and Dominique Lapierre, *Is Paris Burning?* New York: Simon and Schuster, 1965.

35. Claude Chambard, *The Maquis*, Indianapolis: Bobbs-Merrill, 1970, ch. 11–12.

36. M.R.D. Foot, *Resistance*, New York: McGraw-Hill, 1977, ch. 6.

37. In addition to Foot, ibid., passim, and the individual histories of Allied secret services, see Henri Michel, "The Allies and the Resistance," *YVS*, vol. 5 (1963), 317–332.

38. The story is briefly cited in Yehuda Bauer, *The Jewish Emergence from Powerlessness*, Toronto: University of Toronto Press, 1979, p. 31.

39. Cf. Isaiah Trunk, *Judenrat*, New York: Stein and Day, 1972, ch. 17–19.

40. One such example was discussed in Hershel Edelheit's unpublished diary, "Journal from a Lost World."

41. Cited from Emil Fackenheim, "The Holocaust and the State of Israel: Their Relation," in *The Jewish Return into History*, New York: Schocken Books, 1978, p. 283.

42. Foot, *Resistance*, p. 49.

43. Israel Gutman, *Fighters Among the Ruins: The Story of Jewish Heroism During World War II*, Washington, DC: Bnai Brith Books, 1988, ch. 6–7.

44. Yitzhak Arad, "Jewish Family Camps in the Forests — An Original Means of Rescue," in Israel Gutman and Ephraim Zuroff (eds.), *Rescue Attempts During the Holocaust*, Jerusalem: Yad Vashem, 1977, pp. 333–353.

45. Asael Bielski died a hero's death during the battle of Königsberg in late 1944, but the other three brothers eventually settled in Israel. Cf. Yehiel Granatstein and Moshe Kahanovich (comps.), *לכסיקון הגבורה* (Biographical dictionary of Jewish resistance), Jerusalem: Yad Vashem, 1965, vol. 1, pp. 94–96.

46. Abraham J. Edelheit, "The Soviet Union, the Jews, and the Holocaust," in *HSA*, vol. 4 (1990), 120–121.

47. Isaac Kowalski, *A Secret Press in Nazi Europe*, rev. ed., New York: Shengold, 1978, pp. 271–274.

48. Granatstein and Kahanovich, *לכסיקון הגבורה*, English section, pp. 12–13.

49. Bauer, *Jewish Emergence*, pp. 28–30.

50. Israel Gutman, *The Jews of Warsaw*, Bloomington: Indiana University Press, 1982, pp. 130–132.

51. Ibid., pp. 162–170.

52. Ibid., pp. 170–172.

53. Ibid., pp. 236–243.

54. Ibid., pp. 243–249.

55. Cf. the Bund's report on its decision to join ŻOB, as cited in Philip Friedman (ed.), *Martyrs and Fighters*, New York: Lancer Books, 1954, p. 164.

56. Ibid., pp. 164–166. Cf. David Wdowinski, *And We Are not Saved*, New York: Philosophical Library, 1963.

57. Joseph Kermish, "Arms Used by the Warsaw Ghetto Fighters," *Yad Vashem Bulletin*, # 2 (1958), 5–9.

58. Cf. Gutman, *Warsaw*, ch. 11, and Friedman, *Martyrs*, ch. 13, for a history and a documentary account (respectively) of the Small Revolt.

59. Gutman, *Warsaw*, ch. 14.

60. Shmuel Krakowski, *The War of the Doomed: Jewish Armed Resistance in Poland, 1942–1944*, New York: Holmes and Meier, 1984, ch. 13.

61. Foot, *Resistance*, p. 294.

62. Tzipora Hager-Halivni, "The Birkenau Revolt: Poles Prevent a Timely Insurrection," *JSS*, vol. 41 # 2 (1979), 123–154.

63. Krakowski, *War of the Doomed*, pp. 235–260.

64. Henri Michel, *The Shadow War: European Resistance, 1939–1945*, New York: Harper and Row, 1972, p. 178.

65. Cited from Lucien Steinberg, *Not as a Lamb*, Farnborough, UK: Saxon House, 1974, p. 84.

66. Cf. Bauer, *Emergence*, p. 39.

67. Steinberg, *Not as a Lamb*, ch. 10.

68. An example is pictured in the photo section of Anny Latour, *Jewish Resistance in France, 1940–1944*, New York: Holocaust Library, 1981.

69. Abraham Raisky, "We Fought Back in France," *Commentary*, vol. 1 # 4 (1946), 65.

70. Marie Syrkin, *Blessed Is the Match*, rev. ed., Philadelphia: JPS, 1976, p. 306.

71. Raisky, "We Fought Back in France," 65.

72. For the example of Polish forces, see Garlinski, *Poland*, passim; Nigel Thomas, *Foreign Volunteers of the Allied Forces, 1939–1945*, London: Osprey Books, 1991.

73. Lucien Steinberg, "The Participation of Jews in the Allied Armies," Kohn, *Jewish Resistance*, pp. 379–391.

74. As in contemporaneous United States, antisemitism was intense in some U.S. units, although no comprehensive study on the subject has ever been done. For a novelized version of one U.S. Army Air Force officer's perspective, see Frederic Arnold, *Doorknob Five-Two*, Los Angeles: Maxwell, 1984.

75. Cf. Israel Gutman, "Jews in General Anders' Army in the Soviet Union," *YVS*, vol. 12 (1977), 231–296.

76. On the *Jestem Polakiem* affair, see "Back to the Jungle?" in *Jewish Chronicle*, April 19, 1944, p. 8, and "A Challenge to Good Faith," in ibid., April 28, 1944, p. 10. On antisemitism among the London Poles more generally, see Reuben Ainsztein, "The Enemy Within: Antisemitism Among Polish Soldiers in War-Time Britain," *Wiener Library Bulletin*, vol. 13 # 5/6 (1959), 58–59. On conditions in the Polish First Corps, which fought with the Soviet Army, see Kalman Nussbaum, והפך להם לרוע: היהודים בצבא העממי הפולני בברית-המועצות (The Story of an illusion: Jews in the Polish People's Army in the Soviet Union), Tel Aviv: Tel Aviv University Press, 1984, pp. 112–117.

77. Number 10 Inter-Allied Commando operated in both an overt and a covert role. The unit was composed of volunteers from European countries seconded by their respective governments in exile. Sub units of the commando were linguistically separated but were commanded by British

officers. Cf. Ian Dear, *Ten Commando, 1942–1945*, New York: St. Martin's Press, 1987.

78. Foot, *Resistance*, p. 163.

79. Ben-Gurion's oft-quoted statement is cited and placed into political context in Abraham J. Edelheit, "The Yishuv in the Shadow of the Holocaust: Palestinian Jewry and the Emerging Nazi Threat, 1933-1939," Ph.D dissertation, City University of New York, 1992, p. 576.

80. Yoav Gelber, תולדות ההתנדבות (Jewish Palestinian volunteering in the British Army during the Second World War), 4 vols., Jerusalem: Yad Yitzhak Ben-Zvi, 1979–1984.

81. Ibid., vol. 2, provides a comprehensive history of the brigade from inception to demobilization.

82. Ibid., vol. 3, ch. 5–6. For a personal view on the Briha, see Hershel Edelheit, "Journal."

7

JEWISH-GENTILE RELATIONS
IN EXTREMIS

Jews and Gentiles Under the New Order

How did the European peoples react to the murder of their neighbors? Although only a few in-depth studies of the subject exist, it is still possible to generalize about Gentile behavior and the interaction between Jews and Gentiles under the Nazi occupation. When we do so, one fact becomes apparent: There was a slight but perceptible difference between how Jews were treated in Eastern and in Western Europe. Obviously, such a difference would affect the chances a Jew had to escape or evade the Nazis.[1] A statistical analysis of Jewish victimization makes the reality behind this generalization even more clear: Although two-thirds of European Jewry was murdered by the Nazis, in half the European states, 50 percent or more of the Jewish population survived.[2]

Broadly, historians divide Europe along two sets of axes: north-south and east-west. In both cases, the first axis (north or east) represents the lower survival rate and the second (south or west) represents the higher survival rate. Despite glaring exceptions to each model — the 80 percent murder rate for Dutch Jewry cuts deep into the otherwise higher survival rate for Western Europe, and Yugoslavia's 60 percent loss rate does the same for Southern Europe — a combination of both models holds as a valid generalization. To fully validate each model, four other factors must be considered.[3]

First, the nature of Nazi occupation agencies must be taken into account. One of the reasons that Dutch Jews were deported so easily was that Holland was organized as a Reichsprotektorat, thus being placed under direct German civilian (meaning SS and Gestapo) control. Neighboring Belgium remained under military jurisdiction throughout the occupation, whereas Denmark, although occupied, retained its own civilian government (operating under Nazi "advice") until 1943. These differing styles of occupation meant that, respectively, 80 percent of Dutch Jewry, 50 percent of Belgian Jewry, and virtually no Danish Jews perished. A similar consideration operated in mixed occupation territories. France, for example, was partly occupied and partly left under a local, collaborationist regime, with a small sector of southern France (Nice) under Italian control. Again, the result was clear, with more than two-thirds of French Jewry surviving.

Second, the length of Nazi occupation influenced the survival rate of Jews. Most of Italian Jewry survived because Italy remained a sovereign state until September 1943. Tunisian Jewry survived largely intact because Tunisia was occupied by the Nazis only for five months (November 1942 to April 1943) and the time was insufficient to undertake mass murder operations.[4] Still, length of occupation cannot be considered an independent variable. After all, both France and Belgium were occupied for the same length of time, from the summer of 1940 until the summer of 1944. In this case, however, the already-mentioned factor of occupation style affects the Jewish survival rate, regardless of length of occupation. Indeed, it may be fairly noted that the length of Nazi occupation played no role on the survival rate of Soviet Jewry: Most Soviet Jews were murdered at the outset of the occupation. A related factor was the speed of Allied liberation. France was liberated by Anglo-American forces in just three months (June to August 1944), but the Red Army required more than eight months (June 1944 to January 1945) to liberate Poland.

Third, the existence of an easily reached safe haven influenced chances of Jewish survival. Half of Norwegian Jewry survived by slipping across the Swedish border when roundups and deportations began. Likewise, French Jews could cross over into Spain, Switzerland, and the Italian zone. One unique "underground railroad" operated from Holland via Belgium and France, ultimately ending in Spain.[5] Some Italian Jews could cross, with relative ease, to Allied lines in southern Italy in September and October 1943. Such easy access to havens did not exist for the bulk of European Jewry. Jews in Germany, Czechoslovakia, and Poland had virtually no place to run and possessed only a minuscule number of possible places where they could hide.

Finally, the size of the Jewish population and the Jews' relative acculturation/ assimilation influenced their chances for survival. Danish Jewry was saved, ultimately, because of its small population and its high degree of assimilation. Danish non-Jews considered Jews to be co-nationals and utterly rejected antisemitism. The well-known tale that King Christian X wore a Yellow Star of David — causing all Danes to wear the star as a symbol of solidarity with Jews — is but a legend; nevertheless, the legend is indicative of West European attitudes. In contradistinction, the masses of Polish Jewry did not blend in well with their non-Jewish neighbors. The Jews of Poland were only minimally assimilated; their make-up, dress, manner, and language kept them distinctly apart. In a land of ingrown anti-

semitism — the Catholic Church had taught for centuries about the Christ-killer in their midst — Jews dressed in long black caftans, with black hats, white fringes protruding from their shirts, long beards, and side curls; Jews speaking a distinct language — Yiddish — did not fare well with the average Pole. The label *Żydek* was clearly tagged to this phenomena in their midst. Under these circumstances, Jews could hardly vanish and blend into the scenery. The Nazi murder scheme was too immediate to allow a prolonged, difficult changeover of a way of life centuries old. Even if most Orthodox Jews had shaved off their beards and side curls, the women had let their hair grow in and thrown away their wigs, changing their dress to blend in with the rest of the population, masses of Jews could not suddenly proclaim themselves mutes. Jews used to speaking Yiddish, the *mame-loshen*, all of their lives could not begin to speak enough good Polish to fool any of the Nazis or their local helpers.[6]

Thus, the example of Jewish-Gentile relations in Poland was typical of relations in Eastern Europe under the Nazi impact. Although the largest number of individual heroes in all Europe — some three thousand *Hasidei Umot ha-Olam* (Righteous Among the Nations) — can be counted in Poland, Polish Jewry was effectively isolated for the duration of the war. Antisemitism rose in Poland during the war, and most of the underground accepted the propriety of postwar limitations upon Jewish rights in a liberated Polish state.[7] Most Poles remained indifferent to the Jews' plight; some, in fact, were happy with the Nazi solution to the Jewish problem. Mordechai Tenenbaum-Tamaroff, leader of the Jewish underground in Bialystok, summarized the Jewish perspective on Polish-Jewish relations in his diary in the following terms:

If it had not been for the Poles, for their aid — passive and active — in the solution of the Jewish problem in Poland, the Germans would never have dared to do what they did. It was they, the Poles, who called out *Yid* at every Jew who escaped from the train transporting him to his death, it was they who caught the unfortunate wretches, who rejoiced at every Jewish misfortune — they were vile and contemptible.[8]

Moreover, some Poles, such as supporters of the Oboz Narodowo-Radicalny (ONR), the National Radical Camp, actively helped the Nazis, seeing Jews and not the Nazis as the main threat to Poland.[9]

Jews were never accepted into the resistance movements in Eastern Europe, except by Communist or Socialist undergrounds. The Armia Krajowa (AK), the Polish home army, refused to give the assistance that would have allowed the Jews to defend themselves. Only a very small number of weapons were transferred, and only begrudgingly. The general staff of the AK characterized any action on behalf of Jews as premature and contrary to Poland's long-term interests. During the massive deportations of Jews, the underground had no reaction. When the Jews finally resisted, the underground made only a few half-hearted attempts to assist the Jewish fighters in their desperate last stand. During the height of the Warsaw ghetto uprising, Poles held Easter picnics outside the ghetto walls, watching and gawking as the Jews fought their last battle.[10]

Conditions were similar throughout Eastern Europe. In Lithuania, Latvia, Estonia, Belorussia, and the Ukraine, Jews initially feared their neighbors as much as, or more than, the Germans, since the neighbors were usually more brutal than even the Gestapo. It is worth remembering that two Einsatzgruppen totaling only 1,350 men were able to exterminate almost all the Jews throughout the Ukraine and Crimean peninsula in just six months. At every turn the Einsatzkommandos received the enthusiastic aid of hundreds and thousands of Ukrainian volunteers who were trained by the SS at the Trawniki camp and then operated as auxiliaries in the hunt for and extermination of European Jews.[11] In none of these countries, save Czechoslovakia, were Jews welcomed into the resistance. Jewish partisans often had to hide their Jewishness, not out of shame, but out of fear of their would-be

"comrades."

Vichy France and the Jews

This is not to imply that no antisemitism existed in Western Europe. On the contrary, the reality of intense antisemitic agitation in Western Europe must be emphasized. Despite antisemitism, however, West European Jews survived in larger numbers because they were more readily able to blend into the local scenery or they were hidden by sympathetic neighbors. Given the population and other considerations, the French case may be seen as typical of conditions in Western Europe. During the interwar years France's reputation for antisemitism almost equaled Poland's.[12] As a matter of fact, modern secular antisemitism in the reborn Poland derived largely from the exiled Polish intelligentsia living in France, where they had absorbed ideologies from French antisemitic circles.[13] As in Poland, antisemitism became a staple for the French Radical Right and took on the airs of a full-blown Jewish problem.

Antisemitic parties such as Action Française repeatedly drove home the idea of an imminent Jewish threat to France. The outbreak of World War II and France's rapid defeat complicated, but did not fundamentally alter, this situation. Northern France was placed under direct Nazi occupation. Southern France was placed under the control of a collaborationist government led by Marshal Philippe Pétain. Between 1940 and 1942 the Vichy regime actively aped Nazi antisemitism, legislating Jews into second-class citizenship and detaining thousands who had entered the country during the 1930s. As the Nazis converted from a policy of persecution to a policy of active extermination, some members of the Vichy government vacillated briefly, but eventually, the French — at least French officialdom — cooperated. Over the course of 1942 and 1943, nearly 100,000 French Jews were rounded up and "resettled east." Virtually all of them were refugee Jews who had entered the country during the 1930s. Almost all of them were rounded up by the French police, with little or no SS involvement; in many instances the roundup was done solely on French volition and without German prodding. A few "lucky" ones found themselves in forced-labor camps in Vichy-controlled North Africa. The vast majority were sent to Auschwitz, where almost all of them perished.[14]

Whereas the official situation in France was thus dissimilar to conditions in Poland, the popular response to Jewish persecution was even more clearly different. Despite the collaborationists, despite Nazi plans, nearly two-thirds of French Jewry survived, thanks to the actions of the French people and the underground. Many of these survivors undertook as simple an act as crossing from northern France into the Vichy zone (before the latter was occupied in November 1942). When the Vichy zone also became dangerous, these Jews — with the help of many symphatetic French non-Jews — crossed into the Italian zone, finding another temporary haven.[15] At every turn, hunted Jews found their neighbors — and in some cases even total strangers — willing to assist them.

A case in point was the self-appointed ambassador to the Jews, Father Pierre Marie Benoît. A Capuchin monk, Benoît was appalled at the treatment of Jews by Nazis and collaborationists in his native Marseilles. Under his guidance, the monastery became a center for Jewish rescue, sheltering Jews in the basement until they could be smuggled over the border to either neutral Spain or Switzerland. Between July and September 1943 Benoît concentrated on a daring plan to rescue all of the Jews in southern France by transporting them to Allied-controlled North Africa. The plan failed, however, because the Allies did not follow through: The Italian surrender led to a rapid German occupation that took everyone — except local rescue activists — by surprise.[16]

Germans and Jews in the Nazi Era

As complex as Polish-Jewish or Franco-Jewish relations in the Nazi era may seem, relations between Germans and Jews are even more complex. The facts do not lend themselves to easy evaluation. For the most part, historians have emphasized the generalized quiescence about Nazi crimes, even though they note that antisemitism appeared (ex post facto) to be very shallow in Germany during the early 1930s.[17] These historians therefore maintain that Germans did not accept Nazi antisemitism and thus cannot be held collectively guilty of Nazi crimes. Although the factual basis for this view is correct, the conclusions derived from the facts miss a fundamental point: The German public — including the plurality that voted the Nazi party into power in the first place — did not, by and large, protest the persecution of German (and later European) Jewry. Yet indications exist that such protests would have been efficacious. Most particularly, the experience of the Euthanasia Program points to the fact that the regime was sensitive to public opinion. During 1940 Germany's hospitals were emptied of patients with mental or physical handicaps. The patients were officially being transferred to facilities where they supposedly would get better treatment; in fact, however, the patients were taken to one of the six euthanasia centers, camouflaged sanatoriums, where they were murdered. Initially, the program was kept a secret, but the true policy eventually became known and elicited strong protests by masses of Germans, including authorities of both Protestant and Catholic churches. As a result of this storm of protest, the Euthanasia Program was (officially, at least) terminated.[18]

No similar protest or for that matter any kind of protest was ever heard on behalf of Jews. Not even the German resistance movement, composed as it was of dedicated anti-Nazis, unequivocally protested Nazi antisemitism. To be sure, the college students and intellectuals associated with Die Weisse Rose movement did protest the mistreatment of Jews.

As an example, we wish to mention that 300,000 Jews have been bestially murdered in Poland since the German occupation. This is the most horrible of crimes, unparalleled in all human history. . . . Why is the German people so apathetic in the face of such revolting, inhuman crimes? Almost no one takes any note of it. The facts are known, but are set aside as mere documents. And the German people goes on in a stupor, giving these Fascist criminals the courage and opportunity to continue their berserk rampages, which they indeed do. . . . Will the German finally awaken from his stupor, protest as only he can against this clique of criminals, sympathize with the hundreds of thousands of victims, and sense his guilt? . . . For there are none free of guilt. Each is guilty, guilty, guilty![19]

Die Weisse Rose, however, was a minority on this issue. The plotters who, when defeat was imminent in 1944, attempted to kill Hitler did not seek an end to the Final Solution, even at that late date when the majority of European Jewry under Nazi occupation were already murdered. To the contrary, they anticipated the maintenance of concentration camps and the continued incarceration of all inmates in them — in order to avoid embarrassment for Germany. Granted, these anti-Nazi circles did advocate an end to gassing and favored closing the crematoria. But they did not advocate a fundamentally philosemitic policy. It would appear that, for most German resisters, low-level antisemitism was acceptable — as long as it did not include any overtly illegal action.[20] Indeed, it should be recalled that one of those accused, tried, and apparently executed in connection with the bomb plot was Arthur Nebe, former commander of Einsatzgruppe B, who was responsible for mass murder of Jews in eastern Poland and Belorussia.[21]

The Attitude of the Christian Churches

How did the leaders of churches — both Protestant and Catholic — in their official capacity as shepherd of the people and voice of morality, react to the slaughter of millions of innocent souls? By and large, the clergy's attitude reflected that of their congregations. In places where local non-Jews made efforts to save their Jewish neighbors, the church leaders usually were involved in rescue efforts. The converse also held true: In places where rescue efforts failed, local church figures generally remained aloof and did not become involved in rescue efforts. Specific conditions, of course, varied from country to country and also changed with time. Examples of each kind of behavior abound, and a number have already been cited. As important as local churches were, however, national and international church agencies played an even more important, and controversial, role in Jewish-Gentile relations.

In particular, the Vatican adhered to a position of official non-commitment to public work on behalf of Jews. The well-known hypothesis of papal silence — reflected for instance in Rolf Hochhuth's controversial play, *The Deputy* — does, after all, reflect one element of the historical record.[22] Efforts to defend Pope Pius XII's reputation have been largely based on his indirect, quiet diplomatic efforts in the Balkans and Slovakia.

The Slovak Republic may be seen as a testing ground for Vatican diplomacy. After all, Slovak leaders from the president, Josef Tiso, to the prime minister, Vojtech Tuka, and most of the governing bureaucracy, were Catholics. Of course, one cannot predict whether direct Vatican pressure would have done any good, but the Holy See could have exerted much pressure — including the threat of excommunication for collaboration in Nazi crimes — to try to change Slovak policy regarding Jews. In fact, many Catholics have been excommunicated throughout the history of the church for much lesser infractions than murder. Moreover, the notion that Tiso had no choice but to surrender the Jews to the Nazis or else to be faced with a greater evil for the rest of the Slovak people should not be taken as valid, since the Nazis did temporarily halt deportations in 1943 in response to Slovak misgivings.

Instead of reinforcing those misgivings by bold, public diplomacy, the Vatican chose to continue its policy of silent efforts to wean the Slovak government away from collaboration. Furthermore, papal activity in southeastern Europe was primarily concentrated on rescuing Jews by birth or family who were Catholics through conversion. It must thus be reemphasized: The Vatican as an institution did little to promote the rescue of *Jews* during the Nazi era.[23] Even among Vatican officials who advocated a more public response, the justification was exclusively practical: Helping Jews would improve the Vatican's reputation, while also benefiting newly baptized Catholics. Thus, Monsignor Domenico Tardini, head of the Vatican's section for extraordinary ecclesiastical affairs, wrote that action on behalf of Slovak Jewry would "make known to the world that the Holy See fulfills its duty of charity." In contrast, such action would not be useful for "attracting the sympathy of Jews in case they are among the victors (given the fact that the Jews — as much as can be foreseen — will never be too friendly to the Holy See and to the Catholic Church)."[24]

By and large, the same generalization holds true for Protestant churches in Northern Europe. Most Lutheran church leaders, for example, made their peace with the Glaubensbewegung deutscher Christen (Faith Movement of German Christians), the Nazi German church, and did not protest the persecution of the Jews. Even those leaders who opposed the Nazis — such as Dietrich Bonhöffer and Martin Niemöller — usually protested only the persecution of Jews by race (the Arier Paragraph), since the National Socialist racial definition was seen as antithetical to the church's prerogative to convert Jews. The German Evangelical Church's hierarchy never issued any public protest against Nazi antisemitism at its highest level.[25]

As can be gathered from previous chapters, the only churches that do not fit into this generalization were in Scandinavia and the Low Countries. The Danish and Norwegian churches rejected all attacks on Jews, part and parcel of their rejection of Fascism and Nazism — and actively participated in all rescue operations. The Norwegian church was particularly vociferous in rejecting all forms of antisemitism throughout the war. The Danes and Norwegians especially emphasized the close relationship between Christianity and Judaism, a sacred relationship that required Christians to help their fellow human. The same held true in Belgium and Holland. In the case of Holland, the Dutch Reformed Church was especially well disposed toward Jews but was unable to effect their rescue due to the nature of Nazi control. Of Eastern European churches, only the Bulgarian Orthodox Church spoke out against the persecution of Jews. This position was based on traditional theological rejections of Jews: Jews were considered guilty of deicide, but that fact did not permit punishment by a human agency; only divine punishment was considered valid for the past, present, or future sins of the Jews.[26] Nevertheless, the Bulgarian Orthodox Church had much to do in persuading King Boris and a majority of the government to halt the deportations of Bulgarian Jewry.

The ambivalent response of Christians to the Jews' suffering may be explained in light of four considerations: first, the church's two-millennia-old "teaching of contempt," which was reflected even in the statements of Christian anti-Nazis. Second was an inordinate, if legitimate, concern among church figures for the status of their institutions. Fear that the Nazis would silence the churches led to an unwillingness to act on behalf of Jewry. Third, for the defense of church prerogatives — closely related to the previous issue — a defense of converts considered Jews by race was more than sufficient. Finally, the church leaders must be evaluated against the ideological background of their time. In this case, many church figures accepted the widely popular antisemitic identification of Jews with communism. Since communism had persecuted the churches, Nazism could be seen as a defense against atheism. Jews, being the fathers of Bolshevism, were "merely" being punished for their sins. Ultimately, the Holocaust was a test for all humanity; by and large, European churches failed that test.

The same generalization holds for most European and Middle Eastern Muslims. The nascent Arab-Israeli conflict influenced Muslims, who soon began to absorb the worst elements of Nazi antisemitic ideology.[27] As a result, anti-Jewish violence in the Arab world — and in Palestine as well — increased during the 1930s; these events culminated in Arab hopes to effect a "final solution" of their own in 1941.[28] After the failure of Arab nationalists to undermine Britain's strategic position in the Middle East, the mufti of Jerusalem, Haj Amin al-Huseini, fled to the Third Reich in 1942. While in Berlin, the mufti sought to encourage Hitler to speed up the Final Solution and tried to create a Muslim legion to fight as part of the German military. The legion was largely composed of Muslims from Bosnia and the USSR but never really achieved the recruitment goals set for it. Similarly, it cannot be unequivocally stated that the mufti's proddings influenced the Nazis in any way, although it is clear that he based his actions on more than just fear of "Zionist domination."[29]

Fascism and the Jewish Question

Before the outbreak of World War II about 25 percent of European Jewry lived under Nazi, Nazi-inspired, or Fascist regimes. The attitude of these regimes toward Jews and the Jewish question influenced the Jews' chances for survival and are thus worthy of investigation. Contrary to what might be expected, European Fascists had no consistent policy on Jewish issues. Conditions thus varied from country to country and even from party to party.

The rise of Italian fascism initially had very little impact upon Italian Jewry. Italian fascism was notably free of antisemitism, despite some glimmerings of antisemitic agitation among a small circle of Fascists. More than 200 Jews participated in the March on Rome that catapulted Mussolini into power in 1922. Other prominent Jewish Fascists, included Aldo Finzi (a member of the Fascist grand council), Guido Jung (minister of finance from 1932 to 1935), Maurizio Rava (governor of Italian Somaliland and a former head of the *Squadristi*), and Margherita Sarfati (one of the *Duce*'s many mistresses). Many others simply joined the movement for patriotic or personal reasons from 1922 to 1938. This phenomenon continued throughout the 1920s and into the mid-1930s. Characteristically, Benito Mussolini offered to "mediate" between world Jewry and the Nazi regime in 1933. His proposal, however, reflected more on Mussolini's personality, and his conscious campaign of self-aggrandizement, than any realistic effort to spare Jewry; it was, of course, not followed up.[30] After the Nazi-Fascist rapprochement, *Il Duce* increasingly fell under Hitler's influence and was willing to sacrifice Jews to the Nazi Moloch.

Mussolini's lieutenants, including his son-in-law and foreign minister, Count Galeazzo Ciano, were considerably less motivated to cooperate with the Nazis. In particular, they were repelled by Nazi antisemitism and fearful of the potential loss of Italian sovereignty. As a result, they refused to aid in the extermination of European Jewry. The Italian occupation authorities in France and Yugoslavia played an especially prominent role in rescuing Jews. Ignoring Italy's official anti-Jewish policies, the generals often warned Jews of impending danger, thus allowing at least some Jews to escape before the SS got them.[31] Some officers and their men went a step further, actively rescuing Jews and giving or selling them weapons with which to defend themselves. In at least one case Italian troops in Russia used force, firing upon men of an Einsatzkommando, in order to save Jewish lives.[32]

Even today these facts cause wonder and interest. How can we explain the actions of Nazi Germany's closest ally? We must look at two facts: There had been virtually no anti-semitic movement of note in modern Italy and, given the failure of totalitarianism in Fascist Italy, there was always some possibility of ignoring orders when morality and honor were at issue. This is not to deny the existence of a Jewish problem in Fascist Italy. In 1938 a series of very clearly antisemitic laws was published. Jews were virtually excluded from both the armed forces and the government apparatus. Yet compared with the *Endlösung*, these laws were but trifles. Of all the European nations during the war, it can safely be said that only Denmark did more than Italy to help Jews.[33]

In many ways the Balkan governments were the exact opposite of the Italians. Antisemitism had been a political issue in Romania from the days of the Congress of Berlin (1878). Despite minority treaties, legislation in Romanian Bukovina, Bessarabia, and Transylvania deprived Jews of their civil rights. Under the short-lived quasi-Fascist government of Octavian Goga (1937–1938), more than one-third of Romanian Jewry was stripped of its citizenship. Official discrimination against Jews in all branches of the government, the professions, and economic life was stronger in Romania than in virtually any other East European country and grew with the rise of Ion Antonescu's government in 1940.

With the Nazi rise to power, the Iron Guard, Romania's Fascist party, came to the forefront of political and social life. A rabidly antisemitic group, the Iron Guard drew support from the Orthodox Church as well as from a variety of nationalist and chauvinist groups. Like the Poles, their slogan was "Romania for the Romanians!" Upon gaining influence, the Iron Guard proceeded to re-create Nazism's Jewish policy on a smaller scale. They denied Jews citizenship, making it possible to discharge them from their jobs and to nationalize their businesses. Soon public manifestations of antisemitism became clearly discernable. Taking their cue from the Nazis, the Romanian Fascists proved eager to help with the Final Solution. Only the timely intervention of Romanian political concerns in 1944 — specifically, Antonescu's efforts to withdraw from the war — prevented the extermination of all Romanian Jewry.[34]

Fascism in Hungary played a similar, but more limited, role. A Fascist party, the

Arrow Cross, was organized and operated along Nazi lines. The Fascists played almost no role in the Hungarian state, however, until the war. The regent of Hungary, Miklos Horthy, refused to surrender the crown to the legitimate heir, but until 1939–1940 Horthy's power base lay outside the Fascist bloc. By 1941 Horthy had fallen under Hitler's influence and had begun to lead Hungary into the anti-Bolshevik and antisemitic crusade. During this period Jews in Hungary and Hungarian-occupied territory suffered greatly. Despite his antisemitic credentials, Horthy was never totally committed to any particular solution for the Jewish problem. Seeing the war as lost in 1944, Horthy tried to use the Jews as a way to contact the Allies and find an honorable way out of the war for Hungary. Unfortunately, the United States and England did not react quickly enough and allowed the Nazis time to recover. In the spring and early summer of 1944, the Germans unleashed the Arrow Cross and quickly deported most of the nearly 1 million Jews in Hungary to Auschwitz-Birkenau. At every point in the deportation of Hungarian Jewry, the Nazis received decisive assistance from the Arrow Cross and from members of other Hungarian Fascist parties.[35]

Francisco Franco and, to a lesser degree, Antonio de Oliveira Salazar, anticipated that by extending aid to Jews, even in a small way, they would enhance their own position in the postwar era. The Spanish hope to legitimize Fascist rule was, paradoxically, based upon the philosemitic use of antisemitism. They clearly believed the Jews to be in power in Washington, London, and Moscow. Many Spaniards saw the expulsion of the Sephardim in 1492 as a national calamity and felt that now was the time to right that terrible wrong. Legislation was approved declaring Jews of Sephardi origin who could prove that their ancestors were exiles to be Spanish citizens. Because much leeway was provided for local consular officials as to what constituted "proof," those officials saved a small number of Jews using this proviso. Others were allowed temporary refuge on Spanish soil. As long as they could prove that they would leave as soon as possible, no Jew — Sephardi or Ashkenazi — was turned away. Still others were saved from the clutches of death by members of the Spanish Blue Legion in Russia. Under the pretext that camp workers were needed to maintain their quarters, dozens of Jews were thus saved and eventually smuggled to freedom.[36]

Hasidei Umot ha-Olam

The unhappy reality that European Jewry was mercilessly ground to dust by the Nazis without arousing more than a minor riposte from most European non-Jews should not denigrate the heroic actions of the few who did try to help save Jews. Despite manifold dangers to themselves and their families, despite the general apathy toward Jews and antipathy to those who would help them, hundreds of men and women in every European country did all that they could to save Jews. Some succeeded; others did not. In many cases the would-be rescuers and their charges were discovered (usually through betrayal) by the Gestapo and were murdered. Nevertheless, the actions of these few courageous men and women proved that, even in the darkest of days of mass inhumanity, the bonds of humanity had not completely broken. Given the widely differing geographical, religious, ideological, and personal backgrounds of the rescuers, it is difficult to generalize about them. Yet, it is clear that non-Jewish rescuers of Jews during World War II may be divided into three typologies: altruists, subversives, and mercenaries.

Altruists, those who rescued Jews because of moral or religious concerns, have received the most attention in recent years. In general, altruistic rescuers tended to be religiously pious, spiritual individuals, who were deeply committed to the concept of human brotherhood. In Western Europe many of the rescuers were clergy or persons closely connected with the church. In one well-known case — that of Le Chambon-sur-Lignon — an entire village of Huguenots (French Protestant sectarians)

was involved in a systematic rescue operation. To be sure, there were numerous rescuers who were not pious in the traditional sense of the term; they behaved altruistically because of their commitment to humanism and their rejection of Nazi racism.[37]

Subversives, those who rescued Jews for nationalistic considerations, must be viewed in the context of European resistance. Since the persecution of Jews was part and parcel of Nazi occupation policy, it followed that those committed to combating the Nazis would also seek to subvert the Final Solution. In Western Europe, such activities were particularly prominent in Holland and Belgium; the legendary case of Denmark has already been cited.

Rescue of Jews as a part of resistance activities also played a prominent role in Poland, although the actual results of such activity are open to widely differing interpretations. Specifically, two agencies existed that became involved in rescuing Jews: the Armia Krajowa (AK) Department of Civil Resistance, headed by Stefan Korbonski, and the Rada Pomocy Żydom (better known as the Zegota council), chaired by Zofia Kossak-Szczucka. Both were active, to one degree or another, in helping Jews evade the Nazis, primarily by finding appropriate hiding places and/or obtaining false identity papers for those able to "pass" as an Aryan. However, the number of Jews actually helped by the two organizations was relatively small, never more than a few thousand. Korbonski's department was not exclusively focused on Jews. Rescue was only one of a wide range of activities, which included propaganda, the SWIT underground radio station, and an underground court system.[38] Zegota, in contrast, was exclusively focused on rescuing Jews but was hampered by a lack of adequate funds and by official lack of interest in the operation. When Zegota began its operation in September 1942, it lacked recognition from any authoritative leaders in the Polish government in exile or the AK. Such recognition — and the financial commitment it implied — was granted only in December 1942. Official recognition did not immediately lead to official financing, meaning that the council was never able to attain its massive goals. In the end, Zegota rescued about 4,000 Jews.[39]

Mercenaries, those who rescued Jews for personal gain, are, perhaps, the least studied group of the rescuers. Plainly, mercenaries acted on behalf of Jews in order to get paid. When the money ran out, the would-be rescuer betrayed his or her charges and reaped whatever reward the Gestapo offered for information on Jewish fugitives. It is impossible to say with any certitude how many mercenary rescuers became betrayers; actually, it is impossible to clearly delineate how many mercenary rescuers there were to begin with. One thing is clear, however; such individuals were considered a danger not only to Jews but to the general underground as well; the latter routinely pronounced death sentences on informers, regardless of what information they passed to the Nazis.[40]

The quintessential *Hasid Umot ha-Olam* undoubtedly was Raoul Wallenberg. The son of a well-known Swedish banking family, Wallenberg had established an early reputation as a playboy. But as a Swedish diplomat working for the American War Refugee Board (created by President Franklin D. Roosevelt in 1944) in Budapest, Wallenberg showed another side of his personality: seriousness and dedication in attempting to rescue the Jews of Budapest. In his mission, Wallenberg used his charm and charisma, as well as a good dose of bluff and circumspection, to cajole the Hungarian Fascists into permitting him to protect some Jews from deportation. In doing so, Wallenberg also gained the support of a few other diplomats in Budapest, including Carl Lutz, of the Swiss legation, and Giorgio Perlasca, an Italian national who had been appointed caretaker for the Spanish legation. Thanks to their tireless efforts, nearly 100,000 Jews were still alive in Budapest when the Red Army arrived.

Wallenberg sought to secure Soviet assurances for the security of the system of safe houses he had developed. After

Protective pass issued by the Swedish legation in Budapest
Courtesy of Dr. Randolph L. Braham

entering negotiations with the Soviets, Wallenberg disappeared, apparently arrested by the NKVD under the suspicion of being a U.S. spy. Wallenberg's precise fate is, of course, unknown; rumors rampant in the 1980s of his still being alive — and still incarcerated in a *gulag* — do not square away with the official (although much delayed) Soviet admission that Raoul Wallenberg died in 1947.[41]

Jewish tradition speaks of thirty-six saintly individuals who live in each generation and for whom God permits the world to continue to exist. There were, of course, more than thirty-six individual non-Jewish rescuers; nevertheless, they fit into the traditional Jewish definition of *Hasidei Umot ha-Olam*, the Righteous Persons of the Nations. In light of the great tragedy that befell European Jewry, individuals who did lend a hand were indeed the noble few, and they certainly displayed courage and heroism that is worthy of emulation.

Notes

1. Cf. Helen Fein, *Accounting for Genocide*, New York: Free Press, 1979, ch. 3.

2. Ibid., pp. 34–37.

3. In addition to ibid., see the sources listed supra in Ch. 5.

4. Yaron Tsur, "יהודי טוניס בתקופת הכיבוש הנאצי — קהילה מפוצלת בימי משבר" (The Jews of Tunis under Nazi occupation: A divided community in times of crisis), *Yahdut Zemanenu*, vol. 2 (1984), 153–175.

5. Haim Avni, "The Zionist Underground in Holland and France and the Escape to Spain," in Israel Gutman and Efraim Zuroff (eds.), *Rescue Attempts During the Holocaust*, Jerusalem: Yad Vashem, 1977, pp. 555–590.

6. For background on prewar Polish-Jewish relations, see Celia S. Heller, *On the Edge of Destruction*, New York: Schocken Books, 1980.

7. Cf. Israel Gutman and Shmuel Krakowski, *Unequal Victims: Poles and Jews During World War II*, New York: Holocaust Library, 1986, pp. 58–65. Of thirteen Polish underground parties still active in 1944, seven advocated Jewish emigration and two advocated "getting rid of the Jews," presumably a euphemism for continued extermination. Only four parties — the Socialists, the Trade Unionists, Liberal Democrats, and Liberal Pilsudskiites — advocated equal rights for Jews in a postwar Poland. Ibid., p. 107.

8. Mordechai Tenenbaum-Tamaroff, *דפים מן הדלקה* (Pages from the Holocaust), Tel Aviv: Hakibbutz Hameuchad, 1947, pp. 49–50.

9. Gutman and Krakowski, *Unequal Victims*, pp. 216–218.

10. Ibid., ch. 5.

11. B. F. Sabrin, *Alliance for Murder: The Nazi-Ukrainian Nationalist Partnership in Genocide*, New York: Saperdon/Shapolsky, 1991.

12. Hannah Arendt, "From the Dreyfus Affair to the France of Today," *JSS*, vol. 4 # 3 (1942), 195–240.

13. Cf. Pawel Korzec, "Antisemitism in Poland as an Intellectual, Social, and Political Movement," in Joshua A. Fishman (ed.), *Studies on Polish Jewry, 1919–1939*, New York: YIVO, 1974, English section, pp. 18–29.

14. For an overview on Vichy policy regarding Jews, see Michael R. Marrus and Robert O. Paxton, *Vichy France and the Jews*, New York: Basic Books, 1981. On the deportations, see Claude Levy and Paul Tillard, *Betrayal at the Vel D'Hiv*, New York: Hill and Wang, 1969.

15. Léon Poliakov and Jacques Sabille, *Jews Under the Italian Occupation*, Paris: Editions du Centre, 1959, pp. 17–44.

16. James Rorty, "Father Benoit, Ambassador of the Jews: An Untold Chapter of the Underground," *Commentary*, vol. 2 # 6 (1946), 507–513.

17. William S. Allen, *The Nazi Seizure of Power: The Experience of a Single German Town*, rev. ed., New York: Franklin Watts, 1984, was among the first to note the apparently paradoxical relationship between NSDAP electoral success and the failure of Nazi ideology to penetrate deeply into German society; Sarah Gordon, *Hitler, Germans, and the "Jewish Question,"* Princeton: Princeton University Press, 1984, has followed up on Allen's findings.

18. Philippe Aziz, *Doctors of Death*, Geneva: Fermi Publishers, 1976, vol. 4. ch. 2.

19. Leaflet of spring 1942, cited in Philip Friedman, "Was There an 'Other' Germany During the Nazi Period?" in his, *Roads to Extinction: Essays on the Holocaust*, Philadelphia: JPS, 1980, p. 446.

20. Max Spangenthal, "The Jewish Question and the German Resistance Movement," *Yad Vashem Bulletin*, # 19 (1966), 60–63. As an example, we may note that almost all of the plotters accepted the principles behind Nazi antisemitic legislation. Cf. Hermann Graml et al., *The German Resistance to Hitler*, Berkeley: University of California Press, 1970, pp. 112–113.

21. Nebe was implicated in the bomb plot and attempted to escape by faking his own suicide. He

was caught in late 1944, apparently after being betrayed, and was executed in January or February 1945. Heinz Hohne, *Der Orden unter dem Totenkopf: Die Geschichte der SS*, Gütersloh: Sighert Mohn, 1967, p. 537. A colleague, Hans B. Gisevius, who was involved in the bomb plot and acted as an agent for the American OSS, managed to escape to Switzerland. Cf. Hans B. Gisevius, *To the Bitter End*, Boston: Houghton-Mifflin, 1947.

22. Rolf Hochhuth, *The Deputy*, New York: Grove Press, 1964. For a scholarly, but no less critical, account of papal inaction see Saul Friedländer, *Pius XII and the Third Reich: A Documentation*, New York: Knopf, 1966.

23. John Morley, *Vatican Diplomacy and the Jews During the Holocaust*, New York: Ktav, 1980, pp. 207–209.

24. Note of April 7, 1943, cited in ibid., pp. 92–93. Parentheses in original.

25. Gordon, *Jewish Question*, pp. 214–260.

26. Fein, *Accounting*, pp. 114–118.

27. Robert Wistrich, *Hitler's Apocalypse: Jews and the Nazi Legacy*, New York: St. Martin's Press, 1985, ch. 8.

28. Cf. *Jewish Week*, Sept. 5, 1991, p. 24.

29. Joseph B. Schechtman, *The Mufti and the Führer*, New York: Thomas Yoseloff, 1969, passim, and Lukasz Hirszowicz, *The Third Reich and the Arab East*, London: Routledge and Kegan Paul, 1966, ch. 11, 13.

30. Meir Michaelis, *Mussolini and the Jews*, Oxford: Clarendon Press, for the Institute of Jewish Affairs, 1978, pp. 58–60.

31. Poliakov and Sabille, *Jews Under*, passim, and Ivo Herzer (ed.), *The Italian Refuge: Rescue of the Jews During the Holocaust*, Washington, DC: Catholic University of America Press, 1989.

32. Jonathan Steinberg, *All or Nothing: The Axis and the Holocaust, 1941–1943*, London: Routledge and Kegan Paul, 1990, pt. 1.

33. Susan Zuccotti, *The Italians and the Holocaust: Persecution, Rescue, Survival*, New York: Basic Books, 1987, pp. 272–287.

34. I. C. Butnaru, *The Silent Holocaust: Romania and Its Jews*, Westport, CT: Greenwood Press, 1992, concentrates on the ideological factors in Romanian antisemitism. For a documentary history of the Holocaust in Romania, see Jean Ancel (comp.), *Documents Concerning the Fate of Romanian Jewry During the Holocaust*, 12 vols., New York: Beate Klarsfeld Foundation, 1986.

35. Randolph L. Braham, *The Politics of Genocide: The Holocaust in Hungary*, 1st ed., 2 vols., New York: Columbia University Press, 1980, passim.

36. Haim Avni, *Spain, the Jews, and Franco*, Philadelphia: JPS, 1982, ch. 4–6.

37. Cf. Samuel P. Oliner and Pearl Oliner, *The Altruistic Personality*, New York: Free Press, 1988.

38. Stefan Korbonski, *The Polish Underground State*, New York: Hippocrene Books, 1981, ch. 10.

39. Gutman and Krakowski, *Unequal Victims*, ch. 7.

40. Korbonski, *Polish Underground State*, pp. 140–143.

41. Per Anger, *With Raoul Wallenberg in Budapest*, New York: Holocaust Library, 1981.

8

INTERNATIONAL RESPONSES

Responses to the Refugee Crisis

As massive a system as that developed by the Nazis for the purpose of eradicating European Jewry could hardly have been kept secret for long. Try as they might, the Nazis could not have kept the murder of 6 million people from being discovered. Eventually some word would leak out to the free world. One might have thought that the Western Allies at war with Germany would have utilized all means at their disposal in order to end the massacres quickly and save at least a remnant of European Jewry. But Allied reactions to Jewish suffering and even to the wholesale murder of Jews at the hands of the Nazis and their collaborators was slow.

During the 1930s — when Nazi Germany sought to solve the Jewish problem by emigration — most countries turned a deaf ear to pleas for the absorption of more refugees. No country had been immune to the negative impact of the economic depression; fears of new economic crises that would derive from any mass immigration drove almost every country in Europe, the Americas, and the Pacific to restrict refugee immigration.

A few examples should suffice to explain the problems experienced by Jews escaping Germany. Although it had an otherwise liberal and tolerant reputation regarding Jews, Holland attempted to keep Jewish (and, to a lesser degree, non-Jewish)

refugees from remaining in the country. No impediments were initially placed on refugees who used Holland as a transit point, but after 1934 the Dutch made concerted efforts to keep Jewish refugees — except for select individuals possessing economic assets in Holland — out of the country altogether and to make the residence of those who did enter the country as brief as possible.[1] In 1939 the Dutch set up a central detention center for illegal Jewish immigrants in the town of Westerbork.[2] Again, the basis of this policy was an effort to convince Jewish refugees to use Holland only as a transit point. Jews seeking refuge in Belgium met a similar response.

Canada's policy on Jewish refugees was even simpler and was considerably less sympathetic. For the entire period from 1933 to 1939 (and well into the 1940s), Canada's doors were closed to refugees and especially to Jewish refugees from Germany. Restrictive Canadian immigration laws were tightened throughout the 1930s, so that, by 1938, it was virtually impossible for European Jews to enter Canada. As late as 1945 a government official, when asked how many Jewish refugees Canada was willing to accept, could declare, "None is too many."[3]

Even in the few lands where immigration was possible, such as certain South American countries, only individuals with specific skills — primarily doctors and other medical professionals — were given visas.[4] Argentina had actively sought immigrants for most of the period between independence (1816) and the depression. At one point, indeed, the Argentine government even appeared willing to grant an unprecedented degree of autonomy to immigrants who founded settlements in sparsely populated regions. Although the Argentine government did not specify a desire to absorb Jewish immigrants, it also did nothing to prevent a massive influx of Eastern European Jews during this period.[5] Conditions changed radically after 1930. The September 6, 1930, coup brought Argentina under the rule of a military junta with close ties to the Axis (especially Fascist Italy). Another coup on June 4, 1943 — led by colonel Juan Peron and others — put Argentina even more strongly into the rightist camp. Although the fear that the Axis appeared to be losing the war kept Argentina neutral, the new government did not relent on its position regarding refugees until 1945. After the war, a small number of Jewish refugees, in addition to dozens of escaped Nazi war criminals and their collaborators, were belatedly admitted into the country.[6]

The United States — which had passed extremely restrictive immigration quotas in 1924 — similarly sought to restrict refugee immigration. Loosening the immigration quotas was extremely unpopular throughout the interwar period. Even American Jewry, fearful of further whetting the antisemitic torrent that had developed in the late 1920s and early 1930s, supported maintaining the quota system, despite its glaring unfairness.[7] Nevertheless, it has been estimated that the United States issued 1 million fewer immigrant visas than existing quotas would have allowed for the entire period between 1933 and 1941.[8]

Throughout this period only the Yishuv actively sought Jewish mass immigration. Palestine, however, was not ruled by the Jews; the territory was controlled by Great Britain under the terms of a League of Nations mandate for the purpose of creating a Jewish national home. Nearly 250,000 Jews entered Palestine between 1933 and 1939. Arab refusal to accept Jewish rights to the Holy Land, however, and British concern for imperial and strategic interests led to a curtailment — by

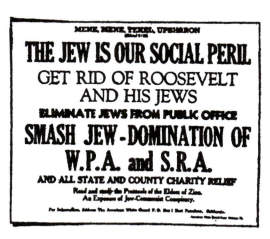

Two antisemitic propaganda tools of the 1930s: a sticker (left) and a handbill (right)
Reprinted from: John L. Spivak, *Secret Armies*, New York: Modern Age, 1939.

the British Palestine administration — of Jewish legal immigration. This policy of curtailment led to British attempts to restrict immigration through the granting of ever-more-restrictive immigrant schedules (as the quotas were called). Although Zionists sought legal means to sidestep the new restrictiveness — for example, using the *Ha'avara* agreement to permit Jewish refugees to immigrate as capitalists — their options were limited. Even the use of illegal means, known as Aliya Bet ("illegal" immigration), could not become a means of mass rescue since neither sufficient physical (ships, sailors, and other commodities for transporting large masses) nor financial resources were available to the World Zionist Organization.[9] Moreover, neither the Yishuv nor world Jewry had enough powerful friends willing to oppose British policy in the Middle East.

In light of the situation in Palestine, the British government slightly relaxed immigration restrictions to England proper. This policy was viewed as the only means to behave in a humanitarian way while avoiding a potential outbreak of violence in the Middle East, which would harm Britain's strategic interests. Even so, the results were rather small, with only 49,500 refugees — including non-Jewish German and Austrian political refugees — entering Great Britain. Further, this figure must be kept in context, since Jewish emigration from Germany, Austria, and Bohemia-Moravia (the Czech Protectorate) totaled an estimated 400,000.[10] Similar restrictions applied to Australia and New Zealand, both large and sparsely populated. The Jew in need of a safe haven was simply classified as persona non grata.[11]

Under these conditions, it is understandable why a refugee crisis existed during the 1930s. Jews and non-Jewish anti-Nazis required a safe haven but could not find one. Here and there a few individuals sought to aid the refugees but discovered that the intense apathy shown by most countries simply could not be overcome. Such was especially the case of James G. McDonald, the American appointed high

"Keep Palestine's doors open": A poster of the Keren Kayemmet le-Israel
Authors' Collection

commissioner for refugees by the League of Nations in 1933.[12] After two years of futilely trying to find even a temporary haven for refugees, McDonald resigned. "The moral authority of the League of Nations and of State Members of the League," he wrote, "must be directed towards a determined appeal to the German government in the name of humanity and of the principles of public law in Europe." The letter, with more than forty pages of supporting documentation, was published in the *New York Times* but failed to effect more than a minor ripple in refugee policy.[13]

Moreover, antisemitism rose precipitously in Europe and the Americas during the 1930s. Fascist and quasi-Fascist parties in the United

States, Great Britain, South Africa, and Switzerland were as intensely antisemitic as the Nazi party itself. Leaders such as Oswald Mosley, Father Charles E. Coughlin, and Benno W. Schaeppi spread racial and religious hatred for Jews on every possible level and by every conceivable medium. Thus, although these Fascists never attained power, they had a significant effect on local politics and especially on the attitudes of local Jewish communities.[14]

Between July 6 and 15, 1938, thirty-two Western nations met in Evian-les-Bains, France, at the invitation of President Franklin Delano Roosevelt. The international conference focused mainly on two issues: to try to find a solution for the growing refugee problem and to establish a worldwide organization whose aim would be to work for an overall solution to the ever-worsening refugee situation. With the Nazi annexation of Austria and the brewing crisis in Czechoslovakia, things got out of hand and something had to be done. Participating nations were assured in advance that no mandatory changes in quota laws would be enacted, but instead, voluntary changes would be requested. At no time were Jewish refugees specified by the participants, who preferred to deal with refugees in the abstract. Even under these conditions, representative after representative simply noted that his or her country was too overloaded to accept any further refugees. Little in the way of rescue was achieved.[15] The conference did agree to create an Inter-Governmental Committee on Refugees, with headquarters in London. The body, however, had no power and few resources.[16]

Moreover, only one country extended a substantive offer of refuge at the Evian Conference. The Dominican Republic offered to allow 100,000 Jews to colonize the area near Santo Domingo — the so-called Sossua project — in return for a large Jewish monetary contribution to ensure that the refugees would not become a public charge. Although $1,423,000 was invested (in reality little more than a large bribe for Dominican politicians) by the American Jewish Joint Distribution Committee (JDC) through 1944, Dominican President Rafael Trujillo permitted the admission of a mere 500 German Jewish refugees. Even that trickle was stopped in 1940, when the JDC refused Trujillo's demands for more than ten times what it had already paid.[17]

That the conference had failed was realized almost immediately. A headline in the *Philadelphia Record*, for example, stated, "Humanitarianism suffers a new blow as Evian parley fails to provide system for aiding Europe's unhappy exiles."[18] It is little wonder then that the outcome of the Evian Conference played into the hands of skilled Nazi propagandists, who gloated about the failure to find a refuge. *Münchner Nachrichten*, for example, wrote:

Obviously Germany was not represented in this noteworthy conference. Nor are we concerned with the decisions that were reached there, since the Jewish question has been thoroughly settled as we are concerned and is being resolved step by step. . . . *If the Jews in Germany are so dear to their hearts, they can certainly have them.* We are delighted to give them up, and we will not even ask any price for them.[19]

Jewish feelings of helplessness must be kept in context. As can be seen in Table 8.1, slightly more than half of all Jewish migrants from Eastern and Central Europe — the total number of whom was 400,000 — immigrated to Palestine. The next most frequent destination, the United States, accepted less than half Palestine's number, accounting for only 23 percent of the total.[20]

TABLE 8.1: Jewish Immigration to Palestine and the United States, 1933–1939

Year	To Palestine	To U.S.A.	Year	To Palestine	To U.S.A.
1933	30,327	2,372	1937	10,536	11,352
1934	42,359	4,134	1938	12,868	19,736
1935	61,854	4,837	1939	27,561	43,450
1936	29,727	6,252	Total	215,232	92,133

Source: D. Gurevich, *Statistical Handbook of Jewish Palestine*, Jerusalem: JAE, 1947, p. 116.

These figures further indicate America's limited role in solving the "refugee crisis." Immigration to the United States did not overtake *aliya* until 1937, despite the disparity in absorptive capability of the two countries (and ignoring the fact that Palestine's immigration policy was established in London, not Jerusalem). In 1937 and 1938, moreover, the differential between the two destinations was not by any means decisive: merely an 8 percent difference in 1937 and 33 percent in 1938. Only in 1939 does a vast difference become obvious, as immigration to the United States was nearly twice Palestine's total.

The well-known case of the SS *Saint Louis* adds to the picture of American indifference to Jewish suffering. On May 13, 1939, the German luxury liner *Saint Louis* departed from Hamburg with 937 German Jews on board. Destined for Cuba, all the German Jews had visas that assured them of the right to land. Since the JDC had offered to guarantee that the refugees would not become a public charge, it appeared that a temporary haven had been found, at least for some German Jews. When the *Saint Louis* arrived in Havana harbor, however, Cuban dictator Ramón Grau San Martín reneged on his promises, allowing only a small number of the refugees to disembark. The ship departed from Havana on June 2, attempting to enter U.S. territorial waters between June 4 and June 6. On each occasion, the ship was forced out by U.S. Coast Guard vessels. Finally, on June 6, 1939, the *Saint Louis* returned to Europe. Only last-minute decisions by Great Britain, Holland, and Belgium prevented the refu-

gees from returning to certain incarceration in Nazi concentration camps.[21]

With the outbreak of war, the refugee crisis became even more acute. The fear that spies might be infiltrated among refugees was cited as reason for continued obstruction of rescue. Similarly, the effort to win the war and not waste resources was touted as the only patriotic response to the Jewish catastrophe in Europe. Yet precisely as the nations sought less involvement in "Jewish" issues, the threat to Jewry became even more ominous.

Uncovering the Final Solution

When the Nazis began systematically murdering European Jewry, they also launched an elaborate deception plan in order to mask the actual meaning of deportations. This plan served three purposes: to dull potential resistance by Jews; to weaken the anxiety of local non-Jews — who might otherwise aid their Jewish neighbors; and to hide the reality from the Allies in order to prevent them from interfering with the murder process. More broadly, this deception scheme also served to turn the Final Solution into what Himmler termed — in a speech before a gathering of the Higher SS and Police Leaders (HSSPF) in Posen in 1942 — the great, unwritten chapter in German history.[22]

Despite Nazi efforts to maintain secrecy, some information did filter out to the West. Much of what was published, however, was framed in the form of rumor or as deriving from reliable, but anonymous, sources.[23] News reportage of this sort was possible only until the U.S. entry into World War II but had been

The *Saint Louis* in Havana harbor
Courtesy of the U.S. Holocaust Memorial Museum

problematic from 1933 on. Although initial Nazi anti-Jewish excesses had been extensively covered, after 1933 the suffering of Jews ceased to be front-page news.

A clear differentiation must be made, however, between the general press and the Jewish press. The latter continued to cover the situation extensively throughout the 1930s, slacking off after 1939 because of the cutting of communications when the war broke out, and then resuming extensive (although, not always accurate) coverage in 1943 and 1944.[24] But Jewish newspapers were bereft of any influence outside the Jewish community. In advocating rescue, therefore, they were limited to preaching to the converted. Influential American papers like the *New York Times*, the *Washington Post*, and the *St. Louis Post-Dispatch* largely remained aloof, and neither reported on the persecution of German Jewry extensively in the 1930s nor advocated rescue. At the same time, almost all the major American newspapers continued to support strict adherence to immigration quotas, in some cases as late as 1948.[25]

In contrast to the situation in the United States, the British press was slightly more forthright in publishing news about Nazi mistreatment of German (and later all of European) Jewry. Nevertheless, willingness to report the news and advocacy of rescue remained an unbridged chasm in Britain, as in the United States. Numerous studies have noted the general ambivalence expressed by

British politicians toward the rescue issue, reflecting their fear that a Jewish tidal wave would inundate Britain, Palestine, or both.[26] In both the United States and Britain, the primary problem was a lack of Jewish influence within the corridors of power, rather than a lack of precise information on Nazi actions. This most singularly demonstrates the weakness of Jewry at the time: The Jews could not turn their communal agenda into the agenda of any country or any discernible group anywhere in the diaspora.

The U.S. entry into the war rendered further publication based on public sources unreliable, although occasionally reports on specific massacres appeared, which did open the possibility of governmental investigation into Nazi war crimes. Some information, mostly intercepts of telegrams regarding deportations, was collected by Allied intelligence services.[27] Such information had little effect on Allied policy and appears to have gotten no further than the lowest levels of the bureaucracy.[28] Further information was available through couriers such as Jan Karski, who reported extensively on conditions in Nazi- and Soviet-occupied Poland.[29]

Taken together, these sources clearly pointed to extensive Jewish suffering but did not necessarily point to the actual Nazi policy of systematic extermination. Uncovering the real meaning of the Final Solution was actually more difficult and may not have been uncovered had it not been for a well-connected German businessman, Eduard Schulte. While on a business trip to Switzerland, Schulte passed information regarding Nazi plans to exterminate European Jewry to Gerhard Riegner, director of the World Jewish Congress (WJC) Swiss branch.[30] Although the information he received was unverified, it was sufficiently ominous to convince Riegner that other Jewish leaders, notably WJC President Stephen S. Wise, should be informed. Riegner, therefore, crafted a telegram that included all the data received from Schulte as well as all necessary precautions regarding authenticity and sent it to Wise and

to Jewish leaders in England, in July 1942. When U.S. State Department officials received the telegram, they sought to suppress it, considering that it was unsubstantiated. Some officials believed that the cable was a "wild rumor."[31] Wise received a copy of the Riegner cable on August 28, 1942 — ironically from British sources — but, in a controversial move for which he has been much criticized after the war, agreed to keep the information private until it could be verified. Wise's actions should be kept in context. Having no status within the government, he could rely only on the good graces of the State Department to receive information from Europe. Therefore, he felt compelled — correctly or otherwise — to accede to a blackout, hoping thereby to protect his access to further information.[32]

For the next three months, U.S., British, and neutral sources sought to verify the information contained in Riegner's telegram. By mid-November these sources not only had confirmed the substance but had discovered an even more horrifying reality: that 2 million Jews had already been murdered. The process of uncovering the Final Solution culminated in an Allied declaration of December 12, 1942, publicly warning that those guilty of atrocities would be punished.[33] Now the question arose of how to turn that Allied threat into a coherent rescue policy.

Allied War Strategy and the Jewish Problem

The sad reality is that no single country was willing to become the Jews' protector. The Allies were not willing to divert any resources away from the war in order to defend the Jews, even in cases where targets had military significance, such as Auschwitz and its rail lines.[34] Only in a few cases were radio messages beamed to Europe by the BBC, warning that what the Nazis termed "resettlement" in fact meant death. Even these broadcasts were stopped by the British government so as not to create anti-Jewish resentment in the occupied territories by appearing to devote too much time to the Jews.[35]

In short, the attitude of the Allies toward the

Jews was an apathetic one. Whereas the Nazis viewed killing Jews as a paramount goal of the war, the Allies never considered the Jewish question as a factor in the formulation of their war strategy; it was merely a side issue to be settled with the end of hostilities.

Generalizations regarding Allied apathy especially held true for the British. His Majesty's Government feared that any act on behalf of Jews in Europe would aid the Zionists, and the Mandatory policy encapsulated in the 1939 White Paper undid Britain's commitment to establish a Jewish national home. The British government, therefore, tried to ignore the Jewish problem for as long as possible, hoping it would go away. A statement wrongly attributed to Lord Moyne (Eric Arthur Guinness), the Briitsh minister resident in Cairo, but apparently made by a senior member of the British Palestine administration, indicates much: Told unofficially of Joel Brand's mission and Eichmann's offer to ransom 1 million Jews for 10,000 trucks, the Englishman responded, "But what will we do with one million Jews?"[36] Official government opinion was little better: An anonymous cabinet member responded, on the record, to the Eichmann offer by hoping that if His Majesty's Government joined the negotiations, the Germans would not "offer to unload an even greater number of Jews on our hands."[37] By then, Britain had virtually sealed all escape routes. In particular, the blockade placed on Palestine — to seize ships bearing "illegal" immigrants — was even strengthened, as Aliya Bet became European Jewry's only practical escape route. In any case, in 1944, outside of the Jewish community in Hungary and the few Jews still lingering in concentration camps, there were hardly any Jews left alive in Nazi-occupied Europe.

The majority of governments in exile located in London also reflected a generally indifferent picture. They expressed sincere regrets at the Jews' suffering; but with the exception of a few small-scale activities, the governments in exile were unable to take concrete steps of any sort. Some, such as the Polish government in exile, could not, or would not, curb antisemitic incidents among their own troops or censor openly anti-Jewish articles in newspapers under their own sponsorship. Almost all the Eastern European governments in exile had some sort of antisemitic law proposed in their legislative plans for the postliberation era.[38]

Not even the Soviet Union — itself a principal victim of barbarous Nazi attacks — undertook any systematic efforts to save Jews. Although perfectly willing to use the Nazi threat to European Jewry for propaganda purposes, by means of the Jewish Anti-Fascist Committee, for example, the Soviet Union did no more than the Western powers to save European Jews. In fact, Soviet policy consistently placed Jews in an ambiguous and dangerous position. The Comintern had not paid much attention to Nazi antisemitism during the 1930s. The Soviet or Communist press did not report on anti-Jewish excesses. Russian Jews therefore never knew of the threat that rapidly approached them. To make matters worse, the Soviets signed a nonaggression pact with Nazi Germany in August 1939. At that point the Russian borders were closed to anti-Nazi refugees, and some agitators were handed over to the Gestapo by its Soviet counterpart, the NKVD. One might have expected that upon the German invasion this policy would change. In an ad hoc fashion, local Soviet authorities evacuated some Jews from the danger zone. By and large, however, they left Jews to their fate. The Supreme Soviet was willing to make pronouncements but did as little or less than the Anglo-Americans.[39]

In the United States, rescue was approached without a sense of urgency. To be sure, the administration framed its policy around a public sense of concern, assuring the press and populace that everything possible was being done to rescue European Jewry. The Roosevelt administration's primary argument, however, was that a speedy Allied victory would be the best way to effect rescue; far from being effective, U.S. government policy was actually a prescription for inaction.[40]

Allied inaction was most apparent on April 19, 1943. On the same day that the Warsaw ghetto uprising began, representatives from Britain and the United States met at the Bermuda Conference. The conference's ostensible goal was to investigate means of rescue. While the small remnant of Warsaw Jewry — the ground burning under them — fought their last battle, the gentlemen in Bermuda exchanged trivial pleasantries; their real goal was to deflect public pressure by appearing to do something while, in fact,

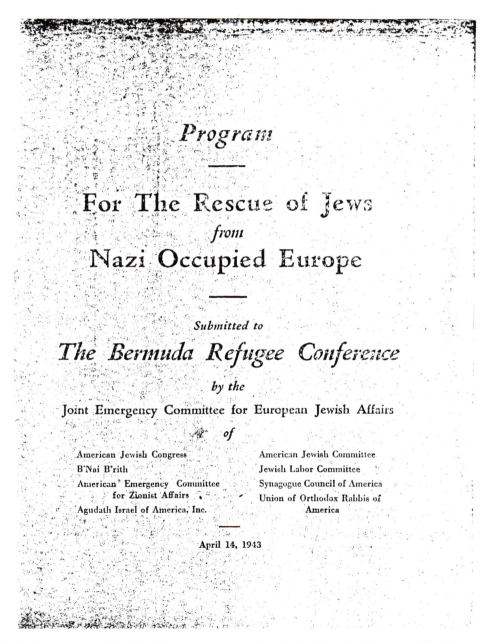

Facsimile front page of the Jewish rescue proposal submitted to the Bermuda Conference
Authors' Collection

making no real policy changes.[41] Not until 1944, when political pressure at home increased during an election year, did the U.S. administration act. Even then decisive action was undertaken only after Secretary of the Treasury Henry Morgenthau became involved. In late December 1943 Morgenthau had instructed two of his assistants, Randolph Paul and John Pehle, to investigate the State Department's handling of rescue issues. In January, Paul and Pehle reported back in a scathing memorandum entitled "The Acquiescence of This Government in the Murder of European Jews."[42] Morgenthau proceeded to take this document to Roosevelt and suggested the creation of a U.S. rescue agency. Roosevelt agreed, signing an executive order on January 22, 1944.[43] The creation of what came to be known as the War Refugee Board (WRB) finally brought the rescue issue to the fore, at least on paper. In reality, the creation of the WRB came too late to save most European Jews and in practice accomplished very little.[44]

Allied behavior raises a complex question regarding rescue: Why did the Allies, engaged in a life or death struggle with the Third Reich, not consider aiding Nazism's premier victims? During the war, public figures who opposed rescue action relied on claims regarding the difficulties of allocating resources during wartime and the need to help civilian victims without aiding the Nazi war effort. Since the war, however, it has become increasingly clear that such claims were a smoke screen used to mask the bureaucratic cupidity, the inertia, and the cases of outright antisemitism that prevented the Allied powers from rescuing Jews in a timely fashion.[45] The same naval resources allocated to transporting German prisoners of war across the Atlantic — on empty troopships that had brought U.S. troops to England — could also have been used to bring refugees to a safe haven. The same Allied policy that permitted breaking the blockade on Nazi-occupied Europe in order to feed famine victims in Greece could have permitted the transfer of sufficient finances to give a chance of success to Jewish rescue advocates. What was lacking was *not* the ability to rescue but the will to effect rescue. Looking at European Jewry's predicament from this perspective, we may conclude that — by their inaction — the Allies became silent partners, albeit indirectly, in the destruction of European Jewry.

The Neutrals: "The Lifeboat Is Full"

Conditions affecting rescue were more complex in the neutral countries. Throughout the 1930s Switzerland sought to restrict the entry of Jewish refugees. Arguing that the country was surfeited, the Swiss government thus reversed a century-old humanitarian policy.[46] Indeed, the Swiss went as far as to demand that the Germans stamp Jews' passports with a letter *J*, as a de facto means of denying entry to all but a selected group of refugees.[47] By 1942 the Swiss borders had been virtually sealed off to Jewish refugees, although Switzerland maintained a liberal policy regarding the entry of escaped Allied prisoners of war and German deserters. Furthermore, in 1939 and 1940 Jewish refugees who entered Switzerland were returned to the Reich.[48] When the war started (September 1, 1939) only 7,100 refugees had legally been permitted into Switzerland.[49] By 1942 this number had grown slightly, and it continued to grow by very small increments through 1943. Only in July 1944 did the Swiss government reverse its policy and permit the entry of all Jewish refugees. The result was not quite a torrent of refugees, although Swiss action was responsible for the rescue of thousands of French Jewish youth.[50] In addition, Swiss diplomatic representatives — most notably Karl Lutz (in Budapest) — were given permission to give Swiss entry visas to Jews endangered by the Nazis.

Sweden's policy regarding Jews began in much the same way as Switzerland's. Before the war that meant that Sweden sought to restrict entry of refugees, especially from Germany and Eastern Europe.[51] When the war broke out, the Swedish government initially intended to continue its restrictive policy: As of

August 1941 more than half of all requests for entry visas by political or racial refugees had been rejected.[52] In 1942, however, Swedish policy changed. Unwilling to actively aid Jews, which might be seen by the Nazis as a breach of Sweden's neutrality, the government was appalled by the increasing evidence of Nazi murder. For the next three years, therefore, Sweden adopted a policy that might be termed positive passivity: The Swedes would do nothing to encourage the entry of refugees but also would not prevent them from entering Sweden once they arrived. By this means most Norwegian and Danish Jews were rescued. In 1944, moreover, this passive policy was converted into an active rescue policy. Swedish representatives, including Raoul Wallenberg and Count Folke Bernadotte used every means available to rescue Jews. Bernadotte used contacts with RFSS Heinrich Himmler's chiropractor, Dr. Felix Kerstein (himself a Swedish citizen), to negotiate the rescue of some 20,000 Jews incarcerated in Nazi concentration camps in March and April 1945.[53]

The same policy of business as usual pervaded international rescue organizations and other humanitarian agencies. The International Red Cross, for example, had conveniently declared Jews stateless and hence outside its sphere of activity, thus easing the way for the Nazis to carry out their designs. The International Red Cross inadvertently helped to spread Nazi propaganda by giving Terezin the air of respectability, although it was merely an antechamber for Auschwitz. Having finally come to an agreement with the Nazis on the inspection of the concentration camps, the International Red Cross was willing to see only Nazi-selected sights. Of course, these sights had been carefully selected and prepared by the Germans. The International Red Cross refused to investigate anything it was not actually shown.[54]

In evaluating the behavior of Europe's neutrals and international organizations we must keep in mind three considerations. First, none of these entities fully lived up to its humanitarian reputations. In particular,

all failed during the 1930s to exert sufficient pressure in order to effect the rescue of threatened Jews when rescue was possible. Second, all of them placed their interest in maintaining neutral status above any moral or ethical concerns. That reality changed only very slowly, with the Swedes modifying their attitude first. Finally, it is clear that the neutrals mirrored Allied policy toward Jews. Had the Anglo-Americans placed rescue on a higher level of priority that they did, the neutrals likely would have followed suit. Clearly, the Swiss changed their policy toward Jewish refugees after the United States took the lead by creating the War Refugee Board.

Responses of Free-World Jewry

If the general apathy, callousness, and sloth of the free world can be considered problematic, the attitude of free-world Jewry can be considered no less so. Although deeply concerned by events in Europe, Jews in the United States, Britain, and Palestine were unable to effect a cogent rescue policy. Powerlessness, disunity, lack of clear policies, and lack of accurate information created this condition, but these factors worked differently in each community.

The Yishuv was in the forefront of efforts involving the resettlement of refugees from Nazi Germany and elsewhere during the 1930s. During the ten years of the Fifth Aliya (1929–1939), more than 250,000 Jews entered Palestine, including nearly 100,000 from Germany. The Yishuv, however, was saddled with a weak economy, Arab hostility, and the machinations of a British administration that tried to keep Jews out of Palestine while officially helping to create the Jewish National Home. Although committed to Zionism through the Balfour Declaration and the League of Nations Mandate, the British had come to the conclusion that imperial interests and Jewish interests no longer coincided. In the early 1930s the Mandatory government therefore sought to keep Jews out of the country, even if that meant liberalization of immigrant quotas to Britain itself.[55]

In 1939 the split between the Yishuv and the

Mandatory government became final. On May 17, 1939, the British issued a new White Paper that repudiated the Jewish national home. Jewish immigration to Palestine was to be limited to 15,000 per annum for five years; thereafter, further Jewish immigration would be contingent upon Arab approval. Similarly, Zionist land acquisition would be severely curtailed in nearly 90 percent of the territory of western Palestine. To make matters worse, the Mandatory government declared its intention to create in 1949 an independent Arab state in Palestine.[56]

The outbreak of war in September forced the Zionists to cancel plans for a revolt and make a terrible decision on the issue of priorities. A truce was declared with the British in order to fight the greater threat. Zionist policymakers hoped to win a fairer solution for the Yishuv in postwar settlements. Meanwhile Zionist policy was, as we have seen, to "fight Hitler as if there was no White Paper" and to "fight the White Paper as if there was no Hitler," as Ben-Gurion said. Given the Yishuv's limited resources, it was not really possible to do both, although rescue efforts were made. Once the Yishuv received confirmed information on the Final Solution, in November 1942, the Jewish Agency Executive (JAE) began to consider a variety of rescue proposals. Many of the proposals centered on helping Jews escape from the Nazis. The JAE demanded that the gates of Palestine be opened to Jews seeking refuge, requested that the Allies retaliate in order to stop the massacres, urged the Allied governments to take other actions to stop or slow down the murder process, and urged the formation of a Jewish army to fight against the murderers.[57]

In 1943 the JAE's secret militia, the Hagana, proposed a defense plan for East European Jewry, but the plan was rejected. Similarly, when the Warsaw ghetto uprising began, the Hagana sought to recruit a "suicide commando" to parachute into the ghetto to stiffen the resistance. Although 500 potential fighters volunteered, the mission was considered too risky and was never carried out.[58]

Moreover, the Yishuv in general and the Jewish Agency in particular sought recognition for their status as the sole legitimate spokespersons and representatives of world Jewry. The British, however, did not see the issue through Zionist eyes. The British obstructed every opportunity for rescue work, fearing that a bold move to rescue Jews might succeed and create more potential candidates for immigrant certificates, thus creating pressure for a pro-Zionist solution to the Palestine impasse.[59]

The Zionist establishment reacted by cooperating with the British on common issues, primarily relating to the war against Nazi Germany, while preparing for the eventual struggle with Britain or the Arabs. Meanwhile, the Zionist movement aimed to establish a postwar Jewish commonwealth through the Biltmore Program of May 1942. More radical Zionists, especially the Revisionist Zionist followers of Ze'ev Jabotinsky, evaluated the situation in much the same manner as the Jewish Agency, opting for cooperation with the British while preparing for future revolt. The Revisionist underground, the Irgun Zva'i Leumi (IZL), thus followed the Hagana, in placing all resources into the anti-Nazi war effort. Not all Zionists agreed, however, that this path was the best for Jews. A splinter group from the IZL, led by Abraham Stern, came to exactly the opposite conclusion: Calling itself Lohame Herut Israel (LEHI), this group continued the armed struggle against the British throughout the war and even tried to contact and make a deal with the Nazis. Rebuffed and repudiated by the majority of the Yishuv, LEHI took to assassinations and terrorism to achieve its goals. The Yishuv, however, was too weak to change the situation during the war. Diplomatic and military efforts notwithstanding, the situation in 1945 was exactly the same as it had been in 1939, except that 6 million Jews — who could have been saved — were dead.[60]

Unlike those of the Yishuv, Anglo Jewry's efforts on behalf of rescue were hampered, almost from the beginning, by the specific nature of both the community and its public context. Specifically, Anglo Jewry, more than any diaspora Jewish community, was plagued by a continuing crisis surrounding potential antisemitic claims of Jewish "dual loyalty." Such fears were slightly less significant between 1933 and 1939, although historians are divided as to the efficacy of the Anglo-Jewish response during those years.[61] Once World War II broke out, Anglo Jewry was placed in a quandary. Adherence to the Allied war effort appeared to clash with the needs of world Jewry. The problem was particularly acute for English Zionists but ultimately affected the actions of almost every Anglo-Jewish organization. As a result, Anglo Jewry had considerable difficulty in formulating a rescue policy and, bereft of actual policy options, could not get His Majesty's Government to rise above the anti-Zionist orientation that doomed European Jewry.[62] Under the prevailing circumstances, Anglo Jewry's problem continued in the immediate postwar years and was not resolved until the State of Israel was established.[63]

The most powerful Jewish community, however, was in the United States. Here too, issues of Jewish interest met with considerable difficulties. The U.S. government, as already noted, was less than enthusiastic about rescue and thus left American Jewry without any alternative and, in effect, without a policy. Moreover, those leaders — such as Stephen S. Wise, Abba Hillel Silver, and Israel Goldstein — who could see the parameters for a rescue policy were largely without any real power. Jews in positions of power were, to a large degree, unwilling to become involved. Bernard Baruch, for example, offered only one rescue proposal during the entire Nazi era: European Jews should find a haven in Angola. But when the proposal was rejected, Baruch eschewed any further involvement in Jewish affairs.[64]

True, American Jewry did possess the resources to emerge from the condition of powerlessness that was forced upon it by the economic depression, but the community remained politically and ideologically disunited. Zionists, non-Zionists, and anti-Zionists each called for different approaches

to the Jewish problem. The problem went even further: American Jewry was split not only on strategy but on tactics as well. Some leaders, for example, urged public advocacy of the Jewish agenda, whereas others opposed doing anything that would embarrass the Roosevelt administration. So enamored of President Roosevelt were the masses of American Jews that voting against him was never a serious option that could have been used to force the rescue issue to the fore. A popular, but unattributed, saying at the time was that American Jews "have three *velts* (worlds): *dos velt* (this world), *yene velt* (the hereafter), and Roosevelt."[65]

It is, however, too easy to criticize the American Jewish leadership, especially in hindsight. As viewed at the time, no simple answers were available: Jews had no reply for the naysayers who claimed that European Jewry's best interests would be served by a maximal war effort; Jews had no alternative haven to Palestine — even their enemies conceded that point — but feared politicizing a humanitarian issue. Moreover, during an extremely popular and successful administration, Jews had no alternative to Roosevelt. The president knew that reality and manipulated the American Jewish community for his own ends.[66]

Again, the problem did not simply cease in 1945. Postwar realities, however, transformed American Jewry: The self-conscious community that was unable to articulate its leadership position during the war finally came of age after the war.[67]

Rescue: Too Little, Too Late?

European Jewry was thus ground to dust between the twin millstones of Nazi antisemitism and Allied apathy. The tragedy was that in its hour of need, European Jewry could find neither savior nor safe haven. Whatever rescue action was undertaken by the Allies occurred after the bulk of European Jewry had been brutally murdered. It is possible that the War Refugee Board, if created in late 1942 or early 1943, could have saved 2 to 3 million Jews instead of the 100,000 to 150,000 that were actually saved with its help or by its efforts. It is possible that had the Allies shown resolve, the Nazis would have abandoned the Final Solution altogether. But because the Allies moved only in 1944 the possibilities will remain merely conjectures. Powerless to affect their fate, the Jews both inside and outside of Europe could only watch with horror at the unfolding tragedy and prepare for the denouement of the Jewish war that Hitler had started.

Notes

1. Dan Michman, "The Committee for Jewish Refugees in Holland (1933–1940)," *YVS*, vol. 14 (1981), 205–232.

2. Westerbork was eventually taken over by the Nazis and was used as a transit camp for the deportation of Dutch Jews. On the history of Westerbork, see Jacob Boas, *Boulevard des Misères: The Story of Transit Camp Westerbork*, Hamden, CT: Archon Books, 1985.

3. Cf. Irving Abella and Harold Troper, *None Is Too Many: Canada and the Jews of Europe, 1933–1948*, New York: Random House, 1982, ch. 2.

4. Michael R. Marrus, *The Unwanted: European Refugees in the Twentieth Century*, New York: Oxford University Press, 1985, pp. 135–141.

5. Haim Avni, *Argentina and the Jews: A History of Jewish Immigration*, Tuscaloosa: University of Alabama Press, 1991, ch. 3.

6. Ibid., ch. 5.

7. David S. Wyman, *Paper Walls: America and the Refugee Crisis, 1938–1941*, New York: Pantheon Books, 1985, pt. 4.

8. Arthur D. Morse, *While Six Million Died: A Chronicle of American Apathy*, New York: Hart Publishing, 1968, pp. 134–149.

9. Abraham J. Edelheit, "The Yishuv in the Shadow of the Holocaust: Palestinian Jewry and the Emerging Nazi Threat, 1933–1939," Ph.D. dissertation, City University of New York, 1992.

10. A. J. Sherman, *Island Refuge: Britain and Refugees from the Third Reich, 1933–1939*, Berkeley: University of California Press, 1973, pp. 259–272.

11. Cf. Michael Blakeney, *Australia and the Jewish Refugees, 1933–1948*, Sydney: Croom Helm Australia, 1985.

12. James G. McDonald, *My Mission in Israel, 1948–1951*, New York: Simon and Schuster, 1951, pp. xii–xiv.

13. *AJYB*, vol. 38 (1936/1937), 193–195.

14. As a means to judge the extent of antisemitism, see the citations in Robert Singerman (ed.), *Antisemitic Propaganda: An Annotated Bibliography and Research Guide*, New York: Garland, 1982.

15. Edelheit, "Yishuv," pp. 428, 449–451; and Selig Adler-Rudel, "The Evian Conference," *LBIYB*, vol. 13 (1968), 235–273.

16. Wyman, *Paper Walls*, pp. 32–33, 50–51.

17. Cf. Yehuda Bauer, *American Jewry and the Holocaust: The American Jewish Joint Distribution Committee, 1939–1945*, Detroit: Wayne State University Press, 1981, pp. 200–201.

18. Cited from Deborah E. Lipstadt, *Beyond Belief: The American Press and the Coming of the Holocaust*, New York: Free Press, 1988, p. 96.

19. Cited in Alfred A. Häsler, *The Lifeboat Is Full*, New York: Funk & Wagnalls, 1969, pp. 28–29. Emphasis added.

20. The figures are based on D. Gurevich (comp.), *Statistical Handbook of Jewish Palestine*, Jerusalem: The Jewish Agency, 1947, p. 116.

21. Gordon Thomas and Max M. Witts, *The Voyage of the Damned*, New York: Stein and Day, 1974.

22. The speech is cited, with deletions, in Lucy S. Dawidowicz, *A Holocaust Reader*, New York: Behrman House, 1976, pp. 132–134.

23. Lipstadt, *Beyond Belief*, p. 139, provided the classic example: the November 1941 deportation of Viennese Jews to an unknown destination, which was reported as a "mere" rumor.

24. The most extensive study of the American Jewish press is Haskel Lookstein, *Were We Our Brothers' Keepers?* New York: Hartmore House, 1985.

25. Cf. Leonard Dinnerstein, *America and the Survivors of the Holocaust*, New York: Columbia

University Press, 1982, pp. 1–8.

26. Andrew Sharf, *The British Press and the Jews Under Nazi Rule*, London: Oxford University Press, 1964.

27. Walter Laqueur, *The Terrible Secret: Suppression of the Truth About Hitler's Final Solution*, Boston: Little, Brown, 1980, pp. 84–86.

28. Ibid., pp. 64–66, 86.

29. Ibid., pp. 229–238. Karski's secret mission was not primarily about Jews, however, and although he (and other couriers) did pay much attention to the Nazi assault on Polish Jewry, the Polish government in exile watered down these reports in 1940 and 1941 to emphasize Poles' suffering under both Soviet and German occupation. Not until 1942 and 1943, when the London Poles realized they could capitalize on Jewish sympathy, did the murder of European Jewry become central to the Polish government's propaganda activities. Cf. David Engel, *In the Shadow of Auschwitz: The Polish Government-in-Exile and the Jews, 1939–1942*, Chapel Hill: University of North Carolina Press, 1987.

30. Walter Laqueur and Richard Breitman, *Breaking the Silence*, New York: Simon and Schuster, 1986.

31. Laqueur, *Terrible Secret*, p. 79.

32. David S. Wyman, *The Abandonment of the Jews: America and the Holocaust*, New York: Pantheon Books, 1984, pp. 42–55.

33. Ibid., pp. 74–76. The full text of the Allied declaration was published in *Zionist Review*, Dec. 24, 1942, 4–5.

34. The most recent survey of the issues involved in the proposed bombing of Auschwitz is Martin Gilbert, "The Question of Bombing Auschwitz," in Israel Gutman and Avital Saf (eds.), *The Nazi Concentration Camps: Structure and Aims, the Image of the Prisoner, the Jews in the Camps*, Jerusalem: Yad Vashem, 1984, pp. 417–473. It may be added that Auschwitz III (Monowitz, the synthetic-fuel factory using slave labor from the Auschwitz main camp) was bombed — as a military target — on August 20, 1944. Although only a few of the 125 USAAF aircraft strayed off the target, some actually dropped their bombs on Auschwitz I, to the glee of the inmates. Cf. *The Book of Alfred Kantor*, New York: McGraw-Hill, 1971, pp. 91–102.

35. Bernard Wasserstein, *Britain and the Jews of Europe, 1939–1945*, Oxford: Clarendon Press, 1979, pp. 297–298.

36. Cf. Bernard Wasserstein, "New Light on the Moyne Assassination," *Midstream*, vol. 26 # 3 (1980), 30–38.

37. Wasserstein, *Britain*, p. 252.

38. The question of Jewish rights was, for instance, debated at length in the *Polish Fortnightly Review*, Sept. 1, 1941. The debate took the entire issue.

39. Abraham J. Edelheit, "The Soviet Union, the Jews, and the Holocaust," *HSA*, vol. 4 (1990), 113–134.

40. Wyman, *Abandonment*, ch. 5.

41. Ibid., ch. 6.

42. A complete copy of the report is reprinted in Michael Mashberg (comp.), "Documents Concerning the American State Department and the Stateless European Jews, 1942–1944," *JSS*, vol. 39 # 1/2 (1977), 163–174.

43. Ibid., pp. 174–182.

44. Wyman, *Abandonment*, ch. 12–14.

45. Cf. Henry Feingold, "Who Shall Bear Guilt for the Holocaust? The Human Dilemma," *American Jewish History*, vol. 68 # 3 (1979), 261–282.

46. Marrus, *The Unwanted*, pp. 14–26.

47. Häsler, *Lifeboat*, pp. 33–35.

48. Ibid., pp. 84–90.

49. Ibid., p. 115.

50. Ibid., pp. 285–313.

51. See, for example, the documents cited in Steven Koblik, *The Stones Cry Out: Sweden's Response to the Persecution of the Jews, 1933–1945*, New York: Holocaust Library, 1988, pp. 167–180.

52. Ibid., pp. 181–182, 190–191.

53. Ibid., ch. 4.

54. Meir Dworzecki, "The International Red Cross and Its Policy vis-à-vis Jews in the Ghettos and Concentration Camps in Nazi-Occupied Europe," in I. Gutman and E. Zuroff (eds.), *Rescue Attempts During the Holocaust*, Jerusalem: Yad Vashem, 1977, pp. 71–110.

55. Edelheit, "Yishuv," ch. 6.

56. Ibid., ch. 10.

57. Cf. Dina Porat, *The Blue and Yellow Stars of David*, Cambridge: Harvard University Press, 1990, pt. 3; and Dalia Ofer, *Escaping the Holocaust*, New York: Oxford University Press, 1990, pt. 2.

58. Yehuda Bauer, "הצנחנים ותכנית ההתגוננות" (The paratroopers and the defense plan), *Yalkut Moreshet*, # 1 (1963), 86–94.

59. Wasserstein, *Britain*, pp. 346–349.

60. Porat, *Blue and Yellow*, ch. 14.

61. Cf. Geoffrey Alderman, *Modern British Jewry*, Oxford: Clarendon Press, 1992, pp. 301–304.

62. Wasserstein, *Britain*, p. 351.

63. Alderman, *Modern British Jewry*, p. 319. In August 1947 antagonism over the Palestine issue spilled over into anti-Jewish rioting in Britain's larger cities.

64. Cf. Henry Feingold, *The Politics of Rescue*, New Brunswick, NJ: Rutgers University Press, 1970, pp. 102–105.

65. No source for this quote has ever been found, although very similar sentiments were, apparently, quite common in the Yiddish-language press at the time. For the perceived Jewish defection to the Republicans as a factor in administration rescue politics, see Rafael Medoff, *The Deafening Silence*, New York: Shapolsky Books, 1987, pp. 173–181.

66. Herbert Parzen, "The Roosevelt Palestine Policy," *American Jewish Archives*, # 26 (1974), 31–65.

67. Zvi Ganin, *Truman, American Jewry, and Israel, 1945–1948*, New York: Holmes and Meier, 1979, ch. 1.

9

AFTERMATH AND RECOVERY

Effacing Nazi Atrocities

World War II, unleashed by Nazi Germany on September 1, 1939, with a ferocity unequalled in the annals of modern warfare, had rebounded against the Third Reich by 1944. The Reich reached its high point in summer 1942. In April 1943, German forces in North Africa surrendered. Soon, Sicily and Italy were invaded, Fascist leader Benito Mussolini was removed from the Italian government, Italy withdrew from the Axis, and the Italians surrendered on September 8, 1943. On the Eastern Front, initial Nazi gains were checked and turned back. In 1942 the Germans lost more than 300,000 men in the Battle of Stalingrad. At Kursk in the summer of 1943, a Wehrmacht attempt to regain the initiative failed after the world's largest tank battle. By January 1944, the Nazis had been pushed back and would soon be fighting on Polish, rather than Russian, soil. By August, the Red Army was almost at the gates of Warsaw, although the complete liberation of Poland was to take another five months. Simultaneously, the Anglo-American forces opened the so-called Second Front, invading France and bringing about the liberation of much of Western Europe. Despite some setbacks — such as the German counter-attack known popularly as the Battle of the Bulge — the Allied tide inexorably pushed on to Berlin and the final victory.

On May 5, 1945, U.S. and Soviet troops met near the German town of Torgau. Five days previously, the Soviets had completed the occupation of Berlin. Hitler, the madman who had set both the war and the Holocaust into motion, killed himself on April 30. Finally, on May 8, 1945, Admiral Karl Dönitz, named as Führer in Hitler's will, signed unconditional surrender papers. World War II was over in Europe.[1]

The hour of liberation, however, arrived too late for hundreds of thousands of the Nazis' victims. As Allied armies began the long trek to Berlin, the Nazis instituted a plan to efface all records of the crimes they had committed. Known by its code name, Aktion 1005, this operation entailed the exhumation and burning of the corpses of Jews murdered in the Soviet Union, Poland, and Yugoslavia. In its heyday, the Nazi killing machine left behind a wide swath of murder sites filled with machine-gunned Jews and, on occasion, other victims as well. Some of these pits contained thousands of corpses, some hundreds, and some only dozens. Aktion 1005 — which was mostly concerned with the larger killing sites — was overseen by a special commando of SS and SD, largely veterans of the Einsatzgruppen (who were responsible for the original murders), under the command of SS-Standartenführer Paul Blobel. Originally organized for the obliteration of the large mass of corpses specifically in the Chelmno death camp (Auschwitz and the other death camps had crematoria), Blobel established his headquarters in Lodz and developed a method of cremating the exhumed bodies on huge pyres. Deeming the initial undertaking successful, Aktion 1005 Sonderkommandos were then dispatched to Babi Yar, Ponary, the Ninth Fort (outside Kovno), Janowska (outside Lvov), Syret, Grabowka (outside Bialystok), Sajmište, as well as to the Einsatz Reinhard camps — among others. The actual exhumation and burning of the corpses was done by Jewish and, to a lesser degree, non-Jewish inmates. Most of the inmates were "recruited" from the Lublin-Janowska camp complex and were themselves killed when their horrible task was completed.

Aktion 1005 was marked by the Germans' systematic and methodical approach but was not fully successful for three reasons: First, some murder sites had already been liberated before a Sonderkommando could be sent to the area by the Aktion 1005 staff. Thus, the liberating forces came upon the murder site still intact. Second, Soviet military operations occasionally interfered with the Sonderkommando obliteration program, necessitating a quick German withdrawal from the murder site before the task could be completed. Third, stubborn efforts by the Leichenkommando — the official title given to Jewish inmates doing the actual work — to sabotage the operation had some impact in slowing down the destruction of evidence. Inmate escapes or other acts of physical resistance, therefore, guaranteed that Aktion 1005 operations were never wholly successful.[2] To counteract Jewish sabotage efforts, the SS pursued its long-held policy of repeatedly "pruning" the Leichenkommando, using Ukrainian or other native prisoners attached to a Sonderkommando. Although officially treated as inmates, these locals were selected as overseers and auxiliary guards because of their collaboration in the Nazi scheme, including in the disposal of the Jewish Leichenkommando after it was no longer needed. As a "reward" upon completion of the operation, most of them were sent to concentration camps or to labor battalions in Germany, some of them were discreetly disposed of, and a few were given the plot of land of the cleared murder site to live on.[3]

The Death Marches

Simultaneously, the Nazis acted to ensure that no living witnesses would fall into Allied hands. As the battlefronts approached the concentration camps, the SS liquidated the camps and forced the inmates on death marches deeper into the Third Reich. There were hardly any camps established on the territories of the Soviet Union; those camps that did exist were of extremely short duration, and most of the Jewish inmates were killed on the spot by Einsatzgruppen commandos. Most of the inmates of the Kauen (Kovno) concentration camp and its subcamps were dispatched to the Ninth Fort or to Ponary, where they were murdered outright; a smaller number of Jews who possessed trades still deemed important to the crumbling Nazi war machine were sent to KL Klooga (Estonia) or to the Latvian concentration camp at Kaiserwald.

Officially, the death marches began toward the end of 1944 and continued until May 8, 1945, the last day of the Third Reich. In reality, however, the SS already had begun to dismantle East European camps in the spring and summer of 1944. Although some 90 percent of the hundreds of camps that had existed in Poland — the *Juden Zwangsarbeitslager* — were, by then, long liquidated and most of their inmates shipped to death camps, the first target of the SS was the liquidation of the remaining labor camps in Poland. The only difference was in tactic: Whereas during 1942 and 1943 most of the Jews in the liquidated camps were slaughtered outright or sent to the death camps, in 1944 the Jewish inmates were spared outright killing and instead were driven in the direction of the Reich. Thousands of non-Jewish inmates who had taken the Jews' place in the SS slave labor empire, and who were housed in the camps emptied of Jews, especially in the aftermath of Operation Erntefest (November 1943), were also shipped to Germany but under slightly better conditions.

As the noose around the Reich became tighter and tighter, inmates by the thousands —

even within the Grossreich itself — were sent on forced marches in various directions: from Germany to the Czech Protectorate and Austria, from Pomerania to the Baltic coast, and — near the end — back into Germany.[4] Harassed without end, prisoners were forced to wander in circles, after days or weeks coming back from point A to point Z and vice versa. Chaos was the general rule; thousands of inmates died from exhaustion, diphtheria, typhus, and other diseases. Since no preparations had been made for their accommodations, many a camp commandant refused to accept the newcomers or even distribute a morsel of bread or a drop of water. Without supplies, starved for days and weeks on end, the already-high inmate death toll increased tenfold, especially during the winter of 1944–1945. Although the SS still tried to salvage something of its slave labor empire, silencing the voices that could lay bare Nazi crimes was the order of the day.[5]

Until the final minute (and, in a few cases, even beyond), thousands of inmates succumbed to the last acts of Nazi barbarity. Hundreds of lightly clad prisoners literally froze to death in open fields where they had been forced to stand overnight. Others were crowded into barns and incinerated when their SS guards lit fires — ostensibly to warm themselves — too close to the straw huts. Any prisoners trying to escape were shot, as were many other inmates lucky enough to live through the night but killed at the whim of their guards with sunrise. Long columns of inmates from different camps merged, separated, and then merged again; always, a corpse-strewn path of death appeared behind the marchers.

In those final hours, even the inmates sometimes succumbed to their baser instincts. Corpse stripping was not unusual and sometimes was undertaken while the unlucky victim was still alive. Additionally, cases of cannibalism — although rare — were reported. Finally, willy-nilly, the death marches came to an abrupt end. The SS guards, more and more restricted in the area they could run with their chattel, gave up one by one, abandoning their prisoners during the night or early in the morning, thus leaving the exhausted, frozen, and starving wretches to their own fate.[6] The long, Nazi-imposed nightmare came to an end.

Liberation: The Surviving Remnant

During the military operations that led to the final destruction of the Third Reich, Allied forces liberated many of the most notorious death factories as well as those slave labor and concentration camps that had not previously been liquidated. On July 24, 1944, the Red Army liberated the notorious Majdanek death camp, where 360,000 victims perished, the majority being Jews. In its wake, a number of lesser-known camps in central and southern Poland, some with only dozens or fewer survivors, were also liberated. Lublin, Lvov, Bialystok, and Dvinsk, among other localities, were also liberated during this period. A sad few Jews in hiding ventured out in the open for the first time in years. By the beginning of the final Soviet offensive (January 1945), aside from the Hasag complex of slave labor camps in Częstochowa, only three major camps were still under Nazi control east of the Oder River: Auschwitz, Plaszow, and Stutthof. The Hasag (Hugo Schneider Aktiengesellschaft) camp complex was liquidated by hastily retreating SS personnel on January 16, 1945, with some of the inmates taken on a death march. The rest, 3,758 Jews, were freed by the Soviets when they liberated the four camps the next day, January 17. The final liquidation of Plaszow came on January 14, 1945, with all remaining inmates being transported to Auschwitz, only to become, on January 17, part of some 66,000 prisoners driven on foot away from the fast-approaching Red Army. In Auschwitz, only 7,650 inmates — considered by the SS to be breathing their last breath — were left behind.[7] Early, on January 27, 1945, the last of the SS personnel disappeared; by mid-afternoon Soviet troops had arrived and secured the camp. Within a week of liberation only 2,000 of the liberated inmates were still alive.[8] The same pattern was replayed at Stutthof. On

Survivor explaining the crematoria at Buchenwald to an American soldier
Courtesy of the Fred R. Crawford Witness to the Holocaust Project, Emory University

January 21, 1945, 6,000 to 7,000 Jews from Stutthof *Nebenlager* were taken on a death march, driven into the Baltic Sea at Palmnicken, and machine-gunned to death. On January 25, because of rumors of the imminent arrival of Soviet forces, 50,000 inmates, mostly Jewish women previously evacuated from Auschwitz and the Baltics, were taken on a death march; at least 30,000 perished. The final evacuation of Stutthof, however, came three months later, on April 25: Close to 5,000 sick and starving prisoners were marched in no particular direction. Stutthof was first liberated on May 1, 1945, by Soviet forces who found 120 very ill, barely alive, walking skeletons.[9] This pattern was repeated when Gross-Rosen (May 8), Sachsenhausen (April 27), and Ravensbrück (April 29) were liberated by the Red Army. Very few of those liberated had the physical strength to survive.[10]

The first camp liberated by the Western Allies and identified as such was Natzweiler-Struthof (in Alsace). A small number of transit camps in France and Holland had been liberated during the summer and autumn of 1944, but — since they were empty — they had not been identified as concentration camps. Natzweiler, in contrast, was liberated by Free French Forces and was identified as a slave-labor camp where brutal medical experiments had also been carried out. When liberated, however, the camp was empty.[11] Even so, the camp with its camp hospital (revir), gas chamber, and crematoria gave Allied troops and Western journalists a foretaste of what they would shortly uncover. It was to Natzweiler where Professor August Hirt, director of the Anatomical Institute at Strasbourg, had had seventy-three Jewish men and thirty Jewish women transferred from Auschwitz. After gassing them and stripping them of all flesh, Professor Hirt used the skeletons as a collection of Jewish types and characteristics with which to study race theory.[12]

On April 4, 1945, armored cavalry units of the U.S. 4th Armored Division discovered Ohrdruf, a small camp near Gotha. U.S. troops were unprepared for what they found. "Cadaverous refugees" was the term used by the American Jewish journalist Meyer Levin, who accompanied the 4th Armored Division. Levin reported that the survivors — the few survivors — were "skeletal, with feverish sunken eyes, shaven skulls."[13] Eight days later the commanders of the U.S. XX Corps invited Generals Dwight D. Eisenhower, George S. Patton, and Omar N. Bradley — the three most senior U.S. commanders — to visit Ohrdruf. All three generals were visibly shaken by the experience; Patton, despite his nickname "old blood and guts," became physically ill.[14]

Similar scenes were replayed at every camp liberated by American and British troops: Buchenwald, freed by men of the 9th Infantry Division on April 11, 1945; Nordhausen, freed by men of the 104th Infantry ("Timberwolves") and 3rd Armored ("Spearhead") Divisions, also on April 11; Dachau, freed by the 42nd and 45th Infantry Divisions on April 29; Woeblin, freed by the 82nd Airborne ("All Americans") Division on May 2; Gunskirchen, freed by the 71st Infantry Division on May 4; Mauthausen and Ebensee, freed by the 11th Armored Division on May 5 and 6, 1945.[15] In each camp a relatively small number of survivors were discovered among a virtual sea of corpses. American and British troops reacted with horror. In almost every case, the liberators forced local Germans to view the sites where the Nazi government had committed crimes in the name of the German people. Now, when brought under Military Police escort to the liberated camps, most expressed horror; a few even shed some tears. Previously, the daily march of sick looking

Generals Eisenhower, Patton, and Bradley view the corpses of Nazi victims at Ohrdruf
Courtesy of the Fred R. Crawford Witness to the Holocaust Project, Emory University

columns of pajama-clad inmates on their way to or from backbreaking labor had never elicited a response; local civilians never questioned the foul smell that polluted the otherwise crystal-clear country air; German civilians living in proximity to the now-liberated camps professed ignorance as to what was going on in those evil places, claiming to have seen nothing, heard nothing, and known nothing.[16] This time, at least, the innocence-professing gentry, including the SS, their helpers, and some of the apprehended murderers themselves were forced to bury the thousands of corpses strewn throughout the camp precinct and inside the filthy and epidemic-infested barracks.

The same condition held true in Bergen-Belsen, liberated by the men of the 63rd Anti-Tank Regiment of the Royal Artillery on April 15, 1945.[17] During their first ten days in Belsen, the British buried thousands of the dead, but despite heroic efforts by medical personnel, they could not prevent a mass outbreak of typhus. Between April 19 and May 5, close to 11,000 of the 60,985 inmates liberated at Belsen died of typhus. Although the epidemic was finally brought under control, in early June the old camp was burned as an emergency measure by the British.[18] Hundreds of less-notorious camps, still accounting for tens of thousands

Dachau: U.S. troops patrolling the newly liberated camp's perimeter
Courtesy of the Fred R. Crawford Witness to the Holocaust Project, Emory University

"Dead SS bastards from the concentration camp Dachau"
Courtesy of the Fred R. Crawford Witness to the Holocaust Project, Emory University

of victims of all nationalities, races, and religions, were also liberated by Allied forces just before the total collapse of Nazism.

The survivors — estimated at between 60,000 and 100,000 — made survival their first priority, followed by communal rehabilitation, education, and preparation for emigration. This *she'erit ha-pleta* (surviving remnant) may be divided into two groups: those originating from Western Europe and those from Eastern Europe. By and large, the West European Jewish survivors were willing to return to their countries of origin and, despite some initial difficulties, successfully reorganized their communities. This was most particularly true in France, Belgium, and Holland, despite the difficult problem of Jewish war orphans in the latter country.[19]

Conditions in Eastern Europe were much less conducive to returning and resulted in the re-creation of only temporary communities. Before the Nazi onslaught, Poland had the largest Jewish community in Europe. At least 90 percent of Polish Jewry was decimated, and with it hundreds of communities were wiped out permanently. To be sure, a significant Polish-Jewish element — especially those returning from the Soviet Union — sought the renewal of Jewish life in Poland. The environment, however, was not conducive for success. In 1944 *Narod* (The populist), the organ of the Polish Christian Socialist Party, published an editorial that declared: "The Jewish problem must be resolved through the gradual emigration of those Jews who after the German extermination policy still remain alive."[20] The *Narod* editorial eschewed antisemitic violence, opting for the peaceful and gradual relocation of Jewish survivors, preferably to Palestine. Other Polish nationalist groups were neither as discreet nor as tactful as the Christian Socialists. Between November 1944 and October 1945, at least 351 Jews were murdered by anti-Communist partisans in Poland. At the time there were fewer than 80,000 Jews living in Poland — in addition to approximately 175,000 Polish Jews then in the Soviet Union.[21]

Postwar Polish antisemitism reached its height on July 4, 1946. A blood libel after the disappearance of a Christian child led to a pogrom in the city of Kielce. In the resulting attack on the Jewish community building, forty-two Jews were murdered. The list of participants was significant: In addition to a Catholic clergyman and numerous peasants, participants included factory workers, a foreman, and a number of police officials and internal security agents. The ostensible Socialist credentials of the latter have led to claims that the entire event was staged by Communists in order to discredit the non-Communist Poles.[22] Whether or not that hypothesis is correct, Jews left Poland in the thousands subconsciously fulfilling the Polish nationalists' desires and, initially inadvertently, playing a crucial role in the struggle to create a Jewish state in Palestine.

The small remnant of Polish Jewry was faced with a double dilemma: It was hard enough to stay in blood-soaked Poland where each step Jews took reminded them of Polish Jewry's great losses, and wherever they stepped, they encountered a cemetery. It was harder still to conceive that after surviving the Holocaust they would be hunted again for the simple reason that they had dared to survive. The years of Nazi occupation of Poland, which had brought pain, humiliation, and suffering for the Polish masses seem to have done little to change their attitude toward Jews. Antisemitism, which should logically have ceased with the demise of Nazi Germany, was instead advocated overtly or covertly by a majority of Poles. Thus, the same Polish Primate, August Cardinal Hlond, who had urged an anti-Jewish boycott in a pastoral letter of 1937, now blamed the Jewish victims themselves for the Kielce pogrom and other subsequent outrages. In the cardinal's eyes, Jews remained too pushy, trying to dominate Poland; they had learned nothing from the past.[23]

Conditions in Hungary, Romania, and Bulgaria were similar to those in Poland: The rise of Communist regimes in all three countries complicated the already difficult process of communal rehabilitation. In Hungary, the first postwar regime supported Jewish efforts to rebuild, even permitting intensive Zionist activity. After 1948, however, as the Communists increasingly began to dominate Hungarian politics, conditions changed for the worst. In particular, Communist decrees on the nationalization of schools and an increasing pace of government limitation of religious institutions' autonomy — although not directly structured toward Jews — had the effect of severely diminishing the status and thus the security of the organized Jewish community. Furthermore, antisemitism did not diminish in postwar Hungary; agitation against Jews merely shifted from the upper and upper-middle classes (which had largely supported the quasi-Fascist regimes during the Horthy era) to the peasants, who vented their opposition to government policies by verbal, and sometimes physical, assaults on Jews.[24] Emigration was only briefly an option: Approximately 18,000 Jews left Hungary for Palestine before emigration was virtually halted in 1949. The halt on emigration coincided with the forced dissolution of the Hungarian Zionist Federation and the first arrests of Zionist leaders (for having organized illegal emigration) in May 1949.[25]

On the surface, conditions in Romania seemed the same as those in Hungary. This situation manifested itself more clearly once the Communists had completed their takeover on December 30, 1947.[26] In reality, however, conditions for Romanian Jewry differed significantly in one area as compared to Hungary. The difference was emigration: Although the Romanian Communist regime also severely limited the autonomous sphere of the Jewish community, emigration — including *aliya* — continued until the mid-1950s.[27] Thus, although antisemitism persisted in all strata of postwar Romania, emigration totaled nearly 100,000 Jews. That figure included 29,000 Jews who emigrated, both legally and illegally, to Palestine/Israel.[28] More significant, evidence suggests that the Romanian Communists knew about and supported intense Zionist efforts at Aliya Bet; this effort was concentrated at the Romanian port of Constantsa in addition to Varna (Bulgaria) and southern Italy.[29]

The Bulgarian Jewish experience was much the same, although antisemitism in Bulgaria was much more muted than in Hungary or Roma-nia. The Bulgarian government was only too willing to permit Jews to emigrate — a reality that became clear during David Ben-Gurion's December 1944 visit.[30] Once the war ended, Bulgaria's Black Sea port of Varna became a main focus for Aliya Bet activities. Finally, the Bulgarian Communists did not ban emigration until 1951 — when most Bulgarian Jews had already left.[31]

Briha, Aliya Bet, and the Revolt

As a result of these conditions, a stream of Jews left the blood-soaked soil of Eastern Europe, attempting to reach the safety offered by the Jewish national home. The Jewish survivors thus began a spontaneous flight, dubbed Briha and initially led by former partisan leaders, including Abba Kovner and Yizhak (Antek) Zuckerman. Later, Briha was organized and made systematic and organized with the help of *shelichim* (emissaries) from the Yishuv. Briha operated along two major routes: from Lodz west to Poznan and Szczecin, thence to the American or British zones in Germany; and from Lodz south to Katowice or Krakow through Czechoslovakia, Hungary, or Austria to either Italy or Yugoslavia. A smaller proportion of the potential émigrés ended up in the Black Sea ports of Varna (Bulgaria) or Constantsa (Romania). Groups ending up in Italy were, in 1945 and the first half of 1946, escorted in part by members of the Jewish Brigade for Palestine, a Jewish unit of the Royal Army. Simultaneous with Briha, thousands of liberated Jewish concentration camp survivors in Germany and Austria were also moved with the help of the Jewish Brigade. Taken from their miserable camp environment in small groups and temporarily housed in refugee shelters nearer the Italian border, they were secretly integrated into large transports of Italian prisoners of war returning from the Soviet Union; once in Italy, they were gradually transported (again, with the help of the Jewish Brigade) to the south to await transportation to Palestine.[32]

Briha proved that the survivors had not lost their spirit, despite their sufferings. The movement of so many Jews with one goal on their minds also placed the Palestine issue into a new perspective. With war's end, Zionists demanded a revision of the White Paper policy but the Labour Party government of Clement Atlee and Ernest Bevin refused to consider any changes. In August, 1945 the Twenty-Second World Zionist Congress called for the immediate admission of 100,000 Jewish refugees to Eretz-Israel. When the British refused, a revolt was begun by all four of Palestine's Jewish undergrounds: the Hagana, Palmah, Irgun Zva'i Leumi (IZL, the National Military Organization), and Lohame Herut Israel (LEHI, the Fighters for Israel's Freedom, also known as the "Stern Gang"). Each of the undergrounds approached operations in a different way. IZL and LEHI, in particular, emphasized urban guerrilla operations (earning them the British appellation of terrorists) and highly publicized attacks on targets important to the British Palestine administration. Perhaps the most famous such operation was the bombing of the King David Hotel in Jerusalem, an operation carried out by IZL on July 22, 1946, and justified by the fact that the hotel was used as the headquarters for the British administration.[33]

For various reasons, the Hagana and Palmah eschewed such tactics, concentrating on *ha'apala* ("illegal" immigration; lit. "striving") and on attempting to publicize the plight of refugees in order to gain universal support for Jewish aspirations. Despite the different approaches and the fact that the underground movements often clashed (sometimes violently) amongst themselves over strategy and tactics, their cumulative efforts eventually brought sufficient pressure to bear on the British to force them to relinquish their mandate and to quit the country.[34]

Briha and *ha'apala* were especially important weapons in the struggle, for although the British could probably defeat the Jewish insurgents, there was no weapon in their arsenal powerful enough to defeat the moral weapon wielded by the *ma'apilim* (immigrants; lit. "strivers") as they defied the might of the British Royal Navy, Air Force, and Army. The *aliya* war began in September 1945 and was primarily undertaken by the Mossad le-Aliya Bet. In all, sixty ships ran the blockade between 1945 and the establishment of the State of Israel on May 14, 1948. On May 13, 1946, two additional ships — the *Eliahu Golomb* and the *Dov Hoz* — were impounded by Italian police authorities while still in port in La Spezia, at the instigation of the British secret service. In the aftermath of the incident, for which Britain was resoundingly condemned, the Palestine Mandatory government was forced to allow the La Spezia internees into Palestine legally.[35]

Of those ships that ran the blockade, only a few succeeded in reaching the coast. Most ships

Two scenes from an anti-British protest by Holocaust survivors in Milan, Italy, in 1946
Authors' Collection

were caught by the Royal Navy, after having been spotted and identified by Royal Air Force patrols. At first, the *ma'apilim* thus captured were kept in the Atlit prison, but in the summer of 1946 a new policy, of deportation to Cyprus, was instituted. This policy had little effect on Mossad operations. Although headquartered in France, the Mossad was run in a decentralized fashion, with agents operating principally at ports in France, Italy, Yugoslavia, Romania, and Bulgaria.[36] Three ships sailed from other ports: *Ha-Hayal ha-Ivri* (the Jewish Soldier) sailed from Belgium, *Chaim Arlosoroff* from Sweden, and *Shivat Zion* (Return to Zion) from Algeria.

These ships proved to be the Zionists' crucial weapon. Whenever a ship set sail, Mossad agents alerted the foreign press, giving all pertinent details. Although such information might have been useful to the British, the agents realized that maximum publicity on the plight of the *ma'apilim* was their only weapon. In any case, the Mossad agents were not giving the British any information they could not easily obtain from other sources. Indeed, the British were able to infiltrate agents on to a number of blockade runners.[37] Try as they might, however, there was one thing the British could not do — break the spirit of the *ma'apilim* or their escorts from the Hagana and Palmah.

In July 1947 the Mossad planned its most ambitious operation, timed to coincide with the arrival of the United Nations Special Committee on Palestine in Eretz-Israel. A river excursion liner, the *President Warfield*, was loaded with more than 4,500 refugees and set sail from Marseilles, France. The ship was soon renamed *Exodus 1947*. Captured after a brief but sharp fight in which three *ma'apilim* were killed, the *Exodus* was transported to Haifa. Although recognizing that adverse publicity would hurt Britain's chances of retaining the Mandate, the Palestine administration decided to alter standard policy and did not deport the *Exodus* to Cyprus. Instead, the *ma'apilim* were transferred to three deportation ships, which set

sail to return the refugees to France. In Marseilles, however, the French government refused to permit the disembarking of passengers against their will. Since the *ma'apilim* refused to disembark and began a hunger strike in protest of their deportation, a standoff ensued.

At this point the British blindly pursued their course to its logical end. Unwilling to let the *Exodus* passengers enter Palestine and unable to disembark them in France, His Majesty's Government decided to make them into an example that, it was hoped, would destroy the Mossad for good. In early September, the British cabinet unanimously decided to disembark the *Exodus* passengers in Germany, by force if necessary. This decree was carried out, in full public view, on September 8, 1947. Still, the passengers refused to disembark. British Military Police were obliged to apply coercive measures — including the use of tear gas — to force the refugees off the deportation ships and onto the blood-soaked soil of Hamburg. The *Exodus* affair was thus a pyrrhic victory. British arms had proved that they could force a group of unarmed Jews to do whatever the government pleased; in doing so they lost all claim to morality, and only a few months later the United Nations would strip Great Britain of the Mandate altogether. The weapon of morality won a victory for perhaps the first time in history.[38]

Exile in Cyprus

In the summer of 1946 the British government had opted to return to a policy of deportation of *ma'apilim*, in this case to the crown colony of Cyprus. In this way the British hoped to stem the tide of *ha'apala*, while maintaining control over Palestine's coastal waters and also appearing to behave "properly" in response to civil resistance. The appearance of propriety was important to the Labour government, for at the same time this decision was taken, a concerted effort to co-opt the U.S. administration was also being undertaken.[39] Thus, the British proposed that a joint Anglo-American Committee of Inquiry be established to investigate the various claims and counter-claims over Palestine. The British hoped that the committee would support the continuation of British rule and, especially, the continuation of White Paper restrictions on immigration. This goal became impossible when the committee reported its findings and accepted, in a modified form, the Zionist demand for the admission of 100,000 Jews to Palestine.[40] Foreign Minister Bevin countered by linking any further Jewish immigration to a surrender of the Jewish insurgent forces, thus nullifying the report and leaving no further room for a negotiated settlement. The British also attempted an amateurish counterpropaganda campaign, trying to prove that the Mossad men were terrorists who coerced Jewish refugees into undertaking the dangerous trip to Palestine rather than returning to their real homes in Eastern Europe. The evidence gathered by the Anglo-American committee and the wide reportage by press sources put an end to these lies and reinforced the perception of British apathy to the fate of Holocaust survivors.[41]

In the end, what was left was the rather sad spectacle of British soldiers forcibly removing *ma'apilim* and then shipping them off in boats that were little better that the ones in which they arrived, to concentration camps in Cyprus. To be sure, these camps were not the Nazi camps liberated by the Allied armies in 1945; nevertheless, they were concentration camps and the very idea behind the deportations created adverse publicity for the British. Had Joseph Goebbels, the Nazi propaganda minister, not committed suicide in the Hitler bunker on April 30, 1945, and been imprisoned instead, he might well have scored a propaganda victory like the one gained after the Evian Conference fiasco.

For the *ma'apilim*, exile on Cyprus had one small compensation. From Cyprus, after a period of detention, one could immigrate to Eretz-Israel legally. As a goodwill gesture, the British government agreed in October 1946 to resume granting up to 1,500 immigrant certificates per month, with some of

those certificates to be automatically set aside for internees.[42]

Externally, the camps were run by the Royal Army; theoretically, the army also supervised the internal running of the camps. To prevent escapes Royal Army patrols guarded the perimeters of the camps, which were surrounded by barbed wire fences mounted with search towers. Internally, however, the camps were run autonomously, with a Central Committee established to administer daily affairs. The Central Committee acted in concert with appointed representatives of American Jewish philanthropic agencies, primarily the American Jewish Joint Distribution Committee (JDC), and with *shelichim* (emissaries) from Eretz-Israel.[43] Most of the latter were members of the Hagana, the Mossad, or both. To help rehabilitate the detainees and to prepare them for their new lives in Eretz-Israel special classes were established in displaced persons' camps throughout Europe, and the Organization for Rehabilitation and Training (ORT), with the help of the JDC, established vocational training schools.

It is perhaps surprising that there were so few escape attempts from the Cyprus camps. Because of the dangers involved in any escape attempt, mass escapes were especially discouraged, although in one case a tunnel was dug through which some 300 *ma'apilim* escaped.[44] Individual escapes, however, were encouraged by the Mossad because they were simpler and less dangerous. Approximately 8,500 *ma'apilim* were even spirited away through the use of forged documents, a program called Aliya Dalet.[45]

Escape was one aspect of the Cyprus exile; there was another: In one case the Zionists actually brought two ships directly to Cyprus. These two ships, the Mossad's largest, were the *Pan York* (*Azmaut*) and *Pan Crescent* (*Kibbutz Galuyot*). Between them they carried 15,239 *ma'apilim*. Hoping to reduce potential casualties, in case of resistance when the British boarded the ships, the Mossad agreed to sail them directly to Cyprus. If this was a defeat, it was only a minor one, for in the end these two ships, along with the *Exodus 1947*, were to be the straws that broke the back of Britain's rule in Palestine.[46]

Political demonstrations were also a staple of detainee life in Cyprus. The *ma'apilim* refused to be cowed by the British and exercised their right to protest their plight on every occasion possible. Protests were primarily comprised of demonstrations, which sometimes became violent, and on one occasion a hunger strike. These demonstrations were given wide coverage in the press — when possible — and the invariable British overreaction to demonstrations was yet another weapon in the Zionist cause. Thus, if the Cyprus episode proved anything, it was the bankruptcy of the British government in attempting to prevent Jewish refugees from freely immigrating to a country that — according to internationally recognized agreements signed by His Majesty's Government — was theirs by right.[47]

From Holocaust to Rebirth

Although it is necessary to be wary of an argument of *post hoc, ergo propter hoc* the linkage between the Holocaust and the State of Israel is clear on the most simple, chronological level: The horrifying events in Europe preceded the new redemption and the creation of the third Jewish commonwealth. On the causal level as well the line between the Holocaust and the re-creation of Jewish statehood is clear. To be sure, Zionist activities stretching back to the 1880s had placed the Jewish national home on a sound footing. As a result, the eventual emergence of a Jewish state was almost inevitable. Yet, the unprecedented nature of Jewish suffering during the Holocaust considerably speeded up the process that led to Israel's independence and the Jewish emergence from powerlessness.

Most Zionist leaders, after all, consciously eschewed the use of specific terminology relating to long-range goals. Indeed, in 1933 the Eighteenth World Zionist Congress had rejected a resolution calling for the creation of a Jewish state, proposed by Jabotinsky. Only a minority of Zionists considered statehood to be an immediately achievable goal as late as 1936 and 1937, when the British Peel Commission proposed partition as the only solution to the Palestine impasse.[48] As a result of the British White Paper of 1939 and the failure of Zionist diplomacy, however, the majority of Zionists reversed themselves and approved the statehood resolution passed by the Extraordinary Zionist Conference held at the Biltmore Hotel on May 10 and 11, 1942. Unconfirmed rumors regarding the persecution of European Jewry made clear to those assembled that European Jewry was in the throes of a great catastrophe. Thus, Article 2 of the resolution offered "a message of hope and encouragement to [our] fellow Jews in the ghettos and Concentration Camps of Hitler-dominated Europe, and our prayers that their hour of liberation may not be far distant." The resolution further offered warm greetings to Jewish fighting men and women and sent a proposal of peace and goodwill to the Arabs. Yet the conclusion of the resolution was unambiguous: "The conference declares that the new world order that will follow victory cannot be established on foundations of peace, justice, and equality unless the problem of Jewish homelessness is finally solved." Consequently, the resolution urged "that Palestine be established as a Jewish commonwealth integrated into the structure of the new democratic world."[49]

In 1945 Zionists redoubled their efforts to rescue the remnant. The tragic realization that Jewish suffering could have been prevented played a major role in Zionists efforts to convince the world of the justice of the Jewish cause. This was especially true in the clear change in American Jewish attitudes: Although most American Jewish organizations had been non- or even anti-Zionist until the Nazi era, only a small minority retained non- or anti-Zionist attitudes after 1945.[50] The experience of the American Jewish Committee is indicative. In 1943 the committee withdrew from the American Jewish Conference because of the latter's approval of the Biltmore Resolution. By 1946, however, the committee had revised its position and strongly supported the creation of the State of Israel.[51]

The impact of the Holocaust on the UN decision to create the State of Israel is equally clear. It is true that the major powers — the United States, the Soviet Union, and France — supported the Zionists, not for idealistic reasons, but for considerations of foreign policy. Still, some UN General Assembly members — especially the South American states — made their decision to vote for partition on an emotional basis: They felt guilty about the lack of timely action on behalf of Jewish refugees during the 1930s and 1940s. In some cases, they still hoped to steer Jewish refugees from their countries to the Middle East. Other states without strategic interests in the Middle East — South Africa, for instance — also made their decision on a moral basis. In their accounting of the pros and cons of Jewish statehood, the Holocaust played a special role. Ultimately the immediate historical background to the UN decision proved decisive.[52]

With the creation of the State of Israel, the Jewish world entered a new era. Whereas Jews had been objects of history, tempest-tossed by events they could not control, for 2,000 years, the Jewish state had now become a subject of history. Jews assumed responsibility for their future as well as for the preservation of the memory of the past. Nevertheless, even fifty years later, the full implications of the Holocaust can only tentatively be gauged.

Members of the staff of the World Jewish Congress, held in Montreaux, Switzerland, in June 1948
Authors' Collection

Notes

1. Peter Calvocoressi and Guy Wint, *Total War: The Story of World War II*, 1st ed., New York: Pantheon Books, 1972, pt. 5.

2. For the memoir of a member of the Jewish Leichenkommando, see Leon W. Wells, *The Death Brigade*, New York: Holocaust Library, 1978, pt. 5.

3. Shmuel Spector, "מבצע 1005' לטשטוש רצח המיליונים במלחמת-העולם השנייה'" (Aktion 1005: Effacing the murder of millions during World War II), *Yahadut Zemanenu*, vol. 4 (1987), 207–225.

4. Yehuda Bauer, "The Death Marches, January–May 1945," *Modern Judaism*, vol. 3 # 1 (1983), 1–21.

5. For an eyewitness testimony by a survivor of the death marches, see Hershel Edelheit, "Journal from a Lost World."

6. Ibid.

7. Jon Bridgman, *The End of the Holocaust: The Liberation of the Camps*, Portland, OR: Areopagitica Press, 1990, p. 24.

8. Ibid., pp. 25–26.

9. Ibid., pp. 27–28.

10. Ibid., pp. 28–29.

11. Robert H. Abzug, *Inside the Vicious Heart*, New York: Oxford University Press, 1985, ch. 1.

12. Hirt's experiments were reviewed in Philippe Aziz, *Doctors of Doom*, Geneva: Fermi Publishers, 1976, vol. 3, pp. 214–250.

13. Abzug, *Vicious Heart*, p. 21.

14. Ibid., p. 27.

15. In addition to the already-cited works by Abzug and Bridgman, see Brewster Chamberlain (ed), *The Liberation of the Nazi Concentration Camps*, Washington, DC: United States Holocaust Memorial Council, 1987, pp. 69–81.

16. Cf. Gordon J. Horwitz, *In the Shadow of Death*, New York: Free Press, 1990, ch. 2, 8.

17. Bridgman, *End of the Holocaust*, p. 49.

18. Ibid., p. 55.

19. On France and Holland, see David Weinberg, "The Reconstruction of the French Jewish Community after World War II," and Joseph Michman, "The Problem of Jewish War Orphans in Holland," in Israel Gutman and Avital Saf (eds.), *She'erit Hapletah, 1944–1948: Rehabilitation and Political Struggle*, Jerusalem: Yad Vashem, 1990, respectively, pp. 168–186, and 187–209.

20. Cited in Lucjan Dobroszycki, "The Jewish Community in Poland, 1944– 1947: A Discussion of Postwar Restitution," in Gutman and Saf, *She'erit Hapletah*, p. 5.

21. The figures are cited from Yehuda Bauer, *The Jewish Emergence from Powerlessness*, Toronto: University of Toronto Press, 1979, pp. 64–65.

22. Ibid. Cf. Michael Checinski, *Poland: Communism, Nationalism, Antisemitism*, New York: Karz-Cohl, 1982.

23. Israel Gutman, *היהודים בפולין אחרי מלחמת העולם השנייה* (The Jews of Poland after World War II), Jerusalem: Merkaz Zalman Shazar, 1985, ch. 2, 6.

24. Nathaniel Katzburg, "Between Liberation and Revolution: Hungarian Jewry, 1945–1948," in Gutman and Saf, *She'erit Hapletah*, pp. 123–137.

25. Ibid., pp. 138–141. Small numbers of Jews managed to filter out of Hungary throughout the 1950s, especially after the 1956 Hungarian Uprising.

26. On the Communist takeover in Romania, see Hugh Seton-Watson, *The East European Revolution*, 3rd ed., London: Methuen, 1961, pp. 202–211.

27. Katzburg, "Liberation and Revolution," p. 141.

28. Jean Ancel, "*She'erit Hapletah* in Romania During the Transition Period to a Communist Regime, August 1944–December 1947," in Gutman and Saf, *She'erit Hapletah*, pp. 160–161.

29. On Romania, see ibid. On Bulgaria and Italy, see Zeev (Venia) Hadari, *1945–1948* פליטים *מנצחים אימפריה: פרשיות עליה ב'* (Refugees defeat an Empire: Chapters in the history of Aliya Bet, 1945–1948), Beersheba: Ben-Gurion University of the Negev Press, 1985, pp. 187–192, 210–225.

30. Tuvia Friling, "Meeting the Survivors: Ben-Gurion's Visit to Bulgaria, December 1944," *Studies in Zionism*, vol. 10 # 2 (1989), 175–195.

31. Cf. Antony Lerman (ed.), *The Jewish Communities of the World: A Contemporary Guide*, 4th ed., New York: Facts on File, 1989, p. 23.

32. Edelheit, "Journal," provided a graphic description of this movement.

33. On the attack per se, see Thurston Clarke, *By Blood and Fire*, New York: Putnam, 1981. An incisive analysis of British failure to suppress the revolt, which unfortunately makes no refernce to aliya bet, is contained in Bruce Hoffman, *The Failure of British Military Strategy Within Palestine, 1939–1947*, Ramat Gan: Bar-Ilan University Press, 1983.

34. Cf. Shimon Golan, *מרות ומאבק בימי מרי* (Allegiance amidst struggle), Tel Aviv: Yad Tabenkin Press, 1988, pp. 315–348.

35. Hadari, פליטים, pp. 226–232.

36. Ibid., pp. 61–69.

37. Cf. Ze'ev (Venia) Hadari and Ze'ev Tzahor, *Voyage to Freedom: An Episode in the Illegal Immigration to Palestine*, London: Vallentine, Mitchell, 1985, p. 115.

38. Aviva Halamish, *אקסודוס — הסיפור האמיתי* (Exodus: The true story), Tel Aviv: Am Oved, 1990.

39. Cf. Miriam J. Haron, "United States-British Collaboration on Illegal Immigration to Palestine, 1945–1947," *JSS*, vol. 42 # 2 (1980), 177–182.

40. J. C. Hurwitz, *The Struggle for Palestine*, New York: Norton, 1950, ch. 15.

41. Arieh J. Kochavi, "The Displaced Persons' Problem and the Formulation of British Policy in Palestine," *Studies in Zionism*, vol. 10 # 1 (1989), 31–48.

42. Michael J. Cohen, *Palestine and the Great Powers, 1945–1948*, Princeton: Princeton University Press, 1982, p. 160.

43. Morris Laub, *Last Barrier to Freedom*, Berkeley, CA: Judah L. Magnes Memorial Museum, 1985, passim.

44. Ibid., pp. 31–32.

45. Hadari, פליטים, pp. 346–348.

46. Ibid., pp. 195–209.

47. Laub, *Last Barrier*, pp. 47–51.

48. Abraham J. Edelheit, "The Yishuv in the Shadow of the Holocaust: Palestine Jewry and the Emerging Nazi Threat, 1933-1939," Ph.D. dissertation: City University of New York, 1992, ch. 6.

49. "The Biltmore Resolution," cited in Walter Laqueur (ed.), *The Israel-Arab Reader*, 2d ed., New York: Bantam Books, 1971, pp. 77–79.

50. Nahum Goldmann, "The Influence of the Holocaust on the Change in Attitude of World Jewry to Zionism and the State of Israel," in *Holocaust and Rebirth: A Symposium*, Jerusalem: Yad Vashem, 1973, pp. 77–103.

51. Naomi W. Cohen, *Not Free to Desist: The American Jewish Committee, 1906–1966*, Philadelphia: JPS, 1972, ch. 11–12.

52. David Horowitz, "The Holocaust as Background for the Decision of the United Nations to Establish a Jewish State," in *Holocaust and Rebirth*, pp. 141–158.

PART 2

DICTIONARY OF HOLOCAUST TERMS

One of the milk cans used to hide the *Oneg Shabbat* archive
Courtesy of the U.S. Holocaust Memorial Museum

A

A: Abbreviation for Arbeitsjude. > see: **Arbeitsjude(n)**.

A dalis [דאליס א, Y/H] "Letter D": Jewish work-gang term warning that a German was approaching. The term originates from the abbreviation of *deutscher* and thus meant "a German is coming."

A kop [קאָפ א, Y] "Per head": A Yiddish term for the fifty to one hundred Polish zloty per person ransom money one had to pay to the Jewish ghetto police of Warsaw (and some other large ghettos) during the first period of deportations in order to save him/herself or members of their families — in most cases a futile attempt — sometimes only for hours.

A sho gelebt iz oichet gelebt [א שעה געלעבט איז אויכעט געלעבט, Y] "To have lived even an hour means also to have lived an entire lifetime": A Yiddish phrase used by Jews incarcerated in ghettos, even in the so-called open ghettos in smaller East European towns, and in camps to signal their defiance of an almost-inevitable death. In practice, the philosophy thereby formulated was to maximize meaningful existence for as long as possible. Thus, for example, if individuals or a family could secure a chicken, piece of meat, or any other "luxury," they would consume it as soon as possible, even late at night or early in the morning, rather than save it.

Ablösung [G] "Firing": Nazi term for the discharge of Jewish employers (following the confiscation of Jewish-owned enterprises). After the Nazi occupation of Poland in September 1939, *Ablösung*, to a large extent, also applied to Polish employers. Through semi-legal maneuvering, at least within the Grossreich, the expropriating of the owner's property went with it. > see also: **Arisierung**.

Abschnitte [G] "Cutoff": Term that relates to those sections of the Nazi plans for the Jews that could be implemented overnight and without great difficulty (e.g., moving Jews into ghettos).

Abwanderung [G] "Internal migration": Nazi cover term for the deportations (i.e., Jews from a given locality "voluntarily" migrated).

Achse [G] "Axis":

1. Scope and Definition
The alliance between Nazi Germany, Fascist Italy, and Japan. The first steps in this alliance were taken in October 1935 when the League of Nations strongly opposed the invasion of Ethiopia and imposed sanctions on Italy. The rapprochement was accelerated by the Spanish Civil War (1936–1939), when both Italy and Germany lent military support to Franco's nationalist forces. In May 1939 the alliance between Italy and Germany was cemented by the signing of the Pact of Steel. In September 1940, the alliance became tripartite when Japan

committed itself to the Berlin-Rome-Tokyo Axis. During World War II the term *Axis states* was applied to the client states allied with Germany: Hungary, Romania, Slovakia, Croatia, and Bulgaria.

2. Inter-Axis Relations

Antikominternpact, "Anti-Comintern Pact," signed by Germany and Japan on November 25, 1936. Italy joined the pact on November 6, 1937. The entire pact was temporarily rendered moot by the Ribbentrop-Molotov nonaggression pact of August 23, 1939. After the opening of Operation Barbarossa, the Anti-Comintern Pact returned to the center of Nazi foreign policy.

Stahlpact, "Pact of Steel," signed by Germany and Italy on May 22, 1939. The pact had a ten-year term and served the interests of both parties, although for differing reasons. Hitler sought the pact to guarantee the Southern Front during his upcoming invasion of Poland, hence his concessions on the South Tyrolean border. Mussolini, for his part, hoped that the pact's article on prior consultation would prevent the beginning of war in 1939 or 1940 so that his military rebuilding plans could proceed. Despite the strain caused by the Nazi invasion of Poland the pact remained in force for the duration of World War II.

Adolphe Legalité [G] "Adolf Legality": Early nickname for Adolf Hitler, coined by some Stürmabteilung social revolutionaries, in connection with the Reichswehr trial of September 1930.

Adonenu ha-Nasi [אדוננו הנשיא, H] "Our princely leader": Nickname for Mordechai Chaim Rumkowski, *Judenälteste* of the Lodz ghetto, used by Jewish children in the schools of the ghetto.

Ahnenpass [G] "Ancestry card": Identity document issued to all SS members — and to civilians in need of such a document — who could prove their ancestral purity after publication of the Nuremberg Laws in September 1935.

Akeda [עקדה, H] "The binding of Isaac": biblical term, deriving from Genesis 22, for the ultimate in self-sacrifice by martyrdom. During the Holocaust, *akeda* and the related term, *ala al ha-moked* (עלה על המוקד), "offered on an altar," was used to designate the deaths of Jews in the gas chambers and crematoria.

Aktion(en)/Grossaktion(en)   [G]   "Operation(s)/Large operation(s)":

1. Scope and Definition

Literally meaning "action," with the implication of an operation, *Aktion* was the German term for any nonmilitary campaign. In more the specific sense, an *Aktion* was an operation of any duration undertaken for political, racial, or eugenic ends. Military operations were usually designated by the term *Fall* (case), although *Aktion* was also used to designate military operations of a political character (e.g., Aktion Margarethe, the occupation of Hungary). A *Grossaktion* in this sense would be a large-scale operation, for example, the plan for the liquidation of the Warsaw ghetto in April 1943: The SS expected the *Grossaktion* to last three days and to render Warsaw *judenrein*. Another term used to designate a political or racial operation was *Einsatz*.

2. Code Names

Aktion Brunner, in November/December 1942, entailed the roundup and deportation to the East of a large number of older Jews still living in Berlin.

Aktion Bürckel, named for Joseph Bürckel, Gauleiter of Baden. The operation was carried out by the SS in October 1940 on Bürckel's specific orders. Some 7,500 Jews from the Baden, Palatinate, and Saar areas were hastily rounded up and taken to the border of the unoccupied zone in France. The Vichy government gendarmerie immediately interned them in the Rivesaltes and Gurs camps. Almost all of them were later deported to death centers in the East.

Aktion Erlassentwurf, "Operation Blueprint Release," major deportation operation in Belgium that took place between August 11 and August 29, 1942. Five transports with a total of 5,997 Jews, including 1,017 children, left for the East. Schedule of departures: (1) August 11, 999 Jews, including 147 children; (2) August 15, 1,000 Jews, including 172 children; (3) August 18, 998 Jews, including 287 children; (4) August 25, 1,000 Jews, including 232 children; (5) August 29, 1,000 Jews, including 179 children. Of the total number of victims, only 68 survived.

Aktion Erntefest, "Operation Harvest Festival," the large-scale massacre initiated by the Nazis on November 3, 1943. One of the last *Grossaktionen* in the Lublin (Poland) area, it was geared toward the total elimination of remaining Polish Jewry. Some 42,000 Jews in the Trawniki and Poniatowa slave-labor camps were systematically machine-gunned and thrown into mass graves. As part of Aktion Erntefest, the 18,000 remaining Jews in Majdanek were ordered to dig their own graves before being murdered. On the same day the Lublin-Lipowa prisoner-of-war camp for Jews was also liquidated, with the prisoners taken to Majdanek, where they were shot to death in front of prepared pits behind the crematorium.

Aktion Fabrik, "Operation Factory," deportation *Razzia* in late February/early March 1943 during which 8,000 intermarried Berlin Jews were rounded up, held in warehouses in the city, and later deported to ghettos and concentration camps in the East. As many of the victims were racially Jewish but not religiously so, German Catholic authorities protested the operation strongly. In April 1943, because of the protests, some of the deportees were permitted to return home. This respite proved temporary, however, as most were re-arrested and deported to Auschwitz in August 1944.

Aktion 14f13, code name for the murder of invalid concentration camp inmates. *14f13* was an extension of the Euthanasia Program and also bridged the gap between euthanasia and the *Endlösung*.

Aktion Gitter, term for operation initiated by the Gestapo on August 22, 1944, against minor German functionaries (mainly Catholics of the Zentrumspartei), who were rounded up and imprisoned in a number of Nazi concentration camps.

Aktion Gypsy Baron, and *Aktion Hay*, two code names for the Nazi-initiated kidnappings of non-German children whose features were defined as "Aryan." > see also: **Lebensborn**.

Aktion Heyde (*Invalidenaktion*) > see also: **Aktion(en), Code Names (Aktion 14f13)**.

Aktion Iltis, SS operation initiated in September 1943 for the deportation of Jews of Belgian nationality to death camps in the East.

Aktion Jeckeln, named after its commander, Höherer SS- und Polizeiführer Friedrich Jeckeln. Undertaken in the Riga ghetto, the *Aktion* took place between November 30 and December 7, 1941. During the *Aktion* some 25,000 Jews were transported to the Rumbula Forest and were murdered.

Aktion Kugel, "Operation Bullet," operation undertaken to systematically eliminate escaped Allied prisoners of war who were recaptured. > see also: **Kugelerlass; Prisoners of War**.

Aktion M, the letter "M" standing for *Möbel*, or furniture, the operation being a subsection of Einsatzstab Rosenberg. The major aim of Operation Furniture was the systematic plundering of Jewish apartments in Nazi-occupied Europe of their contents.

Aktion Margarethe, code name for the German occupation of Hungary on March 19, 1944. As part of this operation, Sonderkommando Eichmann entered Budapest and began the deportation of Hungarian Jewry to the death camps.

Aktion 1005, Nazi code name for the systematic effort to obliterate all traces of the *Endlösung*. The operation's code name originated in the numbering of a memorandum from Gestapo Chief Heinrich Müller to Deputy Foreign Minister Martin Luther. Under the command of SS-Standartenführer Paul Blobel, Aktion 1005 began to exhume and burn the corpses that had been buried at the various extermination sites in Eastern Europe from the summer of 1942 on. Most of the dirty tasks of Aktion 1005 were carried out by Jewish prisoners of Sonderkommando 1005. After their usefulness ended these prisoners were also exterminated.

Aktion Petliura, named after the Ukrainian antisemitic leader Simon Petliura, assassinated in Paris on May 25, 1926, by Sholom Schwartzbart, a Jewish student. The *Aktion* was undertaken in Lvov on July 1–3, 1941, by members of the Nachtigall Battalion, a Ukrainian militia operating under the direction of the Gestapo. Seven thousand Jews were slaughtered during the three days' pogrom.

Aktion Reinhard, Nazi code name for the murder of European Jewry. The name was introduced by the leaders of the *Aktion* in memory of RSHA chief Reinhard Heydrich, who had been assassinated in May 1942. The initial aim of Aktion Reinhard was to kill the Jews then living in the five districts of the General Government. Thereafter, the *Aktion* was expanded to include Jews deported to Poland from all parts of Nazi-occupied Europe. As part of the *Aktion* three extermination camps were established: Sobibór (March 1, 1942), Belżec (March 15, 1942), and Treblinka (June 1, 1942). In these three camps approximately 2,000,000 Jews were murdered during the twenty months of operation in 1942 and 1943. > see also: **Endlösung**.

Aktion Silbertanne, "Operation Silver Fir," Nazi code name for the systematic policy of reprisals begun in response to resistance operations in Holland in 1943.

Aktion Sumpffieber, "Operation Swamp Fever," code name for a major antipartisan operation commanded by SS-Obergruppen-führer Erich von dem Bach-Zelewski. The forces arrayed for the operation, totaling over 6,000 men, included the First Waffen-SS infantry brigade. The intention was to clear Belorussia of partisans and other "brigands," which meant mainly attacking Jewish family camps. Although over 10,000 partisans and Jewish civilians were executed during this operation, whose size was paralleled only by the cruelty of the units involved, it did not break the back of either the general or the Jewish partisans, and miraculously many family camps survived.

Aktion T4, code name for the Euthanasia Program, taken from Tiergartenstrasse 4, the address of Reich Chancellery building. > see also: **Euthanasie**.

Aktion Tannenberg, coinciding with the Nazi blitz on Poland, Operation Tannenberg was not specifically conducted against Jews but was geared against the Polish leadership, the Catholic clergy, and certain professionals, from September 1 to October 25, 1939.

Aktion Wolke A1, plan to destroy Dachau (including two adjoining *Judenlager* — Landsberg and Mühldorf) by a Luftwaffe strike, on the eve of the Allied approach.

Aktion Wolkenbrand, SS plan to poison all Jewish and other-nationality inmates in Dachau just before the Allied liberation. An exception was made for non-Jewish American, British Commonwealth, and French prisoners of war.

Ausserordentliche Befriedungsaktion (ABA) "Extraordinary Pacification Operation," code name for the campaign directed against Polish intellectuals. The purpose of ABA was to suppress resistance and instill fear in Polish population by liquidating persons capable of resistance. Plans for ABA were laid in February and March 1940, with the *Aktion* commencing on May 16. Some 6,500 intellectuals and other suspects, including many Jews, were arrested and murdered. Insofar as ABA was supposed to eliminate Polish capabilities to resist before any resistance movements had crystallized, the *Aktion* was a failure.

Aussiedlungsaktion(en), "Resettlement action(s)," a Nazi cover term for the deportation of entire Jewish communities or parts of larger communities to extermination points. The great Nazi lie that the Jews were being transported for resettlement at points east where they would build a new life for themselves worked very well most of the time. When the deportees were faced with the great horror, it was too late to escape the trap. > see also: **Aktion(en)**, **Code Names (Judenreinigungsaktion(en))**.

Donau und Monte Rosa Aktion, operation involving 800 Norwegian Jews — mostly older people, invalids, women, and children. Dragged out from their beds at 4 A.M. on November 6, 1942, they were cramped abroad two freighters, the *Donau* and the *Monte Rosa*, which sailed, respectively, in November 1942 and February 1943, to Stettin. From there some of them were transported to Auschwitz, the rest were put to work in Upper Silesian coal mines.

Intelligenzaktion, Nazi operation undertaken on March 19, 1942, directed at what was left of the Jewish intelligentsia in the Krakow ghetto. The operation netted some fifty prominent Jews, who were taken to Auschwitz and killed.

Judenreinigungsaktion(en), "Jew cleansing action," another, somewhat blunter, term for an *Aussiedlungsaktion*, over the course of which a village or town became completely *judenrein*. The term refers specifically to those *Aktionen* undertaken in towns where the entire Jewish population could be dealt with at one time. > see also: **Aktion(en), Code Names (Aussiedlungsaktion(en))**.

Kinderaktion(en), "Children action(s)," Nazi operations specifically geared against Jewish children, conducted periodically in the ghettos, orphanages, and labor camps. It is estimated that 1,500,000 young lives were cut short during the Holocaust period.

La Grande Rafle, "The Big Sweep," French code name for the 1942 roundup and deportation of German and Austrian Jews residing in Paris. Although the idea for the operation originated with the Nazis, the French police undertook it with great zeal, offering to deport all the Jews from the unoccupied zone (a proposal that never fully came about). The operation commenced on June 16, 1942, and ended the next day. The internees were initially held at the Vélodrome d'Hiver; from there they were transported to transit camps (such as Drancy), and thence to Auschwitz.

Polenaktion, "Polish Operation," term for the deportation of Polish Jews living in Germany that took place in October 1938. Thousands of Jews, some previously stripped of their German citizenship, were rounded up and taken to the Polish-German border and dumped in a no-mans' land at Zbąszyn.

Selbstreinigungsaktionen, "Self-cleansing actions," Nazi term for the bloody pogroms perpetrated against Jews by Ukrainian, Latvian, and Lithuanian Fascists upon German occupation. The Nazis gave these burnings, lootings, beatings, and killings an air of respectability by calling them righteous self-cleaning actions by a wronged native population against the "oppressive Jews."

Sonderaktionen, "Special actions," cover name for murder actions against Jews or others undertaken by the SS or its subsidiary agencies.

Übersiedlungsaktion, "Resettlement action," a removal order that applied to all able-bodied Jewish men in Vienna, issued and enforced in October 1939. All Jewish men within this category were forcefully deported to occupied Poland for compulsory labor.

Umsiedlungsaktion(en), "Internal resettlement action(s)," similar in scope to the *Aussiedlungsaktion(en)*, differing only in operational methods. Instead of the victims being transported to an extermination site, Jews in an *Umsiedlungsaktion* were taken (in most cases) to a larger Jewish community (closed or open ghetto) where — depending on the Nazi time table — they were kept until their turn came.

Jews in a provincial town near Krakow about to be loaded on a death train
Courtesy of the Main Crimes Commission/
U.S. Holocaust Memorial Museum

An *Umsiedlungsaktion* still entailed loss of life for a portion of the community.

Verschönerungsaktionen, "Beautification projects," essentially undertaken for propaganda purposes in the Terezin ghetto and a small number of concentration camps (e.g. Gross Rosen). The biggest single such project was undertaken in Terezin just prior to the July 23, 1944, visit by representatives of the International Red Cross. In the course of the project a series of fake buildings and institutions were erected to give the impression of a healthy community, only to be torn down after the Red Cross representatives left.

TABLE A.1: Chronology of Anti-Jewish *Aktionen*

Date	Locality	Number of Victims	Murdered At[1]
November 1939			
11	Ostrow Mazowiecki (P)	600	MDA
December 1939			
1	Chelm (P)	1,350	MDA
October 1940			
20	Saar (G)	7,500	Gurs
22	Speyer (G)	community	Gurs
22	Mannheim (G)	2,000	Gurs
22	Heidelberg (G)	350	Gurs
February 1941			
20-28	Plock (P)	community	Dzialdowo
22-23	Amsterdam (Ho)	400	Mauthausen
May 1941			
14	Paris (Fr)	4,000	Pithiviers
June 1941			
27	Jassy (Ro)	thousands	MDA
27	Bialystok (P)	hundreds	MDA
28	Kovno (Li)	thousands	MDA
28	Brest-Litovsk (Br)	5,000	MDA
29	Jassy (Ro)	thousands	MDA
29	Lvov (Uk)	hundreds	MDA
30	Dobromil (Uk)	90	MDA

---

[1] As used throughout this table, MDA stands for murdered during *Aktion*.

July 1941

1	Lyakhovichi (Br)	100	MDA
1	Plunge (Li)	hundreds	MDA
2	Lvov (Uk)	7,000	MDA
2	Kamenka (Uk)	hundreds	MDA
2	Novo Selista (Uk)	800	MDA
2	Stryj (Uk)	hundreds	MDA
3	Bialystok (P)	100	MDA
3	Zloczow (Uk)	3,500	MDA
3	Brohobycz (Uk)	hundreds	MDA
4	Lutsk (Uk)	7,000	Lubard Fortress
4	Kovno (Li)	400	Seventh Fort
4	Tarnopol (Uk)	5,000	MDA
6	Skalat (Uk)	600	MDA
6	Chernovtsy (Uk)	3,000	MDA
7	Khotin (Uk)	2,000	MDA
8	Noua Sulita (Ro)	hundreds	MDA
10	Vilna (Li)	123	MDA
10	Chortkov (Uk)	300	MDA
11	Vilna (Li)	hundreds	Ponary
17	Slonim (Br)	1,200	MDA
24	Liepaja (La)	3,000	Skeden
28	Vilkaviskis (Li)	900	MDA
29	Jassy (Ro)	4,000	MDA

August 1941

1	Kishinev (Ro)	400	MDA
4	Ostrog (Uk)	3,000	MDA
5-8	Pinsk (Br)	11,000	MDA
6	Orgeyev (R)	200	Dniester River
7	Kovno (Li)	1,200	MDA
7-8	Kishinev (Ro)	hundreds	MDA
8-9	Dvinsk (La)	thousands	Pogulanka Forest
14	Lesko (P)	community	Zaslaw
19	Mogilev (Br)	4,000	MDA
20-21	Paris (Fr)	4,300	Drancy
25	Tykocin (P)	1,500	MDA
25	Belgrade (Yu)	8,000	Topovske Supe
27-28	Kamenets-Podolski (Uk)	18,000	MDA
28	Czyzewo-Szlacheckie (P)	thousands	MDA
28	Kédainiai (Li)	community	MDA
29	Utena/Moletai (Li)	3,700	MDA

September 1941

4	Berdichev (Uk)	1,500	MDA
6	Zbaraz (Uk)	70	Lubienicki Forest
15	Berdichev (Uk)	18,000	MDA

17	Lomza (P)	3,000	Galczyn Forest
19	Zhitomir (Uk)	thousands	MDA
22	Vinnitsa (Uk)	30,000	MDA
22	Litin (Uk)	community	MDA
24	Vilkaviskis (Li)	community	MDA
28	Kremenchug (Uk)	thousands	Peschanoye
28-30	Kiev (Uk)	33,771	Babi Yar
30	Berezhany (Uk)	700	MDA

October 1941

4	Kovno (Li)	1,500	Ninth Fort
5	Przemyslany (Uk)	500	Brzezina Forest
5	Berdichev (Uk)	community	MDA
11	Edineti (Ro)	thousands	MDA
12	Stanislawow (Uk)	10,000	MDA
13	Dnepropetrtovsk (Uk)	15,000	MDA
16	Dnepropetrtovsk (Uk)	5,000	MDA
21	Koidanovo (Br)	community	MDA
21-23	Kraljevo (Yu)	thousands	MDA
23	Kragujevac (Yu)	thousands	MDA
23-25	Odessa (Uk)	thousands	MDA
24	Romarno (Uk)	hundreds	MDA
24	Vilna (Li)	hundreds	MDA
25	Tatarsk (R)	community	MDA
26	Kleck (Br)	4,000	MDA
28	Kovno (Li)	10,000	Ninth Fort
30	Nesvizh (Br)	4,000	MDA

November 1941

5-6	Rovno (Uk)	17,000	Sosenki Forest
6	Nadvornaya (Uk)	2,500	MDA
7	Bobruisk (Br)	20,000	MDA
7	Minsk (Uk)	13,000	Tuchinka Forest
7-9	Dvinsk (La)	5,000	Pogulanka Forest
9	Mir (Li)	1,500	MDA
14	Zaleszczyki (Uk)	800	MDA
14	Slonim (Br)	9,000	Czepielow
20	Minsk (Uk)	5,000	Tuchinka Forest
23	Odessa (Uk)	30,000	MDA
23	Poltava (Uk)	1,500	MDA
29	Borislav (P)	1,500	MDA
30	Riga (La)	10,000	Rumbula Forest

December 1941

4	Gorodenka (Uk)	2,500	MDA
8	Novogrodek (Br)	4,000	MDA
15-16	Liepaja (La)	3,000	Skeden

21-30	Bogdanovka (Tr)	50,000	MDA
22	Zablotov (Uk)	1,000	MDA

January 1942

21-23	Novi Sad (Yu)	1,500	Danube River

March 1942

1-2	Minsk (Br)	thousands	Koidanovo
3	Dolginovo (Br)	1,500	MDA
3	Baranowicze (Br)	2,300	MDA
7-9	Mielec (P)	hundreds	MDA
9	Cihrin (Tr)	700	MDA
11	Mielec (P)	2,000	Belzec
13	Hulievca (Tr)	650	MDA
16	Lublin (P)	35,000	Belzec
19	Rava-Ruska (Uk)	2,000	Belzec
19-20	Belgrade (Yu)	500	Gas vans
20	Rohatyn (Uk)	2,000	MDA
24	Izbica Lubelska (P)	2,200	Belzec
25	Glebokie (Br)	100	MDA
25	Tarnopol (Uk)	1,000	MDA
31	Stanislawow (Uk)	5,000	Belzec

April 1942

2	Kolomyia (Uk)	1,000	Belzec
3	Tlumacz (Uk)	1,200	MDA
4	Gorodenka (Uk)	1,500	MDA
10	Kuty (Uk)	950	MDA
18	Warsaw (P)	52	MDA
18-28	Radom (P)	hundreds	MDA
29	Lodz (P)	hundreds	Chelmno
30	Diatlovo (Br)	1,200	MDA

May 1942

1	Dvinsk (La)	thousands	MDA
8	Lida (Br)	5,000	MDA
10	Wolozyn (Br)	1,000	MDA
12	Gabin (P)	thousands	Chelmno
12	Ivye (Br)	2,500	MDA
16	Pabianice (P)	4,500	Chelmno
19-21	Brzeziny (P)	3,000	Chelmno
21-23	Chelm (P)	4,000	Sobibór
21-23	Ozorkow (P)	2,000	Chelmno
22-23	Dolginovo (Br)	community	MDA
23	Wlodawa (P)	hundreds	MDA
27	Zamosc (P)	2,000	Belzec

SS oversee the loading of Jews onto a train headed for a death camp
Courtesy of the Main Crimes Commission/U.S. Holocaust Memorial Museum

28	Krakow (P)	6,000	Belzec
29	Radziwillow (Uk)	1,500	MDA

June 1942

1-8	Krakow (P)	7,000	Belzec
2	Kobrin (Br)	3,000	Bronna Gora
3-5	Braslav (P)	3,000	MDA
6	Biala Podlaska (P)	3,000	Sobibór
11-12	Tarnów (P)	10,000	Belzec
14-15	Disna (Br)	community	Piaskowe Gorki
15	Borki (P)	1,800	MDA
19	Glebokie (Br)	2,500	Borek Forest
24	Lvov (Uk)	thousands	Janowska/Piaski
30	Slonim (Br)	15,000	MDA

July 1942

2	Ropczyce (P)	community	Belzec
7	Rzeszow (P)	1,000	Rudna Forest
7-13	Rzeszow (P)	22,000	Belzec
13	Rovno (Uk)	5,000	Janowa Dolina

15	Sasov (Uk)	1,000	Belzec
18	Szarkowszczyna (Br)	community	MDA
21	Nesvizh (Br)	community	MDA
21	Kleck (Br)	community	MDA
22-31	Warsaw (P)	65,000	Treblinka
24	Derechin (P)	community	MDA
26	Luxembourg	24	Terezin
28	Luxembourg	156	Terezin
28-31	Minsk (Br)	30,000	MDA

August 1942

1	Lancut (P)	community	Nechezioli Forest
1-12	Warsaw (P)	81,000	Treblinka
3	Przemysl (P)	12,000	Belzec
4	Sambor (Uk)	4,000	Belzec
5	Pilica (P)	community	MDA
5	Radom (P)	10,000	Treblinka
6	Warsaw (P)	15,000	Treblinka
6	Diatlovo (Br)	community	MDA
6-17	Radom (P)	20,000	Treblinka
7	Novogrodek (Br)	2,000	MDA
9	Radun (Br)	community	MDA
10	Brzozow (P)	800	MDA
10-30	Lvov (Uk)	50,000	Belzec
11-13	Belchatów (P)	5,000	Chelmno
12	Będzin (P)	5,000	Auschwitz
13	Rymanow (P)	3,000	Belzec
13	Mir (Br)	community	Yablonovshchina
13	Grodek (Uk)	community	Belzec
13	Gorlice (P)	700	MDA
13-27	Warsaw (P)	53,750	Treblinka
14	Gorlice (P)	community	Belzec
17-18	Drohobycz (Uk)	2,500	Belzec
19-23	Lutsk (Uk)	17,000	Polanka Hill
20	Falenica (P)	community	Treblinka
21	Minsk Mazowiecki (P)	community	Treblinka
21	Ozorkow (P)	community	MDA
22	Wielun (P)	10,000	Chelmno
22	Losice (P)	community	Treblinka
22	Siedlce (P)	10,000	Treblinka
23	Lvov (Uk)	50,000	MDA
23-24	Zdunska Wola (P)	8,000	Chelmno
24-28	Nowy Sącz (P)	10,000	Belzec
25-26	Miedzyrzec (P)	thousands	Treblinka
27	Wieliczka (P)	8,000	Belzec
27-28	Sarny (Uk)	14,000	MDA
28	Zloczow (Uk)	3,000	Belzec
28	Chortkov (Uk)	2,000	Belzec
28	Miedzyrzec (P)	10,000	MDA

29	Olesko (Uk)	community	Belzec
29-31	Tarnopol (Uk)	4,000	Belzec
30	Rabka (P)	community	MDA

September 1942

1	Stryj (Uk)	thousands	Belzec
1-15	Vladimir Volynski (Uk)	18,000	MDA
2	Majdan Tatarski (P)	2,000	MDA
2-3	Lachva (Br)	community	MDA
3	Dzialoszyci (P)	1,000	MDA
3-4	Warsaw (P)	6,300	Treblinka
5	Lodz (P)	20,000	Treblinka
5-10	Sanok (P)	8,000	Zaslaw/Belzec
6	Gorodenka (P)	community	MDA
6	Wolbrom (P)	2,000	MDA
6-21	Warsaw (P)	47,900	Treblinka
7	Wolbrom (P)	6,000	Belzec
7	Sniatyn (Uk)	community	Belzec
10	Tarnów (P)	8,000	Belzec
13	Checiny (P)	community	MDA
15-16	Kalush (P)	community	Belzec
15-21	Kamenka (Uk)	community	Belzec
16	Jedrzejow (P)	6,000	Treblinka
17	Sokal (Uk)	2,000	Belzec
19-21	Brody (Uk)	2,000	Belzec
22	Wegrow (P)	community	MDA
22	Baranowicze (Br)	3,000	MDA
22	Częstochowa (P)	40,000	Treblinka
23	Szydlowiec (P)	10,000	Treblinka
23-25	Tuczyn (Uk)	1,000	MDA
25	Kaluszyn (P)	community	MDA
29	Serniki (P)	community	MDA
30	Zelechow (P)	community	Treblinka

October 1942

1-2	Luboml (Uk)	10,000	MDA
2	Belzyce (P)	3,000	Majdanek
3	Kolomyia (Uk)	5,000	Belzec
3	Wislica (P)	3,000	Treblinka
3	Radzymin (P)	community	Treblinka
4-6	Wolomin (P)	3,000	Treblinka
5	Radziwillow (Uk)	community	MDA
5	Tolstoye (Uk)	1,000	Belzec
6-27	Miedzyrzec (P)	10,000	Treblinka
9	Radomsko (P)	500	Treblinka
9	Przedborz (P)	4,500	Treblinka
11	Bychawa (P)	community	MDA
11	Lubatrow (P)	community	Sobibór

11-12	Ostrowiec (P)	11,000	Treblinka
13	Zdolbunow (P)	community	MDA
14	Mizocz (Uk)	community	MDA
14	Kobrin (P)	community	MDA
15	Ostrog (Uk)	community	MDA
15	Bereza Kartuska (Br)	community	Brona Gora
15	Brest-Litovsk (Br)	community	Brona Gora
15	Piotrkow Trybunalski (P)	22,000	Treblinka
17	Buczacz (P)	thousands	Belzec
20	Bar (Tr)	12,000	MDA
20-22	Opatow (P)	6,000	Treblinka
21	Szczebrzeszyn (P)	community	Belzec
21	Skalat (Uk)	3,000	Belzec
23	Oszmiana (Li)	500	MDA
24	Wlodawa (P)	community	Sobibór
27-28	Krakow (P)	7,000	Auschwitz
27-31	Przysucha (P)	4,000	Treblinka
28	Pinsk (Br)	16,000	MDA
28	Hrubieszow (P)	2,000	Sobibór
29	Sandomierz (P)	3,000	Belzec
31	Tomaszow Mazowiecki (P)	7,000	Treblinka

November 1942

1	Plonsk (P)	12,000	Auschwitz
2	Bilgoraj (P)	community	Belzec
2	Ostryna (Br)	community	Auschwitz
2	Tarnogrod (P)	3,000	Belzec
2	Brody (Uk)	2,500	Belzec
2-9	Siemiatycze (P)	thousands	Treblinka
2-11	Bielsk (P)	5,000	Treblinka
3	Tomaszow Mazowiecki (P)	7,000	Treblinka
5	Stopnica (P)	400	MDA
6	Stopnica (P)	3,000	Treblinka
6	Romarno (P)	community	Belzec
8	Staszow (P)	community	Belzec
10	Bochnia (P)	hundreds	Belzec
11	Ozery (Br)	community	Auschwitz
15	Tarnów (P)	3,000	Belzec
18	Przemysl (P)	4,000	Belzec
18	Lvov (Uk)	5,000	MDA
24	Mlawa (P)	community	Treblinka
30	Proskurov (Uk)	community	MDA

December 1942

12	Nowy Dwor (P)	2,000	Auschwitz
17	Baranowicze (Br)	3,000	MDA
17	Vineta (P)	3,000	Auschwitz
23	Pinsk (Br)	150	MDA

January 1943

5	Radomsko (P)	community	Treblinka
5-7	Lvov (Uk)	thousands	MDA
6	Lubaczow (P)	community	Belzec
10	Sandomierz (P)	6,000	Treblinka
12-21	Zambrow (P)	20,000	Auschwitz
13	Radom (P)	1,500	Treblinka
17-22	Grodno (Br)	10,000	Treblinka
18	Sokolka (P)	200	MDA
18-22	Warsaw (P)	5,000	Treblinka[2]
20	Ivye (Br)	1,100	Borisow
26	Stanislaw (P)	1,000	MDA
28-31	Pruzhany (Br)	10,000	Auschwitz

February 1943

1-2	Buczacz (Uk)	2,000	Fedor Hill
5-12	Bialystok (P)	20,000	MDA/Treblinka
16-17	Borislav (Uk)	hundreds	MDA
22	Stanislawow (Uk)	community	MDA

March 1943

1	Paderborn (G)	100	Auschwitz
3	Kavalla (Gr)	1,800	Auschwitz
7	Radoszkowice (Br)	community	MDA
9	Salonika (Gr)	hundreds	Auschwitz
11	Skopje (Yu)	7,000	Treblinka
13-14	Krakow (P)	2,000	Auschwitz
15	Salonika (Gr)	2,000	Auschwitz
16	Lvov (Uk)	1,000	Piaski
20	Częstochowa (P)	120	MDA
21	Skopje (Yu)	2,300	Auschwitz
25	Zolkiew (P)	community	Borek Forest

April 1943

22	Amersfoort (Ho)	community	Auschwitz
30	Doroshich (Uk)	800	MDA

May 1943

1	Brody (Uk)	community	Majdanek
2	Miedzyrzec Podlaski (P)	4,000	Treblinka

---

[2] During this *Aktion* the Warsaw ghetto's "Small Revolt" broke out. > see also: **Resistance, Table R.4: Major Ghetto Uprisings**.

2	Lukow (P)	4,000	MDA
7	Novogrodek (P)	7,000	MDA
9	Skalat (Uk)	community	MDA
21	Brody (Uk)	3,000	Majdanek
21	Drohobycz (Uk)	community	Bronica Forest
22	Stryj (Uk)	1,000	MDA
23	Lvov (Uk)	thousands	MDA
23	Przemyslany (Uk)	community	MDA
27	Sokal (Uk)	community	Belzec
27	Tolstoye (Uk)	3,000	MDA

June 1943

1	Lvov (Uk)	10,000	MDA/Janowska
1-6	Sosnowiec (P)	10,000	Auschwitz
5	Vught (Ho)	1,300	Sobibór
6	Tolstoye (Uk)	1,000	MDA
8	Zbaraz (Uk)	community	MDA
12	Berezhany (Uk)	community	MDA
18	Liepaja (La)	thousands	MDA
20	Amsterdam (Ho)	5,000	Auschwitz

July 1943

10	Lvov (Uk)	thousands	Kamenka-Bugskaya

August 1943

2	Salonika (Gr)	350	Bergen-Belsen
6	Vilna (Li)	1,000	Klooga
7	Salonika (Gr)	1,200	Auschwitz
16-20	Bialystok (P)	25,000	Treblinka
24	Bialystok (P)	5,000	Auschwitz
26	Zawiercie (P)	community	Auschwitz

September 1943

1	Vilna (Li)	5,000	Ponary
2	Tarnów (P)	10,000	Auschwitz/Plaszow
2-3	Przemysl (P)	3,500	Auschwitz
11	Przemysl (P)	1,000	MDA
11-14	Minsk (Br)	community	MDA
17-19	Lida (Br)	community	Majdanek
19	Dąbrowa Tarnowska (P)	community	Belzec
28	Amsterdam (Ho)	5,000	Westerbork
28	Split (Yu)	community	Sajmište

October 1943

8	Liepaja (La)	community	Kaiserwald

16	Rome (I)	1,127	Auschwitz
21	Minsk (Br)	2,000	Maly Trostines
25	Dvinsk (La)	community	Kaiserwald
26	Kovno (Li)	3,000	Klooga

November 1943

2	Riga (La)	4,500	Auschwitz
3	Lublin (P)	42,000	MDA
3	Majdanek (P)	18,000	MDA
3	Trawniki (P)	10,000	MDA
3	Genoa (I)	300	Auschwitz
6	Florence (I)	343	MDA/Auschwitz
9	Venice (I)	200	Auschwitz

December 1943

10	Tarassiwka (P)	500	MDA
13	Vladimir Volynski (Uk)	community	MDA
23	Pinsk (Br)	community	MDA

March 1944

2	Nancy (Fr)	hundreds	Auschwitz
11	Split (Yu)	hundreds	Jasenovac
24	Athens (Gr)	800	Auschwitz
24	Rome (I)	335	Ardreatine Caves
27-28	Kovno (Li)	2,500	MDA/Auschwitz

April 1944

| 21-23 | Uzhgorod (Hu) | 25,000 | Auschwitz |
| 28 | Kistarcsa (Hu) | 1,800 | Auschwitz |

May 1944

11	Munkacz (Hu)	33,000	Auschwitz
15	Kosice (Sl)	4,000	Auschwitz
24	Berehovo (Hu)	3,500	Auschwitz

June 1944

| 6 | Corfu (Gr) | 1,800 | Auschwitz |
| 19 | Kistracsa (Hu) | 1,450 | Auschwitz |

July 1944

1-2	Kaposvár (Hu)	6,000	Auschwitz
2-3	Vilna (Li)	3,000	Ponary
4	Koszeg (Hu)	community	Auschwitz

8	Kovno (Li)	thousands	MDA
20	Rhodes (Gr)	2,000	Auschwitz
24	Sárvár (Hu)	1,500	Auschwitz
31	Drancy (Fr)	1,000	Auschwitz
September 1944			
2	Plaszow (P)	2,000	Auschwitz
3	Westerbork (Ho)	1,000	Auschwitz
19	Klooga (E)	3,000	MDA
October 1944			
7-8	Cservenka (Yu)	1,000	MDA
20	Budapest (Hu)	22,000	Auschwitz

Source: Edelheit & Edelheit: *A World in Turmoil*. Wesport, CT: Greenwood Press, 1991.

Aktionshäftlinge [G] "Operation Prisoners": The thousands of German, Austrian, and Czech would-be political troublemakers rounded up and interned just before the start of World War II.

Aktsye [אקציע, Y] "Operation": Jewish term for a Nazi-ordered *Aktion*. An *aktsye* sometimes meant the roping off of a few streets of a town or village and the ordering of the Jews to move immediately within these confines. An *aktsye* also meant the taking away of some of the more-able-bodied Jews for forced labor to slave-labor or concentration camps; killing some of the Jews on the spot, or leading (sometimes transporting) some of them to the cemetery grounds and killing them there; transporting (or marching) all the Jews in a town or village to an already-established ghetto in a larger city, thus giving them a temporary reprieve on life; transporting them in closed cattle cars to one of the six "death" factories. An *aktsye* could also have meant force marching all the Jews (or some of them) to a sometimes prepared spot — an open pit — outside of town, and/or forcing the victims to dig their own graves (in many instances with their bare hands) and machine-gunning them to death. An *aktsye* was usually a combination of all or any of the above.

Aliya [עליה, H] "Immigration to Palestine/Israel": Jewish immigration to the Holy Land was one of the primary goals of the Zionist movement and was at the center of all Zionist ideologies. Prior to the establishment of the State of Israel, five waves of *aliya* came to Palestine: the First *Aliya* lasted from 1881 to 1903; the Second *Aliya* lasted from 1903 to 1914; the Third *Aliya* lasted from 1920 to 1924; the Fourth *Aliya* lasted from 1924 to 1929; and the Fifth *Aliya* lasted from 1929 to 1939. Free Jewish immigration was guaranteed by the terms of the League of Nations Mandate for Palestine, granted to Great Britain on July 24, 1922. The Mandate further stipulated that Jews immigrating to Palestine did so by right and not by sufferance. Even so, immigration became a constant struggle between the Zionists, the British, and the Arabs. In 1933 the high commissioner for Palestine, General Sir Arthur Wauchope, slightly liberalized immigration facilities for European Jewry, but this policy was reversed in 1936 as a result of the Arab Revolt. In 1939 the British government decided to break its commitment to Zionism and issued a White Paper that limited Jewish immigration to 15,000 a year for five years. After that no further Jewish immigration would be permitted without Arab consent. > see also: **Aliya Bet**; **Israel, State of**; **Biltmore Resolution**; **White Paper of 1939**.

Correspondence of a prospective *oleh*
Authors' Collection

TABLE A.2: Legal Jewish Immigration to Palestine, 1933–1945

Year	*Olim*	Year	*Olim*	Year	*Olim*	Year	*Olim*
1933	30,327	1937	10,536	1941	4,592	1945	15,259
1934	42,359	1938	14,675	1942	4,206	1946	18,760
1935	61,854	1939	31,195	1943	10,063	1947	22,098
1936	29,727	1940	10,643	1944	15,552	1948	17,165[1]

TOTAL: 339,011

Source: A. J. Edelheit: "The Yishuv in the Shadow of the Holocaust: Palestinian Jewry and the Emerging Nazi Threat, Ph.D. dissertation, City University of New York, 1992.

[1] This figure covers the period from January 1 to May 14, 1948.

Bond issued to a Labor Schedule immigrant
Courtesy of the Histadrut Archives/Machon Lavon, Tel Aviv

Aliya Bet [ʻעליה ב, H] "Illegal Immigration":

1. Scope and Definition

Despite the Balfour Declaration and the League of Nations Mandate for Palestine that committed Great Britain to assist in the building of a Jewish national home, the Mandatory administration sought a retrenchment from its commitments as a means to ensure Arab quiescence in the Middle East. As a result, increasingly severe restrictions were placed on *aliya* during the years after the Arab riots of August 1929. In response, Zionists began a policy of *ha'apala* (literally, striving), or immigration without the benefit of an immigrant certificate. Whereas the British termed such immigration illegal, the Zionists referred to it as Aliya Bet, second-type *aliya*, as opposed to regular (legal)

aliya.

Systematic Aliya Bet began in the mid-1930s in response to the steadily worsening situation in Europe. By 1937 both the Revisionist Zionists, followers of Ze'ev Jabotinsky, and the Hagana, the underground militia under the authority of the Jewish Agency Executive, established agencies to foster Aliya Bet. The Revisionist agency, Af-Al-Pi (Despite All), was founded in 1937 and the Hagana's agency, the Mossad le-Aliya Bet (Agency for Illegal Immigration; commonly known as the Mossad), began to operate in 1938.

During World War II Aliya Bet became a primary means for rescuing Jews from the Nazis, although operations were severely hampered by a lack of ships, difficulties in finding trained crews, the continuing British blockade of Palestine, and the generally unsafe conditions in the war zones and in the waters around them. After the war, Aliya Bet became the principal weapon in the Zionist rebellion against the Mandatory government. Using public opinion as its main tool, Aliya Bet succeeded in displaying the bankruptcy of British Palestine policy and provided a major cause for the United Nation's ulti-mate decision to create a Jewish state.

While the major focus of aliya bet was the blockade runners that brought *ma'apilim* to the shores of Palestine, two variants on Aliya Bet must also be mentioned: Aliya Gimmel, or as Aliyat Kenaf (airborne *aliya*), in which aircraft replaced ships for three missions that brought 150 *ma'apilim*, and Aliya Dalet, the use of

Call for a hunger strike by the organization of *ma'apilim* in the Yishuv

Courtesy of the Central Zionist Archives, Jerusalem

forged immigrant certificates by which means some 8,500 *ma'apilim* entered Palestine, primarily from Cyprus. > see also: **Aliya; Briha; White Paper of 1939.**

TABLE A.3: Aliya Bet Ships

Ship	Party	No. of *Olim*	Sailed From	Date	Result[1]
Prewar					
Velos I	H	350	Pireaus	7/34	Landed Tel Aviv
Union	R	117	Pireaus	8/34	Landed Tel Aviv
Velos II	H	350	Varna	9/34	Captured/Returned
Af-Al-Pi	R	15	Pireaus	4/37	Landed Herzliya
Af-Al-Pi II	R	54	Dorado	9/37	Landed Binyamina
Poseidon A	H	65	Lorion	1/38	Landed Mizpe ha-Yam
Af-Al-Pi III	R	96	Fiume	3/38	Landed Tantura
Artemisia A	R	128	Pireaus	4/38	Landed Tantura
Poseidon B	R	65	Pireaus	5/38	Landed Tantura
Artemisia B	R	157	Pireaus	7/38	Landed Tantura
Af-Al-Pi IV	R	156	Pireaus	8/38	Landed Binyamina
Af-Al-Pi V	R	38	Pireaus	9/38	
Draga A	R	180	Shusak	10/38	Landed Tantura
Atarto A	M	300	Bari	11/38	Landed Shefayim
Draga B	R	550	Constantsa	12/38	Landed Netanya
Ely	R	340	Galatz	12/38	Landed Netanya
Gepo A	R	734	Tulcea	12/38	Landed Netanya
Delphi	R	250	Constantsa	12/38	
Atarto B	M	300	Ancona	1/39	Landed Shefayim
Katina	R	800	Baltzec	2/39	Landed Netanya
Atarto C	M	300	Naples	2/39	Landed Tel Aviv
Atarto D	M	378	Shusak	3/39	Landed Tel Aviv
Sandu	P	270	Romania	3/39	Captured/Returned
Assimi	Mi	470	Romania	3/39	Captured/Returned
Gepo B	R	750		4/39	Sank, *olim* rescued
Aghia Dezioni	R	400	Fiume	4/39	Landed Nebi Ruben
Atarto E	M	408	Shusak	4/39	Landed Herzliya
Atarto F	M	337	Brindisi	4/39	Landed Herzliya
Ostia	R	699	Italy	4/39	Landed Herzliya
Agia Nicolaus	P	800	Burgas	5/39	Landed Netanya
Karliza Maria	P	350		5/39	
Atarto G	M	400	Constantsa	5/39	Captured/Detained
Demetrius	M	244	Greece	6/39	Captured

---

[1] The following abbreviations are used to designate parties: H = he-Halutz (Mapai's youth division in the diaspora); M = Mossad le-Aliya Bet; Mi = Mizrachi; P = Private; R = Revisionist Zionists (ha-Zohar or ha-Zach). Details of journey, such as port of departure and result, given when known.

Liessel	R	921	Constantsa	6/39	Captured/Detained
Colorado I	M	379	Constantsa	6/39	
Astir	R	724	Rani	6/39	Landed Majdal
Los Perlos	R	370	Constantsa	7/39	
Nikko	R	560	Fiume	7/39	Landed Netanya
Colorado II	M	377	Constantsa	7/39	Captured/Returned
Rudnichar A	P	305	Varna	8/39	Landed Netanya
Dora	M	480	Flisingen	8/39	
Rim	R	600	Constantsa	8/39	Sank, *olim* rescued
Agia Nicolaus B	R	745	Constantsa	8/39	Landed Netanya
Parita	R	850	Constantsa	8/39	Captured/Detained
Osiris	R	650	Varna	8/39	
Cartova	R	650	Varna	8/39	
Tripoli	R	700	Varna	8/39	

Wartime

Prosola	P	654	Varna	9/39	Trans. to *Tiger Hill*
Tiger Hill	M	1,417	Constantsa	9/39	Landed Tel Aviv[2]
Rudnichar B	P	371	Varna	9/39	Landed Herzliya
Naomi Julia	R	1,130	Constantsa	9/39	Captured/Returned
Rudnichar C	P	457	Varna	11/39	Landed Tel Aviv
Hilda	M	728	Baltzec	1/40	Captured/Detained
Sakarya	R	2,400	Constantsa	2/40	Captured/Detained
Pentcho	R	500	Bratislava	5/40	Sank[3]
Libertad	P	700	Varna	7/40	Landed Zichron Yaacov
Pacific	M	1,100	Tulcea	11/40	⎤ Captured and
Milos	M	671	Tulcea	11/40	⎦ transfered to *Patria*[4]
Atlantic	M	1,880	Tulcea	11/40	Captured/Deported
Salvador	P	327	Varna	12/40	Sank[5]
Darien II	M	800	Constantsa	3/41	Captured/Detained
Struma	P	769	Constantsa	2/42	Sank[6]
Vitorul	P	120	Constantsa	9/42	Sank
Milka A	M	239	Constantsa	3/44	Landed Turkey[7]
Marissa A	M	224	Constantsa	4/44	Landed Turkey
Milka B	M	517	Constantsa	5/44	Landed Turkey

---

[2] As the *Tiger Hill* unloaded, it was fired upon by British gunboats; two *olim* were killed.

[3] The *Pentcho* passengers were picked up by the Italian Navy and were interned on Rhodes; many were later deported to death camps in Poland.

[4] After the British announced that the *Patria* was to be sailed to the Mauritius Islands the Hagana attempted to sabotage the ship. The *Patria* sank in Haifa harbor as a result of the explosion with 260 *olim* killed.

[5] The *Salvador* sank in the Dardanelles and 120 *olim* drowned; the remainder later transferred to the *Darien*.

[6] The *Struma* sank under mysterious circumstances in the Black Sea; there were no survivors.

[7] The *olim* from all ships that landed in Turkey were permitted into Palestine legally.

Marissa B	M	318	Constantsa	5/44	Landed Turkey
Kazbek	M	735	Constantsa	7/44	
Bulbul	M	410	Constantsa	8/44	Landed Turkey
Mefkurie	M	344	Constantsa	8/44	Sank[8]
Salah-al-Din	M	547	Constantsa	11/44	
Taurus	M	948	Constantsa	12/44	

Postwar

Dahlin	M	35	Barletta	8/45	Landed Caesarea
Netuna I	M	79	Bari	9/45	Landed Caesarea
Pietro I	M	168	Chiatone	9/45	Landed Shefayim
Netuna II	M	73	Bari	10/45	Landed Shefayim
Pietro II	M	171	Chiatone	10/45	Landed Shefayim
Berl Katznelson	M	211	Greece	11/45	Captured after landing
Hanna Szenesh	M	252	Savona	12/45	Landed Nahariya
Enzo Sereni	M	900	Vado	1/46	Interned in Atlit
Orde Wingate	M	238	Palestrina	3/46	Interned in Atlit
Tel-Hai	M	736	France	3/46	Interned in Atlit
Max Nordau	M	1,666	Constantsa	5/46	Interned in Atlit
Eliahu Golomb	M	1,014	⌉ La Spezia	5/46	⌉ Ships impounded by
Dov Hoz	M		⌋		⌋ Italian authorities[9]
Haviva Reich	M	462	Greece	6/46	Interned in Atlit
J. Wedgewood	M	1,257	Vado	6/46	Interned in Atlit
Biriya	M	999	France	7/46	Interned in Atlit
Hagana	M	2,678	Yugoslavia	7/46	Interned in Atlit
Hayal ha-Ivri	M	510	Belgium	7/46	Interned in Atlit
Yagur	M	754	France	8/46	Interned on Cyprus
H. Szold	M	536	Greece	8/46	Interned on Cyprus
Katriel Jaffe	M	604	Bocca di Magra	8/46	Interned on Cyprus
23 Yorde haSira	M	790	Bocca di Magra	8/46	Interned on Cyprus
A. Shochat	M	183	Bocca di Magra	8/46	Landed Caesarea
Arba Heruyot	M	1,024	Bocca di Magra	9/46	Interned on Cyprus
Palmach	M	611	Bocca di Magra	9/46	Interned on Cyprus
Bracha Fuld	M	806	Bocca di Magra	10/46	Interned on Cyprus
Latrun	M	1,275	France	11/46	Interned on Cyprus
Knesset Israel	M	3,845	Yugoslavia	11/46	Interned on Cyprus
Rafiah	M	785	Yugoslavia	12/46	Sank
La-Negev	M	647	France	2/47	Interned on Cyprus
Maapil Almoni	M	746	France	2/47	Interned on Cyprus
H. Arlosoroff	M	1,348	Trelleborg	2/47	Landed Bat Galim

---

[8] The *Mefkurie* was torpedoed by a German U-Boat that surfaced to machine-gun the survivors; only five passengers survived.

[9] The *Eliahu Golomb* and the *Dov Hoz* were impounded by the Italian police at the instigation of the British before either could sail. The international crisis that followed forced the British to permit all 1,014 of the *olim* (who would have sailed aboard the two ships) to enter Palestine legally.

Ben Hecht	R	600	Port-de-Bouc	3/47	Interned on Cyprus
S. Lewinski	R	823	Metaponto	3/47	Landed Nizzanim
Moledet	M	1,563	Metaponto	3/47	Interned on Cyprus
T. Herzl	M	2,641	France	4/47	Interned on Cyprus
She'ar Yashuv	M	768	Boliasco	4/47	Interned on Cyprus
Hatikva	M	1,414	Boliasco	5/47	Interned on Cyprus
Morde haGetaot	M	1,457	Mola di Bari	5/47	Interned on Cyprus
Yehuda haLevi	M	399	Algiers	5/47	Interned on Cyprus
Exodus 1947	M	4,530	Marseilles	7/47	Returned to Germany
Gesher A-Ziv	M	685	Milliarino	7/47	Interned on Cyprus
Shivat Zion	M	411	Algiers	7/47	Interned on Cyprus
Af-Al-Pi-Chen	M	434	Formia	9/47	Interned on Cyprus
Geula	M	1,388	Burgas	10/47	Interned on Cyprus
Jewish State	M	2,664	Burgas	10/47	Interned on Cyprus
Kadima	M	794	Palestrina	11/47	Interned on Cyprus
Aliya	M	182	France	11/47	Landed Nahariya
HaPorzim	M	167	France	12/47	Landed Tel Aviv
Lo Tafhidenu	M	850	Civitavecchia	12/47	Interned on Cyprus
29 November	M	680	Girolata	12/47	Interned on Cyprus
The U.N.	M	537	Civitavecchia	1/48	Interned on Cyprus
Pan York	M	7,623	Burgas	1/48	⎤ Mossad agreed to
Pan Crescent	M	7,616	Burgas	1/48	⎦ sail to Cyprus[10]
HaLamed Heh	M	274	Palestrina	1/48	Interned on Cyprus
Yerushalayim	M	670	Civitavecchia	2/48	Interned on Cyprus
La Komemiyut	M	699	France	2/48	Interned on Cyprus
Bonim	M	1,002	Yugoslavia	2/48	Interned on Cyprus
Yehiam	M	769	Gaeta	3/48	Interned on Cyprus
Tirat Zvi	M	798	Italy	4/48	Interned on Cyprus
Mishmar Emek	M	782	France	4/48	Interned on Cyprus
Nachson	M	550	France	4/48	Interned on Cyprus
LaNizahon	M	189	Brindisi	5/48	Landed Tel Aviv[11]

Jewish National Fund label depicting the
blockade runner *She'ar Yashuv*
Authors' Collection

---

[10] Given the large number of *olim* on the *Pans*, and especially out of concern that resistance would be met with deadly force, the Mossad agreed to sail the ships directly to Cyprus.

[11] The last three ships arrived after the State of Israel had become independent.

Medinat Israel	M	243	Brindisi	5/48	Landed Tel Aviv
Emek Ayalon	M	706	Brindisi	5/48	Landed Tel Aviv

TABLE A.4: Aliya Bet: Statistical Summary

Period	Ships	Ma'apilim
1933–1939	47	18,968
1939–1945	27	18,502
1945–1948	65	69,856
Total shipborne	137	107,326
Aliya Kenaf	3	150
Aliya Dalet	NA	8,500
Grand total *ma'apilim*		115,976

Source: A. J. Edelheit: "The Yishuv in the Shadow of the Holocaust: Palestinian Jewry and the Emerging Nazi Threat, Ph.D. dissertation, City University of New York, 1992.

Alle Juden herunter! [G] "All Jews downstairs!": A Nazi command that brought shivers to millions of Jews. Man, woman, and child — old and young — knew what this shrill command meant: Some kind of *Aktion* was about to start, with a death sentence for all or some, without recourse or appeal.

Alljuda [G] "All Judah": Alternate Nazi term for "international Jewry, the source of all evil." The term derives from antisemitic propaganda positing an international Jewish conspiracy to destroy Germany.

Alte kämpfer [G] "Veteran fighters": Germans who had joined the National Socialist Party or its subsidiary agencies before 1924.

Altersgetto [G] "Elders' ghetto": Nazi euphemism for Theresienstadt — the former fortress town of Terezin — the model ghetto/camp in Czechoslovakia that served as a transit point to Auschwitz for Czech and German Jewry.

Ältestenrat [G] "Council of Elders": Nazi term for an imposed Jewish community council, in some ways comparable to the prewar Jewish *kehila*. > see also: **Judenrat**.

Altreich [G] "Old Reich": Germany in its pre-*Anschluss* borders. > see also: **Grossreich**.

Amtsleiter [G] "Commissioner": Rank applied to a chief of a ghetto administrative unit. > see also: **Ghetto, Gettoverwaltung**.

Anhaltelager [G] "Temporary detention camp": > see also: **Konzentrationslager System, National Socialist Camp Catgories**.

Anschluss [G] "Linkage": Term for the annexation of Austria by the Third Reich on March 13, 1938. > see also: **Grossreich**.

Ansteckungsgebiet [G] "Contagious zone": A Nazi excuse for sealing off the ghettos in Eastern Europe; by this act they claimed they were protecting the Aryan inhabitants from the carriers of highly contagious diseases.

Antisemitismus [G] "Antisemitism":

1. Scope and Definition
(1) A term coined by Wilhelm Marr in 1879 to represent the systematic hatred of Jews. (2) A pathological hatred of Jews based primarily on the fact that Jews exist and are perceived to be a threat to the established world order. (3) The denial to Jews of such rights and powers

normally granted to other peoples. In modern usage, the term has racist overtones.

2. Antisemitic Organizations

Pre-1933

Action Française, "French Action," founded in 1896 in the wake of the Dreyfus trial. The organization set as its purpose the removal of all Jewish influences on France. During World War II Action Française members openly collaborated with the Nazis. Publication: *L'Action Française* (1908–1944). > see also: **Collaboration**.

Action Nationale, "National Action," Belgian antisemitic and Fascist party, founded by Pierre Nothomb in 1919. Modeling the Party after Action Française, Nothomb adopted an active stance on Jewish issues. In 1925 a youth movement, Jeunesse Nationale, spun off from the main organization. In 1936 the party collapsed when Nothomb accepted a parliamentary seat with the Catholic Party.

Antisemitenbund, "Antisemites' Club," international antisemitic party founded by Wilhelm Marr in 1879. Cells of the Bund spread throughout Germany, Austria, and Hungary, with membership peaking in 1887.

Bund der Landwirte, "Association of Landowners," founded in 1893 and dedicated to defending the German *Volk* from its three enemies: liberalism, socialism, and Judaism. Unlike most contemporaneous antisemitic organizations, however, their opposition to Jews was based on religious, not racial, factors.

Camelots du Roi, "Knights of the King," French antisemitic order founded by a group of college students in 1906. The party's power peaked in 1911, a period when the Camelots saw themselves as the elite corps in an ultimate counterrevolution that would restore the monarchy. The Camelots publicized a crude form of antisemitism and, unlike contemporaneous antisemitic organizations, advocated violent action to "put the Jew back in his place."

Christliche Socialpartei, "Christian Social Party," founded by Prussian court chaplain

Adolf Stöcker in 1879. Within a decade, the party spread throughout Germany and into neighboring countries, including Austria-Hungary, Switzerland, and France. Stöcker's antisemitism was purely religious: He rejected racism but demanded that Jews convert to prove their complete assimilation. The party reached its peak in the 1890s but disappeared entirely before World War I.

Consul, a Prussian secret military order whose objective was political assassination to subvert the Weimar Republic. At its peak Consul numbered 5,000 members, mostly Reichswehr officers who had been relieved of duty after the Kapp Putsch. Among those blamed for the German defeat in World War I and therefore earmarked to be killed was Walter Rathenau, foreign minister of the Weimar Republic. > see also: **Fascism, Fascist Parties and Organizations (Germany)**.

Deutscher Arbeiter Partei (DAP), "German Workers Party," a forerunner of the NSDAP, founded January 5, 1919 in Munich by Karl Harrer and Anton Drexler. DAP received much assistance from the Thule Gesselschaft. On February 24, 1920, the DAP officially became the Nazi Party. > see also: **Fascism, Fascist Parties and Organizations (Germany)**.

Falange, a Polish antisemitic group whose program was similar to the Nazis in regard to the Jews. After the German invasion of Poland (September 1, 1939) the Falange petitioned the Nazis that it be co-opted to govern the Jews.

Ku Klux Klan, antisemitic and anti-democratic party initially founded in 1865 in the United States to oppose granting civil rights to freed slaves. The "old" Klan declined by the turn of the twentieth century but revived, becoming the "new" Klan, after 1920. The Klan was strongest in the southeastern and midwestern United States and used public means — including lynchings and cross burnings — to intimidate its opponents. The Klan declined again in the aftermath of World War II only to be reborn, as a neo-Nazi party, in the 1970s.

Legiunea Arhangehelului Mihail, "Legion of the Archangel Michael," Romanian antisemitic organization founded in 1927 as a breakaway from Alexandru Cuza's Christian Defense League. In the early 1930s the party collapsed, with most members joining the Garda di Fier.

Narodowa Demokracja, "National Democrats," better known as the Endecja or *Endeks* (from the abbreviation ND), antisemitic political party founded by Roman Dmowski in 1909. Nationalistic and rabidly antisemitic, the Endecja advocated strong measures to reduce Jewish influence in Poland. In particular, Endecja participated in an anti-Jewish boycott and in limited pogroms, the purpose of both of which was to encourage Jewish emigration from Poland. Although the party never attained power, the Endecja reached the pinnacle of its influence during the final years of the Polish republic, when the Sanacja government openly adopted the Endecja antisemitic platform.

Paul Reveres, The, U.S. antisemitic party founded on October 17, 1932. Although it was originally conceived as an anti-Communist organization, antisemitism became the Reveres' main focus after 1935. Chairman: Colonel Edwin M. Handley. Publication: *Paul Revere Message* (irregular, 1933–1934).

Rozwoj, Polish antisemitic organization, founded in 1913. Served as the propaganda wing of the Endecja. Strongly advocated an anti-Jewish boycott. Membership: 80,000. Publications: *Rozwoj* (1918–1919), *Gazeta Niedzielna* (Sunday gazette, 1919–1939).

Volksverweering, "People's Defense," Belgian party founded in the early 1930s. Rabidly antisemitic, the party was also highly nationalistic and anti-British. In Wallonia the party operated as Ligue de la Défense du Peuple. The internal contradiction between rabid antisemitism and equally strong nationalism led to collapse under the impact of Nazi occupation. Publications: *Volksaanval, Ami du Peuple*.

Post-1933, European

Gesamtverband deutscher antikommunistischer Vereinigungen, "General Association of German Anti-Communist Societies," founded in 1933. Although focused on international communism, the Gesamtverband engaged in wholesale anti-Jewish propaganda.

Glaubensbewegung deutscher Christen, "Faith Movement of German Christians," a subsidiary agency of the NSDAP. > see also: **NSDAP**.

Internationale Antisémite, "International Antisemite," Nazi front organization headquartered in Geneva, Switzerland, and controlled by Julius Streicher. > see Also: **NSDAP**

National-Socialistike Arbejer Parti (NSAP), "National Socialist Workers Party," Danish antisemitic party established on October 31, 1935. The NSAP spawned the Dansk Antijødisk Liga, the "Danish anti-Jewish League," the only major antisemitic party in modern Danish history. Sued for slander of Jews, the *Kamptegnet* was closed by Danish court order in 1942. In 1943 the entire party dissolved. Publication: *Kamptegnet*.

Oboz Narodowo-Radykalny (ONR or NARA), "National Radical Camp," antisemitic party founded on April 14, 1934. Banned by Marshal Pilsudski on July 10, 1934, NARA was reorganized on February 21, 1937. Advocating the creation of a Fascist regime, NARA adopted all the trappings of Nazi antisemitism and was supported by the Third Reich. A splinter party of the Endecja, NARA offered a more radical solution to Poland's problems and was strongest in cities and among university students. During the Nazi occupation, NARA initially advocated non-resistance against the Nazis and collaboration in the *Endlösung*. In 1943 and 1944, however, NARA partisan units began to cooperate with the AK. One NARA cell participated in the Polish Warsaw uprising of August–September 1944. Publication: *Sztafieta*.

Oboz Zjednoczenia Narodowego (OZN), "Camp of National Unity," popular name for both the colonels' clique that ruled Poland after Marshal Jozef Pilsudski's death and the paramilitary organizations under the colonels' tutelage. OZN oversaw the overtly antisemitic campaign in Poland during the years between 1936 and 1939, in the name of protecting Poles from the deleterious economic impact of Jews. Officially headed by Pulkownik Adam Koc, OZN was actually controlled by President Ignacy Mosciczki and Minister of Defense Marzalek Edward Rydz-Szmigly. Ironically,

OZN was a strong supporter of the Yishuv at the League of Nations because Zionists advocated Jewish emigration from Poland.

Stronnictwo Pracy, "Labor Front," Polish right-wing labor party founded in 1937, when the National Workers and Christian Democratic Parties merged. Its leader was General Josef Haller, infamous for permitting his soldiers to undertake numerous antisemitic rampages during the Russo-Polish War, and General Wladyslaw Sikorski (the later head of the Polish government in exile) was a close associate. Another illustrious Pole living abroad, the pianist-statesman Ignacy Jan Paderewski, although not a direct associate, lent his name to the party.

Post-1933, American

American Christian Defenders, founded in 1934 and also operating under the name the World Alliance Against Jewish Aggressiveness. Christian Defenders was actually a one-man operation, Eugene N. Sanctuary, for the diffusion of antisemitic propaganda. Sanctuary published more than a dozen books under the Christian Defenders imprint, including an English translation of the *Protocols of the Elders of Zion*.

Christian Front > see also: **Antisemitismus, Antisemitic Organizations, (post-1933, American, National Union for Social Justice)**.

Defenders of the Christian Faith, antisemitic political party founded in 1925 by Reverend Gerald B. Winrod. In addition to his attacks on "Jewish Bolshevism," Winrod strongly attacked the Roman Catholic Church and the Roosevelt administration. Publications: *Defender* (circulation 100,000), *El Defensor Hispano* (Spanish-language edition). Winrod was widely known as "the American Streicher."

National Union for Social Justice, American antisemitic and isolationist organization founded by Father Charles E. Coughlin. Active from 1926 to 1942, Coughlin used the organization, his weekly radio program, and the periodical that he edited as forums to attack his enemies. From 1934 on, Coughlin's main attacks were centered on Jewish leaders and institutions that he branded as Communist. In 1938, the National Union changed its name to the Christian Front. Under this guise Coughlin became little more than a mouthpiece for Nazi propaganda. Coughlin's popularity declined after the Japanese attack on Pearl Harbor, and he was removed from the air in 1942 because of his continued advocacy of isolationism.

Graph A.1: Percentage of Antisemitic Organizations in the United States, by Region

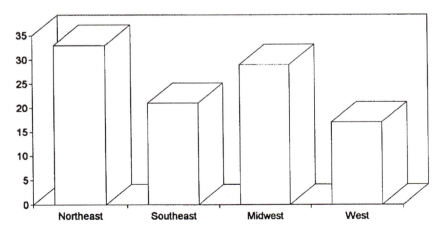

Anus mundi [Latin] "Asshole of the world": Colloquial term for the Auschwitz concentration/extermination camp. > see also: **Arsch der Welt**.

Appell [G] "Roll call": Daily early morning and evening ritual in all the concentration and slave-labor camps within the Holocaust kingdom. Depending on the mood or whim of the

Lagerführer, a roll call that required the inmates to stand at rigid attention on the *Appellplatz* while the prisoners were counted and recounted, inspected, spat at, beaten, and other abuses were inflicted could last for as long as half a day. The roll call was conducted in all kinds of weather; sometimes extra or special roll calls were called for, especially during odd hours, like in the middle of the night or during mealtime. The evening *Appell*s were unusually brutal, at times lasting until "lights-out" time, which meant that the tired, overworked, and starving inmates had to do without their watered-down soup and measly piece of bread.

Appellmacher [G] "Roll caller": A concentration camp inmate whose duty was to count the assembled prisoners and report to the *Blockführer*. This counting went on until all prisoners were accounted for. > see also: **Appell**; **Appellplatz**; **Konzentrationslager System**.

Appellplatz [G] "Roll-call square": principal square in all the concentration and major slave labor camps, where daily roll calls — mornings, evenings, and very often at other times — took place. The *Appellplatz* was also used for executing punishments, ranging from the administration of beatings with whips and truncheons, running of the gauntlet while being pummelled by guards and kapos with wooden bats, frog-jumping, crouching on one's knees for hours — all minor in comparison to the mandatory witnessing of victims hanged or executed by a firing squad for the slightest infringement of camp rules or ripped apart by specially trained dogs just for the sport of it.

Arbeidsinzet [Du] "Labor draft": Dutch term for the drafting and deportation to Germany of Dutch citizens for the German war effort. > see also: **Arbeitseinsatz**.

Arbeit macht frei! [G] "Work makes free": A large sign posted above the main entrance gate to most concentration camps that falsely proclaimed that "work liberates," at least as far as Jews were concerned.

Arbeiterwiderstand [G] "Worker opposition": Leftist opponents of Nazism, whether organized or not. > see also: **Resistance, Resistance Movements (Germany)**.

Arbeitsdienstführer [G] "Work detail leader": An orderly with overall responsibility for the different slave-labor details in a given camp and second in command to the *Arbeitseinsatzführer*, and who also submitted proposals for the appointment of new Kapos.

Arbeitseinsatz [G] "Labor deployment": (1) The concentration camp office responsible to the SS for the organization of the labor details. (2) A Nazi order to the Judenräte holding them responsible for carrying out German orders that required young Jews to report to forced-labor battalions. > see also: **Konzentrationslager System**.

Arbeitserziehungslager [G] "Educational labor camp." > see also: **Konzentrationslager System**.

Arbeitsjude(n) [G] "Jews capable of work": Nazi term for a certain category of Jews in ghettos or concentration camps that could be employed in the German war industry — at least until disposed of. > see also: **Arbeitsmaterial**.

Arbeitskommando aufgelöst [G] "Work detail liquidated": Often, in many concentration and slave-labor camps, work details with Jews that were marched out in the early morning hours were, after finishing their assigned jobs, murdered. To keep their records straight, the term was used by the SS guards in their report to the *Lagerführer* during the evening *Appell*, since the exact number of prisoners had to be accounted for.

Arbeitsmaterial [G] "Work material": Nazi term applying to categories of Jews, in ghettos or camps, capable of doing productive work for the SS or for German private industry. Those designated thus were permitted a brief reprieve before being murdered.

Arbeitspflicht [G] "Work obligation": A decree issued on October 26, 1939, by the Labor Department of the General Government (Poland), making it mandatory for all Poles between the ages of eighteen and sixty to perform public labor.

Arbeitsressorts [G] "Work sections": Workshops set up in the larger Polish ghettos by order of the Gettoverwaltung. The shops were established with capital seized from Jews, and all the workers were Jewish slave laborers.

Arbeitsschein(en) [G] "Work permits": A virtual, although temporary, life certificate for hundreds of thousands of Jews in occupied Eastern Europe. Often changed and manipulated, sometimes by the Judenrat and/or the Jüdischer Ordnungsdienst — but usually at the prodding or whim of the Gestapo — desperate people would go to any length in order to secure an *Arbeitsschein*.

Arbeitsschlacht [G] "Battle of work": Nazi term for the effort to regain full employment in Germany. The program involved creating labor battalions — actually paramilitary units — to engage in construction work. It was partly financed by aryanized Jewish funds. > see also: **Arisierung**.

Arbeitsstatistik [G] "Work statistics": An office within the concentration camp system (run individually by each camp), where records of all the *Arbeitskommandos* (work details) were kept. In addition, a vital statistics index system with individual cards of all the prisoners "officially" admitted to the camp was kept by this office. It also assigned each new prisoner to a working detail.

Arbet vet rateven dos geto [ועט ארבייט ראטעווען דאס געטא, Y] "Work will save the ghetto": Yiddish phrase meaning that the majority of a ghetto's population could be saved through productive work for the Nazi war machine.

Arianisirung [אריאניזיראנג, Y] "Mastering the art of becoming an Aryan": Term for a Jew's ability to furnish himself with false papers and to look like and master the language of the native population in order to pass outside the ghetto as a Gentile and thus escape the fate of a Jew in Nazi Europe.

Arierparagraph [G] "Aryan clause": Nazi regulation barring Jews from membership in German political parties, economic establishments, voluntary associations, and social clubs. It was introduced in April 1933. As the Reich's legislative campaign against German Jewry progressed, the *Arierparagraph* was expanded to include virtually all professions.

Arisierung [G] "Aryanization": Term used to denote the transfer of Jewish-owned businesses to German ownership in the Third Reich and in the countries Germany occupied. This process operated in two phases: the voluntary sale of Jewish-owned businesses in the years between 1933 and 1938, and the period of forced transfer after *Kristallnacht*. *Arisierung* measures were coordinated by the Gauwirtschaftsberater in close cooperation with local economic organizations.

Aroisgefirt [ארויסגעפירט, Y] "Departed": Ghetto euphemism for those deported by the Nazis. Periodically, outside work details returning to the ghetto in the evening found friends or family members missing. Being unaware that an *Aktion* had been carried out during their absence, they inquired about the missing individuals. Although most Jews, at least the adults, knew that those caught in an *Aktion* were taken away to be killed, it was unsafe to volunteer such information openly. Thus, when asked, the answer was a simple *aroisgefirt*.

Arsch der welt [G] "Asshole of the World": German term for Auschwitz. > see also: **Anus Mundi**.

Aryan: Anthropological and linguistic term for those groups speaking Indo-European languages. In the last third of the nineteenth century the term came to be applied to members of the north European races, as opposed to Jews (Semites), orientals, and Negroes. To this basic racist picture of the world, Social Darwinists added the idea of conflict between the races, co-opting the Darwinist idea of survival of the fittest to justify imperialism and antisemitism. In its most radical form this idea justified the Nazis' plan for an apocalyptic racial war that would result in the destruction of Jewry and the reduction of other "lower" races.

Ashmodai [אשמדי, H] "Devil": Nickname for Hitler popular among Orthodox Jews in Eastern Europe. The term is derived from the legendary description of Ashmodai, a sinister-looking creature who always seeks to destroy the righteous. Occasionally, the term was used as *Ashmodai ha-rozeah* (אשמדי הרוצח), "Ashmodai the murderer."

Askari [Slang]: Term for Russian prisoners of war who collaborated with the Nazis. Askaris served as guards and in other capacities in the slave labor and concentration camps. Many were meaner than the SS.

Auf der flucht erschossen [G] "Shot while trying to escape": Nazi justification for certain classes of war crimes: The victim, it was claimed, was killed trying to escape.

Auffangsgesellschaft [G] "Holding company": Agency set up to transfer Jewish property from occupied countries to the Reich. > see also: **Ghetto, Gettoverwaltung.**

Aufräumungskommando [G] "Cleanup unit": Nazi term applied to small detachments of Jews, between a few hundred in the larger ghettos to just a few in the smaller places and sometimes divided into *Aufräumungskolonnen* (cleaning squads). After a *Judenreinigungsaktion*, the detachment of Jews left behind had to gather, sort, and pack all the personal goods the victims had been forced to leave behind (while being loaded on the cattle cars from the *Umschlagplatz*) for shipment into the Reich. As a rule, after finishing this task, the "cleanup unit" either was taken to another town for inclusion in a departing transport or was killed on the grounds of the Jewish cemetery. In rare cases, those in the brigade were transported to a larger ghetto or camp, and thus given a short

AUFRUF

Ich gebe hiermit bekannt, dass alle Personen, die, gemäss der Anordnung der Behörden zur Aussiedlung kommen, sich am 29., 30. und 31. Juli ds. Jhrs. freiwillig zur Abreise melden werden, erhalten pro Person 3 Kg. Brot und 1 Kg. Marmelade.

Sammelpunkt und Produktenverteilung — Stawkiplatz Ecke Wildstrasse.

Der Leiter des Jüdischen Ordnungsdienstes

Warschau, den 29. Juli 1942

Aufruf: Announcement by the chief of the Warsaw Jüdischer Ordnungsdienst
Courtesy of the Żydowski Instytut Historyczny/U.S. Holocaust Memorial Museum

reprieve on life. > see also: **Aktion(en)**, **Code Names (Judenreinigungsaktionen)**; **Umschlagplatz**.

Aufruf [G] "Proclamation": In Nazi-occupied Europe virtually thousands of proclamations were issued by the, sometimes competing, different branches of the German occupation authorities. A very large percentage pertained to European Jewry. Numerous additional proclamations were issued by the Judenräte on German orders.

Ausbürgerung [G] "Revocation of citizenship": Nazi term arising from the Nuremberg Laws. > see also: **Legislation, Anti-Jewish, National Socialist (Third Reich)**.

Auschwitzlüge [G] "Auschwitz lie": Revisionist and neo-Nazi term for the denial of the Holocaust. Circulation of such propaganda is a misdemeanor offense in contemporary Germany.

Ausgemerzt [G] "Exterminated": Nazi term for the wholesale slaughter of entire Jewish communities.

Ausgeraumt [G] "Cleared out": Nazi cover term for the total elimination of the Jews in Europe. Used primarily in the years between 1939 and 1942, the term was a precursor for the two other main terms relating to the solution of the Jewish problem: *Gesamtlösung* and *Endlösung*.

Ausgesondert [G] "Selected": Nazi term for Jews and other categories, indicating that those selected would be liquidated.

Ausgliederung [G] "Separating": Nazi term for the elimination of Jews from all the phases of Aryan society. As a first step came the incarceration of large number of Jews in overcrowded ghettos or special labor camps. > see also: **Ghetto**.

Ausleihzentrale für ungelernte Arbeiter [G] "Lending center for unskilled workers": Nazi term for unskilled Polish laborers to be

drafted for slave labor in Germany.

Auslöschen ewig feindlicher Elemente [G] "Extinguishment of eternally inimical forces": One of the more forcefully expressed Nazi terms for the "special treatment" of European Jewry.

Ausmerzung [G] "Extinction": Nazi term for the unconditional liquidation of world Jewry. Whereas the Nazis had plans for radical eugenic undertakings, whose purpose was to completely transform European civilization, only one group was targeted for complete and irreversible annihilation: the Jews. > see also: **Endlösung**.

Ausschalten [G] "To remove": Nazi cover term for deportation of Jews. Despite the relatively benign connotation of the word, it actually referred to their deportation to death camps or other extermination sites.

Aussenbrigaden [G] "Outside brigades": Jews doing forced labor outside of a camp precinct or ghetto. Fellow Jews considered them lucky, as they had a chance (though a slim one) to acquire something extra to eat or even to escape. > see also: **Aussenkommando**.

Aussendienststelle [G] "Outpost": SIPO (Sicherheitspolizei) or SD branch office in any city or location. The term also applies to a group of concentration camp inmates working and living, for a longer or shorter period of time, outside of the camp.

Aussenkommando [G] "Outside detachment": A group of inmates performing slave labor outside a concentration camp. > see also: **Aussenbrigaden**.

Aussiedlungslager [G] "Deportation camp": Category of temporary concentration camps for those Jews who had escaped initial *Aussiedlungsaktionen* and had returned from hiding, generally during the winter, and were held until they could be transported to extermination camps. > see also: **Konzentrationslager System**.

Aussonderung [G] "Segregation": Nazi cover term applied to orders that all Soviet political commissars and lesser Communist officials be separated from any prisoners of war captured by German forces. Segregation was preparatory to the elimination of all such Communist Party officials. *Aussonderung* also applied to the exclusion of Jews from the general society.

Austauschjuden [G] "Exchange Jews": A category of so-called privileged Jews held by the Nazis as bargaining pawns for exchange.

Auswanderungsdrang [G] "Emigration pressure": Nazi term for the measures used by the Third Reich's government to increase Jewish emigration. These means included special taxes on Jews, Gestapo intervention in Jewish communal affairs, tolerance for Aliya Bet operations from Austria and Czecholslovakia, and, finally, dumping Jews at the borders of Germany's neighbors (especially Poland).

Auswanderungslustige Juden [G] "Jews eager to emigrate": A Nazi propaganda term sometimes used to cover the forceful deportations of entire Jewish communities. As a general rule this term was used during the early stages of Nazi policy, when the German bureaucracy was still eager to get rid of its Jews through emigration.

Ausweis(e) [G] "Identification": An identification card that showed that the bearer was duly employed. During the almost daily *Aktionen* only those bearing *Ausweise* stamped with the seal of the most important shops in the ghettos were (although not always) temporarily spared. Frequent Nazi changes of *ausweis* color, however, meant that even an employee of the most important factory was never really safe from deportation. > see also: **Arbeitsschein**.

B

Badenanstalt für Sonderaktionen [G] "Bathing establishment for special action": SS cover term for the underground gas chambers and crematoria in the extermination camps.

Bandenkampfverbände [G] "Anti-partisan units": Ad hoc anti-partisan units composed of SS, Waffen-SS, Wehrmacht Feldpolizei, and Russian collaborators, commanded by SS-Obergruppenführer Erich von dem Bach-Zelewski. Bach-Zelewski's overall headquarters was founded in 1943 and often also operated against Jewish communities under the guise of anti-partisan operations.

Bandenkinder [G] "Gang children": Captured children of partisans. In some instances, the life of captured non-Jewish children was spared and they were interned in special camps — the *Jugendverwahrlager*.

Banditenbekampfung [G] "Bandit fighting": German term for anti-partisan operations, often used as a cover for anti-Jewish *Aktionen*.

Barackenbau Kommando(s) [G] "Barrack construction unit(s)": Existed in some of the larger concentration camps. Composed mostly of prisoners of war, many of whom collaborated with the Nazis.

Barry [PN] Name of a trained Nazi dog in the Treblinka extermination camp. Barry was especially trained to attack the genitals of naked victims (awaiting their turn at the gas chamber) or of inmates on whom the SS-man Franz "the doll" — the dog's formal owner — had sicced it. > see also: **Herr Rolf**.

Baudienst [G] "Construction service": Polish youngsters forcibly drafted by the Nazis. Because of their antisemitic outlook, the young Poles were, at times, utilized by the Nazis to help with the roundup of Jews in their larger anti-Jewish operations.

Bauhof [G] "Building courtyard": Inmate-labor detachments in the larger concentration camps, especially in Auschwitz, employed in the construction and repair of camp and/or outside facilities. > see also: **Barackenbau Kommando**.

Beauftragter [G] "Administrator": Nazi official who headed the provincial or municipal civil administration in Nazi-occupied Europe. Within their locality, administrators also oversaw, or had SS advisors who oversaw, Jewish affairs.

Beauftragter des RFSS [G] "Representative of the Reichsführer-SS": Official title of Adolf Eichmann, indicating that he was commissioned by Heinrich Himmler to act as his personal representative in all matters regarding the Jewish question.

Befristeter Vorbeugungshäftling [G] "Limited preventive detention prisoner": Inmates incarcerated for a specific period of time. As a rule, no Jew fell within this category; it generally applied to German or Austrian professional criminals, or to other ethnic Germans. > see also: **Berufsverbrecher**.

Bejlisowe mydlo [P] "Beilis soap": Polish term for the soap the Nazis supposedly manufactured from the fat of the murdered victims.

Bekenntniskirche [G] "Confessing Church": Christian opposition group composed of Protestant leaders who opposed the Reichskirche. Led by Pastor Martin Niemöller, the Bekenntniskirche rejected Nazi racial dogma but did not explicitly condemn antisemitism until after World War II. > see also: **Kirchenkampf**.

Bernhard, Fall [G] "Operation Bernhard": Secret SD operation in the Sachsenhausen concentration camp using Jewish inmates — including many with criminal records — to forge British (and later, apparently, U.S. and Swiss) currency. An unknown quantity of this currency appears to have been used by senior SS officials toward the end of the war to purchase goods in neutral countries.

Bernheim Petition, Defense effort against Nazi anti-Jewish legislation presented to the League of Nations in May 1933. Citing the 1922 German-Polish Convention on Silesia that guaranteed minority rights, the Comité des Délégations Juives petitioned on behalf of Franz Bernheim, one of ten thousand Jewish residents in Upper Silesia who suffered under the anti-Jewish laws. In June, the League council declared that the complaint was valid. Because the Germans were interested in the full observance of the Convention, they agreed to nullify all anti-Jewish legislation in Upper Silesia for the duration of the treaty. When the treaty expired in May 1937, all anti-Jewish laws were reapplied.

Berufsverbrecher [G] "Professional criminals": Category of concentration camp inmates primarily composed of German and Austrian criminals. These inmates were considered the "elite" among *Häftlinge* and were usually selected to be kapos or to fill other inmate posts in the camp inner administration. > see also: **Konzentrationslager System**.

Besatzungspolitik [G] "Occupation policy":

1. Scope and Definition

The measures adopted by the German civil or military authorities that controlled the various occupied countries during World War II. Although each occupied country was treated differently, a number of general policies were instituted throughout Europe. In particular, German occupation policy was clear about placing the Jews outside the law and about strong police measures to be used to quell resistance. > see also: **Ghetto; Endlösung; Eingegliederte Ostgebiete; Generalgouvernement**.

2. Nazi Occupation Agencies

Obergericht, "Appellate Court," four courts established in the Generalgouvernement by order of Hans Frank, each having three judges. The courts were located in Warsaw, Radom, Lublin, and Krakow. Although theoretically the *obergericht* was the highest level of justice in the Generalgouvernement, in fact, both Governor General Frank or his Department of Justice could annul any court decision. Moreover, all individuals living in areas under SS jurisdiction — especially Jews — had no recourse whatsoever to the courts.

Reichskommissariat für die besetzen niederländischen Gebiete, "Reich Commission for the Occupied Dutch Territories," Nazi-imposed civilian government run by Germans and Dutch collaborators during World War II. Officially established on May 18, 1940, when Nazi legislation — including all antisemitic legislation — was imposed throughout Holland. Throughout the Nazi occupation the Reichskommissar was Arthur Seyss-Inquart.

Reichskommissariat Ostland (RKO), "Reich Commission for the East," one of the two administrative units of civilian government imposed by the Nazis in occupied areas of the Soviet Union. The RKO included the Baltic Republics and Belorussia, including part of the

Polish territory ceded to the USSR under the Nazi-Soviet pact. The *Reichskommisar* was Heinrich Lohse, who ruled from Riga. He reported directly to Reichsminister Alfred Rosenberg, who had been appointed by Hitler to prepare the territory for ethnic German colonization.

Reichskommissariat Ukraine (RKU), "Reich Commission for the Ukraine," one of the two administrative units of civilian government imposed by the Nazis in occupied areas of the Soviet Union. The RKU included the entire territory of the Ukraine, minus parts of Galicia that had been ceded to the USSR as part of the Nazi-Soviet pact and were now reattached to the General-gouvernement. The *Reichskommissar* was Erich Koch, who ruled from Rovno.

Beseitigt [G] "Eliminated": One among numerous Nazi camouflage terms for having "judiciously" dealt with the Jews, i.e., exterminated them. > see also: **Endlösung**.

Beseitigung [G] "Setting aside": a Nazi term for non-consideration of any outside factors, including the needs of the war effort, in formulating German policy regarding Jews.

Besetzte Ostgebiete [G] "Occupied Eastern territories": Nazi-designated name for a large tract of occupied Soviet territory under the directorship of Alfred Rosenberg. It was there that mass murder of Jews by the fast-moving Einsatzgruppen with the help of local collaborators (June–December 1941) was first carried out. > see also: **Besatzungspolitik, Reichskommissariat Ostland**.

Bet ha-sekila [בית הסקילה, H] "House of stoning": Sephardi term (of Greek Jews) for the wholesale slaughter of European Jewry in the Nazi death camps, ghettos, Jewish cemetery grounds, and other extermination sites.

Betriebsführer [G] "Workplace leader": Nazi term for the manager of a firm, usually the owner. Under work regulations that came into force on January 30, 1934, the *Betriebs-*

führer was responsible for all economic, political, and social activities in his workplace. Until after *Kristallnacht* (November 12, 1938), a Jew could be the *Betriebsführer* for his own firm; thereafter no Jews were permitted to hold such a position, even if their firms were not yet aryanized. > see also: **Arisierung**.

Bibliothek für Sprachen und Musik [G] "Library for Language and Music": Nazi name for the former Rothschild library in Frankfurt am Main, aryanized on January 29, 1934.

Biltmore Resolution: Declaration of Jewish goals adopted at the Extraordinary Zionist Conference held in New York in 1942. The resolution explicitly advocated the establishment of a Jewish commonwealth in Palestine. The conference, so named because it took place in New York's Biltmore Hotel, was attended by many leading Zionist personalities, including Chaim Weizmann, Abba Hillel Silver, Stephen S. Wise, David Ben-Gurion, Israel Goldstein, and Nahum Goldmann. The resolution marked the first time that a majority of Zionists called openly for the establishment of Jewish sovereignty as the ultimate goal of Zionism. The resolution became central to the activities of the American Zionist Emergency Council.

Bindenträger [G] "Armband carriers": Ghetto or camp functionaries who wore a special armband as identification. Among the most prominent *Bindenträger* were members of the Jüdischer Ordnungsdienst.

Biologischer reservat [G] "Biological reserve": Nazi term describing Eastern European Jewry. The principle Nazi goal of *Entjudung*, especially after the Wannsee Conference of January 20, 1942, was the destruction of this biological reserve. After this great reserve was eliminated, world Jewry would, given some time, dry up.

Birkenwald [G] "Brzezinka Forest": A certain area within the Auschwitz-Birkenau concentration camp. Jews selected to be killed were taken to a large barrack-like building situated near a deep trench, where they were gassed and their bodies burned. Birkenwald also served as a shooting place for non-Jewish victims.

Blitzkrieg [G] "Lightning war": Nazi term for the conduct of warfare developed by the Wehrmacht. The objective of this style of war was to attain complete victory in a short time. This style of warfare featured mobility and placed great emphasis on the close co-operation of tanks and dive-bombers to disrupt enemy defenses. These actions were calculated to create shock and disorganization, thereby preventing a reaction by enemy forces.

Blitzpogrom [G] "Lightning pogrom": A forerunner of the *Endlösung*, and, in some ways, its opening stage in Nazi-occupied Europe. The term refers to the rash of atrocities committed against the Jews of Poland by the fast-moving German armies.

Block 10: Area of the Wissenschaftliche Abteilung, the Auschwitz concentration camp scientific department, where so-called medical experiments on women were carried out by Nazi doctors; some of the doctors were associated with reputable German universities.

Block 11: Notorious punishment area in Auschwitz. Here, in the underground cellars, were made the first successful tests in mass extermination with Zyklon B. Six hundred Soviet prisoners of war and some 250 hospital patients were used for that purpose. After the victims were inside and the barracks windows and doors were blocked with heavy layers of dirt, Zyklon B was thrown in through a single opening suffocating all 850 victims.

Block 20: Punitive compound of the Mauthausen concentration camp. At least 6,000 victims lost their lives here during the camp's existence, among them large numbers of Dutch and Austrian Jews.

Block 41: The headquarters for the medical experiment building and the body disposal

plant in the Buchenwald concentration camp.

Blockältester [G] "Block elder": The chief of a "living block" (a single or double row of barracks) in the concentration camps and the larger slave-labor camps. As a rule, especially in the concentration camps, all *Blockältesten* were German, Austrian, or other non-Jewish professional criminals. > see also: **Konzentrationslager System**; **Berufsverbrecher**.

Blockführer [G] "Block leader": The SS non-commissioned officer who was assigned a number of blocks in a concentration camp. > see also: **Konzentrationslager System**.

Blockführerstube [G] "Block commander's guard-house": The office of the SS block commander in a concentration camp. > see also: **Konzentrationslager System**.

Blockschreiber [G] "Block secretary": Inmate selected to be the barracks record keeper. A member of the inner administration of a concentration camp, the *Blockschreiber* was appointed by the SS and was responsible for keeping records on the inmates within his jurisdiction. > see also: **Konzentrationslager System**.

Blocksperre [G] "Block arrest": The prohibition of inmates leaving their block except for work or *Appell*.

Blokowy [P] "Block leader": Polish term for a barracks chief in the Nazi concentration camp system. A woman barracks chief was called a *blokowa*.

Blut und boden [G] "Blood and soil": A Nazi concept — promulgated into the Reich Hereditary Farm Law in September 1933 — stating that only a person of German or cognate blood could be a landowner. The concept animated much Nazi discourse in the pre-*Machtergreifung* era, especially in regard to the condemnation of landownership by Jews. In September 1933, the Nazis turned the concept into law by promulgating the Reich Hereditary Farm Law. > see also: **Eindeutschung**.

Blutige Brigide [G] "Bloody Bridget": An inmate term for the beast of Majdanek, SS staff leader of the *Frauenlager*, Hildegard Lachert.

Blutlich [G] "Blood relation": Nazi neologism signifying membership in the nation. Of course, it followed that membership was limited to Aryans only. > see also: **Volk**.

Blutmischungen [G] "Blood mixings": Nazi racial term for intermarriages or for sexual relationships between Jews and Gentiles. > see also: **Mischling**.

Boycott, Anti-Jewish: First Nazi assault on German Jewry, which began on Saturday, April 1, 1933. The boycott, proclaimed by Joseph Goebbels, and was officially announced as an act of reprisal against Jewish *Greuelpropaganda* (atrocity propaganda). The actual boycott was headed by Julius Streicher and began at 10 in the morning when uniformed SA members were posted in front of Jewish stores, thus preventing would-be customers from entering. As a result of international protests, the Nazis agreed to limit the boycott to only one day, although they threatened to renew it. In fact, the boycott continued unabated and led directly to the *Arisierung* program.

Boycott, Anti-Nazi: Jewish defense mechanism in reaction to the Nazi persecution of German Jewry. On March 19, 1933, the Jewish War Veterans of America announced that its members would boycott German goods and services. Similar boycott groups arose in Poland, the Yishuv, and in France. Ze'ev Jabotinsky, president of Ha-Zohar, declared his support for the boycott in May 1933 and in October organized in Paris the Center for Economic Defense. Following the Anti-Jewish Boycott in Germany, anti-Nazi groups in the United States and other countries joined the boycott. The American Jewish Congress issued its own boycott declaration in August 1933 and founded the Joint Boycott Council with the Jewish Labor Committee in 1935. Despite widespread

ועדת החרם על תוצרת גרמניה.

Poster advocating an anti-Nazi boycott
in the Yishuv
Courtesy of the Jabotinsky Institute Archive, Tel Aviv

support among Jewish communities, the boycott was opposed by many important Jewish organizations, including the American Jewish Committee, B'nai B'rith, the Board of Deputies of British Jews, and the Alliance Israélite Universelle. Because of this disunity, the boycott met with only limited success. Within the Yishuv, support for the boycott was mixed as a result of the Transfer (Ha'avara) agreement. > see also: **Ha'avara**.

Boycottiert die Juden [G] "Boycott the Jews": Slogan for the opening campaign of the Nazi war against German Jewry, officially plastered all over Germany on March 28, 1933. > see also: **Boycott, Anti-Jewish**.

Boznica [P] "God's house": Polish wartime term for a synagogue. Soon after the Nazi occupation of Poland hundreds of synagogues were burned down by special SS units, the Brennkommandos. Later, during the occupation, many of the smaller or unmarked former Jewish prayer houses that were not destroyed were pointed out to the Gestapo by Polish collaborators.

Braune mappe [G] "Brown folder": RSHA code name for the folder holding instructions from Alfred Rosenberg for the treatment of the Jews in the Nazi-occupied territories of the Soviet Union. Rosenberg suggested that the Nazi occupation authorities foment pogroms among the non-Jewish population in order to solve the Jewish problem.

Braunes haus [G] "Brown house": Colloquial name for NSDAP headquarters located at 45 Briennerstrasse, the former Barlow mansion, in Munich. In 1931 the party leadership moved into the building, conferring the name Brown House as its official name. As the NSDAP expanded adjacent buildings were rented or bought and were also included in the complex.

Brenkommando(s) [G] "Arson squads": Special units within the German police, assigned to burn Jewish religious articles, synagogues, and other Jewish institutions in addition to small-scale operations against the non-Jewish population. The purpose of their operation was to sow confusion and terror among the civilian population in newly-occupied Poland.

Brider Yidn [ברידער יידן, Y] "Brother Jews": Title of a broadcast to world Jewry by members of the Jewish Anti-Fascist Committee on August 24, 1941. Used primarily for propaganda purposes, the broadcast emphasized Jewish solidarity and marked the 800th anniversary of the birth of Jewish national-religious poet Judah ha-Levi.

Briefaktion [G] "Letter Operation": Nazi term for the act of compelling certain groups of deported Jews to write letters or postcards to those relatives still at home extolling conditions in the death camps. After completing the letters, the Jews were forced into the gas chambers and murdered. The ruse, however, was largely successful and explains part of the unpreparedness of ghettoized Jews for the deportation experience.

Brigadier [בריגאדיער, Y/Slang] Jewish term for the foreman of a slave labor gang in some ghettos or concentration camps. > see also: **Kapo.**

Briha [בריחה, H] "Flight": The postwar movement of Holocaust survivors from Poland to Displaced Persons' camps in Germany, Austria, and Italy. The avowed aim of Briha was to reach the coasts where the Jews would embark on vessels of the Mossad le-Aliya Bet for the journey to Palestine. Spontaneous Briha began in 1944 and increased as each new Jewish community, or rather the survivors thereof, was liberated. The term applies both to the movement and to the organization that oversaw the operation. In 1945 the Hagana began oversight of the Briha program. > see also: **Aliya Bet.**

Brik fun toyit [בריק פון טויט, Y] "Bridge of death": Term used in the Lvov ghetto designating the Ulica Peltewna railroad bridge. When the ghetto was established, Ulica Peltewna was one of a handful of streets through which Jews were permitted to pass. On many occasions Jews passing to the ghetto area under the bridge were attacked, robbed, and killed by local Ukrainian collaborators.

Brown Shirts: Common name for the Sturmabteilungen, based on their mustard colored uniforms. > see also: **Sturmabteilungen.**

Bücherverbrennung [G] "Book burning": The mass Nazi bonfires on May 10, 1933, in which thousands of copies of books by Jews, Communists, socialists, pacifists, and other "enemies" of the Third Reich were destroyed. The books had been removed from library shelves by student members of the NSDAP and were destroyed with great fanfare. The operation was

Selecting books to be burned
Courtesy of the National Archives/U.S. Holocaust Memorial Museum

carried out under the sponsorship of Nazi propaganda chief Joseph Goebbels. Although only one public book burning was held, this represented the start of a systematic purge of German culture.

Bunawerke [G] "Buna works": Sub-camp of the Auschwitz KL, located three miles (4.8 km) from the main camp and comprising factories run by I. G. Farben Verlag for the production of synthetic rubber. The camp name was derived from the compound Sodium Butadiene, whose chemical symbol NaBu was transposed to Buna.

Bunker(s) [(ס)באנקער, Y] "Bunker": Term used to designate the underground hiding places dug by Jews in many of the East European ghettos.

Bunker, die [G] "The Cellar": Name for the punishment area of Auschwitz I (the main camp), also known as Block 11. The name derived from the narrow, box-like cell into which *Haftlinge* committing infractions were locked. Punishment in the *Bunker* was a death sentence, since the prisoners would be held in the cell without food or water.

Bunker I [1 באנקער, Y] Jewish inmate term for the Birkenau gas chambers and crematoria complex.

C

Camp A: Designation for the Gypsy family camp in Auschwitz-Birkenau.

Capo del Governo [I] "Head of State": title of Benito Mussolini, Italian chief of state, from 1926 on.

Chaim der Shreklecher [דער חיים שרעקלעכער, Y] "Chaim the Terrible": One of a number of nicknames for Mordechai Chaim Rumkowski, *Judenälteste* of the Lodz ghetto.

Chaimki [P] "Chaims": A common term for the currency issued in the ghetto of Lodz, Poland, and nicknamed after Mordechai Chaim Rumkowski, the head of the Lodz Judenrat. A set of postage stamps (valid for internal ghetto use only) was also issued, with German permission, by the Rumkowski administration.

Chapers [כאפערס, Y] "Grabbers": Ghetto term for starved youngsters who, spotting anything resembling food, would snatch the parcel from the hands of the carrier, tear it open, and,

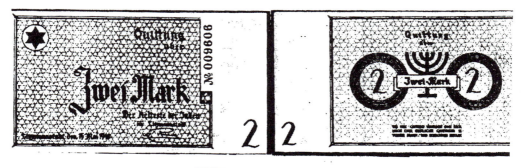

Chaimkis: A two mark note (top) and a ten pfenning postage stamp
Authors' Collection

201

without hesitation, stuff it in their mouths so that it could not be repossessed.

Cheta [Bu] "Guerrillas": common term for Bulgarian partisan units. Organized by the Communists, Cheta units did not discriminate against Jews.

Chopinlager [G] "Chopin camp": Nickname for the warehouse of the Majdanek *Vernichtungslager*, located on Ulica Chopin in Lublin. > see also: **Kanada**.

Choroba glodowa [P] "Starvation disease": The overwhelming hunger that Eastern European Jewry was faced with, especially Jews in the Polish ghettos or slave-labor camps, where they succumbed by the thousands.

Christian der Grausame [G] "Christian the Terrible": SS term for Christian Wirth, whose sadistic cruelty saw no bounds; he was inspector of all the extermination camps.

Churb'n [חורבן, Y/H] "Catastrophe": Yiddish term, with religious overtones, designating the destruction of European Jewry during the Nazi era. > see also: **Holocaust; Shoa**.

Ciklapte kapuste [ציקלאפטע קאפוסטע, Y] "Chopped cabbage": Underground term for badly wounded German soldiers retreating from the Russian front.

Clepsydras [Unknown] "Water clocks": Concentration camp jargon apparently limited to Treblinka and referring to those prisoners destined for death. The *Clepsydra* was a mark on the forehead, usually resulting from a blow to the face or head as punishment for an infraction. The subsequent scar became a mark for imminent death.

Collaboration

1. Scope and Definition
The willful rendering of assistance to the Nazi occupation authorities, the Wehrmacht, and the Third Reich in general. Collaboration may be divided into four components: *Economic*, the least important form of collaboration. Generally identified with shopkeepers, restaurateurs, and other small businesspeople in Nazi-occupied Europe who did business with the occupation authorities out of economic necessity. *Administrative*, the form of collaboration most commonly associated with low-level members of the professional civil service (such as police). Although few in this form of collaboration were ideologically committed to Nazism or fascism, many did their jobs with great enthusiasm. In other cases, notably among railroad workers in Western Europe, outward collaboration was actually a cover for covert resistance activities. *Military*, a form of collaboration associated with those who volunteered for Nazi or Nazi-sponsored military and paramilitary forces. The majority of military collaborators were also political collaborators, although many of those who "volunteered" for the paramilitary Organization Todt were actually kidnapped and treated as slave laborers. *Political*, the form of collaboration associated with many European Fascists who had an ideological affinity with Nazism or, at the very least, thought that national interests would best be served by an alliance with the Third Reich — which they assumed would soon win the war.

It is not possible to quantify the total number of collaborators throughout Europe. This is especially true since the difference between collaboration and resistance — as seen in the first two categories — often was a difference between perception and reality. As with Fascists, collaborators did not always have a consistent attitude toward Jews. In general, economic collaborators were the least antisemitic; and administrative collaboration — at least in regard to Jews — was largely dependent on geographical area. Thus, the collaborationist Danish police, aided rather than prevented the well-known October 1943 rescue operation that saved some 7,000 Danish Jews from deportation. Likewise, the Italian military administration in Italian zones of occupation (France and Yugoslavia) not only did not follow Il Duce's orders but went out of its way to protect and

Ukrainian auxiliaries participating in the suppression of the Warsaw ghetto uprising
Courtesy of the National Archives/U.S. Holocaust Memorial Museum

save Jews. In contradistinction, French police in Nazi-occupied France freely helped the Gestapo in the roundup of Jews; the Polish Blue Police (Granatowa Policja) eagerly hunted Jews hiding on the Aryan side and helped with the *Judenreinigung* policy. Military collaborators reflected a similar situation: Although Italian and Spanish legions on the Russian front were known, in some instances, to have overpowered Einsatzkommandos or otherwise rescued Jews from the clutches of certain death — the Spanish Blue Legion, for instance, saved Jews by claiming they were Spanish citizens — Estonian, Latvian, Lithuanian, Ukrainian, and Croatian paramilitary collaborators helped in the slaughter of hundreds of thousands of Jews. In many instances their cruelty was greater than that of the Germans. Political collaborators were usually strongly antisemitic — their commitment to Nazi victory also reflected a commitment to creating a *judenrein* Europe. > see also: **Fascism**.

2. Collaborationist Organizations

Belgium

Algemeene Schutscharen Vlaanderen, "Flemish General SS," collaborationist organization established September 1940. The Flemish SS was a small body until 1942 when the entire group was absorbed into the Allgemeine SS. Thereafter, the Flemish SS expanded, with both reserve and youth components being created. As of June 1944, the Flemish SS numbered approximately 3,500 members, including 1,600 in the Waffen SS.

Amis du Grand Reich Allemand (AGRA), "Friends of the Greater German Reich," collaborationist organization founded on March 13, 1941 by Alfonse Bougne. AGRA was funded as a cultural organization and set its goal as the fostering the principles of Nazism within Belgium. AGRA comprised a youth group, a protection service, and the Service d'Information Politique (Political Information Service), which paralleled the Gestapo.

Dietsche Militia (DM), "Germanic Militia," police arm of the Belgian Flemish National Union (VNV) Divided into four elements: (1) The Zwarte Brigade, used mostly for counterresistance operations, (2) The Wacht Brigade, a full-time guard detachment used to defend Nazi and Wehrmacht installations, (3) The Motor Brigade, Belgian equivalent of the NSKK, (4) The Hulp Brigade, a part-time auxiliary to help at VNV functions. At its height, DM numbered some 17,000 men. > see also: **Collaboration, Collaborationist Organizations (Zwarte Brigade); Fascism, Fascist Parties and Organizations, (Belgium, Vlaamsch Nationaal Verbond).**

Deutscher Sprach-Verein, "German Language Union," Volksdeutsche fifth-columnist organization active in Belgium. Founded in April 1941, the union advocated the incorporation of Belgium into the Reich.

Legion Vlaandern, "Flanders Legion," SS military unit created on August 6, 1941, on the basis of Flemish members of SS Regiment Nordwest. Largely recruited from among members of the VNV, and especially the Zwarte Brigade. At its height, the legion numbered 405 men and was commanded by Waffen-SS officers. In May 1943 the legion was transformed to SS Freiwillige Sturmbrigade Langemarck.

Légion Wallonie, "Wallonian Legion," Waffen-SS volunteer unit established in August 1941 and commanded by Rex leader Leon Degrelle. At its height the Légion numbered 1,600 men. In action from November 1941 to April 1945 the legion established a reputation for fanaticism unequaled among Waffen-SS units. On June 1, 1943, the legion was attached to the Waffen-SS Wiking Division. In 1945 the legion was rechristened as a Waffen-SS Panzer-Grenadier Division, although it was grossly under strength. In May 1945 most of the legionnaires surrendered to the British Royal Army.

Union des Travailleurs Manuels et Intellectuels (UTMI), "Union of Manual and Intellectual Workers," collaborationist organization founded by Socialist leader Professor Henri de Man. Intending to create a single representative labor movement, de Man took the Socialist rhetoric of National Socialism seriously. As an independent agency, UTMI collapsed in 1941. It was then taken over by the Nazis and used as a front for the abduction of Belgian workers.

Zwarte Brigade (ZB), "Black Brigade," commonly known as Dietsche Militia − Zwarte Brigade. Associated with the VNV, the ZB originally was a volunteer force. After May 1942, however, conscription of eighteen-to-twenty-one-year-olds was begun. At its peak, ZB numbered 12,000 men. > see also: **Fascism, Fascist Parties and Organizations (Belgium, Vlaamsch Nationaal Verbond).**

Belorussia

Belaruskaya Narodnaya Partizanka, "Belorussian National Guerrillas," anti-Communist guerrilla movement founded in the summer of 1941. Despite the willingness of local civilians to collaborate with the Nazis, the movement was never very large. Its members, however, served with the SS on many operations, among others during the murder of Minsk Jewry.

Denmark

Danmarks National-Socialistike Arbejder Parti (DNSAP), "Danish National Socialist Workers Party," founded November 16, 1931, by Frits Clausen. The DNSAP was divided into seventeen *sysseler* (main districts) in addition to storm troop (SA) and youth sections. The DNSAP was not anti-Christian in its orientation and shunned antisemitism. Publications: *Faedrelandet* (Fatherland); *National-Socialisten*.

Freikorps Danmark, "Danish Free Corps," SS formation of 1,164 men established in summer 1941 for operations in the Soviet Union. The unit was only ready for action after March 1942 when it formed one regiment of the Waffen-SS Totenkopf Division. Mauled in operations during the summer of 1942, it was disbanded and reconstituted as SS Grenadier Regiment # 1 Danmark in April and May 1943.

National Socialistike Ungdom (NSU), "National Socialist Youth," Danish Nazi organization established in September 1934. The NSU was open to boys only between the ages of ten and eighteen. From ten to fourteen NSU members were organized into the Skjoldunge (Defense Corps); from fourteen to eighteen in the Vaebnere (Squires). NSU graduates were expected to join the DNSAP's storm troopers at eighteen, but many did not. > see also: **Collaboration, Collaborationist Organizations (Denmark, Danmarks National-Socialistike Arbejder Parti).**

Nye Danmark, "New Denmark," collaborationist party founded in 1943 by Danes who broke with the DNSAP. Joined by the remaining members of the antisemitic NSAP, the Nye Danmark party was a closer copy of the Nazi Party than its progenitor. The party was identical with the Schalburg Corps and was subdivided into the Dansk Folke-Vaern (Danish People's Defense) and the Landstormen (Territorial Assault Men), the equivalent of the SS.

France

Commissariat Général aux Questions Juives (CGQJ), "General Commission on Jewish Affairs," established by the Vichy regime on March 29, 1941, and charged with coordinating all Vichy anti-Jewish policies. The CGQJ played an important role in writing the Statut des Juifs (Statute on the Jews). Chairmen: Xavier Vallat (1941–1942); Louis Darquier de Pellepoix (1942–1943); Charles Mercier du Paty de Clam (1944). Publication: *La Question Juive en France et dans le Monde*. > see also: **Legislation, Anti-Jewish, Axis States (Vichy France).**

Légion des Volontaires Français (LVF), "French Volunteer Legion," Collaborationist military force created July 7, 1941, to participate in the anti-Bolshevik crusade. In all,

the LVF numbered about 13,400 men of whom just 1,700 were deployed at any given time. For most of 1943 the LVF operated as an anti-partisan force in the USSR. During this period the LVF built its reputation as a brutal, but not wholly effective, military force.

Milice Bretonne, "Breton Militia," anti-resistance, anti-Vichy movement created in 1944 to aid the Germans in the Normandy and Brittany regions of France. Popular among Breton separatists, the force consisted of 200 auxiliary police who were armed and paid by the Germans. Known for its savagery, the Milice Bretonne withdrew with the Nazis after D day and continued anti-resistance activities until the end of the war.

Milice Française, "French Militia," French Fascist paramilitary organization formed in January 1942 by Joseph Darnand as part of the Légion Française des Combattants. On January 10, 1943, the Milice was reorganized as an independent agency and was charged with internal security tasks. Most members acted as uniformed police in anti-resistance and anti-Jewish roles, although the Milice also fielded plain-clothes sections. A special section of the Milice, which paralleled the SS, was the Service Spécial de Sécurité. As resistance activites increased, the Milice gained in power and by January 1944, Darnand was admitted into the collaborationist government as minister of security. His Milice, however, failed to stem the tide of resistance activities: Their terror methods merely brought new recruits for the *maquis*.

Organisation Technique (OT), "Technical Service," French collaborationist clandestine agency created by the Milice Française during the winter of 1944. In all, OT recruited and trained eighty agents. Fanatical collaborators, the OT members were parachuted into liberated France to organize anti-Allied resistance. All were captured and most were shot as spies.

Police des Questions Juives, "Jewish Affairs Police," police force set up on March 29, 1941, to enforce the operations of the Commissariat Général aux Questions Juives. In 1944 the majority of the police joined the collaborationist Milice.

Rassemblement National Populaire (RNP),

"National People's Rally," Fascist party founded on February 1, 1941, by Marcel Déat. RNP advocated the creation of a racially pure France ruled by an authoritarian government. RNP raised its own militia, the Légion Nationale Populaire, recruited among ex-servicemen. Membership in June 1942 was 50,000. Thereafter, most RNP members left to join the LVF or the SS and in 1944 the RNP began to cooperate with the Milice.

Service d'Ordre Légionnaire (SOL), "Police Service of the Legion," founded in January 1942 by Joseph Darnand. > see also: **Collaboration, Collaborationist Organizations (France, Milice Française)**.

Service du Travail Obligatoire (STO), "Mandatory Labor Service," Vichy agency created on September 21, 1942, to promote French civilian labor in the Third Reich. Operating without even the pretense of "volunteering," the STO became little more than a front agency for the Organisation Todt.

Holland

Brandenburger(s), special operations unit of the Abwehr that included thirty Dutch fifth columnists who cooperated in an abortive attempt to seize strategic points, including bridges and fortifications, on behalf of the Germans in 1940. > see also: **Wehrmacht**.

Freiwilligen Legion Niederlande (FLN), "Dutch Volunteer Legion," Military force formed for service in the Soviet Union by Dutch collaborators and Dutch Nazi Party (NSB) members on July 27, 1941. Although attached to the Waffen-SS, the FLN did not originally associate with the SS in its publicity. In 1943 the FLN was reorganized into the 4 SS Freiwilligen Panzer Grenadier Regiment, Nederland. As such it was employed in anti-partisan operations in Croatia and the Soviet Union. In December 1944 the unit was enlarged to divisional size; it remained in action continuously until the end of the war. > see also: **Schutzstaffel, Subsidiary Agencies (Waffen SS)**.

Groene politie (Grüne Polizei), "Green Police," common name for the collaborationist police force, so called because of their green uniforms. The Groene Politie was heavily involved in the roundup of Dutch Jewry.

Landstorm, "Territorial Assault," Nazi-created militia, formed to defend Holland from Allied attack.

Landwacht, "Home Guard," collaborationist auxiliary police force formed in 1941 to combat the underground and protect members of the Dutch Nazi Party (NSB).

Nationale Juegdstorm (NJ), "National Youth Troops," Dutch equivalent of the Hitlerjugend, founded in 1934. At its height in 1943 the NJ numbered 18,000 members. Publication: *De Stormmeeuw* (monthly).

National Socialistiche Beweging der Nederlanden (NSB), "Dutch Nazi Party," founded by Anton A. Mussert on December 14, 1931. In 1932 the NSB created its Weer Afdeeling (Storm Troops), but they were banned by the Dutch government in 1935. Upon the Nazi occupation of Holland, the NSB formed the core of a collaborationist administration within the Generalbezirk Nederland. From June 1940 until the liberation, the NSB — or its subsidiary agencies — participated in the roundup and deportation of Jews, in anti-resistance operations, and in military actions against the Soviet Union. Publications: *Het National Dagblad*, the party daily, *Volk en Vaderland*, a weekly, and *Storm*, monthly of the Dutch SS.

National-Socialistische Vrouwen Organisatie (NSVO), "National Socialist Women's Organization," established in 1938 but never a major factor in Dutch life.

Nederlandsche SS, "Dutch SS," NSB subsidiary established September 11, 1940, for police and other routine security duties. On November 1, 1942, the Dutch SS was "germanized," becoming the *Germanische SS en Nederland* (Germanic SS in Holland). At its height the Dutch SS totaled five regiments and was employed, along with one battalion of SS-Standarte Nordwest, to guard the Amersfort, Vught, and Westerbork concentration camps. > see also: **Schutzstaffel, Subsidiary Agencies (SS-Standarte Nordwest)**.

Nederlandse Arbeids Dienst (NAD), "Dutch Labor Service," founded May 21, 1941, as a means to employ demobilized soldiers in construction and clean-up projects. Initially neutral politically, the NAD was nazified in 1942 and was taken over by the NSB. After 1943 the NAD served as a front organization for the transfer of non-Jewish forced laborers to Germany.

Nederlandse Arbeidsfront (NAF), "Dutch Labor Front," Dutch collaborationist organization founded in 1942 and modeled after the DAF.

Nederlandse Unie (NU), "Netherlands Union," semi-collaborationist political group founded in July 1940. The NU's official goal was to foster closer relations between Holland and Germany. The party was catholic and conservative in its orientation but was only moderately antisemitic. Although it numbered 800,000 members in February 1941, the NU failed as a movement: It proved too collaborationist for most of the Dutch and it was too patriotic for the Nazis. The NU disbanded in August 1941.

Verbond van Nederlandsche Journalisten (VNJ), "Union of Dutch Journalists," founded in December 1940 as the propaganda arm of the NSB.

Vrijwillige Hulp-Politie, "Volunteer Auxiliary Police," Dutch body founded in May 1942. Officially an auxiliary police body, the Hulp-Politie was primarily involved in rounding up Jews for deportation east. A subgroup of the Hulp-Politie specialized in ferreting out Jews in hiding.

Vrijwilligerslegioen Nederland (VLN), "Dutch Volunteer Legion," Armed body of the NSB formed to fight with the Wehrmacht in the Soviet Union.

Weer Afdeeling (WA), "Storm Troops," combat arm of the NSB, founded in 1932, disbanded by Dutch government order in 1935, and then re-formed at the behest of the Nazi authorities in 1940. At its height the WA numbered 15,000 men organized into thirteen *Heerbannen* (regional brigades). During the Nazi occupation the WA operated as an unarmed but uniformed police force. Violently antisemitic, the WA participated in numerous anti-Jewish operations throughout Holland. Publication: *De Zwarte Soldaat*.

Hungary

Allambiztonsági Rendészet (AR), "State Security Police," organized in 1939, the AR was the Hungarian equivalent of the Gestapo.

Magyar Zsidótlanitó Különitmény (MZSK), "Hungarian 'Dejewification' Unit," gendarmerie unit that assisted Adolf Eichmann in the deportation of Hungarian Jewry to the gas chambers at Auschwitz, in the summer and fall of 1944. The MZSK leadership included László Endre, László Raky, Lajos Meggyesi, Márton Zöldi, and Péter Hain.

Nyilaskeresztes Part–Hungarista Mozgalom, "Arrow Cross-Hungarist Movement," Fascist party founded by Ferenc Szálasi in 1937. Szálasi's theories were closely related to Nazism, but the racial element was "magyarized." Antisemitism was an inherent part of Arrow Cross ideology. The party drew most of its support from army officers, students, impoverished intellectuals, and segments of the proletariat. The party received approximately 25 percent of the vote in the 1939 elections, but did not participate in the coalition government. On October 15, 1944, the party seized the reins of government in Hungary; Szálasi held power until January 1945.

Latvia

Pērkonkrusts, "Thunder Cross," also known as Kommando Arajs, a Latvian paramilitary unit led by Major Viktor Arajs. Headquartered in Riga, the unit numbered 400 men; it was established soon after the Nazi occupation of Latvia in 1941. Working closely with the Einsatzgruppen and the SD, Arajs became the main organizer of anti-Jewish terror in Latvia. Pērkonkrusts was responsible for the roundup, isolation, and murder of thousands of Latvian, Lithuanian, and Estonian Jews.

Lithuania

Lietuviu Aktyvistu Frontas (LAF), "Lithuanian Activist Front," a nationalist, Fascist, and rabidly antisemitic organization established in Berlin on November 17, 1940. The moving spirit behind the LAF was Lt. Col. Kazys Skirpa, previously Lithuanian ambassador to Germany. The LAF cooperated closely with the Abwehr and other Nazi security organizations. In anticipation of the beginning of Operation Barbarossa, the LAF smuggled orders detailing instructions for an armed uprising into Lithuania. During the course of military operations, LAF members and partisans aided the German seizure of Lithuania by attacking Soviet troops, occupying points of strategic importance, and instigating anti-Jewish pogroms.

Norway

Hirdens Bedriftsvern (HBV), "Hird Factory Guard," anti-resistance unit established by Vidkun Quisling in March 1942. Operating in uniforms, the HBV was oriented toward protecting factories and other installations from saboteurs. At this task the HBV proved a failure: In August 1944 resisters even destroyed HBV headquarters.

Hirdmen, "King's Men," Norwegian storm troopers, modeled on the Nazi SA, founded by Vidkun Quisling on May 17, 1933. In September 1940, when Quisling took over as head of Norway's collaborationist government, Hirdmen were reorganized into regular and militia elements, a naval corps, an aviation unit, and the Førergarden, Quisling's personal bodyguard. Most Hirdmen later joined the Wehrmacht or the Norwegian SS and fought with the Germans during the Russian campaign.

Nasjonal Samling (NS), "National Assembly," Norwegian Fascist party, founded by Vidkun Quisling in May 1933. During the Nazi occupation the NS was the only legal party in Norway, and it pursued a consistently collaborationist policy. The NS had its own militia, patterned on the Nazi SA, and many NS members joined the Wehrmacht or the Norwegian SS, fighting during the Russian campaign.

Norges SS, "Norwegian SS," created out of a regiment of Hirdmen in May 1941. The Norwegian SS were organized into their own legion, attached to the Waffen-SS, for the Russian campaign. Later still, the Norwegian SS became part of the Fifth Waffen-SS Panzer Division (Wiking), which was composed almost exclusively of Scandinavian, Dutch, and Belgian volunteers. > see also:

Schutzstaffel, Subsidiary Agencies (Waffen SS).

O.T. Einsatzgruppe Wiking, "Organization Todt Operational Group Viking," Norwegian labor unit established April 5, 1942, and composed of 3,000 Norwegians. Although the idea of the unit was collaborationist, the laborers were actually treated as prisoners and kept under Gestapo guard while building fortifications in northern Norway.

Poland

Granatowa Policja, "Blue Police," the Polish police force — the only Polish organization not dismantled by the Nazis upon occupation (but cleansed of Jews) — that collaborated with the Nazis. Known by the color of their uniforms, the Blue Police were especially active in helping to oversee the daily police tasks inside most ghettos, in connection with the *Aussiedlungsaktionen* against Jewish communities, and in rounding up single Jews caught hiding outside the ghettos. The Blue Police also participated in the suppression of the Warsaw Ghetto uprising.

Sonderdienst, "Special Service," a collaborationist organization of Volksdeutsche that operated in Nazi-occupied Poland from 1939 on. Many of their members acted as guards in *Zwangsarbeitslager*, with a record of brutal behavior toward the victims. Members of the Sonderdienst also took an active part in the *Aussiedlungsaktionen*.

Russia

Druzhina, "Bodyguard," Russian collaborationist organization founded by the HSSPF of Pskov in April 1942 and led by Lt. Col. V. V. Gil. By March 1943 Druzhina numbered 3,000 men. It is not clear if Gil's defection was sincere or not, for in August 1943 he and 2,500 of his men redefected to Soviet lines. Gil was killed in action in May 1944.

Komitet Osvobozhdeniia Narodov Rosii (KONR), "Russian Liberation Movement," collaborationist organization — also known as the Smolensk Committee — founded by General Andrei A. Vlasov in September 1942. Although not officially recognized by the Germans until September 16, 1943, KONR was a major propaganda factor behind the Russian Liberation Army (ROA). On November 14, 1944, KONR issued the "Prague Manifesto," which called upon Soviet citizens to overthrow communism. On January 28, 1945, KONR took command of ROA (then reduced to two divisions). In May KONR oversaw the ROA mutiny in Prague — when ROA troops fought against the Germans.

Russkaia Natsionalnaia Narodnaia Armiia (RNNA), "Russian National People's Army," also known as the "Osintorf Brigade," a collaborationist military unit created in the Smolensk Oblast in March 1942. In July, RNNA fielded six battalions with 6,000 men. In December 1942, RNNA was absorbed into the Wehrmacht, but its battalions were dispersed in rear-line duties because the troops were considered unreliable.

Russkaia Osvoboditelnaia Armiia (ROA), "Russian Liberation Army," collaborationist force created in January 1943 by uniting all Ostbataillone in the Wehrmacht. In March 1943 ROA became operational, but it never saw action as a unified whole: In April all but two divisions were transferred to the Western Front. On January 28, 1945, ROA became a subsidiary of KONR and thenceforth bore the unofficial name of "Vlasov Army." In May 1945 ROA turned on the Nazis, for example, in the Prague uprising, perhaps to avoid being considered collaborators by the Allies.

Russkaia Osvoboditelnaia Narodnaia Armiia (RONA), "Russian National Liberation Army," also known as the Kaminski Brigade, collaborationist military force raised in Orel in 1941 and commanded by Colonel Bronislav Kaminski. Granted official status in 1942, RONA eventually numbered 20,000 troops. RONA was absorbed into the Waffen-SS in 1944, and one regiment, commanded by Kaminski, was active in suppressing the Polish Warsaw uprising of August and September 1944. At the end of the revolt, Kaminski was court-martialled by order of HSSPF Erich von dem Bach-Zelewski and was executed. RONA was disbanded shortly thereafter.

Wachtbataillone, "Guard battalions," units of former Soviet POWs who offered their services to the SS. Incorporated into the SS, they served as guards in numerous eastern labor camps and in the *Vernichtungslager*, exercising extreme cruelty toward their victims. In addition to their guard duties, in Treblinka and Sobibór (at least), Wachtbataillone members operated the gas chambers.

Slovakia

Freiwillige Schutzstaffel (FS) "Voluntary Defense Squadron," the elite guard of Volksdeutsche, the German minority living in Slovakia. The FS established close collaboration with the Slovak Fascist Hlinkova Garda.

Hlinkova Garda (HG), "Hlinka Guard," collaborationist militia created by the Slovak People's Party on October 8, 1938, and named after Andrej Hlinka, the deceased leader of the Slovak nationalists. The HG acted as the party's internal security force, and it retained that function when Slovakia became independent (March 14, 1939). Throughout, the HG was led by Alexander Mach. From 1941 on some members of the HG were trained in SS camps in Germany. In addition to internal security roles, HG members participated in the deportation of Slovak Jews to extermination sites in Poland during the course of 1942.

Ukraine

Marschketten, "Expeditionary Forces," a term for Ukrainian militia units that operated with the Germans in the southern section of the Generalgouvernement. Their main task was to help German Aussiedlungskommando units in the round-up, terrorizing, robbing, and killing of Jews and the destruction of the Jewish communities in the area.

Nachtigall, "Nightengale," name of the Ukrainian volunteer battalion attached to the Wehrmacht. Nachtigall was responsible for initiating and taking part in many massacres against Jews in German-occupied Soviet territory, among them the rather large pogrom in Lvov on July 1, 1941, that took the lives of thousands of Jews.

Orhanizatsyia Ukrainskych Natsionalistiv (OUN), "Organization of Ukrainian

Nationalists," anti-Soviet movement founded in Berlin in February 1929. OUN was staunchly anti-Communist and, under Nazi influence, antisemitic. In 1941 OUN helped the Nazis form two Ukrainian battalions, Nachtigall and Roland, within the Wehrmacht. OUN Pokhidni Grupy (Mobile Units) provided the Germans with interpreters during their advance through the Ukraine. OUN units performed a variety of anti-Jewish duties throughout the war years.

Roland, name of a military formation attached to the Wehrmacht and made up of Ukrainian nationalists, primarily followers of Stefan Bandera, leader of the OUN. The unit fought on the Russian front from July 22, 1941 on, and was heavily involved in anti-Jewish activities, primarily in eastern Galicia.

SS Galizien, "SS Galicia," official name of a Ukrainian volunteer SS unit organized in 1943. The unit, which began as a battalion in the Waffen-SS, was eventually expanded to divisional size. Members of SS Galizien saw service in almost every major Nazi anti-partisan and anti-Jewish operation in Eastern Europe in 1944 and 1945, displaying great zeal for those undertakings.

Ukrainske Vyzvolne Viysko (UVV), "Ukrainian Liberation Army," auxiliary military unit formed in the Ukraine under Wehrmacht control. Composed of anti-Communists and OUN members, the UVV numbered some 180,000 part-time militia men at its height.

Yugoslavia

Heimwehr, "Home Defense," paramilitary force raised in June 1942 among the Volksdeutsche population of Dalmatia and Slovenia. In all, the Heimwehr provided three infantry regiments with ten battalions, which served in police and anti-guerrilla roles in Serbia.

Hrvatska Zastita, "Croat Militia," paramilitary group founded by Vladko Macek in April 1941. Undertook fifth-column activities on behalf of the Wehrmacht in Dalmatia. Many of the militia men later transferred to the Ustaša.

Ustaša, "Insurgent," Croatian nationalist organization formed by Ante Pavelić in 1930. Pavelić patterned the Ustaša on Italian fascism rather than on Nazism, but his movement also contained a significant antisemitic component. In April 1941 the Ustaša were permitted to form an independent Croatian state — in reality a puppet state under Nazi control. Between 1941 and 1945 the Ustaša carried out a systematic policy of genocide against the Serbs. During that period over half a million Serbs were murdered, along with twenty thousand Gypsies and thousands of opponents of the regime. Additionally, Ustaša members participated in every anti-Jewish *Aktion* in Yugoslavia.

Comnik [קומניק, Y] "End": Slang term for those Jews who risked their lives to engage in business deals, usually desperate efforts to barter for food or medications, with non-Jews in or near ghettos and concentration camps.

Concordat [Latin]: Diplomatic agreement between the Vatican and Nazi Germany negotiated between Franz von Papen and Vatican Secretary of State Eugenio Cardinal Pacelli (who later became Pope Pius XII) and signed on July 20, 1933. The Concordat settled the rights and responsibilities of German Catholics in relation to the regime.

Conducator [Ro] "Leader": Official title of Romanian dictator Ion Antonescu.

Conferences, Antisemitic

Frankfurt, "scholarly" conference held in March 1941 to search for a total solution (*Gesamtlösung*) for the European Jewish problem. Participants included: Alexandru Cuza, Wilhelm Grau, Walter Gross, Alajos Kovács, Sano Mach, Anton A. Mussert, Vidkun Quisling, Alfred Rosenberg, Peter-Heinz Seraphim, and Giselher Wirsing.

Krakow, international anti-Jewish congress, held July 11–15, 1944. Sponsored by Alfred Rosenberg with Hitler's permission. The 402 participants included: Martin Bormann, Leon Degrelle, Hans Frank, Joseph Goebbels, Heinrich Himmler, Amin Al-Husseini, Ernst

Kaltenbrunner, Robert Ley, Anton A. Mussert, Vidkun Quisling, Arthur Seyss-Inquart, and Joachim von Ribbentrop.

Conferences, International

Arcadia, held in Washington, D.C. from December 22, 1941, to January 14, 1942, between Franklin D. Roosevelt and Winston S. Churchill and their chief advisers. Arcadia's aim was threefold: to set up the Combined Chief of Staff that would coordinate all future Allied operations; to set up the instrument for a future United Nations; and to solemnly agree that none of the Allies would enter into separate peace negotiations with Nazi Germany.

Bermuda, held in Hamilton on April 19, 1943, between American and British representatives, ostensibly to find a solution to the wartime refugee crisis. In reality, the Bermuda Conference marked the summit of efforts by officials of both countries to thwart effective action to rescue European Jewry and blunt adverse public opinion. The Bermuda conference exemplifies the extraordinary lengths the United States and Great Britain were willing to go to avoid entanglements on the rescue issue. > see also: **Refugees, Jewish**.

DIE KONFERENZ IN EVIAN.

Die Konferenz hat sich heute, nachdem sie an vier Tagen oeffentliche Sitzungen abgehalten hat, vertagt, und wird ihre Schlusssitzung am Freitag den 15. Juli abhalten. Wir moechten Ihnen im folgenden einen vorlaeufigen Bericht ueber den Verlauf geben.

1.   Die vier oeffentlichen Sitzungen wurden, nach den ueblichen Begruessungen, fast vollstaendig mit Erklaerungen der etwa 30 vertretenen Staaten ausgefuellt. Diese offiziellen Erklaerungen waren fast alle auf den gleichen Ton gestimmt: dass man sich sehr gern an dem humanitaeren Werk beteiligen moechte, dass aber die oekonomischen Verhaeltnisse in jedem einzelnen Staate eine groessere Einwanderung unmoeglich machen. Die einzige Ausnahme bildete die Erklaerung des Vertreters der Vereinigten Staaten, der zu verstehen gab, dass seine Regierung die gesetzlich zulaessige Quota von 27.300 Einwanderern aus Deutschland und Oesterreich voll auszunuetzen bereit sei. Die suedamerikanischen Staaten erklaerten sich grundsaetzlich bereit, Elemente, die in ihre Wirtschaft hereinpassen, d.h. insbesondere Landwirte, zuzulassen, wie ueberhaupt der Grundsatz der Auswahl der Emigranten in allen Erklaerungen eine grosse Rolle spielte.

2.   Diese Erklaerungen der Vertreter von 30 Regierungen waren natuerlich fuer die Oeffentlichkeit im eigenen Lande und in anderen Laendern bestimmt, sie sparten nicht mit Lobpreisungen fuer das eigene Land und fuer dasjenige was es bereits in der Absorption von Einwanderern getan hat. Die Gleichfoermigkeit all dieser Erklaerungen, bei denen auch die Vertreter der kleinsten Staaten laengere Memoranden vorlasen, wirkte ermuedend und war jedenfalls fuer den Fortgang der Verhandlungen nicht foerderlich.

3.   Die Konferenz, oder, wie ihre richtige Bezeichnung ist, "Inter-Governmental Committee", lehnte es ab Vertreter irgendwelcher privaten Organisationen zu empfangen, sondern setzte fuer diesen Zweck ein besonderes Subkomitee ein. Das Argument, das Dr. Goldmann dem amerikanischen Hauptdelegierten Taylor vorbrachte, wonach die Jewish Agency mehr als eine private Organisation sei und daher das Recht beanspruchen koenne vor dem Plenum der Konferenz zu sprechen (in welchem Falle es sich fuer Dr. Weizmann gelohnt haette nach Evian zu kommen) war nicht entscheidend, weil die englische Delegation diesen Antrag haette unterstuetzen muessen. Die englische Delegation, deren Sprecher, Lord Winterton, in seiner Rede Palaestina mit keinem Worte erwaehnt hat, war allgemein, sowohl unter Delegierten wie unter der Presse sehr ueberrascht, war nicht gewillt die Anregung, Dr. Weizmann zu hoeren, aufzugreifen. Daher waren wir der Ansicht - nach Beratungen mit Victor Cazalet und James MacDonald - dass die Reise Dr. Weizmanns nicht zweckmaessig sei.

4.   Die Vernehmungen vor dem Sub-Komitee waren nicht sehr serioes; da man allen etwa 40 Privatorganisationen, ganz gleichgueltig, ob sie gross oder klein waren, das Recht gab, vor der Subkommission zu erscheinen und von 5 bis 10 Minuten zu sprechen, konnte natuerlich von einer eingehenden Eroerterung der Probleme keine Rede sein. Es hat sich bitter geraecht, dass der Vorschlag unserer Londoner Executive beim British Council for German Jewry, vor Evian eine Konferenz der wichtigsten juedischen Organisationen einzuberufen, um eine einheitliche juedische Delegation nach Evian zu schicken wie dies vor vier Jahren bei der Lausanner Konferenz fuer

Facsimile of a report by Dr. Arthur Ruppin on the Evian Conference
Courtesy of the Histadrut Archive/Machon Lavon, Tel Aviv

Dumbarton Oaks, held in Washington, D.C., from August 21 to October 7, 1944, between Allied representatives. The conference laid the groundwork for the UN founding conference in San Fransisco.

Evian, held in Evian-les-Bains, France, from July 6 to 15, 1938, between delegates from thirty-two countries who had been invited by President Franklin D. Roosevelt. The conference was convened to facilitate the emigration of Jewish refugees from the Reich and to create an organization to solve the refugee problem. As the conference proceeded, state after state denied its ability to accept further refugees. Only the Dominican Republic volunteered to contribute unspecified areas for agricultural colonization in return for hefty financial contributions from world Jewry. The conference thus had only one concrete result: the creation of the Intergovernmental Committee on Refugees. > see also: **Refugees, Jewish**.

Montevideo, held in the Uruguyan capital on August 17 and 18, 1942, by members of the Italia Libera movement. The delegates sought Allied recognition of their movement as a legitimate government in exile — a status they did not receive — and discussed postwar plans for a democratic Italy.

Moscow, held in the Soviet capital October 18–30, 1943, between the foreign ministers of three of the Allied states (Vyacheslav Molotov, Cordell Hull, and Anthony Eden). The conference discussed postwar international organization, with emphasis on the fate of Austria.

Munich, held between Hitler, Mussolini, Chamberlain, and Daladier on September 30, 1938. Convened in response to Nazi threats against Czechoslovakia, the conference resulted in the abject abandonment of the Czechs. After Munich, the ultimate development of appeasement, Hitler believed that anything he desired was his for the taking.

Octagon, held in Quebec, Canada, September 10–17, 1944, between Churchill and Roosevelt. The agenda included military questions in addition to considering the Morgenthau Plan.

Potsdam, held in East Berlin from Juy 17 to August 2, 1945, between Churchill, Stalin, and Harry S. Truman. British elections held during the conference resulted in Churchill's replacement by Clement Attlee. The agenda included Soviet entrance into the war against Japan and regulation of relations between the occupying powers in Germany. This conference is often seen as the starting point of the cold war.

Quadrant, held in Quebec, Canada, August 11–24, 1943, between Roosevelt and Churchill. The agenda included discussions of military strategy only.

St. James Palace (1939), held in London February 7–20, 1939 between British, Jewish, and Arab representatives. The purpose of the conference was to find a peaceful solution to the Palestine problem. Arab refusal to meet with Jewish delegates and British insistence on exclusively defending Arab interests brought about a Jewish withdrawal from the talks and ultimately led to the British White Paper of 1939.

St. James Palace (1942), held in London by representatives of the United States, Great Britain, and the governments in exile. The conference focused on Nazi war crimes and on possible postwar responses to such criminal behavior. The conference, however, did not mention Jews as a separate category of victims and failed to establish uniform definitions of the different categories of Nazi crimes.

Sextant, held in Cairo December 2–7, 1943, between Roosevelt and Churchill. The agenda included discussions of military strategy only.

Teheran, held in the Iranian capital from November 28 to December 1, 1943, between the Big Three (Roosevelt, Churchill, and Stalin). The conference concentrated on the issue of a second front only.

Trident, held in Washington, D.C. May 12–25, 1943, between Roosevelt and Churchill. The agenda included discussions of military strategy only.

Yalta, held in the Crimean resort city from February 4–11, 1945, between the Big Three. The conference dealt with postwar zones of occupation in Germany, the United Nations, and the makeup of postwar Poland.

Confino [I] *"Domestic exile"*: Fascist term for one of the milder forms of punishment meted out to dissidents: house arrest.

Consulta Nazionale [I] *"National Consultative Assembly"*: Proto-parliament called by King Umberto II on April 5, 1945, to restore democracy to Italy. The Assembly's task was to prepare the nationwide referendum on the monarchy that took place in April 1946 and that converted Italy into a republic. After that, the Consulta Nazionale disbanded in favor of the Constituent Assembly.

Czerwonka [P] *"Red"*: A dysentery epidemic that claimed hundreds of lives at a time, especially in the larger Eastern European ghettos.

D

D-Lager: Generally the abbreviation for *Durchgangslager* (Transit camp). More particularly, the term refers to the holding pen in Auschwitz used for those women not immediately sent to the gas chambers. Inmates held in the D-Lager were sometimes held for days or weeks before a decision regarding their fate was made by the SS. > see also: **Konzentratsionlager System**.

D II: Code name for the Auschwitz medical office, responsible for the oversight of the various camp doctors. The doctors, in turn, were responsible for the selections of victims from the arriving transports. > see also: **Selektion(en)**.

Das Dritte Reich [G] "The Third Empire":

1. Scope and Definition

Popular Nazi name for their twelve-year rule over Germany. The term was coined in 1923 by Arthur Moeller van den Bruck, a noted Fascist and antisemite, and was rapidly adopted by the NSDAP. In using this term, the Nazis tapped into two meanings, one historical and the other mystical. The historical sense of the term was based on the continuity from the First Reich (the Holy Roman Empire, established in 962 and lasting until 1806) through the Second Reich (the Hohenzollern Empire that existed from 1871 to 1918) to the Third Reich. The mystical meaning developed out of this continuity as well; the Nazis saw the creation of the Reich and its racial apocalypse as the dawn of a messianic era that would usher in the Thousand-Year-Reich.

2. Ministries and Ministers of the Third Reich

Arbeitsministerium, "Labor Ministry," Franz Seldte; *Auswärtiges Amt*, "Foreign Office," Joachim von Ribbentrop; *Besetzte Ostgebieteministerium*, "Occupied Eastern Territories Ministry," Alfred Rosenberg; *Bewaffnung und Munitionsministerium*, "Weapons and Munitions Ministry," Albert Speer; *Ernährung und Landwirtsschaftministerium*, "Nutrition and Agriculture Ministry," Walter Darré; *Finanzenministerium*, "Finance Ministry," Lutz Schwerin von Krosigk; *Innernministerium*, "Interior Ministry," Wilhelm Frick; *Justizministerium*, "Justice Ministry," Otto Thierack; *Luftfahrtministerium*, "Aviation Ministry," Reichsmarshal Hermann Göring; *Ministerrat für die Reichsverteidigung*, "Ministerial Council for the Defense of the Reich," Reichsmarshal Hermann Göring; *Oberkommando der Wehrmacht*, "Commander in Chief of the Army," Generalfeldmarschall Wilhelm Keitel; *Postministerium*, "Postal Ministry," Wilhelm Ohnesorge; *Propagandaleitung*, "Propaganda Administration," Dr. Joseph Goebbels; *Reichskanzlerei*, "State Chancellery," Martin Bormann; *Verkehrsministerium*, "Transportation Ministry," Julius Dorpmüller; *Wirtschaftsministerium*, "Economics Ministry," Walter Funk; *Wissenschaft, Erziehung, und Volksbildungsministerium*, "Science, Education, and Public Instruction Ministry," Bernhard Rust.

Das Kleine Festung [G] "The Small Fortress": Slang name for the Terezin ghetto, or, when used as a proper noun, for the compound in Terezin where prisoners were held before dispatch to extermination or labor camps. The term refers Terezin's nineteenth century origins as a military garrison.

Das Kleine Lager [G] "The Small Camp": Term for the Buchenwald concentration camp annex where some 9,815 German Jews, rounded up by the Gestapo during and just after *Kristallnacht*, were imprisoned. The Small Camp also served as a quarantine area for new prisoners before their transfer to the main camp.

Davenen [דאַוונען, Y] "Praying": Slang Jewish term for movement, used in the sense of making oneself appear to be busy. During a work detail the opportunity to rest sometimes appeared. Resting, however, was fraught with danger if a Nazi overseer or a Kapo appeared. One person would therefore warn idlers to make themselves look busy, by "praying," a code derived from the movements of pious Jews during the prayers.

Davidstern [G] "Star of David." > see also: **Gelbe Flecke**; **Judenstern**.

Denazification

1. Scope and Definition

Denazification was the term used by the Allies for the procedure of cleansing Germany from Nazism and punishing its practitioners. In theory, all four of the big four — the United States, United Kingdom, Soviet Union, and France — were to participate equally in denazification operations. Agreement in principle at the Potsdam Conference led to the beginning of denazification under the auspices of the Supreme Headquarters Allied Expeditionary Forces (SHAEF). Specific guidelines published by the Allied Control Council for Germany on January 12, 1946, established the parameters for this process. Additional regulations, which classified offenders and possible levels of punishment, were published on October 12, 1946. However, the entire program, at least in West Germany, was undermined by the tensions between the United States and the Soviet Union that culminated in the beginning of the cold war.

GRAPH D.1: Flow Chart of Denazification[1]

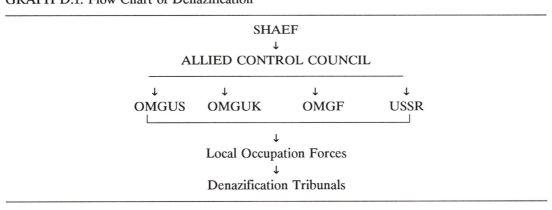

---

[1] The following abbreviations are used: SHAEF = Supreme Headquarters Allied Expeditionary Forces; OMGUS = Office of the Military Government, United States; OMGUK = Office of the Military Government, United Kingdom; OMGF = Office of the Military Government, France.

2. Major Denazification Agencies

Allied Control Commission for Italy (ACCI), established November 10, 1943, to enforce the armistice with Italy. The ACCI ceased to function in 1945, being replaced by the Allied Military Government. Commanders: Lieutenant General Noel MacFarlane, Harold MacMillan, Rear Admiral Ellery Stone.

Allied Control Council (ACC), agency created by the Potsdam Conference to oversee the reconstruction of civilian life in Allied-occupied Germany. The ACC was chaired, ex officio, by the head of Office of the Military Government of the United States but was an executive committee comprising representatives of the Big Four. Lieutenant General Lucius D. Clay acted as chairman of the ACC for its entire period of existence. The other three representatives were Air Marshal Sholto Douglas (UK); Lieutenant General Pierre Koenig (France), and Marshal Vassily D. Sokolovsky (USSR). The ACC ceased to function in 1949.

Central Registry of War Criminals and Security Suspects (CROWCASS), inter-Allied investigative group created by SHAEF in January 1945 to assist in identifying and bringing Nazi war criminals to justice. CROWCASS compiled extensive lists of suspects that led to the systematic investigation of Nazi crimes by the War Crimes Groups attached to the ACC after May 1945. The CROWCASS lists, however, had many omissions, and Allied apathy about prosecutions led to the failure to follow up on many leads.

Counter-Intelligence Corps (CIC), American military department responsible for the investigation, arrest, and detainment of Nazi war criminals. CIC was created as a sub-agency of the G-2 (intelligence) division of the U.S. army. Known as CIC as of January 1, 1942, the unit trained personnel who served in small six-to-ten-man detachments in larger U.S. army units. Although the CIC was effective in ferreting out war criminals, its activities were hampered by the earliest glimmerings of the cold war. As a result, CIC operations were reoriented to counter the Soviet threat, in some cases utilizing the same Nazi war criminals CIC was supposed to arrest.

Office of the Military Government of the United States (OMGUS), name for the U.S. forces occupying Germany and Italy under the terms of the Potsdam agreement.

United Nations War Crimes Commission (UNWCC), agency established in early 1942 to oversee the prosecution of Nazi war criminals. The UNWCC operated through the Judge Advocate General's Departments of each of the Big Four, although, for practical reasons, the Americans and British predominated. The UNWCC was not successful, primarily because of the sloppiness of its investigators, although it and other similar agencies continued to operate until 1949.

War Crimes Groups (WCGs), investigative teams attached to ACC for the identification, arrest, and bringing to justice of Nazi war criminals. Composed of Allied military personnel, the WCGs answered to both the UNWCC and to the Judge Advocate General's office of their respective armies. Somewhat successful in 1945, by 1946 the WCGs found their activities hampered by inter-Allied politics and a desire among certain military and political leaders to end the punishment of Germany.

Depot-Häftlinge [G] "Prisoner-holding pen": SS term for Jews placed in the quarantine camp in Auschwitz-Birkenau until the gas chambers and crematoria could be cleaned out of the remains of previous victims and could be prepared for new ones. These Jews were neither registered nor entered into the camp's record books. In some cases, those selected for labor were also classified as *Depot-Häftlinge* and were murdered. > see also: **D-Lager**.

Der abwehrkampf hat begonnen! [G] "The defensive war has begun!": Nazi anti-Jewish slogan dating to 1933 and exemplifying the rank and file's enthusiasm for Hitler's antisemitic policies.

Der alter bucher [דער אלטער בחור, Y] "The old bachelor": For a Polish Jew to mention Hitler by name during the Nazi occupation was fraught with danger. Hence, this Yiddish nickname.

Der baal darshn [בער בעל-דרשן,] "The preacher": One of at least half a dozen Yiddish terms for Adolf Hitler.

Der doktor [דער דאקטער, Y] "The doctor": Ironic slang expression popular among Polish Jews referring to the Warsaw ghetto. The irony of this expression derived from the fact that a doctor heals the sick and the Warsaw ghetto was, in reality, anything but healthy.

Der eiserne [G] "The Iron One": a nickname for Hermann Göring, reflecting his supposed iron will. > see also: **Hermann Meier**.

Der guter Antisemit [דער גוטער אנטיסעמיט, Y] "The good antisemite": a Yiddish term for a Gentile willing to give shelter to a Jew for a price. As long as the money or goods held out, the Jew was relatively safe. When the Jew had nothing more to give, he was told to leave or, worse, handed over to the Nazis or their helpers.

Der Jude zerstrört das Deutsche wesen [G] "The Jew destroys the German being": Nazi antisemitic slogan during the late 1920s deriving from racial and political ideas popular during the nineteenth century.

Der Jüdischer Napoleon [G] "The Jewish Napoleon": Nickname the Nazis gave to Jakob Lejkin, assistant commandant of the Ordnungsdienst, the Jewish police, in the Warsaw ghetto. A Nazi collaborator and Gestapo informer, Lejkin was ordered killed by the Jewish resistance leadership and sentence was carried out in October 1942.

Der schloss [G] "The Castle": SS term for the reception area of the Chelmno extermination camp. At the castle, the victims were forced to undress (on the pretext of being taken to showers) and were otherwise prepared for their final journey. From there, the victims were forced into mobile gas vans in which they were murdered. From the castle the vans drove to the Waldlager (forest camp) where the bodies were disposed of.

Der schöne Adolf [G] "The handsome Adolf": Nickname for Hitler used by millions of infatuated German (and later Austrian) women and teenagers. > see also: **Der Alter Bucher**, **Der Baal Darshn**.

Der stolzer Jude [G] "The proud Jew": A Nazi nickname for Jacob Gens, chief of the Vilna Jüdischer Ordnungsdienst and later *Judenälteste* of the Vilna ghetto.

Derleben un iberleben [דערלעבן און איבערלעבן, Y] "To live and to outlive (the enemy)": Popular Yiddish phrase among many Jews urging them to take all the suffering and miseries thrown at them in stride, to live to see the day when they could celebrate the destruction of Nazi Germany.

Deutsches Volk! Wehr dich! Kauf nicht beim Juden! [G] "German people, defend yourselves, do not buy from Jews!" Nazi propaganda slogan dating to the April 1, 1933, anti-Jewish boycott. The slogan was printed as part of a poster exhorting Germans not to shop in Jewish stores.

Deutschisierung [G] "Germanization": Nazi ideological term for the Germanization of certain geographical areas. The term had two different meanings and goals, depending on territory: Germanization in Polish and Soviet occupied territory meant some form of removal of the indigenous population, including the possibility of genocide, and left little room for their survival. Germanization in other territories, notably Scandinavia and the Low Countries, was viewed as a "return" of Germanic peoples to the racial fatherland and thus did not imply any action against the population.

Deutschland erwache, Juda verrecke [G] "Germany awake, Judah croak": Early NSDAP slogan, prominently presented in the pages of the *Volkischer Beobachter*, hoping to enlist the German people in Hitler's anti-Jewish crusade.

Di chalutzishe shikse [די חלוצישע שיקסע, Y] "The Pioneering Gentile": Underground nickname for Irena Adamowicz, a Polish Catholic Righteous one, who operated as a courier and aide for Zionist undergrounds throughout Poland and Lithuania. > see also: **Hasidei Umot ha-Olam.**

Di gas on tsirigker [די גאס אן צוריקקער, Y] "The road without return": Yiddish term for the last stretch of road in all six extermination camps that the victims had to tread before being forced into the gas chambers.

Di gele late [די געלע לאטע, Y] "The yellow patch": Colloquial Yiddish term for the armband with a star of David on it that Jews were forced to wear in Nazi-occupied Europe. Although all patches contained a yellow star of David, there was considerable regional diversity in size, shape, and markings. > see also: **Gelbe Flecke; Judenstern; Winkel(en).**

Di kvoreslait fun Treblinka [די קבֿרות-לייט פֿון טרעבלינקא, Y] "The gravediggers of Treblinka": Slang Jewish name for the special unit involved in exhuming and burning the corpses of Jewish victims buried at Treblinka. > see also: **Aktion(en), Code Names (Aktion 1005); Einsatzgruppen, Subunits (Sonderkommando 1005).**

Di roite kommande [די רויטע קאמאנדא, Y] "The red commando": Inmate term for the Treblinka work detail that sorted the personal belongings of the about to be killed victims (after being duped or forced to undress, on the pretense that they were about to be disinfected). So-called, because of the red armbands they had to wear in order to identify them as being part of the work detail. > see also: **Himmelkommando.**

Di shande fun mentshheit [די שאנדע פֿון מענטשהייט, Y] "The disgrace of mankind": Yiddish term for a large majority of the Jewish ghetto police, who quite often willingly helped the Polish Blue Police with the

Nazi ordinance imposing the wearing of the Jewish star
Authors' Collection

roundup of Jews to the *Umschlagplatz* for deportation. > see also: **Jüdischer Ordnungsdienst.**

Di shtarke [די שטארקע, Y] "The strong ones": Yiddish term for members of the Jewish underworld who, while collaborating with the Gestapo, attempted to seize power in the ghettos.

Di voyle [די וווילע, Y] "The smart ones": Members of the Jewish underworld in the Warsaw ghetto who collaborated with the Nazis. These criminals attempted to gain power from the suffering of their own brethren.

Die greuelpropaganda ist eine lügenpropaganda sagen die deutschen Juden selbst [G] "The atrocity propaganda is a lie, German

Jews themselves say": Title of a booklet written in German, French, and English in 1933 (when world opinion still counted to some degree) by Jakow Trachtenberg, a German Jewish Gestapo agent. Goebbels's Propaganda Ministry magnified this so-called denial to the foreign press and scored high points. Some members of the German Jewish leadership apparently adopted the view that by denying mistreatment they would somehow pacify the Nazis.

Die Juden sind unser Unglück [G] "The Jews are our misfortune": Antisemitic slogan coined by German historian Heinrich von Treitschke in 1879. Adopted by the Nazis, the phrase was used extensively in anti-Jewish propaganda from 1920 onward. In particular, the phrase was used as the masthead for *Der Stürmer*.

Die leitung [G] "The leadership": Committee of three, appointed by Eichmann in January 1943, to streamline the Ältestenrat in the Terezin ghetto. The board consisted of Paul Eppstein as chairman, Jacob Edelstein, and Dr. Joseph Löwenherz. In February 1943 the committee was again reorganized, with Edelstein becoming chairman and Benjamin Murmelstein replacing Löwenherz. > see also: **Judenrat**.

Discriminanti [I] "Discriminated against": Italian term for those Jews not exempted from the 1938 racial legislation. Exemptions were limited to war veterans and Jewish ex-members of the Fascist party. > see also: **Legislation, Anti-Jewish, Axis States (Italy)**.

Displaced Persons, Jewish

1. Scope and Definition

With the end of World War II the Allied powers discovered that the Nazis had uprooted between 7 million and 9 million people. Even during the war, however, Anglo-American policy emphasized the repatriation of these Displaced Persons (DPs), and by late 1945, more than 6 million had returned to their homes. Still, that left 1.5 million to 2 million Dps who either refused to or were unable to return to their countries of origin. Nearly 100,000 Jewish DPs were among those still in camps at the end of 1945. Many survivors were not prepared to return to their countries of origin and felt unable to resume their lives in blood-soaked Eastern Europe. Because of the rising tide of antisemitic violence in postwar Eastern Europe, including the Kielce Pogrom, a great number of Jewish refugees soon joined the DPs as they fled Eastern Europe with the Briha. Attempts to resettle the DPs became part of the struggle for a Jewish state after World War II, and the DP problem was only solved after the creation of the State of Israel on May 14, 1948. > see also: **Aliya Bet; Briha; She'erit ha-Pleta**.

2. Types of Displaced Persons Camps

Casern, DP camps converted from former German military installations.

Barrack, DP camps converted from former detention, forced labor, or concentration camps.

Dwelling House, DP camps converted from civilian villages that were temporarily depopulated to make room for refugees.

TABLE D.1: Jewish DPs in the U.S. Zone in Germany, 1945

Camp	Number	Camp	Number
Dachau	2,190	Geretsried	1,800
Ebensee	1,438	Landsberg	5,000
Feldafing	3,309	Munich-Freiman	1,544
Fohrenwald	1,000	Total	16,281

Source: *Department of State Bulletin*, Sept. 30, 1945, pp. 456–463.

GRAPH D.2: DPs in the U.S. Zone in Germany in 1945, by Nationality

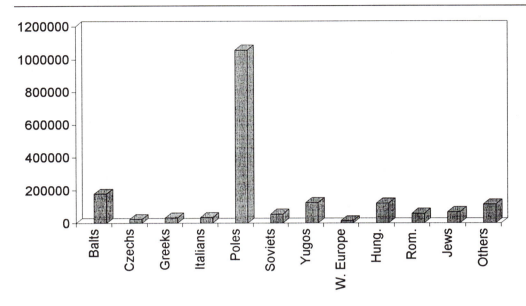

Identity card issued to a Jewish DP after the liberation of Mauthausen

Authors' Collection

TABLE D.2: Jewish DPs in 1946

Zone	Germany	Austria	Italy
American	175,960	22,000	18,000
British	28,000	4,000	NA
French	1,500	1,000	NA
	Berlin 10,000	Vienna 7,000	NA
Total	215,460	34,000	18,000

Source: Z. Warhaftig, *Uprooted: Jewish Refugees and Displaced Persons*, New York: World Jewish Congress, 1946.

3. Jewish DP Organizations

Ichud [איחוד], "Unity," political organization established in September 1945 by the leadership of the Landsberg DP camp. Led by Dr. Samuel Gringauz and David Treger, Ichud operated as both an intermediary between DPs and the U.S. army and as a pressure group for DP emigration to Palestine. Ichud also operated in close contact with the Jewish Agency Executive, especially after David Ben-Gurion's visit to Landsberg on October 22, 1945.

Jewish Relief Unit (JRU), Anglo-Jewish DP aid organization established by the Jewish Committee for Relief Abroad in 1943. The first JRU was activated in Italy in November 1944, caring for Jews at the Bari and Cina Citta refugee camps. Two more JRUs were activated in 1945 to coordinate relief activities in Holland and in the British Zone of Occupation in Germany. At its peak, the JRUs employed 120 civilian personnel, who were seconded to the Allied Military Government. All three JRUs were deactivated in 1951. > see also: **Organizations, Jewish.**

Kibbutz Buchenwald, agricultural training center established at the Buchenwald DP camp in June 1945. Designed to train young survivors for placement in kibbutzim in the Yishuv, Kibbutz Buchenwald was modeled on prewar *hachshara* programs. Additionally, the Kibbutz also served as a center for Jewish political activity on behalf of the Yishuv in the American Zone of Occupation.

Kibbutz Nili, agricultural training center established on the grounds of Nazi party leader Julius Streicher's former estate near Pleikershof, Germany, in mid-1945. In addition to its agricultural training program, the Kibbutz operated a complete DP school program for young survivors.

Merkaz la-Gola [מרכז לגולה], "Center for the Diaspora," agency founded in 1945 by the Jewish Agency for Palestine and operated under the auspices of the Briha. The primary aim of this organization was to move Jews from Germany and Austria to Italy, pending a resolution of further transit plans, usually, their embarkation on a Mossad blockade runner. To move the Jewish DPs, the Merkaz used the Jewish Brigade Group, which was stationed in northern Italy and southern Germany.

4. DP Publications

Dos Fraye Vort [דאס פרייע ווארט], "The Free Word," weekly Yiddish newspaper published at the Feldafing DP camp in the U.S. Zone of Occupation in Germany. Operating under the auspices of a Zionist, Bundist, and Agudas Israel coalition, *Dos Fraye Vort* was edited by M. Gavronsky and appeared from 1945 to 1948.

Landsberger Lager Cajtung, "Landsberg Camp Newspaper," weekly newspaper published at the Landsberg DP camp in the U.S. Zone of Occupation in Germany. The paper appeared from January 8, 1946, until 1948 and was edited by Rudolph Valsonok. The *Landsberger Lager Cajtung* was written in Yiddish but printed in Latin script; the paper was considered the most influential DP newspaper.

Landsberger Szpigel [לאנדסבערגער שפיגעל] "Landsberg Mirror," Yiddish newspaper published in the Landsberg DP camp and printed in Yiddish script. The newspaper was not distributed per se; instead copies were posted at strategic gathering posts throughout the camp.

Unzer Stimme [אונזער שטימע], "Our Voice," organ of the Jewish DPs in the Bergen-Belsen camp. It began publication in August 1945 and continued uninterrupted until the camp closed in 1950. *Unzer Stimme* also used its printing facilities to publish books, pamphlets, and educational materials for DPs throughout Germany.

Dögédula [Hu] "Identification tag": A small metal case carrying the personal papers of members of the Hungarian armed forces, including Jews serving with the Labor Service (Munkaszolgálat). Before 1942 Jewish forced laborers — almost all of them soldiers removed from the army because of the antisemitic decrees of 1938 — wore the tag as part of their military uniform. After 1942 Jews were no longer permitted to wear uniforms and the tag was worn with each individual's personal clothing.

Dolchstosslegende [G] "The stab-in-the-back myth": A contrived version of the history of World War I that gained popularity in Germany during the 1920s. This distortionist claim asserted that Germany had not been defeated on the battlefield but had been betrayed by Jews, Socialists, and Communists.

Dolle Dinsdag [Du] "Mad Tuesday": The events of September 5, 1944. Wild rumors of imminent liberation led to premature celebrations by the Dutch and, in response, to the flight of Dutch Nazis. When the rumors proved false, German occupation authorities undertook severe reprisals.

Dora, Laura, S III [G] Code names for three different underground munitions factories in Germany that employed slave labor and were part of the Dora-Mittlebau concentration camp. V-1 and V-2 rocket components were assembled at these plants under the supervision of German scientists.

Dos draytsentl [דאס דרייצענטל, Y] "The thirteen." > see also: **Trzynastka**.

Dos kleyne geto [דאס קליינע געטא, Y] "The small ghetto": Common term for the southern portion of the Warsaw ghetto that was attached to the main ghetto by a walled throughway at Ulica Zelazna. Representing approximately one-quarter of the ghetto's territory, the Small Ghetto also contained the Walter C. Többens workshop. During the great deportation (July 22, 1942, through September 12, 1942) the Small Ghetto — except for the Többens workshop — was completely depopulated of Jews and the houses were turned over for Polish resettlement.

Drang nach Osten [G] "The urge to the East": Long-standing German concept regarding the inevitability of imperialistic expansion in Eastern Europe. > see also: **Lebensraum**.

Drekfartreter [Y] "Garbage representative": Derogatory Polish Jewish nickname for Hermann Göring. > see also: **Hermann Meier**.

Drittes Lager im Ausland [G] "Third Camp Abroad": Nazi code term for a group of abandoned forts outside Kovno (Lithuania) where the wholesale slaughter of tens of thousands of Jews brought from all over Europe took place. > see also: **Endlösung**.

Durchgangsjuden [G] "Jews in transit": Nazi code term for Jews who, upon arrival in Auschwitz or the other *Vernichtungslager*, were sent straight to the gas chambers without their names being entered in the camp registers.

Durchgangslager [G] "Transit camp." > see also: **Konzentrationslager System**.

Dzialki [P] "Empty lots": The dilapidated buildings that formed the main residences in the Jewish ghettos after 1939. In some cases, the buildings were so far beyond inhabitability that the Jews converted them into vegetable gardens.

E

Effektenkammer [G] "Movable properties chamber": Nazi term for the warehouses where precious metals, jewelry, foreign currency and other valuables taken away from the victims before their extermination were stored. > see also: **Kanada**.

Ehrengericht [G] "Court of honor": A civil court created in Israel, Europe, and the United States after the war to investigate allegations that Jewish leaders and functionaries had collaborated with the Nazis. In addition to such ad hoc courts, four full-time courts were established in Displaced Persons camps, two in Germany (Landsberg and Neu-Ulm) and two in Italy (Trani and Adriatica). If found guilty, the defendant could be banned for a short or long time (or permanently, for particularly heinous offenses) from any participation in the Jewish community.

Ehrenzeichen [G] "Badge of honor": Jewish term for the Yellow Star of David badge that the Nazis ordered all Jews to wear.

Eigenleben [G] "Life of their own": Early Nazi propaganda term that promised German Jewry a restricted but "safe" life outside of German society.

Ein Volk, ein Reich, ein Führer! [G] "One people, one state, one leader": Nazi propaganda slogan used before and after attaining power in Germany (January 31, 1933). The term emphasized the organic nature of German fascism.

Eindeutschung [G] "Germanization": Term used in reference to Poles and Czechs who possessed racial characteristics that the Nazis defined as permitting eventual absorption into the Aryan race. In Poland and the Protectorate of Bohemia-Moravia, this implied the assimilation of racially appropriate elements and the expulsion or murder of those deemed unassimilable.

Eingegliederte Ostgebiete [G] "Incorporated Eastern Territories": Official term for the Nazi-incorporated areas of the former Polish Corridor, Danzig–West Prussia, Pomerania, Wartha, and eastern Upper Silesia. This territory comprised nearly 35,000 square miles — almost a quarter of the land mass of prewar Poland — with a total population of 9,600,000 (including 700,000 Volksdeutsche). The territories were officially incorporated by a *Führererlass* dated October 26, 1939. > see also: **Generalgouvernement**.

Einsatz Otto [G] "Operation Otto": Nazi code term for the launching of new rail links and the improvements of roads in the Generalgouvernement as a prerequisite to the invasion of the Soviet Union. The work program was undertaken with the massive use of Jewish slave labor and some Poles.

Einsatz Reinhard [G] "Operation Reinhard":

Code name for the confiscation of all Jewish property (foreign currency, gold, silver, gems, furs, linens, clothing, underwear, and all other personal belongings) that the victims brought with them on their final journey before being exterminated. The confiscation operation acted as part of Aktion Reinhard, Nazi code name, for the murder of European Jewry.

Einsatzfähig/Einsatzunfähig [G] "Fit/unfit": Nazi term for Jews fit or unfit for work. Each Nazi-ordered Judenrat had to present a list to the *Stadthauptmann* listing all able-bodied Jews in the community (or ghetto) who could perform slave labor. As a rule, at least in the larger ghettos, Jews who were not considered fit were the first to be deported or murdered outright.

Einsatzgruppen [G] "Task Forces":

1. Scope and Definition

The mobile killing squads of the SS during World War II. Einsatzgruppen were initially established in 1938, as part of Fall Grün (the planned invasion of Czechoslovakia) but were disbanded after the Munich Conference. Intended to sow confusion and discontent in the enemy rear, these units were later redesignated Brennkommandos and operated during the Polish campaign. Based on Hitler's declaration of a *Weltanschauungskrieg* against the Soviet Union in March 1941, new Einsatzgruppen were raised (in April) as the primary mobile force to eliminate the "Judeo-Bolshevik threat." These Einsatzgruppen were composed of members of the Sicherheitspolizei (Sipo) — agents of the Gestapo and Kriminalpolizei (Kripo) — and the Sicherheitsdienst. The Einsatzgruppen were organized into Einsatzkommandos and Sonderkommandos, which, in turn, were divided into Einsatzstaben and Einsatztruppen. Organized under the authority of the Reichssicherheitshauptamt (RSHA), the Einsatzgruppen came under the direct jurisdiction of the four Höherer SS- und Polizeiführers (HSSPF), in whose zones they operated.

Beginning on June 22, 1941, the Einsatzgruppen swept through the territories of the USSR immediately behind advancing Wehrmacht troops. In each occupied location a similar scene ensued: Members of an Einsatzgruppe, often with the aid of local *Hiwi*s or of Wehrmacht personnel, ordered all Jews to assemble. The victims were marched to prepared sites, often old Soviet fortifications, made to undress, and then killed by gunfire. By this means the Einsatzgruppen murdered approximately a million Jews and perhaps as many as a half-million Russians (including political commissars, Communist Party officials, partisans, and prisoners of war) during their first sweep (June to December 1941). Psychological difficulties among Einsatzgruppe members, resulting from the mass shootings, led to changes in operational methods, including the use of gas vans and, eventually, fixed extermination camps. Einsatzgruppen, however, continued to operate, in one form or another, virtually until the end of the war.

2. Commanders/Areas of Operation/ Subunits

Einsatzgruppe A, SS-Brigadeführer Franz W. Stahlecker, responsible for the Baltic Republics: 1,000 men divided into Sonderkommandos (SK) 1a, 1b, Einsatzkommandos (EK) 2, 3, 1c.

Einsatzgruppe B, SS-Brigadeführer Arthur Nebe, responsible for Belorussia and the Russian Soviet Socialist Federative Republics (RFSSR): 655 men divided into SK 7a, 7b, EK 8, 9, Vorkommando Moscau.

Einsatzgruppe C, SS-Standartenführer Emil Otto Rasch, responsible for northern and central Ukraine: 750 men, divided into SK 4a, 4b, EK 5, 6.

Einsatzgruppe D: SS-Gruppenführer Otto Ohlendorf, responsible for southern Ukraine and Crimea: 600 men, divided into SK 10a, 10b, EK 11a, 11b, 12.

Sonderkommando Dirlewanger: Named after its commander, SS-Obersturmführer Oskar Dirlewanger. In 1940 Dirlewanger conceived the idea of forming a sharpshooters unit within the Waffen-SS to be composed of German convicts and other desperadoes. Eventually, the unit was increased in size and was renamed

SS-Sturmbrigade Dirlewanger. As such, the unit participated in putting down the 1944 Warsaw uprising.

Sonderkommando Kulmhof: Also known as Sonderkommando Lange and Sonder-kommando Bothmann, after its first and second commanders respectively. This was the SS unit charged with overseeing exter-mination operations at Chelmno.

Sonderkommando 1005: the official name for the SS unit that oversaw the action of Jewish prisoners forced to assist in the exhumation and destruction of evidence of Nazi crimes against the Jewish people. > see also: **Aktion(en), Code Names (Aktion 1005)**.

Sonderkommando Reinhard: the SS administrative unit that oversaw *Aktion Reinhard* in the Generalgouvernement. > see also: **Aktion(en), Code Names (Aktion Reinhard)**.

Einzelaktionen [G] "Individual actions": Term coined by higher-up members of the NSDAP in connection with individual actions against German Jewry. In the early 1930s, unilateral actions against individual Jews by the rank-and-file SA or other anti-semites were considered by the leading Nazis as undesirable or even harmful to Nazi interests, especially in regard to foreign public opinion. > see also: **Wilde Einzel-aktionen**.

Emek ha-bacha [עמק הבכה, H] "Vale of tears": Traditional Jewish martyrdom term used during the Holocaust to refer to the hundreds of extermination sites scattered over Eastern Europe.

Endlager [G] "Final camp": Nazi term for Terezin to indicate that no deportations would be carried out from here. This, how-ever, was a false concept both for external and internal consumption — a propaganda ploy for Hitler's gift to the Jews — the model ghetto Terezin. > see also: **Alters-getto**.

Endlösung der Judenfrage, die [G] "Final

Memorial marker for the Jewish martyrs murdered at Ponary, Lithuania
Courtesy of Isaac Kowalski

Solution of the Jewish Question":

1. Scope and Definition

Nazi cover term for the total extermination of European Jewry. Practical plans for the Final Solution were begun in mid-1941 and cul-minated in the Wannsee Conference of January 1942, where the Nazi bureaucracy formulated detailed plans for the annihilation of all European Jewry. Part of this plan was the deportation of Jews from virtually every Euro-pean country — and eventually the United

States and Great Britain as well — to six specially established *Vernichtungslager* (death camps) in occupied Poland for the exclusive purpose of mass murder.

Historians generally ascribe four phases to the evolution of the Final Solution: from January 30, 1933, to September 15, 1935, the period when the basic groundwork was laid; from September 15, 1935, to September 1, 1939, a period when specific approaches to the problem were formulated; from September 1, 1939, to June 22, 1941, a period of detailed planning and preparation; and from June 22, 1941, to May 5, 1945, the period in which the Final Solution was executed. Historians are divided between so-called Intentionalists, who view the Final Solution as a long-standing goal of Hitler's that was carried out in a uniform, systematic, and decisive fashion, and Functionalists, who deny prior planning for mass murder and note that other routes to the Nazi goal of *Entjudung* had been offered in the years prior to 1941. More recently, an eclectic school has developed that accepts some elements of both schools' arguments, to form a more dynamic conception of how the Holocaust developed. > see also: **Wannsee-konferenz**.

TABLE E.1: European Jewish Population, 1933–1948[1]

Country	1933	1939	1948	# Jews Murdered
Albania	204	204	300	
Austria	250,000	60,000	20,000	60,000
Belgium	44,000	100,000	34,500	25,000
Bulgaria	46,431	48,665	46,500	
Czechoslovakia	400,000	360,000	42,000	200,000
Danzig	9,239	10,448	0	
Denmark	5,947	5,690	5,500	100
Estonia	4,566	4,302	500	1,500
Finland	1,772	1,772	1,800	
France	220,000	300,000	170,000	80,000
Germany	564,379	240,000	40,000	130,000
Greece	72,791	75,000	8,500	65,000
Hungary	475,949	403,000	174,000	500,000
Italy	47,485	57,425	30,000	7,500
Latvia	94,388	95,000	12,000	70,000
Lithuania	155,125	155,000	20,000	140,000
Luxembourg	1,771	3,144	500	1,000
Netherlands	150,000	156,817	28,000	106,000
Norway	1,457	3,000	1,000	800
Poland	2,978,000	3,250,000	105,000	3,000,000
Romania	900,000	850,000	430,000	270,000
Soviet Union	2,672,398	3,020,000	2,000,000	1,000,000
Yugoslavia	68,405	75,000	11,900	60,000

Source: *American Jewish Yearbook*, Philadelphia: JPS, 1933-1948.

---

[1] Only Jewish populations of Nazi, Fascist, or Nazi-occupied countries are tabulated, although the cited figures should be considered approximations.

TABLE E.2: Number of Destroyed Jewish Communities[1]

Country	Number	Country	Number	Country	Number
Austria	37	Greece	28	Netherlands	93
Czechoslovakia	490	Hungary	308	Norway	9
Denmark	1	Italy	9	Poland	1,415
Estonia	11	Latvia	61	Romania	423
France	35	Lithuania	184	Soviet Union	446
Germany	822	Luxembourg	10	Yugoslavia	134

Total: 4,516

Source: Avraham Klevan (ed.): *Jewish Communities Destroyed in the Holocaust*. Jerusalem: Yad Vashem, 1982.

Endziel [G] "Final objective": The National Socialist primary aim, the elimination — by any means — of the Jewish people. Historians have argued over the precise implications of this usage: Intentionalists claim that it proves a long-term plan to murder Jews, whereas Functionalists argue that it merely points toward persecution and does not specify the means to attain the final objective.

Enterdungsaktion [G] "Disinterment operation": Nazi term for the unearthing and burning of the bodies of hundreds of thousands of victims at hundreds of extermination sites throughout Eastern Europe and the Balkans. > see also: **Aktion(en), Code Names (Aktion 1005)**.

Entjudung [G] "De-Judaization": The goal of Nazi antisemitism. As formulated during the 1930s, *Entjudung* operated in two phases: in the short term, the removal of Jews from German economic life, and, in the long term, their complete removal from European civilization. With the outbreak of World War II, this Nazi goal was extended to the rest of occupied Europe. > see also: **Arisierung**.

Entlaust [G] "Deloused": Nazi code term for having permanently cleaned out a pocket of Jews from a given location. > see also: **Endlösung; Judenrein; Wannsee-konferenz**.

Entsprechend behandelt [G] "Appropriately dealt with": Nazi cover term for the murder of Jews. This term was, in most cases, used by the Einsatzgruppen commanders in their weekly (or sometimes daily) reports to the proper authorities in Berlin. > see also: **Erledigt**.

Épuration [Fr], "Purge": French term for the postwar trials of collaborators. The purges began with the Liberation and differed from country to country, depending on the severity of wartime problems associated with collaboration. In France, for example, 39,000 trials of collaborators were held in 1945 and 1946. Of the 1,325 death sentences passed by the courts only about half were carried out. Similarly, Holland and Belgium tried more collaborators, 60,000 and 50,000 respectively, but carried out very few death sentences.

Ereignismeldung [G] "Operational report": Report from the Einsatzgruppenkommanders to the Reichssicherheitshauptamt in Berlin, listing their daily extermination activities (in code) in

---

[1] West European communities include localities with a Jewish population of forty or more; eastern European communities include localities with a population of more than 100 Jews.

the occupied areas of the Soviet Union. >
see also: **Entsprechend Behandelt**.

Eretz ha-damim [ארץ הדמים, H] "Land of
blood": Wartime Jewish term for Nazi Germany, primarily used by Orthodox Jews.

Eretz ha-tumah [ארץ הטמואה, H] "Land of
the unclean": Wartime Jewish term for Nazi
Germany, especially common among Orthodox Jews.

Erfassungsaktion [G] "Seizure actions": A
Nazi term for operations, by the SS in
cooperation with the local Fascist militia, to
seize French, Italian, Bulgarian, Romanian,
Slovak, and Hungarian Jews for deportation
to death camps.

Erholungslager [G] "Recuperation camp":
Nazi technical term for certain categories of
concentration camps that were also designed
as places where exhausted or sick inmates
were sent to recuperate (among others,
Dachau and Bergen-Belsen). In practice,
however, few of those sent to recuperate
ever achieved this goal. > see also: **Konzentrationslager System**.

Erledigt [G] "Finished": Nazi cover term for
the murder of Jews. > see also: **Entlaust**.

Erleichtert [G] "Relieved": Nazi code term
for the liquidation of all or part of a ghetto
population. > see also: **Ausmerzung**.

Ermächtigungsgesetz [G] "Enabling Act":
Legal term for the installation of the Nazi
dictatorship under Adolf Hitler, unanimously
passed by the Reichstag on March 3, 1933.

Ernste Bibelforscher [G] "Serious Bible
researchers": German name for "Jehovah's
Witnesses," most of whom refused to swear
an oath of allegiance to Hitler and were,
therefore, incarcerated in Nazi concentration
camps.

Ersatzhandlungen [G] "Substitute acts": Nazi
term based on unfounded accusations by the

Peoples Tribunals that Jews within the Reich
engaged in sexual acts with German women,
thus making them guilty of the *Rassenschande*
crime according to the Nuremberg Laws.

Erziehungshäftling [G] "Reeducation inmate":
Certain type of political prisoner confined in a
concentration camp for a certain period of
time. No Jew was part of this category.

Eto Evrei, on v targovle rabotaet [R] "He is a
Jew, he works in commerce": Antisemitic
phrase coined by some members of the Soviet
occupation forces in eastern Poland (1939–
1941). For political and propaganda reasons,
ideological antisemitism was strongly discouraged among the Soviet occupation forces, although the Soviets simultaneously sought to uproot Judaism and did not permit the easy entry
of Jewish refugees into the Red Army occupation zone.

Europa, Fall [G] "Europe Plan": The scheme
conceived by the Pracovná Skupina for saving
the lives of the European Jewish remnant by
the payment of a ransom to the Nazis. Encouraged by the apparent success of a $50,000 bribe
(that had been paid to SS-Hauptsturmführer
Dieter Wisliceny) in halting deportations from
Slovakia, the committee members prepared for
a more ambitious ransom scheme: the payment
of a multimillion-dollar bribe to save the remaining Jews of Europe. Negotiations on the
plan continued for nearly a year, from the fall
of 1942 until August 1943. Lack of finances on
the Jewish side and lack of serious intent on
the part of the Nazis doomed this rescue
scheme almost from the very start.

Europäische Neuordnung [G] "The New European Order": Nazi term for the racial and
eugenic apocalypse that was unleashed by the
Third Reich after 1933. Initially, the New
Order was limited to Germany proper, but
after September 1, 1939, the Nazi pattern was
imposed on all occupied countries. Race was
primary within the context of this New Order,
and the Nazis did little to disguise their long-
term intentions: RSHA Chief Reinhard
Heydrich is reputed to have claimed that Nazi

policy was to convert the Poles (and by extension other Slavic peoples) into "two-legged cattle." Of course, there was no room at all in the New Order for the Jews; their fate was obliteration. > see also: **Ausmerzung**.

Euthanasie [G] "Euthanasia":

1. Scope and Definition

Within the context of Nazi eugenics, euthanasia became a term for the systematic murder of those deemed "unworthy of life." Initially, the plan was to sterilize the physically and mentally disabled. After the war began, however, the Nazis converted from sterilization to murder to speed up the eugenic benefits of the program. The first large-scale action seems to have taken place in Pomerania and western Prussia shortly after the Polish campaign. In all, six euthanasia centers were in operation. In August 1941 the Euthanasia Program was officially terminated, due to the resistance of the German people and Church. In practice, however, killings on eugenic grounds — as well as medical experiments on concentration camp inmates — continued to the end of the war. In 1942 most of the euthanasia staff was transferred to the staff of Aktion Reinhard. Throughout its existence (1939–1945) at least 100,000 fell victim to the Euthanasia Program.

2. Euthanasia Centers

Bernburg an der Saale: code-named *Anstalt B*; opened December 1940; closed January 1943; number of victims, 15,000.

Brandenburg an der Havel: code-named *Anstalt B*; opened November 1939; closed November 1940; number of victims, 10,000.

Grafeneck: code-named *Anstalt A*; opened January 1940; closed December 1940; number of victims, 10,000.

Hadamar: code-named *Anstalt E*; opened January 1941; closed 1943; number of victims, 10,000.

Hartheim: code-named *Anstalt C*; opened May 1940; closed 1944; number of victims, 30,000.[1]

Sonnenstein: code-named *Anstalt D*; opened April 1940; closed May 1943; number of victims, 20,000.

3. Code Names Related to Euthanasia

Allgemeine kranken Transportgesellschaft, "General Ambulance Service," a code name for the SS agency responsible for the transporting of the victims to the "sanatoriums" where they faced mercy killing.

Gemeinnützige Krankentransport GmbH, "Charitable Sick Transports Ltd.," code name for the SS agency that brought the victims to euthanasia sites.

Gemeinnützige Stiftung für Anstaltspflege, "Charitable Foundation for Institutional Care," code name for the euthanasia branch that provided the funds to operate the murder institutions.

Evakuiert [G] "Evacuated": Cover term for "deported," another term for taken to an extermination site. > see also: **Aktionen(en)**.

Evionim [אביונים, H] "Paupers": Derisive term for the representatives of the world who met in Evian-les-Bains, France, in July 1938 to find a solution for the refugee crisis. The conference was a complete failure, leading Jews to complain bitterly that they had been betrayed: The world used sympathetic rhetoric but refused to do anything to actually save Jews.

Evipannatrium [G] An experimental injection given to a group of 104 prisoners in the summer of 1941 in the Buchenwald concentration camp. As a result, all 104 victims of this "medical" experiment died within a short period of time.

---

[1] The gassing facilities at Hartheim were also used as an extermination annex for inmates brought from Mauthausen.

F

Fabrik-medizin [G] "Factory medicine": Nazi derogatory term for Jewish medical practice. In Nazi Germany, this could not be tolerated; a *neue deutsche Heilkunde*, a new type of healing, was thus envisioned and promoted. > see also: **Medical Experiments**.

Fascism

1. Scope and Definition

Fascism was a social and political ideology that flourished in Europe during the first half of the twentieth century. This ideology emerged as a synthesis of organic nationalism — an ideology that views the state as an "organic" entity — and virulent opposition to communism. Fascism's guiding principle was the repudiation of liberalism, Marxism, democracy, and parliamentarism. In Fascist theory, the highest order of human organization is the state; every element in society must be subsumed under strict state control and every individual must know his/her place within the state. To explain its rejection of individual liberty, fascism uses the analogy of cells in a living body: Each plays its assigned role without protest and with no extra reward except that reaped by the "whole."

Strengthened by the experience of World War I, fascism emerged as a mass political movement in the 1920s and 1930s. The war disclosed new forms of state control over society and also decisively proved the victory of nationalism over class consciousness.

During those two decades, Fascist parties spread throughout Europe; the ideology attained power in only a few states, most notably in Italy, Spain, and Portugal.

Antisemitism was not an integral element of Fascist ideology, except in Nazi Germany. Nazism, based on race as the defining individual characteristic, could not exist without antisemitism, but fascism — especially as enunciated by Benito Mussolini before 1938 — could. Nevertheless, many Fascist and quasi-Fascist parties adopted antisemitism as a major ideological element under Nazi influence. This primarily manifested itself in Eastern Europe, where authoritarian governments used the Jewish problem as a means of controlling centrifugal forces that threatened to weaken state power. > see also: **Antisemitismus; Nationalsozialistische Deutsche Arbeiter Partei; Collaboration**.

2. Fascist Parties and Organizations

Belgium

Brigade Khaki, "Brown Brigade," Belgian ex-servicemen's organization, founded in 1919. Vehemently nationalistic, the Brigade advocated an isolationist foreign policy that was anti-British, anti-French, and anti-German. Opposed to collaboration, the Brigade disbanded in 1941.

Christus Rex, "Christ the King," Fascist party, more commonly known simply as Rex (or as the Rexists). Breaking away from the centrist Catholic Party in 1935, Rex was led by Leon

Degrelle. Degrelle organized his party to be conservative, nationalistic, and mildly antisemitic. Many of the party's positions were copied directly from Mussolini, and the lack of antisemitism in Italian fascism influenced Degrelle to distinguish between "good Jews" (native Belgians) and all others. Rex openly collaborated with the Nazis throughout the occupation; Degrelle himself led the Belgian Legion in the Soviet Union. > see also: **Collaboration, Collaborationist Organizations (Belgium)**.

Duitschen-Vlaamsche Arbeidsgemeenschap (DEVLAG), "German-Flemish Working Group," founded in 1935. DEVLAG called for the incorporation of Belgium into a greater German Reich. Claiming to be a cultural organization, DEVLAG members were active in fifth-column activities during the German invasion of the Low Countries and later collaborated openly with the Nazis. From 1941 on DEVLAG competed with the VNV for control of the collaborationist government of Belgium; neither party won that struggle since the Nazis played one off against the other as a means of weakening both.

Légion Nationale, "National Legion," Belgian ex-servicemen's organization, founded by Paul Hoornaert in 1922. The Légion was vehemently nationalistic and anti-democratic. The Légion eschewed collaboration; many members — including Hoornaert — joined the resistance and were imprisoned or sent to concentration camps.

Nationaal-Socialistiche Beweging in Vlaandern (NSBiV), "National-Socialist Movement in Flanders," offshoot of the Dutch National-Socialistiche Beweging, founded in the mid-1930s. The NSBiV was forced to merge with the VNV in 1941 and ceased to function.

Verbond Dietsche Nationaal-Solidaristen (VERDINASO or DINASO), "Union for Netherlands National Solidarity," Belgian Flemish separatist party founded by Joris van Severen in October 1931. Modeled on the NSDAP, DINASO sought the partition of Belgium and unity within a global Dutch community. In 1935 the party undertook a massive volte-face. Abandoning partition, DINASO now advocated strong Belgian nationalism. DINASO collapsed in 1941, with some members advocating collaboration with the Germans and others advocating resistance.

Vlaamsch Nationaal Verbond (VNV), "Flemish National Union," Belgian Fascist organization founded in 1933. Pro-German and authoritarian in orientation, the VNV, nonetheless, eschewed antisemitism. During the Nazi occupation the VNV openly collaborated with the Nazis. On May 11, 1941, the Nazis ordered that all other parties in Belgium merge with the VNV. This merger was not fully completed before the end of the war. The VNV was divided into six *gouwen* (districts), subdivided into a total of 900 local sections. For administrative purposes the party was divided into ten departments, including the women's section, the youth section, and the party militia. Total membership in 1942 was 100,000. Publications: *De Schelde* (1933–1936); *Volk en Staat* (1936–1944); *De Nationaal Socialist* (1940–1944).

Bulgaria

Ratnitsi Napreduka na Bulgashtinata (RNB), "Guardians of the Advancement of the Bulgarian National Spirit," a Fascist organization founded in the early 1930s. Pro-Nazi in orientation, the RNB was mildly antisemitic. During the war the RNB openly collaborated with the Nazis even on Jewish affairs.

Suiuz Na bulgarskite natsionalni legioni, "Union of Bulgarian National Legions," Fascist organization established in the late 1930s and popularly known as the Legionnaires. It maintained close contact with German government agencies, including the SS, and accepted the Nazi position on Jewish and other issues. Late in World War II the legionnaires advocated a pro-Nazi coup but were unable to seize the reins of government.

Tsankovites, Bulgarian Fascist movement named after its leader, Aleksandur Tsankov, who founded it in 1923. Militantly nationalist, the Tsankovites were oriented toward Fascist Italy for most of the 1930s. After the beginning of Fall Barbarossa, however, the party shifted its orientation to align more closely with the Nazis. In 1944, prominent Tsankovites entered a Nazi-inspired coalition government with members of the RNB and other Fascist parties.

Czechoslovakia

Nároní obel fašistická (NOF), "National Fascist Community," Czech Fascist party founded in January 1927 by General Rudolf Gajda. Operating on a small scale for the next five years, NOF collapsed after its abortive putsch of January 21/22, 1933. Reorganized after Munich, NOF failed in the elections of May 3, 1939 — receiving 8 seats out of 326 in the National Assembly — and disappeared entirely when the Nazis occupied Bohemia and Moravia in March 1939. Individual NOF members collaborated with the Nazi regime during World War II.

France

Croix de Feu, "Cross of Fire," Fascist league founded in 1927 as a veterans' association. In 1934, Colonel François de la Rocque took over the association and steadily pushed it to the right. At its height, in 1935, Croix de Feu numbered 712,000 members. De la Rocque personally rejected antisemitism, but many members openly embraced Nazi antisemitic propaganda. Government decrees against private legions led to the disbanding of the Croix de Feu in 1936. Publication: *Le Flambeau*.

Jeunesses Patriotes (JP), "Patriotic Youth," university fraternity founded in 1924 that developed into a Fascist party. Led throughout the 1930s by Deputy Pierre Taittinger, JP peaked at a membership of 200,000. The party uniform — a blue overcoat with a blue beret — was later adopted by the collaborationist Milice. JP was not antisemitic and its members included a number of well-known democrats, most notably, former Premier Georges Clemenceau.

Parti Populaire Français (PPF), "French People's Party," Fascist party founded by Jacques Doriot in 1934. In 1938 the PPF had more than 250,000 members. Ideologically, the PPF was closer to Nazism, especially in Doriot's antisemitism, than to Italian fascism. The PPF was also strongly anti-

democratic and anti-Communist. Throughout the 1930s PPF activities were financed by the German Auswartiges Amt. The PPF suspended its activities during the "phony war," but reemerged during the Nazi occupation. The PPF collaborated openly with the Nazis and PPF members played an important role in the Légion des Volontaires Français. > see also: **Collaboration**.

Parti Social Français (PSF), "French Social Party," successor to the Croix de Feu after the 1936 ban on private legions. In 1939 the PSF numbered 3 million members and had eight deputies in the lower house of the French parliament. In 1940 the party name was changed to Progrès Social Français, but the PSF's opposition to collaboration led to its forcible dissolution by the Gestapo in 1942. In 1943 Colonel François de la Rocque was imprisoned in a concentration camp.

Solidarité Française, "French Solidarity," Fascist party founded in 1933 by François Coty. The party advocated a Gallic form of racism and called for the restoration of the monarchy. By advocating a total ban on new immigration Solidarité Française was in effect antisemitic, although no ideological formulation of antisemitism was ever made official. Solidarité Française peaked at 100,000 members in 1934. When Coty died, the party began to decline, and it collapsed altogether in 1936.

Germany

Deutscher Kampfbund, "German Fighting League," founded in Bavaria in 1923. Composed of Freikorps elements that strongly opposed the Weimar Republic, the Deutscher Kampfbund collapsed after the beer hall putsch.

Freikorps, "Free Corps," German veterans' organizations, mostly formed on an ad hoc basis in 1919 and 1920. Numerous Freikorps units crystallized in the first, turbulent years of the Weimar Republic. Although disagreeing on many issues, including attitudes toward Jews, all Freikorps units were strongly nationalistic and anti-Communist. In 1919 the government of Friedrich Ebert was forced to call upon the Freikorps to help put down the Communist-inspired Spartacists revolt. Banding together on a more permanent basis, some Freikorps units formed the nucleus of the Sturmabteilungen (SA) and the Schutzstaffel (SS), the strong-arm bullies of the Nazi Party.

Stahlhelm, "Steel Helmet," founded on December 25, 1918, by the Bund der Frontsoldaten (League of Frontline Soldiers), a strongly anti-Communist and anti-Socialist German veterans' organization. Ironically, Stahlhelm was also vehemently antisemitic, despite the fact that its leader, Alfred Hugenberg, was partly Jewish. Stahlhelm's version of the *Arierparagraph* excluded Jews and Catholics from among its ranks. Immediately after the Nazi seizure of power, Stahlhelm was forcibly integrated into the SA.

Thule Gesellschaft, "Thule Society," radical right-wing group founded in Munich in 1918. Heavily involved in public display of antisemitism, the Thule Gesellschaft introduced the Swastika as a symbol of German nationalists. The society disbanded in 1919, with most members joining the NSDAP.

Great Britain

British Fascisti, short-lived Fascist movement active in England's urban centers. Founded in 1923 in direct response to Mussolini's march on Rome, the British Fascisti hoped to impose a similar dictatorship in England. The Fascisti never gained broad appeal, splitting into rival factions in the mid-1920s and collapsing altogether in 1929. Thereafter, members of the Fascisti joined the British Union of Fascists.

British Union of Fascists (BUF), founded in December 1930 by Oswald Mosley and originally known as the New Party. Initially, Mosley emphasized farsighted social and economic proposals; he combined them, however, with an intense and personal antisemitism. As the decade wore on, Mosley's antisemitism crowded out — and eventually destroyed altogether — the positive elements of the BUF program. By the end of the decade, BUF moved away from Italian fascism and closer to Nazism. Even Nazi symbols were adapted for BUF use. For example, one BUF symbol was a single white

lightning bolt on a black background; it clearly evoked the very similar double lightning bolt symbol of the SS. BUF peaked at 100,000 members in 1938. The party began to decline in 1939 — as war fears grew — and the BUF collapsed altogether in 1940 when Mosley and other leaders were imprisoned for sedition.

Britons, quasi-Fascist and antisemitic organization established on July 18, 1919. Throughout its history the organization was led by Henry H. Beamish, a strong supporter of an anti-Jewish crusade. The centerpiece of the Britons' ideology was belief in a Jewish world conspiracy, alternatively headquartered in Berlin, Moscow, or Washington. The Britons continued to operate until 1948, although the organization never had more than nuisance value.

Imperial Fascist League (IFL), racist and antisemitic party founded in London in 1928. The Fascist element of IFL ideology was weak, however, and provided little more than a cover for antisemitism. Throughout its history, IFL was led by Arnold Leese, who, ironically, saw the BUF as a competitor rather than a potential ally. The entire IFL leadership was interned in 1940, forcing a temporary cessation of activities. Leese renewed his antisemitic rabble-rousing in 1945, merging with the Britons to form the Free Britain Party, which collapsed in 1950. Publications: *The Fascist* (1929–1939); *Free Britain* (1948–1950).

Holland

Het Nationale Front, "The National Front," Dutch Fascist party formed from the Zwart Front in 1937. > see also: **Fascism, Fascist Parties (Holland, Zwart Front)**.

National-Socialistischee Nederlandsche Arbeiders Partij (NSNAP), "National Socialist Dutch Workers Party," the Nazi party of Holland, founded by E.H.R. van Rappard in 1931. Antisemitic in orientation, the NSNAP sought the incorporation of Holland into a greater Germany. The NSNAP collapsed in 1937.

Zwart Front, "Black Front," Dutch Fascist party founded in the early 1930s. Although Catholic in outlook and modeled on Italian fascism, the Zwart Front expressed violent antisemitism. In early 1937 the Zwart Front changed its name to Het Nationale Front.

Hungary

A Zsidókérdést Kutató Magyar Intézet, "Hungarian Institute for Research into the Jewish Question," antisemitic agency founded on April 15, 1944, with SS assistance, as a scientific research institute. Headed by Zoltán Bosnyák and Carl Rekowski. Publication: *Harc*.

Külföldieket Ellenörző Országos Központi Hatóság (KEOKH), "Central National Control Office," established in 1930 to police the entry of all aliens into Hungary. Jews living in the areas incorporated by Hungary between 1938 and 1941 had to register with KEOKH. Many of that category of registrants were deported by the Hungarians in 1941 and 1942 to murder centers in Nazi-occupied territories.

Nyilaskeresztes Part, "Arrow Cross Party," the Hungarian Fascist party, founded by Ferenc Szálasi in 1937. In the 1939 national elections the party captured more than a quarter of the vote and became the most important opposition party. The party advocated a consistently pro-German foreign policy and was virulently antisemitic. On October 15, 1944, Szálasi formed a collaborationist coalition government that actively participated in the deportation of Hungarian Jewry.

Italy

Fasci all'Estero (FA), "Fascists Abroad," agency designed to organize support for the Partito Nazionale Fascista (PNF) among Italians in foreign lands. Created in 1922, the FA was unsuccessful in its goals and was absorbed into the Italian Foreign Ministry in 1935. Chairmen: Giuseppe Bastianini (1922–1926), Cornelio di Marzio (1926–1928), Piero Parini (1928–1935).

Fasci di Combattimento, "Combatant Leagues," militant arm of the PNF, founded by Mussolini on March 23, 1919. Membership mostly comprised members of the Squadristi, who played a critical role in the march on Rome. The Fasci were virtually eliminated after 1925.

Fasci Femminili, "Female Fascists," women's auxiliary unit of the PNF, founded in 1920. Although equivalent to the Squadristi, the organization never played a major role in Italian politics.

Guardia Nazionale Republicana (GNR), "Republican National Guard," term for units of the Volunteer Militia for National Security reorganized after November 20, 1943. The GNR's purpose was to guard members of the Fascist government and to fight partisans. In July 1944 an elite GNR unit, the Brigate Nere (Black Brigade), was created at Mussolini's orders. Also specializing in anti-partisan operations, the Brigate Nere was no more successful than the GNR had been in stemming the anti-Fascist tide.

Milizia Volontaria per la Sicurezza Nazionale (MVSN), "Volunteer Militia for National Security," internal security force established by the PNF to counter both the army and the Squadristi. In 1936 the MVSN was reorganized as a paramilitary force; the MVSN's "Blackshirt Battalions" were attached to regular army units and served on all fronts. In May 1943 all MVSN units were united into a Blackshirt Division, but the entire organization was abolished on December 6, 1943.

Partito Nazionale Fascista (PNF), "National Fascist Party," founded by Benito Mussolini in November 1921. The PNF grew out of the Squadristi and the Fasci di Combattimento, Mussolini's private armies. Although officially a parliamentary party — the PNF secured thirty-five seats in the elections of 1921 — Mussolini's main orientation was toward action. The PNF secured power by the threat of a coup during the so-called March on Rome of October 1922. Thereafter, Mussolini consolidated the PNF's hold on Italy, officially creating a dictatorship in 1925. The PNF ruled from 1922 until deposed — because of internal and external decay — by royal order in July 1943. The PNF was not initially antisemitic and a small but vocal Jewish cadre existed, especially in the North. In 1938 Mussolini changed course by instituting anti-Jewish racial legislation — copied from Nazi Germany. Subsequently Jews were discharged from PNF membership, although Mussolini's anti-Jewish actions were not universally supported even within the PNF.

Partito Fascita Republicano (PFR), "Fascist Republican Party," Fascist puppet party created by the Nazis on Mussolini's behalf in September 1943. The PFR was the ruling party of the Republica Sociale Italiana but had little or no actual popular support and virtually no power.

Republica Sociale Italiana (RSI), "Italian Social Republic," better known as the Sálo Republic, created by Mussolini after he was rescued by the Nazis in September 1943. Outwardly organized as the inheritor of the PNF government, the RSI did not reflect Fascist ideology at all; Nazi control of all aspects of government in the RSI was only thinly veiled.

Servicio Informazioni Militari (SIM), "Military Intelligence Service," primary intelligence agency of the Italian army. In addition to military intelligence tasks, the SIM undertook a variety of covert operations. Among the better known was the support for the Croat terrorist campaign to destabilize Yugoslavia in 1928 and 1929. Covert operations, however, diverted SIM from its main tasks and led to the complete failure of Italian military intelligence during World War II.

Squadristi, "Squadrons," paramilitary arm of the PNF, active between 1920 and 1922. Operating as the shock troops of the PNF, the Squadristi were in the forefront of the campaign to seize control of the streets and thus helped to gain national attention for Fascist goals. Squadristi actions also brought thousands of new recruits to the PNF. The fact that many of the Squadristi saw violence as an end in itself, however, led Mussolini to attempt to instill greater discipline into the movement. The MVSN was created for this task but did not succeed. As a result, the Squadristi were disarmed and disbanded in 1925.

Romania

Garda de Fier, "Iron Guard," the Romanian Fascist party. The Garda developed out of the antisemitic Legiunea Arhangehelului

Mihail in 1929 and, like the legion, was led by Corneliu Codreanu. The Iron Guard was officially disbanded in 1933 but continued to operate as a semi-clandestine movement. After King Carol's 1938 *coup d'état*, all political activity, including that of the Garda, was banned. In 1940, however, the Garda was invited to join the new government. The party, led by Horia Sima and Ion Antonescu, transformed itself into the National Legionary government. Throughout its existence, the Garda was involved in attacks on Jews and willingly participated in the extermination of Romanian Jewry.

Spain

Carlistas, Spanish monarchist group that flirted with fascism. Founded in 1932, the Carlists sought the return of King Alfonso XIII, who had been deposed in 1931. The Carlists fought as allies of the Falange during the Spanish Civil War but did not support the creation of a dictatorship by Francisco Franco. The Carlists ceased to operate independently after 1939.

Falange, "Phalanx," Spanish Fascist organization founded by José Antonio Primo de Rivera in 1934 and committed to overthrowing the Spanish republic. Primo de Rivera was executed on November 20, 1936, and leadership in the Falange fell to Francisco Franco. On the evening of July 17/18, 1936, the Falange, together with a group of senior army officers, engineered a *coup* among discontented troops in Spanish Morocco, which led to the Spanish Civil War. The Falange emerged victorious and was Spain's only legal political party from 1939 until Franco's death in 1975. Despite Franco's close relationship with both Mussolini and Hitler, he kept Spain out of World War II.

Yugoslavia

Hrvatski Savez, "Croat Alliance," separatist and Fascist party founded in 1934 among Croat émigrés living in Belgium. The personnel thus recruited were sent to a clandestine camp at Yank Pustza (Hungary) where they were trained for terrorist operations in Serbia. Most members later joined the Ustašha. > see also: **Collaboration**.

3. Fascist Leaders

Antonescu, Ion (1882–1946): *Conducator* of Romania; tried and executed on June 1, 1946.

Antonescu, Mihai (1907–1946): Deputy prime minister of Romania; drafted aryanization laws; tried and executed on June 1, 1946.

Badoglio, Pietro (1871–1956): Chief of staff of the Italian army; helped depose Mussolini; led Italian co-belligerent government in 1944 and 1945.

Baky, László (1889–1946): Leader of the Arrow Cross Party; tried and executed in January 1946.

Bandera, Stefan (1909–1959): Leader of Ukrainian nationalists; commanded Organization of Ukrainian Nationalists (OUN) during World War II; assassinated by NKVD.

Ciano, Galeazzo (1903–1944): Italian foreign minister and Mussolini's son-in-law; helped depose Mussolini; tried and executed by a Fascist court.

Cuza, Alexandru (1857–1946): Leader of the Iron Guard; responsible for denationalization of Romanian Jewry; died before his trial.

Darquier de Pellepoix, Louis (1897–1980): Head of the Vichy Commissariat Général aux Questions Juives; fled to Spain in 1944 and thus escaped justice.

Endre, László (1895–1946): Assisted in the deportation of Hungarian Jewry; tried and executed in January 1946.

Farinacci, Roberto (1892–1945): Secretary of the PNF and chairman of the Fascist Grand Council; leading antisemite of Fascist Italy; executed by partisans.

Franco, Fransisco (1892–1975): Leader of the Spanish nationalist forces that launched the Spanish Civil War; head of state until his death in 1975.

Horthy, Miklós (1868–1957): Regent of Hungary; initially supported but then halted the deportation of Hungarian Jewry; exiled after World War II.

Jaross, Andor (?–1946): Minister of the interior in the pro-Nazi Sztójay government; responsible for the deportation of Hungarian Jewry; tried by a Hungarian court after World War II and executed.

Laval, Pierre (1883–1945): Prime minister of France; supported limited antisemitic act-ions, including deportations of "foreign" Jews; tried and executed on October 15, 1945.

Mussolini, Benito (1883–1945): *Duce* of Italy and head of state; although not antisemitic, he instituted a series of racial laws in 1938; refused to aid in the physical destruction of European Jewry; entered the war as a member of the Axis; removed from office in 1943, but restored by the Nazis as leader of the puppet Sálo Republic; killed by Italian partisans while trying to escape on April 28, 1945.

Pavelić, Ante (1889–1959): *Poglavnik* of Croatia and head of the Ustaša; instituted intense antisemitic persecutions; responsible for the deaths of thousands of Serbs and Jews; died of injuries after an assassination attempt.

Pétain, Henri Philippe (1856–1951): Head of state of Vichy; accepted antisemitic persecution in France and approved some of its major points; tried for treason and sentenced to death, but sentence was commuted to life in prison.

Quisling, Vidkun (1887–1945): Head of the Nazi puppet government of Norway; tried and executed on October 24, 1945.

Szálasi, Ferenc (1897–1946): Head of state in Hungary after Nazi takeover; responsible for terror against Jews; tried and executed on March 12, 1946.

Sztójay, Döme (1883–1946): Prime minister of the Hungarian puppet regime established in 1944; responsible for the deportation of Hungarian Jewry; tried and executed on March 22, 1946.

Tiso, Jozef (1887–1947): Priest; *Vôdca* of independent Slovakia; supported persecution of Jews and their deportation; tried and executed in August 1946.

Tuka, Voytech (1880–1946): Prime minister of Slovakia; responsible for deportation of Jews; tried but died before his execution.

Ferdinand Roth: Code name for Rabbi Dov Baer Weismandel during the negotiations over Fall Europa. "Mr. Roth" was supposed to be the leader of a major American Jewish organization, with wide-ranging abilities in terms of rescue (i.e., ability to pay large sums in bribes). In reality, however, Weismandel created this fictional character in his correspondence with Nazis during the course of negotiations surrounding attempts at "buying" Jewish lives. > see also: **Europa, Fall**.

Feter Rivn [פעטער ראובן, Y] "Uncle Reuben": Nickname for U.S. President Franklin D. Roosevelt popular among East European Jews during the Nazi era.

Feter(n) [(ן)פעטער, Y] "Uncle(s)": Yiddish slang term, used especially in the Warsaw ghetto, to denote Nazis.

Figuren [G] "Figures": Euphemism denoting the corpses dug up and burned by members of Sonderkommando 1005. This was the only term that prisoner members of the Sonderkommando were permitted to use in relation to their grisly task; any other term was punishable by death.

Fir un fertzik [פיר און פערציק, Y] "Forty-four": Lithuanian Jewish code term for the SS, based on the similarity between the twin thunderbolt SS insignia and the number 44.

Fischen [G] "To fish": Code word for the German attack on the Polish fortress of Westerplatte that dominated the land and sea exits from Danzig.

Fleckfieber [G] "Spotted fever": Nazi code term for the living area specifically allocated to Jews. In order to eliminate all contact between Gentiles and Jews, the Nazis posted large signs at the entrances to the closed (or open) ghettos warning the Aryan population not to enter the area because of danger to their health. > see also: **Ansteckungsgebiet**.

Forzicht mit a vort [פארזיכט מיט א ווארט, Y] "Careful with a word": Slang Yiddish expression for the code words used by Jews

in forced labor groups. Care was always taken in speaking to — or about — work overseers, since an incautious word could lead to interrogation, imprisonment, or death; thus the slogan: Mum's the word.

Foigelach [פויגעלעך, Y] "Birds": Term for Allied bombers, popular among Jews in Nazi ghettos and concentration camps. Despite the fact that the aircraft brought with them the possibility of being hit or killed, the bombers continually raised inmate hopes for survival. > see also: **Kneidlach**.

Freemasons: International secret fraternal order. Founded in the mid-eighteenth century, Freemasons, along with Jews, became the focus for intense suspicion and hatred. From the middle of the nineteenth century on, the idea of a "Jewish-Masonic world conspiracy" became a stock trade item for antisemitic rabble-rousers throughout Europe and, to a lesser degree, in the United States. All Masonic lodges in Germany were forced to close in 1935 and those Masons who did not renounce Freemasonry were incarcerated in concentration camps.

Fremdarbeiter [G] "Foreign laborers":

1. Scope and Definition
Term for the laborers brought to work in the Reich from Nazi-occupied Europe. The Nazis particularly conscripted foreign prisoners of war — especially Russians and Poles — to work in German military industry. The fact that such use of prisoners was in direct contravention of the Geneva Convention did not concern the Nazis, at least not until the tide of war clearly changed. In 1942 and 1943, the Nazis began a policy of selectively kidnapping civilians, especially in Western Europe and Italy, in order to augment construction units of Organization Todt that were involved in building fortifications. The mortality rate among *Fremdarbeiter* was quite high, although not as high as that of Jewish slave laborers.

TABLE F.1: *Fremdarbeiter* in the Grossreich

Country	Number	Country	Number
Belgium	200,000	Italy	300,000
Czechoslovakia	40,000	Poland	1,200,000
France	650,000	Soviet Union	2,000,000
Holland	250,000	Yugoslavia	325,000
Hungary	25,000	TOTAL	4,990,000

Source: E. L. Homze: *Foreign Labor in Nazi Germany*, Princeton: Prineceton University Press, 1967.

Fremdblütig [G] "Foreign blooded": Nazi racial term for persons of non-German heritage, e.g., Jews and Gypsies.

Führerbau [G] "Führer's building": Hitler's headquarters during the late 1930s, located at 12 Königsplatz, Munich. > see also: **Braunes haus**.

Führerbefehl [G] "Führer's order": When used as a general term, an expression for any order emanating directly from Hitler. In specific usage, the "Führer's order" was the authoritative verbal order regarding the extermination of European Jewry.

Führerprinzip [G] "Leadership principle": Nazi term referring to the flow of authority and responsibility. Characteristic of Nazism was the quasi-religious cult of the *Führer*. The *Führerprinzip* functioned as Germany's primary leadership principle, combining political, racial, and bureaucratic conceptions into a totalitarian New Order.

Funktionshäftlinge [G] "Special assignment prisoners": KL term for inmates of German nationality. Given preferential treatment over all other ethnic groups, they literally ran the interior camp administration. > see also: **Konzentrationslager System**.

Fussmarsch [G] "Foot march": Euphemism for a death march, i.e., the removal of prisoners to prevent their liberation by advancing Allied forces. > see also: **Todesmärsche**.

G

Gedankenführungen [G] "Thought guides": Official educational material, distributed among the rank-and-file membership of the Wehrmacht, that expressed virulent anti-semitism.

Gegenrasse [G] "Anti-race": Derogatory Nazi term for Jews. > see also: **Gegenvolk**.

Gegenvolk [G] "Anti-people": Term expressing the Nazi racial theory that classified the Jews as subhuman vermin. The idea behind the term is founded in part on the theory of two "scientific" racists — Count Arthur de Gobineau (1816–1882) and Houston Stewart Chamberlain (1855–1927) — who espoused the idea that racial mixing is ultimately destructive of human civilization. Since Jews, according to the Nazis, are not a race but an anti-race, the goal of Jews is the destruction of Aryan civilization.

Geheime Reichssache [G] "State secret": Those governmental actions of the Third Reich that were to be kept secret ad infinitum. Within this category, the most important secret was to be the *Endlösung*.

Gehsperre [G] "Daytime curfew": Jewish term for the deportation action in the Lodz ghetto that lasted from September 1 to September 12, 1942. During this *Aktion* nearly 16,000 Jews were rounded up and deported to the Chelmno *Vernichtungslager*.

Gelbe Flecke [G] "Yellow patch": One of a variety of outward identification signs Jews were required to wear in occupied Europe by Nazi order. In occupied Lithuania, for example, all Jews regardless of sex or age were ordered to wear a round yellow patch, 10 inches (25.4 cm.) in diameter, with a large "J" imprinted in the center. In other cases, Jews were forced to wear a yellow Star of David. > see also: **Judengelb**.

Geltungsjuden [G] "Current Jews": Those considered to be Jews by Nazi racial definition, regardless of their religious status or nationality. Categories of those considered Jews by race included those deemed full, half, or quarter Jews. > see also: **Mischlinge**.

Gemeinnutz geht vor eigennutz [G] "The common welfare above self-interest": A Nazi pseudo-Socialist slogan, aimed at winning followers for the Nazi economic program. Aryanization of Jewish property fit right in with this slogan. > see also: **Arisierung**.

Gemeinschaftslager [G] "Community camp": Private company camps not belonging to the concentration camp system but employing Jewish slave labor. Jews were rented out to these types of camps by the SS for a mere pittance. A similar camp category, the *Zivilarbeitslager* — not specifically for Jews — proliferated in Nazi-occupied Europe, including the Grossreich, with 8,178 camps of various sizes and duration. > see also: **Konzentrationslager System**.

Generalgouvernement [G] "General Government": (GG)

1. Scope and Definition

Nazi term for the portions of occupied Poland that were not incorporated into the Reich after the end of the Polish campaign. The official name for the GG was General-gouvernement für die Besetzten Polnischen Gebiete (General Government for the Occupied Areas of Poland). The German civil authority was imposed as of October 26, 1939. Hans Frank was appointed General Governor on that date and he established his capital in Krakow. The GG was sub-divided into four districts: Krakow, Warsaw, Radom, and Lublin. In the summer of 1941 Galicia was added to the GG, becoming its fifth district. > see also: **Besatzungspolitik**.

The Generalgouvernement
Courtesy of Dr. Lucjan Dobroszycki

TABLE G.1: Generalgouvernement Districts and Jewish Populations

District	Counties	# Jews	District	Counties	# Jews
Warsaw	10	600,000	Krakow	12	200,000
Lublin	10	250,000[1]	Galicia	16	650,000[2]
Radom	3	300,000	TOTAL	51	2,000,000

Source: S. Segal: *The Nazi New Order in Poland*, New York: A. A. Knopf, 1942.

GRAPH G.1: Jewish Population of the Generalgouvernement, by District

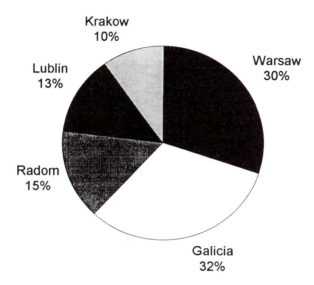

Generalplan ost [G] "General Eastern Plan": Code name for the Nazi plan to enslave the Polish and Soviet peoples that was formulated in late 1941 or early 1942. Based on the assumption of an imminent victory in the war against the USSR, the plan was formulated around a ten-year timetable. In this racial plan there was no room for European Jewry, even as slaves. Of this plan, however, RSHA Chief Reinhard Heydrich is reputed to have remarked that its purpose was to convert the Poles into "two-legged cattle." > see also: **Aktion(en), Code Names (Ausserordentliche Befriedungsaktion)**.

Genickschussspezialisten [G] "Neck shooting specialists": Members of the Einsatzgruppen who specialized in shooting their victims in the neck. Some of the Nazi commanders commented with much satisfaction over a glass of schnapps that by employing this method they were very humane — as the victims died quickly with little or no pain.

Genocide: Term coined in 1943 by Raphael Lemkin to denote consciously undertaken Nazi policies whose intention was the disruption of the physical existence, biological continuity, or spiritual and cultural expression of occupied

---

[1] Including 55,000 deported from the Grossreich.

[2] Population figures as of 1941 and reflecting trends in the territories occupied by the Soviets in 1939.

countries. Although Lemkin referred to the case of Jews, his term did not necessarily imply the total annihilation of the victims of genocide. > see also: **Ausmerzung, Endlösung.**

Genocide Convention: UN-sponsored international treaty banning the murder, torture, forced transfer, or persecution of a group for racial, religious, or political reasons. Formulated under the terms of Article 56 of the UN charter, the convention came into force on January 12, 1951. This has not, however, prevented a number of recurrent, post-Holocaust genocides.

Gesamtlösung [G] "Total Solution": Early term for the Endlösung. The term did not necessarily imply extermination: For example, *Gesamtlösung* was used during the initial stages of the so-called Madagascar Plan. The term did, however, imply comprehensive, methodical, and systematic action against the Jews. In the latter aspect, therefore, *Gesamtlösung* foreshadowed the Endlösung. > see also: **Endlösung, Entjudung.**

Gesetzlose Treiben [G] "Unlawful activities": Individual anti-Jewish actions undertaken by members of the SA. The term was used by Reichsbank President Hjalmar Schacht to decry the anti-Jewish boycott of April 1, 1933; Schacht opposed such actions as likely to inhibit Germany's rearmament plans.

Gesonderte Unterbringung [G] "Ordered destruction": One of the more blunt Nazi terms for the removal of the Jews and their total destruction. > see also: **Ausmerzung.**

Gesundung [G] "Healing": Ideological term used by the Nazis to refer to the result of the *Endlösung*: the healing of the Aryan race after the removal of the Jewish bacilli from its midst.

Geto autobus [בוס אױטאָ געטא, Y] "Ghetto limousine": Yiddish term given to the mobile gas vans coming into the ghettos to pick up victims to be gassed.

Getto Ost [G] "Ghetto East": Official term for the first half of the Rzeszow ghetto as of October 1942. In reality, the "eastern ghetto" took on the air of a compulsory labor camp. Soon thereafter it came under direct SS supervision as *das jüdische Zwangsarbeitslager*. At this juncture men were separated from women — husbands from wives. Any children not yet destroyed were forcefully removed to the *Schmelzgetto* — the other half — where they waited for the next transport to be taken for extermination. The final act for *Getto Ost* came in January 1944, when the bulk of those yet alive were transported to their death, with a fraction taken to the Plaszow concentration camp. > see also: **Schmelzgetto.**

Ghetto

1. Scope and Definition

The term *ghetto* originated in Venice and derived from the closed Jewish quarter (called the *Geto Nuovo*, i.e., the New Foundry) established in 1516. Thereafter, the term came to mean any residential district in which Jews were compelled to live.

During the 1930s, when their policies toward Jews were still in a state of flux, the Nazis and some German Jewish leaders as well spoke of creating a "new ghetto." By this they meant the virtual isolation of the Jews from the German population resulting from vicious Nazi antisemitic propaganda. In contemporary Eastern Europe similar ideas sprouted, primarily from antisemitic political parties, as may be seen by Polish agitation for the creation of so-called ghetto benches in schools and universities. On September 21, 1939, RSHA Chief Reinhard Heydrich penned orders for the civil authorities in the General Government to establish ghettos and Judenräte, pending the *Gesamtlösung* (total solution) to the Jewish question. The Nazis established a total of 356 ghettos in Poland, the Soviet Union, the Baltic Republics, Romania, and Hungary between 1939 and 1945.

There was no uniform pattern in the establishment, method of isolation, or internal regimes of the ghettos. Indeed, two divergent forms of ghettos existed: closed ghettos, those sealed off by walls or other physical means, and open ghettos, those that were not sealed off. Generally speaking, open ghettos were located in small towns, where Jews already lived in close proximity to one another and where it was uneconomical to make those who did not so reside move. Open ghettos were often only temporary measures, with the residents being moved to larger ghettos or being sent directly to their deaths. > see also: **Aktion(en)**.

Closed ghettos, in contrast, were almost always located in larger communities and implied the transfer of all the Jews to a small — usually rundown — neighborhood. In addition to Poland and the Soviet Union ghettos were established in Amsterdam, Budapest, Salonika, and Theresienstadt. The Romanian government established a series of ghettos within the confines of Transnistria, which itself was considered a "reservation" for hundreds of thousands of Jews.

2. The Gettoverwaltung

Gettoverwaltung, "Ghetto Administration," the agency that administered the ghettos of Eastern Europe and, especially, oversaw the activities of the Judenräte. Subsidiary agencies of the Gettoverwaltung, spread throughout Poland, Lithuania, and the occupied Soviet Union included:

Abteilung Umsiedlung, "Department of Population Transfers," agency that oversaw the creation of the Warsaw ghetto, later renamed Transferstelle.

Beschaffungsamt, "Acquisition Office," agency handling the procurement of food and other materials that the Nazis allowed to enter the Lvov ghetto.

Ernährungsamt, "Food Supply Office," allocated food to the Polish ghettos.

Kriminalpolizei Sonderkommissariat Getto, "Criminal Police Special Commission for the Ghetto," special SS unit operational in the Lodz ghetto, founded in 1940, and commanded by Bruno Obersteiner. Primarily involved in confiscating Jewish possessions.

Lautscher Werkstätte, one of two artists workshops set up by the SS in the Terezin ghetto. Primarily dedicated to handcrafts and toys, the workshop operated between March 1942 and September 1943. Throughout its existence the workshop was headed by Oskar Perschke.

Mal und Zeichen Werkstätte, "Graphics and art workshops," print art studio set up by the Nazis in the Kovno ghetto and responsible for designing, printing, and distributing all signs, announcements, and placards for the Germans.

Transferstelle, "Transfer Department," an agency of the German ghetto administration active in the Warsaw ghetto. Officially established on April 14, 1941, the Transferstelle actually began operating in November 1940. Charged with overseeing the economic life of the Warsaw ghetto, the Transferstelle played an important, albeit unofficial, role in preventing food imports into the ghetto.

TABLE G.2: Major East European Ghettos

Ghetto	Jews	Founded	Liquidated
Baranovichi (Br)	10,000	12/12/41	12/17/42
Będzin (P)	27,000	07/01/40	08/01/43
Belchatów (P)	6,000	03/01/41	08/11/42
Berdichev (Uk)	20,000	08/25/41	09/15/41
Berezhany (Uk)	4,000	10/15/42	06/12/43
Bialystok (P)	50,000	08/01/41	08/18/43
Bochnia (P)	3,500	03/15/40	09/43
Brest-Litovsk (Uk)	20,000	11/41	10/15/42
Brody (Uk)	6,000	01/01/43	05/21/43
Budapest (Hu)	70,000	11/13/44	02/13/45

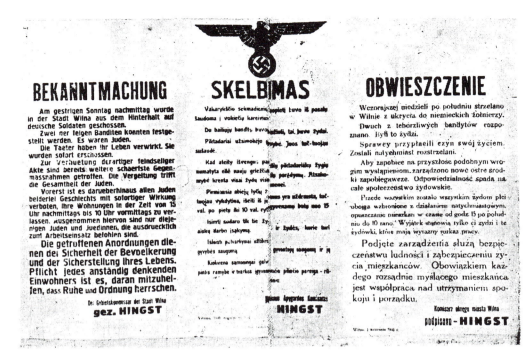

Nazi proclamation ordering the establishment of the Vilna ghetto, September 1, 1941
Authors' Collection

Chernovtsy (R)	50,000	10/11/41	10/43
Chortkov (Uk)	6,000	04/42	12/15/43
Cluj (Hu)	16,000	05/03/44	06/09/44
Częstochowa (P)	48,000	04/09/41	09/22/42
Debrecen (Hu)	9,000	04/28/44	06/21/44
Dés (Hu)	8,000	05/03/44	06/08/44
Diatlovo (Br)	4,000	12/41	08/06/42
Drogobych (Uk)	10,000	10/42	05/21/43
Dvinsk (La)	11,000	07/25/41	05/01/42
Grodno (Br)	25,000	11/01/41	01/22/43
Horodenka (P)	4,000	01/42	07/42
Kaposvár (Hu)	5,000	05/44	07/04/44
Kédainiai (Li)	3,000	07/41	08/28/41
Kharkov (Uk)	21,000	12/14/41	01/05/42
Kherson (Uk)	5,000	08/41	09/16/41
Kielce (P)	27,000	04/41	08/20/42
Kishinev (R)	11,000	07/24/41	10/04/41
Kolomyia (Uk)	18,000	03/25/42	02/02/43
Košice (Cz)	12,000	04/28/44	05/15/44
Kovel (Uk)	14,000	05/21/42	10/6/42
Kovno (Li)	40,000	06/24/41	06/21/43
Krakow (P)	19,000	03/03/41	05/28/42
Lodz (P)	205,000	02/08/40	05/44

Lublin (P)	34,000	03/24/41	03/17/42
Lutsk (Uk)	18,000	12/11/41	08/20/42
Lvov (Uk)	110,000	11/08/41	12/42
Minsk (Uk)	100,000	07/20/41	10/21/43
Piotrkow Trybunalski (P)	18,000	10/08/39	10/13/42
Przemysl (P)	16,000	07/14/41	09/02/43
Radom (P)	30,000	04/07/41	08/16/42
Riga (La)	43,000	08/15/41	11/30/41[1]
Rzeszow (P)	12,500	12/17/41	01/44
Tarnów (P)	15,000	06/19/42	09/02/43
Vilna (Li)	41,000	09/06/41	09/23/43
Warsaw (P)	500,000	10/19/40	05/16/43

Source: Edelheit & Edelheit: *A World in Turmoil*, Westport, CT: Greenwood Press, 1990.

Glaich vi [גלייך ווי, Y] "As if": Term for the attitude common among educators and parents in the larger ghettos: they felt that it was vitally necessary to maintain the appearances of normality as long as humanly possible.

Gleichschaltung [G] "Coordination": A *volkish* idea that the national organism is greater than the sum of its individual parts. These must, therefore, be unified into one monolithic whole that will bring about the rise of the Teutonic order and the "messianic" age. Obviously anything not of the *Volk*, i.e., alien elements, must be gotten rid of, as these will act as a cancer destroying the organism. This primarily meant the Jews. The Nazi Final Solution is only the logical outcome of this policy. For the economic aspect of this > see also: **Arisierung**.

Gmina Żydowska [P] "The Jewish council": Prewar term for the *kahal* and its organs. During the Nazi occupation Poles also used this term to designate the Judenräte.

Gnadentod [G] "Mercy killing": Nazi term for Aktion T-4. > see also: **Euthanasie**.

Goldjuden [G] "Gold Jews": Small commandos in extermination camps composed of Jewish jewelers and watchmakers whose job was to sort, pack, and ship to the SS treasury all valuables taken from the victims murdered in the camps.

Götterdämmerung [G] "Twilight of the gods": Term for the last days of Hitler, the Nazis, and their would-be Thousand-Year Reich.

Governments in Exile

1. Scope and Definition

Although the Nazi occupation of Europe was of unprecedented scope, the continuation of hostilities as well as advances in communications permitted the rise of carryover governments of the occupied Allied and neutral states. Under the circumstances — primarily the almost-total Nazi occupation of their homelands — these governments operated in exile, primarily (though not exclusively), in London. Nevertheless, the exiled governments claimed to be an extension of the legitimate prewar

---

[1] The Riga ghetto was liquidated on this date but was later repopulated by German Jews. These deportees, along with a small number of local Jews left in a small ghetto, eventually numbererd 16,000. Thereafter, *Aussiedlingsaktionen* again depleted the population of the ghetto. The process then began anew and continued until November 1, 1942, when the ghetto was liquidated permanently and the remaining Jews were transferred to the Kaiserwald concentration camp.

administration.

Such claims of legitimacy were clearest in the cases of Holland, Luxembourg, and Norway. In all three the monarchs were present as the heads of state, thus providing continuity with the previous administration. For Belgium, the monarch's absence from London did not impede the legitimacy of the government in exile, since the entire cabinet fled and the king chose to remain in Belgium in order to share his people's trials and tribulations. The same occurred in Denmark, which was not technically at war with the Third Reich and thus never had an official government in exile. Instead, the Danish Consulate General in New York operated as a clearinghouse of Free Danish activities.

The Czech government in exile also retained full legitimacy, since its head of state — President Edvard Beneš — and Foreign Minister Jan Masaryk had been the leaders of Czechoslovakia's pre-Munich government. Somewhat more complicated were the cases of the Greek and Yugoslav governments, both located in Cairo. They continued the prewar governments, but both were seen as illegitimate by wide sections of the populace — ironically, including both resisters (primarily Communist partisans) and (in the case of Yugoslavia) collaborators.

Equally complex was the French situation. Although the French National Committee attempted to present itself as the legitimate inheritor of the mantle of government, many Frenchmen eschewed support of General Charles de Gaulle and viewed the Vichy government of Field Marshall Henri Philippe Pétain as the legitimate government. Once the tide of war clearly changed, a fact exemplified by the French National Committee's move to Algiers on January 1, 1943, a majority of Frenchmen switched their allegiance to de Gaulle. De Gaulle's newfound legitimacy also derived, in large part, from the Nazi occupation of the Vichy zone of France in November 1942.

The most complex situation, however, was that experienced by the Polish government in exile. It was established initially in France, but Nazi operations in Western Europe forced the Poles to move to London. Political considerations soon intervened, however: With the Nazi invasion of the Soviet Union, the Poles reestablished diplomatic relations with Russia (broken when the USSR invaded Poland on September 17, 1939). These relations were always stormy; relations broke down again in April 1943 after the discovery of the Katyn massacres. By 1944 two governments competed for the mantle of legitimacy: the London Poles and the Krajowa Rada Narodowa, more commonly known as the Lublin Committee. The latter took power in Poland as a result of the Soviet liberation and established a Communist government.

2. The London Governments

Belgium, established November 31, 1940, in London. Head of State: Prime Minister H. Pierlot. Agencies: Sureté de l'Etat, "Intelligence Service," headed by Fernand Lepage.

Czechoslovakia, established November 17, 1939, in Paris; moved to London, July 18, 1940. Head of State: Edvard Beneš; Foreign Minister: Jan Masaryk. Agencies: Narodni Osvobozeni, press bureau located in New York.

France, established June 18, 1940, in London. In January 1943, the offices of the French government in exile adopted the title Comité Française de Libération Nationale (CFLN), "French Committee of National Liberation," and moved to Algiers. Head of State: Charles de Gaulle.

Greece, established in May 1941 in Cairo. Head of State: King George II; Prime Ministers: E. Tsedouros (May 1941 to August 1943); S. Venizelos (August 1943 to April 1944); G. Papandreou (April 1944 to May 1945).

Holland, established May 13, 1940, in London. Head of State: Queen Wilhelmina; Prime Minister: P. S. Gerbrandy. Agencies: Radio Oranje, code name for the Dutch radio service. Among other news, it reported the mass extermination of the Jews in Eastern Europe; Bureau Inlichtingen (BI), "Intelligence Bureau," the Dutch secret service that oversaw resistance movements in Holland, established 1943.

Norway, established June 7, 1940, in London. Head of State: King Haakon VII; Prime Minister: Johan Nygaardsvold. Before his escape, the king was authorized by the Norwegian parliament to act on its behalf (in consultation with the prime minister) even without its permission.

Poland, established October 2, 1939, in Paris. In July 1940 the Polish government in exile moved to London. Head of State: Wladyslaw Sikorski (1940–1943); Stanislaw Mikolaiczyk (1943–1945). Agencies: Bureau VI, clandestine communication and supply service; Swit, radio service operating out of London (but claiming to broadcast from Poland), established 1942.

Yugoslavia, established in May 1941 in Jerusalem, moved to Cairo and began official operation on September 13, 1941. Head of State: King Peter I; Prime Minister: B. Purić; Minister of Defense: General D. Mihailović.

3. Communist-Inspired Governments

Krajowa Rada Narodowa, "Polish National Council," popularly known as the Lublin Committee, the Polish pro-Communist government created by Moscow in opposition to the London government in exile.

National Komitee Freies Deutschland, "National Committee of a Free Germany," a pro-Communist organization founded in Moscow.

4. Military Forces of the Exile Governments

Czechoslovak Legion, established in Krakow, Poland, July 11, 1939, moving to France and then to Great Britain after June 10, 1940. Eventually, a division was raised, becoming the Czech First Infantry Division. Component Czech brigades saw service in North Africa and Normandy, but the division per se never saw service. At its height, the Legion numbered some 18,000 men. The exact number of Jews serving in the Legion is unknown, although it has been estimated that as many as one-third of the Legionnaires in France were Jews (at the time the Legion was organized as a reinforced infantry brigade serving with the French Légion

Étrangère).

Forces Belgiques en Grande Bretagne (FBGB), "Belgian Forces in Great Britain," organized on August 12, 1940. In January 1943 FBGB consisted of a reinforced infantry brigade supplemented by miscellaneous support services, for a total of almost 6,000 men. The FBGB saw service in Normandy and northwest Europe between August 8, 1944, and May 1945. In Europe the Belgian forces were increased — by volunteers from Belgian resistance groups — until the FBGB reached divisional strength. Precise data on Jewish participation is unknown, although the fact that Jews served in the FBGB is incontestable.

Forces Libres Français (FLF), "Free French Forces," established in London on July 1, 1940, and led by Charles de Gaulle. Initially composed of miscellaneous units that escaped from France and other battlefronts. FLF forces increased in number steadily until 1944 when the force was reorganized into two army corps with eight divisions and over 150,000 men. FLF forces participated in the campaigns in North Africa and the Middle East, Italy, and, most important, northwest Europe. The French Second Armored Division was given the honor of being the first Allied unit to enter Paris in August 1944. It has been estimated that approximately 10 percent of the personnel of the FLF were Jews.

Nederlandse Legion, "Dutch Legion," established in London on September 24, 1940. On January 11, 1941, the Legion was renamed the Royal Netherlands Brigade; it had one motorized infantry regiment (Princess Irene) and other support services. At its height the Legion numbered some 1,500 personnel. The Brigade saw service in Europe between August 4, 1944, and May 5, 1945 — often serving together with the FBGB. Exact data on Jewish participation is unknown but appears to have been extensive.

Norwegian Brigade, established initially as a training group on September 9, 1940, in London. On March 15, 1941, the force was fixed as a reinforced infantry brigade. One company was parachute trained and provided personnel for the British Special Operations' Executive. At its height the Brigade numbered 4,000 men. On November 11, 1944, one company began guerrilla operations in northern Norway, slowly being reinforced by F Company. On May 9, 1945, the rest of the Brigade followed, as part of the British First Airborne Division, disarming the Germans and providing security for the newly liberated territories. Jewish participation in the Norwegian forces is unknown.

Polski Sily Zbrojne w ZSSR, "Polish Armed Forces in the USSR," original title for the Polish forces raised among prisoners of war held in the Soviet Union. Commanded by General Wladyslaw Anders. At peak strength, the force numbered over 75,000 men organized into two infantry and one armored divisions. The force, renamed Second Polish Corps, left the USSR in August 1942 via Persia (where the Corps remained until July 1943), Iraq, and Palestine. From September 1943 to April 1945 the Corps was engaged in active military operations as part of the U.S. Fifth Army in Italy. It is impossible to establish the precise number of Jews serving in the Corps. The Poles actively sought to disqualify Jewish volunteers under the excuse that they were "unfit for military service." Even those Jews who were accepted faced continuous antisemitism, and many hid their true identities. Jewish soldiers were encouraged to desert, especially when the Corps was in Palestine, and many — including corporal Menachem Begin — did so. The estimated number of Jews who did serve with the Corps in the Italian campaign is 4,000.

Royal Greek Armed Forces in the Middle East, established in Palestine on June 23, 1941. The Greeks initially fielded one infantry brigade. By the end of 1942 this force had been more than doubled, eventually numbering almost 13,000 men. Individual brigades fought in North Africa and Italy, although mutinies in the First and Second Brigades in 1944 brought about their disbandment. At least 135 Jews served in the Greek Armed Forces in the Middle East, primarily in the medical corps.

Royal Yugoslav Guards (RYG), established in Alexandria, Egypt, in January 1942. The force was initially organized as a battalion that became operational on February 19, 1942, and fought in North Africa during the spring and summer. From July 1942 to January 1943 the RYG served in garrison duties in Palestine. Slowly enlarged to a division, the unit became a microcosm of the struggle between Tito and Mihailović. By 1944 dissension was so acute that the British unilaterally disbanded all Yugoslav exile forces. No data exist regarding Jewish participation in the RYG.

Svoboda Army, Czech military force established in Poland in 1939. Fighting briefly during the Polish campaign, the Svoboda Army crossed into Soviet-occupied Poland on September 21, 1939, and was interned *en masse*. In July 1941 the internees were permitted to reorganize a Soviet-sponsored Czechoslovak Legion under the command of General Jan Svoboda. This Legion recognized the authority of the Czech government in London but operated exclusively under Soviet control. At its height the Legion was organized into a complete army corps with over 40,000 men under arms. However, only three brigades of this corps actually saw service: the First and Second Infantry and the Independent Parachute Brigade. The latter was especially active in aiding the unsuccessful Slovak uprising of 1944. Exact figures on Jewish participation in the Svoboda Army are unavailable. It has been estimated that Jews composed between one-third and one-half of all legionnaires in Poland in 1939, with the one-third figure remaining throughout.

5. Jewish Affairs in the Governments in Exile

Belgium: Jewish affairs conducted by the Belgian section of the World Jewish Congress. In 1941 the Belgian government announced its intention to void all anti-Jewish legislation while also condemning collaboration as a form of treason.

Czechoslovakia: Jewish affairs (from 1942) conducted by Ernest Frischer and Julius Friedman, members of the Czechoslovakian State Council. In conjunction with Czech clandestine agencies, they organized rescue activities and sent parcels of food, medicines, and some funds through Portuguese, Swedish, and Swiss representatives to Terezin. The

Czech government in exile also cooperated closely with the Jewish leadership in the Yishuv and the free world.

France: Jewish affairs conducted by René Cassin, René Mayer, and Pierre Mendès-France, all members of the exiled National Assembly. The government was not active on Jewish affairs, however, because of fear of creating antisemitism in occupied France.

Greece: No representatives officially conducted Jewish affairs.

Holland: Jewish affairs conducted by A. H. Drilsma, M. Sluyser.

Norway: No formal representative conducted Jewish affairs; however, the Norwegian government declared all anti-Jewish legislation null and void in one of its first official acts.

Poland: Jewish affairs conducted by Ignacy I. Schwarzbart, Szmuel A. Zygelbojm (1940–1943), and Emanuel Szerer (1943–1945); Ludwig Grossfeld was a member of the Polish State Council. On April 21, 1944, the Polish government in exile established a Council for Rescuing the Jewish Population of Poland, which operated parallel to the Zegota Council. By then, of course, almost no Jews remained alive in Poland.

Yugoslavia: No representatives officially conducted Jewish affairs.

Granatowa Policja [P] "Blue Police": > see also: **Collaboration**.

Greulmeldungen [G] "Atrocity reports": The Nazi broadcasts to neutral countries that denied reports of German atrocities that appeared in the Allied media.

Grossbetreib [G] "Mass operation": Nazi code term for the mass murder program. >

see also: **Aktion(en)/Grossaktion(en)**, **Endlösung**.

Grossraum [G] "Large space": Term for the spatial area claimed by the Nazis for the Aryan race. > see also: **Lebensraum**.

Grossreich [G] "Greater Empire": Nazi term for Germany within the borders that were established during the 1930s as well as the territories incorporated from Poland early in World War II (Danzig–West Prussia, Upper Silesia, and the Warthegau). In addition to Germany proper (and the Polish territories), the Grossreich's borders included the Saar and Rhineland provinces reincorporated in 1935 and 1936; Austria, incorporated as a result of the *Anschluss*; and the Sudetenland, incorporated after the Munich Agreement of September 30, 1938. All these territories had been identified as the "core" of the German *Volk* by nineteenth-century German nationalists and were considered only the first step toward attainment of *Lebensraum*. Additional territory, incorporated as a result of Nazi victories in 1939 and 1940, but whose identification with German culture was more tenuous, included Memel (forcibly taken from Lithuania in 1939) and Alsace-Lorraine and Eupen-Malmédy, incorporated, respectively, from France and Holland in 1940. > see also: **Altreich**; **Lebensraum**.

Groupes francs [Fr] "Freelance groups": French term for Maquis not associated with any of the major political movements. > see also: **Resistance, Resistance Movements (France)**.

Gubernia [P] "Province," Polish-Jewish term for the German-occupied segments of Poland better known as the General Government. > see also: **Generalgouvernement**.

H

Ha'apala [העפלה, H] "Striving": alternative Zionist term for "illegal" immigration. Unlike the term *Aliya Bet*, which emphasizes organized activity, *ha'apala* is used to encompass both organized and spontaneous immigration activity. Furthermore, *ha'apala* emphasizes the actions of the *ma'apilim* as actors in their own rescue. > see also: **Aliya Bet**.

Ha-arurim [הארורים, H] "The accursed ones": Jewish code term for Nazis, reflecting a Hebrew play on words: The Hebrew term for accursed ones is phonetically similar to Aryans.

Anti-*Ha'avara* billfold advocating an anti-Nazi boycott
Courtesy of the Jabotinsky Institute Archive, Tel Aviv

250

Ha'avara [העברה, H] "Transfer": The agreement between German Jewish leaders and the treasury of the Third Reich, under which Jews could emigrate to Palestine and receive a percentage of their capital in the form of German-produced goods. Signed in August 1933, the agreement met with stiff opposition from Jewish groups that advocated an economic boycott of Nazi Germany. German Jews, however, supported the agreement, since it represented the only way for them to get out of Germany without being reduced to penury. In 1935 the World Zionist Congress debated the *Ha'avara* agreement and decided to maintain it, although thenceforth it was placed under the oversight of the Jewish Agency Executive. It has been estimated that as many as 50,000 Jews entered Palestine under

To "Haavara" Ltd., P. O. B. 616, Tel-Aviv

CERTIFICATE

The Trust and Transfer Office "Haavara" Ltd. places at the disposal of the Banks in Palestine amounts in Reichsmarks which have been put at its disposal by the Jewish immigrants from Germany. The Banks avail themselves of these amounts in Reichsmarks in order to make payments on behalf of Palestinian merchants for goods imported by them from Germany. The merchants pay in the value of the goods to the Banks and the "Haavara" Ltd. pays the countervalue to the Jewish immigrants from Germany. To the same extent that local merchants will make use of this arrangement, the import of German goods will serve to withdraw Jewish capital from Germany.

The Trust and Transfer Office,
«HAAVARA» LTD.

We hereby confirm, that in accordance with the above arrangement, we have transferred to-day, by order of Messrs. _____

the sum of (Haavara) RM: _____ in payment of invoice dated _____ as per order dated _____ Countervalue of above amounting to LP. _____ has been received by us.

Dated _____

BANK DER TEMPELGESELLSCHAFT
SIGNATURE OF THE BANK
(Bank of the Temple Society Limited)
FILIALE JA...

The above sum in Reichsmarks has been transferred to the exporter/s of _____ (Germany).

Sample *Ha'avara* certificate
Courtesy of the Jabotinsky Institute Archive, Tel Aviv

Häftling uniform
Authors' Collection

the *Ha'avara* agreement between 1933 and 1939. Even so, the *Ha'avara* corporation experienced considerable difficulties in meeting its payments and was still re-imbursing its German Jewish investors as late as 1951.

Häftling [G] "Prisoner": Term for those forcefully incarcerated in a Nazi con-centration, slave labor, or other type of camp. > see also: **Konzentrationslager System**; **Ka-Tzetnik**.

Hagim u-zemanim le-ason [חגים וזמנים לאסון, H] "Holidays and seasons for dis-aster": Slang modification of the Jewish liturgical expression (the original reads *Zemanim le-Sason*, "seasons for joy") de-noting the fact that the Nazis chose Jewish holidays to impose decrees or undertake *Aussiedlungsaktionen* or other *Aktionen*.

Hakenkreuz [G] "Swastika": The crooked cross taken up by the Nazis as the symbol for their party. Originally thought to be an ancient Aryan runic symbol, more recent scholars have noted that the origin appears to be ancient India. During the 1930s and 1940s, however, the Swastika came to represent pure, unadul-terated evil in Europe and throughout the world.

Halbjude [G] "Half Jew": Nazi term for persons of mixed parentage but possessing at least two Jewish grandparents regardless of their religious affiliation. > see also: **Mischlinge**.

Hallel hagudl [הלל הגדל, Y/H] "Long Hallel": Yiddishized Hebrew title, derived from the Psalms, for the prayer chanted on Jewish holi-days. As work details were spread out over long stretches of road, *Hallel Hagudl* was utilized as a term, especially among orthodox

Jews to warn the laborers that some sort of *Aktion* was about to happen.

Harzburger Front [G] The abortive alliance between the NSDAP, Stahlhelm, and other right-wing German parties that was created during a meeting held at Bad Harzburg, Germany, on October 11, 1931, to coordinate anti-republican activities. The inability of the member organizations to agree on a common platform beyond opposition to the Weimar government led to the collapse of the Harzburg Front within two months.

Hasidei umot ha-olam [חסידי אומות העולם, H] "Righteous Among the Nations":

1. Scope and Definition

Jewish tradition speaks of those who live on a high moral plane and are said to be the "friends of God." According to legend, in every generation thirty-six righteous persons (ל"ו צדיקים) live and it is only for their sake that God allows the world to exist. The traditional term is also used in the Talmud to denote non-Jews who act in accordance with the "seven Noachide laws" and are therefore worthy of eternal life.[1] After the Holocaust the term has come to represent those European non-Jews who risked their lives to save Jews, often with no thought of compensation. In many cases neither the rescuer nor their charges survived; once betrayed or discovered, both received swift punishment in accordance with Nazi "justice": instant death or incarceration in a concentration camp. Since 1957, Yad Vashem, Israel's National Memorial to the Heroes and Martyrs, has honored individuals and groups of hasidei umot ha-olam as a means of commemorating their heroic deeds.

2. Types of Rescuers

Altruists: those who saw rescue of Jews as an end in itself.

Subversives: those who saw rescue of Jews as a means to attain national goals; the goal being to resist the Nazi occupation.

Mercenaries: those who saw rescue of Jews as a means to attain personal goals; the goal being financial gain. Often such rescuers betrayed to the Gestapo the Jews in their charge after they were paid.

3. Individual Righteous

Belgium: André, Joseph; Nèvejean, Yvonne; Taquet, Marie.

Bulgaria: Michaelov, Michael.

Czechoslovakia: Fries, Libuse.

France: Beltrami, Ivan; Benoît, Pierre Marie; Deffaugt, Jean; Donadille, Marc; Guth, Emilie; Orsi, Ermine; Théis, Edouard; Trocmé, André; Trocmé, Daniel.

Germany: Duckwitz, Georg F.; Heine, Fritz; Helmreich, Eberhard; Luckner, Gertrud; Schindler, Oskar; Schmid, Anton.

Great Britain: Coward, Charles.

Greece: Evert, Anghelos.

Holland: Bogaard, Johannes; de Vries, Johannes; Dohmen, Nico; Douwes, Arnold; Mulder, Marguerite; Overduijn, Leendert; Riekirk, Semmy; Steenstra, Luoisa; van Binsbergen, Marion; van der Voort, Hanna; van Mansum, Arie; Weidner, John; Westerweel, Joop.

Hungary: Sztehlo, Gábor.

Italy: Beccari, Arrigo; Brunacci, Aldo; Moreali, Giuseppe; Nicacci, Rufino; Nicolini, Giuseppe.

Japan: Sugihara, Sempo.

Latvia: Klepinin, Dimitri; Lipke, Janis; Lipke, Johanna; Skobtsova, Elizaveta.

Lithuania: Baublys, Petras; Binkiene, Sofija; Borkowska, Anna; Kutorgiene-Buivydaité, Elena; Šimaite, Ona.

Poland: Abramowicz, Natalia; Adamkowska, Maria; Adamowicz, Irena; Arczynski, Marek; Arvanitti, Helena; Barancewicz, Larisa; Bartoszewski, W.; Bazyli, Bogdan; Bereska, Helena; Bieganski, Piotr; Blam, Sara; Boczkowski, Stanislaw; Boczkowski, Zofia;

---

[1] Cf. *Tosefta Sanhedrin* 13:2.

Bogucki, Karol; Bonkowski, Wladyslaw; Buchholz, Janina; Budna-Widerschal, A.; Budnik, Piotr; Bukowinski, Leon; Bussold, Stanislawa; Celka, Szymon; Chacze, Edward; Charmuszko, Pawel; Chelpa, Anna; Chodon Gertner, Marysia; Choms, Wladyslawa; Chmilel, Aniela; Cieply, Jan; Cimek, Jadwiga; Ciemiega, Stefanias; Cywinski, Feliks; Czajkowski, Szymon; Czajkowski, Bronislawa; Czezowski, Tadeusz; Czezowski, Antonina; Czezowski, Teresa; Deba, Magdalena; Deba, Jan; Demel, Jozefa; Demska, Stanislawa; Dudziak, Zofia; Duracz, Jerzy; Dyrdal-Kielbasa, Maria; Dziedzic-Skrzypic, Wiktoria; Egermaier, Waclaw; Egermaier, Leonia; Eliasz, Jan; Falker, Jan; Falker, Maria; Filipowicz, Wanda; Fink, Jozef; Franio, Zofia; Fularski, Antoni; Gaworska, Janina; Gawelczyk, Julian; Gawelczyk, Bronislawa; Gidzinska, Maria; Gill, Jozef; Gill, Janina; Glinka, Stefan; Golowacz, Waclaw; Gorecki, Zbigniew; Gosk, Mieczyslaw; Gosk, Helena; Gosk, Stanislaw; Gregorczyk, Wladyslaw; Grudzinska, Hanna Jozefa; Gut, Marianna; Haifter, Magdalena; Hencel, Ludwik; Hessen, Bronislawa; Horbaczewski, Pawel; Hrekow, Andrzej; Hrekow, Wiera; Hupalo, Franciszka; Iwanski, Henryk; Iwanski, Wiktoria; Jackow, Staszek; Jacyna, Waclaw; Jacyna, Marcelina; Jamiolkowski, Jan; Jamiolkowski, Janina; Janc, Boleslaw; Janc, Helena; Jankiewicz, Tadeusz; Jaromirska, Leokadia; Jaskolka, Wladyslaw; Jaskolka, Maria; Jaskolka, Stanislaw; Jeziorski, Wladyslaw; Jeziorski, Anna; Kakol, Jan; Kakol, Magda; Kanabus, Feliks; Kann, Maria; Karski, Jan; Karsov, Szymaniewska; Karsov, Stanislawa; Klemens, Zofia; Klepacka, Maria; Kmita, Katarzyna; Kmita, Mikolaj, Kmita, Karolina; Koczerkiewicz, Mieczyslaw; Kodasinski, Jozef; Korczeniewska, Helena; Korkuc, Kazimierz; Korniecka, Jozefa; Kostrz, Andrzej; Kowalski, Wladyslaw; Kowalski, Witold; Kowalski, Maria; Krawiec, Maria; Krzemienski, Stanislaw; Krzysztonek, Aniela; Kucharzek, Irena; Kuriata, Mikolaj; Kurjanowicz, Ignacy; Kuropieska, Leopolda; Kurowiec, Dymitr; Kurowiec, Boguslaw;

Kurylowicz, Boguslaw; Kurylowicz, Jan; Kurylowicz, Zofia; Kuzin, Maria; Lasica, Tadeusz; Lintner, Stefan; Lipczynska, Ewa; Lipke Janis, Joanna; Lisikiewicz, Miron; Lozinska, Pelagia; Lozinska, Zuzanna; Lubczynski, Ignacy; Lubicz-Nycz, Bronislawa; Lubicz-Nycz, Izabela; Maciejko, Wojciech; Majewska, Bronislawa; Makara, Rozalia; Malkiewicz, Aniela; Marchwinski, Jozef; Marcinkiewicz, Aleksandra; Markiewicz, Szymon; Markiewicz, Anna; Matysiak, Wladyslaw; Miazio, Emilia; Migden, Apolonia; Mikolajkow, Aleksander; Mikolajkow, Leokadia; Miller, Stefa; Miller, Marcelina; Miluski, Jan; Mirek, Jan; Mirek, Aniela; Misiuna, Wladyslaw; Moycho, Anna; Muzolf, Stanislawa; Myrta, Jozef; Myrta, Katarzyna; Naruszko, Ignacy; Naruszko, Genowefa; Nazarewicz, Kazimiera; Nowak, Franciszek; Nowinski, Waclaw; Oldak, Aleksander; Oldak, Apolonia; Olszanska, Janina; Onowska, Jadwiga; Oppyke, Irene; Osiewicz, Jan; Paszkiewicz, Rozalia; Pastuszynski, Zygmunt; Pawlicka, Janina; Pawlicki, Jan; Pawlowska, Kleopatra; Pekalski, Franciszek; Persiak, Zofia; Peska, Wladyslawa; Pierzycki, Franciszek; Pierzycki, Stanislawa; Pietkun, Jan; Pikulski, Jan; Pikulski, Waclaw; Pilat, Piotr; Pilat, Matylda; Piotrowska, Alicija; Piotrowski, Jozef; Piotrowski, Zofia; Plaskacz, Bronislawa; Podworski, Wladyslaw; Pogorzalski, Julian; Pogorzalski, Stanislaw; Polewka, Franciszek; Polewka, Barbara; Prask, Karol; Przewalski, Jan; Przewalski, Jozefa; Puc, Stanislaw; Pukaite, Genia; Raczynski, Stefan; Reicher Galikowska, Lucia; Renska, Barbara; Rolirad, Henryk; Roslan, Aleksander; Roslan, Mela; Roslaniec, Julian; Rozen, Zofia; Rozen, Katarzyna; Rozwadowski, Dionizy; Rykowska, Jadwiga; Rykowska, Janusz; Rytel, Zygmunt; Rzeczycka, Sylwia; Sadzikowska, Kazimiera; Sawicka, Maria; Schutz, Irena; Schussel, Alfred; Sendler, Irena; Siewierska, Stefa; Slebocki, Halina; Slebocki, Stanislaw; Sloboda, Julia; Sobala, Stefan; Sobczak, Stanislaw; Sobecka, Maria; Socha, Jozef; Sokolowska, Zofia; Spasinski, Stanislaw; Stakowska, Jozefa; Stawski, Stanislaw K.; Stawski, Wanda A.; Strojwas, Anna; Strojwas, Franciszek; Strusinski, Zygmunt; Strusinski, Wiktoria; Strzalecka, Jadwiga;

Strzelec, Stanislawa; Strzelecka, Maria; Swierczynski, Bernard K.; Swietochowski, Wladyslaw; Szczypiorski, Aleksander; Szczypiorski, Antonina; Szelagowski, Wladyslaw; Szemet, Helena; Szepelowski, Wladyslaw; Szlichta, Teodor; Szostak, Stanislaw; Szostak, Zofia; Szymczukiewicz, Witold; Tarasiewicz, Bronislawa; Tarasiewicz, Hieronim; Tarasowa-Cajtag, A.; Tomczak, Natalia; Trojanowski, Andrzej; Twornicki, Janusz; Tymoficzuk, Stanislaw; Ustianowski, Ignacy; Uszczanowski, Antoni; Volinski, Henryk; Wachalska, Anna; Wasilkowski, Jozef; Wasilkowski, Vasilena; Werstler, Antoni; Wiater, Adam; Wiater, Helena; Wiater, Tadeusz; Wieth, Imgrad; Wajcik, Waclaw; Wolfinger, Julia; Wolfinger, Marcus; Wolosianski, Izydor; Wolosianski, Jaroslawa; Woloszyn, Stanislaw; Wozniak, Stanislaw; Wunsche, Jerzy; Zabinski, Antonia; Zabinski, Jan; Zadarnowska, Irena; Zagorski, Waclaw; Zajac, Ewa; Zawadzki, Boleslaw; Ziental, Bronislawa I.; Zukowski, Grzegorz; Zukowski, Wanda; Zwolakowski, Janusz; Zwonarz, Franka; Zwonarz, Jozef.

Portugal: de Sousa Mendes, Aristede.

Russian Republic: Kowalyk (Berger) Jean.

Sweden: Wallenberg, Raoul.

Switzerland: Lutz, Carl.

Ukraine: Fomenko, Witold; Gerasimov, Amfian; Kalenczuk, Fiodor; Melnyczuk, Helena; Zahajkewyz, Orest.

TABLE H.1: Numbers of Recognized Righteous[1]

Country	Cases	Country	Cases	Country	Cases
Albania	3	Greece	117	Soviet Union[3]	363
Austria	69	Holland	3,372	Spain	3
Belgium	476	Hungary	160	Sweden	7
Brazil	1	Italy	142	Switzerland	13
Bulgaria	11	Japan	1	Turkey	1
Czechoslovakia	117	Norway	3	United Kingdom	10
Denmark[2]	11	Poland	3,268	Yugoslavia	76
France	780	Portugal	1	Other	29
Germany	251	Romania	37	Total	9,295

Source: Yad Vashem.

Hebräische volksverderber [G] "Hebrew corruptors": Nazi term deriving from a reference in Hitler's *Mein Kampf* and concentrating on the supposedly deleterious impact of Jews upon the Aryan race. The term refers to Jewish corruptors in two senses: that of racial corruption through intermarriage and that of political and social corruption deriving from Jewish emancipation.

Heckenholt Stiftung [G] "Heckenholt Foundation": A sign on the gas chamber at the Belzec death camp. The sign was part of a cruel hoax, perpetrated to camouflage the chamber's true purpose: Heckenholt was the *SS-Unterscharführer* who operated the gas chamber.

Hermann Meier [Slang]: Derisive nickname for Luftwaffe Chief Hermann Göring. Based on an

---

[1] Includes all individuals recognized as *Hasidei umot ha-olam* by Yad Vashem; The numbers are accurate as of December 31, 1991.

[2] In addition to the eleven individuals noted here, the entire Danish nation is recognized by *Yad Vashem* as a "righteous nation."

[3] This figure includes the totals for all of the former Soviet Republics.

August 9, 1939, promise that if any enemy aircraft were seen over German skies he could be called "Meier," a Jewish-sounding name that played on Göring's involvement in Jewish affairs during the 1930s. As Allied aircraft increased in number over the skies of the Reich, German civilians joked ruefully about this promise.

Herr Rolf [PN] "Mr. Rolf": The name of Plaszow Lagerkommandant Amon Göth's dog, specially trained to attack Jewish inmates on command. Rolf was especially fond of attacking Jewish women after they were forced to undress under the blows of SS whips.

Herrenvolk [G] "Master race": Part of the Nazi ideological terminology emphasizing the belief that Aryans, by the fact of their racial superiority, deserved to rule over the "inferior" races.

Het verzet [Du] "The resistance": Common Dutch term for the Underground or for members of an underground organization. > see also: **Resistance, Resistance Movements (Holland)**.

Hexe [G] "Witch": Common term for frau Ilse Koch, wife of Karl Otto Koch, commandant of the Buchenwald concentration camp.

Hilfsmittel [G] "Auxiliary equipment": Slang Nazi term for gas vans, used in the Soviet Union and Yugoslavia as a means of speeding up the murder operations of the Einsatzgruppen.

Hilfswillige (Hiwis) [G] "Volunteers": Nazi term applied to Soviet prisoners of war and civilians in occupied Eastern Europe who volunteered or were drafted for auxiliary service in the Wehrmacht. In the winter of 1941–1942 guard units made up of *Hiwi*s were added to existing service units. In addition to purely military posts, *Hiwi*s were also assigned to guard ghettos and concentration camps. Eventually the *Hiwi*s were

permitted to carry weapons, eventually being organized into *Ostbataillone*. > see also: **Collaboration**.

Hilufin [חילופין, H/Y] "Exchange": Slang term for items of value used to barter with non-Jews for food at the borders of the ghetto enclosures.

Himmelfahrt [G] "Journey to heaven": Nazi term for victims selected for the gas chambers. After the last of their personal belongings were taken from them, the naked victims were, at times, driven relentlessly through a gauntlet of two rows of guards with whips and clubs towards the "heavenly road" from where there was no escape. > see also: **Himmelstrasse**.

Himmelkommando [G] "Sky commando": An inmate term for the approximately 200-man strong work detail in the Treblinka extermination camp. Like the Red Commando, their job was to retrieve and sort the victims' luggage, which they were forced to leave behind upon alighting from the trains. So-called, because this work detail had to wear sky-blue kerchiefs. > see also: **Di Roite Kommande**.

Himmelstrasse [G] "Heavenly road": Nazi term for a narrow pathway between two walls of entangled barbed wire on the way to the gas chambers. > see also: **Himmelfahrt**.

Hingerichtet [G] "Executed": One among the multiplicity of terms for the killing of Jews. This term was especially used by Einsatzgruppen in reference to their daily tally of victims. > see also: **Endlösung**.

Historikerstreit [G] "Historians' debate": Contemporary term for the debate over the relativization of history of the Holocaust and the Third Reich undertaken by a number of German historians.

Hois komitet(n) [הויס קאמיטעט(ן), Y] "House Committee(s)": Semi-clandestine Jewish self-governing bodies in the Warsaw ghetto. Founded at the initiative of Emmanuel Ringelblum, acting in his capacity as JDC representative in the ghetto. The house committees were responsible for maintaining sanitary conditions and distributing food within each block of houses. As a result of their multiple activities, the house committees became a focal point for resistance to the Judenrat and the Jüdischer Ordnungsdienst.

Holocaust: Term used to designate the Nazi attempt to exterminate and extirpate Jewry. The term originates in the Bible and originally designated a burnt offering that is completely consumed. It came to be identified with the destruction of European Jewry in the United States during the mid-1970s. The parallel Hebrew and Yiddish terms date to the 1940s but are also narrowly defined to mean only the Nazi (and Nazi-inspired) murder of European Jews. > see also: **Endlösung; Shoa; Churb'n.**

Horst Wessel Lied [G] "Horst Wessel Song": Nazi anthem named after a member of the SA who had been killed on February 23, 1930, by a Communist because of a private vendetta. Nazi propagandists converted Wessel into a martyr and turned a poem he published in 1929, set to a march, into the official song of the NSDAP.

Hotel Polski [P] "Polish Hotel": Hotel in Warsaw where the Gestapo kept Jews holding citizenship papers of neutral countries, who were to be exchanged for German citizens interned by the Allies. In late 1943 and early 1944 the internees were transferred to either Vittel (300 persons) or Bergen-Belsen (2,500). When the issuing countries procrastinated in honoring the documents issued by their consulates, most holders of such papers were deported to Auschwitz, where they perished. A further group of 420 persons were murdered in Warsaw's Pawiak prison.

Hots rachmunis [האַטס רחמנות, Y] "Have pity": Yiddish phrase spoken by hundreds of poor, hungry, starving, cold, and destitute Jews — both young and old — while they begged for food or shelter in the larger Polish ghettos.

Humin Kutn [המן קטן, Y] "The Small Haman": Term for Hitler, mostly as expressed by Eastern European Jewry. In light of the fact that just the mention of Hitler's name by Jews was fraught with personal danger, a host of different terms came into wide usage.

Hunde und Juden Verboten! [G] "Dogs and Jews forbidden": Signs appearing in Aryan-owned shops in Nazi-occupied Poland in the autumn of 1939.

Hycler [P] "Dog-shooter": Polish underground term for Adolf Hitler, reflecting the murderous actions of the Nazis in every occupied country.

I

Israel, State of: On May 14, 1948, just three years after the liberation of the concentration camps, the State of Israel was reborn. Historians and theologians have both noted an intimate connection between the two events. On the historical level the Holocaust and the rise of the State of Israel are linked by the chronological reality that one preceded the other and by sharing a clear, if not unequivocal, cause-and-effect relationship. Although it is certain that a Jewish state would have eventually emerged despite Arab opposition and British obstruction, it is equally true that the Holocaust and the fate of European Jewish survivors considerably speeded up the process. This was especially clear during the hearings of the United Nations Special Committee on Palestine in the summer of 1946 and the subsequent UN discussions on the Palestine problem: The horrific event in Europe influenced many states that would have otherwise chosen neutrality (if not hostility) to Jewish aspirations to support partition and the creation of a Jewish state.

The Holocaust plays an important role in everyday life and in ideology in Israel. Sensitivity to military security derives from fears of powerlessness that can be traced back to the years before the establishment of the state: The Yishuv was forced to watch as European Jewry was mercilessly ground to dust but was unable to offer any realistic assistance. This sense of a new state arising to correct a historical injustice played a prominent role in the Entebbe rescue of July 4, 1976 — when Jewish passengers of a hijacked Air France airliner were separated from non-Jewish passengers by German terrorists — and in Prime Minister Menachem Begin's defense of the 1981 attack on Iraq's Ossirak nuclear reactor. In both cases the theme was that another attack, or even a threat of attack, upon Jews — because of their Jewishness — would not go unpunished. Indeed, for this reason, many Israeli leaders deny the validity of distinctions between antisemitism and anti-Zionism: Ultimately both deny to Jews those rights naturally granted to other nations.

On a theological level, a number of Jewish philosophers — Emil Fackenheim, Ignaz Maybaum, Irving Greenberg, and Eliezer Berkovits, among others — concentrate on the dialectical relationship between *hurban* (destruction) and redemption. This theme, which has parallels in the Bible and throughout Jewish thought, recognizes two polar extremes in Jewish history: Destruction — as represented by the pharaonic persecution, the destruction of the First Temple, and finally, the Holocaust — and rebirth — as represented by the Exodus, the return from Babylon in the Persian era, and the creation of the State of Israel. In each case, moreover, both destruction and the subsequent redemption were framed in the form of a renewed covenant between the Jewish people and God and within the Jewish community. > see also: **Yom ha-Shoa; Yishuv.**

J

Jehovahs Pleite [G] "Smashing God": Austrian Nazi term for the destruction of synagogal holy objects (Torahs, etc.) during *Kristallnacht*. The term was used in numerous articles printed in Austrian dailies. The Jewish term *Pleite* which means "flight" was interpreted by the Nazis to mean "smashing," thus implying that God's chosen were kaput.

Jewish Leadership

1. Scope and Definition

As an organized entity, the Jewish community long predated the Nazi persecution of European Jewry. Whether in the context of a *kehila*, *Gemeinde*, or community, Jewish leadership has always played a primary role in securing Jewish rights, status, or — in times of dire emergency — Jewish lives. In modern times, as communal bonds weakened, membership in the Jewish community ceased to be mandatory; nevertheless, the community's role — and especially the leaders' role — in securing the Jewish future took on even more significance. Never was that more true than during the Holocaust, when Jewish leaders in Nazi-occupied Europe and in the free world were confronted with searing decisions that spelled life or death for thousands, hundreds of thousands, or millions of Jews. To date no consensus exists among historians about whether the Jewish leadership active between 1933 and 1945 passed or failed the test presented by Nazism, nor is a consensus likely in the foreseeable future. > see also: **Judenrat**; **Organizations**; **Resistance, Jewish**; **Yishuv**.

2. European

Alter, Abraham M. (1866–1948): Rebbe of the Gur Hasidic dynasty and a founder of Agudas Israel; emigrated to Palestine in 1940.

Alter, Wiktor (1890–1941): Leader of the Polish Jewish Bund; arrested by NKVD and killed on Stalin's orders.

Baeck, Leo (1873–1956): German rabbi and communal leader; incarcerated in Terezin.

Balaban, Mayer (1877–1942): Jewish historian and professor at Warsaw University; shot by the Nazis.

Blum, Léon (1872–1950): French Jewish statesman, Socialist leader, and prime minister (1936–1937); tried by the Vichy regime and incarcerated in a concentration camp.

Brand, Joel J. (1906–1964): Hungarian communal leader; sent in 1944 by Adolf Eichmann to neutral Turkey to negotiate a ransom agreement with the Allies.

Buber, Martin (1878–1965): German Jewish theologian and philosopher; emigrated to Palestine in 1938.

Dubnow, Simon (1860–1941): Dean of East European Jewish historians; political activist who sought to establish Jews as a diaspora nation; murdered by Nazis during *Aktion* in Riga.

Erlich, Henryk (1882–1941): Leader of the Polish Jewish Bund; arrested by NKVD and killed at Stalin's orders.

Federbusch, Simon (1892–1969): Chief Rabbi of Finland and Zionist activist; advocated rescue of East European Jewry from Finland and from the United States (where he moved in 1940).

Filderman, Wilhelm (1882–1963): Romanian Jewish communal activist; actively opposed the antisemitic persecution under the Iron Guard regime; deported to Transnistria in 1943 but was returned shortly thereafter; continued to actively oppose antisemitism; emigrated to France in 1948.

Friedman, Philip (1901–1960): Polish Jewish historian of the Holocaust; organized the Polish Jewish Historical Commission after World War II; professor of Jewish history at Columbia University, YIVO's Center for Advanced Jewish Studies, and the Herzlia Hebrew Teachers College.

Hartglas, Apolinary (1883–1953): Polish Zionist leader; member of the Sejm; emigrated to Palestine in 1940.

Kaplan, Chaim A. (1880–1942): Teacher; diarist of Warsaw ghetto; deported in late 1942 and murdered in Treblinka.

Kasztner, Rezsö (Rudolf) (1906–1957): Hungarian Zionist leader; chairman of the Va'ad ha-Ezra veha-Hatzala in Budapest; engaged in controversial rescue negotiations with the SS during the deportations from Hungary; assassinated in Jerusalem by unknown assailants after a bitter libel trial.

Korczak, Janusz (1878–1942): Polish Jewish writer and educator; headed the orphanage in the Warsaw ghetto; deported with his charges and murdered at Treblinka.

Lévite, Simon (1912–1970): Franco-Jewish Zionist leader; national leader of the Jewish scouts movement; one of the founders of the Armée Juive; representative of Youth Aliya in France.

Maarsen, Isaac (1893–1943): Chief Rabbi of The Hague, Holland; author of scholarly works on biblical subjects; murdered by the Nazis.

Margulies, Emil (1877–1943): Polish Jewish lawyer, politician, and Zionist leader; co-author of the Bernheim Petition; emigrated to Palestine in 1939 and died there.

Mark, Ber (1908–1966): Communist activist and Jewish historian; member of the Jewish Anti-Fascist Committee; delegate to the Lublin Committee; author of historical works on the Jewish resistance movement in Poland.

Menczer, Aron (1917–1943): Youth Aliya activist in Austria and Poland; deported to Theresienstadt and then to Birkenau, where he perished.

Niemirower, Jacob I. (1872–1939): Chief Rabbi of Romania; active in the Zionist movement and a strong opponent of Romanian antisemitism; survived an assassination attempt in 1936; retired in 1939 and died shortly thereafter.

Nissenbaum, Yitzhak (1868–1942): Polish Rabbi and Zionist leader; originated the concept of *Kiddush ha-Hayim* while incarcerated in the Warsaw ghetto; deported to Treblinka, where he perished.

Papenheim, Bertha (1859–1936): German Jewish feminist leader; founder of the Jüdische Frauenbund; arrested by the Gestapo in 1936 and beaten to death.

Prilutsky, Noah (1882–1944): Jewish communal leader and journalist; founder of *Der Moment*; executed by Nazis in 1944.

Pugliese, Umberto (1880–1961): Italian Jewish naval engineer; dismissed from the Italian navy as a result of the 1938 racial laws; incarcerated in Auschwitz but not murdered.

Ringelblum, Emmanuel (1900–1944): Polish Zionist leader and communal activist; historian, teacher, and author; representative of the American Jewish Joint Distribution Committee in Warsaw; founder of the Oneg Shabbat archive; leader of the Jewish Combat Organization (ŻOB); murdered by the Nazis in 1944.

Schiper, Ignacy (1884–1943): Polish Zionist leader and Jewish historian; deported to Treblinka in aftermath of Warsaw ghetto uprising and perished there.

Schwarzbart, Ignacy I. (1888–1961): Polish Zionist and communal activist; representative for Jewish affairs in the Polish government in exile.

Visser, Lodewijk E. (1871–1942): Dutch jurist and communal leader; chief justice of the Dutch Supreme Court; chairman of the Jewish Coordinating Committee, an anti-Nazi coalition group; opposed the Joodse Rad; died before

Nazis could arrest him for his protest activities.

Warburg, Max (1867–1946): German Jewish banker and communal leader; active in Zionist affairs; one of the initiators of the *Ha'avara* agreement; emigrated to the United States in 1938.

Weltsch, Robert (1891–1982): German Zionist leader and journalist; originator of the stirring cry "Wear the Yellow Badge with Pride;" emigrated to Palestine in 1938; leader of the Hitachdut Olei Germania; helped organize the Leo Baeck Institute.

Zeitlin, Hillel (1871–1942): religious scholar, journalist, and writer; shot during the deportation from the Warsaw ghetto.

Zygelbojm, Szmuel Artur (1895–1943): Socialist leader and communal activist; representative of the Bund at the Polish government in exile in London; committed suicide to protest the plight of Polish Jewry.

3. Free World

Bergson, Peter H. (pseud. of Hillel Kook, b. 1915): Revisionist Zionist leader in Palestine and the United States; organized the Yishuv's anti-Nazi boycott; member of the Irgun delegation in the United States; founder of the Emergency Committee to Save the Jewish People of Europe.

Ehrenburg, Ilya G. (1891–1967): Soviet Jewish journalist; leader of the Jewish anti-Fascist Committee.

Fefer, Itzik (1900–1952): Soviet Jewish poet; member of the Jewish anti-Fascist Committee; murdered at Stalin's orders, during postwar purge of Jewish culture.

Goldmann, Nahum (1895–1982): Zionist leader and Jewish communal activist; president of the World Jewish Congress; fled Germany in 1933; active in promoting Jewish causes in New York, London, and Paris before, during, and after World War II.

Goldstein, Israel (1896–1986): American Zionist leader and Rabbi; active in Jewish communal organizations; strong advocate of immediate rescue.

Halprin, Rose L. (1896–1978): American Zionist leader; president of Hadassah; advocate and supporter of Youth Aliya.

Hertz, Joseph Hermann (1872–1946): Chief Rabbi of the British Commonwealth; scholar and author; initiated numerous rescue actions.

Jabotinsky, Ze'ev Vladimir (1880–1940): founder and leader of the Revisionist Zionist movement; advocated anti-Nazi boycott and the evacuation of East European Jewry; died during a trip to the United States.

Lemkin, Raphael (1901–1959): Jurist and legal scholar; born in Poland but migrated to the United States in 1941; formulated the concept of genocide in a brief to the U.S. State Department.

Litvinov, Maksim M. (1876–1951): Jewish Communist Party official; foreign minister of the Soviet Union; ambassador to the United States.

Marks, Simon (1888–1964): Anglo-Jewish businessman and communal activist; member of the Jewish Agency London Executive; vice-president of the English Zionist Federation.

Mayer, Saly (1882–1950): Swiss Jewish communal activist; representative of the JDC in Switzerland; active in ransoming Jews from the Nazis in 1944 and 1945.

Morgenthau, Henry, Jr. (1891–1967): American Jewish political leader; secretary of the treasury in the Roosevelt administration; advocate of rescue plans and the creation of the War Refugee Board; president of the UJA and other American Jewish organizations.

Neumann, Emanuel (1893–1980): American Zionist leader; member of the Jewish Agency Executive and chairman of Jerusalem Executive, 1931–1935; advocate of rescue and of creation of a Jewish state; president of the Zionist Organization of America.

Proskauer, Joseph (1877–1971): American Jewish jurist and communal leader; president of the American Jewish Committee; active in postwar efforts to resettle Jewish Displaced Persons.

Schonfeld, Solomon (1912–1982): English Rabbi; powerful advocate of rescue, especially during and after World War II.

Schwartz, Joseph J. (1899–1975): Director of the JDC European activities; educator and Jewish communal activist; actively supported armed Jewish undergrounds, rescue and ransom efforts, and Aliya Bet.

Silver, Abba Hillel (1893–1963): American Zionist leader, rabbi, and communal activist; president of the Zionist Organization of America and co-chairman of the American Zionist Emergency Council; strongly supported the anti-Nazi boycott, rescue, and the creation of a Jewish state.

Warhaftig, Zorah (b. 1906): Polish Zionist leader and communal activist; Rabbi and member of Polish Mizrachi; organized the Polish anti-Nazi boycott; fled to Lithuania and thence to the United States; among the organizers of the Institute of Jewish Affairs of the World Jewish Congress; involved in rescue and relief activities during and after World War II; member of the Jewish Agency Executive and the provisional government of the State of Israel.

Wise, Stephen S. (1874–1949): American Rabbi, Zionist leader, and communal activist; founder and first president of the American Jewish Congress and the World Jewish Congress; co-chairman of the American Zionist Emergency Council; supported rescue activities but opposed public Jewish protests during World War II.

Joint Juden [G] "Joint Jews": Nazi term describing some American and/or Swiss Jews as representatives of the American Jewish Joint Distribution Committee.

Jud kaput! [G/Slang] "Jew finished": Term that a large number of local antisemites (especially Ukrainians) called out while greeting the Wehrmacht when entering a conquered place.

Juda Verrecke! [G] "Judah, croak!": Nazi propaganda slogan advocating anti-Jewish violence utilized during Nazi parades and marches especially before the *Machtergreifung*.

Juden sind hier nicht erwünscht! [G] "Jews not wanted here!": Slogan on signs that appeared throughout Germany after the *Machtergreifung* in 1933. These signs were temporarily removed during the winter and summer Olympic Games of 1936, both of which took place in Germany. Also appeared as *Juden unerwünscht*.

Judenälteste [G] "Jewish elder": Nazi term for the chairman of a Jewish council. > see also: **Judenrat**.

Judenbegünstigung [G] "Befriending Jews": Nazi legal term for Gentiles who disobeyed the laws by helping or aiding Jews in any fashion and by whatever means. In many instances these Gentiles put their own and their families' lives on the line. > see also: **Hasidei umot ha-olam**.

Judenberater [G] "Jew adviser": German term for the civilian representative, usually a member of the Auswärtiges Amt staff, who was seconded to the Foreign Ministry of German client states as an adviser on the Jewish Question.

Judendelikt [G] "Offending Jews": Generic Nazi term for those Jews who disobeyed anti-Jewish laws, especially relating to racial infractions.

Judeneinsatz [G] "Jew operation": Special division for Jewish labor within the Labor Departments in the major cities of Nazi-occupied Europe.

Judenfresser [G] "Jew Eater": Nickname for Julius Streicher used by other Nazis that emphasized his virulent antisemitism.

Judenfreund [G] "Friend of Jews": Nazi term for those caught helping Jews. Individuals convicted of this crime were forced to wear an armband with the caption *Judenfreund* on it. > see also: **Judenbegünstigung**.

Judengelb [G] "Jewish star": Widely used term for the Jewish badge that the Nazis introduced (actually reintroduced). In the Middle Ages Jews had been compelled to wear a variety of distinctive items of clothing and/or to mark their clothes with a round, yellow badge of shame. The Nazis reintroduced this method of marking and segregating Jews, and other

Judengelb
Authors' Collection

enemies of the Reich, throughout Europe. >
see also: **Winkel(en)**.

Judenhäuser [G] "Jewish houses": The
buildings into which German Jews were
forced to move and from which all Aryans
were relocated. In occupied Eastern Europe,
the local SS command often made similar
arrangements, thereby converting a small
number of buildings into an "open" ghetto.

Judenjagd [G] "Jew hunt": Nazi term for
hunting Jews, applied primarily to the period
of deportations from smaller ghettos in
Poland and Russia. Some Jews would be
able to hide or escape the *Aktion*, thus
necessitating a hunt for Jewish fugitives.

Judenleihgebühr [G] "Fee for the loan of
Jews": Fee paid by German corporations for
"renting" Jewish slave laborers from the SS.
The sum was supposed to be RM 0.70 per
day per head, but companies often refused
to pay for weak or sickly laborers. Theoretically, the income was to go to the local
Ältestenrat der Juden for the upkeep of the
ghettos, although, in fact, the money went
into *SS-Gettoverwaltungs* bank accounts.

Judenmehl [G] "Jewish flour": The second- or
third-rate flour, usually moldy, provided to the
ghettos by the *Gettoverwaltung* for baking
bread.

Judenrat [G] "Jewish council":

1. Scope and Definition
The Judenrat was a Nazi-controlled structure
imposed upon the Jewish communities of Nazi-
occupied Europe. The first Judenräte were imposed by Reinhard Heydrich's September 21,
1939, orders as a prerequisite for the ghettoization of Polish Jewry. As with ghettos, Judenräte did not have a unvarying structure; each
was tailored to conditions in the specific ghetto
or locality. As the Nazis occupied other European countries, Judenräte, or similar institutions were also organized. Once the Judenräte were established, the Nazis wasted no time
in presenting them with demands: drafting Jews
for forced labor, taking a census of the Jewish
population, evacuating apartments and handing
them over to Germans, paying fines or
ransoms, and confiscating valuables owned by
Jews.

In most cases, Judenrat members, and the
ghetto inhabitants as well, believed that by
complying with German demands they could
prove the importance of the Jewish community
to the German war effort. By this means they
hoped to moderate Nazi assaults and gain time
to secure the survival of at least part of the
community. With the deportations that began
in late 1941, however, this policy proved to be
a failure. > see also: **Arbet vet rateven dos
geto**.

At every turn in their existence, Judenrat
members had to make a decision whether to
comply with German demands. In most cases,
the Judenräte supplied the required quota of
able-bodied men for slave labor. Similarly,
most Judenräte also cooperated in handing
over lists of the Jewish population that were
later used for deportations. With the implementation of the Nazi policy of mass extermination, however, the Judenräte were left with
few options for maneuvering between the needs
of the Jewish community and German demands
for deportees to fill the trains heading "east."

AELTESTE der IUDEN | דער עלסטער פ' יידן
in Litzmannstadt   אין ליצמאנשטאט

✡

Identitäts-Karte

Ser. C Nr.

אידענטישקייטס-קארט

Nr.

Identity card issued by the Judenrat in Lodz
Courtesy of Dr. Lucjan Dobroszycki

At that point, Judenrat members had to face the decision of compliance with or resistance to Nazi orders. > see also: **Organizations**.

Depending on size and specific local conditions, a typical Judenrat was composed of the following departments: Birth Certificates; Commerce and Industry; Complaints; Economics; Emergency Affairs; Finance and Budget; General Operations; Health and Hospitals; Housing; Insurance; Labor; Legal; Police; Population Registration; Post Office; Production; Real Estate; Social Welfare; Statistics; Taxation; and Vocational Training. These main departments were further subdivided into offices that carried out the Judenrat's daily affairs. Furthermore, the list shows the very narrow sphere of "self-government" that the Nazis permitted Jews.

2. Major *Judenältesten*

Asscher, Abraham (1880–1950): co-chairman of the Joodse Rad in Holland; deported to Bergen-Belsen but survived; tried by a Jewish court of honor and found guilty.

Barasz, Efraim (1892–1943): chairman of

the Judenrat in Bialystok; supported the resistance movement but also hoped to make the ghetto productive in order to survive; murdered by the Nazis in Poniatowa camp.

Baur, André (1904–1943): vice president of Union Générale des Israélites de France-Nord (UGIF); hoped to use the UGIF to buffer French Jewry but refused to cooperate with Nazi deportation orders; deported and murdered at Auschwitz.

Bieberstein, Marek (?–1944): chairman of the Judenrat in Krakow; arrested by Gestapo on false charges; deported to Plaszow, where he perished.

Cohen, David (1882–1967): co-chairman of the Joodse Rad in Holland; deported to Theresienstadt but survived; tried by a Jewish court of honor and found guilty.

Czerniakow, Adam (1818–1942): chairman of the Warsaw Judenrat; initially cooperated in deportations but committed suicide upon finding out that deportation meant death.

Edelstein, Jakob (1903–1944): chairman of the Judenrat in Theresienstadt; attempted to maintain the integrity of the community; deported to Auschwitz, where he perished.

Elkes, Elchanan (1879–1944): chairman of the Ältestenrat in Kovno; supported the underground and efforts to get Jews into hiding; deported to Landsberg, where he died of medical complications.

Gens, Jakob (1905–1943): chairman of the Judenrat in Vilna; viewed by the inhabitants of the ghetto as a self-styled messianic figure and ghetto dictator; had an ambivalent attitude toward the underground; supported deportations but tried to mute their scope; murdered by the Nazis on the eve of the ghetto liquidation.

Lambert, Raymond-Raoul (1894–1943): chairman of UGIF-Sud; opposed Nazi and Vichy anti-Jewish activities; strongly protested deportations and refused to cooperate with authorities in roundups of Jews; deported and murdered in Auschwitz.

Löwenherz, Josef (1884–1946): head of the Jewish community of Vienna, Austria; forced to provide lists for deportation but attempted to whittle down the number of deportees; died shortly after liberation.

Merin, Moses (1906–1943): chairman of the Judenrat in Sosnowiec and eastern Upper Silesia; considered to be a self-styled messianic figure and ghetto dictator; supported deportations of Jews with few protests; deported and murdered in Auschwitz.

Mushkin, Eliyahu (?–1942): chairman of the Judenrat in Minsk; supported the underground movement and aided in escapes to partisan units; arrested and murdered by Gestapo.

Rumkowski, Mordechai Chaim (1877–1944): chairman of the Judenrat in Lodz; considered to be a self-styled messianic figure and ghetto dictator; supported deportations of Jews with few protests; deported to Auschwitz, where he perished.

Stahl, Heinrich (1868–1942): president of the Jewish community of Berlin; deported to Theresienstadt and made deputy chairman of Judenrat; died in Theresienstadt.

Stern, Samu (1874–1947): chairman of Zsidó Tanács of Hungary; sought to mute the anti-Jewish persecutions but went into hiding after Nazi occupation of the country.

3. Imposed Nationwide Jewish Institutions

Association des Juifs en Belgique (AJB) "Association of Jews in Belgium." Organized November 25, 1941. Chairman: Rabbi Salomon Ullmann.

Centrala Evreilor "Jewish Center," Romania. Organized February 1942; superseded the *Federatia Uniunilor de Comunitati Evreesti* (Union of Jewish Communities). Chairman: Nandor Ghingold.

Joodse Rad "Jewish council," Holland. Organized February 13, 1941. Chairmen: Abraham Asscher, David Cohen.

Jüdische Selbstverwaltung, "Jewish Self-administration," term for the short-lived system of Jewish councils in the occupied Soviet territories of the Ukraine and Belorussia.

Obshtini "Community Councils," governing bodies imposed by the Bulgarian government in all localities containing fifty or more Jewish families. Parallel to the Nazi-imposed Judenräte, the Obshtini also undertook religious, financial, and social functions.

Reichsvertretung der Juden in Deutschland, "Reich Representation of Jews in Germany." Organized in 1933 as a voluntary Jewish representative agency. In 1939 the agency became a Judenrat, with the Gestapo-imposed name *Reichsvereinigung der Juden in Deutschland* (Reich Association of Jews in Germany); President: Rabbi Leo Baeck; Chairman: Otto Hirsch.

Union Générale des Israélites de France (UGIF) "General Union of the Jews of France." Organized November 29, 1941. For organizational purposes the UGIF was divided into UGIF-Nord, in the Nazi-occupied zone, and UGIF-Sud, in Vichy (southern) France. Chairmen: UGIF-Nord — André Baur, Marcel Stora; UGIF-Sud — Raymond-Raoul Lambert.

Ustredna Zidov "Jewish Center," Slovakia. Began operating in Bratislava September 26, 1940. Chairmen: Heinrich Schwarz, Arpad Kondor.

Zentrale der Ältestenräte der jüdischen Kultusgemeinden Ost-Oberschlesiens "The Central Council of the Jewish Councils in Eastern Upper Silesia," regional Judenrat established December 1939 on the line of the Centralverein in Germany; with headquarters in

Sosnowiec. Also known as the Centrala, it oversaw thirty-seven Jewish communities with a total Jewish population of 100,000. Chairman: Moses Merin.

Zsidó Tanács "Council of Jewish Elders," Hungary. Began to operate in Budapest in March 1944 on Eichmann's orders. Chairman: Samu Stern. Additionally, local councils were also formed in Hungary's cities.

Judenrein [G] "Clear of Jews": Nazi term for the result of the Final Solution: the clearing out of all Jews from a specific locality. > see also: **Endlösung**.

Judenrepublik [G] "Jew-Republic": Derogatory term for the Weimar Republic, used by the right-wing opponents of democracy, especially by the NSDAP. The use of the term dates almost to the foundation of the republic and was meant to imply that the new government was just as illegitimate as the short-lived Bavarian Soviet Republic of 1919: Both were condemned as being imposed by Jews in order to destroy the German nation and prepare the way for a Bolshevik takeover.

Judenschwein [G] "Jewish pig": Derogatory term used by the SS in addressing Jews.

Judenstern [G] "Jewish star": Identification badge that Jews had to wear to set them apart from their non-Jewish neighbors. A throwback to the Middle Ages, when Jews had to wear a distinctive mark, the Nazis used a number of different types of the badges. In the East European ghettos, the most common badge was a blue armband stamped with the six-pointed Star of David. In the concentration camps, in Western Europe, and throughout Eastern Europe as well, Jews had to wear a yellow six-pointed star marked with the letter *J* (or the local equivalent) for *Jude*. > see also: **Judengelb**; **Winkel(en)**.

Judentransport [G] "Jewish transport": Marking on segregated trolley cars and other means of public transportation in Nazi Germany after the Nazis began their anti-Jewish campaign.

Judenvernichtungsbrigade [G] "Jew annihilation brigade": Colloquial term for the Einsatzgruppen. > see also: **Aussiedelungskommando**.

Judenzug [G] "Jew train": One of the hundreds of trains bringing Jews from around Europe to the extermination camps in Poland. Deportation trains were handled by a special office within the Reichsbahn (railway service) that coordinated departures and arrivals with Adolf Eichmann's office. Between 1940 and 1942 these trains were not given top priority and often had to stop to let troop transports pass. After 1943, however, Jewish deportation trains received top priority and military trains had, on a number of occasions, to wait for them to pass. > see also: **Umsiedlerzüge(n)**.

Jüdische Stunde [G] "Jew hour": Term for the wartime limitation on the amount of time German Jews were permitted to be on the streets to shop.

Jüdischer Ordnungsdienst [G] "Jewish Order Service": Nazi term for the Jewish ghetto police, also referred to by the Jews as the Jewish police. Police units were established by the Nazis in the larger ghettos as a means of controlling the Jewish masses. The size and organization of the Jewish police force depended on the size of the ghetto. The Jewish police carried out a number of different duties, carrying out both Nazi orders and the policies of the local Judenrat. Of special importance, in the early stages of the deportations, was the participation of the Jewish policemen; many believed that the experience at the *Umschlagplatz* would have been much worse if the Jewish police were not present. However, the existence of the Jüdischer Ordnungsdienst often lulled Jews into a false sense of security regarding Nazi claims that deportations were to work camps in the "east." > see also: **Judenrat**.

Jüdischer Wohnbezirk [G] "Jewish residential district": The generic German term for a ghetto, whether open or closed. As a rule, all

Polish policeman checks identity papers as a member of the Jüdischer Ordnungsdienst looks on
Courtesy of the Simon Wiesenthal Center Beit HaShoah Museum of Tolerance Archives/Library, Los Angeles, CA

"Jewish residential districts" were strictly off-limits to the Aryan population and any infractions were severely dealt with. > see also: **Ghetto.**

Jüdisches Siedlungsgebiet [G] "Jewish settlement region": Official Nazi term for the Terezin (Theresienstadt) ghetto/camp. Established on November 24, 1941, as a deportation point for a special category of elderly Jews (*Altersgetto*), some of whom the Nazi leadership deemed important enough for special consideration. Prior to the first arrivals, about 7,000 non-Jews were removed from the town. The first Jews sent to Terezin came from Bohemia and Moravia; they were soon followed by others from around the Grossreich, including *Mischlinge* and some groups of children. Deportations to Terezin continued throughout the war, as did transports leaving the ghetto/camp for Auschwitz. An estimated 152,000 Jews passed through Terezin before it was liberated by Soviet troops (May 8, 1945). > see also: **Das Kleine Festung.**

K

K44: Code name for the Nazi-sponsored international anti-Jewish congress that opened in Berlin in the fall of 1944. > see also: **Conferences, Antisemitic.**

Kammeradenwerk [G] "Work on behalf of comrades": Another term for ODESSA, the agency helping Nazi criminals escape from justice. > see also: **Organization des Ehemaligen SS-Angehörigen.**

Kampfpartei [G] "Fighting party": Early term for the NSDAP, emphasizing the participation of World War I veterans in the party hierarchy and its militancy. After the change in Nazi tactics that resulted from the abortive Beer Hall Putsch (November 8, 1923), this term was rarely used.

Kanada [Geographic Name] "Canada": Inmate and guard nickname for the warehouses in Auschwitz where the personal property taken from the thousands of victims destined for the gas chambers (and from those given a temporary reprieve) was sorted, packed, and stored. > see also: **Konzentrationslager System.**

Kapo [Slang] "Foreman": Derived from the Italian word *capo*, or chief, the term was used in Nazi concentration camps to designate an inmate appointed by the SS to head a labor *Kommando* of other prisoners. The majority of Kapos behaved in a brutal fashion toward other prisoners, and some

were feared more than the SS.

Karaites: Sectarian Jews who follow the religious teaching of Anan Ben-David. The sect emerged in the eighth century in Babylonia, spreading from there throughout the Middle East and southern Russia. In the early nineteenth century Russian Karaites demanded equal civil rights, and several scholars claimed that the sect's origins were not Jewish. For various reasons, this claim was accepted and the Karaites were accorded the same rights as the Russians. The Nazis first broached the problem of the Karaites when they published the regulations for enforcement of the Nuremberg Laws. Members of the small Karaite community in Germany requested exemption from the anti-Jewish laws, since they claimed that they were not of Jewish origin. On January 5, 1939, this claim was indeed accepted and the Karaites were exempted from the anti-Jewish laws. With some variations, this policy remained in force throughout Nazi-occupied Europe until 1945.

Kaserniert [G] "Kept in barracks": Nazi term for keeping certain Jewish workers employed by the Wehrmacht in some of the larger ghettos — even those ghettos that were liquidated. This Nazi exception was not, however, permanent. With time, those Jews too were liquidated.

Ka-tzetnik [קאצעטניק, Y]: Jewish term for an inmate in a Nazi concentration camp. No name, address, or any other identification, just a number and classification. > see also: **Winkel(en)**.

Kehile [קהילה, Y] "Community": Deriving from the Hebrew word *kahal*, a term for the prewar Jewish community — the *gmina* (polish) or *Kultusgemeinde*. > see also: **Judenrat**.

Kenigs gens [קיניגס געגדז, Y] "King's Goose": Semi-humorous nickname for Jakob Gens, the *Judenälteste* of the Vilna ghetto. The name was a pun on Gens's name but also reflected his iron handed policies in the ghetto.

Kenyérmezo: [Hu/Slang] Name of a fictitious place that Hungarian gendarmerie used in order to pacify large numbers of anxious Jews during the deportations to Auschwitz.

Keret [Hu] "Guards": Term for the Hungarian army officers who were in charge of the Jewish *Munkaszolgálat* laborers. Most of the officers believed they had — if they did not in fact have — a mandate to ensure that as few of their laborers as possible ever returned. In this the officers succeeded: Of nearly 24,000 laborers, only about 7,000 returned in 1942 and 1943.

Kibbutz Galuyot [קיבוץ גלויות, H] "Ingathering of the Exiles": Talmudic term for the messianic era when all Jews will return to the Holy Land. During the war the term was used as a tragic irony: The Nazis concentrated all Jews in one place (Poland) — in some cases telling their victims that they were soon to be transported to Palestine — in order to kill them. Before and after the war, the term was also used by Zionists to designate plans for mass *aliya*. In 1947, the term was used as the code name for the Mossad blockade-runner *SS Pan York*. > see also: **Aliya Bet, Ships**.

Kiddush ha-Hayim [קידוש החיים, H] "Sanctification of life": Used during the Holocaust

to refer to those Jewish responses to Nazi persecution that encouraged Jewish survival and creativity. The term is generally attributed to Rabbi Yitzhak Nissenbaum, one of the main leaders of the Mizrachi movement in Poland. A wide range of activities could be included within the idea of *Kiddush ha-Hayim*, including various self-help and communal activities designed to nourish both the Jews' bodies and their souls. Although these actions cannot themselves be categorized as resistance to the Nazis, they were all designed to promote group integrity and self-respect. In this way the idea of *Kiddush ha-Hayim* also contributed greatly to the development of Jewish resistance to the Nazis.

Kiddush ha-Shem [קידוש השם, H] "Sanctification of God's Name": This term for religious martyrdom was prominent in the Jewish lexicon in the exilic era. The long epoch of Jewish martyrdom dates back to the Greek era in the second century B.C.E. and the subsequent persecutions of the Roman era. The religious faith of Jews was repeatedly tested during the Middle Ages, and at times, entire communities were obliterated in mass acts of *Kiddush ha-Shem*. In most instances the choice of accepting *Kiddush ha-Shem* was voluntary; the options provided by the surrounding society and by *halacha* contributed to the choice made by each local Jewish community. Although the Nazis eliminated the element of choice for the victim, most Rabbinic leaders in Eastern Europe maintained that whenever a Jew was persecuted for his identity, his suffering was, ipso facto, an act of *Kiddush ha-Shem*.

Kindertransporte [G] "Children's transports": Convoys of trains or trucks made up entirely of Jewish children caught during Nazi roundups and transported to the death factories. The term was also used in some instances to denote convoys of children from Germany or other occupied countries that were able to leave Europe for temporary or permanent shelter (e.g., Youth Aliya transports to Palestine).

Kirchenkampf [G] "Church struggle": Although the Nazi party platform professed religious freedom — beyond the struggle against Jews and "Jewish materialism" — the reality was far different. From 1933 on, the Reich's government made numerous efforts to apply the principles of *Gleichschaltung* to both Protestant and Catholic churches. In turn, Nazi efforts to undermine the churches led to a defensive measure known collectively as the "German church struggle." In July 1933 the Nazis signed a concordat to regulate relations between the Reich and the Vatican, but the Nazis observed this agreement primarily in the breach. Nevertheless, the Vatican did not protest Nazi actions beyond very general condemnations of Nazi racism. The task of protecting religious freedom in the Third Reich thus fell to the Protestant denominations and primarily to the Evangelical Church. As a result, the Nazis imprisoned hundreds of ministers, including Pastors Martin Niemöller and Dietrich Bonhöffer; the latter was murdered by the Sicherheitsdienst in April 1945. One aspect of the *Kirchenkampf* has significance for the Holocaust: Those protesting Nazi interference in church affairs especially rejected racial definitions and sought to protect Jewish converts. In some (rare) cases, protesting ministers also sought to use false conversions as a means of rescuing Jews, seeing such acts as the culmination of the church's struggle for independence.

Kirkens grunn [N] "Foundations of the Church": A pastoral letter by the Lutheran Church of Norway, dated April 5, 1942. The letter rejected Nazism and racism and protested Vidkun Quisling's efforts to nazify the churches in Norway.

Kleinterror [G] "Small terror": Nazi term for the first stage in the extermination process of European Jewry. In occupied Poland, the term mainly applied to the uprooting of smaller Jewish communities by ordering them moved into certain designated areas; chasing those Jews living in areas near the San and Bug rivers (the dividing line between German- and Russian-occupied Poland) to Soviet-occupied eastern Poland; or

moving larger Jewish communities into overcrowded ghettos that lacked sanitary facilities and other essential life requirements.

Kneidlach [קנײדלעך, Y] "Dumplings": Jewish term for the cluster of bombs that Allied planes dropped on Nazi installations. > see also: **Foigelach.**

Knochenmühle [G] "Bone-crushing machine": A specially built machine installed in the Chelmno extermination camp by Schriever AG, Hanover. The machine was used to crush the bones of the hundreds of thousands of already gassed victims.

Knokploegen [Du] "Action groups": Dutch term for street gangs. Initially referring to the toughs employed by the Nationaal Socialistisch Beweging against its opponents, after 1941 the term was applied to active resistance groups. In particular, it was used in reference to those groups that attacked collaborators or Nazi offices in order to destroy records. Some of these groups were largely composed of Jews. Moderately successful in their attacks, the *knokploegen* were hampered by effective Nazi anti-resistance tactics.

Knopffabrick [G] "Button factory": a German nickname for the Sobibór extermination camp. The Nazi lie to the victims was that, once in Sobibór, they were going to produce buttons.

Kohnhelerowki [P]: Polish slang term for the Kohn-Heller Company in the Warsaw ghetto, whose wagons were contracted by the ghetto administration to transport the old and sick people to the Jewish cemetery grounds, where they were murdered. Initially, to smooth the path for their daily *Aussiedlungsaktionen*, the Nazis claimed that the elderly could not survive the rigorous trip to the East, where the deported Jews would start a new life. In reality, the Nazi claim was a cruel hoax perpetrated to keep Jews off guard and inhibit resistance.

Kommandatura [R] "High command": The four-power Allied military government for Berlin established soon after the Nazi surrender. Each of these powers — the United States, Soviet Union, Great Britain, and France — assumed responsibility for a sector of occupied Berlin. > see also: **Denazification**.

Kommando Berta [G]: "Commando Bertha": A labor gang from the Buchenwald KL incarcerated at the Rheinmetall munitions factory in Düsseldorf. The detail contained between 250 and 600 slave laborers.

Kommandobefehl [G] "Commando order": *Führer* order dated October 18, 1942, permitting the immediate execution of captured Allied Special Operations personnel, whether or not they were in uniforms.

Kommissarbefehl [G] "Commissar order": Order issued by the Wehrmacht regarding the elimination of all political commissars of the Red Army who fell into German hands. Fall Barbarossa was conceived as not only a military operation but an ideological war as well. As a result, the attack was to include the annihilation of the carriers of communism and of all racial enemies of the Reich. Two weeks before Barbarossa was initiated, the Oberkommando der Wehrmacht (OKW) issued the *Kommissarbefehl* and gave specific instructions for the means of carrying the order out. > see also: **Einsatzgruppen**.

Konter-aktsia [קאנטער-אקציע, Y] "Counter operation": Slang term for spontaneous Jewish acts of resistance during an *Aussiedlungsaktion*.

Konzentrationslager (KL) System [G] "Concentration camp system":

1. Scope and Definition

Although states have always had some means of incarcerating enemies, the first use of the term *concentration camp* was during the Boer War (1899–1902). Initially, the term had no sinister connotations and was used to denote

The concentration camp system
Courtesy of the Fred R. Crawford Witness to the Holocaust Project, Emory University

the camps established by Major General Lord Kitchener into which the Afrikaaner civilian population was transferred as a means to cut off the Boer Commandos from their supply lines. The first of the camps opened in early 1901; within a year the camps were overflowing, with 110,000 internees, in addition to 32,000 Boer troops incarcerated in prisoner of war camps.[1] After the Bolshevik *putsch* (October/November 1917) in Russia, the new administration also created detention camps for the thousands of counterrevolutionaries and "déclassé" persons. These coalesced into the Soviet concentration camp system, known under the Stalinist acronym, Gulag.[2]

In 1933 the Nazis followed suit, creating a system of incarceration for opponents. The early Nazi camps were hastily built and were known as *wilde Lager* (wild camps). These camps were closed after a few months; in October 1933 the first regulations for camp administration were published. Initially overseen by the police and therefore under the nominal control of Hermann Göring, the camps were transferred to the authority of the SS after the "Night of the Long

Knives." On July 4, 1934, the SS-Hauptamt created the Inspectorate of Concentration Camps, headed by Theodor Eicke. At first the inmates were exclusively political prisoners, mostly German Communists and Socialists. After 1937, however, asocials and "habitual criminals" were included as well.

The total number of prisoners in the Nazi camps will probably never be known with exactitude. Estimates vary, though Eugen Kogon's estimate of 2,151,200 is considered the most reliable.[3] To this figure must be added approximately 4 million Jews murdered in the six Nazi *Vernichtungslager* (extermination camps), 220,000 Gypsies, and about 6 million Soviet prisoners of war. In all, Kogon lists 7,820,000, of whom no more than 700,000 survived.[4]

Until 1936 an inmate could be released from the concentration camps; in fact 75 percent of those held in 1933 were released by January 1936. Thereafter, inmate release — except under exceptional circumstances — was not permitted. Jewish men incarcerated after *Kristallnacht* could be released only if their families could prove to the local Gestapo that they would be emigrating shortly.

Concentration camp money
Authors' Collection

---

[1] A. C. Martin, *The Concentration Camps*, Cape Town: Howard Timmins, 1958.

[2] A good summary of the Leninist camp system was provided in James Bunyan, *The Origins of Forced Labor in the Soviet State, 1917–1921*, Baltimore, MD: Johns Hopkins University Press, 1967.

[3] Eugen Kogon, *Der SS-Staat, das System der deutschen Konzentrationslager*, Frankfurt a/M: Europäische Verlagsanstalt, 1946, ch. 19.

[4] Ibid., Kogon includes Jews and Gypsies, but not Soviet POWs in this figure.

TABLE K.1: National Socialist Camp Categories

Anhaltelager	[AnL]	Confinement camp
Arbeiterziehungslager	[AEL]	Worker education camp
Arbeitslager	[AL]	Labor camp
Auffangslager	[AuL]	Absorption camp
Aussenlager	[AusL]	External camp[1]
Durchgangslager	[DL or DuLag]	Transit camp
Durchgangshaftlager	[DHL]	Transit prison camp
Durchgangslager für Juden	[DLJ]	Transit camp for Jews
Firmenlager	[FL]	Company camp[2]
Frauenlager	[FrL]	Women's camp
Geisellager	[GlL]	Hostage camp
Gemeinschaftslager	[GL]	Communal camp
Gestapohaftlager	[GHL]	Gestapo prison camp
Haftlager der Werbestelle	[HW]	Camp for enlisted men
Hauptlager	[HL]	Main camp
Internierungslager	[IL]	Internment camp
Judenarbeitslager	[JAL]	Labor camp for Jews
Judenaufangslager	[JAuL]	Jewish reception camp
Judenlager	[JL]	Jewish camp
Konzentrationslager	[KL]	Concentration camp
Krankenlager	[KrL]	Hospital camp
Kriegsgefangenenlager	[KGL]	Prisoner of war camp
Lager der Gestapo	[LdG]	Gestapo camp
Lager für Ausländische Juden	[LAJ]	Camp for foreign Jews
Nebenlager	[NL]	Subcamp
Polizeihaftlager	[PHL]	Police detention camp
Provisorisches DuLag	[PDL]	Provisional transit camp
Restgetto	[RG]	Resort camp[3]
Sammellager	[SaL]	Assembly camp
Schutzhaftlager	[SchHL]	Protective custody camp
Sicherungslager	[SiL]	Security camp
Sonderkommando 1005	[SK 1005]	Special mobile camp
SS-Sonderlager	[SS-SL]	SS special camp
Stammlager	[SL]	Main camp
Strafgefangenenlager	[SGL]	Prisoner disciplinary camp
Straflager	[SL]	Punishment camp
Übergangslager	[UL]	Temporary detention camp

---

[1] *Aussenlager* were camps attached to major KLs but external to their compounds.

[2] *Firmenlager* and *Judenlager* were camps under the jurisdiction of German or *Volksdeutsche* companies, outside of the KL system. The camps were incorporated into the SS camp system in late 1943.

[3] Camps located in the precincts of a recently liquidated ghetto and holding Jewish stragglers from different villages in the region that had been made *judenrein* by Nazi *Aktionen* in addition to would-be escapees from various transports.

Umsiedlungslager	[UmL]	Resettlement camp
Vernichtungslager	[VL]	Extermination camp[4]
Wohnlager	[WL]	Residence camp
Zivilarbeitslager	[ZivAL]	Civilian work camp
Zwangsarbeitslager	[ZAL]	Forced labor camp
Zweiglager	[ZL]	Branch camp

Source: Weinmann, Martin, with Anne Kaiser and Ursula Krause-Schmitt. *Das national-sozialistische Lagersystem*. Frankfurt am Main: Zweitausendeins, 1990.

TABLE K.2: The Inner Structure of a KL

SS External Administration

Lagerkommandant	Camp Commander
Adjutant	Deputy Commander
Lagerführer	Camp Leader
Rapportführer	Reporting Officer
Verwaltungsführer	Administrative Officer
Arbeitsdienstführer	Work Recording Officer
Arbeitseinsatzführer	Work Detail Leader
Kommandoführer	Labor Group(s) Supervisor
Blockführer	Block Officer
Lagerarzt	Camp Doctor
Sanitätsdienstgefreiter	Medical Orderly
Bewachungsmannschaft	Guard Detail

Prisoner Internal Administration

Lagerälteste	Senior Camp Prisoner
Blockälteste	Senior Block Prisoner
Blockarzt	Prisoner Block Doctor
Stubenälteste	Senior Rooms Prisoner
Blockschreiber	Prisoner Block Clerk
Oberkapo	Head Kapo
Kapo	Chief Work Overseer
Vorarbeiter	Work Foreman
Pfleger	Medical Attendant
Leichenträger	Corpse Bearers
Stubendienste	Room Orderlies
Lagerpolizei	Prisoner Camp Police
Feuerwehr	Prisoner Fire Brigade

Source: Weinmann, Martin, with Anne Kaiser and Ursula Krause-Schmitt. *Das national-sozialistische Lagersystem*. Frankfurt am Main: Zweitausendeins, 1990.

---

[4] This term was not used officially; *Vernichtungsanstalt* (Extermination Institution) and *Vernichtungsstelle* (Extermination Place) were also used as unofficial terms for VLs.

2. KLs and Their Subcamps

KL Auschwitz, established May 26, 1940; evacuated January 18, 1945; liberated by the Soviets January 27, 1945, with 7,650 inmates; Lagerkommandants: Rudolf Höss, Arthur Liebehenschel, Josef Kramer, Albert Schwarz, Fritz Hartjenstein, Richard Baer; approximate number of registered inmates 400,000; number of inmates at one time, 11,000 to 155,000; camp makeup: Auschwitz I, *Stammlager* (main camp). Auschwitz II– Birkenau, *Vernichtungslager* established October 8, 1941, with five departments in addition to the gas chambers/crematoria: *Quarantänelager für neuangekommene Häftlinge* (quarantine camp for newly arrived prisoners); *Familienlager* (family camp, the so-called Theresienstädter lager); *Zigeunerlager* (camp for Gypsies); *Effektenlager* (confiscated property storage camp, the so-called Lager Kanada); *Arbeitserziehungshäftlingelager* (inmate camp for work reeducation); and the *Frauenlager* (women's camp, transferred from Auschwitz I, with prisoners from Ravensbrück). Auschwitz III–Monowitz, established May 31, 1942, as an *Arbeitslager* (work camp) with two major German slave-labor firms, Krupp and Siemens-Schuckert, as employers. Auschwitz IV–Buna, established September 4, 1943, with I.G. Farben Bunawerke as employer of numerous battalions of slave labor. Of the total registered number (some 400,000) who passed through Auschwitz and its *Nebenlager* only about 65,000 survived. Furthermore, an estimated 1 million Jews were murdered in the Birkenau gas chambers, although they were never registered as inmates of Auschwitz.

Nebenlager

Name	Opened	Closed	Inmates
Bierun	1943	1/45	1,000
Bobrek	1940	2/10/45	800
Budy	12/1942	1/45	400
Chorzow	3/1944	1/45	200
Czechowice	10/1944	1/45	600
Czernice	9/19/44	1/20/45	800
Dziedzice	8/20/44	12/44	100
Friedenshütte	1943	2/45	300
Goleszow	1941	1/19/45	1,200
Jaworzno	4/43	1/20/45	4,500
Kobior	1942	1943	200
Lapiewniki-Śląskie	9/44	1/15/45	200
Lagisza Cmentarna	1943	1/11/45	3,000
Ledziny-Lawki	1943	1/45	1,000
Libiaz Maly	1942	1/12/45	1,000
Myslowice	10/43	1/22/45	1,400
Pieskretscham	10/43	3/45	1,000
Siemianowice	1943	1/23/45	1,600
Sosnowiec	3/43	1/17/45	600
Stara Kuznica	1942	1945	500
Swietochlowice	6/42	1/31/45	1,300
Trzebinia	1942	1/21/45	700

KL Bergen-Belsen, established March 27, 1944; liberated April 15, 1945, with approximately 60,985 survivors, of whom about 15,000 perished after liberation; Lagerkommandants: Rudolf Haas, Josef Kramer; average number of inmates 95,000, of whom about 35,000 perished; camp makeup: *Sternlager* (camp for Jewish inmates); *Neutralenlager* (for Jewish prisoners from neutral countries); *Einweisungslager* (camp for Jewish women, primarily from Poland and Hungary); *Erholungslager* (recuperation camp for sick inmates brought in from other concentration camps). Between August 1941 and March 1944, Bergen-Belsen was the location of Stalag XIC for Soviet POWs; on July 15, 1943 this camp became an *Aufenthaltslager* for the exchange of foreign Jews.

KL Buchenwald, established July 15, 1937; liberated by Americans April 11, 1945, with approximately 21,000 survivors. Lagerkommandants: Karl Otto Koch, Hermann Pister; number of inmates at one time, 2,500 to 86,000; camp makeup: *Polensonderlager* (special camp for Poles); *Kinderlager* (children's camp); *Zigeunerlager* (camp for Gypsies); *Internierungslager für Prominente* (detention camp for dignitaries); *Genickschussanlage* (neck shooting establishment, where thousands of Soviet POWs were murdered); *Arbeitserziehungshäftlingelager* (work education prisoner camp); *Italienische Militärinterniertelager* (detention camp for members of the Italian military); average number of inmates passing through Buchenwald and its *Nebenlager*: 240,000.

Nebenlager

Name	Opened	Closed	Inmates
Abteroda	7/30/44	3/27/45	220
Allendorf	8/17/44	3/27/45	1,000
Altenburg	8/02/44	3/23/45	2,000
Annaburg	1/13/45	3/16/45	100
Arolsen	11/14/43	3/29/45	120
Aschersleben	8/15/44	4/10/45	600
Aumale	3/15/44	8/44	300
Bad Salzungen	1/10/45	4/10/45	450
Bensberg	6/29/44	3/29/45	50
Berga	11/13/44	4/10/45	1,600
Berlstedt	12/17/40	3/29/45	250
Billroda	3/19/44	4/03/45	500
Birkhahn	9/24/44	3/11/45	500
Blankenburg	8/25/44	10/28/44	500
Bochum	6/28/44	3/21/45	1,350
Böhlen	7/26/44	1/13/45	800
Colditz	12/44	3/31/45	700
Crawinkel	11/44	3/20/45	7,000
Dernau	8/26/44	12/13/44	180
Dessau	7/25/44	11/44	50
Dortmund	10/02/44	3/45	650
Duderstadt	11/12/44	3/18/45	750
Düsseldorf (4 camps)	6/25/44	1/13/45	1,000
Eisenach	9/29/44	2/17/45	400
Elsnig	10/16/44	3/16/45	750
Eschershausen	9/15/44	3/26/45	500
Essen	8/28/44	3/45	650
Flössberg	12/28/44	4/10/45	1,200
Gandersheim	10/05/44	4/10/45	500
Gelsenkirchen	7/06/44	9/20/44	2,000

Goslar	11/18/40	11/08/41	100
Hadmersleben	6/44	4/10/45	1,400
Halberstadt	8/44	4/11/45	900
Halle	8/02/44	2/28/45	540
Harzungen	4/01/44	10/28/44	2,000
Herzberg	8/15/44	4/10/45	1,700
Hessich-Lichtenau	8/13/44	3/22/45	7,100
Holzen	2/45	4/01/45	2,000
Jena	10/04/44	4/10/45	800
Kassel	12/42	3/29/45	170
Köln	2/13/42	4/05/44	500
Köln-Niehl	8/13/44	2/45	100
Langensalza	10/21/44	4/03/45	1,300
Langenstein	4/44	4/10/45	3,600
Leipzig	6/09/44	3/14/45	4,600
Leopoldshall	1/13/45	4/10/45	150
Lippstadt	8/02/44	3/18/45	500
Lützkendorf	7/15/44	1/18/45	900
Magdeburg	6/18/44	2/45	1,200
Markleeberg	9/07/44	3/11/45	1,000
Meuselwitz	10/06/44	4/10/45	1,450
Mülhausen	5/04/44	3/17/45	500
Neustadt	9/12/44	4/06/45	400
Niederorschel	9/06/44	4/10/45	500
Niedersachsenwerfen	5/12/44	10/28/44	2,500
Oberndorf	11/19/44	1/21/45	300
Örtelsbruch	9/21/43	3/45	700
Ohrdruf	11/44	4/10/45	11,700
Osterode	9/28/44	10/28/44	300
Penig	11/44	3/22/45	700
Plömnitz	8/44	4/10/45	1,000
Raguhn	2/12/45	3/29/45	200
Rothenburg	10/25/44	3/29/45	80
Schlieben	7/25/44	3/22/45	1,000
Schönau	8/22/44	3/26/45	300
Schönebeck	6/44	3/28/45	1,200
Schwerte	4/24/44	1/13/45	700
Sömmerda	9/20/44	3/22/45	1,200
Sonneberg	9/15/44	4/10/45	400
Stassfurt	9/15/44	4/10/45	700
Suhl	7/14/43	10/01/43	80
Taucha	9/12/44	3/11/45	1,450
Thekla	9/27/43	4/10/45	1,400
Tonndorf	9/27/43	3/29/45	100
Torgau	9/07/44	3/28/45	300
Tröplitz	6/06/44	4/10/45	4,300
Unna	7/26/43	2/29/44	50
Wansleben	4/44	4/10/45	600
Weferlingen	8/23/44	3/29/45	500
Weimar	9/27/43	2/28/45	2,000

Wernigerobe	9/27/43	4/10/45	800
Westeregeln	11/19/44	4/10/45	500
Witten-Annen	9/17/44	4/45	700
Wolfen-Bitterfeld	7/44	3/22/45	335

KL Dachau, established March 22, 1933; liberated by Americans April 29, 1945, with approximately 27,400 survivors; Lagerkommandants: Theodor Eicke, Hans Loritz, Martin Gotfried Weiss; number of inmates at one time, 4,800 to 160,000, representing forty different nationalities; between September 27, 1939, and February 18, 1940, all inmates were transferred to Mauthausen, and Dachau was an *Ausbildungslager der Waffen-SS* (training camp for the Waffen-SS); a gas chamber and crematorium were installed in 1942. Of the total number of inmates, approximately 32,000 perished.

Aerial view of Dachau
Courtesy of the Fred R. Crawford Witness to the Holocaust Project, Emory University

Nebenlager

Name	Opened	Closed	Inmates
Allach	5/17/44	4/15/45	3,800
Augsburg	4/14/42	7/28/42	450

Bad Tölz	8/40	4/18/45	180
Blaichach	9/02/44	5/14/45	700
Burgau	1/45	4/14/45	1,000
Eching	4/10/44	4/23/45	500
Emmetting	5/26/44	4/05/45	250
Fischen	11/06/44	4/14/45	250
Friedrichshafen	2/23/43	4/27/44	850
Germering	5/09/44	9/06/44	50
Horgau	12/44	4/14/45	1,500
Karlsfeld	8/17/44	4/14/45	1,100
Kaufbeuren	5/23/44	4/20/45	500
Kaufering	8/27/44	4/14/45	13,000
Kempten	10/11/44	4/23/45	500
Kottern	1943	4/20/45	750
Landsberg	8/07/44	4/14/45	2,300
Landshut	12/20/44	2/06/45	500
Lauingen	11/06/44	4/25/45	900
Mühldorf	9/04/44	4/28/45	4,600
Neustift	10/13/42	4/14/45	50
Nurnberg	5/12/42	3/22/45	100
Ottobrunn	5/24/44	4/17/45	600
Radolphzell	5/19/41	1/16/45	50
Rothschwaige	9/04/44	3/31/45	350
Salzburg	12/11/42	4/14/45	100
Saulgau	4/08/44	4/14/45	400
Stephanskirchen	12/11/44	3/31/45	250
Trostberg	11/44	4/14/45	700
Türkheim	10/44	4/28/45	2,500
Überlingen	9/02/44	4/19/45	700

KL Flossenburg, established May 3, 1938; evacuated April 20, 1945; liberated by Americans April 23, 1945, with some 2,000 inmates. Lagerkommandants: Jacob Weiseborn, Egon Zill, Max Koegel, Karl Künster; number of inmates at one time, 5,000 to 18,000; camp makeup: *Abteilung für sowjetische Kriegsgefangene* (department for Soviet prisoners of war); *Abteilung für Sonderhäftlinge* (department for special inmates). Flossenburg with a mix of (mostly) East European inmates had a very high death rate: those not able to withstand the excruciatingly long hours at the stone quarries were executed by an injection of phenol. Indstrial works at Flossenburg — or its *nebenlager* — included factories for armaments, aircraft, and mineral oil extraction.

Nebenlager

Name	Opened	Closed	Inmates
Altenhammer	12/28/44	4/13/45	400
Ansbach	3/13/45	4/01/45	500
Chemnitz	10/44	4/13/45	500
Dresden	5/25/44	2/13/45	500
Eisenberg-Jezeri	6/21/43	4/13/45	50
Floeha	4/19/44	4/13/45	600

Freiberg	8/44	4/11/45	1,000
Ganalcker	2/21/45	4/45	500
Grafenreuth	9/19/43	4/13/45	100
Graslitz	10/44	4/13/45	850
Gröditz	11/17/44	4/13/45	750
Gundelsdorf	10/44	4/45	100
Hainichen	10/44	4/13/45	450
Helmbrechts	12/44	3/45	1,000
Hersbruck	7/25/44	4/45	4,800
Hertine	10/44	4/13/45	600
Hohenstein-Ernstthal	1/45	4/13/45	400
Hradischko	6/02/44	11/22/44	30
Janovice	8/44	4/13/45	200
Johanngeorgenstadt	12/04/43	4/13/45	900
Königstein	12/27/44	2/13/45	750
Leitmeritz	7/08/44	4/13/45	5,000
Lengenfeld	10/09/44	4/13/45	800
Mehltheuer	10/44	4/13/45	300
Meissen	10/07/43	5/25/44	150
Mielec	3/09/42	8/44	2,000
Mittweida	10/44	4/13/45	400
Mockethal	1/14/45	4/13/45	120
Moschendorf	9/03/44	4/13/45	100
Muelsen	2/44	4/13/45	700
Neurohlau	9/43	4/13/45	1,000
Nossen	1/07/45	4/13/45	400
Nuremberg	2/13/43	3/22/45	300
Obertraubling	2/24/45	3/22/45	600
Öderan	10/44	4/13/45	450
Plattling	2/20/45	4/45	500
Pocking	1/45	4/45	400
Porschdorf	2/13/45	4/13/45	250
Pottenstein	10/12/42	4/13/45	340
Rabstein	9/09/44	4/13/45	600
Rathen	11/15/44	3/17/45	550
Rochlitz	10/27/44	3/27/45	350
Saal	12/05/44	3/06/45	600
Schönheide	2/28/45	4/13/45	50
Siegmar-Schönau	11/25/44	1/45	400
Steinschönau	9/22/44	1/21/45	50
Svatava	10/44	3/27/45	1,250
Theresienstadt	5/31/44	5/08/45	1,000
Venusberg	1/17/45	4/13/45	900
Wilischtal	10/44	4/13/45	280
Wolkenburg	10/44	4/13/45	350
Würzburg	4/43	3/22/45	50
Zschachwitz	11/11/44	4/13/45	1,000
Zschopau	11/29/44	4/13/45	400
Zwickau	9/13/44	4/13/45	700

KL Gross-Rosen, established on May 1, 1941; evacuated February 13, 1945; liberated by the Soviets May 8, 1945, with only a handful of survivors; however, in the large number of *Nebenlager* there were some 12,000 Jewish survivors; Lagerkommandants: Johannes Hassebröck, Wilhelm Gideon, Arthur Rödl; From August 2, 1940, when the camp was originally built, until May 1, 1941, Gross-Rosen was an *Aussenlager* of Sachsenhausen; inmates in Gross Rosen were primarily engaged in quarrying stones for the SS-Deutsche Erd-und Steinwerke GmbH; number of inmates (including sub-camps) at one time 1,500 to 125,000; of the total number of inmates, about 40,000 perished.

Nebenlager

Name	Opened	Closed	Inmates
Aslau	6/20/44	3/19/45	1,200
Buchwald-Hohenwiese	4/11/44	2/18/45	50
Dörnhau	5/44	5/08/45	2,200
Erlenbusch	6/44	4/03/45	500
Eule	4/44	1/13/45	1,300
Falkenberg	4/44	1/01/45	1,300
Faulbrück	2/44	7/44	120
Friedland	9/09/44	5/09/45	500
Gabersdorf	10/44	5/08/45	380
Gebhardsdorf	10/44	3/45	500
Gellenau	3/02/43	3/45	1,500
Görlitz	5/43	1/44	2,000
Gräben	2/44	12/44	500
Grafenort	3/45	5/09/45	400
Halbstadt	10/07/44	5/08/45	2,000
Hohenelbe-Vrchlabi	3/44	5/06/45	400
Kaltwasser	8/44	1/45	2,000
Kittlitztreben	4/43	2/05/45	2,000
Kratzau	1943	5/45	2,800
Kruszwica	11/03/42	4/27/43	120
Kurzbach-Grünthal	9/20/44	1/31/45	250
Langenbielau	3/44	5/08/45	2,000
Langenhorn	9/44	4/04/45	500
Laskowitz	3/44	1/29/45	8,000
Leszno	3/41	8/43	300
Lissa	1/43	8/44	150
Mährisch-Weisswasser	11/44	5/08/45	900
Märzbachtal	11/06/43	2/14/45	400
Märzdorf	9/44	5/08/45	400
Mittelsteine	8/23/44	4/45	400
Oberaltstadt	1941	5/08/45	1,200
Parschnitz	1941	5/08/45	2,000
Schotterwerk	5/44	5/08/45	2,000
Waldenburg	9/44	5/08/45	600
Wolfsberg	5/44	3/03/45	3,000
Wüstegiersdorf	3/44	5/08/45	16,000

KL Hertogenbosch, established January 5, 1943; closed September 5, 1944; also known as KL Vught; Lagerkommandants: Hans Hüttig, Adam Grünewald; camp makeup: *Schutzhaftlager* (protective custody camp, until 1/13/43); *Judenhaftlager* (Jewish prisoner camp, from 1/16/43); *Juden-durchgangslager* (Jewish transit camp, from February 1943), *Geisellager* (hostage camp, added in February/March 1943), *Studenten-lager* (camp for students, opened in

August 1943), *Polizeiliches Durchgangslager* (police transit camp, June 1944), *SD Lager* (security service camp); eight Gestapo prisons also belonged to KL Herzogenbusch; average number of inmates 29,500.[5]

KL Kovno, established June 5, 1943, on the grounds of the Kovno ghetto, Ortsteil Vilijam-pole; evacuated July 25, 1944; number of inmates at one time, 8,000 to 14,000, of whom at least 6,000 to 8,000 perished.

Nebenlager

Name	Opened	Closed	Inmates
Aleksotas	6/43	7/15/44	550
Proveniskiai	1941	1944	6,000
Siaulia	8/17/43	7/21/44	1,000
Vilnius (Vilna)	1942	1945	600
Zezmariai	4/42	1944	450

KL Krakau-Plaszow, established as a *Zwangsarbeitslager für Juden* toward the end of October 1942; transformed into a KL on January 11, 1944; evacuated January 14, 1945; liberated by the Soviets January 15, 1945. In September 1944 an unknown number of AK combatants were "temporarily" housed in Plaszow; most were executed

within the next months; Lagerkommandant: Amon Leopold Göth; number of inmates at one time, 2,000 to 25,000; camp makeup: *Politische und jüdische Häftlinge* (political, mostly Poles, and Jewish prisoners); *Zigeuner* (Gypsies); Heinkel-Flugzeugwerke, aircraft factory, principal employer of prisoner slave labor.

Nebenlager

Name	Opened	Closed	Inmates
Bierzanow I	1943	10/44	1,600
Bierzanow-Plaszow	7/42	11/10/43	1,000
Biesiadka	7/01/42	8/43	700
Huta Komarowska	4/41	7/25/44	700
Kosirze	3/41	12/42	150
Krakow-Kabelwerk	8/26/42	3/14/43	300
Krakow-Podgorze	4/15/42	7/44	400
Mielec	3/09/42	8/44	2,000
Mogila Baulager	1/44	1/16/45	300

---

[5] Although all camps and prisons in Holland were considered *Nebenlager* of Hertogenbosch, no precise data is currently available on these camps. Most were opened in the summer of 1942 and all closed by September 1944.

Wieliczka	3/44	9/44	6,000
Zablocie	4/43	10/44	1,200
Zakopane	7/41	9/42	200

Konzentrationslager der Waffen-SS Lublin, better known as KL Majdanek; established on Himmler's orders on February 16, 1943; evacuated July 1944; liberated by the Soviets July 22, 1944, with 500 inmates; Lagerkommandants: Karl Otto Koch, Hermann Florstedt, Martin G. Weiss, Max Koegel; average number of inmates, 24,000; camp makeup: *Kriegsgefangenenlager der SS* (prisoner of war camp, as of October 1941); *Vernichtungslager* (extermination camp); *Kinder und-Halbwüchsigen-Sammellager* (children and adolescent assembly camp); functioned as headquarters for Aktion Reinhard and Aktion Erntefest; inmates employed by Deutsche Ausrüstungswerke; Waffenfabrik Steyr-Daimler-Puch AG; total number of inmates, 500,000 of whom 360,000 perished.

Nebenlager

Name	Opened	Closed	Inmates
Blizyn	3/08/43	6/31/44	4,000
Budzyn	10/42	7/06/44	3,000
Hrubieszow	10/39	1944	2,000
Lublin-Chopinstrasse	9/16/42	7/06/44	100
Lublin-Chelmska	11/42	1944	4,500
Lublin-Lipowa	11/03/43	1944	2,500
Pulawy	6/43	6/44	2,000
Radom	1/17/44	1944	2,000

KL Mauthausen, established August 8, 1938; liberated by Americans May 5, 1945; Lagerkommandants: Albert Sauer, Franz Ziereis; number of inmates at one time, 2,600 to 120,000; Mauthausen, classified as a *Straflager* (penal camp), was the headquarters for Aktion 14F13 (euthanasia operation at Schloss Hartheim) in Austria and for the Kugel Aktion, the execution of escaped Allied POWs. Inmates employed by Deutsche Erd- und Steinwerke at the Wienergraben quarry and by Messerschmitt AG; of a total number of 200,000 inmates (including *Nebenlager*), approximately 120,000 perished, among them 40,000 Jews. > see also: **Euthanasie**.

Nebenlager

Name	Opened	Closed	Inmates	
Amstetten	3/45	5/45	2,500	
Ebensee	11/18/43	5/06/45		1,700
Eisenerz	4/07/44	12/44	300	
Grossraming	3/43	1945		1,000
Gunskirchen	3/45	5/04/45		17,000
Gusen I	3/21/41	5/05/45		7,500
Gusen II	3/11/44	5/05/45		12,000
Gusen III	12/16/44	5/05/45		275
Hinterbrühl	9/21/44	4/07/45		2,700
Hirtenberg	9/44	1945		800

Leibnitz-Graz	3/24/44	3/27/45	450
Lenzing	10/30/44	3/27/45	500
Linz I	5/15/44	3/27/45	
Linz II	4/18/44	3/27/45	5,300
Linz III	4/11/44	3/27/45	
Loibl-Pass	4/01/44	3/27/45	950
Melk	4/30/44	3/27/45	8,300
Passau I	3/44	11/44	150
Passau II	10/19/42	5/45	80
Peggau	12/01/44	3/27/45	300
Sankt Valentin	10/06/44	3/27/45	1,000
Schwechat	3/18/43	3/27/45	2,700
Styr-Münichholz	2/42	3/27/45	2,000
Wells	12/44	4/23/45	1,000
Wiener Neudorf	3/17/44	4/15/45	2,500
Wiener Neustadt	7/22/44	2/02/45	500

KL Mittelbau/Dora, established October 28, 1944; evacuated (death march) April 1, 1945; liberated by Americans April 9, 1945, with a handful of survivors; from August 27, 1943, to October 28, 1944, Mittelbau was an *Aussenlager* of Buchenwald; Lagerkommandants: Otto Förschner, Richard Baer; approximate number of inmates 34,000; underground armaments factories of Mittelwerk Gmb, producing V-2 rockets.

Nebenlager

Name	Opened	Closed	Inmates
Adorf	11/20/44	3/17/45	250
Berga	10/28/44	1/13/45	450
Bischofferode	11/04/44	3/23/45	60
Bleicherobe	10/26/44	3/05/45	50
Ellrich	5/02/44	3/26/45	130
Harzungen	4/01/44	10/28/44	2,000
Hohlstedt	1/16/45	3/27/45	300
Ilfeld	1/09/45	3/25/45	200
Kleinbodungen	10/02/44	3/23/45	500
Niedergebra	11/05/44	3/23/45	50
Niedersachsenwerfen	10/28/44	3/45	2,500
Nordhausen	5/44	3/27/45	2,200
Osterode	10/28/44	3/27/45	300
Regenstein	2/01/45	3/20/45	400
Rossla	8/31/44	3/27/45	80
Salza	8/27/43	9/28/44	12,000
Stempeda	4/44	4/02/45	500
Trautenstein	9/18/44	3/22/45	50

KL Natzweiler, also known as KL Struthof; established May 1, 1941; evacuated September 1944; Lagerkommandants: Egon Zill, Fritz Hartjenstein, Hans Hüttig, Heinrich Schwarz, Josef Kramer; approximate number of inmates, 44,600 of which at least 12,000 perished (including 25 satellite camps); camp makeup: *Sammellager für Nacht und Nebel*

Häftlinge (assembly camp for Night and Fog prisoners); camp for French resistance prisoners (both categories of prisoners were almost immediately executed); *Versuchs-* *abteilung der Reichsuniversität Strassburg* (Anatomy Institute of the University of Strassbourg, under professors August Hirt and Otto Bickenbach); gas chamber.

Nebenlager

Name	Opened	Closed	Inmates
Colmar	3/19/44	9/44	500
Dormettingen	1/45	3/45	3,000
Echterdingen	11/44	1/20/45	600
Ellwangen	8/43	4/07/45	100
Frankfurt am Main	8/44	3/25/45	1,600
Geisenheim	12/44	4/11/45	200
Geislingen	11/29/44	4/10/45	230
Goslar	10/20/44	4/45	50
Hailfingen	2/44	4/18/45	600
Haslach	9/44	1/45	250
Heppenheim	7/01/43	3/23/45	60
Hessental	4/01/44	4/45	800
Iffezheim	3/02/44	4/07/45	125
Kochendorf	11/01/44	2/45	1,600
Leonberg	3/44	3/30/45	1,150
Longwy-Thil	5/10/44	9/44	800
Markirch	2/25/44	2/45	2,000
Neckarbischofsheim	9/44	3/45	120
Neckargerach	1/44	3/45	1,000
Sandhofen	9/44	3/03/45	1,000
Schömberg	2/44	4/17/45	600
Schörzingen	2/44	4/23/45	500
Unterriexingen	1/44	4/45	300
Vaihingen	8/43	4/19/45	2,500
Wasseralfingen	10/44	2/45	400

KL Neuengamme, originally established as a *nebenlager* of KL Sachsenhausen (September 1938); reclassified as a KL on June 4, 1940; evacuated April 29, 1945; approximate number of inmates: 36,000; Lagerkommandants: Martin G. Weiss, Max Pauly; camp makeup: *Schonungsblock (Sterblager für Kranke und Entkräftete Häftlinge)* (Beauti- fication block, where sick and weak prisoners died); *Spital* (Hospital, where tuberculosis experiments were carried out on Jewish children); *Schiesstand* (Shooting place, murder site for Soviet POWs); *Arrestbunker* (gas chamber, used for Soviet POWs); of a total of some 100,000 inmates (including *Nebenlager*) approximately 56,000 perished.

Nebenlager

Name	Opened	Closed	Inmates
Aurich	10/22/44	12/23/44	2,000
Beendorf	12/28/44	3/07/45	4,500

Fallersleben	9/44	4/06/45	600
Farge	11/22/43	4/08/45	5,000
Fuhlsbüttel	7/43	4/29/45	800
Hildesheim	2/19/45	4/06/45	60
Kaltenkirchen	8/44	3/17/45	65
Ladelund	10/15/44	12/14/44	2,000
Langenhorn	9/44	4/04/45	500
Meppen	1/16/45	3/25/45	2,000
Porta Westfalica	4/10/44	4/12/45	1,100
Schwesing	10/04/44	12/22/44	2,000

KL Ravensbrück, established May 15, 1939; evacuated April 23, 1945; liberated by the Soviets with 3,500 survivors, April 30, 1945; Lagerkommandants: Max Koegel, Fritz Suhren; approximate number of inmates at one time, 24,500 to 70,000; camp makeup: *Frauenlager* (women's camp); camp for men established April 1941; *Ausweichlager* (draft dodger camp); *Jugendschutzlager* (youth protection camp); *Schönungslager* (beautification camp); gas chamber and crematoria. Medical experiments conducted in the camp by Professor Karl Gebhardt, including gangrene and sterilization. Inmates employed by Siemens; total number of inmates (including *nebenlager*): 107,000.

Nebenlager

Name	Opened	Closed	Inmates
Barth	11/05/43	1945	2,000
Hennigsdorf	10/10/44	4/45	850
Retzow	2/45	5/01/45	2,000
Schwarzenfrost	3/44	5/01/45	1,000
Velten	3/43	5/11/45	800

KL Riga/Kaiserwald, camp established in 1942; declared a KL March 15, 1943; closed June 22, 1944; Lagerkommandant: SS Obersturmführer Zauer; approximate number of inmates at one time, 4,000 to 15,000; camp makeup: AEG Telefunken labor commando.

Nebenlager

Name	Opened	Closed	Inmates
Eleja-Meitenes	1942	5/44	1,500
Salaspils	3/42	7/06/43	7,000
Walgunde	1941	9/41	500

KL Sachsenhausen, established September 23, 1936; liberated by the Soviets, with some 3,000 survivors, April 27, 1945; Lagerkommandants: Hermann Baranowski, Hans Loritz, Walter Eisfeld, Anton Kaindl; approximate number of inmates, at one time, 10,000 to 35,000; approximate number of victims that passed through, 135,000; categories of inmates included: politicals, (Communists, Socialists, and Centrists), criminals, Jehovah's Witnesses, asocials, homosexuals; AWOL members of the Wehrmacht and Waffen-SS; Czechs, Dutch, French, Italian, Belgian, Norwegian; Polish and Soviet prisoners of war; Gypsies, and Jews, 1,800 of whom were sent to the camp in the aftermath of *Kristallnacht*. Sachsenhausen had 61 *Nebenlager* and *Baubrigaden* with thousands of inmates slaving for, among others, Heinkel, Deutsche Machinenfabrik AG, and Klinker. A substantial number of victims lost their lives through overwork, starvation, and medical experiments; approximately 11,000 Soviet POWs were shot in the neck in the execution building; and thousands more were gassed in specially constructed gas vans.

Nebenlager

Name	Opened	Closed	Inmates
Drögen-Nindorf	5/03/41	12/30/41	230
Glau-Trebbin	1/02/43	1945	170
Küstrin-Fasterweide	5/17/43	1944	300
Oranienburg	2/18/43	1945	4,200
Prettin	10/04/41	7/01/43	65
Riga	3/24/43	5/27/43	300
Wewelsburg	9/01/41	4/02/45	480
Wittenberg	9/10/44	1945	500

KL Stutthof, established January 13, 1941; evacuated January 25, 1945; liberated by the Soviets May 1, 1945; classified as a *Straflager* (Punishment camp) Lagerkommandants: Max Pauly, Paul Werner Hoppe; average number of inmates at one time, 3,000 to 52,000, representing sixteen nationalities (the majority being Poles) of a total 115,000 inmates, 22,000 were transferred to other camps and more than 65,000 perished.

Nebenlager

Name	Opened	Closed	Inmates
Bocion	8/44	1/45	1,600
Brusy	12/42	3/45	400
Chorabie	1944	1/19/45	1,700
Cieszyny	8/44	1/28/45	1,600
Danzig	8/44	1945	800
Danzig-Neufahrwasser	10/11/39	1945	5,000
Garczyn	8/39	1945	400
Gdynia	1944	1945	600
Graudenz	8/39	1942	5,000
Grenzdorf	11/39	1942	2,000
Grodno	1944	1/15/45	1,500
Kokoszki	1944	1945	1,500
Kolkau	2/45	5/09/45	1,300
Krzemieniewo	9/15/44	1/18/45	450
Lauenburg	4/01/42	1945	100
Malki	4/44	1/28/45	1,000
Mierzynek	9/06/44	1/14/45	3,600
Nawitz	2/05/45	3/09/45	750
Niskie-Brodno	8/44	1/45	500
Praust	1944	1945	500
Szerokopas	8/44	1/45	1,700

| Thorn | 5/29/41 | 7/18/43 | 2,500 |

KL Vaivara, established in September 1943 as a Soviet prisoner of war camp; became *Stammlager* (main camp) for some *nebenlager* and *aussenkommandos*; closed June 28, 1944; Lagerkommandants: Hans Aumeier, Helmut Schnabel; the camp was guarded by a unit of the Estonian SS; approximate number of inmates, 20,000.

Nebenlager

Name	**Opened**	**Closed**	**Inmates**
Klooga	9/43	9/19/44	3,000

GRAPH K.1: Number of Inmates in Major KLs, 1939 and 1942

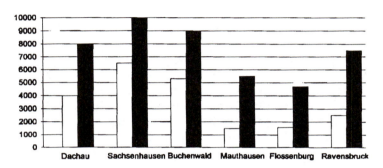

Note: the left bar represents 1939 and the right bar represents 1942.

TABLE K.3: KL Commandos

A. Aussenkommandos

Camp	Commandos	Camp	Commandos
Auschwitz	40	Mauthausen	55
Buchenwald	140	Mittelbau	25
Dachau	94	Natzweiler	56
Dora	24	Neuengamme	67
Flossenburg	86	Ravensbrück	26
Gross-Rosen	77	Riga	15
Hertogenbosch	15	Sachsenhausen	57
Kovno	2	Stutthof	28
Krakau-Plaszow	8	Vaivara	10
Lublin	3	TOTAL	828

B. Unterkommandos

Camp	Commandos	Camp	Commandos
Buchenwald	14	Gross-Rosen	20
Dachau	9	Mauthausen	12
Flossenburg	5	Mittelbau	8

Natzweiler	7	Riga	2
Neuengamme	3	Stutthof	4
		TOTAL:	84

Source: Weinmann, Martin, with Anne Kaiser and Ursula Krause-Schmitt. *Das national-sozialistische Lagersystem*. Frankfurt am Main: Zweitausendeins, 1990.

TABLE K.4: Independent Camps

Jüdische Zwangsarbeitslager (Forced-labor camps for Jews)

Name	Opened	Closed	Inmates
Austria			
Bruck	10/44	3/25/45	2,000
Donnerskirchen	12/44	4/22/45	700
Schachendorf	11/44	3/28/45	4,000
Schattendorf	7/44	3/30/45	1,200
Vienna	6/24/44	4/07/45	500
Bulgaria			
Somovit	5/42	7/43	500
Tabakova	7/43	1944	500
Czechoslovakia			
Bystrice (2 camps)	6/44	5/05/45	1,500
Chrastva	8/44	5/09/45	1,500
Edersgruen	5/39	12/42	350
Karvinna	12/42	9/20/43	800
Sv. Jur	1941	5/45	500
Vrchlabi Horni	1940	1942	300
Zacler	6/42	5/45	120
Estonia			
Kivioeli	9/05/43	8/20/44	1,800
Germany			
Annaberg	12/40	8/30/44	800
Auenrode	12/39	4/10/41	700
Bad Kudowa	8/44	5/08/45	1,600
Birawa	5/43	5/44	350
Birnbaümel	1944	1/45	1,000
Blechhammer	1940	12/44	2,000
Bolkenhain	1940	10/43	350
Brande	9/40	8/43	1,500

Breslau-Güntherbrücke	7/43	12/43	300
Breslau-Neukirch	9/44	2/14/45	600
Faulbrück	2/44	7/44	120
Finkenheerd	12/41	7/43	800
Frankfurt am Oder	8/42	11/44	3,000
Freiburg	11/43	11/44	600
Freiwalden	8/42	3/44	400
Fürstenberg	4/42	8/28/43	300
Geppersdorf	10/40	4/42	500
Gogolin	2/40	1944	300
Gräditz	6/42	10/44	2,000
Gross Masselwitz	1/41	3/44	1,500
Gross Pogul	8/42	12/44	200
Gross Sarne	5/40	4/45	1,500
Grossbeeren	10/43	5/45	2,000
Grunow-Spiegelberge	12/13/40	1942	600
Hohenwarte	1938	12/44	150
Kersdorf	1940	1943	100
Kleinmangersdorf	10/20/40	6/44	1,800
Klettendorf	10/30/41	10/44	800
Kreuzsee	12/16/40	9/43	500
Kurzbach	9/20/44	1/31/45	250
Reichswald	1939	2/25/42	50
Sackenhoym	3/28/41	4/44	300
Sagan	2/41	3/44	100
Sakrau	11/15/40	1943	400
Selchow	8/40	7/43	400
St. Annaberg	9/40	9/41	350
Wulkow	4/44	10/44	200
Zillerthal	10/43	5/44	900

Hungary

Balf	9/01/44	3/25/45	2,500
Csepel	5/42	11/08/44	2,000
Hajduhadhaz	9/08/40	1944	4,000
Koeszeg	4/17/44	12/07/44	600
Pestfuerdoe	5/44	12/44	3,000
Puspoek Ladany	10/02/42	10/01/43	250
Szentkiralyszabadja	1940	1945	4,000
Szolnok	9/01/42	10/07/44	600

Libya

Bukbuk	5/42	11/06/42	350
Giado	5/42	1/43	2,600
Sidi Azaz	5/42	1/43	1,000

Lithuania

Batcum	1942	1944	1,000
Linkaiciai	1942	3/44	180
Siaulia	7/43	7/21/44	400
Vilna	1942	1945	600

Norway

Beisfjord	6/22/42	10/42	900
Jonsvannet	7/15/42	9/01/42	600

Poland

Abramovice	1940	1942	300
Andrychow	9/42	11/43	120
Andrzejow	1/43	9/43	500
Będzin	5/30/40	8/43	300
Biala Podlaska	1941	12/17/42	3,000
Biechow-Dolne	4/42	10/42	200
Bodzechow	10/01/42	2/16/43	200
Boryslaw	12/42	8/06/44	3,500
Brzeziny Sląskie	2/41	2/42	400
Budzyn	7/42	5/44	3,000
Chruslice	8/19/41	5/05/44	600
Czarkow	12/42	11/44	1,100
Częstochowa (4 camps)	9/22/42	1/16/45	1,300
Dąbrowa Gornicza	1940	8/43	1,200
Dąbrowice	1942	1944	300
Dąbrowka Wielka	3/42	9/42	300
Dębica	7/42	4/43	1,600
Debiec	4/42	11/43	1,200
Deblin	1942	7/23/44	2,000
Dorohusk	1940	1941	300
Dubin	6/41	8/43	200
Dukla	8/13/42	11/15/42	150
Dzieczyna	4/43	9/43	150
Falencia	8/15/42	5/07/43	100
Frysztak	7/41	11/41	2,000
Glogow	7/20/42	10/25/42	300
Golonog	4/42	10/42	250
Goslawice	3/44	1/20/45	7,000
Grudzielec	8/42	3/43	100
Hohensalza	1941	1943	430
Holdunow-Smardzowice	3/42	4/43	500
Irena	5/41	6/43	1,000
Janikowo	11/40	3/44	300
Janowska	9/41	11/19/43	6,000
Jedlinsk	12/42	2/44	2,000
Jesionka	6/42	10/42	300

Jozefow	4/01/40	3/01/42	800
Kaczkowice	1941	7/44	5,000
Kielce	9/02/42	8/20/44	500
Klimonty	3/01/42	7/42	1,000
Klobuck	4/41	7/43	800
Kobylnica	4/42	8/43	370
Konskowola	1940	1/43	400
Krosno	8/25/42	1/27/44	120
Krzyzowniki	8/40	10/43	1,000
Lakta	9/41	8/43	100
Lasowice	1940	1/15/45	2,000
Laziska Gorne	3/42	12/42	150
Lazy	1941	1/44	400
Legionowo	1941	1943	100
Leki	1941	1943	350
Lesiow	1942	1/45	700
Lesna Podlaska	1940	1941	400
Limanowa	8/18/42	11/05/42	200
Lipie	10/42	4/43	100
Malaszewice Duze	10/42	2/44	1,000
Malazewicze	10/42	5/44	800
Markuszow	5/30/42	9/02/42	100
Mogila	1/44	1/16/45	300
Nadstawy	7/41	8/43	100
Naguszewo	9/15/44	12/44	480
Narty	4/41	10/41	300
Nowy Dwor	5/42	11/42	120
Nowy Targ	8/30/42	5/23/43	100
Ossowa	1941	1943	1,000
Ostrowiec	4/01/43	8/03/44	2,000
Parzymiechy	1942	1945	300
Pawlowo	6/41	8/43	120
Pionki	3/41	9/44	3,000
Piotrkow	8/01/43	11/28/44	700
Piotrowo	1941	12/43	5,000
Poniatow	7/43	11/44	3,000
Poniatow	10/41	7/44	18,000
Poznan (four camps)	1941	9/43	5,000
Prokocim	1942	10/43	1,700
Przemysl	11/42	10/43	1,200
Przyelodzko	12/40	8/41	400
Przylek	7/42	12/43	300
Pulawy	1942	1943	200
Pustkow	11/39	6/44	6,000
Rachanie	4/43	8/43	1,000
Radymno	10/42	3/43	200
Rogoznica	5/41	3/15/44	400
Rossosz	1/26/40	10/01/40	250
Rozan	5/43	8/43	350
Roznow	7/42	12/42	100

Rozwadow	5/42	10/42	1,100
Rydzina	6/41	10/43	100
Rytro	2/43	2/44	100
Sandomierz	10/42	1/44	350
Sedziszow	1940	12/42	450
Siedlce	1940	3/43	2,000
Skarzysko Kamienna	8/42	7/44	8,000
Slomniki	1940	1942	300
Spytkowice	9/42	2/43	350
Stadien Miejski	1942	1/43	1,000
Stalowa Wola	10/42	9/44	1,000
Starachowice	10/42	7/44	5,000
Stawiszyn	7/41	1/42	100
Stezycka	4/43	6/43	150
Strzeszyn	10/42	1/44	500
Swarzedz	1941	1943	1,200
Szenejki	4/41	10/42	300
Tyszowce	1940	10/41	500
Wilanow	4/42	12/01/42	400
Wlodawa	10/42	4/30/43	600
Wolanow	1940	7/43	1,000
Wymyslow	1942	11/43	200
Zagagie	6/42	7/43	300
Zarzecze	11/39	4/40	800
Zbaszyn	5/24/41	6/30/43	200
Zdroje	1942	1943	2,000
Zebrzydowice	8/42	3/44	200

Romania

Nagy Banya	1940	10/43	5,000
Telegd	7/05/44	3/06/45	250

Soviet Union

Borisov	1/43	3/43	800
Mogilev	7/43		250
Raho	1941		1,000
Smolensk	7/42		250

Yugoslavia

Bor	6/42	10/28/44	10,000

3. The Vernichtungslager

Belzec, established as part of Aktion Reinhard on November 1, 1941; Lager-kommandants: Christian Wirth; Gottlieb Hering. Full-scale extermination operations were begun on March 17, 1942. In June 1942 the gas chambers were enlarged and were switched from carbon monoxide to Zyklon-B. In December 1942, murder operations at Belzec ceased after the murder of between 500,000 and 600,000 victims. Thereafter, Belzec's mass graves were opened as part of

Aktion 1005. Except for a small number of Gypsies, the majority of Jewish victims were from the General Government, with some from Germany, Austria, and Czechoslovakia.

Chelmno (Kulmhof in German), established as the first death camp, with murder operations commencing on December 7–8, 1941. Lagerkommandants: Herbert Lange; Hans Bothmann. The camp was divided into two parts: the Schloss (castle), where arriving inmates were "prepared" for their trip, and the Waldlager (forest camp) where their bodies were interred. The two parts of the camp were separated by 2.5 miles (4 km), over which three gas vans transported the victims while carbon monoxide gas was piped into a sealed chamber at the vehicle rear. By the time they arrived at the Waldlager, the victims were already dead. Chelmno ceased operations in March 1943 but began again on June 23, 1944. The camp was abandoned permanently on January 17, 1945, and was liberated by the Red Army shortly thereafter. Total number of victims estimated at between 152,000 and 310,000. In addition to Soviet POWs and some Poles and Czechs, the majority of Jewish victims were from Lodz and the Warthegau; others came from Austria, Germany, Czechoslovakia, and Luxembourg.

Sobibór, established as part of Aktion Reinhard in March 1942. Lagerkommandant: Franz Stangl. Full-scale murder operations commenced in mid-April 1942, halting in July for repairs to the railway lines and enlargement of the camp's gas chambers. Murder operations resumed in October 1942. For the duration of their operations, the Sobibór gas chambers used carbon monoxide gas. On October 14, 1943, as the camp was readying for conversion to a KL, inmates, led by Liéutenant Aleksandr Pechersky (a Soviet Jewish POW) and Leon Feldhendler (a Polish Jew), revolted; 300 managed to escape of whom 50 survived the war. Thereafter, the Nazis attempted to erase the traces of the killings and dismantled the camp entirely. Total number of victims estimated at between 225,000 and 250,000. All the victims were Jews, the majority from eastern Galicia and the General Government; others came from France, Holland, the Soviet Union, Slovakia, Germany, and Austria.

Treblinka, established as part of Aktion Reinhard in May 1942, on the site of a previous KL established in 1941. Lagerkommandants: Imfried Eberl; Franz Stangl; murder operations commenced on July 23, 1942. Murder operations were undertaken in part of the camp, dubbed the "upper camp" by the Germans. Between August and October 1942 the three gas chambers at Treblinka were enlarged, although the camp continued normal operations. For the duration of their operations, the Treblinka gas chambers used carbon monoxide gas. Between March and July 1943 systematic efforts to erase the traces of murder at Treblinka commenced. On August 2, 1943, the remaining inmates revolted and attempted to flee; 750 Jews participated of whom 70 survived the war. Total number of victims is estimated at between 700,000 and 900,000. Except for a small number of Gypsies, all the victims were Jews, the majority from Warsaw and the General Government; others came from Greece, Slovakia, Bulgaria, and Yugoslavia.

TABLE K.5: Total Number of Nazi and Axis Camps

Country	Camps	Country	Camps	Country	Camps
Austria	89	Germany	1,470	Lithuania	12
Belgium	10	Holland	25	Norway	30
Czechoslovakia	47	Hungary	16	Poland	453
Denmark	2	Italy	9	Romania	4
Estonia	1	Latvia	6	Russia	5
France	73	Libya	9	Yugoslavia	14

Table K.6: Number of Victims of the Major VL/KL

Camp	Low Estimate	High Estimate
Auschwitz-Birkenau	1,200,000	2,500,000
Belzec	500,000	600,000
Bergen-Belsen	35,000	50,000
Buchenwald	50,000	60,000
Dachau	30,000	35,000
Chelmno	152,000	310,000
Gross-Rosen	35,000	40,000
Janowska	30,000	40,000
Majdanek	120,000	200,000
Mauthausen	71,000	120,000
Sachsenhausen	30,000	35,000
Sajmište	47,000	54,500
Sobibór	225,000	250,000
Stutthof	65,000	85,000
Treblinka	700,000	900,000

Source: E. Kogon: *Der SS-Staat, das System der deutschen Konzentrationslager*, Frankfurt A/M, 1946.

Konzentrierungspunkte [G] "Concentration points": Areas to which Jews were to be deported and confined until such a time as the Nazis would decide their fate. As a result of this policy, orders were issued by Reinhard Heydrich (October 1939) for the creation of ghettos in the *Generalgouvernement*.

Koriim [כורעים, H] "Bowing": Word taken from the daily prayer *Aleinu*. The term was passed along orally and meant that the people on the labor details should not stand around but should appear busy because the Schachmeisters, Kapos, SS, or other Nazi officials were on their way and about to make an inspection.

Krankenbehandler [G] "Healer of the sick": Nazi term for Jewish physicians. According to Nazi legislation, Jewish doctors and dentists were forbidden to practice medicine within the Reich, could not provide medical care of Aryans, and could only take care of fellow Jews under the new title of *Krankenbehandler*. This law was adopted for all European countries occupied by the Germans.

Krimchaki: Sectarian Jews who settled in the Crimean peninsula, as early as the second century B.C.E. Despite the similarities between them and the neighboring Tatar tribes, the Krimchaks were always identifiable as Jews and were considered such by the Russian and Soviet authorities. When Einsatzgruppe D arrived in the Crimea in 1941, the Nazis encountered the problem of the peninsula's heterogeneous ethnic population. Initially, Krimchaks were not treated as Jews, in much the same way that Karaites were exempted from antisemitic persecution. That situation rapidly changed, however, and in November the entire Krimchak community was rounded up, with a series of *Aktionen* decimating the community. > see also: **Karaites, Tati**.

Kristallnacht [G] "Crystal night": Common term for the pogrom conducted throughout Germany, Austria, and the Sudetenland on November 9 and 10, 1938. The pogrom was officially justified as a spontaneous popular response to the assassination of Ernst vom Rath, the third secretary of the German embassy in Paris, by Herschel Grynszpan. The term was coined by journalists after the

The New York Times.

Copyright, 1938, by The New York Times Company.

NEW YORK, FRIDAY, NOVEMBER 11, 1938.   P

NAZIS SMASH, LOOT AND BURN JEWISH SHOPS AND TEMPLES UNTIL GOEBBELS CALLS HALT

BANDS ROVE CITIES

Thousands Arrested for 'Protection' as Gangs Avenge Paris Death

All Vienna's Synagogues Attacked; Fires and Bombs Wreck 18 of 21

Jews Are Beaten, Furniture and Goods Flung From Homes and Shops — 15,000 Are Jailed During Day—20 Are Suicides

EXPULSIONS ARE IN VIEW

Plunderers Trail Wreckers in Berlin—Police Stand Idle —Two Deaths Reported

By OTTO D. TOLISCHUS

Headlines of the *New York Times* report the *Kristallnacht* pogrom

Courtesy of the New York Public Library

pogrom and refers to the shattered windows of Jewish storefronts.

Despite efforts to portray the pogrom as spontaneous, the reality was quite different. Vom Rath died on the afternoon of November 9. By that evening, orders had been conveyed throughout the country that the hour for action against the Jews had arrived. In accordance with these orders, SA members were to whip crowds into a frenzy and then unleash them upon the Jewish population: Synagogues were destroyed and burned, Jewish-owned stores were smashed and looted, Jewish homes were assaulted, and individual Jews were physically attacked. Ninety-one Jews were killed during the pogrom, and more than 900 synagogues were demolished. In the aftermath of the pogrom 30,000 Jews were rounded up and were incarcerated in concentration camps.

The pogrom was followed by a new series of administrative actions designed to speed up the aryanization of Jewish property and the expulsion of Jews from the Reich. These acts also resulted in the complete isolation of Jews from the general population. In addition, a fine of 1 billion reichsmarks was imposed on the Jewish community under the pretext of reparation for the murder of vom Rath, and the state ordered the confiscation of insurance payments, while Jewish store owners remained liable for repairs.

Kriyas yam suf [קריעת ים סוף, H/Y] "The parting of the Red Sea": Jewish term for the Allied invasion of Normandy, June 6, 1944.

Krol Chaim [P] "King Chaim": A nickname bestowed upon Mordechai Chaim Rumkowski, *Judenälteste* of the Lodz ghetto. > see also: **Chaim der Shreklecher; Chaimki.**

Kugelerlass [G] "Bullet decree": Nazi term for the November 1944 order by Gestapo chief Heinrich Müller for the summary execution of escaped and recaptured Allied prisoners of war that fell into any one of a number of categories. > see also: **Prisoners of War**.

Kulturboden [G] "Cultural soil": Nazi term for the territory between the Baltic and Black seas that they saw as forming an integral part of the Grossreich. > see also: **Lebensraum**.

Kultusgemeinde [G] "Religious community": German term used in the pre-Nazi era to denote the established Jewish community (the Kehila) and/or its governing board. During the Nazi era the term was used to denote Judenräte, primarily in Austria and Bohemia and Moravia. > see also: **Judenrat; Kehile**.

Kurfurstendam [geographic name]: Street forming Berlin's main business district. The Jewish-owned shops on the street were heavily damaged and looted during *Kristallnacht* pogrom of November 9/10, 1938.

L

La Carlinque [Fr] "The body": French term for the Gestapo.

La douce France [Fr] "Sweet France": French nickname for Marshal Philippe Pétain. > see also: **Collaboration**.

Lagerschutz [G] "Camp guards": Auxiliary police units organized in 1940 by the Nazis to guard concentration camps in Poland. Composed mainly of Ukrainians and Belorussians, the *Lagerschutz* also included some Polish volunteers and was well known for cruelty to prisoners.

Lapanka [P] "To take": Polish term for Nazi manhunts designed to seize Polish slave laborers. In 1942, 1943, and 1944 *Lapanka*s also served as a means of terrorizing the Polish population and deterring resistance. Individuals caught in these raids would be released only if they could prove they worked for the German war effort.

Lateran Pact(s): Treaties signed between the Vatican and the Partito Nazionale Fascista on February 11, 1929, that regulated the relationship between the Holy See and the Italian government. > see also: **Concordat**.

Lebedige toite [לעבעדיגע טויטע, Y] "Living dead": Yiddish term for the hungry, sick, helpless, and destitute Jews languishing in the ghettos and camps awaiting the final *Aktion* that would haul them away to their deaths.

Lebensborn [G] "Fountain of life": Nazi code name for the SS agency involved in the systematic kidnapping of non-Jewish children in Eastern Europe in order to "re-Germanize" them. *Lebensborn* also refers to the kidnapped children themselves, as they were viewed as a potential accretion to the Aryan racial stock of the German people. As most *Lebensborn* records disappeared after World War II, it is impossible to detail the actual number of *Lebensborn* kidnappings, and the agency's other activities are, at best, murky. > see also: **Schutzstaffel, Main Offices (RUSHA); Volk.**

Lebensmittelkarten [G] "Ration cards": Cards issued in Nazi Germany on August 27, 1939, five days before the blitz on Poland. Alien workers and Gypsies within the Reich were given cards with smaller allotments; Jews, still smaller rations. In countries under Nazi occupation the ration card system was also installed, granting a smaller allotment to Poles and other ethnic groups (excluding Volksdeutsche). Jews were on the bottom of the list, having to cope with a starvation diet of 200 to 300 calories per day.

Lebensraum [G] "Living space": A vital part of German and, especially, Nazi, ideology, justifying military aggression and imperialist expansion. The term dates to the very founding of the Second Reich in 1871; it was picked up by the Nazis and became the core of Hitler's ideology. Nazism sought to expand Germany's borders because, it was claimed, Germany was overpopulated and lacked the resources to maintain its people properly. *Lebensraum* was to be gained by a war of expansion and eugenic genocide in the East; an organic element of this policy was the extermination of the Jews. > see also: **Todesraum.**

Lebensrechtsmitteln [G] "Right to live cards": Ghetto term for a specially stamped card — at times distributed to a select group of people — that in German eyes were important enough to remain alive for the time being.

Lebensscheinen [G] "Life certificates": Nazi term that was held dear to most of East European Jews under German occupation. The possession of a valid *Lebensschein* meant the difference between buying time (sometimes a few months, a few weeks, a few days, or even, at times, just a few hours) or immediate deportation to the extermination sites.

Lebensunwertes Leben [G] "Life unworthy of life": Nazi term for those afflicted with incurable diseases, the mentally ill, and those with hereditary diseases. To cleanse Germany of those undesirable elements, a law for the prevention of hereditary diseases was passed on July 14, 1933, establishing euthanasia centers for the destruction of the bearers of hereditary diseases by medical means. Jews, regardless of their state of health, automatically fell within this category. > see also: **Euthanasie; Endlösung.**

Legislation, Anti-Jewish

1. Scope and Definition

The NSDAP program adopted on February 24, 1920, contained the seed for the antisemitic legislation that began in April 1933. The Nazis went through three phases in their anti-Jewish legislation: First,

between April 1933 and September 1935, the Nazis severely limited the sphere of economic activity permitted to German Jews. Second, between September 1935 and 1937, the Nazis defined the racial component of their legislation and reduced Jews to the status of *Reichsangehörigen* — subjects of the state, or something less than second-class citizens. Third, between 1937 and September 1939, the Nazis completely eliminated German Jews from the economy.

With the outbreak of war and the Nazi occupation of much of Europe, existing legislation was extended and made more systematic. In effect, legislation announced in this period laid the legal precedents for the Final Solution. Of special importance, in this regard, were the introduction of the Jewish badge throughout Europe and the October 1941 ban on Jewish emigration.

All the Axis-allied states also enacted their own anti-Jewish legislation. Some of these states, notably Hungary and Romania, already had anti-Jewish laws promulgated during the late 1920s. The majority of Axis-allied states, however, adopted antisemitic legislation under Nazi influence. In these states anti-Jewish legislation was intimately related to collaboration and, generally, involved reversing emancipation and limiting the Jewish role in the economy. Here too, legislation provided the justification for the eventual deportation of Jews, although some countries officially distinguished between "foreign" Jews, whose deportation was desirable, and "native" Jews, whose deportation was not always desirable. > see also: **Endlösung.**

2. National Socialist Legislation

Third Reich
April 7, 1933: *Gesetz zur Wiederherstellung des Berufsbeamtentums*, "Law for the restoration of professional civil service."

April 7, 1933: *Gesetz über die Zulassung zur Rechtsanwaltschaft*, "Law regarding admission to the legal profession."

April 7, 1933: *Gesetz über die Neuwahl von*

Schöffen, Geschworenen und Handelsrichten, "Law regarding new election of assessors, jurors, and commercial judges."

April 11, 1933: *Erste Verordnung zur durchführung des Gesetzes zur Wiederherstellung des Berufsbeamtentums,* "First decree to implement the law for the restoration of professional civil service."

April 22, 1933: *Gesetz über das Schlachten von Tieren,* "Law regarding the [ritual] slaughter of animals."

April 22, 1933: *Verordnung über das Schlachten von Tieren,* "Decree regarding the [ritual] slaughter of animals."

April 22, 1933: *Gesetz über die Zulassung zur Patentanwaltschaft,* "Law regarding the admission to patent attorneyship."

April 22, 1933: *Gesetz über die Neubildung von Steuerausschüssen,* "Law regarding the reconstitution of boards of tax assessors."

April 22, 1933: *Verordnung über die Zulassung von Ärzten zur Tätigkeit bei den Krankenkassen,* "Decree regarding the admission of physicians service in the National Health Insurance."

April 25, 1933: *Gesetz über die Überfüllung von deutschen Schulen und Hochschulen,* "Law regarding the overcrowding of German schools and schools of higher education."

April 25, 1933: *Verordnung zur Durchführung des Gesetzes gegen die Überfüllung von deutschen Schulen und Hochschulen,* "Decree to implement the law against the overcrowding of German public schools and schools of higher education."

May 4, 1933: *Zweite Verordnung zur Durchführung des Gesetzes zur Wiederherstellung des Berufsbeamtentums,* "Second decree to implement the law for the restoration of professional civil service."

May 6, 1933: *Dritte Verordnung zur Durchführung des Gesetzes zur Wiederherstellung des Berufsbeamtentums,* "Third decree to implement the law for the restoration of professional civil service."

May 9, 1933: *Gesetz über die Zulassung der Kriegsteilnehmer zur ärztlichen Tätigkeit bei den Krankenkassen,* "Law regarding the admission of war veterans to medical activity in the National Health Insurance."

May 19, 1933: *Erste Verordnung zur Durchführung des Gesetzes über Ehrenämter in der sozialen Versicherung und der Reichsversorgung,* "First decree to implement the law regarding honorary posts in the social insurance and the state pension."

June 2, 1933: *Verordnung über die Tätigkeit von Zahnärzten und Zahntechnikern bei den Krankenkassen,* "Decree regarding the participation of dentists and dental technicians in the National Health Insurance service."

June 30, 1933: *Gesetz zur Änderung von Vorschriften auf dem Gebiete des allgemeinen Beamten-, Besoldungs- und Versorgungsrecht,* "Law to change provisions regarding the law on officials, salary, and insurance."

July 14, 1933: *Gesetz über die Einziehung volks- und staatsfeindlichen Vermögens,* "Law regarding the confiscation of national wealth in the hands of state enemies."

July 14, 1933: *Gesetz über den Widerruf von Einbürgerungen und die Aberkennung der deutschen Staatsangehörigkeit,* "Law regarding revocation of naturalization and the annulment of German citizenship" (revoked the citizenship of Jews who entered Germany after August 1914).

July 20, 1933: *Gesetz zur Änderung einiger Vorschriften der Rechtsanwaltsordnung, der Zivilprozessordnung und des Arbeitsgerichtsgesetzes,* "Law to change some provisions of the lawyer decree, the code of civil procedure, and the labor court law."

July 26, 1933: *Verordnung zur Durchführung des Gesetzes über den Widerruf von Einbürgerungen und die Aberkennung der Staatsangehörigkeit*, "Decree to implement the law on the revocation of naturalization and annulment of [German] citizenship."

August 5, 1933: *Verordnung über die Einziehung volks- und staatsfeindlichen Vermögens*, "Decree regarding the confiscation of national wealth in the hands of state enemies."

September 22, 1933: *Drittes Gesetz zur Änderung des Gesetzes zur Wiederherstellung des Berufsbeamtentums*, "Third law to change the law to restore the civil service law."

September 22, 1933: *Gesetz über die Errichtung der Reichskulturkammer*, "Law regarding the establishment of the State Chamber of Culture."

September 26, 1933: *Zweite Verordnung über die Einziehung volks- und staatsfeindlichen Vermögens*, "Second decree regarding the confiscation of national wealth in the hands of state enemies."

September 26, 1933: *Patentanwaltsgesetz*, "Patent attorneyship law."

September 28, 1933: *Zweite Verordnung zur Änderung und Ergänzung der zweiten Verordnung zur Durchführung des Gesetzes über die Wiederherstellung des Berufsbeamtentums*, "Second decree to change and supplement the second decree to implement the law regarding the restoration of the civil service."

September 29, 1933: *Reichserbhofgesetz*, "Law regulating peasant holdings (homestead law)."

October 1, 1933: *Zweite Verordnung zur Durchführung des Gesetzes über die Zulassung zur Rechtsanwaltschaft und zur Patentanwaltschaft*, "Second decree to

implement the law regarding the admission to the attorney and patent attorney association."

October 4, 1933: *Schriftleitergesetz*, "Law regarding editors."

October 19, 1933: *Verordnung zur Durchführung des Reichserbhofgesetzes*, "Decree to implement the peasant holdings law."

November 20, 1933: *Verordnung über die Zulassung von Ärzten, Zahnärzten und Zahntechnikern zur Tätigkeit bei den Krankenkassen*, "Decree regarding the admission of doctors, dentists and dental technicians to participate in National Health Insurance service."

December 19, 1933: *Verordnung über das Inkrafttreten und die Durchführung des Schriftleitergesetzes*, "Decree regarding the effective date and the implementation of the editor law."

January 24, 1934: *Gesetz zur Ordnung der nationalen Arbeit*, "Law to systematize national labor" (banned Jews from any role in the Deutsche Arbeitsfront).

March 23, 1934: *Gesetz über Reichsverweisungen*, "Law regarding state expulsions."

May 17, 1934: *Verordnung über die Zulassung von Ärzten zur Tätigkeit bei den Krankenkassen*, "Decree regarding the admission of doctors to participate in the National Health Insurance."

May 29, 1934: *Verordnung zur Durchführung des Gesetzes über Reichsverweisungen*, "Decree to implement the law regarding state expulsions."

July 3, 1934: *Gesetz über Änderungen auf dem Gebiete der Reichsversorgung*, "Law regarding changes in the jurisdiction of state pension."

July 22, 1934: *Ausbildungsordnung für Juristen*, "Training decree for jurists."

September 13, 1934: *Verordnung zur Durchführung der Ausbildungsordnung für Juristen*, "Decree to implement the training decree for jurists."

October 16, 1934: *Steueranpassungsgesetz,* "Tax adjustment law."

December 13, 1934: *Gesetz über den Ausgleich bürgerlich-rechtlicher Ansprüche,* "Law regarding the compensation of civil-legal claims."

February 13, 1935: *Dritte Verordnung über die Zulassung von Zahnärzten und Dentisten zur Tätigkeit bei den Krankenkassen,* "Third decree regarding the admission of dental surgeons and dentists to participate in the National Health Insurance."

May 9, 1935: *Verordnung über die Zulassung von Zahnärzten und Dentisten zur Tätigkeit bei den Krankenkassen,* "Decree regarding the admission of dental surgeons and dentists to participate in the National Health Insurance."

May 21, 1935: *Wehrgesetz,* "Military service law."

May 29, 1935: *Verordnung über die Musterung und Aushebung im Jahr 1935,* "Decree regarding the induction examination and conscription in the year 1935."

June 26, 1935: *Gesetz über den Reichsarbeitsdienst,* "Law regarding the state labor service."

July 25, 1935: *Verordnung über die Zulassung von Nichtarien zum Wehrdienst,* "Decree regarding the admission of non-Aryans to military service."

July 26, 1935: *Durchführungsvorschriften zur Verordnung über die Laufbahn für das Amt des Richters und des Staatsanwalts,* "Implementation of regulations to the decree regarding the career for the office of judges and district attorneys."

September 15, 1935: *Reichsbürgergesetz,* "State citizenship law."

September 15, 1935: *Gesetz zum Schutze des deutschen Blutes und der deutschen Ehre,* "Law for the protection of German blood and German honor."

September 26, 1935: *Durchführungsbestimmungen zur Verordnung über die Gewährung von Kinderbeihilfen an kinderreiche Familien,* "Implementation of decisions to the decree regarding the granting of children's allowances to large families."

November 14, 1935: *Erste Verordnung zum Reichsbürgergesetz,* "First decree supplementing the state citizenship law."

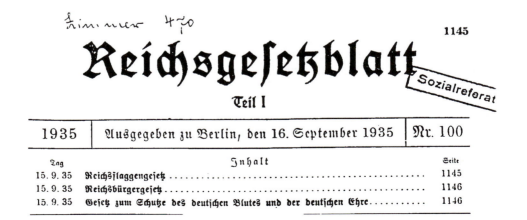

Reichsgesetzblatt issue for September 16, 1935, containing the Nuremberg Laws

Courtesy of YIVO, the Yiddish Scientific Institute, New York

November 14, 1935: *Erste Verordnung zum Gesetz des deutschen Blutes und der deutschen Ehre*, "First decree supplementing the law for the protection of German blood and honor."

November 14, 1935: *Verordnung zur Ausführung des Gesetzes über Titel, Orden und Ehrenzeichen*, "Decree to implement the law regarding title, decoration, and medals."

December 13, 1935: *Reichsärzteordnung*, "State physician classification."

December 13, 1935: *Verordnung zur Ausführung des Gesetzes zur Verhütung von Missbräuchen auf dem Gebiete der Rechtsvertretung*, "Decree to implement the law for prevention of abuse in the area of legal representation."

December 21, 1935: *Zweite Verordnung zum Reichsbürgergesetz*, "Second decree to the state citizenship law."

January 7, 1936: *Verordnung über die Verhältnisse der Landespolizei*, "Decree regarding the conditions of the state police."

January 31, 1936: *Verordnung über die Heranziehung der deutschen Staatsangehörigen im Auslande zum aktiven Wehrdienst und zum Reichsarbeitsdienst*, "Decree regarding the mobilization of German nationals abroad for active military service and for state labor service."

February 7, 1936: *Gesetz über das Reichstagswahlrecht*, "Law regarding the right to vote for the Reichstag (parliament)."

February 24, 1936: *Dritte Durchführungsverordnung zur Verordnung über die Gewährung von Kinderbeihilfen an kinderreiche Familien*, "Third implementation decree to the decree regarding the granting of children's allowances to large families."

February 26, 1936: *Erste Verordnung zum Gesetz über die Verpachtung und Verwaltung*

öffentlicher Apotheken, "First decree to the law regarding the leasing and administration of public pharmacies."

April 3, 1936: *Reichstierärzteordnung*, "State veterinary order."

June 16, 1936: *Wehrgesetz*, "Defense law."

June 29, 1936: *Verordnung über die geschäftsmässige Hilfeleistung in Devisensachen*, "Decree regarding businesslike assistance in foreign exchange matters."

July 7, 1936: *Verordnung über öffentlich bestellte Wirtschaftsprüfer im Genossenschaftswesen*, "Decree regarding certified public accountants in public associations."

October 14, 1936: *Reichsgrundsätze über Einstellung, Anstellung und Beförderung der Reichs- und Landes-beamten*, "Reich principles regarding the hiring, employment, and promotion of Reich and district officials."

December 1, 1936: *Gesetz zur Änderung des Gesetzes über die Devisienbewirtschaftung*, "Law to change the law regarding the foreign exchange control."

January 26, 1937: *Verordnung über den Handel mit Vieh*, "Decree regarding the trading of livestock."

January 26, 1937: *Reichsbeamtengesetz*, "Reich officials law."

March 19, 1937: *Zweite Durchführungsverordnung zum Reichsjagdgesetz*, "Second decree to implement the state hunting law."

March 19, 1937: *Reichsnotarordnung*, "Reich notary public order."

March 19, 1937: *Gesetz zur Änderung des Reichsarbeitsdienstgesetzes*, "Law to change the Reich's labor service law."

April 22, 1937: *Erste Verordnung zur Durchführung des Reichsluftschutzgesetzes*, "First decree to implement the Reich air defense law."

June 30, 1937: *Gesetz über Massnahmen im ehemals oberschlesischen Abstimmungsgebiet,* "Law regarding actions in the former Upper Silesian voting district."

August 31, 1937: *Sechste Durchführungs-bestimmung zur Verordnung über die Gewährung von Kinderbeihilfen an kinder-reiche Familien,* "Sixth implementation regulation to the decree regarding the granting of children's allowances to large families."

September 8, 1937: *Verordnung über die Zu-lassung von Ärzten zur Tätigkeit bei den Krankenkassen,* "Decree regarding the admission of doctors to the National Health Insurance service."

October 8, 1937: *Bestallungsordnung für Apotheker,* "Licensing order for pharmacists."

October 8, 1937: *Verfahrenordnung für die Apotheker-berufsgerichte,* "Procedural order for the pharmacist trade courts."

November 5, 1937: *Gesetz über erbrechtliche Beschränkungen wegen gemeinschaftswidrigen Verhaltens,* "Law regarding law of inheritance limitations because of antisocial behavior."

January 5, 1938: *Gesetz zur Änderung des Gesetzes über Massnahmen im ober-schlesischen Abstimmungsgebiet,* "Law to change the law regarding actions in the Upper Silesian voting district."

January 5, 1938: *Gesetz über die Änderung von Familien- und Vornamen,* "Law regarding the changing of family and first names."

January 12, 1938: *Fünfte Verordnung über die Zulassung von Zahnärzten und Dentisten zur Tätigkeit bei den Krankenkassen,* "Fifth decree regarding the admission of dental surgeons and dentists to participate in the National Health Insurance."

January 15, 1938: *Verordnung zur Durchführung des Gesetzes über Massnahmen in ober-schlesischen Abstimmungsgebiet,* "Decree to implement the law regarding actions in Upper Silesian voting districts."

January 20, 1938: *Berufsordnung der öffentlich bestellten Vermessungsingenieure,* "Trade order for publicly mandated surveyors."

February 5, 1938: *Vierte Verordnung zur Änderung des Gesetzes über das Versteigerer-gewerbe,* "Fourth decree to change the law regarding the auctioneers' profession."

February 6, 1938: *Gesetz zur Änderung des Einkommensteuergesetzes,* "Law to change the income tax law."

February 6, 1938: *Zweite Verordnung zur Durch-führung des Einkommensteuergesetzes,* "Second decree to implement the income tax law."

February 6, 1938: *Zweite Verordnung zur Durch-führung des Steuerabzugs vom Arbeitslohn,* "Second decree to implement the tax deduction for wages."

February 12, 1938: *Gesetz über das Versteigerer-gewerbe,* "Law regarding the auctioneers' profession."

March 18, 1938: *Gesetz über die Herstellung von Waffen,* "Law regarding the manufacture of firearms."

March 28, 1938: *Gesetz über die Rechts-verhältnisse der jüdischen Kultusvereinigungen,* "Law on the legal status of Jewish religious organizations."

March 29, 1938: *Zweite Verordnung zur Durch-führung des Grundssteuergesetzes für den ersten Hauptveranlagungszeitraum,* "Second decree to implement the real estate tax law for the first chief assessment period."

March 30, 1938: *Gesetz über Mietbeihilfen,* "Law

regarding rent assistance."

April 22, 1938: *Verordnung gegen die Unterstützung der Tarnung jüdischer Gewerbebetriebe,* "Decree against helping in the concealment of ownership of Jewish enterprises."

April 23, 1938: *Drittes Gesetz zur Änderung der Vorschriften über die Gebäudeentschuldungssteuer,* "Third law to change the regulations regarding the tax write-offs on buildings."

April 24, 1938: *Verordnung über die Anmeldung des Vermögens von Juden,* "Decree on the registration of Jewish property."

April 26, 1938: *Anordnung auf Grund der Verordnung über des Vermögens der Juden,* "Regulation on the basis of the decree regarding Jewish property."

May 19, 1938: *Erste Verordnung zur Ausführung des Personestandsgesetzes,* "First decree to implement the personal status law."

June 14, 1938: *Dritte Verordnung zum Reichsbürgergesetz,* "Third decree supplementing the state citizenship law."

June 18, 1938: *Verordnung zur Durchführung der Verordnung über die Anmeldung des Vermögens von Juden,* "Decree to implement the decree regarding the registration of Jewish property."

July 6, 1938: *Gesetz zur Änderung der Gewerbeordnung für das Deutsche Reich,* "Law to change the trade law for the German state."

July 23, 1938: *Dritte Bekanntmachung über den Kennkartenzwang,* "Third notice regarding the identification card requirement."

July 25, 1938: *Vierte Verordnung zum Reichsbürgergesetz,* "Fourth decree supplementing the state citizenship law."

July 27, 1938: *Personenstandsgesetz in der Fassung vom 27.7. 1938,* "Personal status law as formulated on July 27, 1938."

August 17, 1938: *Gesetz über die Bereinigung alter Schulen,* "Law regarding the restoration of old schools."

August 17, 1938: *Zweite Verordnung zur Durchführung des Gesetz über die Änderung von Familiennamen und Vornamen,* "Second decree supplementing the law regarding the change of family names and first names."

September 4, 1938: *Gesetz über die Zulassung zur Patentanwaltschaft,* "Law regarding the admission to patent attorneyship."

September 27, 1938: *Fünfte Verordnung zum Reichsbürgergesetz,* "Fifth decree supplementing the state citizenship law."

September 28, 1938: *Erste Verordnung über die Berufsmassige Ausübung der Krankenflege,* "First decree regarding the practice of health care professionals."

October 5, 1938: *Verordnung über Reisepässe,* "Decree regarding travel permits."

October 6, 1938: *Verordnung über die Teilnahme der Juden an der kassenärztlichen Versorgung,* "Decree regarding Jewish participation in the medical insurance system."

October 31, 1938: *Erstes Gesetz zur Änderung des Bürgersteuergesetzes,* "First law to change the citizen tax law."

October 31, 1838: *Sechste Verordnung zum Reichsbürgergesetz,* "Sixth decree supplementing the state citizenship law."

November 11, 1938: *Verordnung über den Waffenbesitz von Juden,* "Decree regarding weapon ownership by Jews."

November 12, 1938: *Verordnung über eine Sühneleistung der Juden deutscher Staatsangehörigkeit,* "Decree regarding an atonement fine for Jewish subjects of the German state."

November 12, 1938: *Verordnung zur Ausschaltung der Juden aus dem deutschen Wirtschaftsleben*, "Decree to eliminate the Jews from German economic life."

November 12, 1938: *Verordnung zur Wiederherstellung des Strassenbildes bei jüdischen Gewerbebetrieben*, "Decree regarding the restoration of storefronts of Jewish places of business."

November 16, 1938: *Erlass des Führers und Reichskanzlers über das tragen von Uniformen*, "Order of the Führer and Chancellor regarding the wearing of uniforms."

November 19, 1938: *Verordnung über die öffentliche Fürsorge der Juden*, "Decree regarding public assistance for Jews."

November 21, 1938: *Durchführungsverordnung zur Verordnung über die Sühneleistung der Juden*, "Regulation implementing the decree regarding the Jews' atonement fine."

November 23, 1938: *Verordnung zur Durchführung der Verordnung über die Ausschaltung der Juden aus dem deutschen Wirtschaftsleben*, "Decree to implement the decree regarding the elimination of Jews from German economic life."

November 28, 1938: *Polizeiverordnung über das Auftreten der Juden in der Öffentlichkeit*, "Police decree regarding the appearance of Jews in public."

November 29, 1938: *Erste Verordnung zur Durchführung und Ergänzung des Brieftaubengesetzes*, "First decree to implement and supplement the carrier pigeon law."

December 3, 1938: *Verordnung über den Einsatz des jüdischen Vermögens*, "Decree regarding the utilization of Jewish property."

December 5, 1938: *Siebente Verordnung zum Reichsbürgergesetz*, "Seventh decree supplementing the state citizenship law."

December 12, 1938: *Gesetz über die Devisenbewirtschaftung*, "Law regarding foreign exchange control."

December 14, 1938: *Zweite Durchführungsverordnung zur Verordnung zur Ausschaltung der Juden aus der deutschen Wirtschaftsleben*, "Second implementation decree to the decree to eliminate the Jews from German economic life."

December 21, 1938: *Hebammengesetz*, "Midwife law."

December 31, 1938: *Zweite Verordnung über Mietbeihilfen*, "Second decree regarding rent assistance."

January 16, 1939: *Verordnung zur Durchführung des Verordnung über den Einsatz des jüdischen Vermögens*, "Decree to implement the decree regarding the utilization of Jewish property."

January 17, 1939: *Achte Verordnung zum Reichsbürgergesetz*, "Eighth decree supplementing the state citizenship law."

January 31, 1939: *Erste Verordnung zur Durchführung des Gesetzes über die Rechtsverhältnisse der jüdischen Kultusvereinigungen*, "First decree to implement the law regarding the legal status of the Jewish religious associations."

February 8, 1939: *Verordnung über die Neugestaltung der Reichshauptstadt Berlin und der Hauptstadt der Bewegung München*, "Decree regarding the reorganization of the state capital, Berlin, and the capital of the [Nazi movement], Munich."

February 17, 1939: *Gesetz zur Änderung der Einkommensteuergesetzes*, "Law to change the income tax law."

February 18, 1939: *Erste Durchführungs-*

verordnung zum Gesetz über die berufs-mässige Ausübung der Heilkunde ohne Bestallung (Heil-praktikergesetz), "First implementation decree to the law regarding the professional practice of medicine without public appointment (non-medical practitioner law)."

February 21, 1939: *Dritte Verordnung auf Grund der Verordnung über die Anmeldung des Vermögens von Juden*, "Third ordinance on the basis of the decree regarding the registration of Jewish property."

February 27, 1939: *Einkommsteuergesetz*, "Income tax law."

March 3, 1939: *Verordnung zur Verordnung über die Anmeldung des Vermögens von Juden*, "Decree to the decree regarding the registration of Jewish property."

March 7, 1939: *Verordnung zur Änderung der Verordnung zur Musterung und Ausbildung*, "Decree to change the decree to the induction examination and training."

March 10, 1939: *Durchführungsbestimmungen zum Lohnsteuergesetz*, "Implementation decisions concerning the wages tax law."

March 17, 1939: *Durchführungsbestimmungen zum Einkommensteuergesetz*, "Implementation decisions concerning the income tax law."

March 18, 1939: *Vierzehnte Verordnung zur Durchführung und Ergänzung des Gesetzes über den Ausgleich bürgerlich-rechtlicher Ansprüche*, "Fourteenth decree to implement and supplement the law regarding the settlement of civil-legal claims."

March 23, 1939: *Zweite Durchführungsverordnung zum Gesetz über die Hitler-Jugend*, "Second implementation decree to the law regarding the Hitler Youth."

March 29, 1939: *Verordnung zur Ausführung des Reichsjagdgesetzes*, "Decree to implement

the state hunting law."

April 26, 1939: *Verordnung über das Erbhofrecht*, "Decree regarding the right to ancestral estates."

April 30, 1939: *Gesetz über Mietverhältnisse mit Juden*, "Law on leases entered into with Jews."

May 8, 1939: *Verordnung zur Durchführung des Gesetzes über die Reisevermittlung*, "Decree to implement the law regarding travel agencies."

June 12, 1939: *Bekantmachung der neuen Fassung des § Abs. 2 Nr. 5 der Reichsärzteordnung*, "Announcement of the new wording of paragraph two, section five, of the state doctors' order."

July 4, 1939: *Zehnte Verordnung zum Reichsbürgergesetz*, "Tenth decree supplementing the state citizenship law."

July 28, 1939: *Verordnung über die gerichtliche Zuständigkeit nach der Verordnung gegen die Tarnung jüdischer Gewerbebetriebe*, "Decree regarding legal jurisdiction according to the decree against the concealment of ownership of Jewish enterprises."

August 4, 1939: *Verordnung zur Durchführung des Gesetzes über die Rechtsverhältnisse der jüdischen Kultusvereinigungen*, "Decree to implement the law regarding the legal status of Jewish religious associations."

September 1, 1939: *Verordnung zur Bestallungsordnung für Apotheker*, "Decree to the appointment order for pharmacists."

September 1, 1939: *Erste Verordnung zur Durchführung des Luftschutzgesetzes*, "First decree to implement the air defense law" (ordered Jews to pay a special air-defense tax).

September 19, 1939: *Verordnung über die Teilnahme an der kassenärztlichen und kassendentistischen Versorgung*, "Decree regarding participation in the medical and dental health insurance system."

October 19, 1939: *Zweite Verordnung zur Durchführung der Verordnung über die Sühneleistung der Juden*, "Second decree to implement the decree regarding the Jews' atonement fine."

October 31, 1939: *Verordnung zur Änderung des Vermögenssteuergesetzes*, "Decree to change the property tax law."

November 15, 1939: *Erste Verordnung über die berufsmässige Ausübung der Säuglings- und Kinderpflege und die Errichtung von Säuglings- und Kinderpflegeschulen*, "First decree regarding the professional exercise of infant and child care and the establishment of infant and child care schools."

November 15, 1939: *Zweite Verordnung über die berufsmässige Ausübung der Säuglings- und Kinderpflege*, "Second decree regarding the professional exercise of infant and child care and the establishment of infant and child care schools."

November 30, 1939: *Verordnung über die Vertragshilfe des Richters aus Anlass des Krieges*, "Decree regarding contractual assistance to judges because of the war."

November 30, 1939: *Verordnung über das Kriegsausgleichsverfahren*, "Decree regarding war compensation procedure."

January 18, 1940: *Zweite Verordnung zur Durchführung der Verordnung über den Einsatz des jüdischen Vermögens*, "Second decree to implement the decree regarding the utilization of Jewish property."

February 16, 1940: *Verordnung zur Ergänzung der Ersten Verordnung zur Ausführung des Gesetzes zum Schutz des deutschen Blutes und der deutschen Ehre*, "Decree to supplement the first decree to realize the law to protect German blood and German honor."

February 17, 1940: *Erste Verordnung über die Berufstätigkeit und Ausbildung medizinisch-technischer Assistentinnen*, "First decree regarding the professional activity and training of medical-technical assistants."

March 4, 1940: *Verordnung über den Wehrersatz bei besonderen Einsatz*, "Decree regarding the recruitment for special tasks."

April 16, 1940: *Verordnung zur Ergänzung des Gesetzes zur Wiederherstellung des Berufsbeamtentums*, "Decree to supplement the law for the restoration of the civil service."

May 4, 1940: *Vierte Anordnung auf Grund der Verordnung über die Anmeldung des Vermögens von Juden*, "Fourth regulation on the basis of the decree regarding the registration of Jewish property."

June 10, 1940: *Verordnung über die Nachprüfung von Entjudungsgeschäften*, "Decree regarding the verification of the de-Judaization of businesses."

June 12, 1940: *Verordnung zur Durchführung der Fünften Verordnung zum Reichsbürgergesetz*, "Decree to implement the fifth decree on the state citizenship law."

June 28, 1940: *Satzung des Reichsluftschutzbundes*, "Statute on the state air defense league."

August 1, 1940: *Verordnung über den Nachweis der deutschblütigen Abstammung*, "Decree regarding the proof for German racial descent."

September 10, 1940: *Verordnung zur Änderung und Ergänzung des Gesetzes über die Mietverhältnisse mit Juden*, "Decree to change and supplement the law regarding leases with Jews."

September 17, 1940: *Verordnung über das Vermögen von Angehörigen des ehemals polnischen Staats*, "Decree regarding the property of citizens of the former Polish state."

November 14, 1940: *Erste Verordnung zur Durchführung über die Nachprüfung von Entjudungsgeschäften*, "First decree to implement the verification of the de-

Judaization of businesses."

November 30, 1940: *Kriegsschäden-Verordnung,* "War damage decree."

December 9, 1940: *Verordnung über Kinderbeihilfen,* "Decree regarding children's allowances."

December 27, 1940: *Verordnung zur Durchführung der Verordnung über den Einsatz des jüdischen Vermögens,* "Decree for the implementation of the decree regarding the utilization of Jewish property."

March 7, 1941: *Zweite Verordnung zur Durchführung und Ergänzung des Gesetzes über die Vermittlung der Annahme an Kindesstatt,* "Second decree to implement and supplement the law regarding arranging the adoption of infants."

March 27, 1941: *Verordnung über die Firmen entjudeter Gewerbebetriebe,* "Decree regarding the companies of de-Judaized enterprises."

April 25, 1941: *Fünfte Verordnung zur Durchführung der Verordnung über den Einsatz des jüdischen Vermögens,* "Fifth decree to implement the decree regarding the utilization of Jewish property."

April 25, 1941: *Verordnung über die Neugestaltung der Reichshauptstadt Berlin und der Hauptstadt der Bewegung München,* "Decree regarding the reorganization of the state capital, Berlin, and the capital of the [Nazi] movement, Munich."

May 6, 1941: *Verfahrensanordnung der Reichskammer der bildenden Künste als Ankaufsstelle für Kulturgut,* "Procedural order for the state chamber for the graphic arts as an acquisition point for cultural assets."

May 29, 1941: *Erlass des Führers und Reichskanzlers über die Verwertung des eingezogenen Vermögens von reichsfeinden,* "Ordinance of the Führer and Chancellor regarding the utilization of the seized property of enemies of the state."

May 31, 1941: *Zweite Verordnung zur Ausführung des Gesetzes zum Schutz des deutschen Blutes und der deutschen Ehre,* "Second decree to implement the law for the protection of German blood and German honor."

July 20, 1941: *Verordnung des Reichsministers des Innern über die Behandlung der Kriegsschäden von Juden,* "Decree of the interior minister regarding the treatment of war damages of Jews."

September 1, 1941: *Polizeiverordnung über die Kennzeichnung der Juden,* "Police decree regarding identification badges for Jews."

September 1, 1941: *Zweite Verordnung über die Neugestaltung der Reichshauptstadt Berlin und der Hauptstadt der Bewegung München,* "Second decree regarding the reorganization of the state capital, Berlin, and the capital of the [Nazi] movement, Munich."

October 3, 1941: *Verordnung über die Beschäftigung von Juden,* "Decree regarding the employment of Jews."

October 31, 1941: *Verordnung zur Durchführung der Verordnung über die Beschäftigung von Juden,* "Ordinance supplementing the decree regarding the employment of Jews."

November 11, 1941: *Zweite Verordnung zur Durchführung der Verordnung über die Nachprüfung von Entjudungsgeschäften,* "Second decree to implement the decree regarding the verification of the de-Judaization of businesses."

November 25, 1941: *Elfte Verordnung zum Reichsbürgergesetz,* "Eleventh decree supplementing the state citizenship law."

December 4, 1941: *Verordnung über die Strafrechtspflege gegen Polen und Juden in den eingegliederten Ostgebieten,* "Decree regarding the application of the penal code to Jews and Poles in the incorporated Eastern Territories."

December 7, 1941: *Einkommenssteuer-durchführungsverordnung*, "Income tax implementation decree."

January 31, 1942: *Zweite Verordnung über die deutsche Volksliste und die deutsche Staatsangehörigkeit in den eingegliederten Ostgebieten*, "Second decree regarding the German nationality register and German citizenship in the incorporated Eastern Territories."

May 17, 1942: *Verordnung zur Ausführung des Gesetzes über den Schutz erwerbstätiger Mütter*, "Decree to implement the law regarding the protection of gainfully employed mothers."

June 12, 1942: *Dritte Verordnung über die Neugestaltung der Reichshauptstadt Berlin und die Hauptstadt der Bewegung München*, "Third decree regarding the reorganization of the state capital, Berlin, and the capital of the [Nazi] movement, Munich."

August 22, 1942: *Sechste Verordnung zur Durchführung der Verordnung über den Einsatz des jüdischen Vermögens*, "Sixth decree to implement the decree regarding the utilization of Jewish property."

September 25, 1942: *Dritte Durchführungsverordnung zum Gesetz über die Rechtsverhältnisse der jüdischen Kultusvereinigungen*, "Third implementation decree to the law regarding the legal status of Jewish religious associations."

April 25, 1943: *Zwölfte Verordnung zum Reichsbürgergesetz*, "Twelfth decree supplementing the state citizenship law."

July 1, 1943: *Dreizehnte Verordnung zum Reichsbürgergesetz*, "Thirteenth decree supplementing the state citizenship law."

September 1, 1944: *Verordnung zur Durchführung der Dreizehnten Verordnung zum Reichsbürgergesetz*, "Ordinance to implement the thirteenth decree supplementing the state citizenship law."

Source: *Reichsgesetzblatt*, Berlin: 1933-1945.

Danzig[1]

July 22, 1939: *Verordnung betr. die Entjudung der Danziger Wirtschaft und des Danziger Grundbesitzes*, "Decree concerning the dejudaizing of the Danzig economy and Danzig real estate."

August 24, 1939: *Verordnung über die Einsetzung von Staatskommissaren bei lebenswichtigen Unternehmungen*, "Decree regarding the appointment of state commissioners at vital enterprises."

September 4, 1939: *Verordnung betr. die Beschlagnahme polnischen Vermögens in Danzig*, "Decree concerning the confiscation of Polish property in Danzig."

September 13, 1939: *Verordnung betr. das Schlachten von Tieren (Schächtverbot)*, "Decree concerning the slaughtering of animals (ban on ritual slaughter)."

September 18, 1939: *Verordnung über die Meldepflicht polnischer Staatsangehöriger*, "Decree regarding the registration of Polish nationals."

September 27, 1939: *Verordnung zur Ausführung der Verordnung über die Beschlagnahme polnischen Vermögens in Westpreussen*, "Decree to implement the decree regarding the confiscation of Polish property in West Prussia."

October 22, 1939: *Dritte Verordnung über die Beschlagnahme polnischen Vermögens in Westpreussen*, "Third decree regarding the

---

[1] Danzig laws are listed for the period before the city was incorporated into the Reich; thereafter, all German anti-Jewish laws came into force.

Verordnungsblatt
für die Zivilverwaltung
in den dem
Gauleiter Forster
als Chef der Zivilverwaltung
unterstellten besetzten Gebieten

Nr. 5	Ausgegeben Danzig, den 13. September	1939

Tag	Inhalt	Seite
13. 9. 1939	Verordnung betr. das Schlachten von Tieren (Schächtverbot)	15
13. 9. 1939	Verwaltungs-Verordnung betreffend Requisitionen	15

Bestellungen auf das Verordnungsblatt nimmt die unterzeichnete Geschäftsstelle entgegen.

Geschäftsstelle
für das Verordnungsblatt für die Zivilverwaltung
in den dem Gauleiter Forster als Chef der Zivilverwaltung
unterstellten besetzten Gebieten
Danzig, Neugarten 12/16.

7
Verordnung
betr. das Schlachten von Tieren (Schächtverbot).
Vom 13. September 1939.

Für die dem Gauleiter Forster als Chef der Zivilverwaltung unterstellten besetzten Gebiete verordne ich auf Grund des § 2 der Bekanntmachung vom 7. September 1939 (Verordnungsblatt S. 1) Folgendes:

§ 1

Warmblütige Tiere sind beim Schlachten vor Beginn der Blutentziehung vollständig zu betäuben.

§ 2

Wer dieser Verordnung zuwiderhandelt, wird mit Gefängnis bestraft.

§ 3

Diese Verordnung tritt mit der Verkündung in Kraft.

Danzig, den 13. September 1939.

Der Chef der Zivilverwaltung
Albert Forster
Gauleiter

8
Verwaltungs-Verordnung
betreffend Requisitionen.
Vom 13. September 1939.

Für die dem Gauleiter Forster als Chef der Zivilverwaltung unterstellten besetzten Gebiete verordne ich auf Grund der Bekanntmachung vom 7. September 1939 (Verordnungsblatt S. 1) folgendes:

Requisitionen jeder Art dürfen nur nach folgenden Grundsätzen vor sich gehen:
  a) Von deutschstämmiger Bevölkerung darf nur gegen bar gekauft werden,
  b) von polnischstämmiger Bevölkerung können unbedingt lebensnotwendige Gegenstände gegen Ausstellung eines Beitreibungsscheines requiriert werden.

First page of the Danzig *Verordnungsblatt* containing the anti-shechita law
Courtesy of the New York Public Library

confiscation of Polish property in West Prussia."

October 23, 1939: *Verordnung über Änderung von Familiennamen und vornamen in Westpreussen*, "Decree regarding change of family names and first names in West Prussia."

November 18, 1939: *Allgemeine Anordnung über die Sicherung jüdischen Vermögens*, "General order regarding the securing of Jewish property."

Source: *Verordnungsblatt des Reichsstatthalters in Danzig-Westpreussen*, Danzig: 1939.

3. Axis States

Bulgaria
January 23, 1941: *Zakon za zashtitata na natsiiata* (ZZN), "Law for the Defense of the Nation."

April 26, 1942: *Zakon Komisarstvo za evreiskite vuprosi* (KEV), "Law creating a Commissariat for Jewish Questions."

August 26, 1942: *Zakon za vuzlagane na Ministerskiia suvet du vzeme vsichki merki za urezhdane na evreiskiia vupros i svurzantine s nego vuprosi*, "Law to charge the Council of Ministers to take all measures for solving the Jewish question and matters connected with it."

October 25, 1942 : *Zakon za burzo urezhdane vuprosi v osvobodenite zemi*, "Law for the rapid settlement of urgent problems in the liberated territories."

Source: *Durzhaven Vestnik*, Sofia: 1941-1942.

Croatia
April 19, 1941: *Zakonska odredba broj 19182-1941 o sačuvanju hrvatske narodne imovine*, "Legal ordinance # 19182-1941 regulating the ownership of Croatian national property."

April 30, 1941: *Zakonska odredba broj XLV-68 Z. p. 1941. o rasnoj pripadnosti*, Legal ordinance # 45-68 of year 1941 appertaining to racial origins."

April 30, 1941: *Zakonska odredba broj XLIV-67-Z. p. 1941. o zaštiti arijske krvi i časti Hrvatskog naroda*, "Legal ordinance # 44-67 of year 1941 regarding the defense of Croatian blood and honor."

Source: *Zbornik zakona i naredaba Nezavisne Države Hrvatske*. Zagreb: 1941.

Hungary
May 18, 1938: *1938. évi XV. törvénycikk a társadalmi és a gazdasági élet egyensulyának hatályosabb biztositásáról*, "Law number 15 of 1938 for the more effective protection of social and economic balance" (first anti-Jewish Law).

March 11, 1939: *1939. évi II. törvénycikk a honvedelemröl*, "Law number 2 of 1939 on National Defense" (established Jewish forced labor).

March 27, 1939: *1939. évi IV. törvénycikk a zsidok közéleti és gazdasági térfoglalásának korlátozásáról*, "Law number 4 of 1939 concerning the restriction of the participation of Jews in public and economic life" (second anti-Jewish Law).

August 2, 1941: *1941. évi XV. törvénycikk a házassági jogról szóló 1894: XXXI. törvénycikk kiegészitéséröl és modositásáról, valamint az ezzel kapcsolatban szükséges fajvédelmi renelkezékröl*, "Law number 15 of 1941 supplementing and amending law number 31 of 1894 relating to marriage and to the necessary racial provisions relating thereto."

Source: R. Braham: *The Politics of Genocide*, New York: Columbia University Press, 1981.

Italy
June 10, 1938: *Il divieto di matrimoni di italiani e italiane con elementi appartenenti alle razze camite, e altre razze non ariane*, "The prohibi-

---

Zakonska odredba o rasnoj pripadnosti

Na prijedlog ministra unutarnjih poslova propisujem i proglašujem

ZAKONSKU ODREDBU
o rasnoj pripadnosti

Točka 1.

Arijskog porijetla je osoba, koja potječe od predaka. koji su pripadnici europske rasne zajednice ili koji potječu od potomaka te zajednice izvan Europe.

U koliko za stanovite službe ne postoje druge odredbe, arijsko se porijetlo dokazuje krsnim (rodnim) i vjenčanim listom predaka prvog i drugog koljena (roditelja te djedova i baka). Kod pripadnika islamske vjerske zajednice, koji ne mogu pridonijeti navedene isprave, potrebno je pismeno posvjedočenje dvojice vjerodostojnih svjedoka, koji su poznavali njihove predke, da medu njima nema osoba nearijskog porijetla.

U dvojbenim slučajevima donosi odluku ministarstvo unutarnjih poslova na prijedlog rasnopolitičkog povjerenstva.

Točka 2.

Osobe, koje pored arijskih predaka imaju jednog predka drugog koljena Židova ili drugog europskog nearijca po rasi izjednačuju se obzirom na sticanje državljanstva s osobama arijskog porijetla.

Osobe sa dva predka drugog koljena Židova po rasi takodjer mogu biti obzirom na državljanstvo izjednačene s osobama arijskog porijetla, u koliko to u točki 3. nije drugačije odredjeno.

— 109 —

Zaštita arijske krvi i časti Hrvatskog naroda

Na prijedlog ministra unutarnjih poslova propisujen i proglašujem

ZAKONSKU ODREDBU
o zaštiti arijske krvi i časti Hrvatskog naroda

Točka 1.

Brak Židova i inih osoba, koje nisu arijskog porijetl s osobama arijskog porijetla, je zabranjen. Isto tako j zabranjen brak osobe, koja pored arijskih predaka ima jednog predka drugog koljena po rasi Židova ili drugog europskog nearijca s osobom, koja je po rasi jednakog porijetla.

Koje osobe vrijede kao Židovi ili nearijci odredjuje zakonska odredba o rasnoj pripadnosti.

Točka 2.

Posebna dozvola za sklapanje braka potrebna je u slijedećim slučajevima:

1. za brak osobe sa dva predka drugog koljena Židova po rasi s osobom, koja imade jednog predka drugog koljena europskog nearijca po rasi, ili s osobom koja je arijskog porijetla;

2. za brak osobe, koja imade medju precima pripadnike drugih neeuropskih rasa s osobom isto takvog porijetla, ili s osobom, koja imade jednog ili dva predka drugog koljena Židova po rasi ili jednog predka drugog koljena Ciganina po rasi, ili s osobom arijskog porijetla;

— 113 —

The Croatian racial laws
Courtesy of the New York Public Library Slavic Division

---

tion of marriage of male and female Italians with those belonging to the Hamitic or other non-Aryan races."

September 5, 1938: *Provvedimenti per la difesa della razza nella scuola fascista,* "Provisions for the defense of the race in the Fascist school."

October 16, 1938: *Gli Ebrei esclusi dall'Insegnamento e dalle Scuole,* "The Jews are forbidden to teach in public schools."

November 15, 1938: *Integrazione e coordinamento in unico testo delle norme gia' enamate per la difesa della razza nella scuola Italiana,* "Integration and coordination of one test of the norms already set for the defense of the race in the Italian school."

November 17, 1938: *Provvedimenti per la difesa della razza Italiana,* "Provisions for the defense of the Italian race."

February 9, 1939: *Norme relative ai limiti di proprietà immobiliare e di attività industriale e commerciale per i cittadini Italiani di razza ebraica,* "Regulations relating to limitations on real estate and industrial and commercial activity of Italian citizens of the Jewish race."

June 29, 1939: *Disciplina dell'esercizio delle professioni da parte dei cittadini di razza ebraica,* "Regulations for the excersize of professions on the part of citizens of the Jewish race."

March 6, 1942: *Disposizioni sulla precettazione civile,* "Provisions for the civilian service."

January 4, 1944: *Nuove disposizioni concernenti i beni posseduti dai cittadini di razza ebraica (Decreto Legislativo del Duce)*, "New regulations concerning property belonging to citizens of the Hebrew race (legislative decrees of the Duce)."

Source: *Gazetta ufficiale d'Italia*, Rome/Sálo: 1938-1944.

Romania

January 22, 1938: *Decret-Lege Privitor la Revizuirea Cetăteniei*, "Decree-Law on the Revision of Citizenship."

October 6, 1940: *Decret-Lege au Fost Numiti Comisari de Românizare la Numeroase Intrepinderi Comerciales i Industriale*, "Decree-Law regarding the Assignment of Commissioners for Romanianization in numerous Commercial and Industrial Establishments."

October 7, 1940: *Trecerea Proprietătilor Rurale evreeşti în Patrimoniul Statului*, "Concerning the Transfer of all Jewish Rural Property to State Control" (amended on August 6, 1942, to transfer responsibility from the Ministry of the Interior to the CNR).

October 7, 1940: *Decret-Lege pentru Reglementarea Situaţiei evreilor in Invăţământ*, "Decree-Law for Regulating the Jews' Status in the Educational System" (instituted numerus nullus).

October 18, 1940: *Decret-Lege Privitor la Reglementarea drepturilor Avocaţilor evreei*, "Decree-Law on the regulation of the Rights of Jewish Lawyers."

January 20, 1941: *Taxelor Militare Datorate de evreei*, "Jewish Military Tax Decree."

November 14, 1941: *Decret-Lege pentru Reglementarea Situaţiei Avocaţilor din Bukovina de Nord şi Basarabia*, "Decree-Law Regarding the Status of [Jewish] Lawyers in Northern Bukovina and Bessarabia."

November 16, 1941: *Decret-Lege pentru Infiinţareaşi Organizarea Inspectoratului General al Taberelor şi Coloanelor de Muncă Obligatorie de Folos Ubştesc*, "Decree-Law Regarding the Establishment of a General Inspectorate for Compulsory Labor Camps and Colonies for Public Benefit."

December 1, 1941: *Decret-Lege Privitor Reglementarea Concesiunilor de Farmacii Aparţinând Evreilor*, "Decree-Law Regarding the Annulment of Licenses for Urban and Rural Pharmacies owned by Jews."

January 7, 1942: *Decret-Lege de Modificarea Legii de Reglementarea pe Timp de Război*, "Decree-Law Amending the Law for Labor Service in Wartime."

February 1, 1942: *Decret-Lege Bunurile Evreeşti Părăsite Administrarea Ler va fi Preluată de Către CNR*, "Decree Law Stating that Abandoned Jewish Property will be administered by the National Center for Romanianization."

March 12, 1942: *Decret-Lege Fiinţarea Unui Impozit Excepţional de Reintregire*, "Decree-Law Establishing an Exceptional Tax [on Jews] in Addition to the Reintegration Loan."

March 23, 1942: *Decret-Lege pentru Prelungirei Centratlor de Închiriere*, "Decree-Law on the Extension of Leases."

April 23, 1942: *Decret-Lege pentru Combatera Camuflajului Bunurilior Evreeşti*, "Decree-Law on Combating the Concealment of ownership of Jewish Property" (amended August 18, 1943).

August 23, 1942: *Decretul-Lege pentru evreii nu mal au dreptul să Angajeze personal de Servicu Creştin*, "Decree-Law that Jews may no longer employ Christian housekeepers" (amended September 14, 1942).

September 19, 1942: *Decret-Lege Aspura Instituirii pedepsei cu Moartea, pentru cei trimişi in Transnistria, care se intorc in ţară în mod fraudulos*, "Decree-Law instituting the death penalty for Jews sent to Transnistria who return to the country illegally."

November 12, 1942: *Decret-Lege pentru sancţionarea falsurilor Comise de evrei şi Străini sau în Folosul Lor*, "Decree-Law regarding the sanctions for infringements committed by Jews and foreigners or for their benefit."

March 5, 1943: *Decret-Lege pentru sanctionarea evreilor nesupuşi la chemare*, "Decree-Law regarding sanctions against Jews who have evaded forced labor."

May 3, 1943: *Decret-Lege Modificarea Legii asupra Organizării Naţunii*, "Decree-Law modifying the law on national [and territorial] organization" (new rules for forced-labor mobilization for Jews).

September 4, 1943: *Decret-Lege pentru Reglementarea Situaţiei Imobilelor preluate dela Centrul Naţional de Românizare*, "Decree-Law regarding the regulation of the status of buildings taken over from the National Center for Romanianization."

September 4, 1943: *Decret-Lege Modificarea Legii pentru Românizarea Personalului în Îtrepinderi*, "Decree-Law modifying the law regarding the Romanianization of personnel in enterprises" (instituted fines for Romanians hiring Jews).

September 25, 1943: *Decret-Lege Modificarea Legii pentru Românizarea Personalului în Îtrepinderi*, "Decree-Law modifying the law regarding the Romanianization of personnel in enterprises" (instituted quotas for non-Romanians employed by private companies).

Source: J. Ancel (ed.): *Documents Concerning the Fate of Romanian Jewry during the Holocaust*. New York: Klarsfeld Foundation, 1986, vol. 8.

Slovakia
April 24, 1939: *Vládne nariadenie ovylúčeni židov z verejných služieb*, "Government

decree regarding the exclusion of Jews from public service."

June 21, 1939: *Vládne nariadenie o úprave vojenskej povinnosti židov*, "Government decree regarding the regulation of military duty for Jews."

January 18, 1940: *Branný zákon Slovenskej republiky Snem Slovenskej republiky sa usniesol na tomto zákone*, "Military service law of the Slovak Republic."

May 29, 1940: *Nariadenie s mocou zákona o dočasnej úprave pracovnej povinnosti Židov a Cigánov*, "Decree with legal force regarding preliminary regulation of the work obligation for Jews and Gypsies."

June 5, 1940: *Nariadenie s mocou zákona o daňových úlavách na opravy domov*, "Proclamation with legal force prohibiting the employment of Christian persons in Jewish households."

June 19, 1940: *Nariadenie s mocou zákona o zákaze rituálnych porážok a o povinnosti omračovat niektoré zvieratá pred zabitim*, "Decree with legal force regarding the prohibition of ritual slaughter and regarding the obligation of marking of certain animals before slaughter."

July 4, 1940: *Zákon o dočasnej úprave exekúcií a konkurzov, zavedených na návrh židov*, "Law regarding the preliminary regulation of the proposition for initiating and enforcing Jewish insolvency."

August 30, 1940: *Nariadenie s mocou zákona o súpise židovského majetku*, "Decree with legal force regarding the seizure of Jewish capital."

August 30, 1940: *Nariadenie s mocou zákona o úprave niektorých právnych pomerov Židov vo veciach školstva a vzdelania*, "Decree with legal force regarding the regulation of certain legal positions of Jews in regard to the educational system and education."

September 3, 1940: *Ústavný zákon ktorým sa*

643

Slovenský zákonník

Čiastka 52. Vydaná dňa 10. septembra 1941. **Ročník 1941**

OBSAH: **198.** Nariadenie o právnom postavení Židov.

198.
**Nariadenie
zo dňa 9. septembra 1941**
o právnom postavení Židov.

Vláda Slovenskej republiky podľa § 1 zákona č. 210 1940 Sl. z. nariaďuje:

VŠEOBECNÉ USTANOVENIA.

Vymedzenie pojmu.

§ 1.

(¹) Za Žida podľa tohto nariadenia sa bez ohľadu na pohlavie pokladá:
a) kto pochádza najmenej od troch podľa rasy židovských starých rodičov;
b) židovský miešanec, ktorý pochádza od dvoch podľa rasy židovských starých rodičov [§ 2, písm. a)], ak
1. dňa 20. apríla 1939 bol alebo po tomto dni sa stal príslušníkom izraelitského (židovského) vyznania,
2. po 20. apríli 1939 vstúpil do manželstva so Židom [písm. a)],
3. pochádza z manželstva so Židom [písm. a)], uzavretého po 20. apríli 1939,
4. pochádza z nemanželského styku so Židom [písm. a)] a narodil sa ako nemanželské dieťa po 20. februári 1940.
(²) Za židovského starého rodiča podľa rasy v smysle ustanovení tohto nariadenia má sa pokladať ten, kto patril k izraelitskému (židovskému) vyznaniu.

§ 2.

Za židovského miešanca podľa tohto nariadenia sa pokladá:
a) kto pochádza od dvoch podľa rasy židovských starých rodičov (§ 1, ods. 2], ak sa podľa § 1, písm. b) nepokladá za Žida,
b) kto pochádza od jedného podľa rasy židovského starého rodiča (§ 1, ods. 2].

§ 3.

(¹) Pokračujúce, poťažne na pokračovanie príslušné úrady, súdy a orgány ve-

Cena Ks 8.40.

rejnoprávnych korporácií a ustanovizní majú v prípadoch, v ktorých je to pre ich rozhodnutie (opatrenie a pod.) nevyhnutne potrebné, žiadať od strany potvrdenie o tom, že nie je Žid, poťažne židovský miešanec.
(²) Úrady, súdy a orgány (ods. 1), nemajú žiadať potvrdenie podľa ods. 1 v prípade, ak je im z predložených dokladov alebo inač známe, že strana nie je Žid, poťažne židovský miešanec.
(³) Potvrdenia podľa ods. 1 vydávajú obecné (obvodné) notárske úrady — v Bratislave Štátny matričný úrad — príslušné podľa bydliska.
(⁴) Pre osoby, ktoré nemajú na území Slovenskej republiky bydlisko, vydáva potvrdenie (ods. 1) Štátny matričný úrad v Bratislave.
(⁵) V pochybných prípadoch, či je niekto Žid, židovský miešanec, alebo nie, rozhoduje Ministerstvo vnútra. O rozhodnutie môže žiadať tak strana, ako aj úrad, súd alebo orgán verejnoprávnej korporácie, poťažne ustanovizne.
(⁶) Matričné výťahy potrebné pre vydanie potvrdenia podľa ods. 1, výslovne na ten cieľ vydané a ako také označené, nepodliehajú kolkom ani poplatkom. Výšku odmeny, ktorú sú oprávnení vyberať cirkevní matrikári za tieto výťahy, určí minister vnútra vyhláškou.

§ 4.

Za židovské sdruženie podľa tohto nariadenia treba považovať:
a) verejnú obchodnú spoločnosť, ak aspoň polovica spoločníkov sú Židia (židovské sdruženia) a súčasne ak aspoň polovica účasti na zisku spoločnosti patrí Židom (židovským sdruženiam).
b) komanditnú spoločnosť, ak aspoň polovica komanditistov a aspoň polovica verejných spoločníkov sú Židia (židovské sdruženia), alebo ak aspoň polovica účasti na zisku spoločnosti patrí Židom (židovským sdruženiam),

Židovsky Kodex
Courtesy of the New York Public Library Slavic Division

vláda splnomocňuje, aby čimila opatrenia vo veciach arizácie, "Amendment to the law that authorizes the government to concern itself with the disposition of aryanization matters."

September 3, 1940: *Zákon ovýkupe nehnutelnosti, na exekučnej dražbe Židmi*

kúpených, "Law regarding the acquisition of real estate arising from public sale of Jewish property."

September 12, 1940: *Nariadenie o vylúčeni Židov z oprávneni viest slovenské motorové vozidlá a o povinnosti Židov-držitelov slovenských motorových vozidiel mat vodiča motorového vozidla nežida*, "Decree regarding the exclusion of Jews from motor vehicle licenses and the obligation of Jewish motor vehicle owners to employ non-Jewish chauffeurs."

September 16, 1940: *Nariadenie o Ústrednom hospodárskom úrade*, "Decree regarding the central economic office."

September 16, 1940: *Nariadenie o zákaze zastupovania advokátom (verejným notárom) vo veciach arizačných*, "Decree regarding the prohibition for lawyers (and notary publics) to act as representatives in aryanization matters."

September 28, 1940: *Nariadenie ktorým sa obmedzuje volnost nakladat s majetkom Židov a židovských sdruženi*, "Decree regarding the restriction of the rights of ownership of Jews and Jewish organizations."

October 18, 1940: *Nariadenie o židovských viazaných účtoch a úschovách*, "Decree regarding Jewish bank accounts and safes."

November 30, 1940: *Nariadenie ktorým sa obmedzuje volnost nakladat s majetkom Židov*, "Decree regarding limitations on the rights of ownership of Jewish property."

November 30, 1940: *Nariadenie o povinnosti Židov vrátit zisk, nadobudnutý odpredajom nehnutelností, kúpených na exekučnej družbe*, "Decree by which Jews will be obligated to return profits that they gained through the sale of investments in real estate."

November 30, 1940: *Nariadenie o niektorých opatreniach v obore priamych daní, dane z obratu, dávky z majetku a prírastku na majetku a populatkov u židovských daňových a poplatkových subjektov*, "Decree regarding specific instructions regarding the sales, capital, and value-added taxes and the remission of fees by Jews liable for taxes and

payment of fees."

February 14, 1941: *Nariadenie o nútenom predaji lekárskych a zubotechnických nástrojov, pristrojov, zariadeni a pomôcok Židov*, "Decree regarding the compulsory sale of medical and dental instruments, equipment, and facilities temporarily belonging to Jews."

April 25, 1941: *Nariadenie o niektorých opatreniach v obore priamych daní u židovských daňových subjektov*, "Decree regarding specific instructions for the framework of the direct taxes by Jewish taxpayers."

June 25, 1941: *Vyhláška Ministrstva národnej obrany o zákaze cestovania do cudziny*, "Interior Ministry proclamation regarding the marking of Jewish residences."

August 21, 1941: *Nariadenie o zákaze prijimania nežidovských osôb do Židovských nemocnic a liečebných ústavov*, "Decree regarding the prohibition against admitting non-Jews in Jewish hospitals and sanatoriums."

September 9, 1941: *Nariadenie o mimoriadnej dávke zo židovského majetku*, "Decree regarding the extraordinary valuation of Jewish property."

September 9, 1941: *Nariadenie o právnom postaveni Židov (Židovský Kodex)*, "Law regarding the judicial status of the Jews (Jewish Codex)."

May 15, 1942: *Ústavný zákon o vystahovani Židov*, "Constitutional law regarding Jewish emigration."

July 2, 1942: *Zákon o obmedzeniach Židov pri osvojeni*, "Law regarding limitations on Jewish acquisitions."

July 13, 1942: *Vyhláška Ministra Financií o zaisteni dalšich hodnôt na úhradu mimoriadnej dávky zo židovského majetku*, "Notification of the Minister of Finance regarding the official memorandum on the reevaluation of Jewish property rights."

October 8, 1942: *Zákon o príroči pre pohladávky a nároky vočištátu, vzniklé prechodom židovského majetku na štát,* "Law regarding a moratorium on claims of debt owed by the state to Jews."

October 22, 1942: *Zákon o Hlinkovej slovenskej ludovej strane,* "Law regarding the Hlinka Slovak People's Party."

December 22, 1942: *Zákon ktorým sa mení zákon o príroči pre pohladávky a nároky voči štátu, vzniklé prechodom židovského majetku na štát,* "Law referring to the law regarding the legality of state use of Jewish property."

Source: *Slovenský Zákonník,* Bratislava: 1938-1942.

Vichy France

August 27, 1940: *Loi portant abrogation du décret-loi du 21 avril 1939, modifiant la loi du 29 juillet 1881 sur la liberté de la presse,* "Law repealing the executive order of April 21, 1939, altering the law of July 29, 1881, about freedom of the press."

September 10, 1940: *Loi prévoyant la nomination d'administrateurs provisoires des entreprises privées de leurs dirigeants,* "Law providing for the naming of temporary administrators as replacements for managers in private enterprises."

October 3, 1940: *Loi portant statut des Juifs,* "Law dealing with the statute on the Jews."

October 4, 1940: *Loi sur les ressortissants étrangers de race juive,* "Law regarding foreign nationals of the Jewish race."

October 7, 1940: *Loi portant abrogation du décret du Gouvernement de la défense nationale du 24 octobre 1870 et fixant le statut des Juifs indigènes des départements de l'Algérie,* "Law repealing the executive order of the government of national defense of October 24, 1870, and establishing the status of native Jews in Algerian departments."

October 11, 1940: *Loi portant suspension de la procédure instituée par les articles 3 à 11 de la loi du 4 février 1919 en ce qui concerne les Israélites indigènes de l'Algérie,* "Law suspending the procedure instituted by articles 3 through 11 of the law of February 4, 1919, concerning native Jews in Algeria."

November 16, 1940: *Loi portant réorganisation des corps municipaux,* "Law regarding the reorganization of municipal bodies."

November 17, 1940: *Loi relative á la surveillance des camps,* "Law relating to the supervision of camps."

November 20, 1940: *Décret portant statut des Juifs d'Algérie,* "Decree regarding the status of Algerian Jews."

December 26, 1940: *Décret portant règlement d'administration publique pour l'application de la loi du 3 octobre 1940 portant statut des Juifs,* "Decree regarding public administrative rules for the application of the law of October 3, 1940, regarding the statute on the Jews."

January 16, 1941: *Décret pour application de la loi du 10 septembre 1940 prévoyant la nomination d'administrateurs provisoires des entreprises privées de leurs dirigeants,* "Decree for the application of the law of September 10, 1940, providing for the naming of temporary administrators as replacements for managers in private enterprises."

January 18, 1941: *Loi instituant un stage obligatoire dans les chantiers de la jeunesse,* "Law initiating an obligatory period in youth camps."

February 2, 1941: *Loi relative aux pouvoirs des administrateurs provisoires des entreprises privées de leurs dirigeants,* "Law relating to the powers of temporary administrators replacing managers of private enterprises."

February 5, 1941: *Décret sur Radiodiffusion nationale,* "Decree on national radio broadcasting."

STATUT DES JUIFS

Généralités

Loi du 29 mars 1941 créant un commissariat général aux questions juives. (*J. O.*, 31 mars, n° 1450).

Art. 1er. — Il est créé, pour l'ensemble du territoire national, un commissariat général aux questions juives.

Art. 2. — Le commissaire général aux questions juives a pour mission :

1° De préparer et proposer au chef de l'Etat toutes mesures législatives relatives à l'état des juifs, à leur capacité politique, à leur aptitude juridique à exercer des fonctions, des emplois, des professions ;

2° De fixer, en tenant compte des besoins de l'économie nationale, à la date de la liquidation des biens juifs dans les cas où cette liquidation est prescrite par la loi ;

3° De désigner les administrateurs séquestres et de contrôler leur activité.

Art. 3. — Le commissaire général est désigné par arrêté du ministre secrétaire d'Etat chargé de la vice-présidence du conseil.

Loi du 19 mai 1941 modifiant l'art. 2 de la loi du 29 mars 1941 créant un commissariat général aux questions juives. (*J. O.*, 31 mars, n° 2169).

Art. 1er. — L'art 2 de la loi du 29 mars 1941 est modifié comme suit :

« Le commissaire général aux questions juives est chargé de :

« 1° Proposer au Gouvernement toutes dispositions législatives et réglementaires, ainsi que toutes mesures propres à mettre en œuvre les décisions de principe arrêtées par le Gouvernement relativement à l'état des juifs, à leur capacité civile et politique, à leur aptitude juridique à exercer des fonctions, des emplois, des professions ;

« 2° Assurer la coordination nécessaire entre les différents secrétariats d'Etat pour l'application de ces diverses dispositions et décisions, et suivre cette application ;

« 3° Pourvoir, en tenant compte des besoins de l'économie nationale, à la gestion et à la liquidation des biens juifs, dans les cas où ces opérations sont prescrites par la loi ;

« 4° Désigner les agents chargés desdites opérations et contrôler leur activité ;

« 5° Provoquer éventuellement à l'égard des juifs, et dans les limites fixées par les lois en vigueur, toutes mesures de police commandées par l'intérêt national ».

— 1 —

The Statut des Juifs

Courtesy of YIVO, the Yiddish Scientific Institute, New York

February 12, 1941: *Décret modifiant le décret du 20 novembre 1940 portant statut des Juifs d'Algérie*, "Decree altering the decree of November 20, 1940 regarding the status of Algerian Jews."

March 9, 1941: *Décret étendant aux colonies les dispositions du décret du 26 décembre 1940, pris pour l'application de la loi du 3 octobre 1940 portant statut des Juifs*, "Decree extending to the colonies the terms of the decree of December 26, 1940, to be used for the application of the law of October 3, 1940, regarding the statute on the Jews."

March 29, 1941: *Loi # 1.450 créant un Commissariat général aux questions juives*, "Law # 1,450 creating a General Commissariat for Jewish affairs" (Statut de Juifs).

April 3, 1941: *Loi # 1.499 modifiant ou complétant la loi du 3 octobre 1940 portant statut des Juifs*, "Law # 1,499 altering or completing the law of October 3, 1940, regarding the statute on the Jews."

April 11, 1941: *Loi # 1.594 modifiant et complétant la loi du 3 octobre 1940 portant statut des Juifs*, "Law # 1,594 altering and completing the law of October 3, 1940, regarding the statute on the Jews."

April 26, 1941: *Loi # 1.833 permettant le blocage de certains comptes en banque*, "Law # 1,833 permitting the blocking of certain bank accounts."

May 12, 1941: *Loi # 2.005 relative aux pensions des ouvriers des établissements militaires et industriels de l'Etat licenciés en vertu . . . de la loi du 3 octobre 1940 portant statut des Juifs*, "Law # 2,005 relating to pensions of workers in military and industrial establishments licensed by the state by virtue . . . of the law of October 3, 1940, regarding the statute on the Jews."

May 19, 1941: *Loi # 2.169 modifiant l'article 2 de la loi du 29 mars 1941 créant C.G.Q.J.*, "Law # 2,169 altering article 2 of the law of March 29, 1941, creating the C.G.Q.J."

June 1, 1941: *Loi # 2.181 interdisant la détention, l'achat et la vente d'armes et de munitions par les Juifs indigènes d'Algérie*, "Law # 2,181 forbidding the ownership, purchase, and sale of arms and ammunition by native Jews of Algeria."

June 2, 1941: *Loi # 2.332 remplaçant la loi du 3 octobre 1940 portant statut des Juifs*, "Law # 2,332 replacing the law of October 3, 1940, regarding the statute on the Jews."

June 2, 1941: *Loi # 2.333 prescrivant le recensement des Juifs*, "Law # 2,333 prescribing the census of Jews."

June 19, 1941: *Décret # 2.605 organisant les services du C.G.Q.J.*, "Decree # 2,605 organizing the services of the C.G.Q.J."

June 21, 1941: *Loi # 2.570 réglant les conditions d'admission des étudiants juifs dans les etablissements d'enseignement supérieur*, "Law # 2,570 regulating the conditions of admission of Jewish students to institutions of higher education."

June 28, 1941: *Décret # 2.778 modifiant l'article 7 du 20 novembre 1940 relatif au statut des Juifs d'Algérie*, "Decree # 2,778 altering article 7 of November 20, 1940, regarding the statute on the Jews of Algeria."

July 13, 1941: *Loi # 2.919 portant prolongation du délai prévu par la loi du 2 juin 1941 prescrivant le recensement des Juifs*, "Law # 2,919 prolonging the time provided by the law of June 2, 1941, prescribing the census of Jews."

July 16, 1941: *Décret # 2.956 réglementant, en ce qui concerne les Juifs, la profession d'avocat*, "Decree # 2,956 regulating the profession of attorney with respect to Jews."

July 16, 1941: *Décret # 2.957 réglementant, en ce qui concerne les Juifs, les fonctions d'officier public ou ministériel*, "Decree # 2,957 regulating the functions of public or ministerial officers with respect to Jews."

July 18, 1941: *Décret # 3.052 étendant à l'Algérie la loi du 2 juin 1941 prescrivant le recensement des Juifs*, "Decree # 3,052 extending to Algeria the law of June 2, 1941, prescribing the census of Jews."

July 22, 1941: *Loi # 3.086 relative aux*

entreprises, biens et valeurs appartenant aux Juifs, "Law # 3,086 relating to enterprises, goods, and securities belonging to Jews."

July 28, 1941: *Décret # 3.188 portant règlement d'administration publique pour l'application de l'article 5 de la loi du 2 juin 1941 portant statut des Juifs,* "Decree # 3,188 regarding public regulations for the application of article 5 of the law of June 2, 1941, regarding the statute on the Jews."

August 11, 1941: *Décret # 3.474 réglementant, en ce qui concerne les Juifs, la profession de médecin,* "Decree # 3,474 regulating profession of physicians with respect to Jews."

August 14, 1941: *Loi # 3.462 modifiant la loi du 10 septembre 1940 prévoyant la nomination d'administrateurs provisoires des entreprises privées de leurs dirigeants,* "Law # 3,462 altering the law of September 10, 1940, providing for the naming of temporary administrators as replacements for managers in private enterprises."

August 14, 1941: *Décret # 3.475 fixant le délai prévu par l'article 3 du décret du 28 juillet 1941 portant règlement d'administration publique pour l'application de l'article 5 de la loi du 2 juin 1941 portant statut des Juifs,* "Decree # 3,475 determining the period provided by article 3 of the decree of July 28, 1941, regarding public regulations for the application of article 5 of the law of June 2, 1941, regarding the statute on the Jews."

August 18, 1941: *Décret # 3.536 modifiant les dispositions du décret du 16 janvier 1941 portant application de la loi du 10 septembre 1940 prévoyant la nomination d'administrateurs provisoires des entreprises privées de leurs dirigeants,* "Decree # 3,536 altering the dispositions of the decree of January 16, 1941, regarding the application of the law of September 10, 1940, providing for the naming of temporary administrators as replacements for managers in private enterprises."

August 23, 1941: *Décret # 3.592 portant application à l'Algérie la loi du 21 juin 1941 réglant les conditions d'admission des étudiants juifs dans les etablissements d'enseignement supérieur,* "Decree # 3,592 regarding application to Algeria of the law of June 21, 1941, ruling on the conditions of admission of Jewish students into institutions of higher education."

September 1, 1941: *Loi # 3.591 portant modification de la loi du 29 mars 1941 créant C.G.Q.J.,* "Law # 3,591 regarding modification of the law of March 29, 1941, creating the C.G.Q.J."

September 13, 1941: *Décret # 3.938 étendant aux fonctionnaires tributaires de la caisse des retraites de l'Algérie certaines dispositions de la loi du 3 avril 1941 modifiant ou complétant la loi du 3 octobre 1940 portant statut des Juifs,* "Decree # 3,938 extending to civil servants contributing to the Algerian pension fund some regulations of the law of April 3, 1941, altering or completing the law of October 3, 1940, regarding the statute on the Jews."

September 14, 1941: *Loi # 3.981 portant statut général des fonctionnaires civils de l'Etat et des établissements publics de l'Etat,* "Law # 3,981 regarding the general status of civil servants of the state and of public establishments of the state."

September 24, 1941: *Décret # 4.133 réglementant en ce qui concerne les Juifs, la profession d'architecte,* "Decree # 4,133 regulating the profession of architect with respect to Jews."

October 20, 1941: *Décret # 4.448 portant règlement d'administration publique pour l'application en Algérie de l'article 5 de la loi 2 juin 1941 portant statut des Juifs,* "Decree # 4,448 regarding the ruling of the public administration for the application in Algeria of article 5 of the law of June 2, 1941, regarding the statute on the Jews."

October 20, 1941: *Décret # 4.428 modifiant le décret du 19 juin 1941 organisant les services du C.G.Q.J.,* "Decree # 4,428 altering the decree of June 19, 1941, organizing the services of the C.G.Q.J."

October 28, 1941: *Loi # 4.550 complétant l'article 2 de la loi du 4 octobre 1940 sur les ressortissants étrangers de race juive,* "Law # 4,550 completing article 2 of the law of October 4, 1940, regarding foreign nationals of the Jewish race."

November 2, 1941: *Loi # 4.268 interdisant toute acquisition de fonds de commerce par les Juifs sans autorisation,* "Law # 4,268 prohibiting to Jews all acquisition of commercial funds without authorization."

November 5, 1941: *Décret # 4.630 réglementant en ce qui concerne les Juifs, la profession d'avocat en Algérie,* "Decree # 4,630 regulating the profession of attorney in Algeria with respect to Jews."

November 5, 1941: *Décret # 4.631 réglementant en ce qui concerne les Juifs, la profession d'médecin en Algérie,* "Decree # 4,631 regulating the profession of physician in Algeria with respect to Jews."

November 5, 1941: *Décret # 4.631 fixant les conditions d'admission des étudiants juifs dans les établissements d'enseignement supérieur en Algérie,* "Decree # 4,631 determining the conditions of admission for Jewish students in institutions of higher education in Algeria."

November 13, 1941: *Loi # 4.769 rendant applicables aux colonies les lois du 2 juin 1941 portant statut des Juifs et préservant l'recensement des Juifs,* "Law # 4,769 making applicable to the colonies the laws of June 2, 1941, regarding the statute on the Jews and the census of Jews."

November 17, 1941: *Loi # 4.865 modifiant la loi du 22 juilliet 1941 relative aux entreprises, biens et valeurs appartenant aux Juifs,* "Law # 4,865 altering the law of July 22, 1941, relative to enterprises, goods, and securities belonging to Jews."

November 17, 1941: *Loi # 4.866 modifiant la loi du 2 juin 1941 portant statut des Juifs,* "Law # 4,866 altering the law of June 2, 1941, regarding the statute on the Jews."

November 19, 1941: *Décret # 5.062 relatif aux personnels en service outremer visés par l'article 7 de la loi du 2 juin 1941 portant statut des Juifs,* "Decree # 5,062 relating to personnel in foreign service referred to by article 7 of the law of June 2, 1941, regarding the statute on the Jews."

November 25, 1941: *Loi # 4.978 sur le Jury,* "Law # 4,978 on the jury" (Jews cannot serve on juries).

November 29, 1941: *Décret # 5.004 réglementant, en ce qui concerne les Juives la profession de sage-femme en Algérie,* "Decree # 5,004 regulating the profession of midwife in Algeria with respect to Jews."

November 29, 1941: *Loi # 5.047 instituant une Union générale des Israélites de France,* "Law # 5,047 instituting a General Union of Jews in France."

December 2, 1941: *Décret # 5.069 déférant aux tribunaux militaires et aux commissions disciplinaires les Juifs indigènes des territoires du Sud de l'Algérie,* "Decree # 5,069 assigning to the military tribunals and to disciplinary commissions the native Jews of the South Algerian territories."

December 17, 1941: *Loi # 4.668 modifiant l'article 2 de la loi du 2 juin 1941 relative au statut des Juifs,* "Law # 4,668 altering article 2 of the law of June 2, 1941, relating to the statute on the Jews."

December 19, 1941: *Loi # 5.275 modifiant les articles 2 et 3 de la loi du 21 juin 1941 réglant les conditions d'admission des étudiants juifs dans les établissements d'enseignement supérieur,* "Law # 5,275 altering articles 2 and 3 of the law of June 21, 1941, regulating the conditions of admission for Jewish students to institutions of higher education."

December 26, 1941: *Décret # 5.338 réglementant, en ce qui concerne les Juives la profession de sage-femme,* "Decree # 5,338 regulating the profession of midwife with respect to Jews."

December 26, 1941: *Décret # 5.339 réglementant, en ce qui concerne les Juifs la profession de pharmacien,* "Decree # 5,339 regulating the profession of pharmacist with respect to Jews."

December 31, 1941: *Loi # 5.535 relative à l'enseignement privé juif en Algérie,* "Law # 5,535 relative to Jewish private education in Algeria."

January 16, 1942: *Loi # 141 accordant à l'U.G.I.F. la faculté d'emprunt dans la limite d'une somme de 250 millions de francs,* "Law # 141 granting to the U.G.I.F. the power to borrow up to the limit of 250 million francs."

January 26, 1942: *Décret # 234 pris pour l'application de l'article 10 de la loi du 2 juin 1941 portant statut des Juifs (conditions de la réintégration en cas de dérogation aux interdictions),* "Decree # 234 taken for the application of article 10 of the law of June 2, 1941 regarding the statute on the Jews (conditions of reintegration in case of annulment of prohibitions)."

February 3, 1942: *Décret # 279 relatif à la réglementation, en ce qui concerne les Juifs de l'exercise de la profession d'officier ministériel en Algérie,* "Decree # 279 regulating the profession of ministerial officer in Algeria with respect to Jews."

February 3, 1942: *Décret # 356 portant réglement d'administration publique pour l'application de l'article 7 de la loi du 2 juin 1941 portant statut des Juifs (durée de perception du traitement après cessation de fonction),* "Decree # 356 regarding the public administrative ruling on the application of article 7 of the law of June 2, 1941, regarding the statute on the Jews (the duration of receipt of salary after the suspension of function)."

February 7, 1942: *Décret # 348 fixant, en ce qui concerne les colonies, les conditions d'application de l'article 2 de la loi du 17 novembre 1941 sur les Juifs,* "Decree # 348 determining the conditions of application with respect to the colonies of article 2 of the law of November 17, 1941, about the Jews."

February 10, 1942: *Loi # 280 relative aux changements de noms, à la révision de certains changements de noms, et à la réglementation des pseudonymes,* "Law # 280 relative to name changes, reviewing of certain name changes, and to the regulation of pseudonyms."

February 14, 1942: *Décret # 450 portant création Union générale des Israélites d'Algérie,* "Decree # 450 regarding the creation of a General Union of Jews of Algeria."

February 18, 1942: *Loi # 254 fixant le statut des Juifs indigènes d'Algérie et abrogeant les lois des 7 et 11 octobre 1940,* "Law # 254 determining the status of native Algerian Jews and abrogating the laws of October 7 and 11, 1940."

February 20, 1942: *Décret # 511 portant réglement d'administration publique pour l'application de l'article 7 de la loi du 2 juin 1941 portant statut des Juifs, concernant les fonctionnaires tributaires de la caisse intercoloniale de retraites,* "Decree # 511 regarding the ruling of the public administration on the application of article 7 of the law of June 2, 1941, regarding the statute on the Jews, concerning civil servants who contribute to the intercolonial pension fund."

February 24, 1942: *Décret # 588 portant application aux colonies de la loi du 21 juin 1941 réglant les conditions d'admission des étudiants Juifs dans les établissements d'enseignement supérieur, telle qu'elle a été modifiée par la loi du 19 décembre 1941,* "Decree # 588 regarding the application of the law of June 21, 1941, to the colonies, regulating admission conditions for Jewish students into institutes of higher education as modified by the law of December

19, 1941."

February 26, 1942: *Décret # 164 fixant les conditions du transfert à l'U.G.I.F. des biens des associations juives dissoutes par la loi du 29 novembre 1941*, "Decree # 164 determining the conditions of transfer to the U.G.I.F. of property of Jewish associations dissolved by the law of November 29, 1941."

March 5, 1942: *Décret # 687 relatif à l'acquisition de fonds de commerce par les Juifs (application aux colonies de la loi du 2 novembre 1941)*, "Decree # 687 relative to the acquisition of commercial funds by Jews (application to the colonies of the law of November 2, 1941)."

March 21, 1942: *Loi # 415 relative à l'U.G.I.F. (ressources)*, "Law # 415 relating to the U.G.I.F. (resources)."

April 12, 1942: *Décret # 1.126 réglementant aux colonies, en ce qui concerne les Juifs, la profession d'avocat et les fonctions d'officier public ou ministériel*, "Decree # 1,126 regulating the profession of lawyer and the functions public or ministerial officer in the colonies with respect to Jews."

April 17, 1942: *Décret # 1.206 fixant les conditions d'application, en Algérie, de l'article 2 de la loi du 17 novembre 1941 modifiant l'article 5 de la loi du 2 juin 1941 portant statut des Juifs*, "Decree # 1,206 determining the conditions of application, in Algeria, of article 2 of the law of November 17, 1941, altering article 5 of the law of June 2, 1941 regarding the statute on the Jews."

May 6, 1942: *Loi # 545 modifiant la loi du 29 mars 1941 créant C.G.Q.J.*, "Law # 545 altering the law of March 29, 1941, creating the C.G.Q.J."

May 6, 1942: *Décret # 1.366 nommant M. Monier secrétaire général aux questions juives*, "Decree # 1,366 naming M. Monier secretary-general for Jewish affairs."

June 5, 1942: *Décret # 1.631 réglementant, en ce qui concerne les Juifs, la profession dentaire*, "Decree # 1,631 regulating the profession of dentist with respect to Jews."

June 6, 1942: *Décret # 1.301 réglementant, en ce qui concerne les Juifs, la professions d'artiste dramatique, cinématographique ou lyrique*, "Decree # 1,301 regulating the dramatic arts, cinematographic, and musical professions with respect to Jews."

June 30, 1942: *Loi # 651 relative aux délais de surenchère en matière de ventes de biens appartenant à des Juifs*, "Law # 651 relative to delays in bidding in matters of the sale of goods belonging to Jews."

July 2, 1942: *Loi # 648 interdisant aux Juifs d'exploiter en Algérie des débits de boissons*, "Law # 648 prohibiting Jews from engaging in the sales of beverages in Algeria."

July 15, 1942: *Loi # 687 modifiant l'article 1 de la loi du 18 janvier 1941 instituant un stage obligatoire dans les chantiers de la jeunesse*, "Law # 687 altering article 1 of the law of January 18, 1941, instituting an obligatory period in youth camps."

August 10, 1942: *Loi # 767 réprimant l'évasion des internés administratifs et la complicité en matière d'évasion*, "Law # 767 preventing the escape of administrative internees and complicity in matters of escape."

September 11, 1942: *Loi # 865 interdisant aux Juifs l'exercice de certaines fonctions, en Algérie, outre les fonctions prévues à l'article 2 de la loi du 2 juin 1941 portant statut des Juifs*, "Law # 865 forbidding Jews the practice of certain occupations, in Algeria, in addition to those listed in article 2 of the law of June 2, 1941, regarding the statute on the Jews."

October 19, 1942: *Loi # 911 fixant, en Algérie, les conditions d'admission des élèves juifs dans les établissements publics d'enseignement autres que les établissements d'enseignement supérieur,*

"Law # 911 determining in Algeria admission conditions for Jewish pupils into public educational institutions other than institutions of higher education."

October 19, 1942: *Loi # 931 portant modification des articles 4 et 6 de la loi du 18 février 1942 fixant le statut des Juifs indigènes d'Algérie*, "Law # 931 regarding the alteration of articles 4 and 6 of the law of February 18, 1942, determining the status of native Jews of Algeria."

November 9, 1942: *Loi # 979 relative au séjour et à la circulation des Juifs étrangers*, "Law # 979 relating to the residence and movement of foreign Jews."

December 3, 1942: *Loi # 1.063 modifiant la loi du 10 août 1942 réprimant l'évasion des internés administratifs et la complicité en matière d'évasion*, "Law # 1,063 altering the law of August 10, 1942, preventing the escape of administrative internees and complicity in matters of escape."

December 11, 1942: *Loi # 1.077 relative à l'apposition de la mention "Juif" sur les titres d'identité délivrés aux Israélites français et étrangers*, "Law # 1,077 relating to putting the word of 'Jew' on identity documents issued to French and foreign Israelites."

June 25, 1943: *Loi # 366 modifiant les articles 4, 5 et 13 de la loi du 22 juillet 1941 relative aux entreprises, biens et valeurs appartenant aux Juifs*, "Law # 366 altering articles 4, 5, and 13 of the law of July 22, 1941, relative to enterprises, goods, and securities belonging to Jews."

June 28, 1943: *Loi # 356 prorogeant le délai prévu à l'article 1 de la loi du 17 novembre 1941, modifiant celle du 22 juillet 1941 relative aux entreprises, biens et valeurs appartenant aux Juifs*, "Law # 356 prolonging the anticipated time period in article 1 of the law of November 17, 1941, altering the law of July 22, 1941, relative to enter-

prises, goods, and securities belonging to Jews."

March 23, 1944: *Loi # 172 relative au fonds de solidarité destiné à venir en aide aux Juifs indigents*, "Law # 172 relative to solidarity funds destined for the subvention of Jews in need."

June 5, 1944: *Décret # 1.477 relatif au traitement du Commissaire général aux questions juives et du Secrétaire général aux question juives*, "Decree # 1,477 relative to the salary of the general commissioner for Jewish affairs and of the secretary-general for Jewish Affairs."

Source: *Journal Officiel de l'Etat français*, Paris/Vichy, 1940-1944.

4. Nazi-occupied Europe

Belgium

May 20, 1940: *Verordnung über die ordnungsmässige Geschäftsführung und Verwaltung von Unternehmungen und Betrieben in den besetzten Gebieten der Niederlande, Belgiens, Luxemburgs und Frankreichs*, "Decree regarding the orderly management of business and administration of enterprises and professions in the occupied territories of Holland, Belgium, Luxembourg, and France."

October 28, 1940: *Verordnung über Massnahmen gegen Juden*, "Decree regarding measures undertaken against Jews" (1. Jews who had fled from Belgium were forbidden to return; 2. Jews had to report their presence in Belgium and thereby establish a register of Jews; 3. All Jewish undertakings had to be reported; 4. Jews were forbidden to establish new businesses and had to mark all shops that belonged to them as Jewish owned).

October 28, 1940: *Zweite Verordnung über das Ausscheiden von Juden aus Ämtern und Stellungen*, "Second decree regarding the exclusion of Jews from offices and professional positions."

May 31, 1941: *Verordnung zur Ergänzung der*

Juden-Verordnung, "Decree to supplement the Jew decree."

August 29, 1941: *Verordnung über Aufenthaltsbeschränkungen von Juden*, "Decree regarding residential limitation of Jews."

November 14, 1941: *Polizeiverordnung des Feldkommandanten in Lille über Massnahmen gegen Juden für den Bereich der Stadt Lille*, "Police decree of the field commandant in Lille regarding measures undertaken against Jews for the area of the city of Lille" (forbade Jews: 1. to frequent public inns; 2. to utilize public parks; 3. to frequent public bathhouses).

November 25, 1941: *Verordnung über die Errichtung einer Vereinigung der Juden in Belgien*, "Decree regarding the establishment of an Association of Jews in Belgium."

December 1, 1941: *Verordnung über das jüdische Schulwesen*, "Decree regarding the Jewish school system."

Besetzte Ostgebiete
August 13, 1941: *Zeitweilige Richtlinien für die Behandlung der Juden in Gebiet des Reichskommissariats Ostland*, "Provisional instructions for the treatment of the Jews in the Reichskommissariat Ostland."

Eingegliederte Ostgebiete
November 1, 1939: *Erlass über die Gliederung und Verwaltung der (eingegliederten) Ostgebiete*, "Ordinance regarding the organization and administration of the (incorporated) Eastern Territories."

France
May 20, 1940: *Verordnung über die ordnungsmässige Geschäftsführung und Verwaltung von Unternehmungen und Betrieben in den besetzten Gebieten der Niederlande, Belgiens, Luxemburgs und Frankreichs*, "Decree regarding the orderly management of business and administration of enterprises and professions in the occupied territories of Holland, Belgium, Luxembourg, and France."

September 27, 1940: *Verordnung über Massnahmen gegen Juden*, "Decree regarding measures undertaken against Jews" (included: 1. definition of who was a Jew; 2. Jews were forbidden to leave the occupied zone; 3. all Jews had to register with the Police Prefecture by October 20, 1940; 4. Jewish-owned shops had to put up signs by October 31, 1940, identifying them as such; 5. Jewish community leaders had to obey all instructions given by the authorities in charge and had to keep the authorities informed of any changes within the Jewish community).

October 18, 1940: *Zweite Verordnung über Massnahmen gegen Juden*, "Second decree regarding measures undertaken against Jews" (decree dealt with economic undertakings).

April 26, 1941: *Dritte Verordnung über Massnahmen gegen Juden*, "Third decree regarding measures undertaken against Jews" (decree dealt with definition of who is a Jew).

May 28, 1941: *Vierte Verordnung über Massnahmen gegen Juden*, "Fourth decree regarding measures undertaken against Jews."

September 28, 1941: *Fünfte Verordnung über Massnahmen gegen Juden*, "Fifth decree regarding measures undertaken against Jews."

December 17, 1941: *Verordnung über eine Geldbusse der Juden*, "Decree regarding a monetary fine for Jews."

February 7, 1942: *Sechste Verordnung über Massnahmen gegen Juden*, "Sixth decree regarding measures undertaken against Jews."

March 24, 1942: *Siebente Verordnung über Massnahmen gegen Juden*, "Seventh decree regarding measures undertaken against Jews" (based on third decree, further defining who is a Jew).

May 29, 1942: *Achte Verordnung über Massnahmen gegen Juden*, "Eighth decree regarding measures undertaken against Jews" (decree imposed the Jewish badge on all Jews, from six years old).

July 8, 1942: *Neunte Verordnung über Massnahmen gegen Juden,* "Ninth decree regarding measures undertaken against Jews" (decree stipulated that: 1. Jews were forbidden to frequent public institutions; 2. Jews had to limit shopping in pubic markets to the hours of 3 to 4 PM; 3. the exceptions to rule # 2 were shopping places marked for Jews only).

December 2, 1942: *Verordnung über den Verfall des Vermögens von Juden deutscher oder ehemals deutscher Staatsangehörigkeit zu Gunsten des deutschen Reiches,* "Decree regarding the forfeiture of property belonging to Jews of German or of former German nationality to the benefit of the German state."

September 15, 1943: *Verordnung über den Verfall des Vermögens von Juden, die Angehörige des ehemaligen polnischen Staates waren, zu Gunsten des Grossdeutschen Reiches,* "Decree regarding the forfeiture of property of Jews who were nationals of the former Polish state to the benefit of the greater German state."

September 15, 1943: *Verordnung über den Verfall des Vermögens von Juden, die Angehörige des Protektorat Böhmen und Mähren waren, zu Gunsten des Grossdeutschen Reiches,* "Decree regarding the forfeiture of property of Jews who were nationals of the Protectorate of Bohemia and Moravia to the benefit of the greater German state."

Source: *Trial of the Major War Criminals before the International Military Tribunal: The Official Text.* Nuremberg: USGPO, 1947-1949.

Generalgouvernement (Poland)
October 12, 1939: *Erlass der Führers über die Verwaltung der Besetzten polnischen Gebiete,* "Führer's decree regarding the administration of occupied Polish territory" (imposed German law on the Generalgouvernement, including the Nuremberg Laws).

October 26, 1939: *Verordnung über die Einführung der Arbeitspflicht für die polnische Bevölkerung des Generalgouvernements,* "Decree regarding the establishment of labor obligation for the Polish people in the General Government" (although the decree was not specifically anti-Jewish, Jews were included).

October 26, 1939: *Verordnung über die Einführung des Arbeitszwangs für die jüdische Bevölkerung des Generalgouvernements,* "Decree regarding the establishment of forced labor for Jews in the General Government."

October 26, 1939: *Verordnung über das Schächtverbot,* "Decree regarding the prohibition of Jewish ritual slaughter."

November 20, 1939: *Anordnung # 4 des Leiters der Abteilung Devisen im Amte des Generalgouvernements,* "Regulation # 4 of the director of the division of foreign exchange in the office of the General Government" (ordinance established control on Jewish bank accounts, real estate holdings, and other capital investments).

November 23, 1939: *Verordnung über die Kennzeichnung von Juden und Jüdinnen im Generalgouvernement,* "Decree regarding the identification badges of Jews and Jewesses in the General Government."

November 23, 1939: *Verordnung über die Aushebung der Steurbefreiung bei jüdischen Korporationen,* "Decree regarding the abolishment of tax exemptions of Jewish corporations" (also abolished other privileges for Jewish community councils).

November 23, 1939: *Verordnung über die Bezeichnung der Geschäfte im Generalgouvernement,* "Decree regarding the regulation of businesses in the General Government" (also provided for the marking of Jewish stores).

November 28, 1939: *Erlass über die Verwaltung*

Decree of October 28, 1942, for the creation of twelve ghettos in the General Government
Courtesy of YIVO, the Yiddish Scientific Institute, New York

der polnischen Gemeinden, "Ordinance regarding the administration of Polish communities."

November 28, 1939: *Verordnung über die Einsetzung von Judenräten*, "Decree regarding the appointment of Jewish councils" (amended January 20, 1940 to make *Judenräte* responsible for Jewish forced labor).

December 11, 1939: *Erste Durchführungsvorschrift zur Verordnung über die Einführung des Arbeitszwanges für die jüdische Bevölkerung des Generalgouvernements*, "First implementation provision to the decree regarding the initiation of forced labor for the Jewish population in the General Government"

(four riders were attached to this law: 1. registration of all Jews between the ages of 12 and 60 years old; 2. curfew — Jews barred from leaving their homes between 9 P.M. and 5 A.M. without obtaining special permission; 3. all Jews entering the General Government had to immediately report to the police; 4. all Jews residing in the General Government were forbidden to change their residencies without explicit permission of the proper authorities).

December 15, 1939: *Verordnung über die Beschlagnahme und Abgabe von Rundfunkgeräten*, "Decree regarding the confiscation and surrender of radios and wireless sets."

December 16, 1939: *Verordnung wegen Arbeits-*

losenhilfe in die Generalgouvernement, "Decree concerning the payment of unemployment relief in the General Government" (further modified on November 9, 1940, to bar Jews from getting such benefits).

December 20, 1939: *Verordnung über Unterstützungen am Militärentenempfänger des ehemaligen polnischen Staates und ihre Hinterbliebenen (Kriegsopferverordnung: Juden erhalten keine unterstützung),* "Decree regarding assistance to military beneficiary receivers of the former Polish state and their survivors (war victims decree: Jews receive no assistance)."

January 22, 1940: *Erste Durchführungsvorschrift zur Verordnung vom 15. November 1939 über die Errichtung einer Treuhandstelle für das Generalgouvernement,* "First implementation provision to the decree of November 15, 1939, regarding the establishment of a trust company for the General Government."

January 24, 1940: *Verordnung über die Beschlagnahme von privaten Vermögen in Generalgouvernement (Beschlagnahmverordnung),* "Decree regarding the confiscation of private capital in the General Government (confiscation decree)."

January 24, 1940: *Verordnung zur Änderung der Verordnung vom 15. November 1939 über die Errichtung einer Treuhandstelle für das Generalgouvernement,* "Decree to change the decree of November 15, 1939, regarding the establishment of a trust company for the General Government."

January 24, 1940: *Verordnung über die Pflicht zur Anmeldung jüdischen vermögens im Generalgouvernement,* "Decree regarding the duty of registration of Jewish property in the General Government" (subsidiary clauses canceled all debts owed to Jews and restricted Jewish real estate ownership).

January 24, 1940: *Verordnung über den*

Aufbau der Treuhandstelle für das Generalgouvernement, "Decree regarding the building of the trust company for the General Government."

January 26, 1940: *Verordnung über die Benutzung der Eisenbahn durch Juden in Generalgouvernement,* "Decree regarding the use of the railroad by Jews in the General Government."

February 19, 1940: *Zweite Verordnung über die kennzeichnung von Juden und Jüdinnen in Generalgouvernement,* "Second decree regarding the identification badges of Jews and Jewesses in the General Government."

March 1, 1940: *Anordnung # 6 des Leiters der Abteilung Devisen im Amt des Generalgouverneurs,* "Regulation # 6 of the director of the division of foreign exchange in the office of the General Governor."

March 1, 1940: *Anordnung # 7 des Leiters der Abteilung Devisen im Amt des Generalgouverneurs,* "Regulation # 7 of the director of the division of foreign exchange in the office of the General Governor" (regulated Jewish finances; forbade Jews to buy or sell gold or silver without special license).

March 7, 1940: *Zweite Verordnung über die Sozialversicherung im Generalgouvernement (Unterstützungen und Verfahren),* "Second decree regarding social security in the General Government (assistance and procedures)" (barred Jewish doctors from treating Aryan patients).

March 16, 1940: *Zweite Verordnung über den Aufbau der Abteilung Treuhandstelle für das Generalgouvernement,* "Second decree regarding the building of the trust company department for the General Government."

April 25, 1940: *Erste Durchführungsvorschrift zur Verordnung vom 28. November 1939 über die Einsetzung von Judenräten,* "First implementation provision to the decree of November 28, 1939, regarding the appointment of Jewish councils."

June 7, 1940: *Zweite Durchführungsvorschrift zur Verordnung vom 28. November 1939 über die Einsetzung von Judenräten,* "Second implementation provision to the decree of November 28, 1939, regarding the appointment of Jewish councils."

July 24, 1940: *Verordnung über die Bestimmung des Begriffs "Jude" im Generalgouvernement.* "Decree regarding the determination of the concept 'Jew' in the General Government" (further expanded Nuremberg racial laws in occupied Poland).

August 31, 1940: *Verordnung über ein Glucksspielmonopol im Generalgouvernement,* "Decree regarding a gambling monopoly in the General Government."

August 31, 1940: *Verordnung über das jüdische Schulwessen im Generalgouvernement,* "Decree regarding the Jewish school system in the General Government."

August 31, 1940: *Verordnung über die Behandlung feindlichen Vermögens,* "Decree regarding the treatment of enemy property."

September 19, 1940: *Verordnung über die Beschäftigung weiblicher Personen in jüdischen Haushalten,* "Decree regarding the employment of female persons in Jewish households."

September 24, 1940: *Verordnung über das Eigentum an dem Vermögen das früheren polnischen Staates,* "Decree regarding the ownership of property in the former Polish state" (article 22 of this decree detailed the ownership of property in the Protectorate of Bohemia and Moravia).

December 20, 1940: *Verordnung über die Einführung einer Arbeitskarte in Generalgouvernement,* "Decree regarding the introduction of work cards in the General Government" (Jews were to receive special work certificates).

February 20, 1941: *Verordnung über die*

Benutzung Öffentlicher Verkehrsmittel durch Juden im Generalgouvernement, "Decree regarding the use of public conveyances by Jews in the General Government."

April 19, 1941: *Erlass für die Nominierung ein Kommissar für den jüdischen Wohnbezirk,* "Ordinance for the nomination of a commissioner for the Jewish residential district."

April 19, 1941: *Verordnung über den jüdischen Wohnbezirk im Warschau,* "Decree regarding the Jewish residential district in Warsaw" (created a commission to oversee the Jewish ghettos and the *Treuhandstelle Ost*).

June 13, 1941: *Zweite verordnung über die Einführung von Kennkarten im Generalgouvernement,* "Second decree regarding the introduction of identification cards in the General Government."

September 12, 1941: *Verordnung über die Bewirtschaftung von Gold, sonstigen Edelmetallen, Edelsteinen, Perlen, sowie daraus gefertigten Waren,* "Decree regarding the control of gold, precious metals, precious stones, pearls, as well as products made from them" (article 8 barred sale of precious metals or jewels to Jews).

October 15, 1941: *Dritte verordnung über Aufenthaltsbeschränkungen im Generalgouvernement,* "Third decree regarding residence restrictions in the General Government" (also applied to Poles).

November 21, 1941: *Anordnung über die Einstellung der Beförderung von Päckchen und Paketen von jüdischen Auflieferern,* "Regulation regarding the stopping of shipment of parcels and packages from Jewish senders."

December 15, 1941: *Neunte Durchführungsverordnung zur Verordnung über die Arbeitsbedingungen und den Arbeitsschutz im Generalgouvernement,* "Ninth implementation decree to the decree regarding the working conditions and the worker protection in the General Government."

October 28, 1942: *Polizeiverordnung über die Bildung von Judenwohnbezirken in den Distrikten Warschau und Lublin*, "Police decree regarding the structure of the Jewish living quarters in the districts of Warsaw and Lublin."

Source: *Verordnungsblatt für das General-gouvernement*, Krakow: 1939-1942.

Holland
May 20, 1940: *Verordnung über die ordnungs-mässige Geschäftsführung und Verwaltung von Unternehmungen und Betrieben in den besetzten Gebieten der Niederlande, Belgiens, Luxemburgs und Frankreichs*, "Decree regarding the orderly management of business and administration of enterprises and professions in the occupied territories of Holland, Belgium, Luxembourg, and France."

July 30, 1940: *Verordnung zur Vermeidung von Tierquälerei beim Viehschlachten*, "Decree to avoid cruelty to animals during the slaughter of cattle."

September 13, 1940: *Verordnung zu recht-lichen und finanziellen Verhältnissen*, "Decree on legal and financial conditions."

June 28, 1942: *Polizeilicher Arbeitseinsatz-gesetz*, "Police labor deployment law."

Luxembourg
May 20, 1940: *Verordnung über die ordnungs-mässige Geschäftsführung und Verwaltung von Unternehmungen und Betrieben in den besetzten Gebieten der Niederlande, Belgiens, Luxemburgs und Frankreichs*, "Decree regarding the orderly management of business and administration of enterprises and professions in the occupied territories of Holland, Belgium, Luxembourg, and France."

Protectorate of Bohemia and Moravia
November 25, 1939: *Notdienstverordnung*, "Emergency labor decree."

September 19, 1941: *Polizeiverordnung über die Kennzeichnung der Juden*, "Police decree

regarding the marking of Jews."

Source: *Trial of the Major War Criminals before the International Military Tribunal: The Official Text*. Nuremberg: USGPO, 1947-1949.

Leibedike megila [לעבעדיקע מגילה, Y] "Lively scroll": Ghetto or camp term when Jews got a hold (by smuggling in a newspaper or other means) of news that was bad for the Germans, such as their being defeated on a battlefield or a big Allied air raid.

Leichen [G] "Corpses": Nazi term for the prisoners of Sonderkommando 1005. By order of their SS guards they were only referred to as *Leichen*. > see also: **Einstazgruppen, Subunits (Sonderkommando 1005).**

Leichenhalle [G] "Mortuary": The hall adjacent to the (old) Auschwitz crematorium where the Nazis experimented with killing by Zyklon B.

Leichenkeller [G] "Corpse cellar": One of many SS terms for the gas chambers and crematoria in Auschwitz-Birkenau.

Leichenkommando [G] "Corpse bearers": Nazi term for the prisoner detachment that was charged with removing the bodies from the gas chambers and transporting them to the crematorium, or with stacking them on huge pyres for burning. As a rule, the *Leichenkommando* was itself disposed of periodically, being replaced by some of the thousands of victims that arrived daily.

Leistungspolen [G] "Meritorious Poles": Nazi term for an exclusive group of Poles that could, in time, earn redemption and thus be spared the fate to come for other Poles.

Leon [PN]: Nom de guerre for Yitzhak Wittenberg, the commander of the Communist underground in the Vilna ghetto.

Libe zihcht a dire [ליבע זיכט א דירה, Y] "Love is looking for an apartment": A musical comedy written by J. Jurandot and performed in the Warsaw ghetto. The title contained more than a grain of truth. In actuality, ghetto life was much more bearable for a couple than for the single person.

Libels, Anti-Jewish

1. Scope and Definition

Over the centuries Jews have suffered from the deleterious impact of three anti-Jewish libels: (1) The blood libel, which claims that Jews use Christian blood to make wine for Kiddush (the ritual sanctification prayer before meals on Sabbath and holidays) or, more commonly, to bake *matzot* (unleavened bread) for Passover; (2) the ritual murder libel, which claims that before Easter, Jews re-create the crucifixion by ritually slaughtering a Christian child;

(3) the desecration of the Host libel, which claims that Jews seek to — or actually do — desecrate the wafer used in the transubstantiation rite, by stabbing it and drawing blood. During the Middle Ages any or all of these libels could be the cause for attacks upon individual Jews or — for instance, in York on March 17–18, 1190 — the martyrdom of entire Jewish communities. These libels have continued until modern times, with the last recorded major blood libel precipitating the Kielce Pogrom in Poland on July 4, 1946. Moreover, a fourth libel, that a Jewish shadow government seeks world dominion, has become a continuing motif in antisemitic rhetoric since the hoax was first propounded in 1911 in the *Protocols of the Elders of Zion*. > see also: **Antisemitismus**; **Pogrom**.

TABLE L.1: Notable Blood Libels

Date	Location	Date	Location
05/26/1171	Blois, France	03/12/1421	Vienna, Austria
03/14/1191	Bray, France	06/02/1453	Breslau, Germany
06/16/1221	Erfurt, Germany	06/23/1475	Trent, Italy
02/03/1235	Bischofsheim, Germany	07/04/1480	Venice, Italy
12/28/1235	Fulda, Germany	11/01/1504	Pilsen, Czechoslovakia
03/27/1247	Valréas, France	07/10/1510	Berlin, Germany
08/25/1255	Lincoln, England	05/25/1556	Sochaczev, Poland
04/02/1279	Rothampton, England	01/18/1670	Metz, France
03/29/1283	Mulrichstadt, Germany	02/05/1840	Damascus, Syria
04/19/1283	Mainz, Germany	04/04/1878	Sachkhere, Romania
10/12/1285	Munich, Germany	04/13/1891	Corfu, Greece
09/22/1287	Lahstein, Germany	06/29/1891	Xanten, Germany
04/24/1288	Troyes, France	04/01/1899	Polna, Czechoslovakia
08/21/1321	Chinon, France	03/28/1900	Konitz, Germany
03/05/1332	Überlingen, Germany	06/22/1911	Kiev, Ukraine
09/30/1337	Degendorf, Germany	08/17/1915	Atlanta, Georgia
04/26/1343	Germersheim, Germany	09/14/1928	Petrovo Selo, Yugos.
1/12/1349	Friedrichshafen, Germany	09/22/1928	Messina, New York

Source: S. Wiesenthal: *Every Day Remembrance Day*, New York: Henry Holt, 1987.

Liberation of Concentration Camps

1. Scope and Definition

Unlike the liberation by Allied armies of towns, cities, and villages of Nazi-occupied Europe, the liberation of the large number

of Nazi concentration camps and the hundreds of the smaller slave-labor camps was not an event of joyous celebrations and parties; rather it was an event of awesome shock for both the liberators and liberated. Allied soldiers entering the camps saw thousands of corpses scattered

U.S. Army doctor with survivors at Mauthausen, shortly after liberation
Courtesy of the Fred R. Crawford Witness to the Holocaust Project, Emory University

across the camps' perimeters, along with scores of other corpses and hundreds of dying, packed like sardines inside the barracks. The stench of the rotten flesh and the dying lying in their own excretion; the heavy soot blackening the skies from the still smoldering, partly burned bodies; the handful of survivors — half-naked skeletons — barely moving in their filthy, shredded uniforms. The visions in Dante's *Inferno* could not even come near to describe this hell on earth, built to near perfection at the cost of millions of lives during the twelve-year existence of the SS state.

Among the liberated were victims of every nationality: Poles, Czechs, French, Dutch, Belgians, Austrians, Germans, and Italians; different ethnic groups from Yugoslavia and the Soviet Union; individuals from neutral countries, Switzerland, Spain, and Sweden; American, Soviet, British, and British Commonwealth prisoners of war; Gypsies; and a handful of Jews.

Although the nominal official number of liberated concentration camp inmates was 219,595, only a proportion of them survived in the long term. Thus, in Dachau almost 40 percent of the liberated died within days of liberation. In Mauthausen 3,000 inmates died during the first week of liberation alone, although the numbers dropped off sharply thereafter. Figures for other camps were less dramatic but were similar. In Gusen, for example, 2,000 of the liberated died in the first week, but the figure dropped almost to zero one month later. Most of those who succumbed died of the aftereffects of disease, malnutrition, or exhaustion. > see also: **Konzentrationslager System; Displaced Persons, Jewish; Todesmärsche.**

TABLE L.2: Liberation of the Concentration Camps

Camp	Liberated by	Date	# Survivors
Auschwitz	Red Army	1/27/45	7,650
Bergen-Belsen	Royal Army	4/15/45	60,985
Buchenwald	U.S. Army	4/11/45	21,900
Dachau	U.S. Army	4/29/45	27,400

Dora	U.S. Army	4/09/45	handful
Ebensee	U.S. Army	5/06/45	3,500
Flossenburg	U.S. Army	4/23/45	2,000
Gross-Rosen (and *Nebenlager*)	Red Army	5/08/45	11,800
Gunskirchen	U.S. Army	5/04/45	18,000
Gusen	U.S. Army	5/05/45	20,000
Kaufering	U.S. Army	4/27/45	handful
Majadenek	Red Army	7/23/44	1,000
Mauthausen	U.S. Army	5/05/45	17,290
Neuengamme	Royal Army	4/29/45	handful
Ohrdruf	U.S. Army	4/04/45	handful
Oranienburg	Red Army	5/04/45	5,000
Ravensbrück	Red Army	4/30/45	3,500
Sachsenhausen	Red Army	4/27/45	3,000
Stutthof	Red Army	5/01/45	120
Terezin	Red Army	5/02/45	17,000

Source: Edelheit and Edelheit: *A World in Turmoil*, Westport, CT: Greenwood Press, 1991.

Lipa [Slang] Jewish underground term for forged Aryan papers that could mean the difference between life and death for Jews in Nazi occupied countries.

Lokshen [לאקשן, Y/Slang] "Noodles": Jewish term popular in Eastern Europe for U.S. dollars, especially gold coins that could be bartered for food, medicines, or other commodities.

Louse Promenade [G/Slang] "Lice promenade": term for the strip of hair left on a concentration camp prisoner's head after all other hair was removed. The pattern of hair was left on the prisoner's head as a means of identifying potential escapees.

Lublin Reservat [G] "Lublin Reservation": The Nazi plan dating to late 1939 or early 1940 to concentrate all European Jews in one locale, a reservation similar to those used in the United States to segregate Native Americans, in the Lublin-Nisko region of Galicia. The planned reservation did not come to fruition, as the Nazi hierarchy decided that the resources needed to transport Jews to Lublin, mostly railroad rolling stock, would be better used transporting Wehrmacht troops to the Western Front.

Lufthunnen [G] "Air barbarians": Derogatory term coined by Propaganda Minister Joseph Goebbels in 1944 after the massive air raids by Allied bomber crews. Goebbels conveniently forgot to mention that mass terror bombing was a Luftwaffe specialty during the early years of the war, when Germany was on the offensive.

Lügen und Geld die Waffen Des Judentums [G] "Lies and money are the Jews' weapon": Title of an elementary school curriculum introducing German youngsters to antisemitism.

Luxembourg Agreement(s): Reparations agreement signed on September 10, 1952, between Jewish representatives, most prominently Nahum Goldmann, and the government of the Federal Republic of Germany. The agreement culminated two years of direct negotiations and came after six years of Jewish advocacy of the return of heirless Jewish property and the payment of compensation to Holocaust survivors. The agreements do not speak of payment for those murdered by the Nazis — no amount of reparations could ever efface the guilt of their murderers — but grant a small stipend to those who suffered physical and mental losses due to Nazi imprisonment and other actions. > see also: **Wiedergutmachung**.

M

Machtergreifung [G] "Seizure of power": The Nazi assumption of power that took place on January 30, 1933. One of a number of related terms, *Machtergreifung* refers to the revolutionary element of the Nazis' apocalyptic revolution. > see also: **Machtübernahme**.

Machtübernahme [G] "Taking over of power": Refers to the gaining of power by Adolf Hitler through "legal" means and the installment of the NSDAP in the leadership position. > see also: **Machtergreifung**.

Madagaskar, Fall [G] "Madagascar Plan": Proposal for the expulsion of the European Jews to the island of Madagascar. During the interwar years, British, Dutch, and Polish antisemites all proposed expelling Jews to Madagascar. In 1937 the Poles even went as far as to send a commission to study the feasibility of mass Jewish immigration, but the proposal went no further. In 1940, with France only recently defeated, the Nazis turned to Madagascar as a possible dumping ground for European Jewry. The plan proved impractical because of the Reich's failure to conquer Great Britain and was abandoned. However, the abortive scheme helped to pave the way psychologically and organizationally for the *Endlösung*. > see also: **Lublin Reservat**.

Malá pevnost [Cz] "Small fortress": Czech term for the Terezin ghetto camp. > see also: **Das Kleine Festung**.

Malachei chabala [מלאכי חבלה, H] "Angels of destruction": Rabbinic term for the Gestapo, SS, or other Germans — either individuals or groups — who were responsible for massacres of Jews.

Malachi [מלאכי, PN]: Nom de guerre of Mordechai Anielewicz, overall commander of the ŻOB during the Warsaw ghetto uprising, based on the Hebraization of his last name. The name also has religious implications, referring to the biblical prophet Malachi. > see also: **Resistance, Jewish Underground Organizations (Poland)**.

Maquisards [Fr] "Maquis members": Popular French term for partisan fighters, regardless of their political orientation or military organization. > see also: **Resistance, Resistance Movements (France)**.

Max Heiliger [G] "Saintly Max": Nazi term for a special SS Reichsbank account ordered opened by Heinrich Himmler on September 23, 1940. According to this order, all valuables confiscated from Jews (foreign currencies, gold and silver items, and precious jewelry) and gold teeth removed from murdered victims would be deposited into the fictitious Max Heiliger account for the benefit of the SS.

Mayim [מים, H] "Water": Jewish inmate term for the watery soup fed to concentration camp inmates once a day, everyday. This pitiful soup became the mainstay of inmates, since it was their only source of nutrition. If an inmate's soup contained one or two pieces of potato peel, that was considered a luxury.

Me ne frego [I] "I don't care": Motto of the Squadristi that shows their utter contempt for all forms of authority, even that of the Partito Nazionale Fascista. > see also: **Fascism, Fascist Parties and Organizations (Italy, Squadristi)**.

Mechutonim [מחותנים, Y] "In-laws": Bitter Polish-Jewish term for the British Mandatory government that indirectly aided the Nazis by preventing Jews from entering Palestine. While Jews thought that the British accepted the League of Nations' Mandate in order to help build the Jewish National Home, they now discovered that Britain cared little for the victims of Nazism.

> see also: **White Paper of 1939**.

Medical Experiments

1. Scope and Definition

During World War II Nazi doctors conducted at least seventy distinct experimental medical projects on unwilling concentration camp inmates. Although exact figures are not available, it has been estimated that seven thousand persons were subjected to these medical experiments. Two broad categories of experiments may be discerned: (1) those whose objectives were compatible with medical practice but whose implementation violated the law, and (2) those whose purpose was irreconcilable with the accepted norms of medical research. The Nuremberg Trials, however, did not distinguish between these two forms, since it is clear that in gathering their research Nazi doctors did not follow the norms of moral scientific inquiry.

TABLE M.1: Nazi Medical Experiments in Concentration Camps

Experiment	Doctor	Camp	Victims
Castration	Clauberg	Auschwitz	thousands
Female genital organs	Clauberg	Auschwitz	400
Gangrene	Gebhardt	Ravensbrück	NA
High altitude	Ruff	Dachau	90
Mustard gas	Hirt	Natzweiler	NA
Phosgene	Bickenbach	Natzweiler	40
Pressure chamber	Rascher	Dachau	NA
Sterilization	Clauberg	Auschwitz	NA
Sulfanilamide	Gebhardt	Ravensbrück	74
Tuberculosis	Heissmeyer	Bullenhauser Dam	120
Twins	Mengele	Auschwitz	800
Typhus	Hoven	Buchenwald	NA
Uterus	Wirths	Auschwitz	NA

Source: Elie A. Cohen: *Human Behavior in the Concentration Camp*, New York: Norton, 1953.

Mihme mehr [מומע מער, Y] "Aunt more": Jewish term popular among victims in Nazi ghettos and camps of Eastern Europe for the United States. The term reflects a dualistic attitude toward America and American Jewry: East European Jews looked toward the United States for aid and

rescue but felt disappointed that more was not done to effect rescue on a mass scale.

Minus malum [Latin] "The lesser evil": Term coined by a number of clerical apologists (including Josef Tiso) that tried to explain the collaborationist policy of the Tiso government in Slovakia: If Tiso sacrificed the Jews to the Nazis, they reasoned, the Nazis would spare Slovakia from greater calamities.

Mischlinge [G] "Hybrids": Nazi term for part Jews under the racial definitions of the Nuremberg Laws. The Nazis recognized different degrees of *Mischlinge*, not all of whom were considered Jewish. *Mischlinge* of the first degree were those who had two Jewish grandparents, were not Jewish by religion, and were not married to a Jewish spouse as of September 15, 1935. *Mischlinge* of the second degree were those with one Jewish grandparent. Generally, Nazi policy permitted the absorption of second degree *Mischlinge*, whereas those of the first degree were equated with Jews.

Mischrasse [G] "Mixed race": Nazi racial term for the Poles, who were viewed as a hybrid group and unworthy of consideration as Aryans. In this vein, Reinhard Heydrich is reputed to have argued that Nazi policy was to reduce the Poles to "two-legged cattle."

Mithot meshunot [מיתות משונות, H] "Unnatural deaths": Hebrew term, primarily used in rabbinical *Responsa*, for the various forms of murder European Jewry were faced with under Nazi occupation.

Mitläufer [G] "Fellow traveler": German who supported the NSDAP's policies but did not join the party.

Munkaszolgálat [Hu] "Labor Service System": Military-related system of forced labor for those considered "politically unreliable" by the Hungarian regime. Ultimately encompassing 100,000 men, the Munkaszolgálat included Jews, Communists, and foreign nationals living in Hungary. Organized into *Munkaszolgálatos Század* (Labor Service Companies), which were established in 1939 and organized on paramilitary lines. The Labor Servicemen were largely employed in building roads and fortifications for the Hungarian armed forces, although the *Munkaszolgálat* also was used as a system of anti-Jewish persecution. The *Keresztény Munkaszolgálatos Század* (Christian Labor Service Company), was a special unit of the Labor Service composed of Christians of Jewish descent. Under Hungarian racial laws they were considered to be Jews.

Muselmann [G] "Muslim": Concentration camp slang term referring to an inmate on the verge of death from starvation, exhaustion, and despair. It appears that the term originated with the similarities between a concentration camp victim and the image of a Muslim prostrating himself in prayer.

Musterlager [G] "Model camp": Nazi term for a number of camps, among them Dachau and the Westerbork (Holland) transit camp. > see also: **Konzentrationslager System**.

Musterprotektorat [G] "Model protectorate": Nazi term for Denmark, which — since it was not at war with Germany when occupied by the Wehrmacht — was to be treated more gently by the military occupation authorities.

N

Na Piaski [P] "To the sands": Polish term for those victims sent to the Piaski extermination site — located at the juncture of the Jewish and Christian cemeteries on Ulica Janowska in Lvov — for execution. Thousands of victims were murdered there and the exact figure will probably never be known. The term derives from the fact that the Piaski had been a sand quarry before the war and implies that the subject of the conversation would soon be joining the host of other victims.

Nacht und Nebel [G] "Night and Fog": Term used in a *Führerbefehl* of December 7, 1941, regarding the methods to be used in suppressing resistance movements in Nazi-occupied Europe. Prisoners arrested under this directive were to simply disappear into the "fog of the night," and even their death was not to be divulged.

Nansen Passport(s) [PN]: Internationally recognized document issued by the League of Nations to stateless refugees during the 1920s. The passport was named for Fridtjof Nansen, the League of Nations overseer for refugee problems from 1919 to 1921. Efforts after 1933 to secure Nansen Passports, by then also known as Nansen Certificates, for Jewish refugees fleeing Nazi Germany failed because of the general unwillingness of Western countries, especially the United States, to recognize the legal validity of such documents.

Nationalsozialistische Deutsche Arbeiterpartei [G] (NSDAP) "National Socialist German Workers Party":

1. Scope and Definition

The Nazi party originally founded as the Deutsche Arbeiterpartei (German Workers Party) in 1919. Despite the rhetorical use of the term socialism in the name of the party, the NSDAP was not a Socialist party in the accepted meaning of the term. Rejecting class struggle — the rallying cry of all Socialists since Marx — the Nazis instead posited the existence of a world racial conflict between the *Herrenvolk*, the Aryans, and the *Gegenvolk*, the Jews. The fixation with the Jews became central to Nazi ideology and was to increasingly dominate NSDAP, and (after 1933) government, decisionmaking. After more than a decade in the political wilderness, the Nazi Party came to power on January 30, 1933, and rapidly began to effect Hitler's *Neue Ordnung*. > see also: **Das Dritte Reich**; **Endlösung**; **Schutzstaffel**.

2. Nazi Party Structure

A. Leadership Categories
Führer - supreme leader
Stellvertreter - deputy
Reichsleiter - state leader
Gauleiter - regional leader

Kreisleiter - district leader
Ortsgruppenleiter - group leader
Zellenleiter - cell leader
Blockleiter - bloc leader
Mitglieder - single member

B. Regional Organization

Gau - region under a *Gauleiter*
Kreis - district (or large town) under a *Kreisleiter*
Ortsgruppe - 1,500 to 3,000 families under a *Ortsgruppenleiter*
Zelle - 4 to 6 blocks (approx. 200 families) under a *Zellenleiter*
Block - 30 to 50 families under a *Blockleiter*

3. Nazi Leaders

Bach-Zelewski, Erich von dem (1899–1972): *SS-Obergruppenführer*; *Höherer SS- und Polizeiführer* for Army Group Center; head of *Bandenbekämpfung*; sentenced to ten years imprisonment but never served.

Barbie, Klaus (1913–1991): *SS-Hauptsturmführer*; head of Gestapo Section IV and SD in Lyons, France; responsible for deportations of Jews and for the murder of resistance leader Jean Moulin; captured after evading justice for twenty-five years, sentenced to life imprisonment, died in prison.

Berger, Gottlob (1896–1975): *SS-Obergruppenführer*; *Leiter der SS-Hauptamtes*; suppressed Slovak uprising (1944); sentenced to twenty-five years imprisonment, of which he served three.

Blobel, Paul (1894–1951): *SS-Standartenführer*; responsible for massacre at Babi Yar; head of Sonderkommando 1005; convicted and hanged on June 8, 1951, at Landsberg Prison.

Bormann, Martin (1900–?): *Chef der NSDAP Kanzlerei*; secretary to Hitler; deputy *Führer*; precise fate unknown.

Bouhler, Philipp (1899–1945): *SS-Obergruppenführer*; head of Aktion T-4; committed suicide.

Brack, Viktor (1904–1948): *SS-Oberführer*; organized Aktion T-4; worked on setting up the gas chambers and extermination camps;

convicted and hanged on June 2, 1948, at Landsberg Prison.

Brandt, Karl (1904–1948): *SS-Gruppenführer*; Hitler's doctor; involved with illegal medical experiments; convicted and hanged on June 2, 1948, at Landsberg Prison.

Brunner, Aloïs (1912–1992?) *SS-Sturmbannführer*; assistant to Eichmann and responsible for deportations of Jews from Austria, Greece, France, and Slovakia; escaped justice and living in Syria, although he is rumored to have died in 1992.

Canaris, Wilhelm (1887–1945): Admiral; head of the Abwehr; implicated in anti-Nazi resistance; executed by Nazis in April 1945.

Clauberg, Karl (1898–1957): Medical doctor; conducted illegal medical experiments; sentenced to twenty-five years but was released in 1955 after serving ten.

Daluege, Kurt (1897–1946): *SS-Obergruppenführer*; deputy *Reichsprotektor* of Bohemia and Moravia and responsible for the massacre at Lidice; convicted and hanged in Prague on October 20, 1946.

Dönitz, Karl D. (1891–1980): *Grossadmiral* of the Kriegsmarine; became *Führer* upon Hitler's death; sentenced to ten years.

Eichmann, Adolf (1906–1962): *SS-Obersturmbannführer*; director of Amt IVB4 and IVD4 of the RSHA; director of Dienststelle Eichmann; responsible for deportations of Jews to death camps; escaped to Argentina, captured and taken to Israel. After a lengthy trial before the Jerusalem District Court he was convicted and hanged on June 1, 1962.

Eicke, Theodor (1892–1943): *SS-Obergruppenführer*; commander SS-Totenkopfverbände; commandant of Dachau; inspector of concentration camps; chief of the WVHA; commander Waffen-SS Totenkopf Division; killed in an airplane crash.

Forster, Albert (1902–1948): *Gauleiter* of Danzig; responsible for mass deportations of Jews and Poles; convicted and executed in Danzig on April 28, 1948.

Frank, Hans (1900–1946): President of the Academy for German Law; responsible for drafting key elements in Nazi anti-Jewish legislation; Governor General of Poland; responsible for the extermination of Polish Jewry;

convicted and hanged in Nuremberg on October 16, 1946.

Frick, Wilhelm (1877–1946): Interior minister; responsible for the anti-Jewish legislative campaign; co-developer of the concentration camp system; convicted and hanged in Nuremberg on October 16, 1946.

Funk, Walter (1890–1960): Minister of finance; responsible for the aryanization program and for looting occupied countries; sentenced to life imprisonment at Nuremberg but released in 1957 due to ill health.

Globocnik, Odilo (1904–1945): *SS-Gruppenführer*; HSSPF in Lublin and Trieste; responsible for carrying out Operation Reinhard; committed suicide in May or June 1945.

Glücks, Richard (1889–1945): *SS-Gruppenführer*; inspector of concentration camps; director of WVHA Amt D, responsible for extermination camps and medical experiments in occupied Poland; disappeared and presumed to have committed suicide.

Goebbels, Joseph (1897–1945): Minister of propaganda; *Gauleiter* of Berlin; organizer of the *Kristallnacht* pogrom; committed suicide with his family in the *Führer* bunker on May 1, 1945.

Göring, Hermann (1893–1946): *Reichsmarschall* of the Luftwaffe; minister for the four-year plan; responsible for the aryanization program and for the implementation of the Final Solution; convicted at Nuremberg and sentenced to death but committed suicide before sentence could be carried out.

Heydrich, Reinhard (1904–1942): *SS-Obergruppenführer*; *Chef der Sicherheitspolizei und der SD* and later of the RSHA; *Reichsprotektor* of Bohemia and Moravia; responsible for the Wannsee Conference and for the Final Solution; assassinated by British agents in Prague on May 27, 1942.

Himmler, Heinrich (1900–1945): *Reichsführer SS und Chef der deutschen Polizei*; responsible for carrying out the Final Solution and numerous war crimes; minister of the interior and head of the replacement army; committed suicide to avoid capture on May 23, 1945 at Lueneburg Heath.

Hitler, Adolf (1889–1945): *Führer* of the NSDAP; founder and destroyer of the Third Reich; largely responsible for Nazi ideology and especially for Nazi antisemitism; launched the war of conquest that eventually crushed the Reich and removed the NSDAP from power; committed suicide in his bunker under the Reich chancellery on April 30, 1945.

Höss, Rudolf (1900–1947): *SS-Hauptsturmführer*; commandant of Auschwitz and responsible for the operation of the gas chambers and crematoria at Auschwitz-II Birkenau, where millions perished; convicted by a Polish court and hanged at the place of his crimes on April 16, 1947.

Jäger, Karl (1888–1959): *SS-Standartenführer*; headed Einsatzkommando 3 of Einsatzgruppe-A; in charge of the extermination of Lithuanian Jewry; evaded justice until 1959, when he was arrested; committed suicide before his trial.

Jeckeln, Friedrich (1895–1946): *SS-Obergruppenführer*; HSSPF in the Soviet Union and Baltic Republics; responsible for the murder of Jews and Communist Party officials in that region; convicted and hanged in the former ghetto of Riga on February 3, 1946.

Jodl, Alfred (1890–1946): *Generaloberst der Wehrmacht*; chief of OKW and responsible for the Western Front; signed the unconditional surrender papers for the German armed forces; convicted and hanged at Nuremberg on October 16, 1946.

Kaltenbrunner, Ernst (1903–1946): *SS-Obergruppenführer*; HSSPF in Donau; *Chef der RSHA* after assassination of Heydrich; convicted and hanged at Nuremberg on October 16, 1946.

Kappler, Hubert (1907–1978): *SS-Obersturmbannführer*; HSSPF for Rome; responsible for the Ardreatine Caves massacre; sentenced to death but sentence commuted to life imprisonment, escaped in 1977 and died shortly thereafter.

Katzmann, Fritz (1906–1957): *SS-Gruppenführer*; HSSPF in Lvov and Radom; responsible for the extermination of Galician Jewry; escaped justice but apparently died in unclear circumstances in 1957.

Keitel, Wilhelm (1882–1946): *Generalfeldmarschall*; *Chef der OKW* and responsible for the Eastern Front; wrote the Commissars'

Order, the Bullet Decree, and the Night and Fog Order; convicted and hanged at Nuremberg on October 16, 1946.

Krüger, Friedrich W. (1894–1945): *SS-Obergruppenführer*; HSSPF in Krakow, responsible for the entire Generalgouvernement; oversaw the *Aktion Reinhard* extermination camps and the liquidation of the Polish ghettos; commanded Waffen-SS Mountain Division Nord and other formations; committed suicide on May 9, 1945.

Ley, Robert (1890–1945): *Chef der Duetsche Arbeitsfront* [DAF]; organizer of Kraft durch Freude program; founder of Adolf Hitler-Schulen; convicted at Nuremberg, he committed suicide while awaiting sentencing.

Luther, Martin (1895–1945): Head of Abteilung-D of the German Foreign Ministry; heavily involved in planning and carrying out the Final Solution; imprisoned by the Nazis in Sachsenhausen, where he died.

Mugrowski, Joachim (1905–1948): *SS-Gruppenführer*; *Chef der SS-Hygeine Institut*; responsible for medical and technical experiments connected to the Final Solution; convicted and hanged at Nuremberg on June 2, 1948.

Müller, Heinrich (1900–?): *SS-Gruppenführer*; *Chef der Gestapo*; responsible for overseeing the Final Solution and other war crimes; rumored to be still at large.

Nebe, Arthur (1894–1945): *Chef der KRIPO*; commander Einsatzgruppe-B; involved in the murder of Jews in Belorussia during World War II; thereafter involved with the anti-Nazi resistance; executed by the Nazis on April 3, 1945.

Ohlendorf, Otto (1907–1951): *SS-Gruppenführer*; commander Einsatzgruppe-D; responsible for the murder of Jews in the Ukraine and Crimea; convicted and hanged in Landsberg Prison on June 8, 1951.

Pohl, Oswald (1892–1951): *SS-Obergruppenführer*; *Chef der Wirtschafts- und Verwaltungshauptamt*; responsible for the operations of the concentration camp system and for numerous crimes against humanity; convicted and hanged in Landsberg Prison on June 8, 1951.

Prützmann, Hans (1901–1945): *SS-Obergruppenführer*; HSSPF in Kiev; responsible for the Babi Yar massacre; organized the Werewolf organization during the waning days of the Third Reich; committed suicide in May 1945.

Reichenau, Walter von (1884–1942): *Generalfeldmarschall*; was a moving factor behind the Wehrmacht's oath to Hitler; commanded the troops who occupied Sudetenland and the rest of Czechoslovakia; saw active service in the Polish, French, and Russian campaigns; responsible for adoption of notions that war in the East was an ideological war and thus was responsible for military cooperation with the Einsatzgruppen; died of a heart attack on January 17, 1942.

Ribbentrop, Joachim von (1893–1946): Foreign minister of the Third Reich; signed the Soviet-German non-aggression pact; wholly immersed in the Final Solution, especially in gaining Axis cooperation in the extermination program; convicted at Nuremberg and hanged on October 16, 1946.

Röhm, Ernst (1887–1934): *Chef der SA*; killed by SS during the Night of the Long Knives purge on June 30, 1934.

Rommel, Erwin (1891–1944): *Generalfeldmarschall*; commander of the Deutsche Afrika Korps (DAK); commander of forces on the Western Front; implicated in the anti-Nazi conspiracy he committed suicide in August 1944.

Rosenberg, Alfred (1893–1946): *Reichsminister für Ostland*; chief Nazi racial ideologue; head of Einsatzstab Rosenberg and involved in pillaging Jewish and other valuables in the occupied countries; convicted and hanged in Nuremberg on October 16, 1946.

Sauckel, Fritz (1894–1946): *Gauleiter* for Thuringia; plenipotentiary for labor deployment and responsible for the use of slave laborers throughout the Reich; convicted and hanged in Nuremberg on October 16, 1946.

Schacht, Hjalmar (1877–1970): Minister of economics; president of the Reichsbank; general plenipotentiary for the war economy; involved in efforts to release German Jews in return for the payment of a ransom; loosely connected with the anti-Nazi resistance and imprisoned by the Nazis; tried at Nuremberg and acquitted.

Schellenberg, Walter (1910–1952): *SS-Brigadeführer*; director of SD-Ausland; involved in numerous counterintelligence and anti-resistance operations; tried at Nuremberg, convicted, and pardoned.

Six, Franz W. (1909–?): *SS-Brigadeführer*; head of Amt VII of the RSHA; commander of Einsatzgruppe-B; sentenced in April 1948 to twenty years but served only seven.

Skorzeny, Otto (1908–1975): *SS-Standartenführer*; junior officer in Leibstandarte Adolf Hitler and Das Reich Waffen-SS divisions; organizer and commander of Waffen-SS commando unit used to rescue Mussolini; tried and acquitted, later fled to Spain where he died.

Speer, Albert (1905–1981): Reich minister of armaments; architect who laid plans for the new Berlin; responsible for the use of slave laborers throughout Germany; sentenced to twenty years imprisonment, which he served.

Streicher, Julius (1885–1946): Publisher of *Der Stürmer*; *Gauleiter* of Franconia; major proponent of Nazi antisemitic ideology and organizer of the anti-Jewish boycott of April 1, 1933; heavily involved in creating the Nuremberg Laws and in aryanization; removed from party offices by Göring; convicted at Nuremberg and hanged on October 16, 1946.

Stroop, Jürgen (1895–1952): *SS-Gruppenführer*; responsible for anti-partisan operations in Galicia and Ukraine; responsible for the liquidation of the Warsaw ghetto and for putting down Jewish armed resistance there; HSSPF in Greece and responsible for deportations of Jews to Auschwitz; convicted and hanged in Warsaw on March 6, 1952.

Wirth, Christian (1885–1944): *SS-Sturmbannführer*; commissioner of KRIPO; member of *Aktion T-4* staff; set up and commanded the Belzec extermination camp; served as inspector of extermination camps within the WVHA; transferred to Trieste; killed by partisans in Fiume in May 1944.

Wolff, Karl (1900–1984): *SS-Obergruppenführer und General der Waffen-SS*; Hitler's chief of staff; HSSPF in Italy and directed the puppet Sálo Republic; involved in deportations of Jews, primarily to Treblinka; acted to arrange the surrender of Axis forces in northern Italy; turned state's evidence at Nuremberg; sentenced to fifteen years but served seven.

4. Nazi Organizations

Abteilung II Raum "Department of Space," within the Reichskommissariat Ostland, headquartered in Riga, Latvia. Involved primarily in finding places for German colonists in the Baltic states and western Belorussia.

Ahnenerbe Forschungs- und Lehrgemeinschaft, "Society for Research into the Teaching of Ancestral Heritage," founded July 1, 1935, for research into the racial prehistory of the German *Volk*. In 1944 Ahnenerbe contained some forty research departments.

Akademie für Deutsches Recht, "Academy for German Law," Founded by Hans Frank on June 26, 1933. The academy, whose members represented a cross-section of the Reich's political leadership, sought responsibility for rewriting the entire corpus of German law. However, except for the Nuremberg Laws, the academy did not fully play its intended role. Publications: *Jahrbuch der Akademie für deutsche Recht*.

Antijüdische Aktion, "Anti-Jewish Action," third name for Joseph Goebbels's antisemitic research institute. Founded originally as the Institut zum Studium der Judenfrage, its name was changed in 1939 to Antisemitische Aktion but was changed again in 1943 to pacify pro-Axis Arabs who, considering themselves Semites, resented the Nazi term.

Antisemitische Aktion, "Antisemitic Action," official name for Joseph Goebbels's Institut zum Studium der Judenfrage after December 1939. Located on Berlin's Potsdamer Strasse 17, the institute was part of the propaganda ministry. Antisemitische Aktion was later renamed Antijüdische Aktion.

Auslandsorganization (AO), "Foreign Organization," an agency of the NSDAP, established May 8, 1933, that was charged with the supervision of Germans abroad. AO also opposed the *Ha'avara* agreement.

Aussenpolitisches Amt (APA), "Foreign Policy Bureau," founded on April 1, 1933, and headed by Alfred Rosenberg. Owing to different tactics, APA found itself in a futile competition with the German Foreign Ministry. APA's major accomplishments were its worldwide contacts with international Fascist parties.

Bund Deutscher Mädel (BDM), "League of German Girls," the female equivalent of the Hitlerjugend, established in 1930. BDM's objectives were based on the Nazi ideology of the woman's role in the Reich: she was to be a mother and the nurturer of a generation of racial warriors.

Deutsche Arbeitsfront (DAF), "German Labor Front," affiliate organization of the NSDAP, established May 10, 1933, and comprising all former labor unions and guilds, professional organizations, and business corporations. The DAF was led by Robert Ley.

Eher Verlag, Nazi publishing house active between 1925 and 1945. The company's operations were largely financed through the *Arisierung* campaign.

Einsatzstab Rosenberg, "Operational Staff Rosenberg," created by Alfred Rosenberg to plunder the cultural and artistic treasures of the Jews. The unit's first activity of this kind was carried out in France by Sonderstab Bildende Kunst (Special Operational Staff for the Arts), created by Hitler's order on September 17, 1940. Concurrent with the activity in France, Einsatzstab Rosenberg carried out a furniture expropriation action (Aktion Möbel) in the Netherlands and in Belgium, similar to that which Rosenberg had begun previously in Germany.

Felddägerkorps, "Field Dagger Corps," early SA shock formation dissolved in 1935 after the *Nacht der Langen Messer*. Members of the Felddägerkorps were later absorbed into the German police.

Fideikommissariat, "Estate Commission," established November 15, 1939 and charged with the aryanization of Jewish-owned factories, warehouses, and businesses in Nazi-occupied Poland.

Forschungsabteilung Judenfrage, "Research Department for the Jewish Question," a sub-agency of the Reichsinstitut für Geschichte des neuen Deutschlands, established in spring 1936.

Glaubensbewegung deutscher Christen, "Movement of German Christian Believers," Nazi-oriented religious organization founded by Wilhelm Kube in 1927. Advocated the aryanization of German Christianity and the removal of Jewish influences. In 1933 the movement became the semi-official religious organization of Germany, a move that splintered the German churches and presaged the "German church struggle." > see also: **Kirchenkampf**.

Haupttreuhandstelle Ost, "Main Trust Office East," established by Hermann Göring as a public corporation; its sole purpose was to legitimize the administration of seized Jewish and Polish properties.

Hilfspolizei, "Auxiliary Police," recruited from other NSDAP agencies and given policing duties. Organized to assist the Hauptamt Ordnungspolizei (ORPO), the Hilfspolizei were not under the *Reichsführer-SS*'s authority, although some sub-police groups (for example, the Bahnschutzpolizei) were incorporated into the SS after 1939.

Hitlerjugend (HJ), "Hitler Youth," the NSDAP youth movement originally founded as part of the SA in 1922. In 1926 the name was changed to HJ. From 1931 on, Baldur von Schirach led HJ, and he converted the organization into a primary tool for ideological and racial indoctrination. As a result, HJ members absorbed Nazi ideology and many grew up to become instruments of the *Endlösung*.

Institut der NSDAP zur Erforschung der Judenfrage, "Nazi Party Institute to Research the Jewish Question," one of many institutions in the Third Reich to investigate the Jewish question. Established April 15, 1939, under the sponsorship of Alfred Rosenberg, the institute had its headquarters in Frankfurt am Main.

Institut für deutsche Ostarbeit, "Institute for German Work in the East," founded in April 1940 in Krakow. Dedicated to the study of Polish Jewry, with the goal of proving Nazi racial theories.

Institut für Erbbiologie und Rassenforschung, "Institute of Hereditary Biology and Race Research," founded in 1934 at the University of

Frankfort am Main by Dr. Otmar Freiherr von Verschuer. The institute was dedicated to research on racial and heredity issues, including a project on twins headed by Josef Mengele and later transferred to Auschwitz.

Institut zum Studium der Judenfrage, "Institute to Study the Jewish Question," founded by Joseph Goebbels in 1936 as part of the Propaganda Ministry. Dedicated to publishing works on issues related to the Jews, as viewed through the prism of Nazi ideology. In December 1939 the institute's name was changed to Antisemitische Aktion, but its method of operation remained the same. Publications: *Mitteilungen über die Judenfrage* (1937–1940); *Die Judenfrage in Politik, Recht, Kultur und Wirtschaft* (1940–1942): *Die Judenfrage* (1942–1945). > see also: **Nationalsozialistische Deutsche Arbeiterpartei, Nazi Organizations (Antijüdische Aktion; Antisemitische Aktion).**

Institut zur Erforschung des jüdischen Einflusses auf Das deutsche kirchliche Leben, "Institute for the Study of Jewish Influence on German Church Life," one of five anti-Jewish research centers established April 4, 1939, and headed by Walter Grundmann.

Kraft durch Freude (KdF), "Strength Through Joy," the leisure organization of the German Labor Front, established November 27, 1933. KdF was designed to convince the working class that their interests and those of the NSDAP coincided. This was accomplished by a variety of KdF activities, including subsidized trips to vacation resorts. In reality, KdF's goals were the strict regimentation of German society in preparation for war.

Landwacht, "Country Guards," rural auxiliary police established in 1942. Members of the Landwacht were drafted from among the ranks of former SA members.

Nationalpolitische Erziehungsanstalten (NAPOLA), "National Political Educational Institutes," Nazi Party cadet training schools established April 14, 1933. Originally intended to have an exclusively Nazi curriculum, in 1939 NAPOLA schools were reorganized to align with more traditional school curricula. In 1944 thirty-five

NAPOLA schools existed, including thirteen in the occupied or incorporated territories.

Nationalsozialistisches Kraftfahrkorps (NSKK), "National Socialist Motor Transport Corps," paramilitary formation of the Nazi Party. Officially created to encourage interest in motor vehicles, the NSKK was actually a cover for the training of recruits for the Wehrmacht's armored divisions. From 1939 onward, NSKK operated as an auxiliary of the Wehrmacht, providing transport services and, in some case, rear area security detachments. Foreign volunteers were accepted into all NSKK detachments, although in 1943 and 1944 some foreign "volunteers" were actually civilians kidnapped to fill out membership rolls. At its height NSKK had 500,000 German men and women in uniform, organized into 100 regional transport regiments.

Organisation Todt (OT), "Todt Organization," Nazi-sponsored paramilitary labor battalions named after Fritz Todt and established in 1938. Primarily involved in the construction of military facilities, OT units also operated in a rear-area security role, especially on the Eastern Front. In 1944 OT fielded eighteen regional Einsatzgruppen: eight in Germany, four in occupied Soviet territory, and one each in Poland, France, Norway, Yugoslavia, Italy, and Czechoslovakia. These units received the Einsatzgruppe designation since they were mobile and operated as needed. They were especially active in occupied countries and used foreign laborers, including Jewish (and other) slave laborers. Headed by: Fritz Todt (1938–1943); Albert Speer (1943–1945).

Rassenpolitisches Amt der NSDAP, "Racial Policy Office of the National Socialist German Workers Party," propaganda agency established by Rudolf Hess May 1, 1934. Of special importance were the agency's guidelines relating to racial legislation.

Reichsinstitut für Geschichte des neuen Deutschlands (RfGdND), "Reich Institute for the History of the New Germany," established by Walter Frank July 1, 1935. Main focus of the RfGdND was to interpret modern German history according to Nazi ideology, with special focus on the Jewish question.

Stosstrupp Adolf Hitler, "Shock Troop Adolf

Hitler," founded by Hitler in 1922 as his personal bodyguard. It became the nucleus for the SS. > see also: **Schutzstaffel**.

Sturmabteilungen (SA), "Storm Troopers," NSDAP shock troops, commanded by Ernst Röhm and noted for virulent antisemitism, antidemocratic activities, the rejection of law and order, corruption, and bids for personal power. The SA's concept of warfare against political enemies was designed to control the streets and gain power and prestige for the NSDAP. The SA was divided into twenty-one districts, with independent mobile squads and an independent high command. With Hitler's rise to power, the SA perceived itself as the dominant power in the Third Reich. When Röhm openly voiced discontentment with the slow pace of Hitler's social revolution, he and the SA leaders were massacred by Himmler's SS in a purge that began on June 30, 1934. Thereafter, the SA declined in power and was finally incorporated into the SS in 1935.

Untersuchungs- und Schlichtungsausschuss (USCHLA), "Investigation and Arbitration Committee," the internal party mediation bureau established February 27, 1925. In the beginning of 1934 USCHLA became the Supreme Party Court of the NSDAP.

Verband deutscher Vereine im Ausland, "Alliance of German Organizations Abroad," a Nazi umbrella organization established in 1934 to serve all ethnic Germans residing outside the Reich, with headquarters in Berlin. It published and distributed an NSDAP propaganda journal, *Heimatbrief* (Letter from Home).

Vermögensverwaltungs- und Rentenanstalt, "Property Administration and Annuities Institute," Nazi agency responsible for the aryanization of all Jewish property in Holland. Officially, Jewish owners of the property were supposed to be paid the price "agreed upon" in twenty-five yearly installments. In reality, the Jewish owners received no payment at all.

Volksdeutsche Mittelstelle (VOMI), "Ethnic German Assistance Office," founded in 1936 by Rudolf Hess and administered by the SS. VOMI's purpose was to coordinate policies regarding ethnic Germans and win them over to National Socialism. Among other things, VOMI sponsored the Sudeten crisis (1938–1939), and the drive for re-Germanization of the Eastern Territories.

Zentrale für Handwerkslieferungen, "Central for Workshop Acquisition," a German marketing institute with Munich headquarters, which bought up for a mere pittance complete factories in the Polish ghettos that as a bonus also included free Jewish slave labor.

Zentralforschungsinstitut, "Central Research Institute," established on the brink of the Third Reich's collapse, this superagency combined all the Nazi anti-Jewish institutes within the Reich, under the auspices of Goebbels's Propaganda Ministry.

Nationalsozialistische Judenhetze [G] "Nazi Jew hatred": National Socialist term of incitement against the Jewish people, the main focus of Nazi racial doctrine.

Nazi Crimes Against Non-Jews

1. Scope and Definition

As befits the totalitarian model of the state that Hitler sought to create, the Nazis persecuted numerous groups beside Jews. In the 1930s, the main targets of Nazi political repression were Communists, trade unionists, Socialists, and all others who refused to be cowed by Nazi terrorization. The latter also included German individuals found guilty of *Rassenschande*. By the thousands those falling within these categories were incarcerated in the ever-growing numbers of concentration camps run by the SS and Gestapo. With the start of World War II, thousands of others — the retarded, crippled, the deaf and mute, those with hereditary diseases, and those considered by Nazi dogma to be useless mouths — were dragged away under the cover of "mercy killing" and were disposed of at euthanasia centers. The campaign against the Soviet Union accelerated Hitler's *Weltanschauungskrieg*, and further categories were added to the above. Soviet prisoners of war and Communist Party officials; Polish political, ideological, and economic leaders; resisters, commandos, and escaped

Allied servicemen; certain religious groups, homosexuals, and so-called asocials; and other racial groups, including especially European Gypsies.

All of these categories suffered numerous indignities; ultimately thousands and even hundreds of thousands perished owing to direct or indirect Nazi action. For example, 6 million Soviet prisoners of war died in Nazi captivity through a systematic policy of malnutrition, overwork, and physical extermination. The same may be said to hold true for Europe's Gypsy population, which had the dubious distinction of being gassed in the same Vernichtungslager as Jews. Nevertheless, a fundamental difference between these crimes and the Nazi policy toward Jews also existed. Specifically, although the Nazis systematically pursued the persecution of all the aforementioned groups, they never acted in as methodical a fashion toward those groups as they did in the pursuit of the Jews. The Nazis never spoke of making any racial, national, or politico-economic group extinct other than the Jews. Thus, some Gypsies were murdered; others were not persecuted at all. Soviet POWs were grossly mistreated and millions were murdered; Hundreds of thousands, however, were permitted to join German auxiliary units (both Wehrmacht and SS), becoming persecutors rather than victims. > see also: **Ausmerzung; Collaboration; Euthanasie; Konzentrationslager System; Medical Experiments; Resistance; Zigeuner.**

TABLE N.1: Chronology of Criminal Acts

Location	Date	# of Victims
Ardreatine Caves (I)	3/24/44	335 (includes Jews)
Auschwitz-Birkenau (P)	9/03/41	600 Soviet POWs
Auschwitz-Birkenau (P)	3/23/43	1,700 Gypsies
Auschwitz-Birkenau (P)	8/02/44	3,000 Gypsies
Dachau	11/11/40	55 Polish intellectuals
Kalavryta (Gr)	12/13/43	All males of village
La Risiera (I)	10/09/43	3,000 Italian POWs
Le Paradis (Fr)	5/27/40	100 British POWs
Lezaky (Cz)	6/10/42	47 men, women, and children
Lidice (Cz)	6/09/42	198 males
Malmédy (Belgium)	12/17/44	115 American POWs
Oradour-sur-Glane (Fr)	6/10/44	642 men, women, and children
Sabac (Yu)	10/12/41	Hundreds of Gypsies
Vercors (Fr)	7/14/44	Hundreds of partisan POWs
Wawer (P)	12/27/39	107 Poles

Source: Edelheit & Edelheit: *A World in Turmoil*, Westport, CT: Greenwood Press, 1991.

Nazi Hunters

1. Scope and Definition

Investigators seeking to bring Nazi war criminals to justice. In 1942 the Allies officially committed themselves to a policy of prosecuting all Nazi war criminals to the fullest extent of the law. In the immediate aftermath of World War II, the Allied military governments established agencies to find those guilty of war crimes and bring them to justice. > see also: **Denazification.**

Exigencies of cold war politics, however, meant that a large number of war criminals managed to escape or evade justice. In their zeal to fight Communist-inspired totalitarianism, the United States and Great Britain looked aside as war criminals escaped; in some cases the war criminals were employed by Allied secret services or other military or research agencies. There was an elaborate underground system arose to usher hundreds of Nazis out of harm's way. As a result, a few individuals, many of them survivors of the Nazi horror, have sought to bring war criminals to justice. The work of the Nazi hunters came to the fore after the capture of Adolf Eichmann by Israeli secret service agents. Generally unpaid for their long and painstaking hours of documentation and research, the Nazi hunters listed herein have all been animated by one belief: that justice delayed is justice denied.

2. The Hunters

Allen, Charles R., Jr.	United States
DeVito, Tony	United States
Friedman, Tuvia	Israel
Gray, James M.	United States
Harel, Isser	Israel
Holtzman, Elizabeth	United States
Horowitz, David	United States
Kaplowitz, Seymour	United States
Klarsfeld, Beate	France
Klarsfeld, Serge	France
Kremer, Charles	United States
Malkin, Peter J.	Israel
Mendelsohn, Martin	United States
Rockler, Walter J.	United States
Ryan, Allen A., Jr.	United States
Schiano, Vincent	United States
Silton, Paul B., Rabbi	United States
Steinberg, Elan	United States
Weiss, Avi, Rabbi	United States
Wiesenthal, Simon	Austria

Nero-Befehl [G] "Nero order": The scorched-earth order given by Hitler on March 19, 1945, when the Red Army was knocking on the walls of Berlin and the Western Allies were overrunning the Third Reich. Hitler's reasoning for the order was that since the *Volk* let itself be defeated, Germany had no right to be.

Neu-kasher [G/H] "Newly kosher": German-Jewish term for meat not slaughtered according to Jewish ritual, which some Jews bought, soaked, and salted (as if it were

kosher) to maintain the outward trappings of Jewish ritual.

Nezhelatelni [Bu] "Undesirable": Bulgarian term for a certain category of Jews to be denaturalized and deported.

Nichteinsatzfähige [G] "Unusable material": Nazi term for old and sick Jews, certain Jewish women, and small children who were unable to work. Overall, those victims the Nazis deemed as *nichteinsatzfähige* were among the first to be killed — either on the spot, on the grounds of the Jewish cemetery, or in prepared pits outside the town or village. Seldom were they included within the transports taken to the extermination camps.

Nirtzah [נרצה, H/Y] "Conclusion": When an *Aktion* or some sort of special inspection came to an end or was broken off for some unknown reason, the name of the concluding prayer of the *Hagada* in the traditional Passover *seder* — *Nirtzah* — was used as a term to tell the Jews that they could, for the time being, breathe easier.

Novemberjuden [G] "November Jews": The 30,000 Jews arrested and interned in the Buchenwald and Dachau concentration camps in connection with *Kristallnacht*. > see also: **Kristallnacht**.

Novemberverbrecher [G] "November criminals": Early Nazi derogatory term for the Weimar Republic, its leaders, and German Jewry — the corruptors of the German *Volk*.

Nur für Ostjuden [G] "Only for Eastern Jews": German Jewish term that harbored a misconception. Many German Jews who were deported to forced-labor camps in Poland, the Ukraine, Latvia, or Lithuania clung to the false assumption that after a while they would be exonerated and allowed to return to the *Vaterland*. Thus, all the massacres going on around them were meant "for Eastern Jews only."

Nürnberger Gesetze, die [G] "The Nuremberg Laws": The two racial laws promulgated on

September 15, 1935, at a special Reichstag session held during the Nuremberg party rallies. Although limited in number, the laws had wide-ranging repercussions for the German Jewish community. The first of the two laws, the *Reichsbürgergesetz* (State citizenship law), effectively rendered German Jewry stateless by declaring Jews to be subjects of the German state. The second law, *Gesetz zum Schutze des deutschen Blutes*

und der deutschen Ehre (Law for the protection of German blood and German honor), had broader applications since it defined who was a Jew, who was an Aryan, and who was a *Mischling*. Both laws became the basis for all subsequent Nazi antisemitic legislation in Germany and, during World War II, throughout occupied Europe. > see also: **Legislation, Anti-Jewish, National Socialist Legislation (Third Reich)**.

1146　　　　　　Reichsgesetzblatt, Jahrgang 1935, Teil I

Reichsbürgergesetz.
Vom 15. September 1935.

Der Reichstag hat einstimmig das folgende Gesetz beschlossen, das hiermit verkündet wird:

§ 1

(1) Staatsangehöriger ist, wer dem Schutzverband des Deutschen Reiches angehört und ihm dafür besonders verpflichtet ist.

(2) Die Staatsangehörigkeit wird nach den Vorschriften des Reichs- und Staatsangehörigkeitsgesetzes erworben.

§ 2

(1) Reichsbürger ist nur der Staatsangehörige deutschen oder artverwandten Blutes, der durch sein Verhalten beweist, daß er gewillt und geeignet ist, in Treue dem Deutschen Volk und Reich zu dienen.

(2) Das Reichsbürgerrecht wird durch Verleihung des Reichsbürgerbriefes erworben.

(3) Der Reichsbürger ist der alleinige Träger der vollen politischen Rechte nach Maßgabe der Gesetze.

§ 3

Der Reichsminister des Innern erläßt im Einvernehmen mit dem Stellvertreter des Führers die zur Durchführung und Ergänzung des Gesetzes erforderlichen Rechts- und Verwaltungsvorschriften.

Nürnberg, den 15. September 1935,
am Reichsparteitag der Freiheit.

Der Führer und Reichskanzler

Adolf Hitler

Der Reichsminister des Innern

Frick

Gesetz zum Schutze des deutschen Blutes und der deutschen Ehre.
Vom 15. September 1935.

Durchdrungen von der Erkenntnis, daß die Reinheit des deutschen Blutes die Voraussetzung für den Fortbestand des Deutschen Volkes ist, und beseelt von dem unbeugsamen Willen, die Deutsche Nation für alle Zukunft zu sichern, hat der Reichstag einstimmig das folgende Gesetz beschlossen, das hiermit verkündet wird:

§ 1

(1) Eheschließungen zwischen Juden und Staatsangehörigen deutschen oder artverwandten Blutes sind verboten. Trotzdem geschlossene Ehen sind nichtig, auch wenn sie zur Umgehung dieses Gesetzes im Ausland geschlossen sind.

(2) Die Nichtigkeitsklage kann nur der Staatsanwalt erheben.

The Nuremberg Laws
Courtesy of YIVO, the Yiddish Scientific Institute, New York

O

Oberjude/obman [G] "Head Jew/head man": Two Nazi terms for the head of a Jewish council. > see also: **Judenrat**.

Obermajdan [G]: Fictitious term given by the Nazis to the Treblinka railway station in order to completely camouflage all of the approaches to the extermination site. Obermajdan had the air of a respectful, sleepy little village and thus confused the victims, on their arrival, as to their actual fate.

Odessa > see also: **Organization der ehemaligen SS-Angehörigen**.

Odzydzenie Polski [P] "De-Judaizing Poland": The antisemitic policy that many advocates of a rapprochement with Germany felt that Poland ought to pursue: the total racial purification of the country and the complete removal of all Jewish influences in the economy, culture, and politics.

Okkupationskommando [G] "Occupation commando": Nazi term for German occupation authorities. > see also: **Besatzungspolitik**.

Ölsardinenmanier [G] "Sardine method": Nazi term for the mass killing of Jews by numerous Einsatzkommandos. The first victims were forced to lie down flat at the bottom of the pit and were then shot to death. The second batch of victims were then forced to lie down on top of the first layer of corpses, with the heads of these victims facing the feet of those already dead. The third layer followed on top of the second, again in reverse order. Depending on the number of victims killed, the "sardine method" was repeated until the pit was filled to capacity.

Onderduikers [Du] "Divers": Colloquial Dutch term for those who went into hiding when sought by the Nazis. *Onderduikers*, including many Jews and British and U.S. airmen who had been shot down, received assistance from the Dutch underground, which tried to secrete them out of Holland. > see: **Resistance, Resistance Movements (Holland)**.

Oneg shabbat [עונג שבת, H] "Sabbath delight": Code name for the secret Warsaw ghetto archive that was established and administered by Emmanuel Ringelblum. The materials collected by the archivists were sealed inside metal containers and milk jugs and were hidden in three locations within the ghetto precinct. On September 18, 1946, one part of the archive was uncovered in the ruins of a house at 68 Ulica Nowolipki. Another fragment was found (nearby) four years later, on December 1, 1950, but the third part of the archive has apparently been irretrievably lost. Most of the material is currently held by the Żydowski Instytut Historyczny in Warsaw, with smaller portions held by Yad Vashem and the U.S. Holocaust Memorial Museum.

Operation Musy [PN]: Rescue plan for

European Jewry named after Jean M. Musy, a prominent Swiss supporter of the Third Reich. The plan, worked out between Musy and Heinrich Himmler on January 12, 1945, stipulated that the Nazis would transport 1,200 Jews to Switzerland every fortnight; in return anti-Nazi propaganda would cease and Himmler's "humanitarian" deed would be given wide publication. An initial transport of 1,210 departed from Theresienstadt on February 5, 1945, and arrived safely. Himmler's desire for publicity — derived from his desire to ingratiate himself with the Allies in order to survive politically in a post-Hitler Germany — backfired, however: Hitler became aware of published reports of the operation and forbade its continuation.

Organizations

1. European Jewish, Pre-Nazi

Austria

Israelitische Allianz zu Wien, "Vienna Jewish Alliance," an independent Jewish organization with similar aims to the Paris-based Alliance Israélite Universelle, established in 1873. The Allianz main focus was on combating antisemitism, helping Jewish World War I victims, and organizing and maintaining educational institutions in Galicia and Bukovina. The Allianz was liquidated by Austrian Nazis after the *Anschluss*.

Israelitische Kultusgemeinde, "Jewish Religious Community," central communal and welfare organization of Austrian Jews, established in 1890. After 1938 the community continued to operate under Gestapo supervision until it was disbanded after the last deportations of Austrian Jewry. Chairman: Josef Löwenherz (1936-1942).

Jüdische Volkspartei (JVP), "Jewish People's Party," the political arm of the Austrian Zionist movement, founded in 1906. During the 1920s, JVP candidates ran in all Austrian elections. Major aim was the protection of Austrian Jewry's rights. Party abolished in 1934 by order of the Austrian government. Publication: *Wiener Morganzeitung*.

Organisation für jüdische Wanderfürsorge, "Organization for the Jewish Migrant Welfare," philanthropic agency established in Vienna in 1930. After 1933 the organization provided a wide range of aid to German Jews transmigrating through Austria. Ceased to function after the *Anschluss*.

Belgium

Consistoire Central Israélite (CCI), "Central Jewish Consistory," religious and communal organization patterned on the Franco-Jewish consistory and established in 1830. The CCI operated in Antwerp, where the majority of Belgian Jewry resided. CCI operations ceased in 1941 — when the Nazis founded the Association des Juives en Belgique — but resumed upon liberation in 1945.

Solidarité Juive (SJ), "Jewish Solidarity," Communist-oriented Jewish mutual aid society established in the late 1930s. SJ had chapters in all of Belgium's urban centers, drawing its membership from among Jewish immigrants from Poland and Romania. SJ continued its activities underground during the occupation of Belgium but ceased to function as an independent body after the liberation.

Czechoslovakia

Ben-Guria, Jewish nationalist college fraternity established in 1931. Sponsored the El Al Zionist high school society. Disbanded by the Gestapo in 1939.

Demokratische Flüchtlingsfürsorge (DF), "Democratic Refugee Welfare," refugee aid agency established in 1933. DF mainly cared for Jewish and other political refugees from Germany and operated until the Nazi occupation and dismantlement of Czechoslovakia.

Flüchtlingshilfe, "Refugee Help," Czech refugee aid organization sponsored by the Women's International Zionist Organization and dedicated to helping German Jewish refugees. Established after the Nazi *Machtergreifung* in 1933.

Jewish Transport and Colonization Company, Slovakian Jewish organization established in 1939 to facilitate Jewish emigration from Slovakia with part of their property. > see also: **Ha'avara**.

Jüdische Akademische Verbindung Barissia, "Barissia Jewish Students' Association," established in 1903. Purpose was to organize Jewish college students for self-defense. Was active in the revival of the Verband Zionistischer Akademiker and collected money for the Keren Kayemet le-Israel. Publications: *Barissenblätter, Schriften zur Diskussion des Zionismus.*

France

Alliance Israélite Universelle (AIU), "Universal Jewish Alliance," founded in 1860 as a social organization to aid Jews in distress throughout the world, headquartered in Paris. AIU was especially active in aiding German Jewish refugees during the 1930s. The outbreak of World War II, and especially the Nazi occupation of France, disrupted AIU activities, although some branches continued to operate. AIU resumed its full activities in 1945.

Comité d'Assistance aux Réfugiés (CAR), "Aid Committee for Refugees," established by "native" French Jews in April 1933 as a coordinating committee for refugee aid. In contradistinction to other French Jewish organizations, the CAR cooperated closely with numerous immigrant Jewish agencies. The CAR disbanded in July 1935 after a series of disputes over the disbursement of aid to refugees.

Comité de Bienfaisance Israélite de Paris, "Jewish Welfare Committee of Paris," philanthropic agency established in 1855 to aid Jewish immigrants and refugees. During the 1930s the committee actively sought jobs for indigent Jewish refugees. In late 1933 the committee combined with other charities to create the Comité de Coordination des Oeuvres de Bienfaisance Israélites à Paris.

Comité de Coordination des Oeuvres de Bienfaisance Israélites à Paris, "Coordinating Committee for Jewish Charities in Paris," established in the early 1930s to oversee all Jewish philanthropic work. Under Nazi occupation, the Comité de Coordination became the springboard for the UGIF. After World War II the committee resumed its activities, with American Jewish Joint Distribution Committee financing. > see also: **Organizations, Jewish, (European Jewish, Nazi era, Nazi and Fascist Sponsored).**

Comité de Défense des Juifs Persécutés en Allemagne, "Committee for the Defense of Persecuted Jews in Germany," apolitical Jewish self-defense agency established in December 1933. Composed of "native" French Jews, the committee opposed the Socialist orientation of the Ligue Internationale contre l'antisémitisme and was supported by more conservative elements among Franco-Jewry. The committee ceased to function in 1940 and was never reestablished.

Consistoire Central des Israélites de France, "Central Consistory of Jews of France," Jewish religious and communal organization established in 1808. In 1935 the consistory numbered seventy-two communities. During the 1930s the consistory turned its attention to the aid of Jewish refugees. Consistory activities in northern France ceased in June 1940 and in the Vichy zone in November 1942. The consistory was reorganized in 1945.

Éclaireurs Israélites de France (EIF), "Jewish Scouts in France," social and educational organization founded in February 1923 by Robert Gamzon. Officially apolitical, the EIF became increasingly Zionist in its orientation during the 1930s. In 1930 EIF had 1,200 members, doubling its membership by 1940. During World War II, EIF operated underground, providing many members for all-Jewish and mixed *maquis.* The EIF was a major component of the Armée Juive and the Organisation Juive de Combat. > see: **Resistance, Jewish Underground Organizations (France).**

Ligue Internationale contre l'Antisemitisme (LICA), "International League Against Antisemitism," Franco-Jewish defense agency founded in 1927. From 1933 to 1939 LICA advocated a strong French response to Nazi antisemitism and worked to open France's borders to German Jewish refugees. LICA was moderately Socialist in its orientation and supported the Popular Front government of Léon Blum. In January 1937 LICA changed its name to *Ligue Internationale contre l'racisme et l'antisemitisme.* The organization operated in the underground during World War II. It reverted to LICA in 1945.

Organisation de Sécours aux Enfants (OSE), "Aid Operations Organization for Children," international health and nutrition agency dedicated to the welfare of children, established in Russia in 1912 but headquartered in Paris throughout its existence. OSE operated as OZE in Eastern Europe and as TOZ in interwar Poland. OSE and its subsidiaries attempted to maintain operations during World War II but faced increasing difficulties as the Final Solution progressed. OSE, but not its East European subsidiaries, resumed operations in 1945.

Union des Femmes Juives de France pour la Palestine (UFJ), "Federation of Jewish Women of France for Palestine," the French federation of the Women's International Zionist Organization established in 1924. With the German occupation of France, UFJ went underground, taking on the main task of helping to save Jewish children. Toward this goal, UFJ created a special branch, the *Service Clandestin de Placement d'Enfants de la WIZO* (WIZO's Clandestine Service for the Placement of Children). About 1,250 children were placed with non-Jewish families and thus saved from deportation to the death camps. The UFJ also participated in aliya bet after World War II.

French Colonies

Conseil de la Communauté Israélite (CCI), "Council of the Jewish Community," umbrella organization of Tunisian Jewry, established in 1881 and centered in Tunis. Reorganized and democratized in 1937, the CCI was active in refugee and philanthropic work throughout the 1930s. Upon the Nazi occupation of Tunisia in November 1942, the CCI became the Judenrat for Tunisian Jewry.

Germany

Akademie für die Wissenschaft des Judentums, "Academy for the Science of Judaism," academic institution established in 1919 to aid in the advancement of Jewish scholarship. Liquidated in 1934 by order of the Gestapo.

Centralverein deutscher Staatsbürger Jüdischen Glaubens (CV), "Central Union of German Citizens of the Jewish Faith," founded 1893 as a self-defense organization. Membership (1924) 72,500. Publication: *CV Zeitung*. Transformed into the Centralverein der Juden in Deutschland by Nazi order in 1935. Disbanded, again by Nazi order, on November 10, 1938.

Deutscher Vortrupp Gefolgschaft deutscher Juden, "German Vanguard of German Jewish Followers," German Jewish anti-Zionist organization founded by Hans Joachim Schöps in 1933, who considered themselves Jews by religion only. The Vortrupp thus hoped to protect Jewish rights in Germany by proving Jews to be an integral part of the German *Volk*. As an answer to Nazi anti-Jewish propaganda that Jews are only in the professions or business, Schöps also promoted a plan to have Jewish youth work in agriculture. All was futile, however, since none of the Vortrupp's plans were put into operation, it being highly unlikely that Hitler ever became aware of them.

Gesellschaft zur Förderung der Wissenschaft des Judentums, "Association to Further the Scientific Study of Judaism," scholarly organization founded in 1902. Purpose was to enhance the scholarly study of Judaism by sponsoring research and publication. Liquidated by the Gestapo in November 1938. Publication: *Monatsschrift für die Geschichte und Wissenschaft des Judentums*.

Hagibor [הגיבור], "The Mighty," German Jewish sports association, established during the 1920s. Hagibor was dismantled by Gestapo order on October 14, 1933, and its property was confiscated.

Hilfsverein der deutschen Juden, "Relief Organization of German Jews," assimilationist and anti-Zionist philanthropic agency founded in 1901. Officially dedicated to helping improve the political and social position of Eastern European and Middle Eastern Jewry, the Hilfsverein actually concentrated on aiding Jewish transmigrants from Russia and Romania to leave Germany in an expeditious manner. Name changed to Hilfsverein der Juden in Deutschland in 1935, but permitted to carry on emigration work. Disbanded in 1939. Publication: *Russische Korrespondenz* (G/F/E).

Hochschule für die Wissenschaft des Judentums, "College for the Scientific Study of Judaism," established in 1872 as the Rabbinical Seminary of the German Reform movement. Chancellor in 1933 was Leo Baeck. The center continued to operate during the early Nazi period and became a focal point for spiritual resistance. Closed by Nazi order July 19, 1942, at the time of the liquidation of Berlin Jewry.

Jüdische Jugendhilfe, "Jewish Youth Help," social and educational agency established by Recha Frier in 1932. Initially organized for vocational training, the agency became the German arm of Youth Aliya in 1933. As such, the agency continued to operate — although with increasing Gestapo interference — until 1938. > see also: **Yishuv, Yishuv Organizations (Aliyat Yeladim va-No'ar)**.

Jüdischer Frauenbund, "Jewish Women's Association," social and friendly organization established by Bertha Pappenheim and Sidonie Werner in 1904. In 1933 the Frauenbund had 30,000 members throughout Germany. Operations were, in effect, curtailed in 1936, and the Frauenbund ceased to exist as an independent agency in 1938. Its last members were murdered in 1943. Chairwomen: Bertha Pappenheim (1904–1936); Hannah Karminski (1936–1943).

Reichsbund jüdischer Frontsoldaten, "National Association of Jewish War Veterans," fraternal organization founded in 1919. Purpose was to counter antisemitic propaganda and instill a patriotic attitude in German Jews. During the 1920s the Reichsbund oversaw a small, and ultimately unsuccessful, Jewish paramilitary organization. Liquidated at Gestapo order on November 10, 1938. Publication: *Der Schild*.

Verband National deutscher Juden, "Association of National-German Jews," assimilationist organization established in 1921. The Verband advocated a right-of-center political platform and supported the total assimilation and de-nationalization of German Jewry. Leaders of the Verband also argued that Jews ought to accept the truth of some antisemitic accusations. Liquidated by order

of the Gestapo in late 1935. Chairman: Max Naumann (1921–1935). Associated youth group: Das Schwarzes Fähnlein (the Black Squad); publication: *Der National-deutscher Jude*.

Verein zur Abwehr des Antisemitismus, "Association for Combating Antisemitism," self-defense organization founded in Germany and Austria in 1890. Although financed by German Jewish organizations, the Verein was largely composed of philosemitic German public figures. Operating primarily through the press, the Verein was active in defending Jews against antisemitic defamations although it fought a losing battle, during the 1920s, against Nazi propaganda. The Verein disbanded under Gestapo pressure in 1933.

Vereinigung für das liberale Judentum in Deutschland (VLJD), "Union for Liberal Judaism in Germany," religious organization founded in 1908 and including Reform rabbis and laypersons. Membership peaked in 1933 at 10,000; growth was slow because many liberal Jews found the VLJD's orientation too conservative, whereas traditional Jews found it too radical. The VLJD ceased to function as an independent body in 1933. Chairman: Rabbi Hermann Vogelstein (1908–1933); President: Caesar Seligman (1928–1933). Publication: *Liberales Judentum*.

Zentralwohlfahrtstelle der Deutschen Juden, "Central Welfare Agency of German Jews," charitable organization established in 1917 to aid needy German and foreign Jews. The Welfare Committee operated, in effect, as the German branch of the American Jewish Joint Distribution Committee and continued to operate as such during the interwar era. One of the founding members of the Reichsvertretung (Reich Representation) in 1933, the Welfare Committee ceased to function in 1938.

Zionistische Vereinigung für Deutschland (ZVfD), "German Zionist Organization," founded in October 1897, but becoming a mass movement only after 1913. During the Nazi era, the ZVfD was permitted to operate with less Gestapo interference than other Jewish organizations, since it advocated Jewish emigration. The ZVfD was a vocal supporter of the Ha'avara agreement that permitted Jews to emigrate to Palestine with a portion of their capital. The ZVfD ceased to function after *Kristallnacht*. President: Siegfried Moses (1933–1937). Publication: *Jüdische Rundschau*. > see also: **Ha'avara Agreement**; **Yishuv**.

Hungary

Magyar Izraelita Nők Országós Szövetsége (MINOSZ), "National Association of Hungarian Jewish Women," although not officially affiliated with WIZO, MINOSZ worked closely with it, helping to save Jewish refugees from the hands of local Fascists and Nazis. MINOSZ gave liberal financial support to *aliya* and to *hachshara* programs.

Italy

Associazione Donne Ebrea d'Italia (ADEI), "Association of Jewish Women in Italy," friendly society established in the 1920s. In 1931 ADEI joined with the Italian Federation of WIZO to become ADEI-WIZO. In cooperation with Delegazione assistenza emigranti ebrei, ADEI-WIZO conducted extensive relief work for Jewish refugees from Nazi Germany and Eastern Europe. It also supported aliya bet activities during the late 1930s.

Comitato Italia-Palestina (CIP), "Italy-Palestine Committee," Zionist group established in 1928 to facilitate contacts between Italy and the Yishuv. Membership included numerous Jewish communal leaders and a small group of influential members of the Partito Nazionale Fascista. Sole chairman: Leone Carpi. Publication: *L'idea Sionistica*.

Poland

Algemeiner Yidisher Arbeiterbund in Lita, Poilen un Rusland (אלגעמיינער ײדישער ארבעטער באנד אין ליטע, פוילן און רוסלאנד, Bund), "General Jewish Workers' Union in Lithuania, Poland, and Russia," a moderately anti-Zionist Jewish Socialist party. Bund-sponsored groups, spread throughout Eastern Europe, formed one of the pillars of the Jewish resistance to the Nazis (both active and passive) along with the Zionists and Jewish Communists.

Brit ha-Hayal [ברית החיל], Revisionist Zionist paramilitary organization founded by a group of Jewish veterans of the Polish army in the 1930s and active in the ghetto undergrounds.

Centrala Opieki nad Sierotani (CENTOS), "National Federation for the Care of Orphans," philanthropic agency established in 1924. In 1931 CENTOS looked after 10,000 orphans, with slightly less than half of the budget coming from the American Jewish Joint Distribution Committee. CENTOS peaked in 1938 when it cared for 15,000 orphans, operated a series of health clinics and schools, and had 60,000 paying members. Operating budget was 6 million zlotys. CENTOS continued to operate legally under the Nazi occupation, but ceased to function when the mass deportations to death camps began. Publications: *Dos Shutzloze Kind, Undzer Kind*.

Centrale Yidishe Shul-Organizatsye (צענטראלע ײדישע שול-ארגאניזאציע, CYShO), "Central Yiddish School Organization," educational institution, founded in 1921, with affiliates throughout Poland. In 1929 CYShO-affiliates had 24,000 students in 216 schools, including a teachers college. Non-Zionist and secular in orientation, CYShO was neutral on all other political and social issues facing Polish Jewry.

Organizacja Centralna Opieki nad Dzieckim Żydowskiem w Polsce, "Central Organization for the Protection of Jewish Children in Poland," established in 1926. The organization ceased functioning in 1939.

Tarbut [תרבות], "Culture," Zionist school system established in Eastern Europe before World War I. In interwar Poland, Tarbut had 260 schools in addition to 4 teachers colleges. All instruction in Tarbut schools was done in modern Hebrew. The schools were ordered closed as a result of the Nazi occupation, although many continued to operate illegally.

Towarzyctwo Zdrowia Ludnosci Żydowskiej w Polsce (TOZ), "Health Association of the Jewish People in Poland," welfare organization established in 1921 by the JDC. Primarily oriented to promoting better health care and nutrition among impoverished Polish Jews. > see also: **Organizations, European Jewish, Pre-Nazi (Poland, Centrala Opieki nad Sierotani)**.

Yidisher Visenshaftlicher Institut (ייִדישער וויסנשאפֿטלעכער אינסטיטוט, YIVO), "Institute for Jewish Research," school dedicated to the scientific study of Yiddish language and literature, Jewish folklore, and Eastern European Jewish history, founded in Vilna in August 1926. Library contained 100,000 published items, including over 2,500 periodicals, and more than 100,000 manuscripts. YIVO sections opened in Buenos Aires and in New York in 1937, with the surviving operation transferred to the latter in 1945. Publications: *Historishe Shriften*; *Ekonomishe Shriften*; *YIVO Bletter*; *YIVO Annual for Jewish Social Science.*

Zukunft (צוקונפֿט), "Future," youth movement associated with the Bund. Active in organizing self-defense units during the interwar years, the movement continued to operate underground during the Nazi occupation.

Romania

Associatia Culturale a Femeilor Evree, "Cultural Association of Jewish Women," a WIZO affiliate in Romania, established in 1919. Among other, the Associatia ran kindergartens, organized professional re-orientation courses, and assisted refugees who managed to flee Poland.

Switzerland

Comité des Délégations Juives (CDJ), "Committee of Jewish Delegations," Jewish public body founded in 1919 to represent Jewish interests at the League of Nations. During the 1930s the CDJ was active in defending German Jewish interests, for example, by sponsoring the Bernheim Petition, defending the rights of East European Jewry, protecting the League's Minority Rights Treaties, and seeking safe havens for Jewish refugees. In 1936 the CDJ became a founding member of the World Jewish Congress. At that point the CDJ ceased to function, becoming the Swiss section of the WJC. > see also: **Bernheim Petition**; **Organizations, Jewish, (International, World Jewish Congress)**.

Verband jüdischer Frauen für Kulturarbeit in
Palästina*, "Association of Jewish Women for Cultural Work in Palestine," a branch of Swiss WIZO established in 1927. In the 1930s and 1940s it was actively engaged in refugee relief work.

2. European Jewish, Nazi Era

Anti-Nazi/Fascist Political Organizations

Comité General de Defense (CGD), "General Defense Committee," semi-clandestine political agency, founded in 1943 and designed to protect the interests of immigrant Jews living in France. Based on a loose federation of Zionist, Bundist, and Communist organizations, the CGD sought a positive role for immigrant Jews in the Franco-Jewish community. In 1944 — at the initiative of the Zionists — CGD combined with the Consistory to create the Conseil Représentatif des Juifs de France, after which CGD ceased to operate.

Conseil Représentatif des Juifs de France (CRIF), "Representative Council of Jews of France," Jewish communal body created during a semi-clandestine meeting in January 1944. Organized to unify French Jewry, CRIF was a coalition of Zionist parties, the Consistory, and immigrant Jewish groups (including Jewish Communists). More a conglomerate than a unified body, CRIF provided Jews with a single voice to defend their interests. CRIF continues to operate as the representative body of Franco-Jewry.

Evreiski Antifashistski Komitet > see also: **Organizations, Jewish, Nazi Era (Anti-Nazi/Fascist Political Organizations, Yidisher Antifashistisher Komitet).**

Faraynigter Yidisher Komitet far di Milchume Antkegen di Farfolgung fun Yidn in Deutshland (פֿאראייניקטער ייִדישער קאמיטעט פֿאר די מלחמה אנטקעגן די פֿארפֿאלגונג פֿון ייִדן אין דייטשלאנד), "United Jewish Committee for the War Against Persecution of Jews in Germany," chartered in 1934, with headquarters in Warsaw, the aim of this organization was to gather and print information of the Nazi policies against Jews and other so-called inferior races.

Komitet Koordinacny (KK), "Coordinating Committee," the underground body that coordinated the activities of all the Jewish political parties in the Warsaw ghetto on behalf of the Jewish National Committee. > see also: **Resistance, Jewish, Underground Organizations**.

Pracovná Skupina, "Working Group," formed by Gisi Fleischmann and Rabbi Dov Baer Weismandel on February 25, 1942, for the purpose of aid and rescue efforts. The group was primarily responsible for initiating the negotiations with Slovak and German authorities that have come to be known as the "Europa Plan." > see also: **Europa, Fall**.

Schweizerischer Hilfsverein für jüdische Flüchtlinge in Ausland, "Swiss Aid Organization for Jewish Refugees Abroad," rescue agency operating in Geneva from 1941 through 1944. Sole chairman: Isaac Sternbuch.

Yidisher Antifashistisher Komitet (ייִדישער אנטיפאשיסטישער קאמיטעט, YAK), "Jewish Anti-Fascist Committee," Soviet propaganda and information agency established in Moscow in 1942. YAK addressed itself primarily to American Jewry in an effort to gain support for the Soviet Union. Although officially an independent agency, in fact, YAK operated as an arm of the Soviet propaganda machine. YAK became the de facto communal organization for Soviet Jewry during the war, and hopes were high that the committee would be permitted to continue its operations thereafter. These hopes were dashed in 1948 when Stalin ordered YAK disbanded and its leaders killed. Chairman: Shlomo Mikhoels (1942–1948). Publication: *Eynikeyt*.

Cultural and Self-Help Agencies

Delegazione assistenza emigranti ebrei [DELASEM], "Delegation for the Assistance of Emigrants," an umbrella of Jewish organizations founded in 1933. DELASEM officially ceased to operate in 1939 but actually continued as a clandestine organization. The assistance DELASEM provided in the war years, under difficult conditions, helped save thousands of Jews from all over Nazi-occupied Europe.

Jüdischer Kulturbund, "Jewish Cultural Association," founded May 1933 to develop Jewish culture and art and to promote Zionism among German Jews. The association carried out its programs through lectures, exhibitions, plays, concerts, and discussion groups. Membership: 50,000, including over 1,700 artists and writers, in over 100 German cities and towns. Publications: *Monatsblätter des Kulturbundes deutscher Juden* (after November 1938, *Monatsblätter des jüdischen Kulturbundes*). Throughout the Nazi era the organization was strictly regulated by the Gestapo.

Komitet far di Promotsye oif Yidishe Halutsishe Kolonizastye in Madagaskar un Kenya (קאמיטעט פאר די פראמאצעע אויף ייִדישע חלוצישע קאלאניזאצעע אין מאדאגסקאר און קעניע) "Committee for the Promotion of Jewish Pioneering and Colonization in Madagascar and Kenya," emigration organization, established in December 1938 by Polish Jews, but at the urging of the Polish government. Advocated the evacuation of Polish Jewry to Madagascar or to other colonies.

Kulturbund deutscher Juden, "Cultural Organization of German Jews," a fraternal organization of artists, actors, singers, and others in the cultural and entertainment field who, because of being Jewish, lost their jobs and social standing within German society with the Nazi *Machtergreifung*. Under the Nuremberg Laws, when German Jews lost their citizenship, the Gestapo ordered a change in the organization's name.

Tkuma (תקומה), "Rebirth," Hebrew cultural agency founded in 1940 in the Warsaw ghetto. Organized lectures and educational programs on subjects that included Hebrew language and literature, Jewish culture, and political issues affecting Jewry.

Yidishe Soziale Aleinhilf (ייִדישע סאציאלע אליינהילף, YISA), "Jewish Social Self-help," philanthropic agency founded in September 1939. In October 1939, YISA changed its name to ŻTOS and, later still, to Jüdisches Hilfs-Komitet. In all these guises, YISA oversaw Jewish survival efforts by funneling money from the American Jewish Joint Distribution Committee to organizations working in the ghetto. YISA also oversaw the so-called house committees and the cultural and educational activities of Tkuma and Yidishe Kultur Organizatsye.

Zentralausschuss für Hilfe und Aufbau, "Central Committee for Aid and Reconstruction," came into being because of the economic boycott the Nazis initiated on April 1, 1933, against German Jewry. Though there were many factions and interests among German Jews, all the major Jewish organizations came to its support, and it thus became the principal agency directing economic aid.

Zsidó Munkaközösség, "Jewish Work Collective," Revisionist Zionist organization established in Budapest in August 1939. Primarily operating as a propaganda agency, the collective published ten booklets on the Jewish problem and on possible solutions to it. Included in that total were two so-called Yellow Papers, detailing conditions specific to Hungarian Jewry and written for Hungary's ruling elements. The collective ceased to operate in June 1942 at the instigation of the Hungarian government. Between 1941 and 1944 the Collective also operated a clandestine arm, known as the Zsidó Közvéleménykutató-Állomás, the "Jewish Public Opinion Research Station."

Nazi- and Fascist-Sponsored

Comité de Recrutement de la Main-d'Oeuvre Juive, "Central Committee for the Recruitment of Jewish Workers," Nazi cover agency for the conscription of Jewish slave laborers in Tunisia, established on December 10, 1942, and under the direct command of the SD commander in Tunis, Walter Rauff. Over 3,000 Jewish laborers were recruited by the committee. From January to March 1943 the committee also operated as an Einsatzkommando for the deportation of Tunisian Jews to death camps in Poland.

Jüdische Soziale Selbsthilfe (JSS), "Jewish Self-Help," Nazi-approved philanthropic agency active in the Polish ghettos. > see also: **Organizations, Jewish, European Jewish, Nazi Era (Nazi- and Fascist-Sponsored, Żydowska Samopomoc Spoleczna).**

Palästina Treuhandgesellschaft zur Beratung deutscher Juden (GmbH), "Palestine Trust Company to Advise German Jews, Inc.," German Jewish corporation responsible for transfer of Jewish capital to Palestine under the Ha'avara agreement. > see also: **Ha'avara.**

Żydowska Samopomoc Spoleczna (ŻSS), "Jewish Self-help Society," Nazi-approved Jewish relief organization supported by the JDC, founded in January 1940. Distributed relief parcels to Jews in East European ghettos, thereby acting as a conduit for Żydowskie Towarzystwo Opieki Spolecznej. ŻSS also was permitted to operate within the context of the Naczelna Rada Opiekuncza (Central Council for Care), ŻSS's Polish (non-Jewish) counterpart. After the United States entered the war, both ŻSS and ŻTOS began to cooperate with the Coordinating Committee of the Warsaw ghetto underground.

Żydowskie Towarzystwo Opieki Spolecznej (ŻTOS), "Jewish Mutual Aid Society," semilegal Jewish welfare agency operating as the JDC front organization in Poland from September 1939 to the end of December 1941. Primarily responsible for maintaining soup kitchens and children's welfare agencies, ŻTOS was unsuccessful in its operations outside of the Warsaw ghetto. Chairmen: Emmanuel Ringelblum, Yitzhak Gitterman (1939–1941).

3. Jewish, Free World

Australia

Australian Jewish Welfare Society (AJWS), philanthropic agency established in 1937 to offer assistance to Jewish refugees. Since Australians, as a rule, remained largely hostile to mass immigration, the AJWS never pressured the government to increase immigration. Instead, the agency adopted a quiet diplomatic policy that ensured the entry of a small, but steady, number of Jewish refugees. Only after 1945 and the realization that a policy of quiet diplomacy had failed did AJWS begin to advocate public protests against the continued refusal to admit Jewish refugees.

Canada

Canadian Jewish Congress (CJC), political body established in 1919. Parallel agency to the

American Jewish Congress and working for the same goals, the CJC was a founding member of the World Jewish Congress in 1936. Chairman: Samuel Bronfman (1936–1959). Publication: *Congress Bulletin*.

Jewish Immigrant Aid Society of Canada (JIAS), philanthropic agency aiding Jewish refugees, established in Toronto in 1919. A founding member of the Canadian Jewish Congress, JIAS also was a founding member of the World Jewish Congress. Given the unfriendly atmosphere toward Jews, however, JIAS was unable to prod the government to open Canada to Jewish immigration until after 1948. chairman: Samuel Guttman.

United Jewish Refugee Agency (UJRA), umbrella agency of Canadian Jewish philanthropies, established in May 1941. Given the difficulties experienced in trying to open Canada to Jewish refugees, UJRA's leadership hoped that pooling their resources would provide them more leverage with the government. This hope proved futile, however, as the government staunchly refused to consider the entry of any Jewish refugees during the war.

United Jewish Refugee and War Relief Agencies, philanthropic agency established in 1939. Dedicated to assisting Jewish war refugees in Europe and elsewhere. Affiliated with the CJC. Chairman: Samuel Bronfman.

Zionist Organization of Canada, umbrella agency for Zionist organizations in Canada, founded in 1892. Dedicated to organizing Canadian Jewry for the creation of a Jewish commonwealth in Mandatory Palestine. The organization acted as a full member of the World Zionist Organization and cooperated closely with the Zionist Organization of America. Chairman: Michael Garber (until 1946). Publication: *The Canadian Zionist*.

South Africa

Hebrew Order of David (HOD), Jewish philanthropic agency offering assistance to Jewish immigrants and refugees in South Africa, established in 1904. In addition to its charitable activities, HOD also was involved in combating assimilation. HOD was headquartered in Johannesburg and had a peak membership of 3,000.

Jewish Board of Deputies, official representative body of South African Jewry, founded in 1912. During the 1930s the board was active in opposing the antisemitic and pro-Nazi propaganda of the Greyshirt Movement and in promoting Jewish refugee immigration. In 1937 the government enacted the Alien Act, which effectively terminated German Jewish immigration despite Board of Deputies' protests. Chairmen: Cecil Lyons (1935–1940); Gerald N. Lazarus (1940–1945). Publication: *South African Jewish Affairs*.

SA Jewish Ex-Service League, fraternal organization of Jewish war veterans, founded in 1925. Heavily involved in combating antisemitism, the league advocated strong anti-Nazi measures including an anti-Nazi boycott. Publication: *The Judean*.

South African Zionist Federation (SAZF), political body established in 1905. Organized geographically, the SAZF was always an outspoken supporter of Zionist and Jewish unity as well as Jewish statehood. The Holocaust considerably strengthened the SAZF, which peaked in membership at 15,000.

United Kingdom

Anglo-Jewish Association (AJA), non-Zionist communal body established in 1871. Dedicated to the protection of Jewish rights in England and abroad, the AJA opposed the hierarchical organization of the Board of Deputies. AJA was a sponsor of the Jewish Colonization Association but was opposed to Zionism. Chairman: Leonard Stein (1939– 1949). Publications: *AJA Annual Report*, *AJA Review*.

Association of Jewish Refugees (AJR), political organization of Central and Eastern European Jewish refugees in England, established in London in 1940. Deriving in part as a protest against the 1940 internment of Jewish refugees as "enemy aliens": the AJR dedicated itself to protecting the rights of Jewish refugees and to advocacy for the rescue of European Jewry. After World War II the AJR worked with Jewish displaced persons. In July 1948 the AJR became a founding member of the United Restitution Organization. > see also: **Displaced Persons, Jewish**; **Wiedergutmachung**.

Board of Deputies of British Jews, Jewish representative body founded in 1760. Official representative body of Anglo Jewry, which also sought to safeguard Jewish interests in England and abroad. Among its multiple activities, the board also oversaw the Chief Rabbinate of England. In 1936 the board became a founding agency of the World Jewish Congress and, therafter, cooperated with the Jewish Agency for Palestine. Chairmen: Neville Laski (1933–1939), Selig Brodetsky (1939–1948).

Central British Fund for German Jewry (CBF), philanthropic agency established in May 1933. Dedicated to financing the resettlement of German Jewish refugees, primarily (though not exclusively) in the Yishuv. All Anglo-Jewish organizations were affiliated with the fund, which succeeded in raising considerable sums. Chairman: Lionel de Rothschild.

Central Council for Jewish Refugees, overall coordinating committee of Anglo-Jewish organizations, established in 1939. The Central Council succeeded the Central British Fund but was not able to place rescue on the British government's agenda. In 1943 the Central Council was transformed into the Central British Fund for Jewish Relief and Rehabilitation and continued to operate until the early 1950s. The fund was a founding member of the Conference on Jewish Material Claims Against Nazi Germany. > see also: **Wiedergutmachung**.

Chief Rabbi's Religious Emergency Council, founded March 1938 by Chief Rabbi Joseph Herman Hertz. The organization's main aim was to assist in the rescue of Jewish refugees. After the Final Solution became known, the organization advocated granting British protection to all European Jews. This proposal was rejected by the British Foreign Office.

Council for German Jewry, alternative name for the Central British Fund, used between 1938 and September 1939.

English Zionist Federation (EZF), founded in 1897 as a component of the World Zionist Organization. Oriented toward Chaim Weizmann's moderate Zionist demands, the EZF was hard-pressed by the Nazi persecution. In 1933, the EZF became one of the sponsors of the Central British Fund but continued to emphasize the need to create an open-door policy for *aliya*.

Federation of Women Zionists of Great Britain and Ireland, a British affiliate of WIZO. Took leading role in organizing and giving aid to German and Austrian Jewish refugees. Helped to establish the Women's Appeal Committee; oversaw children and Youth Aliya; helped organize the Central British Fund for Jewish Refugees; sponsored the entry into Britain of 1,000 boys and girls from the German Zionist movement; and set up and maintained the Whittinghame Farm School for 200 children.

Jewish Fellowship (JF), anti-Zionist organization established in London on November 7, 1944. Parallel to the American Council for Judaism, JF sought to define Jews exclusively as a religious group and denied the need for a Jewish state. JF collapsed in November 1948, since the newly established State of Israel rendered the political orientation of the JF irrelevant.

Jewish People's Council Against Fascism and Antisemitism (JPC), left-wing activist self-defense agency established in 1936 specifically to counter the British Union of Fascists. Although widely viewed as a Communist front group, the JPC was open to members of all political and religious orientations; they were linked by their anti-Fascist orientation. The JPC argued strongly, but unsuccessfully, for an Anglo-Jewish anti-Nazi boycott. The JPC disbanded after World War II because of continuing antagonism with other Anglo-Jewish organizations.

Jewish Refugees Committee (JRC), organization established in London in 1933 to aid German and other Jewish refugees in Great Britain. Although organized officially to help only Jewish refugees, the JRC in effect aided all non-Aryans who did not receive assistance from another agency. Operating primarily through sub-committees, the JRC also helped in finding places of resettlement for the refugees. JRC ceased its operations in 1955.

Joint Foreign Committee (JFC), political body

sponsored jointly by the AJA and Board of Deputies. Founded in 1933 to monitor the situation in Germany, the JFC disbanded in 1943 because of disagreements about the Biltmore Resolution.

Polish-Jewish War Emergency Fund, Anglo-Jewish fundraising agency active in relief work for Polish Jewish refugees and operating under the auspices of the Federation of Polish Jews in Great Britain.

United States

Advisory Council on European Jewish Affairs of the World Jewish Congress, think tank founded in 1942 to advise the WJC on European Jewish problems and possible solutions. Sole chairman: Stephen S. Wise. Publications: *Bulletin, Newsletter*.

American Council for Judaism, anti-Zionist organization established in 1942 by breakaway elements of the Central Council of American Rabbis who opposed the CCAR's stand on the Biltmore Resolution. Chairmen: Elmer Berger, Lessing Rosenwald. Publication: *Issues* (1946–1969).

American Council of Jews from Austria, friendly society founded in 1942. Dedicated to helping Jews from Austria in the United States and those still in Austria. Chairman: Ernest Stiassny.

American Council for Warsaw Jews, friendly society founded in 1942. Dedicated to relief work for Warsaw Jewry via sending food packages to Poland. Additionally, the council assisted in establishing priorities for postwar reconstruction. Publication: *Yearbook*.

American Emergency Committee for Zionist Affairs (ECZA), Zionist lobbying group established in 1939 to counteract the White Paper. Primarily organized as a public relations campaign, after the Biltmore Conference (May 1942), ECZA was reorganized and re-emerged as the American Zionist Emergency Council. Chairman: Stephen S. Wise (1939–1942).

American Federation for Lithuanian Jews, friendly society founded in 1937 and dedicated to helping Lithuanian Jewish societies in the United States. Publication: *Lithuanian Jew*.

American Federation of Jews from Central Europe, friendly society founded in 1941. Dedicated to aiding German Jewish refugees in the United States.

American Friends of Polish Jews, fraternal organization founded in 1941 to render aid to Polish Jews and especially to Polish-Jewish refugees. Publication: *Bulletin*.

American Jewish Committee, self-defense agency founded in 1906. Dedicated to protecting Jewish rights throughout the world. Publications: *American Jewish Yearbook, Contemporary Jewish Record* (1940–1945), *Commentary* (monthly since 1945).

American Jewish Conference, umbrella organization for American Jewry, established in August 1943 at the initiative of Henry Monsky of B'nai B'rith in an effort to unite American Jewry. The conference convened in September with three items on its agenda: a proposal to rescue the Jews of Europe, plans for Jewish postwar relief, and a resolution to support the creation of a Jewish commonwealth in Palestine after the war. After the conference passed a resolution approving the Biltmore Resolution, by a majority of 477 to 4 (with 20 abstentions), the American Jewish Committee withdrew from the conference. Despite this setback to Jewish unity, the conference continued to operate until it disbanded (to form the Conference of Presidents of Major American Jewish Organizations) in 1949. > see also: **Biltmore Resolution**.

American Jewish Congress, self-defense agency, founded in 1917. Dedicated to the defense of Jewish rights and interests in the United States and throughout the world. The congress was electrified into action by the rise of the Nazis. In 1933 the congress became a strong supporter of the anti-Nazi boycott movement and advocated open-door policies for Jewish refugees. In 1936, the congress became the catalyst for the creation of a World Jewish Congress. During World War II the congress continued its support for rescue operations, although it was hampered by disputes within American Jewry regarding Zionism and rescue priorities. Chairman: Stephen S. Wise (1917–1949). Publications: *Congress Bulletin, Congress Weekly*.

American Jewish Joint Agricultural Corporation (Agro-Joint), subsidiary arm of the JDC, founded in 1924. Dedicated to promoting Jewish agricultural settlements and to aiding in the resettlement of Jewish refugees.

American Jewish Joint Distribution Committee (JDC), philanthropic agency founded in 1914. Dedicated to providing aid and assistance to suffering Jews, primarily in Eastern Europe. The JDC also financed Agro-Joint. During World War II, local JDC representatives continued to funnel resources into Jewish communities, in some cases against explicit JDC orders to desist from "illegal" actions. After the war, the JDC provided a considerable proportion of the finances for the Mossad le-Aliya Bet. Publication: *JDC Digest.*

American National Committee of the World Union for Preserving Health of Jews — OSE, medical organization founded in 1929 to provide medical and health services to East European Jews.

American ORT Federation, American section of the Organization for Rehabilitation and Training, founded in 1922. Publication: *ORT Economic Review.*

American Zionist Emergency Council (AZEC), political arm of ZOA, established from the American Emergency Committee for Zionist Affairs in 1942. Dedicated to the creation of a Jewish Commonwealth in Mandatory Palestine and the overturning of the British White Paper of 1939. Chairmen: Abba Hillel Silver, Stephen S. Wise (1942–1945). Publication: *Palestine.*

Anti-Defamation League of B'nai B'rith (ADL), self-defense agency founded in 1913. Dedicated to combating the defamation of Jews and Judaism in the United States and throughout the world and to advance understanding and democratic ideals between diverse groups. Publications: *ADL Bulletin, ADL Newsletter, ADL Review.*

Association of Jewish Refugees and Immigrants from Poland, friendly society founded in 1940 to aid Jewish refugees from Poland. Chairman: Jacob Apenszlak (1940–1945).

Association of Yugoslav Jews in the United States, friendly society founded in 1941 to assist Yugoslav refugees, Jews and non-Jews alike.

Conference on Jewish Relations, educational organization founded in 1933 to ascertain the Jewish role in the modern world. Chairman: Salo W. Baron (1933–1988). Publication: *Jewish Social Studies* (1939–1988).

Dominican Republic Settlement Association (DORSA), refugee aid agency founded in 1939, as a result of Dominican offers made at the Evian Conference. DORSA was dedicated to turning into reality the offer to permit the entry of 100,000 Jews.

European Jewish Children's Aid, philanthropic agency founded in 1934, as German Jewish Children's Aid. Affiliated with the National Refugee Service. Dedicated to helping Jewish refugee children up to sixteen years old with the intention of their eventual immigration to the United States Chairman: Herman W. Block (1934–1945).

Federation of Hungarian Jews in America, friendly society founded in 1914. Dedicated to promoting the interests of Hungarian Jews in America and Hungary.

Federation of Polish Jews in America, friendly society founded in 1908. Dedicated to the defense of Polish Jewry and the unification of all American Jews of Polish origins. Reorganized after World War II as the American Federation for Polish Jews. Publications: *Der Verband, Polish Jews.*

Freiland League for Territorial Settlement, anti-Zionist settlement organization founded in 1941. Dedicated to the acquisition of territory for large-scale Jewish colonization, primarily in southern Africa or Australia. Publication: *Oifn Shvel.*

German Jewish Children's Aid, established in 1934 as an umbrella organization by eight independent American Jewish political, social, and welfare agencies. Its aim was to help train and educate German Jewish refugee children in the United States; to help other German Jewish children to immigrate to the United States at the request of their parents or relatives and with the government's permission.

Hadassah, the Women's Zionist Organization of America, Zionist body established in 1912. Dedicated to fostering Zionist ideals in the diaspora, developing medical, social and educational facilities in the Yishuv, and assisting youth aliya. At the end of World War II, Hadassah numbered some 120,000 members. Publication: *Hadassah Newsletter, Hadassah Magazine.* > see also: **Yishuv, Yishuv Organizations (Aliyat Yeladim ve-Noar).**

Hebrew Committee for National Liberation (HCNL), Zionist front group founded in 1939 as the Committee for a Jewish Army of Stateless and Palestinian Jews (CJA). Officially dedicated to promoting a variety of Jewish interests, the HCNL was in reality the American arm of the Irgun Zvai Leumi. In 1942 the CJA became the Emergency Committee to Save the Jewish People of Europe (ECJSPE) which was active in publicizing Nazi atrocities and which worked tirelessly for the creation of the War Refugee Board. In 1944 ECSJPE was transformed into the HCNL, which also oversaw the activities of the American Friends of a Jewish Palestine. Chairman: Hillel Kook (Peter H. Bergson, pseud). Publication: *The Answer.*

Hebrew Sheltering and Immigrant Aid Society (HIAS), philanthropic agency founded in 1885 and reorganized in 1901. Provided financial support for Jewish immigrants in the United States and other countries in the Western Hemisphere.

Institute of Jewish Affairs (IJA), think tank established in 1941 as part of the World Jewish Congress. Undertook research on wartime and postwar Jewish public affairs. Chairman: Jacob Robinson (1941–1948). Publication: *Jewish Affairs.* In the 1960s the IJA was reorganized and moved to London, continuing in its tasks of monitoring antisemitism, the fate of East European Jewry, and assisting the hunt for Nazi war criminals. IJA currently publishes: *Christian-Jewish Relations, Patterns of Prejudice,* and *Soviet Jewish Affairs.*

Jewish Council for Russian War Relief, philanthropic agency founded in 1942. Dedicated to providing charitable relief for the Soviet Union and for Soviet Jewry. Affiliated with Russian War Relief. Publication: *For Soviet Russia.*

Jewish Labor Committee, Jewish socialist political organization, founded in 1934. Dedicated to the promotion of democratic socialism, representing Jewish labor in the American labor movement, and fighting Nazism, fascism, and antisemitism. Chairman: Adolph Held (1938–1945). Publications: *Facts and Opinions, Voice of the Unconquered.*

Jewish People's Committee for United Action Against Fascism and Antisemitism, founded in 1936, dedicated to enlisting American Jewry in the struggle against fascism.

Jewish State Zionists of America (Jewish State Party, JSP), Zionist political party founded in 1933 as the American wing of the international JSP (the so-called Grossman faction of Ha-Zohar). Dedicated to the creation of an independent Jewish state in Mandatory Palestine.

Jewish War Veterans of the U.S.A., friendly society of Jewish veterans, founded in 1896. Dedicated to preserving the memory of Jews who fought in America's wars, and promoting the Jewish war effort in World War II. Publication: *The Jewish Veteran.*

League for Labor Palestine, Socialist-Zionist organization, founded in 1933. Dedicated to assisting the operations of the Histadrut and promoting moderate Labor Zionism. Publications: *Histadrut Bulletin, Jewish Frontier.*

National Commission to Combat Antisemitism, auxiliary agency of the American Jewish Congress, founded in 1944. Publication: *Digest of the Antisemitic and anti-Democratic Press of the United States.*

National Council of Jewish Women, women's organization founded in 1893. Provided educational, social, and financial services for American Jewish women and for Jewish refugees in the United States. Publication: *The Council Woman.*

National Jewish Welfare Board (JWB), philanthropic agency founded in 1917. Dedicated to promoting the social welfare of Jews in the United States, the U.S. Armed Forces, and abroad. Publications: *Honor Roll, The Jewish Center, The Jewish Chaplain, Jews in Uniform, JWB Sentinel, Program Aids, Women's Division Bulletin.*

National Refugee Service (NRS), philanthropic agency founded in New York in 1939.

Offered a wide range of assistance to refugees fleeing racial, religious, or political persecution. In 1946 the NRS merged with a number of other similar agencies to form the United Service for New Americans. In that form, the agency operated through the offices of the National Council of Jewish Women. Publications: *Community Bulletin, Special Information Bulletin.*

Netherlands-Jewish Society, friendly society founded in 1940. Dedicated to aiding Dutch Jews. Publication: *Mededeelingen.*

New Zionist Organization of America, Zionist political party, founded in 1926. American wing of Ha-Zohar/Ha-Zach. Active in promoting an anti-Nazi boycott, but not considered a mainstream Zionist organization. Did not cooperate with the Hebrew Committee for National Liberation. Publication: *Zionews.*

Representation of Polish Jewry, political body for Polish-Jewish affairs active in London and New York. Represented all Polish-Jewish parties except the Bund. Members: Arieh Tartakower, Jacob Apenszlak, Isaac Lewin, Zorach Warhaftig, Kalman Stein, Jacob Kenner, Moses Polakiewicz. The Representation of Polish Jewry was an associate agency of the World Jewish Congress and, from 1943 to 1945, of the Polish government in exile. Publications: *Our Tribune, News Bulletin* (1943–1945).

Union of Orthodox Rabbis of the United States and Canada, Agudath ha-Rabbonim, religious and philanthropic agency founded in 1902. During and after World War I the union cooperated with the American Jewish Joint Distribution Committee in philanthropic activities to aid Yeshiva students. In 1939 the Union established the Va'ad ha-Hatsala, a rescue committee that united Orthodox relief agencies in North America. The union's activities were closely coordinated with those of the Hebrew Committee for National Liberatiion.

Union of Russian Jews, friendly society founded in 1941. Dedicated to the re-establishment of contact with Soviet Jewry. Publication: *The Jewish World.*

United Galician Jews of America, friendly society founded in 1935. Dedicated to aiding Jews in Galicia in cooperation with the JDC. Publication: *Unzer Shtimme.*

United Palestine Appeal (UPA), founded January 1, 1936, in New York. Primarily philanthropic in nature, the UPA also undertook political activity on behalf of *aliya* and settlement projects for Jewish refugees. Chairman: Abba Hillel Silver (1938–1948).

United Romanian Jews of America, friendly society founded in 1909. Dedicated to defending Jewish rights in Romania and to assist Romanian Jews in the United States. Publication: *The Record.*

Zionist Organization of America (ZOA), umbrella agency for all Zionist bodies in the United States, founded in 1897. Dedicated to the creation of a Jewish commonwealth in Mandatory Palestine. Publications: *Dos Yidishe Folk, Inside Palestine, The New Palestine, ZOA Newsletter.*

Other Diaspora

Comité Central Israelita (CCI), "Central Jewish Committee," central representative body of Uruguayan Jewry, established in 1940. Primarily organized around congregations, the CCI acted as a coordinator for the community and was involved in self-defense activities. At its height, membership was 7,200.

Comité Central Israelita de México (CCIM), "Central Jewish Committee of Mexico," representative body of Mexican Jewry, established in 1938. Organized as a self-defense agency, CCIM also sponsored anti-Nazi activities throughout Mexico. CCIM was the only Jewish organization recognized by the Mexican government. During World War II, CCIM advocated an open door policy for Jewish refugees and succeeded in opening Mexico to a small number of Jewish refugees in 1944 and 1945.

Comité Popular Contra el Antisemitismo, "Popular Committee Against Antisemitism," anti-Zionist communal organization, founded in 1933. Leaning toward the left, the Comité Popular was the only Jewish organization not associated with the Delegación de Asociaciones Israelitas Argentinas.

Delegación de Asociaciones Israelitas Argentinas (DAIA), "Delegation of Argentine

Jewish Organizations," Jewish communal umbrella organization founded in 1935. Representing all Argentine Jewish groups, DAIA was active in arguing for an open door policy toward refugees.

International

Agudas Israel (אגודת ישראל), "Association of Israel," Orthodox anti-Zionist party, founded in Poland in 1912; a subsidiary agency, Poale Agudas Israel, was founded in 1922. Aguda rejected the concept of Jewish secular nationalism, insisting that a Jewish state could be created only by divine agency not human activity. Despite this fundamental ideological anti-Zionism, Aguda supported some Jewish immigration to the Yishuv throughout the 1930s. As the Nazi persecution of European Jewry intensified, Aguda strongly urged rescue operations via the creation of temporary havens. Representatives of Aguda served in the provisional government of the Sate of Israel in 1948 and 1949.

He-Halutz (החלוץ), "The Pioneer," Zionist youth training movement associated with Mapai. Founded in the 1920s, he-Halutz provided agricultural training to permit young persons to qualify for labor certificates to Palestine. These efforts increased after 1933 as a means to help German Jews escape the Third Reich. He-Halutz continued its operations underground during the 1940s and the movement was active in Jewish resistance throughout Europe.

HIAS-ICA-Emigdirect (HICEM), united committee for Jewish emigration, established by the 1927 merger of three refugee aid societies. HICEM acted primarily as a catalyst for emigration, apportioning funds provided by the American Jewish Joint Distribution Committee to resettlement projects in Palestine, South America, and Australia. Despite the 1934 secession of Emigdirect, HICEM continued to operate and maintained the same initials.

Mizrachi [מזרחי], "Easterner" (actually the name derived from the abbreviation Merkaz Ruhani, "a spiritual center"), Religious Zionist party, founded in 1902. In 1919 ha-

Poel ha-Mizrachi, a religious but Socialist offshoot, was founded. During the 1930s and 1940s Mizrachi participated in a coalition with Mapai in the Jewish Agency and World Zionist Organization. Both were dedicated to the re-creation of a Jewish national home in the spirit of Jewish law (*halacha*).

Obshchestvo Razpostranienia Truda sredi Yevreyev (ORT), "Organization for Rehabilitation and Training," worldwide Jewish vocational training and philanthropic organization, founded in Russia in 1880. ORT subsidiaries have played an important, and at times critical, role in rehabilitation of Jewish refugees throughout the world. Most notably, ORT schools provided vocational education for Jewish survivors in displaced persons camps throughout Europe.

Reprezentacja Żydowsta Polskiego (RŻP), "Representation of Polish Jewry," international umbrella body linking all Polish Jewish political parties — except for the Revisionist Zionists (who refused to join) — on behalf of relief efforts for Polish Jewry. Main centers of RŻP activity were London, New York, and Tel Aviv.

Women's International Zionist Organization (WIZO), international Jewish women's organization established in London on July 11, 1920. During the 1930s WIZO grew to have chapters in some sixty-two countries worldwide. WIZO established subsidiary agencies for fundraising and political activity in many countries. During the 1930s and 1940s WIZO actively pursued rescue goals in and out of Europe. In order to maintain Jewish unity, WIZO became a member of both the World Zionist Organization and the World Jewish Congress. Membership peaked at 250,000 in fifty federations. Publication: *WIZO Monthly Folder.*

World Jewish Congress (WJC), international Jewish defense agency founded in 1936. The WJC was organized around the postulate that Jews constitute one nation; the organization set its task at defending Jewish interests against Nazism and antisemitism. Of prime importance to the operations of the WJC was the American Jewish Congress, led by Rabbi Stephen S. Wise. During World War II, the WJC operated largely from the United States and was active in promoting rescue and other relief proposals.

World Union of Jewish Students (WUJS), fraternal body founded in Paris in 1924 and encompassing Jewish students from around the world. WUJS was primarily concerned with antisemitic quotas in East European countries and with finding refuges for Jewish scholars. WUJS was also involved in the establishment of Jewish fraternities on college campuses throughout the world and aided in the fundraising for the Hebrew University. In 1940 the organization moved to Switzerland, whence it continued its refugee aid operations. WUJS resumed its activities in Paris, and then in London, in 1948.

World Zionist Organization (WZO), Zionist body created by Theodor Herzl in 1897. The WZO advocated the creation of a Jewish national home in Palestine, a goal that was partly attained with the adoption of the League of Nations Mandate for Palestine in 1922. Thereafter, WZO activity shifted to the consolidation of the Yishuv and its enlargement. During the 1930s the WZO was committed to a policy of rescue by means of mass immigration, especially after 1935. In 1942 the WZO adopted the Biltmore Resolution, which called for the creation of a Jewish state in Palestine after World War II. Presidents: Nahum Sokolow (1931–1935) Chaim Weizmann (1935–1948).

4. Free World, Non-Sectarian

Anti-Nazi and Anti-Fascist

American Kulturkampf Association, founded March 1939, its main purpose being to counteract Nazi propaganda and the spread of Nazism in Western societies.

Church of Scotland, assembly of all Protestant churches in Scotland, organized into presbyteries and regions. During the 1930s the Church council represented 1,400 active clergy members. The Church council passed anti-Nazi and pro-Jewish resolutions at each of its synods between 1933 and 1945. In addition, the Church council sponsored a non-sectarian refugee relief agency that did not attempt to proselytize among those aided.

International Missionary Council (IMC), multinational religious body dedicated to spreading Protestantism throughout the world. Inter alia, its activities included conversion of Jews. In 1937 the IMC strongly condemned racial antisemitism as fundamentally incompatible with Christianity.

Italia Libera, "Free Italy," coalition of exiled Italian opponents of the Fascist regime. Initially founded in London, the movement later moved to New York, where it gained the support of the Italian-American community. The organization disbanded after the Italian armistice of September 1943.

National Committee Against Nazi Persecution and Extermination of the Jews, established in early 1944 in order to rally American public opinion on behalf of rescue of threatened European Jews. Additionally, the committee also sought to combat antisemitism in the United States.

Office of War Information (OWI), established June 13, 1942, to coordinate the domestic and foreign employment of intelligence and other information. Among other roles, the OWI was responsible for censoring published reports on events in Europe. OWI studiously refused to publish atrocity reports dealing with Jews, although after December 1942 it did not censor such reports in American newspapers. As of March 9, 1943, OWI was also responsible for all overt and covert anti-Nazi propaganda in Europe, the Middle East, and North America. OWI ceased functioning on August 31, 1945.

World Alliance for International Friendship Through the Churches, established in 1914 as a multinational peace group. Organized into national councils that elected the 145-member World Alliance. Between 1933 and 1945 the World Alliance worked to aid Jewish refugees and strongly condemned Nazi antisemitism.

World Council of Churches (WCC), international religious body comprising over 200 Protestant, Anglican, and Eastern Orthodox groups in eighty countries. During the 1930s the WCC strongly condemned racial antisemitism. Before World War II individual members of the WCC hierarchy worked on behalf of refugees, with mixed results. In 1939 the WCC became involved in refugee relief activities, working closely with the World Jewish Congress. The WCC played an especially important role in transmitting information on Nazi actions to the free world.

Pro-Nazi/Fascist

Amerika-Deutscher Volksbund, "German-American Bund," founded as the Friends of the New Germany on June 30, 1932. The Bund supplanted the Fascist Teutonia party. After the Nazi seizure of power, the Bund served as a propaganda tool for the Reich. The Bund was reorganized on December 1, 1935, under the leadership of Fritz Kuhn. Actual membership figures for the Bund are not known, although estimated membership was 25,000, organized into three *Gauen*: *Ost* (Eastern U.S.), *Mittelwest* (Midwest), and *Westen* (West). By 1939 these *Gauen* were organized into 71 locals, including 17 in New York City. From 1936 to 1941 the Bund also acted as a funnel for foreign-currency transfers to the Reich, especially under the guise of charitable donations to the Nazis' Winterhilfe fund.

The Bund's activities led to a 1939 investigation by the House Un-American Activities Committee (the so-called Dies Committee). The hearings turned up a number of financial irregularities in the Bund's books and led to Kuhn's conviction and imprisonment. The Bund was disbanded altogether upon U.S. entry into World War II.

The Silver Shirts, American Nazi-style party founded in 1933. In 1934 the Silver Shirts claimed to have 15,000 members. By 1935 the party peaked, although immediate decline was averted by a merger with the Christian Party. Thereafter, the party did decline, although it continued to have a nuisance value until it disbanded after U.S. entry into World War II. Publications: *Liberation, Silver Legion Ranger*.

Refugee and Relief Agencies

Academic Assistance Council, British organization established in April 1933 to assist Jewish scholars expelled from universities in Nazi Germany.

Alaskan Resettlement Corporation for Refugees, founded in 1939 and advocating the settlement of German Jewish refugees in the U.S. territory of Alaska. The corporation collapsed in 1940 when Congress refused to consider the proposal.

American Friends Service Committee (AFSC), a Quaker philanthropic agency, founded during World War I. During the 1930s the AFSC was chaired by Rufus M. Jones and Clarence E. Pickett and actively supported the cause of German refugees, including Jews. From 1940 on, the AFSC provided the majority of financing for the German Emergency Committee, the Non-Sectarian Committee for Refugee Children, and the Non-Sectarian Foundation for Refugee Children. AFSC worked for refugee relief throughout World War II.

Canadian National Committee on Refugees (CNCR), nonsectarian lobbying agency on behalf of Jewish refugees; created in Ottawa on December 6, 1938. The CNCR lobbied with the Canadian government but failed to obtain any easing of limitations on immigration. Throughout its existence, CNCR publicly eschewed any political identification, even to the extent of never publicly condemning manifestations of antisemitism within the Canadian government.

Church of England Committee for non-Aryan Christians, aid organization founded in the spring of 1933 to aid those German refugees considered Jewish by Nazi racial policy but who were Christian by religion.

Food for Freedom, charitable organization founded in 1942, concerned with providing war relief for European countries. After 1945 Food for Freedom organized itself as a fundraising agency for the United Nations Relief and Rehabilitation Agency (UNRRA).

Intergovernmental Committee on Political Refugees (IGCR), established as a result of the Evian Conference in 1938 and charged with finding a solution to the refugee crisis. Although well meaning, the IGCR was unable to offer any real assistance to Jewish refugees, and the beginning of World War II put the organization virtually out of operation. The Bermuda Conference called for the reorganization of the IGCR, but that proposal proved abortive. Although continuing to exist the IGCR, was rendered marginal by the War Refugee Board. The IGCR was disbanded in 1947 and absorbed by the International Refugee Organization.

International Solidarity Fund (ISF), subsidiary agency created by the British Labour Party in association with the Trades Union Council in 1933 to aid Socialist refugees from Nazi Germany. The ISF operated on two levels: gaining entry visas for these individuals and providing them with stipends to cover their living expenses. Although not directly concerned with the plight of Jewish refugees, the trade unionists insisted that aid in opening the doors of Great Britain for persecuted Jews be part of the ISF agenda. The ISF did not, however, possess the financial wherewithal to aid Jewish refugee funds.

Le Comité National de Secours aux Refugies, "National Committee for Aid to Refugees," a non-sectarian philanthropic organization in France established in 1933 and active until the Nazi occupation.

Movement for the Care of Children from Germany (MCCG), ecumenical rescue agency dedicated to aiding German refugee children, established in February 1938. In two years of operation, MCCG was able to save slightly under 9,500 children, including 8,400 Jewish refugee children. All the children were accommodated in foster homes, with British and Scottish families. The MCCG rescue program was interrupted by World War II and did not resume in 1945. Ironically, many of the children had to be evacuated from their foster homes during the Battle of Britain, thus becoming double refugees. Chairmen: Lord Gorell, Herbert Samuel (1938–1945).

Non-Sectarian Foundation for German Refugee Children, an American non-sectarian organization composed of Protestant, Catholic, and Jewish lay leaders founded in early 1940. Its purpose was to implement the Wagner-Rogers Bill pending before Congress, by assuming responsibility for placing German refugee children in foster homes of their own faith throughout the United States.

President's Advisory Committee on Political Refugees (PACPR), consultative body created by President Franklin D. Roosevelt to aid in developing refugee policies for the United States. PACPR membership included Rabbi Stephen S. Wise, president of the American Jewish Congress, and James G. McDonald, the first League of Nations high commissioner for refugees. Although officially created to advise the president, PACPR almost never met with him, dealing with his State Department advisers instead. PACPR became dormant after U.S. entry into World War II and collapsed altogether in 1943.

Refugee Economic Corporation, relief and research agency, founded in 1934. Dedicated to providing economic and social assistance to refugees from political, racial, and religious persecution. Also conducted research on the issue of resettlement.

United States Committee for the Care of European Children (USC), non-sectarian refugee organization founded in July 1940 by Clarence E. Pickett. The USC superseded the Non-Sectarian Foundation for Refugee Children, also established in 1940. In both guises, USC advocated the immigration of unaccompanied refugee children from the Third Reich, beyond U.S. quota restrictions. Among the more prominent USC supporters was Eleanor Roosevelt. USC continued to operate during and after World War II, disbanding in 1953.

War Refugee Board (WRB), U.S. government rescue agency established by executive order of President Franklin D. Roosevelt on January 22, 1944. Roosevelt's executive order vested the WRB with the power to take all necessary measures to rescue those in imminent danger. In reality, however, the WRB was severely circumscribed, since few of the other arms of the federal government agreed to cooperate with it. This was especially true of the War Department, which saw action for rescue as wasteful of resources needed for prosecuting the war, and the State Department, which obstructed WRB activities as a means of covering up its own inaction on rescue. Reflective of the situation was the fact that most of the WRB's financing came from American Jewish sources and not the government. Although it has been estimated that as many as 200,000 Jews were rescued by the WRB, it is clear that the agency was an example of rescue activity being too little and too late.

Organization der ehemaligen SS Angehörigen [G] [ODESSA] "Organization of former SS members": Secret agency that aided SS members in their escape from justice after World War II. ODESSA received considerable assistance from well-meaning, but naive, church figures who sought to help "anti-Communists" escape from the Soviets. > see also: **Kammeradenwerk**.

Organizatsye Hoch [ארגאניזאציע האך, Y] "Hoch organization": Yiddish term for the Lvov Jewish council after its *Judenälteste* Joseph Hoch. > see also: **Judenrat**.

Organiziren [ארגאניזירן, Y] "Organize": Inmate term in the concentration or slave labor camps. One had to organize or scheme — be it day or night — in order to survive perhaps a little longer, sometimes only an extra day or just a few hours. The term also was used in many ghettos.

Ostabzeichen [G] "East mark": Nazi term for an embroidered square inscribed "Ost" that was mandatory for all Soviet citizens to prominently display while performing forced labor within the Reich.

Ostarbeiter [G] "Eastern worker": Non-Jewish laborers drafted (by force or otherwise) for work in the Reich from Eastern Europe and the Baltics. Though at times maltreated, they were not designated for the incinerator.

Ostmark [G] "Eastern Province": Nazi term for Austria after the *Anschluss*. After the Munich Agreement, the term was also used to refer to the Sudetenland. Early in 1942

the NSDAP banned use of the term.

Ostmensch [G] "Eastern man": Nazi term designating an inferior Eastern European Slav. Nazi racial dogma divided the European nationalities into supposedly "superior" and "inferior" groupings. > see also: **Herrenvolk**.

Ostpolitik [G] "Eastern policy": Nazi term affirming the central aim of German foreign policy: to obtain extra space for the German *Volk* by any means. > see also: **Lebensraum**; **Drang nach Osten**.

Ostraum [G] "Eastern space": Nazi term for parts of Poland and the Soviet Union whose citizens would be deported to make place for Germans to settle in their stead and Germanize the land.

Otryad(i) [R], "Detachment(s)": Official term for units of Soviet partisans. Under an order from Joseph Stalin of July 3, 1941, partisan units of between 200 and 1,000 men were to be established to harass the enemy and continue military operations in the occupied territories. As the partisans became better organized, three types of Otryadi emerged: military, composed of soldiers (generally airborne troops) led by regular officers; civil, composed of civilians led by political commissars; and protection, mixed units used to protect partisan bases. > see also: **Resistance**.

Oysrotung [אויסראטונג, Y] "Extermination": Although conversation regarding the mass slaughter of Jews was generally taboo to perhaps millions of victims, and even the imminent danger of the coming *Aktion* and what its actions would mean to thousands were spoken of in the open by only a select few. The Yiddish term *oysrotung* was voiced in the abstract because few of the victims could visualize the physical destruction of an entire people. Hence the Jewish people went to their death with dignity.

P

P [Identity mark]: Badge worn by Polish *Fremdarbeiter*, a category of Poles who supposedly volunteered to work in Nazi Germany.

PJ: Initials for "Polish Jews" RSHA code name for trains bearing Jews from Poland (*polnische Juden*) to the various death camps.

Palestine Express [Slang]: Nickname for the underground escape organization operating in Paris, led by Haim Victor Gerson who was code-named "Captain Vic" by the British. The name derived from the fact that Gerson and many of his agents were active Zionists, a fact that they emphasized especially to British airmen that they helped to escape. The Nazis made an all-out effort to capture Gerson and succeeded in capturing some of the members of the organization. Nonetheless, Gerson eluded the Gestapo and the "express" continued to operate until liberated in 1944.

Parashutistn [פאראשוטיסטן, Y] "Parachutists": Ghetto term for Jewish smugglers who, risking their life if caught, left the ghetto precincts to trade for food items and other life necessities.

Parashutistn Want [פאראשוטיסטן וואנט, Y] "Parachutist wall": Inmate slang for a high cliff overlooking the Mauthausen *Wienergraben* quarry floor, from whence hundreds of Jewish and some other inmates were forced to jump to their deaths.

Paratroopers, Palestinian

1. Scope and Definition

As early as November and December 1942, the Jewish Agency Executive and the leadership of the Hagana and Palmah advocated using military means to rescue European Jewry. Thus, for example, a defense plan was proposed in 1944 under which Jewish volunteers would be infiltrated into northern Romania to form a guarded camp for Jews escaping the Nazi death machine. Since the Hagana lacked the resources to carry out the mission alone, approval and support had to come from the British or the Americans, neither of whom were willing to sponsor such a mission. Shortly after the defense plan was canceled, however, the British Inter-Service Liaison Detachment (ISLD), an arm of the Special Intelligence Service, approached the Jewish Agency with a proposal to train a group of 32 Palestinian volunteers who would be deployed in the Balkans for espionage and other activities. Additionally, ISLD agreed that the paratroopers would be able to fulfill their Jewish and Zionist missions in terms of rescuing Jewish survivors.

Of 250 volunteers, the 32 were chosen. The majority of members came from the German and Balkan sections of the Palmah, composed almost entirely of Jewish refugees and recent *olim* living in the Yishuv. Of those sent to

Zvi Ben-Yaakov

Abba Berdicev

Peretz Goldstein

Haviva Reik

Raphael Reis

Haim Enzio Sereni

Hannah Szenes

Set of labels issued by the Jewish National Fund to commemorate the seven who fell
Authors' Collection

Europe, 12 fell into Nazi hands; 7 of them died in captivity or were executed as spies. Although the mission of the paratroopers thus did not live up to either its military or rescue potentials, it did serve as an important rallying point for European Jews: it proved that despite the apathy of the world, one group — the Yishuv — cared enough to risk life and limb to rescue even a remnant. Since the end of World War II, the mission of the paratroops has attained near legendary status in Israel and among Jewish communities throughout the world. > see also: **Resistance; Yishuv.**

TABLE P.1: The Paratroopers and Their Missions

Barberman, Sara (Yugoslavia)	Kanner, Uriel (Romania)
Ben-Ephraim, Yitzhak (Romania)	Laner, Dan (Austria)
Ben-Yaakov, Zvi (Slovakia)	Lupsko, Ricco (Romania)
Ben-Yosef, Aaron (Bulgaria)	Mekarisko, Yitzhak (Romania)
Berdicev, Abba (Slovakia)	Nussbacher (Palgi), Joel (Hungary)
Berger, Dov (Romania)	Reik, Haviva (Slovakia)
Dafni, Efra (Italy)	Reis, Raphael (Slovakia)
Dafni, Reuven (Yugoslavia)	Rosenberg, Peretz (Yugoslavia)
Doroguer, Zadok (Italy)	Rosenfeld, Yona (Yugoslavia)
Finzi, Shalom (Yugoslavia)	Sereni, Haim Enzio (Italy)
Fishman, Arye (Romania)	Szenes, Hannah (Hungary)
Gokowski, Lova (Romania)	Testa, Nessim (Yugoslavia)
Goldstein, Peretz (Hungary)	Trachtenberg, Szaika (Romania)
Jablodowski, Rehavam (Yugoslavia)	Varon, Yosef (Bulgaria)
Kamacz, Haim (Slovakia)	Wilander, Haim (Austria)
Kaminker, Baruch (Romania)	Zohar, Eli (Yugoslavia)

Source: Hagana History Archive (ATH), Paratrooper Collection

2. The Seven Who Fell

Ben-Ya'akov, Zvi (1922–1944), captured near Banska Bystrica, Slovakia, October 30, 1944, and executed by the Gestapo at Kremnica.

Berdicev, Abba (1918–1944), killed near Bratislava, Slovakia, while trying to lead a group of escaped Allied prisoners of war to safety.

Goldstein, Peretz (1923–1944), captured crossing Hungarian border and deported to KL Oranienburg, where he was executed under the Nacht und Nebel Erlass.

Reik, Haviva (1914–1944), captured near Banska Bystrica, Slovakia, October 30, 1944, and executed by the Gestapo at Kremnica.

Reis, Raphael (1914–1944), captured near Banska Bystrica, Slovakia, October 30, 1944, and executed by the Gestapo at Kremnica.

Sereni, Haim Enzio (1905–1944), captured in Tuscany, Italy, May 15, 1944, and de-ported to Mauthausen, where he was executed on November 18, 1944, under the Nacht und Nebel Erlass.

Szenes, Hannah (1921–1944), captured June 7, 1944, and executed after a trial for treason in Budapest, on November 7, 1944.

Parrout présent et faire face [Fr] "Be present everywhere and stand up": Armée Juive motto, coined by David Knout, one of the founders of the underground. As a teacher and ideologue for the Jewish resistance in France, Knout felt that the underground served a role besides fighting the Nazis. That role, as expressed in this motto, was to foster a sense of Jewish solidarity and a willingness to become involved in Jewish communal affairs.

Partei [פארטיי, Y] "Party": Ghetto term alluding to the Jewish underground. In light of a certain number of planted Gestapo agents and/or Jewish informers, any allusion to an existing resistance cell would have meant instant death and untold misery for scores or hundreds of Jews.

Partisanjäger [G] "Partisan Hunters": Light infantry units created to combat partisans in Eastern Europe. Although drawn almost exclusively from Wehrmacht personnel, the *Partisanjäger* often took part in atrocities committed against unarmed civilians, including Jews.

Peitsche und Zucker [G] "Whip and sugar": Nazi term for the policy instituted by Reinhard Heydrich and pursued toward the Czech population in the Protektorat. Each of the two items, the whip and the sugar, represented means by which the Nazis hoped to deter resistance in the short-run and to force the Germanization of the Czech population in the long-run.

Pinkert yinglech [פינקערט יינגלעך, Y] "Pinkert boys": Yiddish term for the Warsaw ghetto grave diggers and garbage collectors. The term derives from the name of American detectives (the Pinkerton men) popularized by cowboy films.

Placowke [P] "Place": Slang Polish term for groups of young Jews forced to work for the Nazis, at Judenrat expense, outside the Polish ghettos.

Poglavnik [Croat] "Leader": Croatian title, adopted in 1941, for Ante Pavelić, the "*Führer*" of the puppet state of Croatia during World War II. > see also: **Fascism**.

Pogrom [R] "Attack":

1. Scope and Definition

Common term for physical attacks on Jews, usually accompanied by the destruction of property, murder, and rape. Most commonly, the term has been used to designate the physical attacks visited upon Jews in Czarist — and revolutionary — Russia and Eastern Europe since 1881. Historians have noted three eras of pogroms in Russia: (1) 1881 to 1882, after Narodnik terrorists assassinated Czar Alexander II; (2) 1903 to 1905, when the Russian government used pogroms as a means to release revolutionary tensions building up in Russian society; and (3) 1919 to 1921, when dislocations caused by the Russian Civil War permitted Russians, especially those associated with the counterrevolutionary "Whites," to act without fear of police authorities. Since 1921, the term has meant any attack on Jews, whether systematic or spontaneous, in any country. Interwar Poland, was particularly prone to spontaneous pogroms, very often started when members of Endecja student groups attempted to force Jewish students in the Polish universities to sit on "ghetto benches." The systematic Nazi assault on German Jewry during the night of November 9/10, 1938 — *Kristallnacht* — is possibly the best known-pogrom of the twentieth century. In addition, the Nazis used pogroms — especially in occupied Soviet territory — as a cover for murder operations against Jews. Pogroms were, surprisingly, also encountered in postwar Poland and other parts of Eastern Europe, when a handful of survivors sought to come back to their former homes. > see also: **Antisemitismus; Libels, anti-Jewish; Kristallnacht**.

TABLE P.2: Major Twentieth-Century Pogroms

Date	Location	Killed	Injured
4/19/1903	Kishinev	47	424
8/10/1903	Gomel	8	100
8/13/1904	Ostrowicze	20	19
10/24/1904	Vitebsk	NA	120
11/04/1904	Ovidiopol	11	212
2/15/1905	Gomel	1	300

2/18/1905	Dvinsk	NA	200
2/21/1905	Theodosia	47	50
4/23/1905	Pavlikovka	13	NA
5/11/1905	Zhitomir	29	150
6/30/1905	Lodz	341	500
7/12/1905	Bialystok	10	300
7/23/1905	Kiev	100	406
8/14/1905	Bialystok	60	200
9/04/1905	Kishinev	4	80
9/30/1905	Ekaterinoslav	2	368
10/31/1905	Odessa	800	5,000
10/31/1905	Kiev	60	369
11/01/1905	Kishinev	35	100
11/01/1905	Minsk	100	485
11/01/1905	Simferopol	50	NA
11/02/1905	Yusovka	12	90
11/02/1905	Rostov on the Don	34	159
11/02/1905	Theodosia	12	300
11/03/1905	Elisabetgrad	10	100
11/03/1905	Orsha	30	NA
11/03/1905	Tomsk	1,000	NA
11/04/1905	Kremenchug	20	80
11/07/1905	Kalarash	100	80
6/14/1906	Bialystok	200	700
9/08/1906	Siedlce	32	20
5/07/1919	Braslav	82	12
5/09/1919	Maly Trostinets	400	NA
5/14/1919	Olgopol	20	100
5/28/1919	Maly Trostinets	400	NA
5/31/1919	Cherkassy	700	NA
6/04/1919	Kamenets-Podolski	100	NA
6/15/1919	Jaltichkov	148	NA
7/05/1919	Dunkov	24	150
7/29/1919	Uman	200	NA
10/27/1919	Przemysl	15	NA
11/28/1919	Kielce	15	600
1/17/1920	Wodzislaw	20	20
3/11/1920	Lvov	73	463
4/24/1920	Hodorkov	700	800
6/03/1920	Cholm	8	30
6/06/1920	Jezierani	NA	200
6/06/1920	Dubno	700	NA
8/24/1920	Czelldomolk	10	100
10/09/1920	Vilna	80	NA
5/21/1921	Jaffa	34	NA
6/15/1921	Czapowicz	26	NA
7/16/1921	Zhitomir	43	NA
9/24/1921	Woinilow	10	45
10/01/1921	Bolsowze	21	NA
10/01/1921	Bukazowce	24	NA

8/05/1934	Constantine (Alg)	24	60
3/09/1936	Przytyk	NA	NA
4/15/1938	Dąbrowa	NA	NA
4/29/1938	Vilna	NA	NA
11/09/1938	Kristallnacht	100	NA
11/11/1938	Bratislava	NA	NA

Source: *American Jewish Yearbook*, Philadelphia: Jewish Publication Society, 1903-1938.

Politische Bereitsschaften [G] "Political squads": The groups of full-time Nazi Party rowdies that eventually developed into the SS-Verfügungstruppen. > see also: **Schutzstaffel, Subsidiary Agencies (Waffen-SS)**.

Prinz-Albrecht Palais [PN] "Prince Albert Palace": From 1935 on, the headquarters building of the SS, SD, and Gestapo in Berlin. Commonly referred to as at one address, the agencies were actually housed in three adjacent buildings on Prinz-Albrecht Strasse. Steady expansion of the SS domain meant that the buildings were soon overcrowded and expansion began soon after the outbreak of World War II. By 1943 SS headquarters and those of subsidiaries occupied more than thirty buildings in Berlin. In 1987 the street — heavily damaged during the April 1945 battle for Berlin — was excavated, with the ultimate intention of creating a memorial to the victims of Nazi terror.

Prisoners of War (POW):

1. Scope and Definition

The treatment of POWs has been regulated by both international law and practice for almost as long as there have been wars. In 1929 all the European powers except the Soviet Union signed the Geneva Convention on the Treatment of Prisoners of War. The treaty strictly regulated treatment, punishments, and the use of POWs for forced labor. Despite the fact that Germany signed the Geneva Convention, the Nazis did not fully comply with the treaty. Soviet prisoners were maltreated, underfed, and forced to do menial slave labor. Large numbers were killed outright, including six hundred murdered in a gas chamber experiment at Auschwitz in December 1941 and January 1942. A total of six million Soviet POWs are estimated to have lost their lives in Nazi captivity. Polish prisoners of war experienced a somewhat less brutal fate. In contrast, the Nazis meted out much less severe treatment to POWs originating in the United States and Great Britain. Still, many POWs died in captivity or were killed, including fifty recaptured Royal Air Force officers who had escaped from Stalag-Luft II in 1944 and were murdered on Hitler's explicit orders.

In general, the treatment accorded to Jewish POWs was the same as that accorded to nationals of their countries of origin. Thus American and British Jews captured by the Nazis, as well as members of Jewish units from the Yishuv fighting for the British, were treated relatively well. Polish and Russian Jewish POWs — with the exception of Polish Jewish officers — were murdered by the Nazis. > see also: **Kugelerlass; War Effort, Jewish**.

TABLE P.3: Major Types of POW Camps

Offizierenlager	[Offlag]	Officer POW Camp
Stammlager	[Stalag]	Prisoner of war camp
Stammlager-Luft	[Stalag-Luft]	Air force POW camp

TABLE P.4: Stalags Holding Polish Jewish POWs

ID Number	Camp Name	Location
Stalag IA	Stablack	East Prussia
Stalag IB	Hohenstein	East Prussia
Stalag IIA	Neu Brandenburg	Pomerania
Stalag IIB	Hammerstein	Pomerania
Stalag IID	Stargard	Pomerania
Stalag IIIA	Luckenwalde	West Prussia
Stalag VIA	Hamer	Westphalia
Stalag VIC	Rathorn	Westphalia
Stalag VID	Dortmund	Westphalia
Stalag VIIA	Moosburg	Bavaria
Stalag VIIIB	Lamsdorf	Upper Silesia[1]
Stalag XIA	Altengrabow	Hanover
Stalag XIIA	Limburg	Wiesbaden
Stalag XIIB	Frankenthal	Wiesbaden
Stalag XIIID	Nuremberg	Bavaria
Stalag XVIIA	Kaisersteinbruch	Austria

Source: S. Senft and H. Więcek, *Obozy jenieckie na obsarze Śląskiego Okręgu Wehrmachtu 1939–1945*, Wroclaw: Zaklad Narodowy im Ossolinskinch, 1972.

Privilegierte Gefangene [G] "Privileged prisoners": Nazi term for captured Jewish soldiers of the American and British armies. Generally, captured Jewish soldiers from the occupied countries were not treated according to the Geneva Convention but were liable to the lot that befell European Jewry under Nazi occupation.

Prominenten [G] "Important ones": KL inmate term for German or Austrian convicted criminals who were picked by the SS to run the internal makeup of the concentration camps. In their brutality they even outdid the SS-Totenkopfverbände that guarded the camps. > see also: **Konzentrationslager System**.

Protektsye papirn [פראטעקציע פאפירן, Y] "Protection papers": Yiddish term for visas or other personal documents issued by certain neutral countries identifying the bearer as being under the protection of that country. While such papers did not help save Jews during the early years of the War, by 1944 they were used to good effect by representatives of neutral countries and the Red Cross in saving thousands of Hungarian Jews during Aktion Margarethe.

Protokolle der Weissen von Zion [G] "The Protocols of the Elders of Zion": Infamous antisemitic forgery produced by the czarist secret police and first published in 1911. The text purports to be the protocol of a secret meeting held during the First Zionist Congress and is variously attributed to Theodor Herzl or a member of the Rothschild or Bleichröder families. The speaker details a conspiracy to use liberalism and communism as means to attain Jewish domination of the entire world. The text was reprinted in many different editions and languages. The German and English editions were probably the most influential. In recent

---

[1] Lamsdorf also contained a large contingent of Jewish enlisted POWs from the Royal Army, including many from the Yishuv.

years, an Arabic edition has been published by the Saudi Arabian government.

Publications

1. Scope and Definition

Before World War II, the Jewish world was serviced by a widely ramified and politically sophisticated press. In almost every country the press represented a link within the community and a bridge between communities spread across the globe. Under the circumstances, a fully comprehensive review is impossible. The following data reflect only a sampling of the literally thousands of periodicals that appeared during the years between 1933 and 1945, noting who was responsible for the editing during that period (only). We have limited our selections to major journals for which data was available, listing other verified titles as an addendum to each country.

2. Jewish

Australia

Australian Jewish Herald (AJH), English-language weekly, published by the Jewish community of Melbourne since 1879. During the 1930s and 1940s AJH closely reflected the attitudes of the Australian Jewish Welfare Society. A strong advocate of rescue, AJH was less willing to openly criticize the Jewish communal leadership.

Australian Jewish Historical Society Journal and Proceedings, semi-annual scholarly journal appearing in Sydney since 1939. Peak circulation was 700. Editor: M. Z. Forbes.

Australian Jewish News (AJN), bilingual, English and Yiddish, weekly, published in Melbourne since 1933. AJN was active in advocacy of rescue and was a staunch critic of the apparent timidity of many Australian Jewish leaders. Editor: I. Schnierer.

Austria

Der Jude, "The Jew," Zionist monthly published between 1934 and 1938. Publication ceased at Gestapo order after the *Anschluss*.

Belgium

De Centraale, "The Center," monthly organ of the Belgian Jewish community. Published since 1923, in Yiddish and Flemish. Publication ceased during the Nazi occupation, but resumed (as a quarterly) in 1945.

Bulgaria

Poale-Zion, "Zionist Worker," official Bulgarian-language publication of the Poale-Zion, appearing in Sofia between 1930 and 1939. Publication was interrupted at government order between February 1939 and October 1944. Thereafter publication resumed until July 1948, when the entire staff emigrated to Israel. *Poale-Zion's* editorial policy tended toward the left on internal Zionist affairs but supported Mapai and the Jewish Agency on external issues. Editors: Joseph Reuven (until 1939); Shabbetai Ashkenazi (1944–1948).

Razvet, official Bulgarian-language publication of Ha-Zohar in Bulgaria, appearing in Sofia between 1927 and 1940. From 1935 on, published as a weekly. Editor: Raphael Levi (1935–1940).

Yevreski Ratz, "Jewish Voice," independent Jewish monthly published in Sofia between 1932 and 1941. Given special permission to publish after the government ordered the Jewish press to cease in 1939, *Yevreski Ratz* was halted after the adoption of the Bulgarian racial laws in June 1941. Zionist and nationalist in orientation, *Yevreski Ratz* tried to remain above partisan Jewish politics. Editor: Albert Michael.

Canada

Kanader Adler [קאנאדער אדלער], "Canadian Eagle," Canadian Yiddish newspaper founded in Montreal in 1907 as a weekly. Soon afterwards, the newspaper became a daily, but since 1963 publication has been less regular. Since 1914 the *Adler* has also published the *Canadian Jewish Chronicle* as its weekly English-language edition. Circulation peaked at 18,000. Editor: Israel Rabinovitch.

Other Canadian-Jewish Publications:

Canadian Jewish Review (Montreal), 1921–1966.

Der Yidisher Zhurnal (Toronto), 1915–1967.
Dos Yidishe Vort (Winnipeg), 1910–1969.
Vochnblat (Toronto), 1926–current.

Czechoslovakia

Allgemeine Jüdische Zeitung (AJZ), "General Jewish Newspaper," Orthodox weekly published in German and Yiddish in Slovakia from 1933 to 1939. Publication ceased at the demand of the Tiso government and was never resumed. Pro-Zionist in orientation, AJZ reflected the position of the Mizrachi Party. Editors: David Gross, Moshe Müller.

Jüdische Volksstimme, "Jewish People's Voice," Zionsit weekly published in German in Brno between 1901 and 1939. Publication ceased upon the Nazi occupation and was not resumed. Editors: Max Hickl, Hugo Gold.

Selbstwehr, "Self-Defense," Zionist weekly published in Prague in German and Czech from 1918 to 1938. Considered one of the most prominent Zionist publications in Central Europe, *Selbstwehr* published articles on a wide range of Jewish topics. Editors: Felix Weltsch, Hans Lichtwitz.

Vestnik Zidovskych Nábozenskych Obci v Ceskoslovensku, "Publication of the Jewish Community Council of Czechoslovakia," official *kehila* monthly published in Prague in 1938 and 1939. The Gestapo halted the *Vestnik* in March 1939, but publication resumed in 1945.

Other Czech-Jewish Publications:

Českožidovskykalendar (Prague), 1881–1938.
Judaica (German, Bratislava), 1934–1937.
Zeitschrift für die Geschichte der Juden in der Tschechoslowakei (German/Czech, Brno and Prague), 1930–1938.

France

Di Naye Presse [די נייע פרעסע], "The New Press," Franco-Jewish Communist daily, published in Yiddish in Paris between 1934 and 1939. In 1934 and 1935 the paper followed Communist policy regarding Jews and Judaism, viewing both as archaic and expressing special opposition to Zionism.

Articles repeatedly attacked the organized Jewish community. This policy changed with the adoption of the Popular Front in 1936 and was most singularly represented by the editors' belated support for the Jewish anti-Nazi boycott.

Revue des Études Juives (REJ), "Review of Jewish Studies," scholarly quarterly published in Paris since 1880. REJ ceased publication during the Nazi occupation but resumed in 1945. During the 1960s REJ united with the English quarterly *Historia Judaica* and since then has published bilingual, English and French, issues.

Pariser Tagblatt, "Paris Daily," German-language daily published by Jewish refugees in Paris between 1933 and 1938. Although widely circulated, the transient nature of the refugee community meant that the paper was never able to build up its circulation and the entire project folded for financial reasons in early 1938.

Unzer Stimme [אונדזער שטימע], "Our Voice," Yiddish daily published in Paris between 1933 and 1940. Officially published by the Jewish Socialist Bund in France, *Unzer Stimme* was, in effect, a subsidiary of the Bund's Warsaw daily *Folkstsaytung*.

Other Franco-Jewish Publications:

Le Judaïsme Sephardi (Paris), 1932–1940.
L'Univers Israélite (Paris), 1844–1940.

Germany

CV Zeitung, "CV Newspaper," official monthly of the Centralverein Deutscher Staatsbürger Jüdischen Glaubens, published between 1895 and 1935. Enunciating an assimilationist and anti-Zionist orientation, the *CV Zeitung* was closed at Gestapo order when the Centralverein was transformed into the Reichsvertretung der Deutschen Juden. > see also: **Organizations, European Jewish, Pre-Nazi (Germany); Judenrat.**

Der Israelit, "The Israelite," Orthodox Jewish weekly published between 1860 and 1938. From 1912 on, *Der Israelit* served as the official organ of Agudas Israel. Publication ceased just before *Kristallnacht.*

Der Schild, "The Shield," official publication of the Jewish veterans association, published between 1921 and 1938. Publication ceased after *Kristallnacht*.

Israelitisches Familienblatt, "Jewish Family Paper," independent weekly published in Hamburg between 1898 and 1938. Although published in one community, news from throughout Germany and the entire Jewish world was included. From 1935 the paper was transferred to Berlin and became the official organ of the Reichsvertretung der Deutschen Juden. Peak circulation was 30,000 in 1937. Publication ceased just after *Kristallnacht*. Editor: Ezriel Carlebach.

Jahrbuch für jüdische Geschichte und Literatur, "Yearbook for Jewish History and Literature," scholarly periodical published in Berlin between 1898 and 1938 by the Verein für jüdische Geschichte und Literatur. Edited by Ismar Elbogen, the yearbook was famous for the high caliber of its contributors. Circulation peaked at 5,000. The Gestapo halted publication just before *Kristallnacht*.

Jüdische Rundschau (JR), "Jewish Observer," official weekly of the Zionistische Verein für Deutschland, published between 1897 and 1938. The publication was closed at Gestapo order just after *Kristallnacht*. In 1939 and 1940 JR was replaced by *Jüdische Welt-Rundschau*, a short-lived weekly published in Paris and printed in Tel Aviv.

Other German-Jewish Publications:
Israelitische Gemeindezeitung (Munich), 1924–1938.
Monatsschrift für die Geschichte und Wissenschaft des Judentums (Breslau), 1902–1938.

Great Britain
Di Tsayt (די צייט), "The Times," Yiddish-language daily appearing in London between 1913 and 1950. Pro-Zionist in orientation, the editorial line supported Mapai and the Jewish Agency. In 1944 the newspaper switched to weekly publication. Highly influential on London's East End, *Di Tsayt* halted publication after a majority of Anglo-Jews ceased to read Yiddish.

Jewish Chronicle, authoritative weekly of the Anglo-Jewish community, published in London since 1841. The *Chronicle* was one of the earliest journals to publish details on Nazi anti-semitic actions in 1933 and continued to do so throughout the Holocaust period. Circulation peaked in 1945, at 60,000.

Jewish Standard (JS), English-language fortnightly published in London between 1888 and 1945. Officially independent, during the 1930s JS adopted a Revisionist Zionist orientation that was retained throughout the remaining years of publication. Editor: Abraham Abrahams (1933–1945).

Zionist Review (ZR), official monthly organ of the English Zionist Federation, published between 1917 and 1952. Peak circulation was 16,000.

Other Anglo-Jewish Publications:
Association of Jewish Refugees in Great Britain, Information (London), 1941–current.
Jewish Echo (Glasgow), 1928–current.
Losh un Lebn (London), 1940–current.

Holland
De Joodse Wachter, "The Jewish Watchman," Dutch-language monthly of the Nederlandsche Zionistische Beweging, published between 1905 and 1940. Publication was interrupted by World War II but resumed in 1945.

Other Dutch-Jewish Publications:
Baderech (The Hague; in Dutch language, Hebrew title), 1925–1938.
Berit Halutsim Datiyim (Amsterdam; Hebrew/Dutch), 1935–1939.
Centraal blad voor Israeliten in Nederland (Amsterdam), 1885–1940.
Het Beloofde Land (Amsterdam), 1922–1940.
Nieuw Israeliétisch Weekblad (Amsterdam) 1865–current.

Hungary
Egyenlöség, "Equality," weekly organ of the Neolog (reform) Jewish community in Hungary appearing in Budapest from 1881 to 1938. Publication ceased due to a government ban.

Magyar zsidó szemle, "Hungarian Jewish Review," scholarly journal appearing in Budapest between 1884 and 1948. Publication was disrupted, but never completely halted, during World War II. Editor: Ludwig Blau.

Mult es jövő, "Past and Future," Zionist monthly concentrating on Jewish cultural affairs, appearing in Budapest between 1911 and 1944. Banned by the Gestapo after the German invasion of Hungary. Editor: József Patai.

Other Hungarian-Jewish Publications:
Évkönyv (Budapest), 1897–1944.
Zsidó Szemle (Budapest), 1909–1938.

Italy
La Nostra Bandiera, "Our Flag," organ of the Jewish Fascists, published in Turin during the 1920s and early 1930s. Publication ceased after the promulgation of Italy's racial laws in 1938.

La Rassegna Mensile di Israel, "The Monthly Review of Israel," Orthodox monthly published in Rome between 1925 and 1938. Publication was halted by the government in 1938 but resumed in 1948. Editor: Guido Bedarida.

Latin America
Dos Blat: Revista Familiar Quincenal, "The Sheet: A Family Review," bi-monthly Yiddish/Spanish newspaper published by and for Jewish refugees in Bogota, Colombia, between 1938 and 1960.

Jüdische Wochenschau — La Semana Israelita, "Jewish Weekly Review — The Jewish Week," weekly by and for German Jewish refugees, published in Buenos Aires, Argentina between 1942 and 1948.

Other Latin American–Jewish Publications:
Boletin informativo (Santiago), 1938–current.
Der Argentiner Magazin (Buenos Aires), 1936–current.
Di Prese (Buenos Aires), 1918–current.
Di Yidishe Tsaytung (Buenos Aires), 1914–current.
Foroys (Mexico City), 1940–current.
Havaner Lebn (Havana), 1933–1939.

Poland
Chwila, "Moment," Polish-language daily published by the Zionist organization in Lvov between 1919 and 1939. Highly regarded, the newspaper was respected by non-Zionists and by Zionists of all ideological stripes. Editor: Henryk Hescheles.

Folkstsaytung [פאלקסצייטונג], "People's Paper," official daily organ of the Jewish Bund published between 1921 and 1939. Edited by Alexander Ehrlich and Wiktor Alter. Legal publication ceased in October 1939, but it continued underground irregularly until 1943. Resumed publication as *Naye Folkstsaytung* after World War II until taken over by Communist authorities in 1948.

Grafic Żydowski, "Jewish Graphic," Polish/Yiddish monthly illustrated newsmagazine appearing in Warsaw between 1929 and 1937. Concentrated on photojournalism, with bilingual captions. Publication ceased due to financial difficulties.

Haynt [הײנט], "Today," Yiddish-language daily published in Warsaw between 1908 and September 22, 1939. Zionist in orientation, *Haynt* tended toward the center-left on Jewish issues. During the mid-1930s *Haynt* also published a subsidiary newspaper in Paris under the title *Parisier Haynt*.

Moment [מאמענט], Yiddish-language daily published in Warsaw between 1910 and 1939. Zionist in alignment, *Moment* tended toward the center-right on Jewish issues. In 1938 and 1939, *Moment* adopted a revisionist orientation. Circulation peaked at 60,000 just before World War II.

Other Polish-Jewish Publications:
Arbeter Tsaytung (Warsaw), 1918–1939.
Di Tog (Warsaw), 1938–1939.
Di Woch (Stanislawow), 1934–1939.
Dos Yidishe Togblat (Warsaw), 1929–1939.
Fraye Shriftn (Warsaw), 1926–1937.
Literarishe Bleter (Warsaw), 1924–1939.
Lubliner Togblat (Lublin), 1918–1939.
Maly Przzeglqd (Warsaw), 1926–1939.
Miesięcznik Żydowski (Warsaw), 1930–1935.
Nasz Przglqd (Warsaw), 1923–1939.

Naye Folksblat (Lodz), 1923–1939.
Nowy Dziennik (Cracow), 1918–1939.
Unzer Ekspres (Warsaw), 1926–1939.
Varshever Radyo (Warsaw), 1924–1939.
Yugnt-veker (Warsaw), 1922–1939.

Switzerland

Israelitisches Wochenblatt, "Jewish Weekly,"
independent Jewish newspaper published in
Zurich in German and French since 1901.

Jüdische Rundschau, "Jewish Observer," religious Zionist weekly published in Basel
from 1940 on. Replaced *Jüdische Welt Rundschau* but has been more attuned to Swiss
Jewish issues since World War II.

United States

American Hebrew, English-language
weekly, published in New York between
1879 and 1969. Orthodox in orientation, the
publication has remained officially independent of any political or religious association. Editors: Isaac Landman, Louis Biden.

Anti-Nazi News, published by the Holly-
wood Anti-Nazi League in Defense of
American Democracy. Contained short articles and reviews of news items on Nazi
Germany, fascism in Europe, the Pacific,
and the Americas, including the United
States. The league was affiliated with the
National Committee on Justice for Victims
of Nazism. Published from October 20, 1936,
through February 2, 1940.

Aufbau, "Reconstruction," German Jewish
weekly published in New York since 1934.
Circulation peaked at 30,000 just after
World War II, primarily among German
Jewish refugees who settled in New York.
Editor: Manfred George.

Boro Park and Vicinity Anti-Nazi Bulletin,
published by the United Anti-Nazi Council
of Boro Park. Stated aim of the bulletin was
to organize the people of Boro Park to boycott Nazi goods and services and to combat
antisemitism in all its forms. Published
December 1936 through 1937.

Boycott News Bulletin, published by the
Detroit League for Human Rights. Mainly
exposed businesses that did not adhere to
the American boycott of German goods and
services.

Contemporary Jewish Record (CJR), monthly
published by the Amrrican Jewish Committee
from 1940 to 1945. Oriented toward news
analysis, CJR also included a monthly update
of important events around the Jewish world.
In 1945 CJR was transformed in *Commentary*.
Editor: Elliot Cohen.

Der Yidishe Tog (דער יידישע טאג), "The Jewish Day," Yiddish daily newspaper published in
New York from 1914 to 1953. During the 1930s
and 1940s the *Tog* was actively pro-Zionist in
its orientation. Editors: Samuel Margoshes, B.
Z. Goldberg. In 1953 the *Tog* merged with the
Morgen Zhornal.

Forverts (פארווערטס), "Forward," Yiddish
daily published in New York since 1897.
Socialist in orientation, during the Holocaust
era *Forverts's* editorial opposition to Zionism
mellowed. Peak circulation reached 200,000
after World War I but fell to 80,000 in the
1940s. In the 1930s *Forverts* opened a radio
station, WEVD. Editor: Abraham Cahan.

Jewish Frontier (JF), monthly organ of the
American Friends of Labor Palestine, published since 1934. Oriented toward the
moderate position espoused by Mapai, JF has
been considered influential among liberal and
pro-Zionist circles throughout the United
States. Editor: Hayim Greenberg.

Jewish Spectator (JS), independent monthly
published since 1939 by the School of the Jewish Woman in New York City. Although oriented toward scholarly and educational issues, JS
has been very much a representative of the
personal style of journalism that concerned
itself with both historical and contemporary
Jewish issues. Editor: Trude Weiss-Rosmarin.

Jewish Telegraphic Agency (JTA), press
agency providing wire services for a wide range
of Jewish periodicals, founded in The Hague in
1914. JTA moved to London in 1919 and to
New York in 1922. JTA has published both
daily and weekly news bulletins from 1924 on.
Editor: Boris Smolar.

Morgen Zhornal [מארגן זשורנאל], "Morning
Journal," Yiddish daily published in New York
from 1901 to 1953, when it merged with the
Tog. Combined an orthodox religious orientation with intense support for Zionism.

Circulation peaked before World War II at 111,000. Editor: Jacob Fishman.

National Jewish Monthly (NJM), monthly organ of B'nai B'rith published in Washington, D.C. since 1886. In addition to news reports and editorials, NJM has published updates on international events related to B'nai B'rith. Non-Zionist in orientation during the 1930s, NJM's editorial orientation changed to pro-Zionist after 1942.

New Palestine (NP), official bimonthly organ of the Zionist Organization of America, published in Washington, D.C. between 1921 and 1948. After the establishment of the State of Israel, the title was changed to *The American Zionist*.

Yishuv

Davar (דבר), "Word," Hebrew daily published in Tel Aviv by the Histadrut and Mapai since 1925. Between 1925 and 1944 *Davar's* editor was Berl Katznelson.

Ha'aretz (הארץ), "The Land," independent daily published since 1919. During the 1930s the editor of *Ha'aretz* was Dr. Moshe Glickson.

Jüdische Welt-Rundschau (JWR), "Jewish World Observer," Zionist weekly that repalced the *Jüdische Rundschau*. Published in Paris and printed in Tel Aviv, JWR ceased publication after the Nazi occupation of France in June 1940.

MB, Wochenzeitung des Irgun Olej Merkas Europa, "MB, Weekly of the Organization of Central European Immigrants," German-language newsletter appearing in Tel Aviv since 1933. Initially printed as a mimeographed newsletter, MB has been published as a regular weekly since 1939. After World War II the title was shortened to *Mitteilungsblatt*.

Palestine Post (PP), independent, but pro-Mapai, English-language daily published in Jerusalem since 1933. Originally called *The Palestine Bulletin*, the title was changed in 1933; the title changed again in 1949 to *The Jerusalem Post*. Throughout the Nazi era PP was edited by Gershom Agronsky (later Agron), a prominent supporter of Mapai and the Jewish Agency.

Other Yishuv Publications:

Bamahaneh (Tel Aviv), 1934–current.
Haboker (Tel Aviv), 1935–1965.
Hamashkif (Tel Aviv), 1938–1948.
Hayarden (Jerusalem), 1934–1941.
Jedioth Chadashot (German, Tel Aviv), 1935–current.
Nayvelt (Yiddish, Tel Aviv), 1934–1955.

Yugoslavia

Jevrejski Glas, "Jewish Voice," weekly organ of the Yugoslav Jewish community published between 1928 and 1941. Ceased publication upon the Nazi occupation.

3. Antisemitic, Fascist, and Nazi

Austria

Östreicher Beobachter (OB), "Austrian Observer," official organ of the Austrian Nazi Party, published as the equivalent of the German *Völkischer Beobachter*. Between 1934 and 1938 OB was published as an underground paper. Antisemitism played a prominent role in OB, as it did in its parent publication. After the *Anschluss* OB appeared as the official daily of Ostmark (Eastern Province), Austria's new name. Publication ceased in 1945.

Belgium

Ami du Peuple, "Friend of the People," journal of the Volksverweering organization and appearing during the 1930s. Antisemitic and rabidly nationalistic in orientation. Publication ceased in 1940, since antisemitism and nationalism were incompatible under the exigencies of Nazi occupation.

De Schelde, "The Shield," official journal of the Vlaamsch Nationaal Verbond, appearing between 1933 and 1936. From 1936 to 1944 the journal appeared as *Volk en Staat* (Folk and State). Nationalistic and pro-Nazi in orientation, neither publication enunciated a specifically antisemitic orientation. Publication ceased after the liberation of Belgium. Editor: Antoon Meremans. > see also: **Fascism, Fascist Parties and Organizations (Belgium)**.

Le Pays Réel, "The Real Country," journal of the Rexist movement, published in Brussels between 1935 and 1945. During the 1930s the journal's editorial line was mildly anti-semitic, but that position solidified and became more virulent during the war. *Le Pays Réel* continued to publish during the war and adopted an openly collaborationist orientation. > see also: **Fascism, Fascist Parties and Organizations (Belgium)**.

Bulgaria

Ataka, "Attack," weekly newspaper published by the Bulgarian Nazis. Edited by Khristo Kunchev.

Durzhaven Vestnik, "Official Gazette," journal for the promulgation of decrees and laws passed by the Bulgarian government.

Canada

L'Action Catholic, "Catholic Action," official Catholic Church publication appearing in Quebec from 1931 on. During the 1930s and 1940s the editorial line was openly antisemitic, anti-British, and pro-Fascist.

Action Nationale, "National Action," publication of the French Canadian Patriotic Front, a quasi-Fascist party active in Quebec. Associated broadly with the Action Française, during the 1930s the newspaper advocated secession from Canada and was actively antisemitic in orientation. Editor: Lionel Groulx.

Czechoslovakia

Poledni List, "Midday Scroll," journal with Fascist tendencies and antisemitic overtones, published in Prague from 1926 to April/May 1945. Its editorial articles were especially antisemitic during the Nazi occupation. Editor: J. Střibrným.

Denmark

Kamptegnet, "Combat Journal," journal of the National-Socialistike Arbejer Parti, the only major antisemitic party in modern Danish history. Published in Copenhagen between 1935 and 1942. Circulation was limited to party members only and thus the journal had little influence on Danish society. In 1942 the Danish Jewish community sued the editors for libel and won their case in a Danish court, which ordered

publication ceased.

France

L'Action Française, "French Action," official daily organ of the Action Française, appearing between 1908 and August 1944. Created in the aftermath of the Dreyfus Affair, the paper was overtly antisemitic and *L'Action Française* enunciated a pro-Nazi orientation during the 1940s.

La Libre Parole, "The Free Word," daily antisemitic newspaper published between 1892 and 1940. Founded and edited by Eduard Drumont, *La Libre Parole* was the official publication of his Antisemitic League until his death in 1910. The league was strongly Catholic in its leanings, and Drumont's motto was "France for the French." After 1910 the newspaper's antisemitic orientation became more subdued. Publication ceased with the Nazi invasion of France.

Revue Internationale des Sociétés Secrètes, "International Review of Secret Societies," investigative Catholic news journal seeking to expose the Judeo-Masonic world conspiracy, appearing in Paris between 1909 and 1939. In the early 1920s the Review editors sponsored the publication of a French translation of the *Protocols of the Elders of Zion*. A new edition of the *Protocols* was serialized in the Review during 1934.

Germany

Archiv für Judenfragen, "Archive for Jewish Questions," publication of Joseph Goebbels's Institut zum Studium der Judenfrage, appearing between 1943 and 1945. The publication succeeded *Die Judenfrage*, published by the Institut from 1941 to 1943. Circulation was never very high, despite the high quality of the publication. Editor: Friedrich Löffler.

Blick in die Zeit, "A Look at the Times," monthly political and cultural journal published in Berlin under Nazi auspices between November 1933 and July 1935. Arranged as a collection of press clippings on events in Germany and throughout the world, *Blick in die Zeit* carried the obligatory number of antisemitic articles. Editor: A. Ristow.

Das Schwarze Korps, "The Black Corps,"

official weekly of the SS, published between March 6, 1935, and April 12, 1945. Approximate circulation reached 750,000 in 1944.

Der Angriff, "The Attack," organ published by Joseph Goebbels from July 4, 1927, to April 24, 1945. Between 1927 and 1929 *Der Angriff* was a monthly; in 1929 and 1930 it appeared twice weekly; in 1931 and 1932 daily, and thereafter twice daily. Approximate circulation reached 300,000 in 1944.

Der Judenkenner, "The Jew Knower," Nazi antisemitic periodical published by Julius Streicher on an irregular basis. Known for its rude manner, the *Judenkenner* was aimed primarily at a younger German audience.

Der Stürmer, "The Stormer," popular weekly published by Julius Streicher between 1923 and 1945. Banned by the Weimar government in 1923, *Der Stürmer* reappeared on March 24, 1925. Approximate circulation reached 600,000 in 1940 but declined thereafter. Virulently antisemitic, Streicher oriented *Der Stürmer* toward the most prurient interests of his readership and usually published what amounted to pure pornography.

Der Vierjahresplan, "The Four-Year Plan," official publication of Reichsmarschall Herman Göring's office for the Four-Year Plan, appearing quarterly between 1937 and 1940. After April 1940 the periodical appeared irregularly. Although published in sanitized form, the periodical contained considerable data on the aryanization of German Jewish property.

Der Weltkampf, Monatsschrift für die Judenfrage aller Länder, "The World Struggle, Monthly for the Jewish Question in All Countries," antisemitic publication appearing between 1924 and 1945 under the general editorship of Alfred Rosenberg. From March 1941 on, *Weltkampf* appeared under the aegis of the Institut zur Erforschung der Judenfrage. Despite a veneer of scholarship, *Weltkampf* was not considered to be on the same intellectual level as other Nazi antisemitic periodicals.

Deutsche Wochenschau für Politik, Wirtschaft, Kultur und Technik, "German Weekly for Politics, Economy, Culture, and Technology," weekly published in Berlin between 1935 and 1940. Within the context of its discussion of political and cultural issues, the weekly published articles on the Jewish problem by prominent and not-so-prominent Nazis.

Deutscher Wochendienst (DW), "German Weekly Service," internal periodical of the German Propaganda Ministry, offering guidelines for what periodical editors could or could not publish. Rabidly antisemitic, the DW repeatedly emphasized the theme of a Jewish conspiracy and of racial warfare.

Die Aktion, Kampfblatt für das neue Europa, "The Action: Battle Pages for the New Europe," Nazi propaganda sheet appearing between 1939 and 1945. Primarily aimed at convincing readers in the neutral countries of Germany's legitimate claims, *Aktion* used every opportunity to blame World War II on Jewish financiers and British plutocrats. Editor: Hans Fritzsche.

Die Judenfrage, "The Jewish Question," semimonthly organ of the Institut zum Studium der Judenfrage, published in Berlin between 1937 and 1943. From 1938 on, the periodical appeared as a weekly, and in 1939 its sponsorship officially changed to Antisemitische Aktion, and later still to Antijüdische Aktion. These transformations reflected the changes in agency title; they did not reflect changes in actual personnel or orientation. Editor: Georg Haller. > see also: **National Sozialistische Deutscher Arbeiter Partei, Organizations**.

Forschungen der Judenfrage, "Research on the Jewish Question," official publication of the Reichsinstitut für Geschichte des Neuen Deutschlands, appearing from 1936 to 1945. Quasi-scholarly in its orientation, the publication was partnered with the institute's *Historische Zeitschrift,* Which dealt with "Aryan" studies.

Völkischer Beobachter (VB), "People's Observer," official organ of the NSDAP, published from 1921 to 1945. From 1923 on, VB appeared as a daily. Circulation peaked in 1944 at 1,700,000; it was published in north and south German editions. From 1933 on VB acted as the semi-official organ of the Third Reich.

Weltdienst, "World Service," Nazi news agency and journal that operated under the authority of the propaganda ministry. Between 1940 and 1942 *Weltdienst* also published a Hungarian edition, entitled *Világ-Szolgálat*.

Zeitschrift für Rassenkunde, "Journal for Racial Science," Nazi quasi-scientific journal published in Stuttgart monthly between 1935 and 1939. In addition to articles on antisemitic racial "science," the *Zeitschrift* published frequent monographs on the inequality of the races and especially on the racial status of the Slavs.

Great Britain

Fascist, monthly organ of the Imperial Fascist League, appearing in London between March 1929 and September 1939. Virulently antisemitic, the editorial line became increasingly pro-Nazi in 1935. The journal was considered subversive of the British war effort, and publication was halted upon the outbreak of war. After the war, the journal reemerged as *Free Britain*, appearing between 1948 and 1950. Editor: Arnold S. Leese (1929–1939).

Fascist Quarterly, quasi-scholarly quarterly published by the British Union of Fascists (BUF) in London between January 1935 and January 1940. From 1937 on, the issues appeared as the *British Union Quarterly*. Contributors included many respected British public figures, a fact that indicates that the BUF semmed respectable in some circles. Publication was halted in 1940 because the editorial line of the journal was considered subversive of the British war effort. Editor: Oswald Mosley.

National Worker, antisemitic paper published in London by Colonel Graham Seton-Hutchinson between August 3, 1933, and September 1939.

Italy

La Difesa della Razza, "The Defense of the Race," antisemitic and racist journal published in Rome between 1938 and 1945. Initially planned as a weekly, in reality the journal appeared semi-monthly. Used as a broadcasting medium for Italy's antisemitic laws, the journal also printed the *Manifesto della difesa della Razza*. Circulation peaked at 200,000 Just before World War II. Publication was disrupted in 1943 but resumed in the Sálo Republic on an irregular basis in 1944 and 1945. Editor: Telesio Interlandi. > see also: **Fascism, Fascist Parties and Organizations (Italy).**

Popolo d'Italia (PI), "People of Italy," official daily of the Fascist party. Originally Communist in orientation, PI became virulently nationalist under the guidance of then-editor Benito Mussolini. After the March on Rome, PI became the mouthpiece for the Fascist government. Publication continued uninterrupted until 1943, when Mussolini's downfall led to a temporary halt in publication. Publication resumed in the Sálo Republic but ceased at the end of the war. PI's attitude towards Jews and Nazism paralleled Mussolini's changing attitudes and policies.

Luxembourg

Luxemburger Freiheit, "Luxembourg Freedom," pro-Nazi German-language newspaper published in the principality during the 1930s and 1940s.

Poland

Gazeta Niedzielna, "Sunday Gazette," weekly journal of Rozwoj, the propaganda wing of the Endecja (Endeks) party, published in Warsaw between 1919 and 1939. Circulation peaked at 80,000 during the 1930s.

Gazeta Polska, "Polish Gazette," semi-official government newspaper, published in Warsaw between 1919 and 1939. Virulently antisemitic in orientation, *Gazeta Polska* was primarily employed for the publication of official pronouncements.

Gazeta Warszawska, "Warsaw Gazette," Polish-language daily published in Warsaw from 1774 to 1939. From 1935 on, the newspaper's editorial line became increasingly antisemitic, reflecting the orientation of the Sanacja government.

Glos Narodu, "People's Voice," official organ of the Christian Democratic Party, published in Krakow between 1893 and 1939. Throughout its existence, the newspaper had an antisemitic editorial line; after 1935 its emphasis shifted from religious antisemitism to demands for

Jewish emigration. Publication was halted because of the Nazi occupation but briefly resumed after 1945.

Przegląd Powszechny (PP), "General Review," conservative daily newspaper published from 1884 to 1953. From 1884 to 1936 PP appeared in Warsaw; from 1936 to 1939 it appeared in Krakow. The paper's antisemitism became more pronounced after 1936. Publication officially ceased with the Nazi occupation, although the publishers and editors worked on a number of underground publications. Publication resumed in Warsaw in 1947 and continued until 1953, when it was suppressed by the Communists. Editors: Jan Urban (1933–1936); J. Rotworojnski (1936–1939); Edward Kosibowicz (1947–1953).

Sztafieta, "Courier," official journal of the Oboz Narodowo-Radykalny, published throughout the 1930s. Fascist and antisemitic in orientation, *Sztafieta* ceased publication in October 1939.

Slovakia

Gardista, "Guardist," official publication of the Hlinkova Garda, published in Bratislava between 1938 and 1945. Virulently antisemitic in orientation, *Gardista* avidly supported the deportation of Slovak Jewry. Editors: K. Sidor (1938–1939); A. Mach (1939–1944); O. Kubala (1944–1945).

South Africa

Der Deutsch-Afrikaner, "The German African," pro-Nazi publication appearing in Pretoria during the 1930s. The periodical was dedicated to propagating Nazi and antisemitic ideas in South Africa, South-West Africa (now Namibia), and Mozambique.

United States of America

Dearborn Independent, daily newspaper published by Henry Ford in Dearborn, Michigan, during the 1920s and 1930s. In October 1920 the newspaper serialized The *Protocols of the Elders of Zion*, an act that resulted in lawsuits by American Jewish leaders and the declaration of an anti-Ford boycott. As a result of the decline in Ford Motor Cars sales, the *Independent* published an apology by Ford in 1927. Thereafter, however, the *Independent* continued to publish pro-Nazi and antisemitic articles.

Free American, official journal of the German-American Bund, appearing between 1933 and 1941. Grossly antisemitic, the editorial line of the paper was to blame all international problems on a Jewish conspiracy against Germany. Publication was interrupted in 1938 by the arrest of Bund leader Fritz Kuhn on child molestation charges but resumed thereafter. In late 1941 publication was permanently banned at the order of the U.S. government, since the Bund's pro-Nazi orientation was considered subversive.

Liberation, antisemitic weekly published and edited by William Pelley between 1930 and 1941. In 1933, *Liberation* became the official organ of the Silver Shirts, which Pelley also led. Experiencing considerable financial difficulties in its first years, *Liberation* was raised from the doldrums by the Nazi *Machtergreifung*. Virulently antisemitic, the editorial line was clearly pro-Nazi and isolationist. *Liberation* was ordered to cease publication after the Japanese attack on Pearl Harbor, as its positions were considered subversive.

4. Wartime Nazi-Controlled/Collaborationist

Belgium

De National Socialist (DNS), "The National Socialist," monthly journal published by Vlaamsch Nationaal Verbond (VNV) in Brussels between 1940 and 1944. Overtly collaborationist and antisemitic in its orientation, DNS was issued to all members of the VNV.

Croatia

Nova Hrvatska, "New Croatia," official publication of the Croat collaborationist government, appearing between 1941 and 1945.

Czechoslovakia

Jüdisches Nachrichtenblatt/Żidovkse Listy, "Jewish News Bulletin," weekly published in German and Czech, with Gestapo approval, from December 24, 1939, to 1944.

Denmark

Faedrelandet, "Fatherland," official publication of the Danish Nazi party, appearing in Copenhagen between 1931 and 1945. The same publishing house also published *National-Socialisten* (National Socialist) during the same period. Although pro-German in orientation and openly collaborationist, both journals avoided overt antisemitism.

France

Bulletin de l'U.G.I.F., "Bulletin of the General Union of Jews in France," official journal of the Nazi-imposed Jewish governing body in France, appearing between 1940 and 1944. Published in two editions, one for the German zone and the other for Vichy. Used primarily as a means to broadcast Nazi or French collaborationist declarations regarding Jews. > see also: **Judenrat; Legislation, Anti-Jewish, Axis States (Vichy France)**.

La Question Juive en France et dans le Monde, "The Jewish Question in France and the World," semi-official bi-weekly publication associated with the Commissariat Général aux Questions Juives, appearing between 1942 and 1944.

Journal Officiel de l'Etat Français, "Official Journal of the French State," legislative journal published between January 1, 1941, and August 25, 1944.

Germany

Jüdisches Nachrichtenblatt, "Jewish Newsletter," official organ of the Reichsvereinigung, published between 1938 and 1943. Used primarily to publicize Nazi regulations concerning Jews.

Holland

De Stormmeeuw, "The Young Storm," official monthly journal of the Nationale Juegdstorm (NJ) of the National Socialistische Beweging der Nederlanden, appearing between 1934 and 1945. All NJ members received a subscription, meaning that the circulation peaked at approximately 18,000.

Het Joodsche Weekblad, "The Jewish Weekly," officially permitted organ of the Joodse Rad, published in Amsterdam between April 11, 1941, and September 1943. Used primarily to publish Nazi-imposed antisemitic decrees and laws, the paper had no independent editorial policy.

Menorah, legally published Jewish literary annual published by the Dutch Zionist Federation in 1940 and 1941. Editors: Hugo Heymans, J. Melkman.

Storm, "Storm," official monthly of the Dutch SS, published by the National Socialistiche Beweging der Nederlanden, appearing between 1940 and 1945.

Volk en Vaderland, "Folk and Fatherland," weekly journal of the National Socialistiche Beweging der Nederlanden (NSB), appearing between 1940 and 1945. During the 1930s and 1940s the NSB also published a daily, *Het National Dagblad*.

Hungary

Harc, "Struggle," weekly published by the Institute for Research into the Jewish Question between May 20, 1944, and 1945. Editor: Zoltán Bosnyák.

Nemzet Szava (NS), "Nation's Voice," official mouthpiece of Hungarian Nazi party, appearing between 1937 and 1944. In addition to its radical right-wing orientation, NS adopted a pro-Nazi and virulently antisemitic editorial line.

Lithuania

Lietuviu Archivas: Bulletin für die Erforschung des Bolschewismus und Judentums, "Lithuanian Archives: Bulletin for Research on Bolshevism and Judaism," bi-weekly publication of the antisemitic Lithuanian Studien-Büro, appearing between 1941 and 1944. Printed in German, the paper was apparently oriented toward the neutral press.

Vilner Geto Yediyes (ווילנער געטא ידיעות), "News of the Vilna Ghetto," daily bulletin published between 1941 and 1943. Contained announcements and regulations for the Vilna ghetto.

Poland

Biuletyn Kroniki Codziennej, "Daily Chronicle

Bulletin," official newspaper of the Lodz ghetto, published under the authority of Judenälteste Mordechai C. Rumkowski. Appeared between January 12, 1941, and July 30, 1944. In 1941 and 1942 the Chronicle was written in Polish and thereafter in German.

Das Generalgouvernement, "The General Government," monthly organ of the Nazi occupation authorities, published between 1940 and 1944. Because of the secret nature of the Final Solution, very little was published on a political nature affecting Polish or other Jewry, although some articles were published on the origin and culture of Polish Jewry.

Gazeta Żydowska (GŻ), "Jewish Gazette," Polish-language publication appearing in Krakow between 1940 and 1942. Published by the Nazis, GŻ was designed as a means of control for the ghetto populations in the General Government. Between 1940 and 1941 GŻ appeared twice a week, thereafter thrice.

Krakauer Zeitung, "Krakow Newspaper," official Nazi monthly published by the Propaganda Department of the General Governor's office in Krakow between 1940 and 1943. Although an "official" publication, the periodical was available to the general public and thus avoided information on the Final Solution.

Litsmanshtetishe Geto-Tsaytung, "Lodz Ghetto Newspaper," Yiddish title for the Lodz ghetto chronicle.

5. Anti-Nazi/Fascist

France

Les juifs et les chrétiens, "Jews and Christians," philosemitic church journal published monthly by the French Dominican order, from 1936 to 1940. Although not widely circulated, the journal was extremely influential within French clerical circles; many of its readers became active in rescuing Jews during World War II. Editors: Oscar de Ferenzy, Fr. Roland de Vaux.

Témoignage Chrétien, "Christian Witness," French Catholic journal published between 1914 and 1944. From 1940 on, the journal advocated a clearly anti-Nazi position. During the occupation the journal also published a clandestine version, entitled *Les cahiers du Temoignage chrétien.* Rejecting antisemitism, the editors became more strident in their calls for rescue; as a result the Nazis ordered the journal suppressed in early 1944.

Soviet Union

Eynikeit (אייניקייט), "Unity," Yiddish-language journal of the Jewish Anti-Fascist Committee, published in Kuibyshev between July 6, 1942, and 1948. Publication facilities were moved to Moscow in 1943, after which the journal appeared as a weekly. Contributors to *Eynikeit* included Ilya Ehrenburg and Vasily Grossman. Primarily organized as a vehicle for the furtherance of Soviet propaganda, both in the USSR and abroad. Publication of *Eynikeit* was halted at the height of Stalin's purge of Jewish culture in November 1948. Editor: Shakhne Epstein (1942–1948).

6. Underground, Jewish

Lithuania

Sztandar Wolnosci, "Banner of Freedom," Polish-language organ of the Jewish resistance movement in Vilna, published between 1941 and 1943. Editor: Isaac Kowalski.

Poland

Der Glok (דער גלאק), "The Bell," Yiddish-language organ of the Bund, published in 1942.

Der Ruf (דער רוף), "The Call," Yiddish-language organ of the Żydowska Organizacja Bojowa (ŻOB) in Bialystok, published irregularly in 1942.

Der Shturm (דער שטורעם), "The Storm," Yiddish-language organ of the Bund, appearing in 1942 and early 1943.

Der Weker (דער וועקער), "The Alarm Clock," Yiddish-language organ of the Bund, published in Warsaw in 1942.

Dror (דרור), "Liberty," published in Warsaw by he-Halutz in Yiddish, Hebrew, and Polish editions, between May 1940 and 1943.

Glos Demokraty, "Voice of the Democrat," Polish-language organ of Akiba, published in

Krakow.

Hechalutz Halohem (החלוץ הלוחם), "The Fighting Pioneer," Hebrew-language organ of the Jewish resistance movement in the Krakow ghetto. Published between 1941 and 1943.

Magen David (מגן דוד), "Shield of David," Hebrew and Polish organ of Betar, published in Warsaw on an irregular basis in 1941 and 1942.

Min ha-Metzar (מן המצר), "From the Depths," Hebrew-language paper published in the Lodz ghetto irregularly during the period that the ghetto existed.

Morgen Freiheit (מארגן פרייהייט), "Morning Freedom," Communist Yiddish paper in the Warsaw ghetto, appearing as *Morgen Frei* from February to December 1941 and as *Morgen Freiheit* thereafter. Publication terminated in 1943.

Neged ha-Zerem (נגד הזרם), "Against the Stream," monthly published by ha-Shomer ha-Zair in Warsaw from 1941 to 1943.

Oif Broiz (אויף ברויז), "Ferment," Yiddish news bulletin published in Warsaw by ha-Shomer ha-Zair between May and July 1942. Editor: Mordechai Anielewicz.

Plomienie, "Flames," Polish-language organ of ha-Shomer ha-Zair published from September 1, 1940, to April 1943.

Proletarier Gedank (פראלעטאריער געדאנק), "Worker Thought," organ of the Bund, appearing in Warsaw between October 1940 and 1943.

Przedwiosnie, "Before Dawn," Polish organ of ha-Shomer ha-Zair in Warsaw, published on a monthly basis. Appeared between 1941 and 1942, except from May to July 1942, when it appeared under the alternate title *Zaezewie*, "The Spark."

Slowo Mlodych, "Word of the Young," organ of Gordonia, published in Warsaw between November 1941 and 1943.

Yediot (ידיעות), "News," Yiddish and Hebrew weekly published in the Warsaw ghetto between March and July 1942.

Yugent-Shtime (יוגנט-שטימע), "Young Voice," Yiddish-language organ of the Bund, published in the Warsaw ghetto from 1940 to June 1941. Closed down by the Gestapo after arrest of editor Alter Bass.

Za Naszą i Waszą Wolność, "For Our Liberty and Yours," monthly organ of the Bund in Warsaw, published in 1941 and 1942. Also distributed outside the ghetto. From February 1942 a Yiddish edition, entitled *Tsayt Fragn* (Contemporary Questions), appeared.

Zukunft (צוקונפט), "Future," Yiddish-language organ of the Bund Socialist Youth Organization in the Warsaw ghetto, published between 1940 and 1943.

Romania

Courier (קוריער), Yiddish periodical appearing in the Djurin ghetto in Transnistria irregularly between April and September 1943.

7. Underground, European

Belgium

La Libre Belgique, "Free Belgium," clandestine journal published from August 15, 1940, until liberation.

Czechoslovakia

Hlas Revoluce, "Voice of the Revolution," irregular periodical of the Czech underground in the Mauthausen concentration camp.

Rude Pravo (RP), "Red Law," Communist party daily newspaper, published legally between 1920 and 1938. After Munich, RP appeared as an irregular underground journal that was widely read and very influential. After the liberation of Czechoslovakia, RP resumed regular publication, becoming the semi-official mouthpiece of the government after the Communists seized power in 1948.

France

Cahiers Politiques, "Political Notebooks," underground publication of the Conseil National de la Résistance that appeared in 1943. The *Cahiers* became the epicenter of a small scandal in April 1943, when the editor, Maxime Blocq-Mascart, published an antisemitic editorial. He was later reprimanded, refused a promotion by de Gaulle, and forced to recant the editorial.

Défense de la France, "Defense of France," published by the Gaullist wing of the Forces

Françaises de l'Intéreur between 1941 and 1944.

L'Humanité, "Humanity," daily organ of the French Communist Party, published in Paris since the late 1920s. Upon the outbreak of the Russo-Finnish war, *L'Humanité* began publication as an underground newspaper, initially with an anti-French editorial policy. The paper continued to exist in the underground after the Nazi occupation, although its editorial line changed after the German invasion of the Soviet Union in June 1941. Thereafter, *L'Humanité* strongly advocated active resistance measures and the rescue of Jews. Legal publication resumed in 1944.

Germany

Westdeutsche Kampfblätter, "West German Battle Newspaper," non-Communist, anti-Nazi underground journal appearing in twelve issues between May 1936 and October 1937.

Holland

De Geus onder Studenten, "The Spirit among Students," monthly underground organ of the student body of the Leiden University, published between October 1940 and 1944. Circulation peaked at 8,000.

De Ploeg, "The Plow," monthly underground organ of the student body of Groningen University, published between July 1943 and 1945. Circulation peaked at 4,000.

De Reformatie, "The Reformation," monthly underground organ of the Dutch Reformed Church published between May 1940 and May 1945. Circulation peaked at 1,200.

De Vonk, "The Spark," underground organ of the Internationale Socialisten Bond (International Socialist League), published between January 1941 and 1944. From January 1941 to February 1943, the publication appeared monthly; thereafter it appeared as a fortnightly. Circulation peaked at 20,000, but a special issue on the Nazi introduction of mandatory wearing of the Star of David was distributed in 300,000 copies.

De Waarheid, "The Truth," Dutch Communist organ, published between 1940 and 1945. Circulation peaked at 7,000.

Het Parool, "The Word," monthly underground organ of the Dutch Socialist Party, published between February 1941 and 1945. Circulation peaked at 100,000 in September 1944, when the paper appeared daily.

Ons Volk, "Our Nation," largest Dutch independent underground organ, published between October 1943 and 1945. From October 1943 to September 1944 the publication appeared monthly; thereafter it appeared weekly. Circulation peaked at 120,000.

Op Wacht, "On Guard," underground organ appearing in The Hague between January 1944 and May 1945. Circulation peaked at 12,000.

Oranjebode, "Messenger of Orange," publication of the Dutch Calvinist Church between 1941 and 1943, superseded by *Trouw*.

Trouw, "Truth," monthly underground organ of the Dutch Calvinist church that superseded *Oranjebode* in 1943. Publication continued until 1945 (and thereafter), by which time circulation reached 60,000. Considered to be the most influential of the Dutch underground papers.

Vrij Nederland, "Free Netherlands," monthly underground organ of the Dutch Calvinist church, published in Eindhoven between August 31, 1940, and 1944. Circulation peaked at 40,000. Throughout the same period, a daily news bulletin appeared under the same title with approximately the same circulation. After September 1944 the journal appeared legally as a daily, although publication ceased in 1948.

Italy

Il Partigiano, "The Partisan," irregular journal published by Socialist and Communist partisan groups active in the northern provinces; appearing between 1943 and 1945. Approximate distribution: 5,000 copies weekly.

La Liberazione, "Liberation," semi-clandestine newspaper published by the Comitato di Liberazione Nazionale in Milan in 1943 and 1944. After liberation the newspaper continued to appear legally; publication ceased in 1945.

L'Unità, "Unity," Communist underground newspaper published in northern Italy in 1943 and 1944. *L'Unità* was the most widely read and influential underground journal in Italy.

Poland

Agencja A, "Agency A," biweekly organ of the Spoteczny Komitet Antykommunistyczny (ANTYK) the Civilian Anti-Communist Committee. Sponsored by the Delegatura, the representative body of the Polish government in exile, and the Armia Krajowa, ANTYK was officially dedicated to countering Soviet propaganda. ANTYK's publications, however, actually became a main focus for Polish antisemitic propaganda.

Barykada Wolności, "Liberty's Barricade," biweekly published by centrist members of the Polska Partia Socjalistyczna, associated with the pro-government Polscy Socjaliści movement. The paper maintained a close relationship with Emmanuel Ringelblum and published some items from the *Oneg Shabbat* archive.

Biuletyn Informacyiny, "Information Bulletin," official publication of the Armia Krajowa, appearing between November 1939 and September 1944. Approximate distribution: 50,000 copies weekly. In addition to information on Nazi occupation policy, the *Biuletyn* published extensive reports on the persecution of Polish Jewry.

Glos Warszawy, "The Voice of Warsaw," official organ of the Polska Partia Robotnicza in Warsaw published between 1942 and 1944.

Informator, "Monitor," weekly organ of the Polska Partia Socjalistyczna/Wolnosc-Rownosc-Niepodleglose (Polish Socialist Party/Freedom-Equality-Independence) faction. Pro-government in exile, *Informator* called for active measures to rescue Polish Jewry.

Mloda Polska, "Young Poland," biweekly of the National Party's youth movement. Opposed tolerance for national minorities and declared that by the German extermination of the Jews "victory has been achieved."[1]

Naród, "The Nation," organ of the Christian Labor Party. Advocated mass Jewish emigration from Poland after World War II.

Nowe Drogi, "New Ways," organ of the Democratic Party. Advocated rescue, full equality for Jews in postwar Poland, and punishment of Nazi war criminals.

Polska, "Poland," irregularly published in Warsaw by the Obóz Polski Walczacej. Leaning to the center-right, *Polska* editors called for mass Jewish emigration from Poland after liberation.

Polska Zyje, "Poland Lives," first underground periodical to appear in Warsaw starting in November 1939. The harbinger of the Polish underground press, it terminated in early 1940.

Przez Walkę do Zwycięstwa, "Through Struggle to Victory," official biweekly organ of the Stronnictwo Ludowe, the National Party. Supported the Polish government in exile but opposed overt acts of resistance for fear of German retaliation. Antisemitic in orientation, the paper toned down this attitude after the Warsaw ghetto uprising.

Przebudowa, "Reconstruction," monthly published by the Stronnictwo Ludowe, the National Party. Carrying over antisemitic overtones from prewar years, the magazine advocated mass emigration of Jews from a postwar Poland.

Reforma, "Reform," organ of the Partia Robotnicza, the Christian Labor Party. Pro–government in exile, *Reforma* called for the reorganization of postwar Poland and mass emigration of Jews.

Robotnik, "The Worker," published by the left-wing opposition element of the Polska Partia Socjalistyczna, associated with the Robotnicza Partia Polskich Socjalistów (RPPS). Opposed to the policy of the Polish government in exile, *Robotnik* was pro-Soviet, though non-Communist, in orientation.

Slowa Prawdy, "Words of Truth," biweekly published by the Grupy Katolico-Narodowe.

---

[1] Issue of October 13, 1943, cited from Shmuel Krakowski "Holocaust in the Polish Underground Press," *Yad Vashem Studies*, vol. 16 (1984), p. 267.

Unlike other organs of this Catholic group, *Slowa Prawdy* had an antisemitic orientation.

Szaniec, "Rampart," weekly organ of the Oboz Narodowo Radykalny published from 1942 to 1944. Did not support the government in exile but also opposed the Lublin Committee. *Szaniec* was vehemently antisemitic, anti-Ukrainian, anti-Soviet, and anti-Nazi.

Walka, "Struggle," biweekly published by the Stronnictwo Narodowe, the National Party. Although anti-Nazi, *Walka* also enunciated an antisemitic orientation.

Wiadomości Häftlingowski, "Prisoner News," irregular publication of the prisoners' committee in Buchenwald. Appeared in 1944 and 1945.

Wiadomości Polskie, "Polish News," weekly organ of the Armia Krajowa, published between November 1939 and October 1944. Approximate distribution: 10,000 copies.

Wielka Polska, "Great Poland," biweekly published by the conservative faction of the National Party opposed to Jewish civil rights. *Wielka Polska* advocated Jewish mass emigration.

8. Representatives of Occupied Countries

Governments in Exile: London

Danish Listening Post, published by the national America-Denmark Association (ADA), New York. Mimeographed fortnightly containing news of Denmark, published during the Nazi occupation. Because the legitimate Danish government was unable to flee, the ADA acted as a de facto government in exile.

Dziennik Polski, "Polish Daily," official daily organ of the Polish government in exile's Ministry of Information, appearing between 1940 and 1945. In 1940 and 1941 *Dziennik Polski* paid scant attention to Jewish issues; thereafter its editors almost always managed to put an antisemitic slant on virtually every news item, even those dealing with the persecution of Polish Jewry.

Free France, published by the Free French Press and Information Service, New York, between 1940 and 1944. Mimeographed fort-nightly published by the Free French government, headed by General de Gaulle. Special attention was paid to the actions of the Vichy regime.

Glos Polski, "Polish Voice," organ of the Polish government in exile between November 1939 and July 1940, while it was in Paris. Published articles with antisemitic overtones.

Jestem Polakiem, "I Am a Pole," weekly published by the Polish armed forces in London between 1940 and 1945. The editorial policy permitted inclusion of rabidly antisemitic materials, which resulted in external pressure on the Polish National Council and forced it to publicly dissociate itself from the publication on a few occasions.

La Belgique Indépendante, "Independent Belgium," weekly organ of the Belgian government in exile appearing in London from 1940 and 1945. Separate Flemish and Walloon editions existed, with identical contents.

Netherlands News, published by the Netherlands Information Bureau in New York between 1940 and 1945. Fortnightly collection of mimeographed press releases.

Newsflashes from Czechoslovakia, published by the Czechoslovak National Council of America in Chicago. News weekly on the fate of Czechoslovakia under Nazi occupation.

News from Belgium, published by the Belgian Information Center, New York. A weekly news bulletin reporting in brief on Nazi activities in occupied Belgium, appearing from 1940 to 1945.

News from Czechoslovakia, published by the American Friends of Czechoslovakia in New York. A mimeographed news bulletin issued fortnightly.

Przegląd Prasy Podziemnej (PPP), "Survey of the Polish Underground Press," quarterly compilations of articles appearing in publications in Poland and published by the Polish government in exile in London. Eclectic in its editorial policy, PPP did not publish any new materials.

Governments in Exile: Moscow

Wolna Polska, "Free Poland," weekly published in Moscow during 1944 and 1945 by the Union of Polish Patriots. Briefly became the official journal of the Lublin Committee.

German Exile Press

Aufruf, "Call," published fortnightly in Prague in 1933 and 1934 by the Streitschrift für Menschenrechte.

Das Andere Deutschland, "The Other Germany," German-language monthly published by anti-Nazi exiles in Buenos Aires, Argentina, between 1938 and 1948. In 1944 another periodical by the same title, but otherwise apparently unrelated, was published as a bimonthly in Montevideo, Uruguay.

Deutsche Informationen (DI), "German Informations," German-language anti-Nazi periodical appearing in Paris between 1936 and 1939. Published by a group of Socialist exiles living in France, DI was militantly anti-Nazi and anti-Communist in orientation. After the Munich Agreement the title was changed to *Volksfront*, but publication ceased on the outbreak of World War II.

Deutschland Information, "Germany Information," Communist monthly published in Paris in 1938 and 1939 by the Kommunistische Partei Deutschlands Central Committee.

Einheit, "Unity," fortnightly published in London between 1942 and 1945 by the Sudeten German Anti-Fascist Committee.

9. Research Journals on the Holocaust

Biuletyn Żydowski Instytut Historyczny (BZIH), "Bulletin of the Jewish Historical Institute," Polish quarterly published in Warsaw by the Żydowski Instytut Historyczny since 1948.

Bleter far Yidishe Geshichte (בלעטער פאר יידישע געשיכטע), "Journal of Jewish History," quarterly published by the Żydowski Instytut Historyczny, Warsaw, since 1948.

Dappim le-Heker ha-Shoa (דפים לחקר השואה), "Studies of the Holocaust and the Jewish Resistance," published by Beit Lohamei ha-Getaot and the Haifa University Center for Holocaust Studies, Israel.

Dimensions, monthly published by the Braun Center for Holocaust Studies of the Anti-Defamation League of B'nai Brith, New York, since 1985.

Holocaust and Genocide Studies: An International Journal, scholarly quarterly published by Oxford University Press in association with the United States Holocaust Memorial Museum (Washington, D.C.) and Yad Vashem, the Holocaust Martyrs' and Heroes' Remembrance Authority (Jerusalem), since 1986.

Internet on the Holocaust and Genocide, published by the Institute of the International Conference on the Holocaust and Genocide, Jerusalem. A bi-monthly newsletter of brief Holocaust related items, appearing since December 1987.

Martyrdom & Resistance, bimonthly published since 1974 in New York by the American Federation of Jewish Holocaust Survivors.

Response, published by the Simon Wiesenthal Center, monthly bulletin reviewing the search for escaped Nazis and other activities of the center. Published since 1987.

Simon Wiesenthal Center Annual, scholarly annual published by the Simon Wiesenthal Center for Holocaust Studies, Los Angeles, since 1983.

Together, publication of the American Gathering/Federation of Jewish Holocaust Survivors in New York. Appearing since 1984, *Together* was initially a monthly, but it now appears twice a year.

Voice of the Woman Survivor, published by Warsaw Ghetto Resistance Organization's Women's Auxiliary to the Community of Survivors, Holocaust Resource Centers and Libraries. Quarterly periodical appearing since 1983 containing brief memoirs and historical items.

Yad Vashem Bulletin, quarterly published in Jerusalem by Yad Vashem in Hebrew and English editions between 1957 and 1969. Renamed *Yad Vashem News* in 1969 and still appearing.

Yad Vashem Studies (YVS), annual published since 1957 in Jerusalem in Hebrew and English editions by Yad Vashem.

Yalkut Moreshet (ילקוט מורשת), "Legacy Anthology," Hebrew quarterly with English summaries published by the Moreshet Institute, Kibbutz Givat Haviva, Israel, since 1963.

Q

Quisling [PN/Slang], popular term for a collaborator derived from the name of Norwegian Nazi leader Vidkun Quisling. During the war, Quisling, whose glaring collaboration with the Nazis was viewed as inappropriate in light of German aggression, became the model for a crass and self-serving politician willing to sell his soul to the enemy in return for personal power. > see also: **Collaboration**.

R

Rada Starszych [P] "Council of elders": Polish term for the Jewish community elders. > see also: **Judenrat**.

Rada Żydowska [P] "Jewish Council": Polish term for Judenrat. According to a Nazi decree, all official titles and all other proceedings of the Jewish councils had to be bilingual. The same also held true for all Nazi decrees: They were published in German and Polish. > see also: **Rada Starszych**.

Rassengezetze [G] "Racial laws": Nazi term for those laws that were based upon the categorization of Aryan and non-Aryan. Primarily this term referred to the Nuremberg Laws. > see also: **Legislation, Anti-Jewish, National Socialist Legislation (Third Reich)**.

Rassenschande [G] "Race defilement": Nazi term for any sexual relationship, and under some circumstances for casual contact, between Jews and Aryans. This terminology also applied to married couples, unless one of the partners was a *Mischling*.

Rassenträger [G] "Bearer of race": Nazi term for German youth who would carry on the battle to secure the purity of the Aryan race.

Rasseverrat [G] "Racial treason": Early Nazi term for any form of sexual or social contact between Jews and Aryans. In 1933 this ideology formed the basis for Nazi anti-Jewish legislation. > see also: **Legislation, Anti-Jewish, National Socialist Legislation (Third Reich)**.

Rauberbanden [G] "Bands of brigands": Nazi term for East European partisans, who were condemned as common criminals. > see also: **Resistance**.

Raumgewinn [G] "Winning of space": Term indicating German obsession with extra-territorial space. Nazi policy was to acquire space by any means, including the enslavement or murder of other peoples within reach. > see also: **Drang Nach Osten; Lebensraum**.

Räumungsbefehl [G] "Clearance order": Command issued by Heinrich Himmler in January 1945 regarding the evacuation of inmates from those concentration camps in Eastern Europe that were located on the route of advancing Soviet armies. These prisoners were force-marched into the Reich under the terms of the order, but many perished on the trek. > see also: **Todesmärsche**.

Razzia [I], "Raid": Fascist term for a roundup, often of Jews. The term was also used by the Nazis in relation to anti-Jewish *Aktionen* in Southern and Eastern Europe. > see also: **Aktion(en)**.

Recht ist was dem deutschen Volke nützt [G] "Right is that which benefits the German nation": The principle term on which the Nazi judiciary operated. Although the term appears at first glance to mean simply an ultranationalist underpinning for the legal system, in reality, the result was legal anarchy. In particular, the Nazis manipulated the terms of international law and justified their actions on the basis of the benefit to the German people.

Rechtsberater [G], "Rights consultant": Nazi term for Jewish lawyers who could no longer practice their profession in normal channels. They were limited to representing Jewish clients and even then could not directly argue cases in the courts. > see also: **Legislation, Anti-Jewish, National Socialist Legislation (Third Reich).**

Rechts/links [G] "Right/left": A code term by an official of an *Aussiedlungskommando* during an *Aktion*. By the mere pointing of a finger to right or left, or by the blink of an eye, the fate of thousands of Jews was decided — life or death! Right usually meant staying behind and thus buying some time; left indicated deportation to the slaughterhouse.

Referent für Judenfragen [G], "Representative for the Jewish Question": Title of Adolf Eichmann, who represented the SD Main Office in its relation with European Jewry.

Refugees, Jewish: Those seeking to escape Germany after the Nazi takeover joined a centuries-long tradition of mass refugee movements. However, in the aftermath of World War I, the Bolshevik revolution, and the worldwide economic depression, refugees found a hostile world environment. Countries around the world enacted severe barriers to limit the influx of refugees, if not to prevent their entry altogether.

In the years between 1933 and 1938 most émigrés sought refuge in countries neighboring Germany, principally France, the Netherlands, Switzerland, Czechoslovakia, and Austria. These countries proved difficult havens for Jews, however, and very few German Jewish refugees entered them; those

who did often were admitted on a temporary basis only. Larger numbers of Jewish refugees emigrated to Palestine, the United States, and Great Britain. In this period, the exodus from Germany remained limited, with Jewish emigration totaling only 128,000 (of the nearly 525,000 in Germany at the time). In 1938, the exodus became a mass migration, with entire families uprooting themselves and becoming refugees. Some 36,000 German Jews — and another 63,000 from Austria after the *Anschluss* — left, with the majority going to Palestine and the United States. Fifty thousand Jews escaped Germany in 1939, and 71,500 Jews left between September 1, 1939, and October 1941, when all exits were blocked.

The plight of Jewish refugees did not improve with the outbreak of war. Indeed, the approximately 100,000 Jewish refugees spread across Europe when war broke out suffered greatly. In Western European countries, Jewish refugees were often interned. In France, Holland, and Belgium, such internment became a springboard for eventual deportation and extermination in Eastern Europe. The same fate overtook most of the Jewish refugees who fled Poland into the Soviet Union; only those deported (in 1939, 1940, and 1941) to Soviet concentration camps in Siberia were, ironically, spared from the Nazi onslaught.

Finding a haven outside of the Nazi sphere of influence posed similar difficulties. In Great Britain, large numbers of German Jewish refugees were interned, and almost all of them were later released. Thousands volunteered to serve in the Allied armed forces, considering themselves to be "His Majesty's loyal enemy aliens." Among the latter, members of X-Troop, #10 (inter-Allied) Commando stand out, since almost all of them were Jews from the Reich, who would receive no protection from the Geneva conventions if captured. American policy remained restrictive; the admission of Jews was strongly opposed by the State Department. The climate shifted only in 1944, when Franklin D. Roosevelt finally agreed to establish the War Refugee Board. Even so, the agency was hampered in its operations and did not become a major force for rescue.

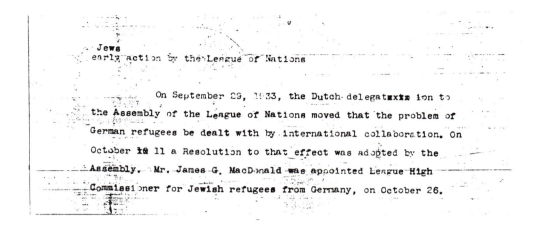

Jews
early action by the League of Nations

On September 29, 1933, the Dutch delegation to
the Assembly of the League of Nations moved that the problem of
German refugees be dealt with by international collaboration. On
October 11 a Resolution to that effect was adopted by the
Assembly. Mr. James G. MacDonald was appointed League High
Commissioner for Jewish refugees from Germany, on October 26.

Appointment of James G. McDonald as League of Nations High Commissioner for Refugees
Courtesy of the Library of Congress, Manuscripts Division

Swiss policy remained restrictive throughout the war and made the rescue of large numbers of Jews difficult. About 21,000 Jews managed to enter Switzerland, but thousands more were turned back at the borders. Sweden began the war with a similar policy but changed that policy in autumn 1943 — in response to the need to rescue Danish Jewry — and thereafter Sweden remained a safe haven for all who could escape the Nazi death machine. Turkey and Spain also sought to restrict the entry of refugees but agreed not to prevent their entry as long as they did not remain permanently in the country. Oddly, one of the few countries that voluntarily became a haven for persecuted Jews during the war was Fascist Italy. Italian forces protected Jews, even against *Il Duce's* express wishes, wherever they found themselves in occupation: in France, Greece, and Croatia.

The refugee problem remained after World War II ended, then transformed into a Displaced Persons problem. > see also: **Aliya Bet; Briha; Displaced Persons, Jewish; Organizations.**

Reichsbürger [G] "Reich citizen": The status of Aryans under the Nuremberg Laws. > see also: **Legislation, Anti-Jewish, National Socialist Legislation (Third Reich).**

Reichsheini [G] "Reich ass": German nickname for Heinrich Himmler. The term, a pun on Himmler's first name, was used affectionately. > see also: **Hermann Meyer.**

Reichskommissariate [G] "Reich commission": The governmental structure imposed by the Nazis in the occupied Soviet territories. The Reichskommissariats fell under the jurisdiction of Alfred Rosenberg's Ministry for Occupied Territories. > see also: **Besatzungspolitik.**

Reichsprotektor [G] "Reich protector": The Nazi official overseeing the government of the Protectorate of Bohemia and Moravia, a thinly disguised military occupation of the Czech lands. From 1939 to 1941 the *Reichsprotektor* was Konstantin Baron von Neurath. He was followed by Reinhard Heydrich, until his assassination by British agents on June 4, 1942, and by Kurt Daluege, who served in this position until the Allies liberated Czechoslovakia in May 1945.

Reichstag [G] "Parliament":

1. Scope and Definition
The German parliament organized along democratic lines under the constitution of the Weimar Republic. During the 1920s and early 1930s the Reichstag was elected by the system

of proportional representation. A minor party in the Reichstag from 1924 to 1930, the Nazi Party steadily gained strength until it became the largest party as a result of the indecisive elections of June 1932. On February 27, 1933, the Nazis instigated a suspicious fire in the Reichstag building, which was conveniently blamed on the Kommunistische Partei Deutschland. On March 23, 1933, the Reichstag voted to approve the Enabling Act that gave Hitler unlimited dictatorial powers. Thereafter, the Reichstag continued to meet but became a mere rubber stamp for Hitler's decisions.

TABLE R.1: NSDAP Reichstag Representation, 1924–1932

Date	Number of Seats	Percent of Vote
May 1924	32	6.6
December 1924	14	2.8
1928	12	2.4
1930	107	19.6
July 1932	230	38.4
November 1932	196	34.3

Source: J.C.G. Röhl, *From Bismarck to Hitler*, New York: Barnes and Noble, 1970, p. 129.

Reichstrunkenbold [G] *"Reich drunkard"*: German term for Robert Ley, founder and leader of the Deutsche Arbeitsfront (DAF).

Reichswehr [G] *"Reich Military"*: The German army permitted by the Treaty of Versailles. Under the terms of the treaty, Germany was allowed an army of 100,000 men, with only defensive weapons. A related term, Schwarze Reichswehr (the Black Reich Military), pertained to units, including air and armored forces, developed by Germany in contravention of the treaty. These illegal developments began, with Swedish and Soviet aid, even before Hitler's appointment as chancellor. Politically, the Reichswehr was a bastion of anti-democratic ferment throughout the Weimar era. In 1935 Hitler dropped all pretenses of observing the terms of the Treaty of Versailles and expanded the military, a fact the was reflected in changing the Reichswehr's name to Wehrmacht. > see also: **Wehrmacht**.

Reinigungskommando [G] *"Cleaning commando"*: Any Jewish forced-labor detachments that were utilized as sanitation companies in Polish cities and towns that had been declared *judenrein*.

Research Institutes, Antisemitic
Dansk Antijødisk Liga, *"Danish Anti-Jewish League,"* research institute founded in 1942. In 1944 the name was changed to Dansk Liga til Fremme af Racebevidstheden (Danish League for the Furtherance of Race Consciousness).

Institut d'Études des Questions Juives, *"Institute for the Study of Jewish Affairs,"* founded May 11, 1941, the institute was reorganized and moved to Paris in 1943. Chairman: C. Serpeille de Gobineau. Publication: *La Question Juive en France et dans le Monde* (1942–1944).

Studien-Büro/Studiju Biuras, *"Research Bureau,"* Lithuanian quasi-governmental agency for studying the Jewish Question. Officially independent, the bureau was actually sponsored by the Nazis. Originally founded in Kaunas in December 1941, the entire operation moved to Vilna in 1942. Publication: *Lietuviu Archivas Bulletin für die Erforschung des Bolschewismus und Judentums.*

Research Institutes, Holocaust
Beit Lohamei ha-Geta'ot (בית לוחמי הגיטאות), *"Ghetto Fighters' House,"* research institute established on Kibbutz Lohamei ha-

Geta'ot (KLH) in 1949. The institute includes a museum, research center, archive, and publishing house. The archive contains a rich collection of material on the Holocaust, emphasizing East European Jewry. In the 1980s a cooperative arrangement with the Holocaust Studies Institute at Haifa University widened the audience for KLH's research. Publication: *Dappim le-Heker ha-Shoa*, an annual published since 1972.

Berlin Documents Center, an archive of material discovered by U.S. Army personnel in southern Germany. The archive contains approximately 30 million files on the leadership of the Third Reich. These files contain personal data on more than 10 million individual NSDAP, SS, and SD members.

Centre de Documentation Juive Contemporaine (CDJC), "Center of Contemporary Jewish Documentation," located in Paris. The CDJC was created in 1943 to preserve evidence of Nazi crimes. Currently, the CDJC houses an archive and research center in addition to a publishing house and the Memorial for the Unknown Jewish Martyr. The archive contains extensive documentation on the persecution of French Jewry by the Nazis and the Vichy authorities. Publication: *Le Monde Juif*, a quarterly published since 1946.

Centro di Documentazione Ebraica Contemporanea (CDEC), "Center for Contemporary Jewish Documentation," located in Milan. The CDEC was established in 1955 as a clearinghouse for information on Italian Jewry. CDEC's archive contains an array of material on Jews in the Italian peninsula from the Risorgimento through the Fascist era, with emphasis on the period from 1938 to 1945.

Główna Komisja Badania Zbrodni Hitlerowskich w Polsce, "Main Commission for Investigation of Nazi Crimes in Poland," established by act of the Polish National Council on March 29, 1945, as a section of the Ministry of Justice. The commission's domains are the investigation of Nazi crimes committed in Poland or against Polish citizens, providing assistance to tribunals dealing with the pursuit of Nazi war criminals, and research and documentation about the occupation period.

Leo Baeck Institute (LBI), dedicated to the study of German Jewish history, life, and letters, founded in 1955. LBI's three main centers are in London, New York, and Jerusalem. Publications: *Leo Baeck Institute Yearbook*, an annual published since 1955; *Bulletin des Leo Baeck Instituts*, a quarterly published since 1956.

A Living Memorial to the Holocaust — Museum of Jewish Heritage (MJH), currently under construction in New York City. MJH operates under the auspices of the New York Holocaust Memorial Commission. MJH is primarily an educational institution but will also have some archival holdings.

Moreshet Institute, "Legacy Institute," located on Kibbutz Givat Haviva. The institute is a memorial and research center dedicated to the study of the Holocaust and Jewish heroism, established in 1963. The institute houses an archive, research institute, and publishing house, with the emphasis on the Polish Jewish experience. Publication: *Yalkut Moreshet*, a quarterly published since 1963.

Památník Terezin, "Terezin Memorial," official memorial, archive, and study center established in 1968. Publication: *Terezínské Listy*.

Rijks Instituut voor Oorlogsdocumentatie, "State Institute for War Documentation," the official Dutch research institute, established on May 8, 1945, in Amsterdam. The institute houses an archive that holds several hundred collections of documents on the Nazi occupation and the persecution of Dutch Jewry as well as a publishing house.

Simon Wiesenthal Center (SWC), research institute established in 1977 in Los Angeles, California. SWC combines a museum and a research and publishing institute. The center has extensive archival and photographic collections on antisemitism, neo-Nazism, and the hunt for Nazi war criminals and opened its museum, Bet ha-Shoa — A Museum of Tolerance, in 1993. Publications: *Simon Wiesenthal Center Annual*, published since 1984, *Response*, a quarterly published since 1987. Additionally, SWC has produced two documentary movies on the Holocaust: *Genocide* (1981, winner of

Model of the U.S. Holocaust Memorial Museum, Washington, D.C.
Courtesy of the U.S. Holocaust Memorial Museum

the Academy Award for best documentary) and *The Shtetl* (1991).

United States Holocaust Memorial Museum (USHMM), national research and memorial institute on the Holocaust, opened in April 1993. The USHMM is a subsidiary agency of the United States Holocaust Memorial Council, created by presidential order in 1979. The museum includes a library and archive, although original scholarship is not the USHMM's central focus; instead, the Museum Learning Center will focus attention on educational programs to increase awareness of, and sensitivity to, the Holocaust among the anticipated 1 million annual visitors to the museum.

Wiener Library, dedicated to the study of German Jewry in the twentieth century, now located in Tel Aviv. The Wiener Library was originally founded in the early 1930s as the research arm of the Centralverein deutscher Staatsbürger jüdischen Glaubens. The library moved to Amsterdam in 1934, and in 1939 it moved again, to London; throughout its moves the compilation of material continued. In 1980, the archive was transferred to Tel Aviv University. Publications: *Wiener Library Bulletin*, published quarterly since 1947; *Journal of Contemporary History*, quarterly published since 1966 and now under the aegis of Sage Publications.

Yad Vashem [יד ושם], "Holocaust Martyrs' and Heroes' Remembrance Authority," Israeli national institution commemorating the Holocaust, established in 1953 in Jerusalem. Yad Vashem contains both a research center and an

Yad Vashem Museum
Authors' Collection

educational institute, in addition to its museum. The archive, with its millions of pages of documentation, is at the center of the Yad Vashem research institute. Since 1968 Yad Vashem has also been a center for international scholarship on the Holocaust: Every four years since then Yad Vashem has sponsored an international scholars' conference on topics related to Holocaust studies. Publications: *Yad Vashem Studies*, an annual published in English and Hebrew editions since 1957; *Yad Vashem Bulletin*, a quarterly published in Hebrew and English editions between 1957 and 1969; *Yad Vashem News*, a quarterly published since 1969.

Żydowski Instytut Historyczny (ŻIH), "Jewish Historical Institute," Warsaw. Originally established in 1944 as the Central Jewish Historical Commission, becoming the ŻIH in 1948. The institute focuses on the history of Polish Jewry, with emphasis on the Holocaust. In addition to its research center the ŻIH contains an archive and a publishing house. Publications: *Bleter far Yidishe Geshichte*, a Yiddish quarterly published since 1948; *Biuletyn Żydowski Instytut Historyczny*, a Polish-language quarterly published since 1948.

Resistance

1. Scope and Definition

Although planned or spontaneous resistance to the Nazis or their henchmen, undertaken by both individuals and groups, was an almost universal phenomenon in Nazi occupied Europe, no single definition of resistance has been formulated by historians. In general, resistance (and Jewish resistance as well) may be fairly assumed to be any illegal anti-Nazi act that carried with it the possibility of the death penalty, aided the Allied war effort directly or indirectly, and — by definition — caused discomfiture to the Nazis. Most such activity was carried out by force of arms; unarmed resistance acts included anti-Nazi propaganda and espionage. Jewish resistance activities may be divided into four functional categories: intelligence, the uncovering and transmission to Jews and to the outside world, of Nazi plans and actions relating to Jews; evasion, the attempt to foil Nazi plans by such means as were available (for example, by obtaining false identity papers); escape, the attempt to permanently avoid the Nazis by hiding in forests or fleeing to safe havens; and subversion, the attempt to halt or delay the *Endlösung* by military means.[1] These categories also hold true, with some modifications, for the general resistance movements that arose in Nazi-occupied Europe.

Organizationally, European resistance movements relied upon a cadre of military personnel who had evaded imprisonment, upon civilians willing to work for national liberation, and upon agents from Allied countries who were parachuted into Nazi-occupied countries for the express purpose of assisting resistance movements. Lacking a sovereign Jewish state and, hence, an army and the assistance of an outside power, Jewish resistance organizations relied on civilians, members and alumni of youth movements, and members of prewar self-defense organizations.

---

[1] We based these categories upon M.R.D. Foot, *Resistance*, New York: 1977, pp. 1–10. Cf. Abraham J. Edelheit, "Ideological Orientations in the Historiography of the Jewish Resistance During the Holocaust," MA Thesis, Yeshiva University, 1981, pp. 23–29, 70–74.

2. Jewish Underground Organizations

Belgium

Comité de Défense des Juifs (CDJ), "Jewish Defense Committee," Belgian resistance movement established in September 1942 by a coalition of Jewish parties and their non-Jewish supporters. The CDJ was primarily involved in rescue operations and only secondarily in subversive activities. In the latter sphere, the CDJ acted as a facilitator, putting Jews willing to fight into contact with underground groups. The CDJ's most prominent activity was hiding some 27,000 Jewish children and perhaps twice as many adults from the Nazis until Belgium was liberated in 1944.

Czechoslovakia

Skid, secret youth group in the Terezin ghetto, composed of adolescents too old to be considered children, but too young to be considered adults. Created in December 1942, Skid served primarily as a cultural and friendship group. Skid was eliminated in 1944 when the adolescents were deported; most perished in Auschwitz. Publication: *Vedem*.

France

Armée Juive (AJ), "Jewish Army," also known as the L'organisation juive de Combat (OJC), resistance organization founded in Toulouse, January 1942, by Abraham Polonski and Lucien Lublin. At its height the AJ numbered some 2,000 fighters. In 1943 AJ commenced operations, primarily concerned with getting members across the Pyrenees into Spain. From there they continued to Palestine, with the goal of joining the Jewish Brigade of the British army. In 1944 AJ concentrated on creating Maquis that took action against informers, collaborators, and Gestapo agents in Toulouse, Nice, Lyons, and Paris. These Maquis also participated in the growing operations of the Forces Françaises de l'Intérieur in southern France. In addition to its combat operations, AJ undertook a highly successful rescue operation, using funds provided by the American Jewish Joint Distribution Committee to save Jewish children threatened with deportation.

Comité de la rue Amelot, "Committee of Amelot Street," underground organization, composed mainly of immigrant Jews, organized by Léo Glaeser and David Rapaport on June 15, 1940. Organized to provide false identity papers and maintain social aid to Jews in hiding. Eventually, a number of other organizations joined with the Amelot committee to form the Fédération des Sociétés juives de France.

La Colonie Scolaire (LCS), "The Educational Summer Camp," umbrella organization for passive resistance in northern France. Operating as a legally chartered day camp for Jewish children, LCS oversaw the activities of the Comité de la rue Amelot.

La Sixieme, "The Sixth," underground organization active in Paris and devoted to providing Jews with false identity papers.

L'organisation juive de Combat (OJC), "Jewish Fighting Organization," resistance movement also known as the Armée Juive (AJ). The OJC reflected the period of history in which AJ Maquis were joined by non-Zionist groups, including the Union des Juifs pour la Résistance et Mutuel Secours, which provided people and financial support for the Jewish underground. Considered part of the Armée Secrète, OJC Maquis were strongest in southern France and participated actively in the August 1944 Allied campaign known as Anvil-Dragoon.

L'Union des Juifs pour la Resistance et Mutuel Secours, "Union of Jews for Resistance and Mutual Aid," resistance movement founded by Polish Jewish émigrés living in France in 1941. The Union numbered between 3,000 and 7,000 members at its height, with some 1,500 combatants. The main purpose of the Union before 1944 was smuggling Jews out of France to avoid deportation to death camps in the East. After 1944, the Union concentrated on active resistance operations, undertaken in concert with Maquis of the Forces Françaises de l'Intérieur. Before D day, the Union united with the Armée Juive to form the Organisation juive de Combat and continued to operate within the context of that organization.

Main Forte (MF), "Strong Hand," title of the group that supervised the operations of the Armée Juive. Between 1940 and 1944 MF was also responsible for arranging the transfer of AJ members to Spain and thence to Palestine to join the Jewish Brigade group.

Union des Juifs pour la Résistance et l'Entr'aide (UJRE), "Jewish Union for Resistance and Mutual Aid," Jewish Communist underground founded in 1944. Operating in southern France, UJRE Maquis associated with the Forces Françaises de l'Intérieur, despite their ideological affinity for the Francs-Tireurs et Partisans. UJRE Maquis participated in the liberation of Marseilles and other French cities in August 1944.

Germany

Gruppe Herbert Baum, "Herbert Baum Group," German Jewish Communist underground group, established in Berlin in 1937. For its first five years the group was involved in anti-Nazi propaganda and educational activities, primarily among the dwindling number of Jewish youth who survived in the Nazi capital as slave laborers. On May 18, 1942, Baum and several of his compatriots attempted to torch a Nazi anti-Bolshevik and antisemitic exhibition entitled Das Sowjetparadies. The attack failed, however, and led to the mass arrest of members of the group.

Holland

Oranje Vrijbuiters (OV), "Orange Freebooters," non-Communist Jewish resistance organization operating in Amsterdam. Involved in a wide variety of resistance activities, members of OV seem to have specialized in assassinations and stealing ration cards.

Lithuania

Faraynikte Partizaner Organizatzye (פאראייניקטע פארטיזאנער ארגאניזאציע, FPO), "United Partisan Organization," Jewish underground movement established in the Vilna ghetto on January 21, 1942. After discovering that Jews deported to Ponary — ostensibly for slave labor — had actually been murdered, representatives of Jewish youth movements in Vilna, including Abba Kovner of ha-Shomer ha-Tzair, Nissan Reznik of ha-No'ar ha-Tsiyoni, Josef Glazman of Betar, and Yitzhak Wittenberg of the Communists, met to establish the Jewish resistance movement. The Bund's youth movement joined FPO later in 1942. FPO's primary task was to prepare the ghetto for self-defense and to spread the call for resistance to other ghettos in the vicinity of Vilna. In practice, the FPO command decided not to attempt to fight in the ghetto but concentrated on forming partisan units in the forests. Efforts to contact the Polish undergrounds, both Communist and non-Communist, failed, because the Polish undergrounds had been weakened during the months of Soviet rule in Vilna and had not yet recovered their strength. The first group to leave for the forests, led by Glazman, arrived in the Naroch Forest on July 24, 1943. More groups left thereafter, although they were hampered by repeated Nazi anti-partisan operations. In September 1943, when the Nazis appeared likely to liquidate the ghetto, FPO tentatively planned to change its tactics and fight in the ghetto. However, when the liquidation *Aktion* actually began, FPO units did not receive popular support for an armed uprising. A small revolt, led by the last remaining FPO units, did occur on the day that the final liquidation happened, September 24, 1943. Thereafter all FPO units fought in the forests.

Irgun Brit Zion (ארגון ברית ציון, IBZ), "United Zion Organization," Jewish underground movement established in Kovno by Zionist youth group members in 1940. At its height in 1943, IBZ numbered between 150 and 200 members. IBZ's main activities were in the educational and propaganda spheres, although the leadership also encouraged those members physically capable of joining the partisans to do so. Chairmen: Shimon Grau, Yitzhak Shapira, Avraham Melamed, and Aryeh Cohen. Publications: *Nitzotz, Shalhevet.*

Matzok (מצ'ק), Zionist underground group deriving its name from the Hebrew initials for the Kovno Zionist Center. Matzok's leadership represented a broad coalition of ghetto parties and had the support of the Judenrat leadership, especially the chairman, Dr. Elchanan Elkes, and the ghetto police. Matzok operated in two spheres: getting those who could fight into the forests and finding hiding places for those who could not fight.

Poland

Akiba (עקיבא), underground youth movement established in the Krakow ghetto in 1940. Led by Shimshon and Justyna (Tova) Draenger, Akiba became one of the founding groups of he-Halutz ha-Lohem.

Blok kegn Fashizm (בלאק קעגן פאשיזם), "Anti-Fascist Bloc," Jewish underground movement established at the initiative of Jewish Communists in the Warsaw ghetto. Created in March 1942, the Bloc attracted the support of left-wing Zionist parties. The Gestapo's May 30, 1942, arrest of Communists in the ghetto led to the Bloc's dissolution, but its remnants became the first component groups of the Żydowska Organizacja Bojowa (ŻOB).

Dror (דרור), "Freedom," underground group composed of members of ha-Shomer ha-Zair that was created in the Warsaw ghetto in 1940. In 1942 the Dror faction became one of the founding parties of the ŻOB, and Dror members took part in all major ŻOB operations. > see also: **Resistance, Jewish Underground Organizations (Poland, Żydowska Organizacja Bojowa)**.

Gruppe Bauminger, "Bauminger Group," popular name for the underground group in the Krakow area composed of leftist youth not associated with Akiba or he-Halutz ha-Lohem.

He-Halutz ha-Lohem (החלוץ הלוחם), "The Fighting Pioneer," Jewish underground movement founded in Krakow in August 1942. At its height, the movement numbered 100, most from the Akiva Zionist youth movement. The group cooperated closely with the Żydowska Organizacja Bojowa in Warsaw and with the Polish Socialist and Communist undergrounds in Krakow. Owing

to conditions in Krakow, the leaders decided that priority should be given to attacks outside the ghetto; since Krakow served as the General Government's capital numerous targets were available. In addition the nearby forests promised many possibilities of creating partisan groups, though promises of aid from the Armia Ludowa never materialized. Leaders: Shimshon Draenger, Aharon Liebeskind, Avraham Leibovich (Laban), and Manik Eisenstein.

Organizacja Bojowa Żidowskiej Mlodziezy Chalucowej, "Fighting Organization of Pioneer Jewish Youth," Polish name for he-Halutz ha-Lohem.

Sozialistischer Kinder Farband (סאציאיסל-טישער קינדער פארבאנד, SKIF) "Socialist Youth Group," underground collective for non-Zionist youth movements active in the Warsaw ghetto.

Yidishe Kamf Organizatsye (יידישע קאמף ארגאניזאציע), "Jewish Combat Organization," Yiddish name for ŻOB.

Żydowska Organizacja Bojowa (ŻOB), "Jewish Combat Organization," premier Jewish underground group in Poland. ŻOB was founded in Warsaw on July 28, 1942, as a coalition of Jewish underground parties, led by Mordechai Anielewicz. By October 1942, ŻOB had become sufficiently confident in its strength to begin plans for active defense of the Jewish population and to spread the resistance to other ghettos. Between October 1942 and April 1943, ŻOB cells were established in Bialystok (led by Mordechai Tenenbaum-Tamaroff), Będzin (led by Zvi Brandes), and Krakow (led by Avraham Leibovich). ŻOB organized four major ghetto revolts, the most important of which was the Warsaw ghetto uprising of April 19 to May 16, 1943. In the aftermath of that revolt, about 1,000 ŻOB fighters escaped to the Aryan side of the city, where they continued to fight. This group took part in the Warsaw general uprising in August 1944 as part of the Armia Ludowa.

Żydowski Związek Wojskowy (ŻZW), "Jewish Military Union," Revisionist Zionist underground movement created by members of Betar late in 1942. The ŻZW did not join the ŻOB, although it did coordinate operations and share weaponry with the larger organization. Chairman of the ŻZW committee was Dr.

David Wdowinski, and the military commander was Pawel Frenkiel. Many ŻZW fighters fled to the Aryan side of Warsaw in the aftermath of the ghetto revolt, but most were hunted down and murdered by the SS.

Soviet Union

Jerusalem, popular name (given by non-Jewish Partisans) for the Jewish family camp located in Belorussia and commanded by the Bielski brothers, Tuvia, Aharon, Asael, and Zusia. By the end of 1942 the family camp included over 1,000 persons, of whom 600 were fighters. Despite standing orders to remove all civilians from partisan camps, the Bielskis continued to operate, with the help of a sympathetic commander, in the dual role of resisters and rescuers until liberated. The camp provided the personnel for the Kalinin partisan brigade of the Soviet army.

TABLE R.2: Jewish Partisan Units

Name	Location	Name	Location
51	Slonim	*Hirsh Kaplinski*	Volhynia
106	Naliboki Forest	*Kalinin*	Belorussia
208	Mogilev	*Karyuchin*	Ukraine
406	Zaslavl	*Kruk*	Ukraine
Alerte	Paris	*Kutuzov*	Minsk/Slutsk
Anton Ivanov	Plovdiv	*La Malquière*	Lautrec
Atlas	Belorussia	*Lazo*	Kuidanov
Bandes	Galicia	*Leon*	Vilna
B'nai Ya'ar	Krakow	*Nekomo*	Vilna
Budenny	Zaslavl	*Povirsk*	Ukraine
Carmagnole-Fryd	Lyons	*Ratno*	Ukraine
Dzerzhinski	Kuidanov	*Torchinbrod*	Ukraine
Foroïs	Bialystok	*Yehiel*	Vilna

Source: I. Kowalski (ed.): *Anthology on Armed Jewish Resistance*, 4 vols., Brooklyn, NY: Jewish Combatants Publishers House, 1986-1991.

TABLE R.3: Major Concentration Camp Uprisings

Camp	Date	Camp	Date
Auschwitz II (Birkenau)	10/06–07/44	Lesienice	11/20/43
Chelmno	01/17–18/45	Sobibór	10/14/43
Janowska	11/19/43	Stalowa Wola	12/28/42
Kruszyna	12/16/42	Syret	09/29/43
Krychów	08/16/43	Treblinka	08/02/43

Source: Edelheit & Edelheit: *A World in Turmoil*, Wetport, CT: Greenwood Press, 1991.

TABLE R.4: Major Ghetto Uprisings

Ghetto	Date	Ghetto	Date
Będzin	08/01/43	Mir	08/09/42
Bialystok	08/15–20/43	Miory	06/02/42

Braslaw	06/03/42	Nesvizh	07/21/42
Brody	05/17/43	Nowogrodek	10/14/42
Częstochowa	06/25/43	Otwock	08/19/42
Dabrowica	08/28/42	Parczew	09/19/42
Dworzec	12/19/42	Radomsko	01/05/43
Dzisna	06/14/42	Serniki	09/29/42
Glebokie	06/19/42	Radziwillow	05/29/42
Ilja	03/17/42	Skalat	04/07/43
Jaworow	04/18/43	Slonim	06/29/42
Kamien Koszyrski	08/10/42	Sosnowiec	08/01/43
Kamionka	05/09/42	Stolin	09/11/42
Kielce	12/17/42	Szarkowszczyna	07/18/42
Kleck	07/21/42	Tarnopol	06/20/43
Korzek	09/30/42	Tarnów	09/02/43
Krakow	12/24/42	Tatarsk	10/25/41
Kremenets	09/09/42	Tomaszow Lubelski	02/25/42
Lachva	09/03/42	Tuchin	09/24/42
Lida	06/10/42	Vilna	09/24/43
Luboml	10/01/42	Warsaw	01/18–21/43
Lvov	06/25/43	Warsaw	04/19–5/16/43
Markuszow	05/09/42	Wlodzimierz Wolynski	11/13/42
Minsk	03/02/42	Zdzieciol	08/06/42

Source: Edelheit & Edelheit: *A World in Turmoil*, Wetport, CT: Greenwood Press, 1991.

3. Jewish Resistance Leaders

Abugov, Aleksandr (b. 1913): partisan commander in the Ukraine; later commanded a cavalry reconnaissance unit of the Red Army.

Altman, Tossia (1918–1943): active in Warsaw; ha-Shomer ha-Zair; involved with resistance activities throughout Poland and Lithuania; killed during the Warsaw ghetto uprising.

Anielewicz, Mordechai (1919–1943): active in Warsaw; ha-Shomer ha-Zair; commander in chief of ŻOB; killed during the Warsaw ghetto uprising.

Arad, Yitzhak (b. 1926): active in Vilna; partisan fighter in Rudninkai Forest; active in Briha and Aliya Bet; brigadier general in Israel Defense Forces (IDF); director of IDF education branch; director of Yad Vashem.

Atlas, Yehezkiel (1913–1942): Physician; partisan commander in Lipiczany Forest; killed in combat with Germans near Wielka Wola.

Baum, Herbert (1912–1942): Berlin; Communist leader; involved in anti-Nazi propaganda; arrested by Gestapo and killed.

Bauminger, Zvi H. (1919–1943): active in Krakow; ha-Shomer ha-Zair; led ŻOB in Krakow; killed during Gestapo raid on his headquarters.

Berman, Adolf Abraham (1906–1978): active in Warsaw; Poale Zion Smol; representative to Polish underground and secretary of Rada Pomocy Żydom (Zegota).

Bielski, Tuvia (1906–1987): partisan commander in Belorussia; created "Jerusalem" Jewish family camp in Naliboki Forest.

Blum, Abraham (1905–1943): active in Warsaw; Bundist; commander of ŻOB; killed during the Warsaw ghetto uprising.

Cohn, Marianne (1924–1944): active in France; leader in Jewish youth movements; active in smuggling Jewish children to Switzerland; killed by Milice members.

Draenger, Justyna (Tova) (1917–1943): active in Krakow; Akiva; founder of he-Halutz ha-Lohem; fought with partisans in Wiśnicz Forest; captured and presumed murdered by the Gestapo.

Draenger, Shimshon (1917–1943): active in Krakow; Akiva; founder of he-Halutz ha-Lohem; fought with partisans in Wiśnicz Forest; captured and presumed murdered by the Gestapo.

Dvoretski, Alter M. (1906–1942): *Judenälteste* in Diatlovo; partisan commander in Lipiczany Forest; murdered by non-Jewish partisans.

Edelman, Marek (b. 1921): active in Warsaw; Bundist; commander of ŻOB; crossed to the Aryan side after Warsaw ghetto uprising; fought in the Warsaw general uprising.

Feiner, Leon (1888–1945): active in Warsaw; Bund representative to the Polish underground and to Zegota; died of natural causes.

Fleischmann, Gisi (1897–1944): active in Slovakia; Women's International Zionist Organization leader; leader of Pracovná Skupina; murdered in Auschwitz.

Gamzon, Robert (1905–1961): active in France; commander of the Armée Juive; liberated Castres and Mazamet on August 21, 1944.

Gildenman, Moshe (1898–1958): partisan commander in Volhynia; served in the Red Army from 1943 to 1945.

Gitterman, Yitzhak (1889–1943): active in Warsaw; director of American Jewish Joint Distribution Committee in Poland; leader of ŻOB; killed during Small Revolt.

Glazman, Josef (1913–1943): active in Vilna; Betar; commander of Faraynilte Partizaner Organizatzye (FPO); fought as partisan in Naroch and Rudninkai Forest; killed in action.

Grossman, Haika (b. 1919): active in Bialystok; ha-Shomer ha-Zair; commander of ŻOB group in Bialystok and of partisan unit in forests; active in Briha and Aliya Bet; speaker of the Israeli Knesset during the 1980s.

Kaczerginski, Shmerke (1908–1954): active in Vilna; leader of FPO; poet and partisan fighter in the Naroch Forest.

Kaplinski, Zvi (1910–1942): partisan commander in the Lipiczany Forest; murdered by non-Jewish partisans.

Klinger, Chaika (1917–1958): active in Będzin; ha-Shomer ha-Zair; participated in the Będzin uprising, escaping to Slovakia and thence to Palestine.

Korczak-Marla, Ruzka (1921–1988): active in Vilna; ha-Shomer ha-Zair; member of FPO command; partisan leader in Rudninkai Forest; among the first survivors to reach Palestine in 1944.

Kovner, Abba (1918–1988): active in Vilna; ha-Shomer ha-Zair; commander of FPO and of Nekama partisan unit in Rudninkai Forest; among the founders of Briha and strong supporter of Aliya Bet after World War II; national poet of the Holocaust and rebirth.

Liebskind, Aharon (1912–1942): active in Krakow; Akiva; commander of he-Halutz ha-Lohem; killed during Gestapo raid on his headquarters.

Lubetkin, Zivia (1914–1976): active in Warsaw; Dror; ŻOB representative on Aryan side; survived the ghetto uprising and the Warsaw general uprising; active in Briha and Aliya Bet after World War II.

Pechersky, Aleksandr (b.1909): Soviet army officer; leader of successful Sobibór uprising.

Plotnicka, Frumka (1914–1943): active in Będzin; leader of ŻOB group; killed in action during uprising.

Rayman, Marcel (1923–1944): active in Paris; Communist; organized first Francs-Tireurs et Partisans unit in France; captured and executed by Gestapo.

Robota, Roza (1921–1944): active in Auschwitz; ha-Shomer ha-Zair; contact person for the Jewish underground; hanged after unsuccessful revolt.

Sutzkever, Abraham (b. 1913): active in Vilna; poet and partisan in the Naroch Forest.

Tenenbaum-Tamaroff, Mordechai (1916–1943): active in Bialystok; Dror; leader of ŻOB; killed during revolt.

Wdowinski, David (1895–1970): active in Warsaw; Betar; founder and leader of Żydowski Związek Wojskowy; incarcerated in concentration camp after ghetto uprising.

Weill, Joseph (1902–1988): active in France; involved with rescue of children; fled to Switzerland in 1943.

Weissmandel, Dov Baer (1903–1956): active in

Slovakia; Rabbi; leader of the Pracovná Skupina; escaped from deportation train.

Wilner, Arie (1917–1943): active in Warsaw; ha-Shomer ha-Zair; ŻOB representative to Polish underground; killed during Warsaw uprising.

Wittenberg, Yitzhak (1907–1943): active in Vilna; Communist; leader of FPO; captured by Gestapo and murdered.

Yelin, Chaim (1913–1944): active in Kovno; Communist; partisan commander in Rudninkai Forest; ambushed by Gestapo and murdered.

Zuckerman, Yitzhak Antek (1915–1981): Warsaw; Dror; commander of ŻOB; responsible for supply of arms to the ghetto fighters; survived the uprising and led ŻOB fighters during Warsaw general uprising.

4. Resistance Movements

Albania

Balli Kombëtar, Albanian resistance movement named after its leader. Anti-Communist and anti-royalist in orientation, Balli Kombëtar fielded a number of under-strength battalions between 1940 and 1943. In combat, however, the fighters proved no match for the Italians. After the Italian Armistice the movement was forcibly united with Enver Hoxha's partisans.

Austria

Kampfgruppe Auschwitz, "Battle Group Auschwitz," underground cell created by Austrian Communists incarcerated in Auschwitz in mid-1943. By the end of the year Polish and other inmates joined the group, which reemerged as Związek Organizacji Wojskowej. > see also: **Resistance, Resistance Movements (Poland, Związek Organizacji Wojskowej)**.

Belgium

Armée Belge des Partisans (ABP), "Belgian Partisan Army," Communist resistance group involved in active anti-Nazi operations from mid-1941 to 1944. The ABP specialized in the selective assassination of Nazi administrators and various Belgian collaborators.

Armée de la Libération (AL), "Army of Liberation," Belgian underground movement active in Liège. Founded in 1940, the AL operated, in one form or another, throughout the war.

Armée Secrète (AS), "Secret Army," umbrella agency for the Belgian resistance, recognized by the Belgian government in exile and supported by the British Special Operations Executive (SOE). The AS was active in operations aiding the Allied advance during the period from July to September 1944.

Clarence, Belgian espionage group based in Brussels. Founded by Walthère Dewé, who ran "La Dame Blanche" line in World War I. Dewé was captured and killed on June 14, 1944. The Clarence line shut down shortly thereafter; in its years of operation it transmitted considerable intelligence data.

Comet, code name for the underground escape organization from Belgium through France to Spain. Founded August 1941 by Andrée de Jongh.

Comité d'Entr'aide, "Mutual Aid Committee," escape line with terminals in Belgium and Spain. From Brussels the line passed through Paris and Bayonne to Bilboa and Gibraltar. Over three years the Comité helped more than 700 individuals, including dozens of Jews and hundreds of escaped Allied POWs.

Front de l'Independance (FI), "Independence Front," Communist underground organization, founded March 1941. Strongest in Liège, FI was the parent organization for the Comité de Vigilance des Intellectuels Antifascistes and was closely associated with the Front Wallon. All three organizations encouraged Jews to join their ranks and all had rescue departments.

Front National (FN), "National Front," underground movement founded in September 1941. Cooperated closely with the Comité National des Defense Juive.

Front Wallon (FW), coalition of Communist and non-Communist underground movevments, founded in May 1941. Supported by the Belgian government in exile, FW was primarily active in "civil" resistance, for example, organizing crippling strikes in Liège and other industrial centers.

Groupe C, "Group C," Belgian resistance movement centered in Brussels and founded in late 1940 or early 1941. Consisting mostly of engineering students, Groupe C specialized in sabotaging industrial and strategic targets in Nazi-occupied Belgium.

Légion Belge (LB), "Belgian Legion," founded in 1940. Composed largely of army reserve officers, the LB was closely linked to the Belgian government in exile. Deactivated after mass arrests during 1942, the LB was transformed in 1944 into the Armée Secrète.

Mill, code name for a Belgian espionage cell composed of engineers and other railway employees. Using their knowledge of the Belgian national rail system, Mill was able to provide the Allies with data on all trains moving in and out of the Western Front, including both those transporting troops West and those transporting Jews to death camps in the East.

Mouvement National Belge (MNB), "Belgian National Movement," clandestine group operating on a national level under the authority of the Belgian government in exile and active in sabotage, espionage, and anti-Nazi propaganda. Founded in 1940, the MNB nearly collapsed with the arrest of its leaders, especially Camille Joset, in 1942. By 1944 the organization had recovered sufficiently to play a role in preventing the Nazi destruction of port facilities in Antwerp, thus aiding the Allied advance in September.

Oeuvre Nationale de l'Enfance (ONE), "National Action for Infants," underground movement dedicated to rescuing Jewish children from the Nazis. During the occupation, ONE placed more than 2,000 Jewish children in Christian homes, thus saving their lives.

Zéro, Belgian espionage agency organized in 1940, providing information to the Allies regarding German troop concentrations. Despite the heavy concentration of Gestapo agents, Zero was able to operate until the liberation.

Bulgaria

Naroden Glas, "Voice of the Nation," clandestine Communist broadcasting agency, operational from 1939 to 1944. Primarily involved in anti-government propaganda, its broadcasts in 1942 and 1943 called upon the populace to help save Jews. In 1944 the broadcasts took a patriotic turn, especially following the mysterious death of Czar Boris I after a visit with Hitler.

Otechstven Front (OF), "Fatherland Front," Communist resistance organization founded on July 17, 1942, and headed by Georges Dimitrov. OF formulated very broad goals to attract members of all classes and groups. Despite OF's Communist leanings, the movement was recognized by the Bulgarian National Committee in London and was supported by both the Special Operations Executive and Narodnyy Komissariat Vnutrennikh Del (NKVD). OF allowed Jews of all ideological stripes to join its ranks.

Czechoslovakia

Obrana Naroda (ON), "National Defense," Czech underground army founded in October 1939. The ON command was composed mainly of military personnel and was divided into thirteen territorial divisions. ON collapsed in 1941 when much of its leadership was arrested. Commander: General Josef Bily (1939–1941).

Sparta I and II, Czech underground movements providing important intelligence data to the Western Allies (Sparta I) and the Soviets (Sparta II).

Ústredři Vedeni Odboje Domaciho, "Central Committee for the Internal Struggle," Czech underground umbrella organization working with the Czech government in exile in London.

France

Alliance, underground agency specializing in intelligence gathering founded by Georges Loustuanau-Lacau in July 1940. Used contacts in the Vichy government to obtain data that was later passed on to the British. The organization was also known by its code name, Noah's Ark. At its height, Alliance numbered 2,000 members.

Armée Secrète (AS), "Secret Army," coalition of underground organizations created by Jean Moulin in September 1942. In 1944 the AS included about 80 percent of the resistance groups in France and, in theory if not in practice, commanded both the Forces Françaises de l'Intérieur and the Francs-Tireurs et Partisans.

Ceux de la Libération, "Those for the Liberation," independent underground movement active in northern France. In 1942 the organization was a founding member of the Conseil National de la Résistance, created by Jean Moulin to unite resistance groups under one banner.

Comité d'Action Militaire (COMAC), "Military Action Committee," the combat arm of the CNR that in May 1944 became Force C of the FFI.

Comité Parisien de Libération, "Parisian Committee of Liberation," the FFI command that oversaw the August 1944 Paris uprising.

Conseil National de la Résistance (CNR), "National Council of the Resistance," Movement fusing all the member entities of the French underground into a unified command, created by Jean Moulin on May 27, 1943. CNR superseded the Mouvements Unis de Résistance (MUR) by adding the Communists to the united resistance movement.

Forces Françaises de l'Intérieur (FFI), "French Forces of the Interior," combat arm of the CNR, founded in January 1944 and under the command of the Armée Secrète. Primarily operational in southern France. A coalition of groups, the FFI also included the Armée Juive in its ranks.

Francs-Tireurs, "Sharpshooters," non-Communist resistance movement active in southern France before the creation of the CNR.

Francs-Tireurs et Partisans (FTP), "Sharpshooters and Partisans," Communist underground movement founded in 1941. Primarily concentrated in the departments north of Paris. In May 1943 the FTP agreed to join the CNR, thus uniting all French underground groups. The First and Fourth Detachments of the FTP were largely made up of Transylvanian Jews. The latter, responsible for rail demolition (with quite successful results), was also commanded by a Jew, Joseph Boczov. Commanders: Pierre Villon, Robert Noireau.

Main-d'oeuvre immigrée (MOI), "Immigrant Manpower," French Communist front organization active among immigrants that established Maquis during the Nazi occupation. Among other units established by MOI were a number of all-Jewish combat groups in Paris and other French cities.

Mouvement de Libération Nationale (MLN), "National Liberation Movement," first French underground movement, founded in Marseilles on August 15, 1940, by Henri Frenay. Loyal to the French government in exile, in 1943 the MLN changed its name to Combat. As such, the group joined the CNR and later the AS.

Mouvement National contre le Racisme (MNCR), "National Movement Against Racism," underground organization made up of intellectuals. MNCR's main focus was to help save hunted Jews from falling into Nazi and French collaborators' hands. Of special importance was the placing of Jewish children with willing Christian families.

Mouvements Unis de Résistance (MUR), "United Resistance Movements," unified framework for all non-Communist resistance movements in southern France, founded by Jean Moulin in March 1943. That May MUR signed an agreement with the FTP to coordinate operations, thus creating the Conseil National de la Résistance.

Musée de l'Homme, "Museum of Man," propaganda and espionage organization formed by Boris Vildé in August 1940. The group, one of the earliest French resistance organizations, took its name from the Paris anthropological museum that was the group's headquarters. In March 1941 the group was betrayed to the Gestapo. Most of its members were arrested, tried, and executed.

Noyautage de l'Administration Publique (NAP), "Infiltration of the Public Administration," underground movement whose aim was to infiltrate the Vichy regime and seize the civil administration upon liberation.

Organisation Civile et Militaire (OCM), "Civil and Military Organization," militant non-Communist resistance movement founded by Captain Touny in 1941. Centered in Paris, the OCM was Fascist in political orientation. In 1943 OCM joined the CNR, becoming part of the Armée Secrète.

Organisation de Résistance de l'Armée (ORA), "Army Resistance Organization," clandestine movement within the so-called armistice army in Vichy France. Primarily organized among junior officers, the ORA failed to influence the armistice army as a whole to offer resistance to the Nazis. Nevertheless, ORA's 4,000 members were widely involved in anti-Nazi activities; more than a quarter of them were deported to concentration camps in Germany or killed in action.

Zéro-France, clandestine French movement that concentrated on intelligence gathering. In 1944 Zéro had 1,000 members — of whom about 200 worked for the French railways — and the organization passed to the Allies important information on German troop movements.

Germany

Arbeitsgemeinschaft für Friede und Freiheit, "Union for Peace and Liberty," active resistance movement founded in Berlin by Werner Scharff. Involved in attempts to rescue Jews, the Arbeitsgemeinschaft, which numbered only a dozen members at its height, was broken up when Scharff was arrested and sent to Theresienstadt. Scharff was executed in March 1945.

Die Weisse Rose, "The White Rose," group of anti-Nazi students organized at the University of Munich in February 1943. Weisse Rose undertook a brief anti-Nazi propaganda campaign but was eliminated by the Gestapo in March and April 1943. Most of the leaders of the group, including Hans and Sophie Scholl, were executed. The White Rose was also known as the Scholl Kreis.

Freiburg Kreis, "Freiburg Circle," resistance group at Freiburg University led by Gerhard Ritter. Never became active.

Freiheitsaktion Bayern, "Freedom Action Bavaria," active resistance movement operating in the Munich region. Closely linked to the Dachau International Prisoners' Committee, the organization assisted in that camp's smooth liberation.

Höher Einsatz, "Higher Operation," an illegal bank organization operating as a subsidiary of the Arbeitsgemeinschaft für Friede und Freiheit, providing aid to Jews in hiding.

Kreisau Kreis, "Kreisau Circle," German resistance movement named after Helmuth James von Moltke's estate, where the group held its regular meetings. Composed of German military and political leaders, the circle sought to replace Hitler with a constitutional government, although not with a liberal democracy. Strong supporters of the July 20, 1944, bomb plot, the circle was decimated by the Gestapo after the failure to assassinate Hitler.

Mittwoch Gesellschaft, "Wednesday Club," conservative anti-Nazi group named for the fact that its members gathered on Wednesdays. Although some of the members later became involved in active resistance, the club itself remained a peripheral entity in the German underground.

Rote Kapelle, "Red Orchestra," ethnically mixed Communist intelligence service headquartered in France but employing agents at middle levels of the Wehrmacht and Auswärtiges Amt. Formed by Leopold Trepper, a Jewish Communist, Rote Kapelle accumulated considerable intelligence data regarding German troop dispositions in Western Europe that the Soviets refused to share with the Western Allies. Despite Gestapo penetration, Trepper operated throughout World War II.

Greece

EPON, naval arm of Ethniko Apeleutherotiko Metopo/Ellenikos Laikos Apeleutherotikos Stratos (EAM/ELAS), primarily involved in transporting agents into, and rescued Jews out of, Greece during World War II. Financed jointly by the Special Operations Executive and the Hagana, in 1945 EPON turned all its resources over to the Mossad le-Aliya Bet.

Ethnika Kai Koinonike Apeleutherosi (EKKA), "National and Social Liberation Movement," non-Communist and anti-royalist underground movement founded in 1941 by Georgios Kartalis. In May 1943 EKKA's combat units were forcibly united with EAM/ELAS, although EKKA continued its political activities through 1946.

Ethniko Apeleutherotiko Metopo/Ellenikos

Laikos Apeleutherotikos Stratos (EAM/ELAS), "National Liberation Front/ Greek Popular Liberation Army," Communist resistance movement established in 1941. EAM acted as the political arm of the underground and ELAS as its military arm. Cooperating with the Greek government in exile for the duration of World War II, EAM/ELAS fought against the provisional government during the Greek Civil War.

Ethnikos Demokratikos Ellenikos Synthesmos (EDES), "National Republican Greek League," non-Communist resistance movement founded by Colonel Napoleon Zervas in 1941. With EDES under the direct command of the Greek government in exile, Zervas hoped to avoid conflict with the Communist EAM/ELAS movement. Although he succeeded in this in most parts of the country for the duration of the war, peaceful coexistence ceased with the opening of the Greek Civil War.

Holland

Bureau Inlichtingen (BI), "Intelligence Bureau," secret service agency of the Dutch government in exile, established in 1943, which oversaw resistance movements in Holland. BI's home element was penetrated by the Gestapo in a highly successful German move against British intelligence, known as the "North Pole" fiasco.

Landelijke Knokploegen (LKP), "National Action Groups," established in 1943, dealt with securing ration books, false ID cards, and other papers through attacks on Nazi governmental offices.

Landelijke Organisatie voor Hulp aan Onderduikers (LO), "National Organization for Assistance to 'Divers' [those in hiding]," resistance group dedicated to aiding all persons in hiding from the Nazis.

Nationaal Steunfonds (NSF), "National Assistance Fund," finance section of the Dutch underground which financed resistance activities.

Nederlandse Binnenlandse Strijdkrachten (NBS), "Dutch Forces of the Interior," the officially recognized underground forces in Holland that were supported by the Dutch

government in exile. Operated under the command of Prince Bernhard.

Orde Dienst (OD), "Order Service," armed section of the underground whose missions included the seizure of key government installations and the guarantee of public safety upon the German withdrawal.

Raad van Verzet in Het Koninkrijk der Nederlanden (RvV), "Council of Resistance in the Kingdom of the Netherlands," Dutch underground movement dedicated to espionage and sabotage activities.

Hungary

Magyar Fuggetlensegi Mozgalom (MFM), "Hungarian Independence Movement," anti-Fascist organization founded by Karoly Kiss in 1942. Catholic and anti-Communist in orientation, MFM had no specific foreign policy orientation, although most of its members opposed participation in World War II. In 1943 and 1944 MFM members participated in a number of partly successful efforts to rescue Hungarian Jews.

Italy

Comitato di Liberazione Nazionale (CLN), "Committee of National Liberation," umbrella group for Italian anti-Fascist resistance movements established after the downfall of Mussolini in July 1943 and cemented during the abortive anti-Nazi fighting that September. The CLN was organized as a decentralized structure, with the Comitato Centrale di Liberazione Nationale — located in Rome — having marginal control over all other agencies. The rescue of Jews played a special role within the wide range of CLN activities.

Confederazione Generale Italiana del Lavoro (CGIL), "General Confederation of Italian Labor," framework for trade union reorganization and anti-Fascist resistance created on June 3, 1944. The CGIL brought together all Communist, Socialist, syndicalist, and Catholic trade unions with a total of 3,000,000 members. The CGIL broke up in 1948.

Partito d'Azione (Pd'A), "Party of Action," Milanese resistance cell founded in January 1943. The Pd'A formed one of the main bases of the CLN; eventually three Pd'A partisan brigades were formed: Rosselli, GL, and Italia Liberia. The Pd'A split briefly in 1944 but reunited in 1945 to play an active part in the uprisings that liberated northern Italy from the Nazis and their Fascist sympathizers. Failing to gain mass support in the elections of 1946, Pd'A disbanded.

Partito Democrazia Christiana (PDC), "Christian Democratic Party," anti-Fascist body established on July 25, 1943. The PDC stood for pluralism, individualism, and democracy — all concepts directly opposed to Mussolini's ideas about the corporate state. PDC members joined resistance movements as individuals; the PDC as such had no combat groups since it was a political movement exclusively. Since the end of World War II the PDC has been one of the staunchest supporters of democracy in Italy.

Norway

Militaer Organisasjonen (MILORG), "Military Organization," Norwegian underground military organization providing a framework for the united resistance movement. Led by junior officers of the former Norwegian forces, MILORG concentrated on preparing for an eventual national uprising. At its height MILORG had over 40,000 men under arms; they seized key institutions and disarmed German troops in May 1945 to liberate all of Norway.

Norge Fritt, "Free Norway," Communist resistance movement that engaged in sabotage against German occupation forces. Small in number, the members of Norge Fritt cooperated with the larger MILORG.

Sivilaer Organisasjonen (SIVORG), "Civil Organization," anti-Nazi movement founded, as a counterpart to MILORG, in 1941. Primarily engaged in propaganda and educational activities. SIVORG was recognized and financed by the Norwegian government in exile.

Poland

Akcja Cywilna Pomocy Więźniom, "Civil Action for Help to Prisoners," a clandestine organization established in 1940 by the Polish underground army, Polska Armia Kra-

jowa (PAK or AK).

Armia Krajowa (AK), "Home Army," underground established on February 14, 1942, as a coalition of centrist and right-wing parties all of whom operated under the authority of the Polish government in exile (London) via the Delegatura. AK policy was neither to encourage nor to discourage local attacks on Nazi targets; rather, the AK high command placed its emphasis on building up its strength for a national insurrection. As a direct result of this policy, some AK groups aided Jews and Jewish resistance movements, others stood idly by and did nothing to help Jews, whereas still other member groups actively obstructed rescue of Jews. In the summer of 1944 the AK launched Operation Tempest, a series of small-scale attacks to aid the Soviet advance. These operations culminated in Operation Typhoon, the general uprising in Warsaw that took place in August and September 1944. The controversial halting of Red Army advances before Warsaw allowed the Germans to regroup and doomed Typhoon to failure.

Armia Ludowa (AL), "National Army," successor to the Gwardia Ludowa, created on December 31, 1943. Although maintaining military cooperation with the Armia Krajowa, the AL remained politically loyal to the Lublin Committee rather than the Polish government in exile in London. During the Warsaw ghetto uprising AL units offered some assistance to the ŻOB but were unable to attain more than token achievements. The AL participated actively in the Warsaw uprising of 1944, liberating hundreds of Jewish prisoners in the Pawiak prison and arming them for self-defense.

Gwardia Ludowa (GL), "National Guard," armed combat group of the Polska Partia Robotnica (the Polish Communist party), established in April 1943. The GL agreed to cooperate with the Armia Krajowa but did not amalgamate with it. In December 1943 the GL became the Armia Ludowa.

Narodowe Sity Zborne (NSZ), "National Armed Forces," a peripheral underground movement known for virulent nationalism and antisemitism. The NSZ refused to join the Armia Krajowa but did cooperate with it on anti-Nazi operations during 1944. NSZ units were responsible for numerous attacks on Jews and Jewish partisan units in the Polish and Belorussian forests.

Organizacja Bojowa PPS, "Combat Group of the PPS," social democratic underground movement, founded in early 1940. By the end of the year the Polska Partia Socjalistyczna (PPS) units merged with other democratic undergrounds to found the Polityczny Komitet Porozumiewawczy. In March 1942 that movement dissolved, when its leadership was arrested en masse by the Gestapo. The PPS then joined the AK. Throughout the war, PPS policy remained to offer any assistance possible to Jews in danger. The PPS was thus one of the main supporters of the Rada Pomocy Żydom (Zegota council), although a lack of resources hampered relief activities. During the Warsaw uprising of 1944 remnants of the ŻOB joined PPS battle groups to fight the Nazis.

Orzel, "Eagle," resistance movement especially active in the Majdanek concentration camp.

Polityczny Komitet Porozumiewawczy (PKP), "Political Committee of Agreement," Polish underground coalition established in late 1940. PKP consisted of the PPS, the National Party, and the Peasants Party, In March 1942 the PKP collapsed when its leaders were captured by the Gestapo. Most surviving members then joined with Tajna Armia Polska and other centrist and right-wing parties to found the Armia Krajowa.

Polska Partia Robotnicza (PPR), "Polish Workers Party," founded in January 1942 as a coalition of Socialist and Communist groups. The PPR became the nucleus of the Gwardia Ludowa but did not recognize the authority of the Polish government in exile. > see also: **Resistance, Resistance Movements (Poland, Gwardia Ludowa)**.

Rada Pomocy Żydom (Zegota), "Council for Aid to Jews," Polish underground organization developing from the Tymczasowy Komitet Pomocy Żydom on December 4, 1942. Zegota was organized as a loose democratic coalition of groups supporting action to rescue Jews. The council's activities were overseen by a board composed of five Polish and two Jewish members. From its inception Zegota received the assistance of the Delegatura of the Polish government in exile in addition to funds made available by Jewish agencies. Chronic shortages of funds impeded more extensive operations, although by 1944 Zegota had assisted more than 4,000 Jews.

Tajna Armia Polska (TAP), "Secret Polish Army," Polish underground movement founded by cavalry officers in December 1939. On February 14, 1942, TAP merged with the PPS and other groups that supported the government in exile in London to form the Armia Krajowa. TAP articulated a nationalist policy that had no room for antisemitism, although TAP was not active in rescue operations.

Tymczasowy Komitet Pomocy Żydom, "Provisional Committee for Aid to Jews," rescue organization established September 27, 1942. Created at the initiative of Zofia Kokkak-Szczucka, the committee was composed of democraticly oriented Catholic activists. At its height the committee had 180 persons under its care. In December 1942 the committee was reorganized as the Rada Pomocy Żydom.

Związek Organizacji Wojskowej (ZOW), "United Military Organization," official name for the Auschwitz underground that succeeded Kampfgruppe Auschwitz. ZOW was an arm of the Polish Armia Krajowa, although membership was not limited to Poles. ZOW aided the Jewish Sonderkommando's October 1944 revolt by providing the explosives used to destroy one of the crematoria in Birkenau. ZOW did not, however, use the Sonderkommando revolt as the signal for a general camp uprising; in fact, no camp uprising ever occurred in Auschwitz. > see also: **Resistance, Resistance Movements (Austria, Kampfgruppe Auschwitz)**.

Związek Walki Zbrojnej (ZWZ), "Union of Armed Struggle," unified Polish underground movement created on December 4, 1939, as a means of coordinating the operations of resistance groups that sprang up in the aftermath of Nazi occupation. The ZWZ was subdivided into six regional commands and operated as the home element of the Polish government in exile. On February 14, 1942, the ZWZ changed its name to Armia Krajowa.

Yugoslavia

Četnik(s), "Guerrilla(s)," popular name for the anti-Communist and anti-Nazi guerrilla movement led by Colonel Draža Mihailović. The term is somewhat misleading, however, since Serbian collaborationists also created groups that were called Četniks.

Jugoslovenska Vojska u Otadžbini (JuVO), "Yugoslavian Home Army," official name for the non-Communist resistance movement more commonly known as Četniks. Organized by a group of army officers led by Colonel Draža Mihailović on April 28, 1941,

JuVO became an arm of the Yugoslav government in exile in January 1942, with Mihailović appointed minister of defense. JuVO policy was to avoid direct military confrontation with the Nazis, hoping to avoid reprisals in Serbia, although small-scale operations were conducted. This lack of immediate mass action brought JuVO into conflict with the more activist orientation of the Communist partisans led by Josef Broz (Tito) and by 1943 competition escalated to civil war. To fight the Communists, Mihailović's lieutenants made local accommodations with Italian and Bulgarian occupation forces, a fact that led the Allies to abandon JuVO in 1944.

TABLE R.5: General Partisan Units

Name	Location	Name	Location
# 16	Greece	*Lazo*	USSR
# 54	Greece	*May 1 Brigade*	Belorussia
Bataljone Chlopske	Poland	*Medvedev*	Ukraine
Batya	Ukraine	*Misyora*	Ukraine
Bor	Lithuania	*Molotov*	Polesye
Borba	Lithuania	*Oktyabr*	Belorussia
Boudienny	USSR	*Ośka*	Poland
Brigade # 1	Yugoslavia	*Partisanskaia Iskra*	USSR
Brigade # 3	Yugoslavia	*Petöfi*	Slovakia
Brigade # 7	Yugoslavia	*Smirt Fashizmu*	Ukraine
Brigata Garibaldi	Italy	*Sosnieki*	Poland
Brigata Osoppo	Italy	*Stalin*	Slovakia
Bulayev	Ukraine	*Stella Rosa*	Italy
Dadya Petya	Ukraine	*Tchavdar*	Bulgaria
Jan Zizka	Slovakia	*Voroshilov*	Lithuania
Kaplan	Ukraine	*Wanda Wasilewska*	Poland
Lenin	Ukraine	*Za Pabiado*	Lithuania

Source: Heinz Kuehnrich, *Der Partisanenkrieg in Europa 1939–1945*, East Berlin: Dietz, 1968.

TABLE R.6: Escape Attempts from Nazi Concentration Camps

Year(s)	Attempts	Succeeded	Failed
1933-1939	70	21	49
1940-1941	56	12	44
1942-1943	645	359	286
1944-1945	2,083	1,418	665

Source: K. Dunin-Wasowicz, *Resistance in the Nazi Concentration Camps*, Warsaw: PWN, 1982.

5. Allied Agencies Aiding Resistance

Inter-Service Liaison Detachment (ISLD), the arm of the Secret Intelligence Service that operated in the Balkans. In 1944 the ISLD approached the Jewish Agency and the Hagana with a request for volunteers to parachute into southeastern Europe for espionage and resistance operations. This proposal led to the recruitment, training, and deployment of the thirty-two Palestinian Jewish paratroopers. > see also: **Paratroopers, Palestinian**.

Jedburgh Teams, teams of uniformed Office of Strategic Services (OSS) agents parachuted into Europe to aid resistance groups. Among others, one Jedburgh team aided the Armée Juive in an attack on an armored German train near Lyons in August 1944.

Narodnyy Komissariat Vnutrennikh Del (NKVD), "People's Commissariat for Internal Affairs," Soviet secret police agency operational between 1934 and 1943. From 1943 to 1946 the NKVD operated as the NKGB. In both guises the NKVD offered assistance to Communist resistance movements, primarily in Eastern Europe.

Office of Strategic Services (OSS), U.S. intelligence service derived from the Coordinator of Information in June 1942. Headed by General William Donovan, the OSS acted as both an espionage agency and an active service organization assisting European resisters. The latter task was undertaken, especially in 1944 and 1945, by Jedburgh teams. The OSS cooperated with the British secret services, especially with the Special Operations Executive. Compared to the British, however, the OSS had one advantage: the availability of many potential agents who were already fluent in European languages, including numerous German Jewish refugees.

Secret Intelligence Service (SIS), British espionage agency also known as MI-6 (for Military Intelligence Office 6) and founded in 1909. During the interwar era SIS agents were stationed in key European cities under the guise of passport control officers. As such, they played a crucial — although reluctant — role in the impassioned efforts of German and East European Jews to escape the Nazi and Fascist onslaught after 1933. During World War II, the SIS was exclusively involved in espionage activities and did not aid resistance movements except insofar as they passed information to the Allies regarding German operations. SIS did cooperate with the Jewish Agency for Palestine and with the Hagana in a limited way, especially in the Middle East Intelligence Center, created in 1939.

Special Operations Executive (SOE), arm of the British secret service created in 1940 to aid European resistance movements. Originally called Military Intelligence (Research) (MI[R]), the SOE was under the direct control of the Ministry for Economic Warfare. SOE's senior officer was General Sir Colin McV. Gubbins. SOE was organized geographically, with each department responsible for operations in one country. Other agencies were responsible for recruitment, training, supplies, and transportation. The SOE cooperated with other Allied secret services, notably the OSS, and with the Hagana. The latter planned a number of joint operations with the SOE in the Middle East and southeastern Europe. It has been estimated that a high proportion of SOE field agents were Jews, a fact that caused some consternation for the Palestine Administration.

Restgettos [G] "Residual ghettos": Nazi term for a few special confinement camp/ghettos where a number of Jews who had somehow survived Aktion Reinhard (1942–1943) were gathered. Most of the victims were either liquidated on the spot or were sent to the *Vernichtungslager*.

Restlose Beseitigung jedes passiven oder aktiven Widerstandes [G] "The total elimination of all resistance, passive or active": Oberkommando des Wehrmacht directive of June 4, 1941, empowering Wehrmacht troops to eliminate all resistance in the Soviet Union by whatever means available. This order dovetailed into the *Kommissarbefehl* and thus became a license for mass murder.

Revier [G] "Hospital": Term for the crude

medical facilities in the Nazi concentration camps. Although ostensibly existing to nurture sick inmates back to health, the *Reviere* actually operated as ante-chambers for the murder of all prisoners too ill to work productively. Prisoners murdered thus were killed by an injection of phenol. In many camps, the *Revier* also served as the site for illegal medical experiments conducted on inmates.

Richtlinien [G] "Guidelines": Nazi term for the provisional instructions on how to handle the Jews, Communist party offcicals, and others deemed dangerous to German interests in occupied Soviet territories.

Rishoyim [רשעים, Y/H] "Evil ones": Pun used mostly by Polish Jews for German currency, the Reichsmark, and based on the similarity of the sounds between pronunciation of the first part of the German and the Yiddish term, when pronounced with a Polish-Jewish accent.

Rohstoff [G] "Raw material": Nazi term describing Soviet prisoners of war in the latter part of 1943. Until this point, thousands of captured Soviet POWs had been machine-gunned to death in nightly executions. With forced labor starting to become scarce, however, the Nazis started to see in them a valuable source of raw material to be worked to death.

Roite hiner [רויטע הינער, Y] "Red hens": Jewish ghetto and camp term identifying Soviet bombers and fighter planes. Since open gloating by the imprisoned Jews of Allied bombings of Nazi strategic plants (almost always situated near a camp or ghetto) would have meant severe punishment or even immediate execution, the term *roite hiner* — transmitted by mouth — would indicate that this time the Soviets were inflicting the damage, thus imbuing the helpless Jews with a ray of hope for a better day.

Roiter Fraitig [רויטער פרייטיק, Y] "Red Friday": Jewish term for the date of the second Nazi occupation of Bialystok (June 27, 1941). It was so called because of the hundreds of Jewish victims that were burned alive in one of the city's synagogues.

Rosh tov [ראש טוב, H] "A good head": Slang Jewish term popular in the Warsaw ghetto for Rostov, the site of the first Soviet victory. Used in the sense of a good beginning, the term reflected Jewish optimism that liberation might be around the corner. > see also: **Derleben un Iberleben**.

Rückkehr unerwünscht [G] "Return not desired": Nazi term used to classify a special category of prisoners (other than Jews). Accompanying those individuals was their personal file stamped RU by the Gestapo, indicating that under no circumstances should they be released (after serving their time), but instead should be disposed of. > see also: **Nacht und Nebel**.

Russisches kriegsgefangenen Arbeitslager [G] "Russian prisoner of war labor camp": Nine-block area of the Auschwitz KL that was turned into a camp for Soviet prisoners of war in September 1941. Most of the POWs at Auschwitz perished, including a group of 600 murdered in an early experiment using Zyklon B gas. > see also: **Konzentrationslager System; Prisoners of War**.

S

VI F, 4a [G]: Nazi technical term for one of the many departments under the overall authority of the RSHA. Its main function was to manufacture counterfeit foreign currencies — including U.S. dollars, Swiss francs, British pounds, and South African rands. The counterfeiters were a group of Jewish criminal inmates held at the Sachsenhausen concentration camp.

S-3 [G]: Nazi technical term denoting the Buchenwald "Little Camp." > see also: **Konzentrazionslager System**.

SB [G]: Initials for *Sonderbehandelt*, Nazi term for the disposal of undesirables, "given special treatment."

Sálo Republic [Geographic name]: Popular name for the Republica Sociale Italiana, based on the location of Mussolini's headquarters in the village of Sálo (northern Italy) from September 1943 to April 1945. > see also: **Fascism, Fascist Parties and Organizations (Italy, Republica Sociale Italiana)**.

Sammelplatz/Sammelstelle [G] "Gathering place/Gathering post." > see also: **Umschlagplatz**.

Sauberkeit ist Gesundheit [G] "Cleanliness is health": Motto hung in the false showers, actually gas chambers, in some of the death camps. This Nazi term helped maintain the charade that the murder camps were benign labor facilities up until the very last possible minute, at which time any meaningful resistance or escape was no longer possible.

Säuberung [G] "Cleansing": Nazi term for the rapid depletion of the German universities and graduate schools of Jewish professors, lecturers, instructors, and Jewish student body. During World War II, the term was also used to indicate the cleansing of entire Jewish communities by deporting them to extermination points to be killed. > see also: **Judenrein**.

Säuberungs- und sicherheits Massnahmen [G] "Cleansing and security measures": Nazi term for special Einsatzgruppen units (Oberbayern, Brandenburg, and Thuringen) that, on September 13, 1939, unleashed a brief terror campaign against a number of Polish cities, towns and villages — foremost among them Wloclawek and Bydgoszcz — burning down synagogues and plundering and murdering Jews and Poles alike in order to instill fear and respect for the Nazi conqueror.

Säuberungsziel [G] "Cleanup goal": Term employed by the Einsatzkommandos in their unrelenting hunt for Jews. The faster the Jews were rounded up to be murdered, the faster the Einatszkommando's mission would be accomplished.

Schädlingsbekämpfung [G] "War against vermin": Nazi cover term for Zyklon B, the prussic acid gas that was used to exterminate millions of Jews.

Schandfleck [G] "Badge of infamy": Nazi term for the yellow Star of David the Jews were compelled to wear. > see also: **Judengelb; Sternträger**.

Scheinvolk [G] "Sham folk": Nazi ideological term for the Jewish people, emphasizing the notion that Jews do not constitute a nation, a status that implies a creative force, but instead comprise an "anti-people," whose force is solely destructive and corrosive. It followed that the health of Europe's nations rested upon the removal of this threat. > see also: **Gegenvolk**.

Scheisskommando [G] "Latrine commando": Special work detail in concentration camps. Generally inclusion in the commando was used to punish inmates for even trivial infractions.

Scheisskopf [G] "Shithead": Nazi derogatory term for Jews, used frequently by SS camp guards and their helpers. In many instances *"du scheisskopf!"* went hand in hand with a whack over the head of the Jewish victim.

Scheissmeister [G] "Latrine master": Nazi term for latrine orderlies whose function it was to time how long and how often an inmate would spend in the camp latrine.

Schicksal [G] "Destiny": Nazi ideological term to justify their actions: Following the policy would lead Germany to its destiny. The same term, with a slightly different meaning, was used by Hitler — in the sense of his own personal destiny — to justify indecision.

Schlagt den Weltfiend [G] "Beat the world's enemy": Nazi antisemitic slogan, popular with the SA, inciting pogroms or other acts of anti-Jewish violence.

Schlagt die Juden tot! [G] "Beat the Jews to death": SA propaganda statement popular in the early 1930s during the so-called period of singular or wild actions. > see also: **Einzelaktionen**.

Schlauch [G] "Tube": Nazi colloquial term for the path between the barracks and the gas chamber at Belzec. In this space Jews were forced to leave behind the rest of their personal possessions and take off their clothes; from there too they were urged on by curses and blows to all parts of their bodies to enter the gas chamber. > see also: **Himmelfahrt; Himmelstrasse; Konzentrationslager System, Vernichtungslager**.

Schlucht [G] "Ravine": Normally, a long, deep, narrow gorge cut out by nature, in the Holocaust Kingdom, a ravine became synonymous with the deaths of hundreds of thousands of innocent, civilian victims, mostly Jews.

Schmelz [G] "Junk": Normally, scrap metal to be smelted, but for the Nazis, the inmates to be transferred from a labor camp to an extermination site.

Schmelzgetto [G] "Smelting ghetto": Derogatory term for the so-called ghetto west in Rzeszow, this part of the ghetto — originally inhabited by local Jews — was completely emptied during a bloody liquidation action in September and October 1942. At the beginning of January 1943 Ghetto West was reopened and filled largely with broken families, older persons, women, children, and others considered superfluous by the Nazis that somehow had eluded previous roundups in villages and townlets. Hundreds of others that had been incarcerated in small slave-labor camps were also brought to the Schmeltzgetto to await, with the others, transportation to an extermination site.

Schrifttungspflege [G] "Cultivation of writing": Nazi term for the wholesale surveillance and censorship of literature under the auspices of Alfred Rosenberg's Kampfleague für deutsche Kultur.

Schutzangehörigen des Reiches [G] "Protected subjects of the Reich": Poles living in the territories annexed by the Reich in 1939. The term reflected their second-class status but was merely a technicality that hid their actual status as slave laborers.

Schutzhaft [G] "Protective custody": An official euphemism for removal to concentration camp. > see also: **Konzentrationslager System**.

Schutzhäftling [G] "Prisoner in protective custody": Nazi term for a person kept in Gestapo prison or concentration camp while awaiting trial. > see also: **Konzentrationslager System**.

Schutzmannschaften [G] (Schuma) "Protective details": Generic term for local security forces raised by the Germans for internal security, police, and anti-partisan operations in Belorussia, the Ukraine, and the Baltic Republics. Schuma units were usually small, organized only to battalion size, and operated in the general area of their homes. > see also: **Collaboration**.

Schutzpässe [G] "Protective passports": The specially stamped papers issued to some Jews by representatives of Spanish, Swedish, or Swiss governments indicating that individuals bearing those documents were under the protection of the country whose seal was on the document. Primarily used in Hungary during 1944, these passports saved tens of thousands of Jews.

Schutzschein [G] "Protective certificate": A special "security" slip periodically given to the Judenräte for distribution among Jewish workers. For a Jew trapped in the ghetto it was a matter of life or death to secure a *Schutzschein*. Carrying a picture of the bearer, it was considered a lifesaver; therefore no effort was spared by many to get hold of one either by bribes or other means. However, in order to harass the ghetto dwellers even more, the Gestapo often changed the color of the currently valid *Schutzschein* — from pink to yellow, white, green, or blue.

Schutzstaffel (SS) [G] "Protection Squad":

1. Scope and Definition

The praetorian guard of the Third Reich. The SS was first recruited in March 1923 as a bodyguard unit for NSDAP officials. At the time, the SS was part of the Sturmabteilung (SA), but this relationship changed after the Night of the Long Knives. As a result of the purges and under Heinrich Himmler's careful control, the SS became the primary police agency in the state, controlling the Gestapo, concentration camps, and the Nazi Party security service (the Sicherheitsdienst).

The SS utilized for its own members concepts of racial purity that were more stringent than those of the rest of the party. For example, SS members had to prove their Aryan ancestry back to the year 1700. The racial purity of SS members, along with the unqualified loyalty they showed to Hitler, soon converted the SS into one of the premier organizations of the Third Reich. Moreover, the voluntary nature of the SS and its special uniforms — all black and bearing the "Death's Head" symbol — further increased the sense of elite status and gave SS members a sense of being the avant-garde in Germany's purification.

As a result, the SS took every pain to be in the forefront of solving the Jewish problem; in effect the SS seized the Jewish question as the first step in a radical re-creation process: Hitler and Himmler both spoke of the transvaluation

Schutzpass issued by the Portuguese Embassy in Budapest, Hungary
Courtesy of Dr. Randolph L. Braham

of values and the SS was to play the critical role in this process. By 1941, when the SS takeover was complete, implementation of the Final Solution began, with the invasion of the Soviet Union. To the final days of the Third Reich, the SS remained the foundation of the Nazi regime. > see also: **Konzentrationslager System; Nationalsozialstizche Deutsche Arbeiterpartei.**

2. SS Main Offices

Reichsführer-SS und Chef der deutschen Polizei, "State leader of the SS and chief of the German police," title of Heinrich Himmler as of June 1936. Under his control were twelve main offices of the SS.

1. *SS-Hauptamt,* "Central Office of the SS," founded January 30, 1935, to coordinate general operations of the SS, recruit personnel, and control the local and Germanic SS agencies. Chief: August Heissmeyer (1935–1940); Gottlob Berger (1940–1945).

2. *Reichssicherheitshauptamt* (RSHA), "State Security Main Office," founded on September 29, 1939, by the fusion of the SD and Gestapo. The RSHA was responsible for all SS and police operations as well as internal and external security. Additionally, the RSHA was the agency delegated primary responsibility for carrying out the *Endlösung*. Chief: Reinhard Heydrich (1939–1942); Ernst Kaltenbrunner (1942–1945). The RSHA was divided into seven *Amtsgruppen* (departments): I: Personnel; II: Administration and Supply; III: SD-Inland; IV: Gestapo; V: Kripo; VI: SD-Ausland; VII: Documentation and Research.

3. *Hauptamt Ordnungspolizei* (ORPO), "Uniformed Police Main Office," founded on June 17, 1936. Responsible for all common police, fire, coast guard, and civil defense functions. Chief: Kurt Daluege. ORPO was divided into seven *Amtsgruppen*, by function: I: Schutzpolizei (uniformed police); II: Verwaltungspolizei (administrative police); III: Wasserschutzpolizei (riverine police); IV: Küstenpolizei (coastal police); V: Feuerschutzpolizei (fire police); VI: Civil defense; VII: Technical services. ORPO also oversaw the operation of the Grenzpolizei (border police) and the Bahnschutzpolizei (railroad protection police).

4. *Chef des Persönlichen Stabes der Reichsführer-SS,* "Chief of the Personal Staff of the *Reichsführer-SS*," founded 1936. In addition to controlling those operations directly associated with Himmler, the office oversaw the operations of Hitler's bodyguards and associated agencies. Chief: Karl Wolff.

5. *Wirtschafts- und Verwaltungshauptamt* (WVHA), "Economy and Administration Main Office," founded April 20, 1939. Coordinated the operation of the far-flung SS economic empire, especially in terms of the concentration camps. In March 1942 the WVHA absorbed the independent Inspectorate of Concentration Camps, headed by Theodor Eicke, which became Amt D under the control of Richard Glücks. Chief: Oswald Pohl. WVHA was divided into five *Amtsgruppen*: A: Truppenverwaltung (troop administration); B: Verpflegungs- und Bekleidungswirtschaft (furnishings and food); C: Bauwesen (construction); D: Konzentrationslager (concentration camps); E: Wirtschaftsbetriebe (economic enterprises). > see also: **Konzentrationslager System.**

6. *SS-Personal Hauptamt,* "SS Personnel Office," founded June 1, 1939. Responsible for various administrative functions relating to personnel. Chief: Maximillian von Herf.

7. *Hauptamt SS-Gericht,* "SS Legal Department," founded October 17, 1939. The department was responsible for application of the internal SS penal code, internal SS courts, and the application of disciplinary action against SS members. Chief: Franz Breithaupt.

8. *SS-Führungshauptamt,* "Main Operational Office of the SS," founded on August 15, 1940. Responsible for employment of all SS agencies except the Waffen SS. Chief: Hans Jüttner.

9. *Dienststelle Oberführer Heissmeyer,* "Administrative Department Heissmeyer," founded in 1940. Responsible for services to SS members and their families as well as for the SS school system. Chief: August Heissmeyer.

10. *Stabshauptamt Reichskommissariat für die Festigung des deutschen Volkstums* (RKfDV), "Central office of the Reich Commission for Strengthening the Germanic Peoples," founded on June 15, 1941. The office was responsible

for the repatriation of *Volksdeutsche* and the appropriation to them of property aryanized from Jews. Additionally, the office planned for the creation of German colonies in the Ostland. Chief: Ulrich Greifelt. This office was created to aid the activities of the *Reichskommissar*, a position created by Hitler for Himmler on October 7, 1939.

11. *Hauptamt Volksdeutsche Mittelstelle* (VOMI), "Main Office for the Welfare of Ethnic Germans," founded on January 1, 1937. The office was responsible for the welfare of ethnic Germans and their nazification. Chief: Werner Lorenz.

12. *Rasse- und Siedlungshauptamt* (RUSHA), "Race and Resettlement Main Office," founded on January 30, 1935. The office was to coordinate all SS racial and resettlement activities while also controlling the racial purity of SS members. Chief: Richard Hildebrandt.

3. Subsidiary Agencies

Abteilung Bothmann, "Bothmann Section," euphemistic term for the SS killing squad operating at the Chelmno extermination camp. Commanded by Hans Bothmann, the squad was recruited in late 1941, largely from the staff of the euthanasia program. >: see also: **Konzentrationslager System.**

Adolf Hitler Schulen (AHS), "Adolf Hitler Schools," established in 1937 as political training schools for future Nazi leaders. Similar to NAPOLA, the AHS were less military oriented.

Allgemeine SS, "General SS," the common term for all SS agencies not included in the Waffen-SS.

Bahnschutzpolizei, "Railroad Protection Police," an NSDAP auxiliary police taken over by the SS in 1942.

Dienststelle Eichmann, "Eichmann Administrative Office," also known as Sonderkommando Eichmann, SS agency established March 19, 1944, and sent to Hungary to expedite the ghettoization, deportation, and extermination of the last Jewish community that remained largely intact. > see also: **Aktion(en), Code Names (Aktion Margarethe).**

Eins-A Abteilung, "Division I-A," section of the Prussian police for special investigations that was reformed into the Gestapo in 1933.

Eins-C Dienst, "Office I-C," early name for the SD, derived from the office number at SS headquarters. The office was also known as Unterabteilung I-C.

Germanische Sturmbann(e) (GS), "Germanic Battalion(s)," ethnic units of the SS composed of collaborators from Holland, Denmark, Norway, and Switzerland. After six weeks of training, GS members were enrolled in the Allgemeine SS and, thereafter, in the Waffen-SS.

Hygiene-Institut der Waffen-SS, "Hygiene Institute of the Waffen-SS," research center established by a group of Nazi scientists in the Buchenwald concentration camp. The institute's primary research focus was into the pathology and serology of typhus fever. Despite the intense research on human guinea pigs — most of whom perished as a direct result of the experiments — no scientifically useful data was ever collected.

Jagdkommandos, "Hunting Commandos," organized in occupied Poland by HSSPF Friedrich Wilhelm Krüger in the beginning of 1940, the Jagdkommandos were early versions of the infamous Einsatzgruppen that operated against Russian Jewry from June 22, 1941. Motorized and well armed, they hit different and hard to reach locations at speed of lightning, bringing with them terror and death. The Jagdkommandos were also employed in seeking out and destroying Polish partisan units.

Jagdverbände, "Hunting Associations," SS sabotage units that operated behind Allied lines, mostly the Soviet Union. Jagdverbände were also employed in occupied Eastern Europe in partisan-dominated areas.

Leibstandarte-SS Adolf Hitler (LAH), "Hitler's Bodyguard Unit," established on March 17, 1933, and commanded by Josef (Sepp) Dietrich. In 1940 LAH was expanded into a division and became part of the Waffen-SS.

Nationalpolitische Erziehungsanstalten (NAPOLA), "National Political Educational Institutes," established as part of the Ministry of Education in 1933, but taken over by the SS in 1937. NAPOLA schools were essentially cadet-training centers for students between twelve and eighteen years of age. Chief: A. Heissmeyer.

Ordensburg, "Order Castle," finishing school for future Nazi leaders, all of whom were graduates of the Adolf Hitler Schulen.

Reichszentralstelle für jüdische Auswanderung, "Reich Central Bureau for Jewish Emigration," office created by the SS to encourage Jewish emigration from Germany. Established in January 1939, the Reichszentralstelle was the logical development of the office created by Adolf Eichmann in Vienna. All emigration offices ceased to function in October 1941, when further Jewish emigration was banned, and became a cover for the *Endlösung*.

SS-Heimwehr, "SS Home Defense Force," local SS defense unit established in 1939 officially to defend Danzig from a Polish attack. Although an NSDAP organ, the SS-Heimwehr operated under Wehrmacht command during the Polish campaign.

SS-Regiment Westland, SS regiment recruited in the Flanders region beginning June 1940. The regiment operated as part of the Waffen-SS Wiking Division.

SS-Standarte Nordwest, unit of the Allgemeine SS raised in Germany among Belgian and Dutch citizens in April 1941.

SS-Totenkopfverbände, "SS Death's Head Associations," established on March 29, 1936, and commanded by Theodor Eicke. The Totenkopfverbände were used to guard concentration camps and prisons. As a result they played a critical role in the *Endlösung*. Later expanded to divisional size, the Totenkopfverbände formed part of the Waffen-SS.

SS-Werterfassung, "SS Valuables Maintenance Agency," agency for collecting, cataloging, and shipping to Germany all valuables left over by deported Jews. Most of the agency's activities were undertaken by Jews supervised by the SS. > see also: **Kanada**.

Sekretariat für das Sicherheitswesen, "Secretariat for Security Affairs," office created by the SS and SD in the General Government as per *Führererlass* of May 7, 1942, for the coordination of all security matters in one office. The local HSSPF, in this case, Friedrich W. Krüger, was ex officio chairman of the committee. As such, he had ultimate authority on all security matters, answering only to Himmler, and could sidestep normal governmental channels. By definition, the secretariat also held ultimate authority on Jewish affairs and could overturn decisions by other agencies — including the Wehrmacht — that might otherwise have impeded the *Endlösung*.

Verfügungstruppen (VT), "Militarized Troops," established by Himmler on June 30, 1934, in connection with the purge known as *Nacht der langen messer*. VT replaced the earlier armed SS formations, *Kasernierte Hundertschaften* (barracks companies) and *Politische Bereitschaften* (political shock troops) that had been founded in 1933. In turn, the VT was replaced by the Waffen-SS.

Volkssturm, "People's Assault Units," established on October 18, 1944, as a last-ditch defense force to protect the Reich. Primarily composed of old men and young children (often members of the Hitlerjugend) who were poorly armed and even more poorly led.

Wachmannsschaft, "Guard Units," early term for the SS units that guarded the concentration camps. Later reorganized as the Totenkopfverbände.

Waffen-SS, "Armed-SS," established as Himmler's private army in November 1939 and replacing the SS Verfügungstruppen. In addition to its military role, the Waffen-SS retained all other SS roles. Indeed, Waffen-SS members played a special role in the *Endlösung* and in other war crimes. From June 1940 on, non-German Aryans could join the Waffen-SS; by 1945 20 of the 38 Waffen-SS divisions were composed largely, if not completely, of non-Germans.

Zentralstelle für jüdische Auswanderung, "Central Bureau for Jewish Emigration," SS office organized by Adolf Eichmann in Vienna in April 1938. The Zentralstelle fell under the dual authority of the SS and the Finance Ministry and was created to expedite the exodus of Jews from the Reich. Eichmann used a carrot and stick approach to accomplish his tasks, and was sufficiently successful that he

TABLE S.1: The Waffen-SS Divisions

1 SS Panzer Division, Leibstandarte Adolf Hitler
2 SS Panzer Division, Das Reich
3 SS Panzer Division, Totenkopf
4 SS Panzer Grenadier Division, Polizei
5 SS Panzer Division, Wiking
6 SS Gebirgs Division, Nord
7 SS Freiwillige Gebirgs Division, Prinz Eugen
8 SS Kavallerie Division, Florian Geyer
9 SS Panzer Division, Hohenstaufen
10 SS Panzer Division, Frundsberg
11 SS Freiwillige Panzer Grenadier Division, Nordland
12 SS Panzer Division, Hitlerjugend
13 Waffen Gebirgs Division der SS, Handschar
14 Waffen-Grenadier Division der SS, Galiz nr. 1 / Halicina
15 Waffen-Grenadier Division der SS, Lett nr. 1
16 SS Panzer Grenadier Division, Reichsführer-SS
17 SS Panzer Grenadier Division, Götz von Berlichingen
18 SS Panzer Grenadier Freiwillige Division, Horst Wessel
19 Waffen-Grenadier Division der SS, Lett nr. 2
20 Waffen-Grenadier Division der SS, Estn nr. 2
21 Waffen Gebirgs Division der SS, Skanderberg
22 Freiwllige Kavallerie Division der SS, Maria Theresia
23 Waffen-Grenadier Division der SS, Kama
24 Waffen Gebirgskarstjäger Division der SS
25 Waffen Grenadier Division, Ungar nr. 1 / Hunyadi
26 Waffen Grenadier Division, Ungar nr. 2
27 SS Freiwillige Grenadier Division, Langemarck
28 SS Freiwillige Grenadier Division, Wallonien
29 SS Freiwillige Grenadier Division, Russ nr. 1
30 SS Freiwillige Grenadier Division, Russ nr. 2
31 SS Freiwillige Panzer Grenadier Division, Böhmen-Mähren
32 SS Panzer Grenadier Division, 30 Januar
33 Waffen Kavallerie Division der SS, Ungar nr. 3
34 SS Freiwillige Grenadier Division, Landstorm Nederland
35 SS Polizei Grenadier Division
36 Waffen Grenadier Division
37 SS Freiwillige Kavallerie Division, Lützow
38 SS Panzer Grenadier Division, Nibelungen

Source: *Handbook on German Armed Forces*, Washington, DC: USGPO, 1944.

was ordered to organize a nationwide office on his Viennese model.

4. SS Enterprises

Deutsche Ausrüstungswerke GmbH (DAW), "German Armaments Works," a large and profitable enterprise utilizing slave labor drafted from all strata of Nazi-occupied Europe, established in 1939 and run by the SS.

Deutsche Erd und Steinwerke GmbH (DEST), "German Earth and Stone Works Ltd.," established in 1938 as an SS enterprise. It used large numbers of concentration camp inmates as cheap labor in the stone quarries and brickworks.

Deutsche Ölschiefer-Forschungs GmbH, "German Shale Oil Research Company Ltd.," SS corporation for fuel production headquartered in the Natzweiler KL.

Deutsche Umsiedlungs-Treuhand GmbH, "German Resettlement Trust Ltd.," corporation affiliated with the Reichskommissariat für die Festigung des deutschen Volkstums and responsible for carrying out the program of repatriating *Volksdeutsche,* transferring property aryanized from Jews to them, and planning for the creation of German colonies in the *Ostland.*

Deutsche Wirtschaftsbetriebe GmbH (DWB), "German Economic Enterprises Ltd.," umbrella corporation created by the Wirtschafts- und Verwaltungshauptamt to control the far-flung SS economic empire.

Gemeinnützige Krankentransport GmbH, "General Purpose Ambulance Service Ltd.," SS front corporation used to transport patients to euthanasia centers.

Mittelwerk GmbH, "Central Works Ltd.," SS construction company located in the Dora KL, Mittelwerk contracted for the slave laborers who dug the tunnels where V-1 and V-2 rockets were built.

Ostindustrie GgmbH, "Eastern Industries Ltd.," an SS enterprise founded in March 1943 by the WVHA in Poland. Under the supervision of Odilo Globocnik, it ran factories in the Lublin area, using Jewish slave labor.

Union, munitions factory operated by the SS for Krupp GmbH in Auschwitz-Buna.

TABLE S.2: SS Ranks and Equivalents

Rank	Equivalent	Rank	Equivalent
Reichsführer	National Leader	*Untersturmführer*	Second Lieutenant
Oberstgruppenführer	Colonel General	*Sturmscharführer*	Sergeant Major
Obergruppenführer	General	*Stabsscharführer*	Sergeant Major
Gruppenführer	Lieutenant General	*Hauptscharführer*	Master Sergeant
Brigadeführer	Major General	*Oberscharführer*	Senior Sergeant
Oberführer	Brigadier General	*Scharführer*	Staff Sergeant
Standartenführer	Colonel	*Unterscharführer*	Corporal
Obersturmbannführer	Lieutenant Colonel	*Rottenführer*	Lance Corporal
Sturmbannführer	Major	*Sturmmann*	Private First Class
Hauptsturmführer	Captain	*Schütze*	Private
Obersturmführer	First Lieutenant	*SS-Mann*	Private

Source: *Handbook on German Armed Forces,* Washington, DC: USGPO, 1944.

Schwarze (שווארצע, Y) "The Black": Yiddish term for Ukrainian and Russian collaborationist camp police in the service of the SS. The term was derived from the black uniforms they wore. > see also: **Collaboration.**

Schwarze Kapelle [G] "Black Orchestra": Term used by the SD for the Wehrmacht officers involved in Operation Valkyrie. Since those involved were not Communists, the term *Schwarze* was used to distinguish them from the Rote Kapelle, the Soviet espionage group. > see also: **Resistance,** **Resistance Movements (Germany).**

Schweinehund [G] "Pig-dog": Derogatory Nazi term used when addressing Jews. When thus addressed by a Nazi (even of the lowest rank) a Jewish victim had to stay in a straight posture with a fixed look. Almost always *Schweinhund* was followed with a hard blow on the victim's head, often repeated more than once.

Selektion(en) [G] "Selection(s)": Nazi term for the process by which members of a transport were chosen: some, generally a small number, for slave labor; the rest, usually the vast majority, being sent to the gas chambers. A similar selection process occurred during *Aussiedlungsaktionen*, generally in smaller towns, with those selected to survive being organized into a "clean-up detail." Continual selections in concentration camps and slave-labor camps removed the ill, the unfit, those for some reason passed over during a previous selection, and those reduced to *Muselmänner*.

Selektsye (סעלעקציע, Y) "Selection": Jewish term for the almost daily selections conducted by the Nazis or their helpers in the ghettos, slave labor, or concentration camps. > see also: **Selektion(en)**.

Septemberites [E/G Slang]: Term for those who joined the NSDAP after September 1930, usually used in the sense of an "opportunist."

Seuchensperrgebiet [G] "Epidemic zone": Nazi term justifying the closure of the large ghettos in Poland after 1939: they claimed that the areas were rife with typhus and other infectious diseases. In point of fact, Nazi policy guaranteed that such statements would become self-fulfilling prophecies, since the Jews in the ghettos subsisted in overcrowded conditions and without proper medical or sanitary facilities, resulting in mass outbreaks of deadly epidemics. > see also: **Ghetto**.

Shabriring [G/Slang] "Informing": term used by Jews — actually derived from the term for selling one's possessions — for the process of ghetto inmates informing to the authorities on other Jews in return for money.

Shadchn (שדחן, Y) "Matchmaker": Inmate term for the *Kapo*s in the death camps, who helped weed out the *muselmänner* and other sick looking prisoners in the periodic SS selections for the gas chamber.

Shaliach/shelichim (שליח/שליחים, H) "Emissary/emissaries": Generic term for

representatives of the Zionist parties sent from Palestine to Europe to inculcate nationalist ideals and party loyalty among Jewish youth groups before and after World War II. The term also refers to anyone carrying out a mission on behalf of the movement or the Jewish people.

Shamayim (שמים, H) "Heaven": Jewish term for SS-Reichsführer Heinrich Himmler. It was especially used in late 1944 and early 1945 during secret negotiations with Himmler's representatives at the Swiss border to save at least a remnant of the Jews.

Shchite (שחיטה, Y) "Ritual slaughter": Corrupted Hebrew word in the Yiddish vocabulary denoting "ritual slaughter." During the Holocaust *shchite* was used as a blunt Jewish term to signify the Nazi-inspired massacre of the Jewish people.

Shechthois (שעכטהויז, Y) "Slaughter house": Jewish term for the number II Vilna ghetto, where Jews who could not secure *Ausweise*, the constantly changing labor cards or life certificates, were held to await their turn to be taken to the Ponary death pits to be killed.

Sheeny [Uk/Slang]: Antisemitic term for Jews, originating with Ukrainians and Belorussians. Since the turn of the century, the term has spread elsewhere, notably to the United States.

She'erit ha-Pleta (שארית הפליטה, H) "The surviving remnant": Biblical phrase (originating in I Chronicles 4:43) used during and after World War II to denote survivors of the Holocaust. > see also: **Displaced Persons, Jewish**; **Briha**.

She'erit ha-Tikva (שארית התקוה, H) "Remnant of hope": alternative term for the *She'erit ha-Pleta* that emphasized the hope of Jews to evacuate postwar Europe for a permanently safe haven — a Jewish state in Palestine — at all costs. > see also: **Yetziat Europa**; **She'erit ha-Pleta**.

Shleppers (שלעפּערס, Y) "Pullers": Ghetto term for the strong-arm squads of the Polish or (at times) Jewish police, who eagerly exercised their powers granted by the Nazis by going after Jewish victims. > see also: **Collaboration, Collaborationist Organizations (Poland, Granatowa Policja); Jüdischer Ordnungsdienst.**

Shmirer (שמירער, Y) "Whitewasher": Yiddish term for Adolf Hitler, who, in Eastern Europe in the 1930s, was widely perceived as a house painter or *kalecher*.

Shoa (שואה, H) "Catastrophe": Hebrew term for the destruction of European Jewry. Deriving from a Biblical term that referred to the destruction of ancient Israel (e.g. Isaiah 10:3), the term has only rarely been used in post-biblical Jewish literature. Some Zionists used the term as early as 1915, to refer to the systematic destruction of Jewish life in wartime Eastern Europe, although using such quotes to prove premonitions of the impending Holocaust is an exaggeration. Since the 1940s the term has been used in Israel to refer to the Holocaust. In this usage it reflects the attempt both to link the modern catastrophe to a biblical antecedent and, given the unprecedented scope of the Nazi persecution of European Jewry, to find a term for destruction that is sui generis. Since 1951 the term has gained semi-official status in Israel since the Knesset designated the twenty-seventh day of the Hebrew month Nissan (ca. April) as Yom ha-Shoa. > see also: **Chrubn; Holocaust; Yom ha-Shoa.**

Shpringers (שפרינגערס, Y) "Jumpers": Yiddish term for those few Jews who somehow managed to jump off the moving trains on the way to the extermination camps. Unfortunately, in the long run, few of the *shpringers* succeeded. Even if the jump was successful, most escapees were soon caught, betrayed by a local peasant, or — in the winter — succumbed to frostbite and starvation. Some of the *shpringers* were even murdered by roving Polish bands, whose members belonged to the Polish underground, the Armia Krajowa.

Sicherheitsverwahrungshäftlinge [G] "Protective custody security prisoners": Category of inmates held in certain designated concentration camps. Some Communists and all officials of the independent trade unions were taken into protective custody in early 1933. > see also: **Konzentrationslager System.**

Sicherungsverwarhte [G] "Preventive detention": Non-Jews sent by the Gestapo to concentration camps after having served out their prison sentences for criminal or civil offenses. > see also: **Konzentrationslager System.**

Siedlungsraum [G] "Resettlement area": Nazi term for their planned Lublin-Nisko reservation scheme of late 1939–early 1940, to resettle Jews brought in from all over occupied Europe. > see also: **Lublin Reservat; Madagaskar, Fall.**

Sippenhaft [G] "Family responsibility": Form of collective responsibility invoked by the Nazis to punish resisters throughout Europe. Under the term of *Sippenhaft*, for example, some 7,000 family members of senior Wehrmacht officers were arrested after the failure of Operation Valkyrie; 5,000 of them were later murdered by the Gestapo.

Slave Labor

1. Scope and Definition

Although the use of civilian slave labor is strictly prohibited by the Geneva Conventions, the Nazi conquests brought with them the systematic use of slave laborers from throughout Europe. In the earliest instance of a labor corvée, both Jews and Poles in the General Government were made liable for *Zwangsarbeit* by a decree of October 26, 1939. In addition, Polish and Jewish — and after June 22, 1941, Soviet — prisoners of war were also pressed into forced labor. By 1942 the program of slave labor extended throughout all the occupied countries. In some cases, collaborationist groups supported such labor drives; in most cases, however, the potential "recruits" had to be obtained in systematic and often brutal manhunts that (after 1943) met with considerable opposition. Despite this opposition,

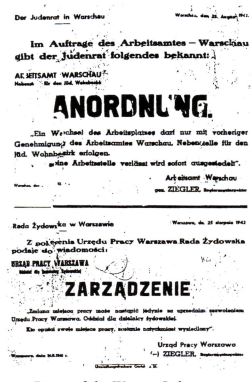

Poster of the Warsaw Judenrat
announcing a slave labor draft
Courtesy of the Żydowski Instytut
Historyczny/U.S. Holocaust Memorial Museum

the total number of forced laborers in Germany was estimated at 7 million in 1945; more than half came from Poland and the Soviet Union.

Jews too provided a large number of slave laborers. Initially, the Judenräte were responsible for providing Jewish laborers on a daily basis. In the Jewish case, however, the Judenräte were also required to provide the Jewish slave laborers with the tools they were to work with and with soup kitchens to feed them. As Nazi policy developed, special labor camps for Jews were established. Thereafter, the use of Jewish slave labor continued in both labor camps and in shops and factories established by German businesses inside the major ghettos. Jews thought that labor for the Nazis provided a chance — to be sure, a slim one — of survival. Initially this appeared to be a justified hope, but by 1943 the logic proved specious: the Nazis reduced the number of Jewish slave laborers in occupied Poland from 700,000 in 1942 to 100,000 in 1943 through the systematic liquidation of Jewish labor camps and the deportation of all Jewish workers to death camps.

From the beginning, slave labor was the exclusive province of the SS, and throughout the war slave laborers provided the SS with the financial resources to create its vast economic empire. > see also: **Konzentrationslager System; Schutzstaffel.**

2. German Corporations Using Slave Labor[1]

Deutsche Gesellschaft für Schädlingsbekämpfung (DEGESCH), "German Vermin-Combatting Corporation," developer of Zyklon B, a highly concentrated prussic acid, specifically formulated for use in pest control. Absorbed by I.G. Farben in 1941, DEGESCH also was involved in other chemicals related work using slave laborers in the Auschwitz IV-Buna camp.

Hugo Schneider Aktiengesellschaft (HASAG), "Hugo Schneider Corporation," major armaments manufacturer for the German military, using slave labor in numerous locations throughout Germany and occupied Poland.

I.A. Topf und Söhne, Erfrut, "I. A. Topf and Sons, Erfrut," construction company that used slave labor to construct the gas chambers and crematoria in the major extermination camps.

Ostdeutsche Bau-Gesellschaft, "East German Building Company," construction company that used slave labor in the construction of concentration camps in Germany and occupied Poland.

Ostdeutsche Bautischlerei-Werkstätte (OBW), "East German Workshops for Carpentry

---

[1] This is a selected list of a few from the hundreds of German and Volksdeutsche firms that used slave laborers during World War II.

Construction," factory founded in the Warsaw ghetto and employing hundreds of workers. The OBW workshop was the first headquarters for the ŻOB.

Rheinmetall, Düsseldorf, munitions manufacturer using between 250 and 600 slave laborers in the Buchenwald KL.

Schmitz Werke, "Schmitz Works," munitions contractors for the Wehrmacht, especially active in the Skarzysko-Kamienna (Poland) Zwangsarbeitslager, employing large numbers of slave laborers.

Sluzba Porzodkowa [P] "Order service": Polish term for the Jewish Ghetto Police, who, nominally, were under the jurisdiction of the Granatowa Policja. All members were required to wear an identifying white armband stamped Sluzba Porzodkowa. > see also: **Jüdischer Ordnungsdienst**.

Sonderaktion [G] "Special action": Nazi cover term for an Einsatzgruppe or Kommando operation; the term equally applied to a special action against Jews in a certain locality or an action against a segment of the local non-Jewish population.

Sonderausgleichabgabe [G] "Special delivery arrangement": Nazi term for a special tax in addition to the regular tax levied on Polish wage earners. During the early occupation period some Jewish workers receiving wages were also liable to this special tax.

Sonderbehandlung [G] "Special handling": Nazi code term for the extermination of European Jewry. Primarily used in reports regarding the liquidation of Jews from a specific transport at one of the *Vernichtungslager*. The term was also used by Einsatzgruppen commanders in their daily reports to Berlin, that is, that such and such group of Jews in such and such village had been dealt with or *sonderbehandelt*.

Sondergericht [G] "Special court": Special Nazi courts that no Jew had recourse to, but that issued death sentences against Jews in occupied Europe for the slightest infraction

of German law. > see also: **Volksgericht**.

Sonderkommando [G] "Special detachment": A commando of Jewish prisoners in the six extermination camps, selected to work in the gas chambers and crematoria. Their task was to pull out the bodies of gassed Jews, search them for any valuables the victims had been able to conceal before being driven into the gas chamber, tear out any gold fillings, and so on, take them on lorries the the crematoria to be incinerated, or bury them in large pits. Periodically, members of a Sonderkommando underwent a selection and were themselves gassed, being replaced by new victims. > see also: **Konzentrationslager System**.

Sonderzüge [G] "Special trains": RSHA code term for the trains bearing Jews to extermination camps. The Nazi zeal to carry out the Final Solution was such that large numbers of transport trains vitally important to the Wehrmacht's pursuit of war were instead requisitioned and put at the disposal of the *Aussiedlungskommandos* (under the overall supervision of Adolf Eichmann) to enable them to continue their tasks.

Sotsialni opasni element [R] "Dangerous social element": Soviet term for certain Jews that Stalin ordered deported to Siberia from Estonia, Latvia, and Lithuania just prior the Nazi attack on Russia. Ironically, most of those Jews deported to Siberia were saved from the Nazi slaughter.

Sperrgebiet [G] "Prohibited area": Nazi term for an area within a given town designated as Jewish. In the larger localities this usually meant a temporary ghetto — a way station on the road to extermination. In most cases no Jew could leave or enter a *sperrgebiet* without special permission. As a rule, the civilian non-Jewish population (including Germans) were also forbidden to enter the area.

Sperrlisten [G] "Blocked lists": Certain privileged Jews who for one reason or another were held in special camps or stations instead of being sent with the transports. Some of the names on the "lists" were temporary, others permanent. Usually the categories of qualification were: spouses of Aryans, *Mischlinge* (half-Jews), converted Jews, important industrialists, Jews of neutral countries, economically useful Jews (diamond cutters and fur workers), disputed cases, Georgian (USSR) Jews, Sephardic Jews, and Karaites. Overall, a large number of Jews on the *Sperrlisten* were, in the end, murdered, as was the case of the Jews held in the Vittel camp. > see also: **Hotel Polski.**

Sperrstempel [G] "Exemption stamps": The Nazi-instituted system by which certain categories of Dutch Jews, those possessing the exemption stamp on their identity cards, were exempted from deportation, at least temporarily. Persons having this stamp — considered a prize by the Dutch Jews — were exempted from deportation because of special considerations such as economic utility. > see also: **Schutzschein.**

Sprachregelung [G] "Language regulation": Nazi term for the agreed cover-up terminology with all their criminal partners in regard to the Final Solution. > see also: **Endlösung.**

Staatsangehörigen [G] "Subjects of the state": Term for those possessing the second-class citizenship status to which German Jewry was reduced by the terms of the Nuremberg Laws. > see also: **Legislation, Anti-Jewish, National Socialist Legislation (Third Reich).**

Stadthauptmann [G] "City Chief Official": German civilian authority in Nazi-occupied Europe. Many of the Stadtshauptmänner were in charge, together with the Gestapo and other Nazi agencies, of the ghettos and some of the camps within their precincts. The German city chief officials were also in charge of the local native mayors and city officials.

Städtische Werkstätten [G] "Municipal workshops": The factories that proliferated all over occupied Poland. Most of the workshops were established by ethnic Germans with an eye for cheap Jewish labor. Not surprisingly, the workshops had considerable support from the Jewish leadership. Most of the reasoning behind their support derived from the concept that employing as large as possible a segment of Jews would save their lives and perhaps those of their families. Of course, as it soon became clear — this was a futile assumption. > see also: **Slave Labor.**

Stahlpakt [G] "Pact of Steel": > see also: **Achse.**

Steckbrief [G] "Warrant": Dispatch issued September 21, 1939, by Reinhard Heydrich, chief of the RSHA, to the Einsatzgruppen operating in occupied Poland. The *Steckbrief* dealt with instructions for setting up the apparatus for the first phase of the Final Solution.

Sterbeurkunde(n) [G] "Death certificate(s)": Forms issued by some concentration camps notifying next of kin that inmates had died during their incarceration. > see also: **Todesfallsaufnahme(n).**

Sternträger [G] "Star carrier": Nazi derogatory term for all Jews under their jurisdiction. Another, similar, term was *Sternjude* (Star Jew); any Jew caught in the street without the prescribed identification was liable to severe punishment, even death.

Stiftung [G] "Foundation": Cover term for the establishments that claimed to be scientific or research agencies but in reality were murder organizations, responsible for the extermination of millions of victims. > see also: **Euthanasie; Konzentrationslager System.**

Strengstens bestraft [G] "Severely punished": Nazi cover term for the murder of undesirables, including partisans, political prisoners, and lawbreakers. Papers stamped with SB were sent along with the prisoner to the concentration camp Gestapo office, specifying that the incarcerated fell within this category. In unusual circumstances, a Jew's papers might also be stamped SB, although this was usually limited to Jewish inmates incarcerated for reasons other than their Jewishness (e.g., professional criminals). > see also: **Rückkehr Unerwünscht.**

Sturmabteilungen (SA) "Stormtroopers": Nazi term for the "Brownshirts," the rabble-rousing shock formations of the NSDAP, founded in 1921. An early SA elite unit was the Stabswache (Guard staff), created in 1923 to act as bodyguards for high NSDAP officials. In 1933 the Stabswache was transferred to the SS and became the nucleus of the Leibstandarte-SS Adolf Hitler. With Himmler's successful plot to undercut and dismantle the SA, followed by the murder of SA chief Ernst Röhm (Night of the Long Knives), the power of the SA was broken, with the organization becoming totally dependent on the SS.

Stürmerkästen [G] "*Stürmer* boxes": Public bulletin boards used by Julius Streicher to publicize the anti-Jewish campaign and to blackmail those Germans who still did business with Jews.

Symphonia Diabolica [Latin] "Devil's Symphony": Concentration camp term for the SS-ordered camp orchestras (e.g. in Mauthausen). The musicians had to play mornings and evenings — when the work details marched out from camp and upon return to camp — during certain *Aktionen*, on certain special occasions , or just for the amusement of the SS.

Szafa gra [P] "The box is playing": Polish term for an official who was ready to take a bribe. Many of these officials were doubly corrupted; not only did they collaborate with the Nazis, but they also worked both sides — bleeding the victims dry — after which they handed them over to the Gestapo or SD.

Szmalcowniki [P] "Blackmailers": Underground term for Poles who collaborated with the Gestapo. Often posing as rescuers, these Poles betrayed the Jews in their charge to the Gestapo as soon as the Jews' money to pay them ran out.

T

Talmud Hundertschaft [G] "The Talmud Hundred Group": A research project into Jewish history and Talmud organized in the Terezin ghetto on Eichmann's orders. This study group of Jewish scholars was charged with the translation of the Talmud into the German vernacular, but they did not succeed; only a short time into the project, most of the assembled scholars were shipped to Auschwitz to be exterminated in the gas chambers.

Tango fun toyt (טאנגא פון טויט, Y) "Tango of death": Yiddish term for a special tune dubbed *tango fun toyt*, composed by Jewish musicians on orders of SS-Untersturmführer Wilhelm Rokita and the SS leadership of the Janowska concentration camp. The tune was played by the camp orchestra early in the mornings when the work details left and when they returned in the evening. The orchestra was also required to play for the sheer amusement of the SS and during special *Aktionen* when victims were driven to Piaski for execution. > see also: **Symphonia Diabloica; Tol fun toyt.**

Tati [R] "Mountain Jews": A Jewish religious group living in the Caucasus. Although religiously Jewish, this group was initially not considered racially Jewish, and thus none of its members suffered from the German occupation. However, after the German defeat at Stalingrad, Nazi policy changed and the Tati were virtually wiped out. > see also: **Krimchaki; Karaites.**

Tätigkeitsberichte [G] "Action reports": Euphemism for the daily reports in bulletin form issued by the four Einsatzgruppen, giving detailed accounts of *Aktionen* undertaken against the "enemy," with exact-total figures of "enemies" eliminated or pacified, with a view toward reaching the goal in the process of the Final Solution. > see also: **Endlösung.**

Tausendjährige Reich [G] "The Thousand-Year Reich": Nazi term for the period they hoped to rule Germany. The Third Reich, unlike the First and Second Reichs, was supposed to last for a millennium. > see also: **Das Dritte Reich.**

Tekifn/Tekifim [תקיפים, Y/H] "Influential ones": Derogatory slang term for those Jews who attained influence in the ghettos, often using their new-found power to persecute other Jews. > see also: **Ehrengericht.**

Tiyul [טיול, H] "Trip": Coded term for the small-scale but systematic escape of Polish and Slovakian Jews to Hungary between 1940 and 1942. In 1944 the Va'ad ha-Ezra veha-Hatzala in Budapest organized the "re-Tiyul" program whereby Jews from Hungary were smuggled into Slovakia and Romania.

Todesfallsaufnahme(n) [G] "Death certificate(s)": Forms issued by some concentration camps during the 1930s and into the middle of 1940, notifying next of kin that inmates had died during their incarceration. The death certificate almost always read "died of heart failure or similar natural causes." From late 1940 to the end of the war, such certificates were a rarity. > see also: **Sterbeurkunde(n)**.

Todeskisten [G] "Death caskets": Nazi term for the Polish ghettos based on Joseph Goebbels's way of characterizing them. This Nazi term, indeed, was not an empty propaganda ploy but mirrored the exact dimensions of life in the ghetto.

Todesmärsche [G] "Death marches":

1. Scope and Definition

The forced marching of heavily guarded prisoners. Marched from one locality to another, often with no rhyme or reason, over long distances and under inhumane conditions, the prisoners were brutally mistreated and in many cases were killed by their guards. Most death marches took place during 1944 and 1945 when the Nazis sought to evacuate concentration camps in order to prevent the prisoners' liberation. In this case, moving the inmates served two purposes: to delay discovery of war crimes and to ensure a continuing supply of slave laborers. Death marches continued until last days of the Reich, and it is estimated that 250,000 victims died during the marches. > see also: **Fussmarsch**.

Table T.1: Major Death Marches

Date	From	Destination[1]	Number
07/28/44	Gesia St. Camp	Kutno	4,400
11/08/44	Budapest	Austria	76,000
12/29/44	Budapest	Austria	thousands
01/01/45	Upper Silesia	Mauthausen	thousands
01/17/45	Auschwitz	Germany	66,000
01/19/45	Althammer	Germany	400
01/21/45	Blechhammer	Gross-Rosen	4,000
01/21/45	Stutthof	Baltic Sea	7,000
01/25/45	Stutthof	Germany	50,000
01/26/45	Neu-Salz	Flossenburg	1,000
02/02/45	Gross-Rosen	Austria	thousands
02/05/45	Gross-Rosen	Bergen-Belsen	40,000
04/01/45	Dora-Mittelbau	Bergen-Belsen	thousands
04/03/45	Nordhausen	Flintsbach	thousands
04/03/45	Buchenwald		30,000
04/04/45	Ohrdruf		thousands
04/06/45	Bergen-Belsen		2,400
04/06/45	Buchenwald		3,100
04/07/45	Buchenwald		40,000
04/11/45	Mauthausen	Ebensee	hundreds
04/13/45	Dachau	Gardelegen	3,000
04/13/45	Rehmsdorf		4,300
04/15/45	Sachsenhausen ⌉		60,000
04/15/45	Ravensbrück ⌋		

---

[1] Destination is given when known; in many cases, death marches took no particular direction and those inmates that survived ended up where they began.

04/25/45	Stutthof	4,000
04/26/45	Dachau	7,000
04/27/45	Buchenwald	1,000

Source: Edelheit & Edelheit *A World in Turmoil*, Wesport, CT: Greenwood Press, 1991.

Todesraum [G] "Death space": Nazi term for the remaining territory in Eastern Europe that would be granted to inferior races once Germany had won the war. For Jews, the term implied the space sufficient for mass burial. > see also: **Lebensraum**.

Jüdische Rundschau's banner headline of April 1, 1933:
"Wear It with Pride, the Yellow Badge"
Courtesy of the New York Public Library, Jewish Division

Tol fun toyt [טאל פון טויט, Y] "Valley of death": Yiddish term for the stretch of land known as Piaski — the valley of death — a valley northwest of Lvov, located near the Janowska camp and in the vicinity of the Jewish and Catholic cemeteries. No exact figures are available as to the number of victims, but it is reliably estimated that they numbered in the tens of thousands.

Toytshtekn (טויטשטעקן, Y) "Death rod": Yiddish term for the throttle used to open the vent into which a German orderly placed Zyklon B, beginning the process of gassing of Jewish victims in the extermination camps.

Tragt ihn mit Stolz, den Gelben Fleck! [G] "Wear It with Pride, the Yellow Badge": Title of an article by Robert Weltsch in the German Zionist newspaper *Jüdische Rundschau* on April 4, 1933. Weltsch called on German Jews not to surrender but to bear the upcoming dark days with pride and dignity.

Transportenblock [G] "Transportation area": KL term for a barrack or two (depending on circumstances) set aside to hold *muselmänner* and other undesirables earmarked for transfer to a death factory or execution site within the camp precinct.

Transportunfähig [G] "Not fit for transportation": Nazi term for the incapacitated elderly, the very young, the feeble, the chronically ill, and the bedridden, whose transportation to extermination sites by routine methods would have proved too bothersome to the Umsiedlungskommandos. Those thus designated were, generally, forced onto trucks, driven to a nearby cemetery, and were then murdered.

Trzynastka [P] "The Thirteen": Polish term for a special Jewish economic unit directly under the authority of the Warsaw gestapo, located at Ulica Leszno 13 within the Warsaw ghetto. The collaborationist Trzynastka was accountable neither to the Judenrat nor to the Jüdischer Ordnungsdienst. Considered the lowest of the low, the group's main function was to spy on fellow Jews, to confiscate vitally needed smuggled goods, and to seek out Jews with counterfeit Aryan papers. This group of thieves and partners to the gestapo crimes was headed by Abraham Ganzweich.

Tshokes (טשאָקעס, Y) "Old bedclothes": Yiddish ghetto term for items sold to Poles outside the ghettos in order to have cash with which to buy food or badly needed medicines.

U

Überfallskommando [G] "Search unit": A special unit of the Jewish ghetto police of Lodz that was organized similarly to the Sonderabteilung.

Übergangslösung [G] "Interim solution": Nazi term for those steps necessary to lead to the *Endziel* of eliminating the Jews. During the 1940s the term took on a more sinister meaning and usually represented an intermediate deportation (e.g., to Terezin) before transport to an extermination center.

Übergangsmassnahme [G] "Transition measure": Term used to explain the purpose of ghettoizing the Jews in a 1940 report by Friedrich Ubelhor. Ghettoization was seen, therefore, as only one stage in the long-term solution of the *Judenfrage*.

Übermensch [G] "Superman": Nazi racial concept depicting themselves as above all and everything. Derived from Friedrich W. Nietzsche's treatise of the same title, the term was given racial and apocalyptic overtones by the Nazis.

Übersiedlung [G] "Resettlement": Nazi cover term for the liquidation of the Jewish population of a given town in occupied Europe. The end result of an *Übersiedlung* was the removal of the Jewish community to a death camp or extermination site. > see also: **Aktion(en)**.

Ud muzal meha-esh [עוד מוצל מהאש, H] "A brand saved from the fire": Often shortened to just *ud* [עוד], this biblical term is from Zechariah 3:2. Used by survivors — especially those who survived in death camps — and reflecting the tragic fortune of those who survived. Occasionally, the term also referred to holy books saved from destruction. In post-Holocaust Israel many survivors named their first son Udi, a derivation of the term *ud*, to reflect the survival of a remnant of the people of Israel.

Umgelegt [G] "Liquidated": One of the many Nazi bureaucratic code terms used by the murderers in their official reports regarding the massacre of Jews and others. In no case were Nazis supposed to use plain terms — although they occasionally did — because the *Endlösung* was supposed to be the great unwritten chapter of German history. As a result a variety of euphemistic terms were used to describe the permanent removal of Jews. > see also: **Einsatzgruppen**.

Umschlagplatz [G] "Transfer place": Term applying to a place or square (in the larger ghettos usually the point near a railway spur), where Jews were ordered to assemble prior to deportation. At the *Umschlagplatz*, the Jewish victims were loaded into the cattle cars that brought them to extermination sites. In smaller or open ghettos, the *Umschlagplatz*, usually the town square, also served as a place for selections conducted by the *Umsiedlungs-kommandos* to determine who would remain behind for the time being; who would be shot on the spot or taken to the Jewish cemetery, or a sometimes-waiting pit outside of town to be killed; and finally, who would be marched off to the nearest rail spur to be loaded in closed boxcars heavily lined with lime — without air, sanitary conditions, food, or water — to suffocate on the long, slow trip to be gassed or machine-gunned on arrival. > see also: **Aktion(en)**.

Umsiedlerzüge [G] "Resettlement trains": Nazi cover term for the numerous trains that left the Grossreich and Nazi-occupied Europe everyday, at all hours, during the *Judenreingungsaktionen* of 1942 and 1943. The trains' destination invariably was one of the six extermination factories. > see also: **Judenzug**.

Umsiedlungskommando [G] "Resettlement detail": The official Nazi "deportation board" composed of members from the RSHA (the Gestapo and SD). These fast-moving squads brought doom to the Jewish inhabitants of Eastern Europe. Each township and place it visited became instantly *judenrein*. > see also: **Aktion(en)**.

Umsiedlungsstab [G] "Resettlement staff": The deportation board officers, in whose hands lay the fate of the Jewish communities. Within the span of a single day an *Umsiedlungsstab* was responsible for the uprooting of as many as two or more Jewish communities. > see also: **Umsiedlungs-kommando**.

Umvolkung [G] "Change of national allegiance": > see also: **Eindeutschung**.

Üntermensch [G] "Inferior man": Nazi racial concept of a non-Aryan. Within this term Jews, Gypsies, and certain categories of Slavs were considered, according to Nazi dogma, as something less than human.

Unternehmung [G] "Undertaking": SS term for an extraordinary operation or, more frequently, for the planning stage of such an operation. > see also: **Aktion(en)**.

Upgefroirene epalech (אפגעפרורענע עפאלעך, Y) "Frozen apples": Phrase popular among Jewish partisans for German soldiers retreating, nearly frozen and frostbitten, from the Eastern Front.

Uprisings, Jewish > see: **Resistance**.

Ur Kasdim [אור כשדים, H] "Ur of the Chaldees": Biblical geographic name (see Genesis 11:28) associated with Abraham. During the Holocaust, the phrase was used to denote a crematorium, an analogy derived from a Jewish legend that had Abraham placed into a fiery chamber (= a crematorium) as punishment for his monotheism.

Usu shoimer (אתא שומר, Y/H) "Enters the watchman": Part of a Hebrew chant often utilized as a term by Orthodox Jews in the labor camps and on outside work details. A transposition of Isaiah 21:12, "The watchman says, the morning enters," the term was used to warn persons of the approach of a guard or Kapo.

V

V: Universal resistance term for the eventual Allied victory over Nazi Germany. Copying Prime Minister Churchill's two-fingered V-for-victory sign, the resisters repeatedly daubed a V (usually in red paint) over German notices.

Verfügungstruppen [G] "Standby troops": Militarized formations of the SS, founded September 24, 1934. Recruited from all elements of the SS, Verfügungstruppen served as conventional troops under Wehrmacht command during the Polish campaign. In addition, Verfügungstruppen were used as guards in the rapidly expanding concentration camp system. > see also: **Schutzstaffel, Subsidiary Agencies (Waffen-SS).**

Vergangenheitsbewältigung [G] "Struggling with the past": Postwar German term for the process by which writers, philosophers, and artists came to grips with the implications of the Third Reich. Whereas the term was used with positive connotations during the 1950s, in recent years it has taken on a negative sense and has come to represent the failure to fully live up to the past.

Vergeltungswaffen [G] "Retaliatory weapons": Nazi term for the V-1 and V-2 rockets produced by slave labor in Peenemunde and in the Dora-Mittelbau concentration camp.

Vernichtungslager [G] "Extermination camp": Technical term for the six murder camps established in the context of the Final Solution. > see also: **Konzentrationslager System; Endlösung.**

Vernichtungsstelle [G] "Extermination place": Blunt Nazi term, used in internal discussions only, pertaining to the six extermination camps. When used as a proper noun the term refers specifically to Auschwitz-Birkenau. > see also: **Vernichtungslager.**

Vernichtungsstelle # 2 [G] "Extermination place # 2": Nazi term for the Ninth Fort, a murder site near Kovno, Lithuania. A number of other abandoned forts in the same area were also utilized by the Nazis as extermination sites, although, in comparison to the Ninth Fort, on a much smaller scale.

Versailler Diktat [G] "Versailles Dictate": Derogatory German term for the Versailles Treaty, which was viewed as grossly unfair for Germany. Hitler used this terminology repeatedly, linking his condemnation of the unfair treaty to a call for revenge against the internal enemies (Jews, Communists, and Socialists) who forced the treaty upon Germany. > see also: **Dolchstosslegende.**

Vertrauensmann [G] "Confidant": An undercover agent; colloquial term for a collaborationist Dutch police agent working for the Sicherheitsdienst (SD) or Gestapo. > see also: **Collaboration.**

Vertrauliche Information der Parteikanzlei
[G] "Confidential information from the party chancellery": The secret circulars distributed to top Nazi echelons. These *Führer* decrees were of such importance that they could not be entrusted to normal applications, such as their publication in the *Reichsgesetzblatt* or other official government journals. It has long been assumed by historians that the order regarding the Final Solution was distributed in this manner, although no extant copies of a written command has ever come to light.

Vertrouwensmannen der Regiring [Du] "Representatives of the government": Individuals designated by the Dutch government in exile as representing the interests of the government in its absence. These individuals also formed the transitional governing bodies during the Allied liberation of Holland. > see also: **Governments in Exile**.

Volk [G] "People": German ideological term referring to the members of the nation, used since the nineteenth century. The term was much modified by the Nazis, who used it primarily in the sense of a community of blood. The Nazis also used *Volk* to represent the basic element of social and intellectual structure (e.g., *Völkish Kultur*). Finally, many Nazis — Hitler especially — used the term in a cosmic sense, ascribing great importance to the *volk*'s health and its racial purity. Derived from the romantic notion that a nation is an organic entity, this usage of the term *Volk* was a primary justification for both the Euthansia Program and the Final Solution.

Volksdeutsche [G] "Ethnic Germans": Individuals of German ethnic origin living outside of Germany. Although they were not German citizens, the Nazi party used the Volksdeutsche as both a fifth column and a propaganda weapon in their goal for *Lebensraum*. Even prior to the *Machtergreifung*, the NSDAP placed considerable stress on Volksdeutsch affairs, for example through the Auslandsorganisation der NSDAP. Many

Volksdeutsche were intimately involved in the persecution of European Jewry during World War II, especially in Eastern Europe. > see also: **Nationalsozialistiche Deutsche Arbeiter Partei, Nazi Organizations (Volksdeutsche Mittelstelle)**.

Volksgericht [G] "People's court": Nazified court system for alleged crimes against the German *volk*, established in April 1934. The courts had two primary provinces of authority: the trial and punishment of persons accused of *Rassenschande* and the trial and punishment of "traitors." A special *Volksgericht* was convened in August 1944 to try the army officers and political figures involved in the July 20, 1944, bomb plot against Hitler.

Volkstod [G] "Racial death": Nazi term for the planned fate of those they considered ideologically inferior. This, in turn, led to the sterilization laws of such categories as the mentally handicapped, manic depressives, schizophrenics, epileptics, and those with other hereditary diseases that the Nazis considered offensive. > see also: **Euthanasie**.

Vornahmen, Jüdische [G] "Forenames, Jewish":

1. Scope and Definition

On August 18, 1938 the Reich Ministry of the Interior published a list in the *Reichsgestzblatt* of first names that Jewish parents were permitted to use for their male or female offspring. This document was considered to be legally binding throughout the Grossreich. The Nazis further legislated the addition of Abraham and Sarah to the names of all adult Jews (male and female respectively) in the Reich.

2. Nazi-Allowed First Names, Males

Abel, Abieser, Abimelech, Abner, Absalom, Ahab, Ahsja, Ahasver, Akiba, Amon, Anschel, Aron, Asahe, Asaria, Ascher, Asriel, Assur, Athalja, Avigdor, Avrum; Bachja, Barak, Baruch, Benaja, Berek, Berl, Boas, Bud; Chaggai, Chai, Chajin, Chamor, Chananja, Chanoch, Chaskel, Chiel; Dan, Denny; Efim, Efraim, Ehud, Eisig, Eli, Elias, Elihu, Eliser,

Eljekim, Elkan, Enoch, Esau, Esra, Ezechiel; Faleg, Feibisch, Feirel, Feitel, Feivel, Feleg; Gad, Gadaleo, Gedalja, Gerson, Gideon; Habakuk, Hagai, Hemor, Henoch, Herodes, Hesekiel, Hillel, Hiob, Hosea; Isaac, Isai, Isachar, Isbeseth, Isidor, Ismael, Israel, Itzig; Jechiel, Jaffe, Jakar, Jakusiel, Jecheskel, Jehu, Jehuda, Jehusiel, Jeremia, Jeroboam, Jesaja, Jethro, Jiftach, Jizchak, Joab, Jochanan, Joel, Jomtob, Jona, Jonathan, Josia, Juda; Kainan, Kaiphas, Kaleb, Korach; Laban, Lazarus, Leev, Leiser, Levi, Levek, Lot, Lupu; Machol, Maim, Malchisua, Maleachi, Manasse, Mordochai, Mechel, Menachem, Moab, Mochain, Mosche, Moses; Nachschon, Nachum, Naftali, Nathan, Naum, Nazary, Nehab, Nehemia, Niesim, Noa, Nochem; Obadja, Orev, Oscher, Osias; Peisach, Pinchas, Pinkus; Rachmiel, Ruben; Sabbatai, Sacher, Sallum, Sally, Salo, Salomon, Salusch, Samaja, Sami, Samuel, Sandel, Sandik, Saul, Schalom, Schaul, Schinul, Schmul, Schneur, Scholem, Sebulon, Semi, Sered, Sichem, Simson; Teit, Tevele; Uri, Uria, Uriel; Zadek, Zedekia, Zephanja, Zeruja, Zevi.

3. Nazi-Allowed First Names, Females

Abigail; Bascheva, Baile, Bela, Bescha, Bihri, Bilha, Breine, Brieve, Brocha; Chana, Cava, Cheiche, Cheile, Chinke; Deiche, Devaara, Driesel; Egele; Faugel, Feigle, Feile, Fradchen, Fradel, Frommet; Geilchen, Gelea, Ginendel, Gittel, Gole; Hadassa, Hale, Hannacha, Hitzel; Jachet, Jachevad, Jedidja, Jente, Jezabel, Judis, Jyske, Jyttel; Keile, Kreindel; Lana, Leie, Libsche, Libe, Livie; Machle, Mathel, Milkele, Mindel; Nacha, Nachme; Peirche, Pesschen, Pesse, Pessel, Pirle; Rachel, Rause, Rebekka, Rechel, Reha, Reichel, Reisel, Reitzge, Reitsche, Rivi; Sara, Scharne, Scheindel, Scheine, Scheva, Schlaemche, Semche, Simche, Slove, Sprinze; Tana, Telze, Tirze, Treibel; Zerel, Zilla, Zimle, Zine, Zipora, Zirel, Zorthel.

Vorzugslager [G] "Preferential camp": One of many alternate Nazi names for the Terezin ghetto/camp. This name, implying that inmates received beneficial treatment, was used for propaganda purposes in neutral countries to hide from organizations such as the International Red Cross Terezin's actual role as an ante-chamber for Auschwitz.

W

Wagon Juden [G] "Wagon Jews": Nazi term for those Jews whose job it was to collect the corpses off the streets in the larger ghettos, i.e., Warsaw, Lodz, Krakow, for burial in a common grave.

Waldgänger [G] "Forest travelers": Nazi term for partisans who fought in the woods of Eastern Europe. > see also: **Bandenkampfverbände**.

Wannsee-konferenz [G] "Wannsee Conference":

1. Scope and Definition

Nazi conference of January 20, 1942, at which plans for the *Endlösung der Judenfrage* were finalized. The meeting was a follow-up to the systematic anti-Jewish operations of the Einsatzgruppen in the Soviet Union and eastern Poland. Only a few substantive decisions were taken at the conference, however, since the plans had been worked out in advance by RSHA Chief Reinhard Heydrich and his staff. The real purpose of the conference was actually to gain the support of all elements of the German bureaucracy for SS domination of the murder process. The only issue that turned out to be controversial was that of the fate of *Mischlinge*, and no complete policy on their fate was worked out during the conference, which lasted merely eighty-five minutes. Only one substantive decision was made: to begin the extermination with Polish Jewry and move

westward from there. In the end, members of the German bureaucracy proved more interested in their own administrative control than in the moral question of consigning some 11 million human beings to death. > see also: **Endlösung**.

2. List of Participants

Josef Bühler, state secretary, Generalgouvernement.

Adolf Eichmann, SS-Obersturmbannführer, head of Amt IVB4 (the Jewish department) of the Gestapo, also known as Dienststelle Eichmann.

Roland Freisler, president of the Volksgerichtshof (People's Court).

Reinhard Heydrich, SS-Obergruppenführer und General der Polizei, head of the RSHA and *Reichsprotektor* Böhmen-Maehren.

Otto Hofmann, SS-Obergruppenführer, Rasse-und Siedlungshauptamt.

Wilhelm Kritzinger, *Staatssekretär* Reichskanzlei (Secretary to the Reich Chancellery).

Herbert Lange, SS-Sturmbannführer, commandant Sonderkommando Lange at the Chelmno extermination camp; commander SD Latvia.

Georg Leibbrandt, director of the Political Department of the Rosenberg Ministry.

Martin Luther, director of the Foreign Office Department Deutschland.

Alfred Meyer, Gauleiter, Secretary of state in the Ministry for Occupied Eastern Territory and deputy to Alfred Rosenberg.

Heinrich Müller, SS-Gruppenführer, head of Amt IV RHSA (Gestapo).

Erich Neumann, Staatssekretär (Reich secretary), responsible for the Four-Year Plan.

Karl Schongarth, SS-Oberführer, *Befehls-* *haber der Sicherheitspolizei und des Sicherheits- dienstes*, head of the SD and Gestapo in the Generalgouvernement.

Franz Stuckart, Secretary of state in Ministry of Interior. Drafted the Nuremberg Laws and their subsequent amendments.

TABLE W.1: Jews to Be Liquidated as per the Wannsee Protocol

A. Germany and Occupied Areas[1]

Altreich (pre-1933 Germany)	131,800
Ostmark (Austria)	43,700
Ostgebiete (Eastern Territories)	420,000
Generalgouvernement (Poland)	2,284,000
Bialystok (Poland)	400,000
Protektorat Bohmen und Mähren (Bohemia and Moravia)	74,200
Estland (Estonia)	Judenfrei
Lettland (Latvia)	3,500
Litauen (Lithuania)	34,000
Belgien (Belgium)	43,000
Danemark (Denmark)	5,600
Frankreich, Besetztes Gebiet (France, Occupied)	165,000
Frankreich, Unbesetzes Gebiet (France, Vichy)	700,000
Griechenland (Greece)	69,600
Niederlande (Holland)	160,800
Norwegen (Norway)	1,300
Subtotal	4,536,500

B. Axis and Other European Areas

Bulgarien (Bulgaria)	48,000
England	330,000
Finnland	2,300
Irland (Ireland)	4,000
Italien, Einschl. Sardinien (Italy & Sardinia)	58,000
Italien/Albanien (Italian-occupied Albania)	200
Kroatien (Croatia)	40,000
Portugal	3,000
Rumanien, Einschl. Besarabien (Romania/Bessarabia)	342,000
Schweden (Sweden)	8,000
Schweiz (Switzerland)	18,000
Slowakei (Slovakia)	88,000
Spanien (Spain)	6,000
Turkei, europaischer Teil (Turkey, European)	55,500
Ungarn (Hungary)	742,800

---

[1] Jews exterminated before January 1, 1942, the last date that statistical evidence had been compiled before the conference, are not included.

UdSSR (Soviet Union)	5,000,000
Ukraine	2,994,684
Weisrusland, Ausschl. Bialystock (Belorussia)	446,484
Subtotal	10,186,968
Totals (A and B)	14,723,468

Source: *Trial of the War Criminals before the Nuremberg Military Tribunals*, vol. 13, Washington, D.C.: USGPO, 1952.

War Crimes Trials

1. Scope and Definition

Under international law, nationals of a belligerent nation could be held responsible for criminal acts committed during the course of military operations. At the end of World War II this principle was applied to those German leaders accused of war crimes, crimes against peace, and crimes against humanity. The initial process of bringing war criminals to justice was undertaken during the three phases of the Nuremberg trials. At the International Military Tribunal, the four powers — the United States, Britain, France, and the Soviet Union — tried a group of 22 "major" German and Austrian war criminals.

Subsequently, "minor" trials were held in each of the occupation zones of Germany. Between 1945 and 1949 trials in the U.S., British, and French zones resulted in the conviction and punishment of an additional 5,025 Germans. Other trials were held, simultaneously or in the next decades, throughout Eastern and Central Europe and particularly in the Federal Republic of Germany. Two major trials have also been held in Israel: that of Adolf Eichmann and that of John (Ivan) Demjanjuk.

2. Major War Crimes Trials[1]

Auschwitz Trial, held in Kraków in November and December 1947. Forty members of the camp administration were tried: twenty-three were sentenced to death; sixteen were sentenced to prison; one verdict is unknown.

Auschwitz (Frankfurt) Trial, three separate trials held in Frankfurt between 1963 and 1966. Twenty-two members of the camp administration were tried: all were sentenced to prison terms.

Barbie Trial, held in Lyons, during summer 1987. Barbie was head of the SD and SS in France. Found guilty he was sentenced to life in prison (he has since died in prison).

Belsen Trial, held in Lüneburg September 17 to November 17, 1945. Forty-eight members of the Bergen-Belsen camp administration were tried: Eleven were sentenced to death (all were executed); twenty-three were sentenced to prison terms; and fourteen were acquitted.

Dachau Trial, held in Dachau November 15 to December 14, 1945. Forty members of the camp administration were tried: Thirty-seven were sentenced to death, although many were sentenced in absentia.

Demjanjuk Trial, held in Jerusalem February 16, 1987, to April 18, 1988. Demjanjuk was accused of being the infamous "Ivan the Terrible," who operated the gas chamber at Treblinka. Found guilty, Demjanjuk was released by the Israeli Supreme Court in late 1993, after new evidence raised some doubts about his identification.

Doctors' Trial, held in Nuremberg October 25, 1946, to August 20, 1947. Twenty-three Nazi doctors tried: Seven were sentenced to death; five were sentenced to life imprisonment; two,

---

[1] Not all the listed sentences were carried out; in most cases sentences were greatly reduced at the discretion of clemency boards.

to twenty years; one, to fifteen years; and one, to ten years; seven were acquitted.

Eichmann Trial, held in Jerusalem April 11 to December 11, 1961. Eichmann, head of the Gestapo's Jewish Affairs section, was tried: Found guilty, he was sentenced to death and was executed.

Einsatzgruppen Trial, held in Nuremberg July 3, 1947, to April 10, 1948. Twenty-four senior SS and SD officers were tried: Fourteen were sentenced to death (four executed); one committed suicide; one was convicted but not sentenced owing to ill health; and eight were sentenced to prison terms.

Erhard Milch Trial, held in Nuremberg November 13, 1946, to April 17, 1947. Milch was sentenced to life imprisonment.

Friedrich Flick Trial, held in Nuremberg February 8 to December 22, 1947. Six industrialists were tried: Three were sentenced to prison terms and three were acquitted.

Hostage Trial, held in Nuremberg May 10, 1947, to February 19, 1948. Twelve senior Wehrmacht officers were tried: One committed suicide; eight were sentenced to prison terms; one was released owing to ill health; and two were acquitted.

I.G. Farben Trial, held in Nuremberg May 8, 1947, to July 8, 1948. Twenty-four members of the board of directors of the company were tried: Thirteen were sentenced to prison terms and eleven were acquitted.

International Military Tribunal, held in Nuremberg November 20, 1945, to October 1, 1946. Twenty-two major Nazi war criminals were tried: Twelve sentenced to death, including one in absentia, ten of them were hanged, and one committed suicide; three were sentenced to life imprisonment, two to twenty years, one to fifteen years, and one to ten years; three were acquitted.

Jurists' Trial, held in Nuremberg January 4 to December 4, 1947. Fifteen Nazi judges were tried: Four were sentenced to life imprisonment; four, to ten years; one, to seven years; and one, to five years; one of the defendants was released owing to ill health; and four were acquitted.

Krasnodar Trial, July 14 to 17, 1943. Thir-

teen collaborators were tried: eight were found guilty and sentenced to death; three were sentenced to twenty years imprisonment; two were acquitted.

Krupp Trial, held in Nuremberg August 16, 1947, to July 31, 1948. Nineteen senior Krupp corporate figures were tried: Eighteen were sentenced to prison terms and one was acquitted. All the sentences were eventually commuted to time served.

Majdanek Trial, held in Düsseldorf November 26, 1975, to June 30, 1981. Sixteen members of the camp administration were tried: two were unfit to stand trial, and one died during the proceedings; nine were sentenced to prison terms ranging from three years to life imprisonment; four were acquitted.

Ministries Trial, held in Nuremberg November 14, 1947, to April 13, 1949. Twenty-one senior Nazi diplomats and governmental officials were tried: Nineteen were sentenced to prison terms and two were acquitted. All the sentences were eventually commuted to time served.

Natzweiler Trial, held in Rastadt May 29 to June 1, 1946. Ten members of the Natzweiler-Struthof camp administration were tried: One was sentenced to death (and was executed); five were sentenced to prison terms; four were acquitted.

Oberkommando Wehrmacht (OKW) Trial, held in Nuremberg November 28, 1947, to October 28, 1948. Fourteen members of the

Rudolf Höss being led to trial as portrayed in a contemporary Italian postcard

Authors' Collection

Wehrmacht high command were tried: Twelve were sentenced to prison terms and two were acquitted. All the sentences were eventually commuted to time served.

Oswald Pohl Trial, held in Nuremberg January 13 to November 3, 1947. Eighteen members of the Wirtschafts- und Verwaltungs Hauptamt were tried: Four were sentenced to death; eleven were sentenced to prison terms; three were acquitted.

RUSHA Trial, held in Nuremberg July 1, 1947, to March 10, 1948. Fourteen SS leaders tried: Thirteen were sentenced to prison terms and one was acquitted. Richard Hildebrandt, sentenced to a prison term, was later extradited to Poland and was executed after a trial on other indictments.

War Effort, Jewish

1. Scope and Definition

Nazi propaganda sought to portray World War II as a Jewish war; to the extent that all segments of Jewry recognized Germany as the premier enemy to Jewish survival, it was. Unlike World War I, when Jews' loyalties were divided — Jews fought and died for both sides during that war — in World War II Jews were clearly oriented toward the Allies. This reality gave the Jews less political power in relation to the Allied governments and meant that, in contrast to

World War I, when both sides openly courted Jewish support, the Jews could, in effect, be taken for granted.

Nevertheless, whether motivated by altruism, patriotism, or a desire for vengeance against the genocidal foe, Jews obeyed the call to the colors in numbers beyond their percentage in every Allied country: for example, 550,000 American Jews, out of a total 5,500,000 Jews, served, a service rate of 10 percent, even though American Jewry made up less than 3 percent of the total population. Similarly, the figure for Soviet Jewish war service was 500,000 of a total Jewish population estimated at 3,000,000, or 16 percent; Soviet Jewry made up less than 1 percent of the total population. The figures for other countries, although perhaps not as startling, are similar.

Of even greater significance was the participation of nearly 35,000 men and women from the Yishuv who served in the British Royal Armed Forces. Despite the White Paper of 1939 that virtually cut off the possibility of Jews entering Palestine, the Jewish Agency formulated a policy of supporting the Allies unequivocally. "We shall fight Hitler as if there was no White Paper," said David Ben-Gurion, "and we shall fight the White Paper as if there was no Hitler." Of special importance for the Yishuv's war effort was the creation, in September 1944, of the Jewish Brigade group within the Royal Army. The brigade became a focal point for

TABLE W.2: Jews in the Allied Armies

Country	Number	Country	Number
Belgium	7,000	Poland	140,000
Czechoslovakia	8,000	Soviet Union	500,000[1]
France	80,000	United Kingdom	91,000[2]
Greece	13,000	United States	550,000
Holland	7,000	Yishuv	35,000

Source: *Encyclopedia Judaica*. Jerusalem: Keter, 1972, vol. 11, p. 1550

---

[1] Excluding Jews in the Polish and Czech Communist exile armies that were established under Soviet tutelage in 1943.

[2] Includes British Commonwealth nations, but not Palestine.

the postwar rescue of survivors and was one of the cores upon which the Israeli army was based.

In sum, Jews served in every Allied army on virtually every battlefield and every front during the war.

Wehrmacht [G] "Armed Forces":

1. Scope and Definition

The armed forces of the Third Reich. The name was officially adopted when conscription was publicly reintroduced on March 16, 1935. As such, the Wehrmacht replaced the Reichswehr and, especially, the officially nonexistent Schwarze Reichswehr. Initially, these forces were organized into twenty-eight divisions and 13 *Wehrkreise* (military districts). At its height, however, the Wehrmacht totaled 13,555,000 personnel in 275 divisions. Nazi indoctrination of Wehrmacht troops began even before it officially existed; indeed, on August 2, 1934, the entire military high command swore an unprecedented oath of personal allegiance to Hitler rather than to the Reich.

Therefore any disapproval of Nazi atrocities committed in the wake of the Polish campaign was muted and was silenced altogether after the spectacular victories on the Western Front in 1940. Hardly any opposition was voiced to Hitler's orders issued in connection with the upcoming *Weltanschauungskrieg* against the Soviet Union.

Theoretically, the Wehrmacht was controlled by the Oberkommando der Wehrmacht (OKW, Armed Forces High Command), which coordinated the activities of the Oberkommando des Heeres (OKH, Army High Command), Oberkommando der Luftwaffe (OKL, Air Force High Command), and Oberkommando der Kriegsmarine (OKM, Navy High Command). All four of the agencies competed against one another in the prosecution of the war and all of them competed against the Waffen-SS, which was Himmler's private army.

In addition to its role as passive witness to the mass murders committed by the Einsatzgruppen, Wehrmacht, especially units of the Feldgendarmerie (Military Police), actively supported these actions. Furthermore, many of the most senior Wehrmacht commanders justified the atrocities committed against Jews, Communists, and partisans in their orders to the troops. In this regard, Wehrmacht standing orders — such as the *Kommissarbefehl*, the *Kommandobefehl*, and the *Kugelerlass* — all expose the illusion that the Wehrmacht officer's corps behaved in a "gentlemanly" or "chivalrous" fashion. Postwar claims that the Wehrmacht was ignorant of the *Endlösung* are largely unsupported by the documentary evidence, especially insofar as such claims concern senior members of the OKW and the OKH staffs.

Only a minuscule group of senior Wehrmacht officers opposed Hitler's destructive policies. This group did not, however, offer a serious policy of resistance to the Nazis until 1944, when a small group of plotters attempted to assassinate Hitler. > see also: **Resistance.**

2. Operational Code Names

Achse, "Axis," operation to disarm the Italian army, commencing September 9, 1943.

Adlerangriffe, "Eagle Attack," first day of the aerial attack on Great Britain, August 15, 1940.

Aïda, Deutsche Afrika Korps offensive eastward, mid-August 1940.

Alarich, the operation to occupy Italy in September 1943.

Alpenveilchen, "Alpine violet," the operation to aid the Italians in Albania and Greece in late 1941.

Anton, the operation to occupy Vichy France, commencing November 10, 1942.

Attila, plan to occupy the Vichy zone to begin November 9, 1942. Replaced by Fall Anton.

Aufbau Ost, "Building East," early plan for the invasion of the Soviet Union, August 5, 1940.

Barbarossa, plan for the invasion of the Soviet Union, carried out beginning June 22, 1941.

Danzig, plan to proceed with offensive operations in the West, November 20, 1939. Superseded by Fall Weserübung.

Eiche, "Oak," operation to free Benito Mussolini from imprisonment in Gran Sasso d'Italia, undertaken by SS paratroopers led by Otto Skorzeny, on September 13, 1943.

Felix, plan for the seizure of Gibraltar through Spain, November 20, 1940. Plan vetoed by Franco.

Frühlingserwachen, "Spring Awakening," German counterattack in Hungary, March 5, 1945.

Gelb, "Yellow," plan for the invasion of France and the Low Countries, carried out beginning May 10, 1940.

Grün, "Green," tentative plan for attack on Czechoslovakia, September 1938. Plan cancelled as a result of the Munich Agreement.

Marita, "Marita," planning for the invasion of Greece that began December 13, 1940, with the offensive commencing on April 7, 1941.

Merkur, "Mercury," code name for the invasion of Crete, commencing April 25, 1941.

Rot, "Red," code name for the attack on the French Somme line, June 5, 1940.

Schwarz, "Black," operation to occupy northern Italy, commencing September 9, 1943.

Seelöwe, "Sea Lion," code name for the abortive plan to invade England in 1940.

Walküre, "Valkyrie," plan by senior officers to kill Hitler and take over the German government, carried out unsuccessfully on July 20, 1944.

Weiss, "White," plan for the invasion of Poland, September 1, 1939.

Weserübung, "Exercise Weser," code name for the invasion of Denmark and Norway, carried out beginning April 9, 1940.

Zitadelle, "Citadel," plan for summer operations in the Soviet Union, beginning July 5, 1943.

Wehrmachtsgut [G] "German Army property": Nazi term to camouflage transports with Jews on their way to the extermination camps. As a rule, most of these markings were on train transports departing from French or Dutch internment camps.

Wehrmachtverpflichtete Werkstätten [G] "Army Service Workshops," Aryan-owned civilian firms undertaking contract work for the Wehrmacht. Jews working at such firms, especially in Poland, were at times reprieved

from deportations. > see also: **Lebensscheinen**.

Wer beim Juden kauft ist ein Volksverräter [G] "Whoever buys from Jews is a traitor to his people": Nazi propaganda slogan that was part of their economic boycott of German Jewry.

Werkschutzkommando [G] "Factory guard commando": Nazi term for unarmed Jewish police guards in many of the factories in the Polish ghettos. Usually commanded by *Volksdeutsche* (ethnic Germans), Ukrainians, or Latvians; under whom (but still over the Jews) were certain Russian prisoners of war and some Poles. These commandos were prominently posted at armaments works (e.g., Skarzysko Kamienna).

White Paper of 1939: statement of British policy on Palestine, commonly called the MacDonald White Paper. Issued on May 17, 1939, the White Paper set severe limitations on the growth of the Yishuv and, consequently, limited the possibility of successfully rescuing European Jewry. In particular, the White Paper limited *aliya* to a total of 15,000 individuals per year (including 5,000 refugees) for a period of five years, after which no new Jewish immigration would be permitted without Arab consent. The Yishuv viewed the White Paper as a direct threat to Jewish rights and, with regard to Jewish refugees fleeing Nazi-occupied Europe, to Jewish survival. Therefore, the Jewish Agency turned to an independent policy, as represented by Aliya Bet and the Biltmore Resolution of May 11, 1942. > see also: **Aliya Bet**; **Biltmore Resolution**; **Yishuv**.

Wiedergutmachung [G] "Reparations":

1. Scope and Definition

Payments made to individual Jews and to the State of Israel as collective heir for property of murdered Jews who have no surviving heirs. The first claims for restitution was made by the Jewish Agency for Palestine on September 20, 1945. In 1953, however, when Chancellor Konrad Adenauer sought to legitimize the Federal Republic of Germany's government, Jewish and Israeli claims finally received their due attention. Between 1953 and 1965, a series of negotiations was undertaken that finally resulted in a reparation agreement that paid minimal compensation to victims of Nazi brutality (or to the State of Israel, in cases where no heirs survived). The payment totalled $845,000,000, of which $110,000,000 went to the Conference on Jewish Material Claims Against Germany.

2. Restitution Agencies

Conference on Jewish Material Claims Against Germany (CJMCAG), umbrella agency for Jewish reparations claims, established on October 25, 1954, in New York. The CJMCAG represents all other Jewish agencies that have interest in the fate of heirless Jewish property. It was established as a trustee agency to oversee the fulfillment of the 1952 Luxembourg agreement on German reparations. Monies obtained by the CJMCAG are, in turn, distributed to Jewish communities by the Joint Distribution Committee in order to benefit relief and rehabilitation efforts for Holocaust survivors and/or other Jewish refugees. A portion of the funds from the CJMCAG was used to finance the Yad Vashem-YIVO documentation project, the Wiener Library, and building the memorial to the unknown Jewish victim, erected in Paris in 1956. In 1956 the CJMCAG absorbed the United Restitution Organization (URO) — which became the legal arm of the CJMCAG. Since the 1960s the CJMCAG has also financed the Memorial Foundation for Jewish culture.

Council for the Protection of German Jewish Rights, London-based subsidiary of the Association of Jewish Refugees that was intimately involved in seeking compensation for Jewish victims of the Nazis and demanding a return to the Jewish community of all heirless Jewish property. In July 1948 the council became a founding member of the United Restitution Organization. > see also: **Organizations, Jewish, Free World (United Kingdom, Association of Jewish Refugees)**.

Jewish Restitution Successor Organization (JRSO), agency incorporated in New York in 1947 to seek the return of heirless Jewish property in the American zone of occupation in Germany and in Berlin. The JRSO used all capital thus gained to relieve the plight of Jewish Displaced Persons and refugees throughout Europe and in Palestine. In July 1948 the JRSO merged with other American, English, and European Jewish agencies to form the United Restitution Organization.

United Restitution Organization (URO), reparation organization for Jewish survivors of the Holocaust, created by the merger of English, American, and European advocates of the restoration of Jewish property. Established in July 1948, the URO has headquarters in New York, London, Bonn, and Tel Aviv. Since 1956 the URO has operated as the legal arm of the Conference on Jewish Material Claims Against Germany and deals exclusively with the issue of reparations to individual survivors.

Wienergraben [G] "Viennese quarry": The granite quarry in Mauthausen, famous for the 186 steps that made the removal of cut stones an ordeal, especially in the winter. The Nazis made this ordeal even worse by hosing down the stairs in the winter and demanding that a rapid pace be maintained. Equally well known was the cliff above the quarry, called in Yiddish *Parashutistn Want* (Parachutist wall) by inmates. Hundreds of Jewish inmates were forced to jump from that cliff to their deaths.

Wilddiebe Kommando [G] "Poachers Commando": The Dirlewanger Poachers, a special extermination commando that operated in Poland and Belorussia. Under the command of Dr. Oskar Dirlewanger — an alcoholic, sex pervert, and convicted criminal — the Wilddiebe was made up of hardened criminals, released from German and Austrian penal institutions for the sole purpose of hunting down and killing any and all Jews they could find. At the successful conclusion of the war, they were to be forgiven, their criminal records wiped clean, and they were to be integrated into society. > see also: **Einsatzgruppen, Commanders/Areas of Operation/Subunits (Sonderkommando Dirlewanger)**.

Wilde Einzelaktionen [G] "Wild individual

actions": NSDAP term for the unsystematic attacks on Jews that characterized the SA's approach to the Jewish problem in the days immediately following the *Machtergreifung*. Hitler rejected single actions as too unmethodical and thus unlikely to rid Germany of the Jews in the long term.

Winkel(en) [G] "Triangle(s)": The Nazi identification marks that every inmate in a concentration camp had to wear. The mark, in the shape of a small triangle, was worn on both the front and back of the inmate's uniform and was color-coded to identify prisoners by their "crime."

The colors and their meaning were: *Red*, German political prisoner (generally Communists); *Yellow*, Jew (actually a six-pointed star produced by overlaying two triangles); *Violet*, Jehovah's Witness; *Blue*, Emigrant; *Green*, Common criminal; *Black*, Asocial; *Brown*, Gypsy; *Pink*, Homosexual. Within these categories, a number of special sub-categories also existed, further defining the prisoners. For example, Jewish criminals wore a six-pointed star that was half yellow and half green. The same was true for Jewish political detainees (in this case, yellow and red).

Additional categories also existed and were signified by letters, or combinations of letters, on the triangles. In most instances, the letter abbreviated the inmate's country of origin, but other combinations also existed. The Letter *k*, for example, signified *Kriegsverbrecher*, a war criminal. A black triangle struck with a white letter *A* signified an *Arbeitserziehungshäftling* (labor discipli-

nary prisoner); a black triangle struck with the word *Blöd* signified a mentally retarded inmate; a green triangle struck with a black letter *S* signified an *strafhaft* (penal) prisoner; a green or yellow triangle struck with a black border signified an inmate guilty of *Rassenschande*; a red triangle struck on a red and white target symbol signified an inmate suspected of trying to escape; finally, a triangle marked *Emigrant* signified those who had illegally left Germany and returned upon changing their mind. These people were apprehended by the Gestapo and despatched to a concentration camp.

Wir fahren nach Polen Um Juden zum dreschen! [G] "We are riding to Poland in order to thrash the Jews": Large painted signs on Wehrmacht transport trains going to Poland in September 1939, loudly advertising German army intentions.

Wirtschaftlich Wertvolle [G] "Valuable for the war economy": The pretext under which some Jews were allowed special privileges in some of the ghettos. Among the special benefits was being one of the last (in most cases with immediate family) to be "resettled."

Wolfsschanze [G] "Wolf's Lair": One of Hitler's headquarters, located outside Rastenburg in East Prussia. It was at this location that the military plotters attempted unsuccessfully to assassinate Hitler on July 20, 1944: A bomb was planted near Hitler by Colonel Claus Schenk von Stauffenberg, one of the leaders of the plot. However, the bomb exploded under a briefing table, which lessened its impact, and Hitler was only slightly injured.

Y

Yaakov der ershter (יעקב דער ערשטער, Y) "Jacob the First": A Jewish term for Jakob Gens, head of the Jüdische Ordnungsdienst and *Judenälteste* of the Vilna ghetto, viewing him as a "Jewish king" — Jacob the First of the Vilna dynasty.

Yale/Yales/Yaleve/Yalevate (יעלה/יעלעס/יעלעווע/יעלעוואטע, Y) "Climbers": Yiddish neologisms (derived from Hebrew) signifying newly important individuals in the ghetto, their wives, and their children.

Yerushalayim d'Lite (ירושלים ד'ליטה, H/Y) "Jerusalem of Lithuania": Jewish term for Vilna, so called as it was a center, if not *the* center, of the Eastern European Jewish intelligentsia.

Yetziat Eropa [יציאת אורופה, H] "Exodus from Europe": Slang Hebrew term for the *Briha*, tapping in on the historical Jewish experience of the exodus from Egypt. The parallelism with previous Jewish experience played an important psychological and ideological role among the survivors and animated many of their activities.

Yevreyski soviet [R] "Jewish council": Russian term for the Jewish councils imposed by the occupation authorities throughout Nazi-occupied Europe. > see also: **Judenrat.**

Yidisher Rat (יידישאר ראט, Y) "Jewish council": Yiddish term for the Nazi-imposed Judenrat. A variation was *Yidnrat*, which means the same thing. > see also: **Kehile**; **Ältestenrat**; **Judenrat.**

Yidn, Farshreibt! (יידן פארשרייבט, Y) "Jews, write it down": A charge attributed to Jewish historian Simon Dubnow. Before he was taken out of the ghetto to be killed (reportedly by a former student of his) in Riga, Latvia, on December 8, 1941, it is reported that Dubnow admonished other Jews near-by to record all that was happening.

Yishuv [ישוב, H] "Settlement":

1. Scope and Definition
Hebrew term for the quasi-independent Jewish political entity in Palestine before the establishment of the State of Israel. The Nazi persecution of European Jewry elicited a strong response from the Yishuv, and it found its main expression in a policy of constructive aid known as rescue *aliya*. The aid program, however, was forced to consider three other elements: first, that the Yishuv did not possess the reins of government. Actual governmental powers were vested in the hands of a British colonial administration that ruled Palestine under the terms of the League of Nations Mandate of July 24, 1922. Second, the Yishuv's resources were limited, considering the relatively small size of the community (176,000

souls in 1933; 450,000 in 1939) and its reliance upon aid from international Jewish bodies. Finally, the Yishuv was hampered by the enmity of the Arab world, which sought to forestall the establishment of a Jewish state. During the 1930s, Arab opposition took the form of terrorism; in 1942, the Mufti of Jerusalem traveled to Berlin to encourage Hitler to speed up the Final Solution.

These three factors, one playing upon the other, came to the fore in 1939, when the British issued a White Paper that repudiated His Majesty's Government's promises to the Jewish people and severely limited *aliya*. During World War II the Yishuv was forced to watch the systematic destruction of European Jewry without being able to offer any real assistance to the victims. After World War II, however, the Yishuv became the central focus for rescue of the surviving remnant of European Jewry. The struggle to open the gates, along with the political and military struggle to reverse the 1939 White Paper, led to a successful revolt that culminated in the establishment of the State of Israel on May 14, 1948. > see also: **Aliya; Aliya Bet; Biltmore Resolution; Israel, State of; White Paper of 1939.**

2. Major Yishuv Organizations

Achdut ha-Am (אחדות העם), "Unity of the Nation," ethnic party of German Zionists in Palestine, founded in 1938. Leaning toward the liberal wing of the Zionist movement, Achdut ha-Am advocated rescue action for Jewish refugees in concert with bi-nationalism.

Af-Al-Pi (עף-על-פי), "Despite All," the Revisionist Zionist agency for "independent immigration" established in 1937. > see also: **Aliya Bet.**

Aliyat Yeladim va-No'ar (עליית ילדים ונוער, YA), "Youth Aliya," organization and movement for the immigration of young people, founded as Jüdische Jugendhilfe in 1932. Initially concentrating on German Jewish youth, YA was the brainchild of Recha Freier. In 1933 the YA idea became the central focus of Henrietta Szold and the

Hadassah organization. YA's plan was to bring young people to Palestine, provide them with vocational training, and thereby permit their permanent settlement. In all, YA was able to rescue some 30,000 Jewish children between 1933 and 1945; activities continued after the war with displaced Jewish children (and indeed continue up to this day). YA was the only legal immigration permitted by the British during World War II.

Committee for the Jews of Occupied Europe (CJOE), also known as the Joint Rescue Committee, rescue department of the Jewish Agency Executive, established in January 1943. The CJOE reflected the Yishuv's intense concern about events in Europe after information on the Final Solution emerged. However, continued British obstruction and a lack of sufficient funding prevented the CJOE from carrying out more than a token rescue task. Chairman: Yitzhak Gruenbaum (1943–1945).

Hagana (הגנה), "Defense," underground militia founded in 1920. Organized geographically, the Hagana operated under the command of the Histadrut, with the support and authority of the Jewish Agency Executive. In 1937 the Hagana formed the Mossad le-Aliya Bet to promote the rescue of Jewish refugees from Nazi-occupied Europe. > see also: **Aliya Bet.**

Hativa Yehudit Lohemet (חטיבה יהודית לוחמת, HIL חי"ל), "The Jewish Brigade Group," military force created within the British army but composed of Palestinian and stateless Jews. HIL was established in September 1944 and played an active role in the Italian campaign. In 1945, HIL was transferred to occupation duties in Germany and Austria. The location of HIL units granted them an ability to aid Holocaust survivors, and one of their more important tasks was in facilitating the Briha. HIL was disbanded by the British in 1946 but provided the core of the soon-to-be-established Israeli Army. > see also: **Aliya Bet; Briha; Displaced Persons, Jewish; She'erit ha-Pleta; War Effort, Jewish.**

Histadrut ha-Zionit ha-Hadasha (הסתדרות הציונית החדשה, ha-Zach הצח), "The New Zionist Organization (NZO)," Revisionist Zionist body established when ha-Zohar seceded from the World Zionist Organization

Makeup of the NZO Executive
Courtesy of the Jabotinsky Institute Archive, Tel Aviv

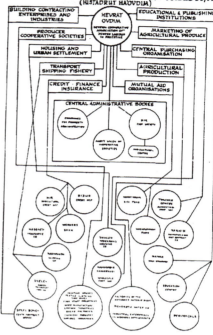

Inner structure of the Histadrut
Authors' Collection

(WZO) in September 1935. Operating as an oppositional group, ha-Zach reflected Jabotinsky's increasing fears of impending catastrophe. As a viable party, however, ha-Zach did not survive Jabotinsky's death in 1940, although the body continued to exist until it reintegrated with the WZO after the establishment of the State of Israel.

Histadrut ha-Ovdim ha-Kelalit shel ha-Ovdim be-Eretz Israel (הסתדרות העובדים הכללית של העובדים בארץ ישראל), "General Federation of Workers in the Land of Israel," more commonly known simply as the Histadrut, socialist Zionist labor organization associated with Mapai and founded in 1920. During the Holocaust, the Histadrut stood in the forefront of attempts to increase *aliya* as a means of rescue and to integrate new immigrants into the general atmosphere of the Jewish National Home. As such, the Histadrut cooperated with the Jewish Agency and other Jewish organizations, although Histadrut operations were, at times, surrounded by controversy.

Hitachdut ha-Zionim ha-Revisionistim (התאחדות הציונים הרביסיונסתים, ha-Zohar, הצהר), "Association of Revisionist Zionists," founded by Ze'ev Jabotinsky in 1925. Ha-Zohar was a strong advocate of the anti-Nazi boycott, opposing the *Ha'avara* agreement. In 1935 Jabotinsky withdrew ha-Zohar from the World Zionist Organization and founded Histadrut ha-Zionit ha-Hadasha.

Hitachdut Olei Czechoslovakia (התאחדות עולי צ׳כוסלובקיה, HOC העצ), "Association of Czech Immigrants," friendly society founded in 1939. During the war HOC coordinated its activities with the rescue committee of the Jewish Agency. HOC later merged with Hitachdut Olei Germania to form Irgun Olei Merkaz Europa.

Hitachdut Olei Germania (התאחדות עולי גרמניה, HOG העג), "Association of German Immigrants," friendly society founded in 1932. From 1933 on, HOG operated as an immigrant aid and absorption agency, closely coordinating its activities with the Jewish Agency and the Va'ad Le'umi. Increasingly politicized after 1935, HOG dovetailed into the unsuccessful Achdut ha-Am party in 1938.

Irgun Olim Bilti Legali'im (ארגון עולים בלתי ליגליים), "Organization of Illegal Immigrants," founded in the early 1930s. The organization advocated unlimited Jewish immigration to Palestine and, as a more immediate measure, the "legalization" of all *ma'apilim* already in the country. > see also: **Aliya Bet**.

Irgun Zva'i Leumi (ארגון צבאי לאומי, IZL אצל), "National Military Organization,"

underground movement founded by dissident Hagana members and members of BETAR in 1931. In 1937 the Irgun formed the Af-Al-Pi organization to promote "independent" aliya. When World War II broke out, the Irgun declared a truce in its operations against the British, and Irgun members participated actively in all anti-Nazi operations of the Yishuv. > see also: **Aliya Bet**.

Jewish Agency (JA), quasi-governmental organization of Yishuv and diaspora Jews interested in building a Jewish National Home. The Executive of the Jewish Agency (JAE) was created under article 4 of the League of Nations Mandate and was organized as a

Jewish Agency proclamation of May 29, 1933, calling for the rescue of German Jewry
Courtesy of the Central Zionist Archives, Jerusalem

דבר מפלגת פועלי א"י
לקונגרס הציוני הכ"א

לא נכנע!

זהו נדר העם להמשיך, להמשיך
בהתאבקותו המדינית, להמשיך
בעבדתו הקונסטרוקטיבית,
להמשיך בעליה, בסרקע,
בהתישבות, בחרושת, בהתגוננות:
להערים על פסודות ולעקף חוקים
לשם ההמשך הזה, ליצור בקרם
מתיחות רוחנית, המטילה את מרות
אי־הכניעה על כל פרט והמטונת
אליה כל מעשה וכל הליכות חיים.

Mapai election poster
for the 21st World Zionist Congress
Courtesy of the Histadrut Archive,
Machon Lavon, Tel Aviv

shadow cabinet. The JA operated under the auspices of, and was responsible to, the World Zionist Organization. Chairman: David Ben-Gurion (1935–1948).

Lohame Herut Israel (לוחמי חרות ישראל, LEHI לחי), "Fighters for the Freedom of Israel," splinter group of the IZL, led by Abraham "Ya'ir" Stern, which disagreed with the truce declared in 1940. LEHI advocated continuing military struggles to establish a Jewish state but remained at the fringes of the Yishuv until after World War II.

Mifleget Poale Eretz Israel (מפלגת פועלי ארץ ישראל, Mapai מפא"י), "Workers Party of the Land of Israel," Socialist Zionist party, founded in 1930, to which the majority of the Jewish Agency Executive belonged. Mapai advocated a moderate Socialist platform that emphasized cooperation with non-Socialist Jewish parties in attainment of Zionist goals. From 1935 on, Mapai began to advocate mass Jewish emigration from

Europe. With the adoption of the Biltmore Program in 1942, Mapai also began to publicly advocate the creation of a Jewish state in Palestine. Chairman: David Ben-Gurion (1930–1948).

Mossad le-Aliya Bet (מוסד לעליה ב'), "Agency for Aliya Bet," the arm of the Hagana for *ha'apala*, founded in late 1937. > see also: **Aliya Bet**.

Palästine Treuhandstelle (PALTREU), "Palestine Trust and Transfer Company, the agency that oversaw the Ha'avara agreement. > see also: **Ha'avara**.

Pidyon Shevuyim (פדיון שבויים), "Redemption of Captives," fund created in 1938 by the Va'ad Leumi to assist with Aliyat ha-Noar. For technical reasons, the fund was not overwhelmingly successful and was terminated at the outbreak of World War II.

Va'ad Leumi (ועד לאומי, VL), "National Council," executive arm of Knesset Israel — the official name of the Jewish millet (community) in British mandatory Palestine, established in 1920 and reorganized in 1926. The Knesset Israel theoretically represented all Jews living in Palestine; its legislative arm being the seventy-member Asefat ha-Nivharim. In reality, the VL was oriented toward internal developments, such as health care and education, leaving all political activities in the hands of the Jewish Agency Executive.

3. Yishuv Leadership During the Holocaust

Arlosoroff, Haim (1899–1933): Labor Zionist leader; from 1929 to 1933, member of the Jewish Agency Executive responsible for "foreign policy"; one of the negotiators of the Ha'avara agreement; murdered by unknown persons on June 16, 1933.

Begin, Menachem (1913–1992): Revisionist Zionist leader and sixth prime minister of the State of Israel; leader of Betar in Poland; joined the Polish armed forces in the USSR but deserted when the force reached Palestine; from 1942 led the Irgun Zva'i Leumi.

Ben-Gurion, David (1886–1973): Labor Zionist leader and first prime minister of the State of Israel; from 1935 to 1948, chairman of the Jewish Agency Executive; established the Yishuv's general policies and priorities on the

Fundraising letter of Pidyon Shevuyim
Courtesy of the Central Zionist Archive, Jerusalem

entire panoply of Jewish and Zionist issues.

Ben-Zvi, Yitzhak (1884–1963): Labor Zionist leader and second president of the State of Israel; during the 1930s and 1940s, chairman of the Va'ad Leumi and president of Asefat ha-Nivharim.

Dobkin, Eliyahu (1898–1976): Labor Zionist leader and member of the Jewish Agency Executive; headed the Histadrut immigration department between 1933 and 1945.

Fishman-Maimon, Judah L. (1875–1962): Rabbi, religious Zionist leader and first minister of religious affairs of the State of Israel; member of the Jewish Agency Executive from 1935 to 1948.

Galili, Israel (1911–1986): Labor Zionist leader; commander of the Hagana from 1935 to 1947; responsible for the creation of the Mossad le-Aliya Bet.

Golomb, Eliahu (1893–1945): leader of the Hagana and a strong supporter of the Mossad le-Aliya Bet.

Gruenbaum, Yizhak (1879–1970): Polish Zionist leader and member of the Jewish Agency Executive; immigrated to Palestine in 1932; during the late 1930s was responsible for the Aliya Department.

Hadari, Ze'ev (Venia Pomerantz; b. 1916): engineer, historian, and rescue activist; member of the Mossad le-Aliya Bet staff in Turkey and

Bulgaria during World War II; from 1946 until 1948 headed the Mossad Paris office.

Herzog, Isaac (1888–1959): Ashkenazic Chief Rabbi of Palestine and Israel; strong advocate of rescue at all costs.

Jabotinsky, Ze'ev (1880–1940): Revisionist Zionist leader; founder of ha-Zohar and ha-Zach; from 1936 supreme commander of the Irgun Zva'i Leumi; viewed antisemitism as "the most significant component" in Nazi ideology and, consequently, supported the anti-Nazi boycott as well as the evacuation of European Jewry.

Katznelson, Berl (1887–1944): Mapai leader and chief ideologue; editor in chief of *Davar*; strongly opposed the fragmentation of the Zionist movement; advocated *aliya* at all costs.

Lewin, Isaac M. (1894–1971): Agudas Israel leader; founder of Aguda in Poland; escaped from Warsaw in 1940; member of the rescue committee of the Jewish Agency, 1943–1947.

Raziel, David (1910–1942): Revisionist Zionist leader; from 1931 until his death commander of the Irgun Zva'i Leumi; worked with British intelligence in the Middle East and was killed during a mission in Iraq.

Senator, Werner D. (1896–1953): non-Zionist member of the Jewish Agency Executive and advocate of a territorialist solution to the German Jewish problem.

Sharett (Shertok), Moshe (1894–1965): Labor Zionist leader, Israel's first foreign minister and second prime minister; fulfilled the former role as member of the Jewish Agency Executive during the 1930s and 1940s.

Szold, Henrietta (1860–1945): Zionist leader in the United States and Palestine; founder of Hadassah; responsible during the 1930s and 1940s for Youth Aliya.

Weizmann, Chaim (1874–1952): Zionist leader and first president of the State of Israel; active in rescue affairs in London throughout the 1930s and 1940s.

Yom ha-Shoa (יום השואה, H) "Holocaust [Remembrance] Day": Official title for the

Israeli national day of commemoration for the Holocaust, on 27 Nisan (generally April). Enacted into law by an act of the Knesset on April 12, 1951, Yom ha-Shoa is commemorated as a solemn day in Israel: All places of entertainment are closed and at noon sirens throughout the country blare, bringing all work to a temporary halt. In the diaspora that day, or the Sunday after Passover, is also commemorated as a solemn day of mourning and reflection. Additionally, 10 Teveth (an already existing fast day, December-January) has been

Poster commemorating Yom ha-Shoa
Authors' Collection

declared by the Chief Rabbinate of Israel to be a day of remembrance for all the martyrs whose day of death (*Yahrzeit*) is unknown.

Yoshev beseter (יושב בסתר, H) "Dwell in secret": Jewish code term for a hiding place, derived from a religious term for God, the "Hidden One." Jews used the term to mean that just as God is hidden (i.e., unfindable in physical terms), they too should hide and not appear at the Nazis' beck and call.

Yunakes (יונאקעס, Y/Slang) Yiddish term for uniformed Volksdeutsche police in the Polish ghettos in the service of the Gettoverwaltung. Officially, the *Yunakes* were organized to act as tariff police; unofficially most of them were intimately involved with the criminal elements in the ghetto, helping them smuggle goods in, for a cut of their income.

Z

Za dom spremni [Croat] "Ready for the fatherland": Motto of the Ustaša, implying their willingness to do anything for Croatia: in particular, the massacre of Jews, Communists, and non-Catholics, especially Serbs.

Zeilappel [G] "Counting formation": Special callups for counting of a camp's inmates. This was done at unusual hours, mostly in the middle of the night, in order to harass and further weaken the victims. It was not, however, a substitute for the early morning and evening *Appell*s.

Zeitenwende [G] "Change of era": Nazi historiographical term to avoid using B.C. or A.D. Thus, they would use *Zw vor* for B.C. and *Zw nach* for A.D.

Zentralstelle [G] "Central office": The assembly point for Amsterdam Jews where they were forced to report before being deported. The Hollandse Schouwburg (Dutch Theatre) was also used at a later date as an assembly point for deportation of Dutch Jewry. > see also: **Umschlagplatz**.

Zhides [Ro] "Jews": Derogatory term used by the Romanian Fascist militias and antisemites to describe Jews.

Zidovsky Kral [Sl] "King of the Jews": Nickname of Dr. Anton Vasek, head of Department #14 for Jewish affairs in the Slovak Ministry of Interior. For the part Vasek played in the deportation of Slovak Jewry, he was found guilty by a Czechoslovak People's Court and executed.

Zigeuner [G] "Gypsy": Common term for quasi-nomadic clans originating in the Middle Ages that were singled out for persecution by the Nazis. Despite their clearly Aryan origins, the Gypsies were considered *Andersblutige*, that is "people of different blood." This concept was legislated in September 1935, when the Nazis explicitly included Gypsies in the Nuremberg Laws. Unlike the case with Jews, however, the Nazis did not maintain a consistent policy regarding Gypsies: most were considered *Mischlinge*, but some, "pure" Gypsies, were considered Aryans and thus exempt from some Nazi racial legislation. These "pure" Gypsies were even permitted to join the Wehrmacht. Regardless of degree of purity, all Gypsies were considered to be asocials; once Nazi policy toward Jews turned more brutal (especially after 1938), Gypsies also experienced considerable persecution. When the Nazis launched the Final Solution, Gypsies were included in the categories of individuals to be permanently removed from society. Here, too, distinctions were drawn between "pure" and "impure" Gypsies; the former were to be spared (although they were to be sterilized) while the latter were to be murdered. Approximately 200,000 Gypsies were murdered during the Holocaust.

TABLE Z.1: The Persecution of the Gypsies

Country	1939 Pop.	Murdered
Austria	11,200	6,500
Belgium	600	400
Bohemia & Moravia	13,000	5,500
Croatia	28,500	28,000
Estonia	1,000	1,000
France	42,000	14,000
Germany	20,000	15,000
Holland	300	200
Hungary	100,000	28,000
Italy	25,000	2,000
Latvia	1,000	1,000
Lithuania	1,000	1,000
Luxembourg	200	200
Poland	50,000	13,000
Romania	300,000	36,000
Serbia	60,000	12,000
Slovakia	80,000	2,000
USSR	100,000	30,000
TOTAL	833,800	195,800

Source: Ian Hancock: *The Pariah Syndrome*, Ann Arbor, MI: Karoma Pub., 1987.

Zog nit kainmul (זאג ניט קיינמאל, Y) "Never Say": Title of a partisan song written by Hirsh Glik, a poet and member of the Faraynikte Partizaner Organizatzye in the Vilna ghetto — killed during an encounter with the Nazi murderers. Set to music as a march, the lyrics were translated into many languages.

Zovhei adam agalim yishakun (זבחי אדם עגלים ישקון, H) "They who sacrifice men kiss calves": Biblical term derived from Hosea 13:2 and calling attention to the fact that the Nazis, who burned humans to death in the gas chambers and crematoria, banned Jewish ritual slaughter (*shechita*) on grounds of its being "inhumane."

ZS [Hu]: Abbreviation for *Zsidó* (Jew), stamped on all documents belonging to Jews in Hungary.

Zugangsbaracke [G] "Entry barrack": The quarantine area of newly admitted inmates in a given concentration camp. The prisoners had to spend from one to two weeks in this enclosure, until all the pertinent administrative work was finished.

Zur Vernichtung durch Arbeit [G] "Destruction through work": Nazi term alluding to an agreement made between Reich Minister of Justice Otto Thierack and Reichsführer-SS Heinrich Himmler on September 18, 1942, whereby all Jews and certain other categories serving in penal institutions were to be transferred to SS custody in order to be worked to death.

Zusammenballung [G] "Crowding together": Nazi term for incarcerating as many Jews as possible into a few large ghettos, in preparation for deportation to extermination camps or extermination sites.

Zusatzarbeit [G] "Overtime": Nazi term used in most slave-labor camps and work ghettos. Although officially there was a set schedule of daily working hours for all inmates — Jews,

ZOG NIT KEINMOL

Zog nit keinmol az du geist dem letztn veg,
Ven himlen blaiene far rhteln bloiye teg.
Kumen vet noch unzer oisgebenkte sho
S'vet a poik ton unzer trot mir zainen do.
Fun greenem palmen land biz vaitn land fun shnel,
Mir kumen on mit unzer pain mit unzer vel;
Vugefaln s'iz a shpritz fun unzer blut
Shpro-tzn vet dort unzer gvure unzer mut.
Es vet die morgen zun begilden unz dem heint
Un der nechten vet farschvinden mitten feint,
Nur oib farzammen vet die zun un der kayar
Vie a farrol zol gayen dus lied fun dor zu dor.
Dus lied geschrieben is mit blut un nit mit blei
Es is nit kein liedel vun a feugel oyf den frei;
Dus hut a folk zuvishen follendicke vent
Dus lied gezungen mit naganis in die hent.

זאָג ניט קיינמאָל!
(פּאַרטיזאַנער הימן פֿון ווילנער געטאָ)

זאָג ניט קיינמאָל אַז דו גייסט דעם לעצטן וועג,
כאַטש הימלען בלייענע פֿאַרשטעלן בלויע טעג;
קומען וועט נאָך אונדזער אויסגעבענקטע שעה,
ס'וועט אַ פּויק טאָן אונדזער טראָט — מיר זיינען דאָ!

פֿון גרינעם פּאַלמענלאַנד ביז ווייסן לאַנד פֿון שניי,
מיר קומען אָן מיט אונדזער פּיין, מיט אונדזער וויי,
און וואו געפֿאַלן ס'איז אַ שפּריץ פֿון אונדזער בלוט,
שפּראָצן וועט דאָרט אונדזער גבֿורה אונדזער מוט.

ס'וועט די מאָרגנזון באַגילדן אונדז דעם היינט,
און דער נעכטן וועט פֿאַרשווינדן מיטן פֿיינט,
נאָר אויב פֿאַרזאַמען וועט די זון און דער קאַיאָר —
ווי אַ פּאַראָל זאָל גיין דאָס ליד פֿון דור צו דור.

דאָס ליד געשריבן איז מיט בלוט און ניט מיט בליי,
ס'איז ניט קיין ליד פֿון אַ פֿויגל אויף דער פֿריי,
דאָס האָט אַ פֿאָלק צווישן פֿאַלנדיקע ווענט
דאָס ליד געזונגען מיט נאַגאַנעס אין די הענט.

טאָ זאָג ניט קיינמאָל אַז דו גייסט דעם לעצטן וועג,
כאַטש הימלען בלייענע פֿאַרשטעלן בלויע טעג;
קומען וועט נאָך אונדזער אויסגעבענקטע שעה —
ס'וועט אַ פּויק טאָן אונדזער טראָט — מיר זיינען דאָ!

מיזרחא — הירש גליק

Text of the Partisan Hymn
Authors' Collection

nonetheless, were required to put in an extra two to five hours daily on a "voluntary basis." This was almost always brutally enforced.

Zwangsarisierung [G] "Forced aryanization": Nazi term for the accelerated aryanization program, ordered by Reichsmarschall Hermann Göring after *Kristallnacht*. > see also: **Arisierung**.

Zwangsentjudungsverfahren [G] "Forced removal of Jews": Nazi term for the total aryanization of Jewish businesses and ostracizing of German Jewry undertaken after *Kristallnacht*. At this time arbitration was no longer available and the Jewish business owner was forced to take whatever renumeration he was offered; his removal from society was almost total.

Zwangsgemeinde [G] "Forced community": Nazi term that applied to localities with a Jewish population that did not belong to any form of Kahal (the prewar Jewish community council). Nazi policy in overrun Europe dictated that all localities where Jews lived had to be represented by a Judenrat, and all Jews — willing or not — had to belong to it. Even the very assimilated (who, up to that period, had hardly considered themselves to be Jewish) were forced to join the ranks.

Zwischenreich [G] "Interregnum government": Derisive Nazi term for the Weimar Republic that became popular after the *Machtergreifung*. The phrase emphasized the illegitimacy of the Weimar government since the republic was not accorded the status of a Reich but represented the interregnum between the legitimate Second and Third Reichs. > see also: **Judenrepublik**.

Żyd [P] "Jew": Term used by Polish antisemites as a slur to describe Polish Jewry. > see also: **Zhides**.

Żydokomuna [P] "Jewish Communism": Antisemitic term very prominent in Polish Fascist daily propaganda usage just prior to the Nazi blitz on Poland and, to some extent, even after the Nazi occupation. The term suggested that all Jews were Communists — and they were therefore responsible politically, economically, and socially for the Polish predicament.

Żydowska Gmina Wyznaniowa [P] "Jewish religious community": Polish prewar term for the Jewish *kehila*.

Zyklon B: commercial name for the chemical hydrogen cyanide (HCN), commonly known as prussic acid. Although Zyklon B was originally developed as an insecticide, the Nazis experimented with it during the Euthanasia Program and, thereafter, used it for the mass extermination of Jews in the *Vernichtungslager*. Zyklon B was manufactured by two firms: Deutsche Gesellschaft für Schädlingsbekämpfung (DEGESCH, the German Vermin combatting Corporation, a subsidiary of I.G. Farben) and Tesch und Stabenow Verlag.

FOR FURTHER READING

I. Primary Sources

A. Archives

Archival records and illustrations pertaining to the Holocaust have been researched in the following collections, although space does not permit the citation of specific record groups and files:
1. Archion Toldot ha-Hagana (Hagana Historical Archive, ATH), Tel Aviv.
2. Ben-Gurion Research Center (BGRC), Kiryat Sde Boker.
3. Central Zionist Archives (CZA), Jerusalem.
4. Fred R. Crawford Witness to the Holocaust Project, Emory University, Atlanta.
5. Histadrut Archive (HIS), Tel Aviv.
6. Jabotinsky Institute Archive (JIA), Tel Aviv.
7. Jewish and Slavic Divisions, New York Public Library (NYPL), New York.
8. Simon Wiesenthal Center Archives and Library, Los Angeles.
9. United States Holocaust Memorial Museum (USHMM), Washington, DC.
10. United States Library of Congress, Washington, DC.
11. YIVO Institute Archives and Library, New York.

B. Press and Periodicals

American Jewish Archives
American Jewish History
American Jewish Year Book
American Sociological Review
Commentary
Congress Bulletin
CV Zeitung
Department of State Bulletin
Holocaust and Genocide Studies (HGS)
Holocaust Studies Annual (HSA)
Jestem Polakiem
Jewish Chronicle
Jewish Social Studies (JSS)
Jewish Week

Leo Baeck Institute Year Book (LBIYB)
Midstream
Modern Judaism
Neged Hazerem
New Leader
New York Times
Romanian Jewish Studies
South African Jewish Affairs
Studies in Zionism
Wiener Library Bulletin
World Review
Yad Vashem Bulletin
Yad Vashem Studies (YVS)
Yahadut Zemanenu (Hebrew with English summaries)

Journal of Contemporary History (JCH)   *Yalkut Moreshet* (Hebrew with English summaries)
Jüdische Rundschau   *YIVO Annual*

C. Published Primary Sources and Collections

Ancel, Jean (comp.). *Documents Concerning the Fate of Romanian Jewry During the Holocaust.*
     12 vols., New York: Beate Klarsfeld Foundation, 1986.
Arad, Yitzhak, Israel Gutman, and Abraham Margaliot (eds). *Documents on the Holocaust.* New
     York: Ktav, 1981.
Arad, Yitzhak, Shmuel Krakowski, and Shmuel Spector (eds.). *The Einsatzgruppen reports:
     Selections from the dispatches of the Nazi death squads' campaign against the Jews, July
     1941–January 1943.* Translated from German by Stella Schossberger. New York:
     Holocaust Library, 1989.
Banzi, Antonio. *Razzismo Fascista* [Fascist racism]. Palermo: Libreria Agate, 1939.
"The Bernheim Petition to the League of Nations," *AJYB*, vol. 35 (1934/1935), 74–101.
Blau, Bruno. *Das Ausnahmerecht für die Juden in Deutschland 1933–1945* [The exceptional law
     for the Jews in Germany, 1933–1945]. Düsseldorf: Verlag Allgemeine Wochenzeitung der
     Juden in Deutschland, 1965.
Brewitz, Walter. *Die Nürenberger Gesetze in ihrer praktischen Auswirkung* [The Nuremberg laws
     in their practical application]. Berlin: Der Weltkampf, 1940.
Churchill, Winston S. *The Gathering Storm.* History of the Second World War, vol. 1. Boston:
     Houghton Mifflin, 1948.
Dawidowicz, Lucy S. (ed.). *A Holocaust Reader.* New York: Behrman House, 1976.
Deeg, Hans P. *Die Judengesetze Grossdeutschlands* [Greater Germany's Jewish laws]. Nuremberg:
     Stürmer, 1939.
Dobroszycki, Lucjan (comp.). *Chronicle of the Lódz Ghetto.* New Haven: Yale University Press,
     1984.
Ehrenburg, Ilya, and Vasily Grossman (eds.). *The Black Book.* Translated from Russian by John
     Glad and James S. Levine. New York: Holocaust Library, 1981.
Elmo, Luciano. *La Condizione Giuridica degli Ebrei in Italia* [The judicial condition of the Jews
     in Italy]. Milan: Baldini & Castoldi, 1939.
Flessner, Volmar. *Rasse und Politik im Staatsbürgerrecht* [Race and politics in state citizenship
     law]. Berlin: Deutscher Rechtsverlag, 1938.
Friedländer, Saul. *Pius XII and the Third Reich: A Documentation.* New York: Knopf, 1966.
Friedman, Philip (ed.). *Martyrs and Fighters.* New York: Lancer Books, 1954.
Genschel, Helmut. *Die Verdrängung der Juden aus der Wirtschaft im Dritten Reich* [The elimination
     of Jews from the economy of the Third Reich]. Göttingen: Musterschmidt, 1966.
Gross, Feliks, and Basil Valvianos (eds.). *Struggle for Tomorrow: Modern Political Ideologies of the
     Jewish People.* New York: Arts, Inc., 1954.
Guett, Arthur. *Die Rassenpflege im dritten Reich* [Race cultivation in the Third Reich]. Dresden:
     Ehlermann, 1940.
Hadari, Ze'ev (ed.). המוסד לעלייה ב': יומן מבצעים פאריס, *1947* [The Mossad for Aliya Bet:
     Operational diary Paris, 1947]. Beersheba: Ben-Gurion University of the Negev, 1991.
Halpern, Israel (ed.). ספר הגבורה (The book of Jewish heroism). 2 vols. Tel Aviv: Am Oved,
     1940-1941.
Handbook on German Armed Forces. Washington, DC: U.S. Government Printing Office, 1944.
Hertzberg, Arthur (ed.). *The Zionist Idea.* New York: Atheneum, 1976.
Hilberg, Raul, Joseph Kermish, Raul Hilberg, and Staniskaw Staron (eds) *The Warsaw Diary of
     Adam Czerniakow.* New York: Stein and Day, 1979.
Hitler, Adolf. *Mein Kampf.* Boston: Houghton Mifflin, 1971.

Huberband, Shimon. *Kiddush Hashem: Jewish Religious and Cultural Life in Poland during the Holocaust*. Hoboken, NJ: Ktav for Yeshiva University Press, 1987.

Katsh, Abraham I. (ed.). *The Warsaw Diary of Chaim A. Kaplan*. rev. ed. New York: Collier Books, 1973.

Kaufmann, Max. *Die Vernichtung der Juden Lettlands* [The destruction of Latvian Jewry]. Munich: Deutscher Verlag, 1947.

Kermish, Joseph (ed.). *To Live with Honor and to Die with Honor: Selected Documents of the Warsaw Ghetto Underground Archives, "O.S." (Oneg Shabbat)*. Jerusalem: Yad Vashem, 1986.

Kowalski, Isaac (ed.). *Anthology on Armed Jewish Resistance 1939–1945*. 4 vol. Brooklyn: Jewish Combatants Publishers House, 1986–1991.

Krueger, Alf. *Die Lösung der Judenfrage in der deutschen Wirtschaft: Kommentare zur Judengesetzgebung* [The solving of the Jewish question in the German economy: Commentaries on Jewry laws]. Berlin: Limpert, 1940.

"Legal Status of the Jews Defined in Orders Issued by Nazis," *Congress Bulletin*, vol. 2 # 4 (1935), 1, 4.

La Legislazione antiebraica in Italia e in Europa: atti del Convegno nel cinquantenario delle leggi razziali [Anti-Hebrew legislation in Italy and in Europe]. Rome: Camera dei deputati, 1989.

Laqueur, Walter (ed.). *The Israel-Arab Reader*. rev. ed. New York: Bantam Books, 1970.

Levin, Dov. בין ניצוץ לשלהבת: "ארגון ברית ציון" במלחמת העולם השנייה [Spark and Flame: Irgun Brit Zion during the Second World War]. Ramat Gan: Bar Ilan University Press, 1987.

Lichtenberger, Henri. *The Third Reich*. Translated from French and edited by Koppel S. Pinson; foreword by Nicholas Murray Butler. New York: Greystone Press, 1939.

Lubetzki, J.. *La condition des Juifs en France sous l'occupation allemande, 1940–1944: La législation raciale* [The Jewish condition in France under the German occupation, 1940–1944: The racial legislation]. Paris: Centre de Documentation Juivé Contemporaine, 1945.

Mendelsohn, John (editor in chief). *The Holocaust: Selected Documents in Eighteen Volumes*. New York: Garland, 1981.

Meyer, Henry C. (ed.). *The Long Generation: Germany from Empire to Ruin*. New York: Walker, 1973.

Molho, Michael, and Joseph Nehama. *In Memoriam: Hommage aux Victimes Juives des Nazis en Grèce*. 2 vols. Salonika: Imp. N. Nicolaides, 1948–1953.

Mussolini, Benito. *The Political and Social Doctrine of Fascism*. New York: Carnegie Endowment for International Peace, 1935.

Nicholson, Harold. *Peacemaking 1919*. New York: Grosset & Dunlap, 1965.

Noakes, Jeremy, and Geoffrey Pridham (eds.) *Documents on Nazism, 1919–1945*. New York: Viking Press, 1975.

Paul, Alexander. *Jüdisch-deutsche Blutmischung: Eine sozial-biologische Untersuchung* [Jewish-German blood adulteration: A social-biological examination]. Berlin: Schötz, 1939.

Poliakov, Léon, and Jacques Sabille. *Jews Under the Italian Occupation*. Paris: Editions du Centre, 1959.

Richer, Bodo. *Die Nürenberger Grundgesetze* [The Nuremberg Laws]. Berlin: Carl Heymann, 1935.

Ringelblum, Emmanuel. *Notes from the Warsaw Ghetto: The Journal of Emmanuel Ringelblum*. Edited and translated by Jacob Sloan. New York: Schocken Books, 1975.

Rothkirchen, Livia. *The Destruction of Slovak Jewry: A Documentary History* (Hebrew/English). Jerusalem: Yad Vashem, 1961.

Rutkowski, Adam. *La Lutte des Juifs en France à l'epoque de l'occupation, 1940–1944: recueil de documents* [The struggle of French Jewry during the occupation, 1940–1944: An anthology of documents]. Introduction by Georges Wellers. Paris: Centre de Documentation Juive Contemporaine, 1975.

Segal, S. *The Nazi New Order in Poland*. New York: Knopf, 1942.

Snyder, Louis L. (ed.). *Fifty Major Documents of the Twentieth Century*. Princeton: Van Nostrand Company, 1955.

Spivak, John L. *Secret Armies: The New Technique of Nazi Warfare*. New York: Modern Age Books, 1939.

Tenenbaum-Tamaroff, Mordechai. דפים מן הדלקה [Pages from the Holocaust]. Tel Aviv: Hakibbutz Hameuchad, 1947.

Trial of the War Criminals Before the Nuremberg Military Tribunals. 42 vols. Washington, DC: USGPO, 1952.

Wagner, Gerhard. *Die Nürenberger Judengesetze* [The Nuremberg Jewish laws]. Munich: Eher, 1937.

Walk, Joseph, Daniel C. Brecher, et al.: *Das Sonderrecht für die Juden im NS-Staat: eine Sammlung der gesetzlichen Massnahmen und Richtlinien. Inhalt und Bedeutung* [The special laws for the Jews in the National Socialist State: A collection of legal measures and guidelines. Contents and meaning]. Heidelberg: Muller Juristischer Verlag, 1981.

Warhaftig, Zorach. *Uprooted: Jewish Refugees and Displaced Persons*. New York: The World Jewish Congress, 1946.

Weismandel, Dov Baer. שאלות ותשובות מן המצר [Responsa from the depths]. New York: The Author, 1953.

Weltsch, R.. "Tragt ihn mit Stolz, den gelben Fleck," *Jüdische Rundschau*, April 4, 1933, p. 1.

World Jewish Congress et al. *The Black Book: The Nazi Crime Against the Jewish People*. New York: Nexus Press, 1981.

D. Autobiographies and Memoirs

Anger, Per. *With Raoul Wallenberg in Budapest*. New York: Holocaust Library, 1981.

Arad, Yitzhak. *Ghetto in Flames*. New York: Holocaust Library, 1982.

Arnold, Frederic. *Doorknob Five-Two*. Los Angeles: Maxwell, 1984.

Biss, André. *A Million Jews to Save*. New York: A. S. Barnes, 1973.

The Book of Alfred Kantor. New York: McGraw-Hill, 1971.

Borzykowski, Tuvya. צוישן פאלנדיקע ווענט [Between falling walls]. Warsaw: Hehalutz, 1949.

Curda-Lipovsky, B. *Terezinske Katakomby* [Terezin catacombs]. Prague: Delnicke Nakladatelstvi, 1946.

Djemal Pasha. *Memoirs of a Turkish Statesman*. London: Hutchinson, 1922.

Edelheit, Hershel. "Journal of a Lost World." unpublished memoir MS.

Gisevius, Hans B. *To the Bitter End*. Boston: Houghton-Mifflin, 1947.

Grossman, Chaika. *The Underground Army: Fighters of the Bialystok Ghetto*. Translated from Hebrew by Shmuel Beeri; edited by Sol Lewis. New York: Holocaust Library, 1987.

Gurdus, Luba K. *The Death Train: A Personal Account of a Holocaust Survivor*. New York: Holocaust Library, 1978.

Heymont, Irving. *Among the Survivors of the Holocaust, 1945: The Landsberg DP Camp Letters of Major Irving Heymont, United States Army*. Cincinnati: American Jewish Archives, 1982.

Konfino, Barukh. עלייה ב' מחופי בולגריה [Illegal immigration from the shores of Bulgaria]. Tel Aviv: Ahiasaf Publishing, 1965.

Korbonski, Stefan. *Fighting Warsaw*. New York: Funk and Wagnalls, 1956.

Kowalski, Isaac. *A Secret Press in Nazi Europe*. rev. ed., New York: Shengold, 1978.

Lambert, Giles. *Operation Hazalah*. Indianapolis: Bobbs–Merrill, 1974.

Landau, Ludwik. *Kronika Wojny i Okupacji* [Chronicle of the war and occupation]. Warsaw: Panstwowe Wydawnictwo Naukowe, 1962.

Laub, Morris. *Last Barrier to Freedom*. Berkeley, CA: Judah L. Magnes Memorial Museum, 1985.

Luber, I.. *Zycie i Smierc Ghetta Warzawskiego* [Life and death in the Warsaw Ghetto]. Rome: Biblioteka Orla Bialego, 1945.

Malkin, Peter, and Harry Stein, *Eichamnn in My Hands*. New York: Warner Books, 1990.

McDonald, James G. *My Mission in Israel, 1948–1951*. New York: Simon and Schuster, 1951.

Perl, William. *The Four Front War*. New York: Crown, 1979.

Smolar, Hersh. *The Minsk Ghetto*. New York: Holocaust Library, 1989.

Speer, Albert. *Inside the Third Reich*. New York: Macmillan, 1970.

Vrba, Rudolf, and Alan Bestig. *I Cannot Forgive*. New York: Grove Press, 1984.

Warhaftig, Zorach. פליט ושריד בימי השואה [Refugee and remnant during the Holocaust]. Jerusalem: Yad Vashem and the Ot va-Ed Foundation, 1984.

Wdowinski, David. *And We Are not Saved*. New York: Philosophical Library, 1963.

Wells, Leon W. *The Death Brigade*. New York: Holocaust Library, 1978.

II. Secondary Sources

A. Encyclopedias and Guidebooks

Czech, Danuta. *Auschwitz Chronicle: 1939–1945*. Foreword by Walter Laqueur. New York: Henry Holt, 1990.

Edelheit, Abraham J. and Hershel Edelheit. *Bibliography on Holocaust Literature*. Boulder, CO: Westview Press, 1986.

——. *Bibliography on Holocaust Literature: Supplement*. Boulder, CO: Westview Press, 1990.

——. *Bibliography on Holocaust Literature: Supplement, Volume 2*. Boulder, CO: Westview Press, 1992.

Edelheit, Hershel, and Abraham J. Edelheit. *A World in Turmoil: An Integrated Chronology of the Holocaust and World War II*. Westport, CT: Greenwood Press, 1991.

Encyclopaedia Judaica. 16 vols. New York/ Jerusalem: Macmillan and Keter, 1972.

Freeman, Michael (comp.). *The Atlas of Nazi Germany*. New York: Macmillan, 1987.

Granatstein, Yehiel, and Moshe Kahanovich (comps.), לכסיקון הגבורה [Biographical dictionary of Jewish resistance]. 2 vols. Jerusalem: Yad Vashem, 1965.

Gurevich, D. (comp.). *Statistical Handbook of Jewish Palestine*. Jerusalem: The Jewish Agency, 1947.

Gutman, Israel (editor in chief). *The Encyclopedia of the Holocaust*. New York: Macmillan, 1989.

Gutman, Israel, and Gideon Greif (eds.). *The Historiography of the Holocaust Period*. Jerusalem: Yad Vashem, 1988.

Kammer, Hilde, and Elisabeth Bartsch. *Nationalsozialismus*. Hamburg: Rowohlt Taschenbuch, 1992.

Klevan, Avraham (ed.). *Jewish Communities Destroyed in the Holocaust*. Jerusalem: Yad Vashem, 1982.

Lerman, Antony (ed.), *The Jewish Communities of the World: A Contemporary Guide*. 4th ed., New York: Facts on File, 1989.

Singerman, Robert (ed.). *Antisemitic Propaganda: An Annotated Bibliography and Research Guide*. New York: Garland, 1982.

Pressac, Jean-Claude. *Auschwitz: Technique and Operations of the Gas Chamber*. New York/ Paris: Beate Klarsfeld Foundation, 1990

Taylor, James, and Warren Shaw (comps.). *The Third Reich Almanac*. New York: World Almanac, 1987.

Weinmann, Martin, with Anne Kaiser and Ursula Krause-Schmitt. *Das national-sozialistische Lagersystem* [The National Socialist camp system]. Frankfurt am Main: Zweitausendeins, 1990.

Wiesenthal, S.: *Every Day Remembrance Day*. New York: Henry Holt, 1987.

Wistrich, Robert. *Who Is Who in Nazi Germany*. New York: Macmillan, 1982.

Zentner, Christian, and Friedemann Bedürftig (eds.). *The Encyclopedia of the Third Reich*. 2 vols. Translated from German by Amy Hackett. New York: Macmillan, 1991.

B. Journal Articles

Adler-Rudel, Selig. "The Evian Conference," *LBIYB*, vol. 13 (1968), 235–273.

Ainsztein, Reuben. "The Enemy Within: Antisemitism Among Polish Soldiers in War-Time Britain," *Wiener Library Bulletin*, vol. 13 # 5/6 (1959), 58–59.

Ancel, Jean. "The Jassy Syndrome," *Romanian Jewish Studies*, vol. 1 # 1 (1991), 35–52.

——. "The Romanian Way of Solving the 'Jewish Problem' in Bessarabia and Bukovina, June–July, 1941," *YVS*, vol. 19 (1988), 227–231.

Arendt, Hannah. "From the Dreyfus Affair to the France of Today," *JSS*, vol. 4 # 3 (1942), 195–240.

——. "The Jew as Pariah: A Hidden Tradition," *JSS*, vol. 6 # 2 (1944), 99–122.

"Back to the Jungle?" in *Jewish Chronicle*, April 19, 1944, 8,

Barkai, Avraham. "German-speaking Jews in Eastern European Ghettos," *LBIYB*, vol. 34 (1989), 247–266.

Bauer, Yehuda. "The Death Marches, January–May 1945," *Modern Judaism*, vol. 3 # 1 (1983), 1–21.

——. "Rescue Operations Through Vilna," *YVS*, vol. 9 (1973), 215–233.

——. "הצנחנים ותכנית ההתגוננות" [The paratroopers and the defense plan], *Yalkut Moreshet*, # 1 (1963), 86–94.

Cang, Joel. "The Opposition Parties in Poland and Their Attitude Towards the Jews and the Jewish Problem," *JSS*, vol. 1 (1939), 241–257.

"Challange to Good Faith, A." *Jewish Chronicle*, April 28, 1944, p. 10.

Cohen, Morris R. "Philosophies of Jewish History," *JSS*, vol. 1 (1939), 39–72.

"Colonies for Poland," *World Review*, vol. 2 (1936), 60–61.

Edelheit, Abraham J. "The Soviet Union, the Jews, and the Holocaust," *HSA*, vol. 4 (1990), 113–134.

Eriksen, Robert. "Theologian in the Third Reich: The Case of Gerhard Kittel," in *JCH*, vol. 12 # 3 (1977), 595–622.

Feingold, Henry. "Who Shall Bear Guilt for the Holocaust? The Human Dilemma," *American Jewish History*, vol. 68 # 3 (1979), 261–282.

Friedman, Philip. "Polish Jewish Historiography Between the Two Wars, 1918–1939," *JSS*, vol. 11 (1949), 373–408.

Friling, Tuvia. "Meeting the Survivors: Ben-Gurion's Visit to Bulgaria, December 1944," *Studies in Zionism*, vol. 10 # 2 (1989), 175–195.

Fry, Varian. "Operation Emergency Rescue," *New Leader*, vol. 48 #25 (1965), 11–14.

Gekhman, E. "Simon Dubnov: How the Famous Jewish Historian Died," *Jewish Chronicle*, # 3950 (1944), 1, 7.

Goldhagen, Erich. "Pragmatism, Function and Belief in Nazi Antisemitism," *Midstream*, vol. 18 # 10 (1972), 52–62.

Gringauz, Samuel. "The Ghetto as an Experiment of Jewish Social Organization," *JSS*, vol. 11 # 1 (1949), 3–20.

Gut, Felix. "The Jewish Star over Luxembourg," *South African Jewish Affairs*, vol. 42 # 11 (1987), 29–30.

Gutman, Israel. "Jews in General Anders' Army in the Soviet Union," *YVS*, vol. 12 (1977), 231–296.

Hager-Halivni, Tzipora. "The Birkenau Revolt: Poles Prevent a Timely Insurrection," *JSS*, vol. 41 # 2 (1979), 123–154.

Haron, Miriam J. "United States-British Collaboration on Illegal Immigration to Palestine, 1945–1947," *JSS*, vol. 42 # 2 (1980), 177–182.

"Hungarian Jews Doomed: Planned Extermination," *Jewish Chronicle*, July 14, 1944, pp. 1, 7.

Jochmann, Werner. "The Jews and German Society in the Imperial Era," *LBIYB*, vol. 20 (1975), 5–11.

Kermish, Joseph. "Arms Used by the Warsaw Ghetto Fighters," *Yad Vashem Bulletin*, # 2 (1958), 5–9.

——. "The Land of Israel in the Life of the Ghetto as Reflected in the Illegal Warsaw Ghetto Press," *YVS*, vol. 5 (1963), 105.

——. "The Underground Press in the Warsaw Ghetto," *YVS*, vol. 1 (1957), 85–123.

Kershaw, Ian. "The Persecution of the Jews and German Popular opinion in the Third Reich," *LBIYB*, vol. 26 (1981), 261-289.

Kochavi, Arieh J. "The Displaced Persons' Problem and the Formulation of British Policy in Palestine," *Studies in Zionism*, vol. 10 # 1 (1989), 31–48.

Lavi, Theodore. "Documents on the Struggle of Romanian Jewry for Its Rights During the Second World War," *YVS*, vol. 4 (1960), 261–315.

Levin, Dov. "On the Relations Between the Baltic Peoples and Their Jewish Neighbors Before, During, and After World War II," *HGS*, vol. 5 (1990), 53–66.

Litani, Dora. "The Destruction of the Jews of Odessa in the Light of Romanian Documents," *YVS*, vol. 6 (1967), 135–154.

Mashberg, Michael (comp.). "Documents Concerning the American State Department and the Stateless European Jews, 1942–1944," *JSS*, vol. 39 # 1/2 (1977), 163–174.

Masson, Jeffrey M. "Hilberg's Holocaust," *Midstream*, vol. 32 # 4 (1986), 51–55.

Michel, Henri. "The Allies and the Resistance," *YVS*, vol. 5 (1963), 317–332.

Michman, Dan. "The Committee for Jewish Refugees in Holland (1933–1940)," *YVS*, vol. 14 (1981), 205–232.

Mosse, Werner E. "Problems and Limits of Assimilation: Hermann and Paul Wallich, 1833–1938," *LBIYB*, vol. 33 (1988), 43–65.

Opler, Morris E. "The Bio-social Basis of Thought in the Third Reich," *American Sociological Review*, vol. 10 (1945), 776–786.

Parzen, Herbert. "The Roosevelt Palestine Policy," *American Jewish Archives*, # 26 (1974), 31–65.

Pinot, B. Z. "Hitler's Entry into Vienna," *Yad Vashem Bulletin*, # 3 (1958), 15–16.

Poliakov, Léon. "The Mind of the Mass Murderer: the Nazi Executioners – and those who stood by," *Commentary*, vol. 12 # 5 (1951), 451–459.

Porat, Dina. "The Transnistria Affair and the Rescue Policy of the Zionist Leadership in Palestine, 1942–1943," *Studies in Zionism*, vol. 6 # 1 (1985), 27–52.

Raisky, Abraham. "We Fought Back in France," *Commentary*, vol. 1 # 4 (1946), 65.

Rorty, James. "Father Benoit, Ambassador of the Jews: An Untold Chapter of the Underground," *Commentary*, vol. 2 # 6 (1946), 507–513.

Rosenstock, Werner. "Exodus 1933–1939: A Survey of Jewish Emigration from Germany," *LBIYB*, vol. 1 (1956), 373–390.

Schechtman, Joseph B. "The Transnistria Reservation," *Yivo Annual*, vol. 8 (1953), 178–196.

Shelah, Menahem. "Sajmište — An Extermination Camp in Serbia," *HGS*, vol. 2 # 2 (1987), 243–260.

Spangenthal, Max, "The Jewish Question and the German Resistance Movement," *Yad Vashem*

Bulletin, # 19 (1966), 60–63.

Spector, Shmuel. "מבצע 1005' לטשטוש רצח המיליונים במלחמת-העולם השנייה" [Aktion 1005: Effacing the murder of millions during World War II], *Yahadut Zemanenu*, vol. 4 (1987), 207–225.

Stanley, John. "The Politics of the Jewish Question in the Duchy of Warsaw, 1807–1813," *JSS*, vol. 44 (1982), 47–62.

Tartakower, Arye. "Adam Czerniakow — the Man and His Supreme Sacrifice," *YVS*, vol. 6 (1967), 55–82.

Tsur, Yaron. "יהודי טוניס בתקופת הכיבוש הנאצי — קהילה מפוצלת בימי משבר" [The Jews of Tunis under Nazi occupation: A divided community in times of crisis], *Yahdut Zemanenu*, vol. 2 (1984), 153–175.

Vago, Bela. "The Intelligence Aspects of the Brand Mission," *YVS*, vol. 10 (1974), 111–128.

Wasserstein, Bernard. "New Light on the Moyne Assassination," *Midstream*, vol. 26 # 3 (1980), 30–38.

Zariz, Ruth. "Officially Approved Emigration from Germany After 1941: A Case Study," *YVS*, vol. 18 (1987), 275–291.

C. Anthologies and Collections of Essays

Alon, Gedalia. *מחקרים בתולדות ישראל* [Studies in Jewish history]. Tel Aviv: Hakibbutz Hameuchad, 1973.

Baron, Salo W., and George S. Wise (eds.). *Violence and Defense in the Jewish Experience*. Philadelphia: Jewish Publication Society, 1977.

Berenbaum, Michael (ed.). *A Mosaic of Victims*. New York: New York University Press, 1990.

Browning, Christopher. *Fateful Months: Essays on the Emergence of the Final Solution*. New York: Holmes and Meier, 1985.

Chamberlain, Brewster (ed.). *The Liberation of the Nazi Concentration Camps*. Washington, DC: United States Holocaust Memorial Council, 1987.

Dagan, Avigdor (ed.). *The Jews of Czechoslovakia*. 3 vols, Philadelphia: JPS, 1968–1983.

Fishman, Joshua A. (ed.). *Studies on Polish Jewry, 1919–1939*. English/Yiddish. New York: YIVO, 1974.

Friedman, Philip. *Roads to Extinction: Essays on the Holocaust*. Edited by Ada June Friedman; introduction by Salo W. Baron. New York and Philadelphia: Conference on Jewish Social Studies/ Jewish Publication Society, 1980.

Furet, François (ed.). *Unanswered Questions: Nazi Germany and the Genocide of the Jews*. New York: Schocken Books, 1989.

Gilbert, Martin. *The Macmillan Atlas of the Holocaust*. New York: Macmillan, 1982.

Gutman, Israel, and Cynthia J. Haft (eds.). *Patterns of Jewish Leadership in Nazi Europe 1933–1945*. Translated from Hebrew by Dina Cohen et al. Jerusalem: Yad Vashem, 1979.

Gutman, Israel, and Livia Rothkirchen (eds.). *The Catastrophe of European Jewry: Antecedents — History — Reflections*. Jerusalem: Yad Vashem, 1976.

Gutman, Israel, and Avital Saf (eds.). *The Nazi Concentration Camps*. Translated from Hebrew by Dina Cohen et al. Jerusalem: Yad Vashem, 1984.

——. *She'erit Hapletah, 1944–1948: Rehabilitation and Political Struggle*. Translated from Hebrew by Ralph Mandel. Jerusalem: Yad Vashem, 1990.

Gutman, Israel, and Efraim Zuroff (eds.). *Rescue Attempts During the Holocaust*. Translated from Hebrew by Moshe Gottlieb et al. Jerusalem: Yad Vashem, 1977.

Hayes, Peter (ed.). *Lessons and Legacies: The Meaning of the Holocaust in a Changing World*. Evanston, IL: Northwestern University Press, 1991.

Herzer, Ivo (ed.). *The Italian Refuge: Rescue of the Jews During the Holocaust*. Washington, DC:

Catholic University of America Press, 1989.

Hirschfeld, Gerhard, and Patrick Marsh (eds.). *Collaboration in France: Politics and Culture During the Nazi Occupation, 1940–1944*. Oxford: Berg, 1989.

Holocaust and Rebirth: A Symposium. Jerusalem: Yad Vashem, 1973.

Katzburg, Nathaniel (ed.). פדות:הצלה בימי השואה [Pedut: Rescue during the Holocaust]. Ramat Gan: Bar Ilan University, 1984.

Klarsfeld, Serge (ed.). *The Holocaust and the Neo-Nazi Mythomania*. Translated from French by Barbara Rucci. New York: Beate Klarsfeld Foundation, 1978.

Kohn, Moshe M. (ed.). *Jewish Resistance During the Holocaust*. Translated from Hebrew by Varda Esther Bar-On et al. Jerusalem: Yad Vashem, 1971.

Pinkus, Benjamin, and Ilan Troen (eds.). סוליד ריות יהודית לאומית בעת החדשה [Jewish national solidarity in the modern era]. Beersheba: Ben-Gurion University of the Negev, 1988.

Porter, Jack N. (ed.). *Genocide and Human Rights: A Global Anthology*. Washington, DC: University Press of America, 1982.

Sabrin, B. F. *Alliance for Murder: The Nazi-Ukrainian Nationalist Partnership in Genocide*, New York: Saperdon/Shapolsky, 1991.

Vago, Bela and George L. Mosse (eds.). *Jews and Non-Jews in Eastern Europe*. Jerusalem: Israel Universities Press, 1974.

Weber, Eugen, and H. Rogger (eds.). *The European Right*. Berkeley: University of California Press, 1965.

D. Books

Abella, Irving, and Harold Troper. *None Is Too Many: Canada and the Jews of Europe, 1933–1948*. New York: Random House, 1982.

Abitbol, Michel. *Les Juifs d'Afrique du Nord sous Vichy* [The Jews of North Africa under Vichy]. Paris: G. P. Maisonneuve et Larose, 1983.

Abzug, Robert H. *Inside the Vicious Heart: Americans and the Liberation of Nazi Concentration Camps*. New York: Oxford University Press, 1985.

Abrahamsen, Samuel. *Norway's Response to the Holocaust: A Historical Perspective*. New York: Holocaust Library, 1991.

Adam, Uwe D. *Judenpolitik im Dritten Reich* [Jewish policies in the Third Reich]. Düsseldorf: Droste, 1972.

Adler, Hans-Günther. *Theresienstadt, 1941–1945: Das Antlitz einer Zwangsgemeinschaft. Geschichte, Soziologie, Psychologie* [Theresienstadt, 1941–1945: The face of a forced community. History, sociology, psychology]. Tübingen: J.C.B. Mohr, 1960.

Adorno, Theodore. *The Authoritarian Personality*. New York: Harper and Row, 1950.

Albrich, Thomas. *Exodus durch Östreich: die jüdischen Flüchtlinge 1945–1948* [Exodus through Austria: The Jewish refugees 1945–1948]. Innsbruck: Haymen-Verlag, 1987.

Alderman, Geoffrey. *The Jewish Community in British Politics*. Oxford: Clarendon Press, 1983.

——. *Modern British Jewry*, Oxford: Clarendon Press, 1992.

Allen, William Sheridan. *The Nazi Seizure of Power: The Experience of a Single German Town 1930–1935*. New York: New Viewpoints, 1973.

Angress, Werner T. *Between Fear and Hope: Jewish Youth in the Third Reich*. New York: Columbia University Press, 1988.

Arad, Yitzhak. *Belzec, Sobibor, Treblinka: The Operation Reinhard Death Camps*. Bloomington: Indiana University Press, 1987.

Arendt, Hannah. *The Origins of Totalitarianism*. New ed. New York: Harcourt, Brace, Jovanovich, 1973.

Aron, Robert. *The Vichy Regime, 1940–1944*. Boston: Beacon Press, 1958.

Ascheim, Steven. *Brothers and Strangers: The East European Jews in German Jewish Consciousness*. Madison: University of Wisconsin Press, 1982.

Avneri, Aryeh L.. ‏מולוס עד טאורוס‎ [From Velos to Taurus]. Tel Aviv: Hakibbutz Hameuchad, 1985.

Avni, Haim. *Argentina and the Jews: A History of Jewish Immigration*. Tuscaloosa: University of Alabama Press, 1991.

——. *Spain, the Jews, and Franco*. Philadelphia: JPS, 1982.

Aziz, Philippe. *Doctors of Death*. 4 vols. Geneva: Ferni, 1976.

Barkai, Avraham. *From Boycott to Annihilation: The Economic Struggle of German Jews, 1933–1943*. Translated from German by William Templer. Hanover: University Press of New England, for Brandeis University Press, 1989.

Barlas, Haim. ‏הצלה בימי השואה‎ [Rescue in the days of the Holocaust]. Tel Aviv: Hakibbutz Hameuchad, 1975.

Bartov, Omer. *The Eastern Front, 1941–1945: German Troops and the Barbarization of Warfare*. New York. MacMillan, 1986.

——. *Hitler's Army: Soldiers, Nazis, and War in the Third Reich*. New York: Oxford University Press, 1991.

Baruch, Nir. ‏הכופר: בולגריה ויהודיה במשך הדורות‎ [The ransom: Bulgaria and its Jews over the generations]. Tel Aviv: Shevilim, 1990.

Bauer, Yehuda. *American Jewry and the Holocaust: The American Jewish Joint Distribution Committee, 1939–1945*. Detroit: Wayne State University Press, 1981.

——. *From Diplomacy to Resistance: A History of Jewish Palestine 1939–1945*. New York: Atheneum, 1973.

——. *The Holocaust in Historical Perspective*. Seattle: University of Washington Press, 1978.

——. *The Jewish Emergence from Powerlessness*. Toronto: University of Toronto Press, 1979.

Bellon, Bernard P. *Mercedes in Peace and War*. New York: Columbia University Press, 1990.

Benardete, Meir J.. *Hispanic Culture and the Character of the Sephardi Jews*. New York: Sepher-Hermon Press, 1982.

Beni, Albert. ‏יהודי בולגריה במאבק נגד הנאצים‎ [Bulgarian Jews in the struggle against Nazism]. Tel Aviv: World Zionist Organization, 1980.

Ben-Sasson, Haim H. ‏פרקים בתולדות היהודים בימי הביניים‎ [Chapters in the history of the Jewish people in the Middle Ages]. Tel Aviv: Am Oved, 1962.

Bettelheim, Bruno. *The Informed Heart: Autonomy in a Mass Age*. New York: Avon Books, 1971.

Billig, Joseph. *L'Hitlérisme et le Système Concentrationnaire* [Hitlerism and the concentration camp system]. Paris: PUF, 1967.

Blakeney, Michael. *Australia and the Jewish Refugees, 1933–1948*. Sydney: Croom Helm Australia, 1985.

Blau, Joseph L.. *Modern Varieties of Judaism*. New York: Columbia University Press, 1964.

Boas, Jacob. *Boulevard des Misères: The Story of Transit Camp Westerbork*. Hamden, CT: Archon Books, 1985.

Borkin, Joseph. *The Crime and Punishment of I.G. Farben*. New York: Free Press, 1978.

Bracher, Karl Dietrich. *The German Dictatorship: The Origins, Structure, and Effects of National Socialism*. Translated from German by Jean Steinberg; introduction by Peter Gay. New York. Holt, Rinehart and Winston, 1970.

Bradley, John. *Lidice: The Sacrificial Village*. New York: Ballantine Books, 1972.

Braham, Randolph L. *The Hungarian Labor Service System, 1939–1945*. Boulder, CO: East European Quarterly, 1977.

——. *The Politics of Genocide: The Holocaust in Hungary*. 1st ed., 2 vols., New York: Columbia University Press, 1980.

Breitman, R. *The Architect of Genocide: Himmler and the Final Solution*. New York: Knopf, 1991.

Bridgman, Jon. *The End of the Holocaust: The Liberation of the Camps*. Portland, OR: Areopagitica Press, 1990.

Browning, Christopher. *Ordinary Men: Reserve Police Battalion 101 and the Final Solution in Poland*. New York: HarperCollins, 1992.

Bunyan, James. *The Origin of Forced Labor in the Soviet State, 1917–1921*. Baltimore: Johns Hopkins University Press, 1967.

Buss, P. and A. Mollo. *Hitler's Germanic Legions*. London: Macdonald and Jane's, 1978.

Butnaru, I. C. *The Silent Holocaust: Romania and Its Jews*. Westport, CT: Greenwood Press, 1992.

Calvocoressi, Peter and Guy Wint. *Total War: The Story of World War II*. first edition, New York: Pantheon Books, 1972.

Chambard, Claude. *The Maquis*. Indianapolis: Bobbs-Merrill, 1970.

Chary, Frederick B.. *The Bulgarian Jews and the Final Solution, 1940–1944*. Pittsburgh: University of Pittsburgh Press, 1972.

Checinski, Michael. *Poland: Communism, Nationalism, Antisemitism*. New York: Karz-Cohl, 1982.

Clarke, Thurston. *By Blood and Fire*. New York: Putnam, 1981

Cohen, Elie A.. *Human Behavior in the Concentration Camp*. New York: Norton, 1953.

Cohen, Michael J. *Palestine and the Great Powers, 1945–1948*. Princeton: Princeton University Press, 1982.

Cohen, Naomi W. *Not Free to Desist: The American Jewish Committee, 1906–1966*. Philadelphia: JPS, 1972.

Cohen, Richard I.. *The Burden of Conscience: French Jewish Leadership During the Holocaust*. Bloomington: Indiana University Press, 1987.

Cohn, Norman. *Warrant for Genocide*. New York: Harper and Row, 1966.

Collins, Larry, and Dominique Lapierre, *Is Paris Burning?* New York: Simon and Schuster, 1965.

Cooper, Matthew. *The Nazi War Against Soviet Partisans, 1941–1944*. New York: Stein and Day, 1979.

Craig, Gordon A.. *The Politics of the Prussian Army, 1640–1945*. London: Oxford University Press, 1955.

Crankshaw, Edward. *Gestapo: Instrument of Tyranny*. New York: Viking Press, 1957.

Curtis, Michael. *Totalitarianism*. New Brunswick, NJ: Transaction Books, 1979.

Dawidowicz, Lucy S.. *The War Against the Jews 1933–1945*. New York: Holt, Rinehart and Winston, 1985.

Dear, Ian. *Ten Commando, 1942–1945*. New York: St. Martin's Press, 1987.

Dekel, Ephraim. *B'riha: Flight to the Homeland*. Translated from Hebrew by Dina Ettinger; edited by Gertrude Hirschler; introduction by Philip S. Bernstein. New York: Herzl Press, n.d.

Delarue, Jacques. *The Gestapo: A History of Horror*. Translated from French by Mervyn Savill. New York: William Morrow, 1964.

Diehl, J. M.. *Paramilitary Politics in Weimar Germany*. Bloomington: Indiana University Press, 1977.

Dinnerstein, Leonard. *America and the Survivors of the Holocaust*. New York: Columbia University Press, 1982.

Dresner, Samuel H. *The Zaddik*. New York: Schocken Books, 1960.

Dubnow, Simon. *Nationalism and History: Essays on the Old and New Judaism*. Philadelphia: Jewish Publication Society, 1958.

Dunin-Wasowicz, K. *Resistance in the Nazi Concentreation Camps*. Warsaw: PWN Polish Scientific Publishers, 1982.

Eck, Nathan. התועים בדרכי המות [Wanderers in the path of death]. Jerusalem: Yad Vashem, 1960.

Edelheit, Abraham J. "The Yishuv in the Shadow of the Holocaust." Ph.D. Dissertation: City University of New York, 1992.

Elazar, Daniel J. *The Other Jews*. New York: Basic Books, 1989.

Engel, David. *In the Shadow of Auschwitz: The Polish Government-in-Exile and the Jews, 1939–1942*. Chapel Hill: University of North Carolina Press, 1987.

Eyck, Erich. *A History of the Weimar Republic*. 2 vols. Cambridge: Harvard University Press, 1967.

Fackenheim, Emil. *The Jewish Return into History*. New York: Schocken Books, 1978.

Feig, Konnilyn. *Hitler's Death Camps*. New York: Holmes and Meier, 1981.

Fein, Helen. *Accounting for Genocide: National Responses and Jewish Victimization During the Holocaust*. New York: Free Press, 1979.

Feinberg, Nathan. האגודות היהודיות למען חבר הלאומים [The Jewish League of Nations Societies]. Jerusalem: Magnes Press, 1967.

——. המערכה היהודית נגד היטלר על במת חבר הלאומים [The Jewish Struggle Against Hitler at the League of Nations]. Jerusalem: Magnes Press, 1957.

Feingold, Henry L.. *The Politics of Rescue: The Roosevelt Administration and the Holocaust, 1938–1945*. New York: Holocaust Library, 1970.

Feldblum, Esther Yolles. *The American Catholic Press and the Jewish State 1917–1959*. New York: Ktav Publishing House, 1977.

Finkelstein, Norman. *Captain of Innocence: France and the Dreyfus Affair*. New York: Putnam, 1991.

Fleming, Gerald. *Hitler and the Final Solution*. Introduction by Saul Friedländer. Berkeley: University of California Press, 1984.

Flender, Harold. *Rescue in Denmark*. New York: Simon and Schuster, 1963.

Foot, M.R.D. *Resistance: European Resistance to Nazism 1940–1945*. New York: McGraw-Hill, 1977.

—— *SOE: The Special Operations Executive, 1940–1946*. London: BBC Publications, 1984.

Friedenreich, Harriet P. *The Jews of Yugoslavia*. Philadelphia: Jewish Publication Society, 1979.

Ganin, Zvi. *Truman, American Jewry, and Israel, 1945–1948*. New York: Holmes and Meier, 1979.

Garlinski, Józef. *Poland in the Second World War*. New York: Hippocrene Books, 1985.

Gelber, Yoav. תולדות ההתנדבות [Jewish Palestinian volunteering in the British army during the Second World War]. 4 vols. Jerusalem: Yad Yitzhak Ben-Zvi, 1979–1984.

Gilbert, Martin and R. Gott. *The Appeasers*. Boston: Houghton Mifflin, 1963.

Golan, Shimon. מרות ומאבק בימי מרי [Allegiance amidst struggle]. Tel Aviv: Yad Tabenkin Press, 1988.

Gold, Mary J. *Crossroads Marseilles, 1940*. Garden City, NY: Doubleday, 1980.

Gordon, Harold. *Hitler and the Beer Hall Putsch*. Princeton: Princeton University Press, 1972.

Gordon, Sarah. *Hitler, Germans and the "Jewish Question."* Princeton: Princeton University Press, 1984.

Graml, Hermann. *Der 9. November 1938, Reichskristallnacht* [November 9, 1938, Crystal Night]. Bonn: Schriftenreihe der Bundeszentrale für Heimatdienst, 1958.

Greenberg, Louis. *The Jews in Russia: The Struggle for Emancipation*. 2 vols. New York: Schocken Books, 1976.

Grunberger, Richard. *The 12-year Reich: A Social History of Nazi Germany 1933–1945*. New York: Holt, Rinehart and Winston, 1971.

Gutman, Israel. *Fighters Among the Ruins: The Story of Jewish Heroism During World War II*. Washington, DC: Bnai Brith Books, 1988.

——. היהודים בפולין אחרי מלחמת העולם השנייה [The Jews in Poland after World War II]. Jerusalem: Zalman Shazar Center for the Furtherance of the Study of Jewish History, 1985.

——. *The Jews of Warsaw, 1939–1943: Ghetto, Underground, Revolt*. Translated from Hebrew by

Ina Friedman. Bloomington: Indiana University Press, 1982.

——, and Shmuel Krakowski. *Unequal Victims: Poles and Jews During World War II*. New York: Holocaust Library, 1986.

Hadari, Zeev (Venia). פליטים מנצחים אימפריה:פרשיות עליה ב',1948–1945 [Refugees defeat an Empire: Chapters in the history of Aliya Bet, 1945–1948]. Beersheba: Ben-Gurion University of the Negev Press, 1985.

——, and Ze'ev Tzahor, *Voyage to Freedom: An Episode in the Illegal Immigration to Palestine*. London: Vallentine, Mitchell, 1985.

Haft, Cynthia J. *The Bargain and the Bridle: The General Union of Israelites in France*. Chicago: Dialog Press, 1983.

Halamish, Aviva. הסיפור האמיתי —אקסודוס [Exodus: The true story]. Tel Aviv: Am Oved, 1990.

Häsler, Alfred A. *The Lifeboat Is Full*. New York: Funk & Wagnalls, 1969.

Heller, Celia. *On the Edge of Destruction*. New York: Schocken Books, 1977.

Heller, Mikhail, and Aleksandr M. Nekrich. *Utopia in Power: The History of the Soviet Union from 1917 to the Present*. New York: Summit Books, 1986.

Henkys, Reinhard. *Die nationalsozialistischen Gewaltverbrechen* [The National Socialist crimes of violence]. Stuttgart: Kreuz-Verlag, 1964.

Hertzberg, Arthur. *The French Enlightenment and the Jews*. New York: Columbia University Press, 1968.

Hilberg, Raul. *The Destruction of the European Jews*. 3 vols. rev. ed. New York: Holmes and Meier, 1985.

——. *Perpetrators, Victims, Bystanders: The Jewish Catastrophe, 1933–1945*, New York: HarperCollins, 1992.

Hildebrand, Klaus. *The Foreign Policy of the Third Reich*. Berkeley: University of California Press, 1973.

Hillel, Marc and Clarissa Henry. *Of Pure Blood*. New York: McGraw-Hill, 1976.

Hirszowicz, Lukasz. *The Third Reich and the Arab East*. London: Routledge and Kegan Paul, 1966.

Hochhuth, Rolf. *The Deputy*. New York: Grove Press, 1964.

Hoffman, Bruce. *The Failure of British Military Strategy Within Palestine, 1939–1947*. Ramat Gan: Bar-Ilan University Press, 1983.

Höhne, Heinz. *Der Orden unter dem Totenkopf: Die Geschichte der SS* [The Order of the Death Head: The story of the SS]. Gütersloh: Sighert Mohn, 1967.

Holborn, Hajo. *A History of Modern Germany, 1940–1945*. Princeton: Princeton University Press, 1969.

Homze, E. L. *Foreign Labor in Nazi Germany*. Princeton: Prineceton University Press, 1967.

Horowitz, Dan and Moshe Lissak. *Origins of the Israeli Polity: Palestine Under the Mandate*. Translated from Hebrew by C. Hoffman. Chicago: University of Chicago Press, 1978.

Horwitz, Gordon J. *In the Shadow of Death*. New York: Free Press, 1990.

Hunt, Linda. *Secret Agenda*. New York: St. Martin's Press, 1991.

Hurwitz, J. C. *The Struggle for Palestine*. New York: Norton, 1950.

Jäckel, Eberhard. *Hitler's Weltanschauung: A Blueprint for Power*. Middletown, CT: Wesleyan University Press, 1969.

Janowsky, Oscar I. *The Jews and Minority Rights*. New York: AMS Press, 1966.

Joes, Anthony James. *Fascism in the Contemporary World: Ideology, Evolution, Resurgence*. Foreword by A. James Gregor. Boulder, CO: Westview Press, 1978.

Juchniewicz, Mieczyslaw. *Poles in the European Resistance Movement 1939–1945*. Translated from Polish by Beryl Arct. Warsaw: Interpress, 1972.

Katzburg, Nathaniel. *Hungary and the Jews, 1920–1943*. Ramat Gan: Bar Ilan University Press, 1981.

Kechales, Haim. קורות יהודי בולגריה [The history of Bulgarian Jewry]. 3 vols. Tel Aviv: Davar Press, 1969.

Kedourie, Elie. *England and the Middle East*. London: Bowes and Bowes, 1956.

Keegan, John. *Waffen-SS: The Asphalt Soldiers*. New York: Ballantine Books, 1970.

Kindermann, G.. *Hitler's Defeat in Austria, 1933–1934*. Boulder, CO: Westview Press, 1988.

Kisch, Guido. *The Jews in Medieval Germany: The Study of Their Legal and Social Standing*. New York: Ktav Publishing House, 1970.

Koblik, Steven. *The Stones Cry Out: Sweden's Response to the Persecution of the Jews, 1933–1945*. New York: Holocaust Library, 1988.

Korbonski, Stefan. *The Polish Underground State*. New York: Hippocrene Books, 1978.

Krakowski, Shmuel. *The War of the Doomed: Jewish Armed Resistance in Poland, 1942–1944*. New York: Holmes and Meier, 1984.

Krausnick, Helmut, Hans Buchheim, Martin Broszat, and Hans-Adolf Jacobsen. *Anatomy of the SS State*. Translated from German by Richard Barry, Marian Jackson, and Dorothy Long. Introduction by Elizabeth Wiskemann. New York: Walker, 1968.

Kuehnrich, Heinz. *Der Partisanenkrieg in Europa 1939–1945* [The partisan war in Europe 1939-1945]. East Berlin: Dietz Verlag, 1968.

Laqueur, Walter. *A History of Zionism*. New York: Holt, Rinehart and Winston, 1972.

——. *The Terrible Secret: Suppression of the Truth About Hitler's Final Solution*. Boston: Little, Brown, 1980.

——, and Richard Breitman. *Breaking the Silence*. New York: Simon and Schuster, 1986.

Latour, Anny. *The Jewish Resistance in France (1940–1944)*. Translated from French by Irene R. Ilton. New York: Holocaust Library, 1981.

Leeds, Christopher. *Italy Under Mussolini*. London: Wayland Publishers, 1972.

Levin, Dov. *Fighting Back: Lithuanian Jewry's Armed Resistance to the Nazis, 1941–1945*. Translated from Hebrew by Moshe Kohn and Dina Cohen; foreword by Yehuda Bauer. New York: Holmes and Meier, 1985.

Levin, Nora. *The Jews in the Soviet Union Since 1917: The Paradox of Survival*. 2 vols. New York: New York University Press, 1988.

——. *While Messiah Tarried: Jewish Socialist Movements, 1871–1917*. New York: Schocken Books, 1977.

Levy, Claude, and Paul Tillard. *Betrayal at the Vel D'Hiv*. New York: Hill and Wang, 1969.

Levy, Richard S.. *The Downfall of the Antisemitic Political Parties in Imperial Germany*. New Haven: Yale University Press, 1975.

Lifton, Robert J. *The Nazi Doctors: Medical Killings and the Psychology of Genocide*. New York: Basic Books, 1986.

Lipscher, Ladislav. *Die Juden in Slowakischen Staat, 1939–1945* [The Jews in the Slovakian state, 1939–1945]. Munich: Oldenbourg, 1980.

Lipstadt, Deborah E. *Beyond Belief: The American Press and the Coming of the Holocaust*. New York: Free Press, 1988.

Littlejohn, David. *The Patriotic Traitors: A History of Collaboration in German Occupied Europe, 1940–1945*. London: Heinemann, 1972.

Lookstein, Haskel. *Were We Our Brothers' Keepers?* New York: Hartmore House, 1985.

Macartney, C. A. *October Fifteenth: A History of Hungary*. New York: Praeger, 1957

Madajczyk, Czeslaw. *Generalna Gubernia w Planach Hitlerowskich* [The General Government in the Hitlerite plan]. Warsaw: Panstwowe Wydawnictwo Naukowe, 1961.

Marcus, Jacob R. *The Rise and Destiny of the German Jew*. New York: Ktav Publishing House, 1973.

Mark, Bernard. *L'Extermination et la résistance des Juifs en Pologne* [The extermination and resistance of the Jews in Poland]. Warsaw: Żydowski Instytut Historyczny, 1955.

Marrus, Michael R.. *The Holocaust in History*. Hanover: University Press of New England, for Brandeis University Press, 1987.

——. *The Unwanted: European Refugees in the Twentieth Century*. New York: Oxford University Press, 1985.

——, and Robert O. Paxton. *Vichy France and the Jews*. New York: Basic Books, 1981.

Martin, A. C.. *The Concentration Camps*. Cape Town, RSA: Howard Timmins, 1958.

Martin, David. *The Web of Disinformation: Churchill's Yugoslav Blunder*. San Diego: Harcourt, Brace, Jovanovich, 1990.

Mason, David. *Salerno: Foothold in Europe*. New York: Ballentine Books, 1972.

McDonald, Callum. *The Killing of SS-Obergruppenführer Reinhard Heydrich*. New York: Macmillan, 1989.

McKale, Donald M.. *The Swastika Outside Germany*. Kent, OH: Kent State University Press, 1977.

Medoff, Rafael. *The Deafening Silence*. New York: Shapolsky Books, 1987.

Meier, Kurt. *Kirche und Judentum: Die Haltung der evangelischen Kirche zur Judenpolitik des Dritten Reiches* [Church and Judaism: The position of the Evangelical church on the Jewish policy in the Third Reich]. Göttingen: Vandenhoeck und Ruprecht, 1968.

Melzer, Emanuel. *1935–1939 יהודי פולין :במלכדת מדיני מאבק* [Political strife in a blind alley: The Jews of Poland 1935–1939]. Tel Aviv: Tel Aviv University Press, 1982.

Mendelsohn, Ezra. *The Jews of East Central Europe Between the World Wars*. Bloomington: Indiana University Press, 1983.

——. *Zionism in Poland*. New Haven: Yale University Press, 1981.

Meyer, Michael A.. *The Origins of the Modern Jew*. Detroit: Wayne State University Press, 1979.

Michaelis, Meir. *Mussolini and the Jews: German-Italian Relations and the Jewish Question in Italy 1922–1945*. Oxford: Clarendon Press, for the Institute of Jewish Affairs, London, 1978.

Michel, Henri. *Les Mouvements clandestins en Europe 1938–1945* [The cladenstine movements in Europe 1938–1945]. Paris: PUF, 1965.

——. *The Shadow War: European Resistance, 1939–1945*. New York: Harper and Row, 1972.

Milano, Attilio. *Storia degli Ebrei in Italia* [Story of the Jews in Italy]. Turin: Giulio Enaudi Editore, 1963.

Minkin, Jacob S.. *The Romance of Hasidism*. New York: Macmillan, 1935.

Moore, Deborah D. *B'nai B'rith and the Challenge of Ethnic Leadership*. Albany: State University of New York Press, 1981.

Morley, John F.. *Vatican Diplomacy and the Jews During the Holocaust 1939–1943*. New York: Ktav Publishing House, 1980.

Morse, Arthur D. *While Six Million Died: A Chronicle of American Apathy*. New York: Hart Publishing, 1968.

Mosse, George L.. *German Jews Beyond Judaism*. Bloomington: Indiana University Press, 1985.

——. *Toward the Final Solution: A History of European Racism*. New York: Harper Colophon Books, 1978.

Mountfield, David. *The Partisans: Secret Armies of World War II*. London: Hamlyn, 1979.

Müller-Hill, Benno. *Tödliche Wissenschaft: Die Aussonderung von Juden, Zigeuner und Geistkranken 1933–1945* [Deadly science: The selection of Jews, Gypsies, and the mentally ill 1933–1945]. Hamburg: Rowohlt, 1984.

Nicholls, A. J.. *Weimar and the Rise of Hitler*. New York: St. Martin's Press, 1979.

Nicosia, Francis R.. *The Third Reich and the Palestine Question*. London: I. B. Tauris, 1985.

Niewyk, Donald I.. *The Jews in Weimar Germany*. Baton Rouge: Louisiana State University Press, 1960.

Nolte, Ernst. *Three Faces of Fascism*. New York: Dell, 1966.

Northedge, F. S.. *The League of Nations: Its Life and Times, 1920–1946*. New York: Holmes and Meier, 1986.

Nussbaum, Klemens. *והפוך להם לרועץ: היהודים בצבא העממי הפולני בברית המועצות* [Story of an illusion: The Jews in the Polish People's Army in the USSR]. Tel Aviv: Diaspora Research Institute, the Society for Jewish Historical Research, 1984.

Ofer, Dalia. *Escaping the Holocaust: Illegal Immigration to the Land of Israel, 1939–1944*. New York: Oxford University Press, 1990.

Oliner, Samuel P., and Pearl Oliner, *The Altruistic Personality*. New York: Free Press, 1988.

O'Neill, Robert J.. *The German Army and the Nazi Party, 1933–1939*. Foreword by Basil Liddell Hart. New York: James H. Heineman, 1966.

Orlow, Dietrich. *The Nazis in the Balkans: A Case Study of Totalitarian Politics*. Pittsburgh: University of Pittsburgh Press, 1968.

Parkes, James. *The Conflict of Church and Synagogue*. New York: Atheneum, 1974.

Penkower, Monty Noam. *The Jews Were Expendable: Free World Diplomacy and the Holocaust*. Urbana: University of Illinois Press, 1983.

Pitt, Barrie. *The Crucible of War*. New York: Paragon House, 1986.

Poliakov, Léon. *די געלע לאטע* [The yellow patch]. Foreword by Justin Godar. Paris: Haynttsaytiker Yidisher dokumentatsye-tsenter, 1952.

——. *Harvest of Hate*. New York: Holocaust Library, 1979.

——. *The History of Antisemitism*, vol. 1. New York: Schocken Books, 1974.

Porat, Dina. *The Blue and the Yellow Stars of David: The Zionist Leadership in Palestine and the Holocaust 1939–1945*. Cambridge: Harvard University Press, 1990.

Posner, Gerald. *Mengele: The Complete Story*. New York: McGraw-Hill, 1986.

Presser, Jacob. *Ashes in the Wind: The Destruction of Dutch Jewry*. Translated from Dutch by Arnold Pomerans. Detroit: Wayne State University Press, 1988.

Pulzer, Peter. *The Rise of Political Antisemitism in Germany and Austria*. Rev. ed. Cambridge: Harvard University Press, 1988.

Ramati, Alexander. *The Assisi Underground*. New York: Stein and Day, 1978.

Rautkallio, Hannu. *Finland and the Holocaust*. New York: Holocaust Library, 1987.

Reitlinger, Gerald. *The SS: Alibi of a Nation 1922–1945*. Foreword by Martin Gilbert. Englewood Cliffs, NJ: Prentice-Hall, 1981.

Rich, Norman. *Hitler's War Aims*. 2 vols. New York: Norton, 1974.

Rings, Werner. *Life with the Enemy: Collaboration and Resistance in Hitler's Europe, 1939–1945*. Translated from German by J. Maxwell Brownjohn. Garden City, NY: Doubleday, 1982.

Roberts, J. M.. *Europe 1880–1945*. New York: Holt, Rinehart, and Winston, 1967.

Robinson, Jacob. *And the Crooked Shall Be Made Straight: The Eichmann Trial, the Jewish Catastrophe, and Hannah Arendt's Narrative*. Philadelphia: Jewish Publication Society, 1965.

Röhl, J.C.G.. *From Bismarck to Hitler*. New York: Barnes and Noble, 1970.

Ross, Robert W.. *So It Was True: The American Protestant Press and the Nazi Persecution of the Jews*. Minneapolis: University of Minnesota Press, 1980.

Roth, Cecil. *A History of the Marranos*. New York: Meridian Books, 1959.

Rudavsky, Joseph. *To Live With Hope, To Die With Dignity*. Lanham, MD: University Press of America, 1987.

Russell, Edward F.L.. *The Record: The Trial of Adolf Eichmann for His Crimes Against the Jewish People and Against Humanity*. New York: Knopf, 1963.

Sachar, Abram L.. *The Redemption of the Unwanted: From the Liberation of the Death Camps to the Founding of Israel*. New York: St. Martin's/Marek, 1983.

Sachar, Howard M.. *The Course of Modern Jewish History*. New York: Dell Publishing, 1977.

Samuel, Maurice. *Blood Accusation*. New York: Knopf, 1966.

Sayer, Ian, and Douglas Botting. *America's Secret Army: The Untold Story of the Counter Intelligence Corps*. London: Grafton Books, 1989.

Schechtman, Joseph B.. *The Mufti and the Führer*. New York: Thomas Yoseloff, 1969.

Scholem, Gershom. *The Messianic Idea in Judaism*. New York: Schocken Books, 1971.

Schleunes, Karl. *The Twisted Road to Auschwitz*. Urbana, IL: University of Chicago Press, 1970.

Schmidt, Matthias. *Albert Speer: The End of a Myth*. New York: St. Martin's Press, 1985.

Schneider, Gertrude. *Journey into Terror*. New York: Ark Home, 1979.

Schoenbrun, David. *Soldiers of the Night: The Story of the French Resistance*. New York, Dutton, 1980.

Senft, S., and H. Więcek, *Obozy jenieckie na obsarze Śląskiego Okręgu Wehrmachtu 1939–1945*. Wroclaw: Zaklad Narodowy im Ossolinskich, 1972.

Seton-Watson, Hugh. *The East European Revolution*. London: Methuen, 1961.

——. *Eastern Europe Between the Wars, 1918–1941*. New York: Harper Torchbooks, 1967.

——. *From Lenin to Khrushchev: The History of World Communism*. New York: Praeger, 1960.

Shabbetai, Karl. *As Sheep to the Slaughter?* New York: World Association of Bergen-Belsen Survivors, 1963.

Sharf, Andrew. *The British Press and the Jews Under Nazi Rule*. London: Oxford University Press, 1964.

Sherman, A. J.. *Island Refuge: Britain and Refugees from the Third Reich 1933–1939*. Berkeley: University of California Press, 1973.

Shirer, William L.. *The Rise and Fall of the Third Reich*. New York: Simon and Schuster, 1960.

Snoek, Johan M.. *The Grey Book*. Introduction by Uriel Tal. New York: Humanities Press, 1970.

Spector, Shmuel. *The Holocaust of Volhynian Jews 1941–1944*. Translated from Hebrew by Jerzy Michalowicz. Jerusalem: Yad Vashem/Federation of Volhynian Jews, 1990.

Steinberg, Jonathan. *All or Nothing: The Axis and the Holocaust, 1941–1943*. London: Routledge and Kegan Paul, 1990.

Steinberg, Lucien. *Not as a Lamb: The Jews Against Hitler*. Translated from French by Marion Hunter. Farnborough, UK: Saxon House, 1974.

Stern, Fritz. *The Politics of Cultural Despair*. Berkeley: University of California Press, 1961.

Sydnor, Charles W. Jr.. *Soldiers of Destruction: The SS Death's Head Division, 1933–1945*. Princeton: Princeton University Press, 1977.

Syrkin, Marie. *Blessed Is the Match*. rev. ed., Philadelphia: JPS, 1976.

Szakowski, Zosa. *Jews and the French Foreign Legion*. New York: Ktav, 1975.

Tagliacozzo, Michael. *La Comunità di Roma sotto l'Imcubo della Svastica: Le Grande Razzia del Ottobre 1943* [The Community of Rome Under the Nightmare of the Swastika: The Great Raid of October 1943]. Milan: N.P., 1963.

Talmon, Jacob L.. *Political Messianism: The Romantic Phase*. Boulder, CO: Westview Press, 1985.

Taylor, A.J.P.. *The Origins of the Second World War*. New York: Atheneum, 1961.

Tenenbaum, Joseph. *Race and Reich: The Story of an Era*. New York: Twayne, 1956.

——. *Underground: The Story of a People*. New York: Philosophical Library, 1952.

Thalmann, Rita, and Emmanuel Feinermann. *Crystal Night 9–10 November 1938*. Translated from French by Gilles Cremonesi. London: Thames and Hudson, 1974.

Thomas, Gordon, and Max M. Witts, *The Voyage of the Damned*. New York: Stein and Day, 1974.

Thomas, Nigel. *Foreign Volunteers of the Allied Forces, 1939–1945*. London: Osprey Books, 1991.

Thompson, Robert S.. *Pledge to Destiny: Charles de Gaulle and the Rise of the Free French*. New York: McGraw-Hill, 1974.

Tomaszewski, Jerzy. *Rzeczpospolita wielu narodów* [A Republic of Many Nations]. Warsaw: Czytelnik, 1985.

Trachtenberg, Joshua. *The Devil and the Jews: The Medieval Conception of the Jew and Its Relation to Modern Antisemitism*. Philadelphia: Jewish Publication Society, 1961.

Trunk, Isaiah. *Judenrat: The Jewish Councils in Eastern Europe Under Nazi Occupation*. Introduction by Jacob Robinson. New York: Stein and Day, 1977.

Tsizling, Neryah, and Ezra Lahad. *לדמותה של שארית הפליטה* [On the nature of the She'erit ha-Pleta]. Kibbutz Lohame ha-Getaot: Ghetto Fighters Publishing House, 1985.

Tuchman, Barbara. *The Proud Tower*. New York: Macmillan, 1966.

Turner, Henry Ashby, Jr.. *German Big Business and the Rise of Hitler*. New York: Oxford University Press, 1985.

Unger, Menashe. *דער גייסטיקער ווידערשטאנד פון ייִדן אין געטאס און לאגערן* [The spiritual resistance of the Jews in the ghettos and camps]. Preface by Elie Wiesel. Tel Aviv: Hamenorah, 1970.

Vital, David. *The Origins of Zionism*. New York: Oxford University Press, 1975.

Wasserstein, Bernard. *Britain and the Jews of Europe 1939–1945*. Oxford: Clarendon Press, for the Institute of Jewish Affairs, London, 1979.

Watt, Richard M.. *Bitter Glory: Poland and Its Fate, 1918–1939*. New York: Simon and Schuster, 1982.

Weber, Eugen. *Action Française*. Stanford: Stanford University Press, 1962.

Weinreich, Max. *Hitler's Professors: The Part of Scholarship in Germany's Crimes Against the Jewish People*. New York: Yiddish Scientific Institute — YIVO, 1946.

Weinryb, Bernard D.. *The Jews of Poland*. Philadelphia: Jewish Publication Society, 1973.

West, Nigel. *MI-6: British Secret Intelligence Service Operations, 1909–1945*. New York: Random House, 1983.

Wischnitzer, Mark. *To Dwell in Freedom*. Philadelphia: Jewish Publication Society, 1948.

Wistrich, Robert. *Hitler's Apocalypse: Jews and the Nazi Legacy*. New York: St. Martin's Press, 1985.

Wright, Gordon. *The Ordeal of Total War*. New York Harper and Row, 1968.

Wyman, David S.. *The Abandonment of the Jews: America and the Holocaust*. New York: Pantheon Books, 1984.

——. *Paper Walls: America and the Refugee Crisis, 1938–1941*. New York: Pantheon Books, 1985.

Yahil, Leni. *The Holocaust: The Fate of European Jewry, 1932–1945*. Translated from Hebrew by Ina Friedman and Haya Galai. New York: Oxford University Press, 1990.

——. *The Rescue of Danish Jewry*, Philadelphia: JPS, 1969.

Zeman, Z.A.B.. *Nazi Propaganda*. Oxford: Oxford University Press, 1973.

Zimmels, H. J.. *The Echo of the Nazi Holocaust in Rabbinic Literature*. New York: Ktav, 1975.

Zinberg, Israel. *A History of Jewish Literature*. New York: Ktav Publishing House, 1978.

Zuccotti, Susan. *The Holocaust, the French, and the Jews*. New York: Basic Books, 1993.

——. *The Italians and the Holocaust: Persecution, Rescue, and Survival*. New York: Basic Books, 1987.

ABOUT THE BOOK AND AUTHORS

This two-part volume combines an accessible overview of contemporary Jewish history with a unique dictionary of Holocaust terms. In addition to assessing the Holocaust specifically, Part 1 of the book discusses the history of European Jewry, antisemitism, the rise and fall of Nazism and fascism, World War II, and the postwar implications of the Holocaust. The authors also consider key historiographical and methodological issues related to the Holocaust.

Part 2 provides a complete dictionary of terms relating to the Holocaust culled from dozens of primary and secondary sources in a range of languages. Included here is a comprehensive set of tables on *Aktionen*, Aliya Bet, anti-Jewish legislation, antisemitic organizations, collaboration, concentration camps, fascism, the Third Reich, the Nazi Party, Jewish and nonsectarian organizations, publications, Judenräte, and resistance movements. Each table is prefaced by a descriptive overview of pertinent issues.

Graphs, photographs, and documents supplement the text, and an extensive bibliography as well as person, place, and subject indexes make this unique work invaluable as a reference tool.

Abraham J. Edelheit is a visiting professor at Kingsborough Community College in New York and is a scholar in residence for the Jewish Association for Services to the Aged. **Hershel Edelheit**, a Holocaust survivor, is director of ERICH (Edelheit Research Institute for Contemporary History), a private nonprofit research institute dedicated to the study of Jewish history in the twentieth century. Together they have edited seven reference books on the Holocaust and modern history, most notably the three-volume *Bibliography on Holocaust Literature* (Westview Press).

NAME INDEX

PLACE INDEX

Abteroda, 276
Adorf, 284
Adriatica, 223
Africa, 143, 155
Albania, 81, 226, 255, 407, 441, 445
Aleksotas, 282
Algiers, 81, 184, 246
Allach, 278
Allendorf, 276
Alsace-Lorraine, 18, 50, 75, 249
Altenburg, 276
Altengrabow, 375
Altenhammer, 279
Althammer, 432
Amersfoort, 174
Amsterdam, *76*, 77-78, 166, 175, 243, 276, 378, 386, 398, 399, 402, 457
Amstetten, 283
Anatolia, 16
Annaburg, 276
Ansbach, 279
Antwerp, 77, 350, 408
Argentina, 126-127, 339, 379, 392
Armenia, 16
Arolsen, 276
Aschersleben, 276
Asia, 15, 68
Aslau, 281
Athens, 80, 82, 176
Atlanta, 332
Augsburg, 278
Aumale, 276
Aurich, 285
Auschwitz, 37, 68-69, 77-78, 80-82, 85, 104, 117, 121, 132, 136, 143, 145-147, 163-165,

171, 173-177, 185, 188, 190, 192, 194, 196-197, 200-201, 207, 214, 216, 222, 257, 260, 264-265, 267-269, 275, 288, 295, 331, 333, 336, 340, 342, 344, 346, 374, 401, 404, 406-407, 413, 416, 424, 427, 431-432, 437, 439, 442
Australia, 52, 68, 128, 357, 361, 364, 376
Austria, 7, 44, 48-49, 52, 75, 81, 108, 128-129, 145, 150, 185-186, 193, 199, 212, 221, 226-227, 249, 255, 260, 265, 283, 289, 294-295, 297, 332, 339, 347, 350, 353, 360, 368, 371, 375-376, 381, 395, 407, 413, 432, 441, 450, 458
Austria-Hungary, 8, 15, 186

Babi Yar, 59, *60*, 144, 168, 339, 341
Babylonia, 4, 268
Bad Salzungen, 276
Bad Tölz, 279
Baden, 162
Balkans, 4, 118, 121, 227, 369, 415
Baltic Republics, 71, 195, 242, 340, 419
Banska Bystrica, 371
Bar, 157
Baranovichi, 169, 172-173, 243
Barth, 286
Bavaria, 30, 232, 375, 410
Będzin, 101, 171, 243, 291, 403-404, 406
Beendorf, 285
Belchatów, 171, 243
Belgium, 16, 50, 61, 77, 114, 119, 122, 126, 130, 149, 152, 162, 183, 203-204, 226-227, 230-231, 235, 238, 246, 248, 253, 255, 265, 294, 325-326, 331, 343, 350, 376, 381-382, 385, 388, 391, 395, 401, 407-408, 441, 444, 458
Belgrade, 95, 167, 169
Belorussia, 23, 59, 101, 116, 118, 164, 195, 204,

SUBJECT INDEX